A Guide
to
Composition
Pedagogies

A Guide
to
Composition
Pedagogies

GARY TATE
Texas Christian University

AMY RUPIPER TAGGART
North Dakota State University

KURT SCHICK
James Madison University

H. BROOKE HESSLER
Oklahoma City University

SECOND EDITION

New York   Oxford
OXFORD UNIVERSITY PRESS

Oxford University Press, publishes works that further Oxford University's
objective of excellence in research, scholarship, and education.

Oxford   New York
Auckland   Cape Town   Dar es Salaam   Hong Kong   Karachi
Kuala Lumpur   Madrid   Melbourne   Mexico City   Nairobi
New Delhi   Shanghai   Taipei   Toronto

With offices in
Argentina   Austria   Brazil   Chile   Czech Republic   France   Greece
Guatemala   Hungary   Italy   Japan   Poland   Portugal   Singapore
South Korea   Switzerland   Thailand   Turkey   Ukraine   Vietnam

Published by Oxford University Press
198 Madison Avenue, New York, New York 10016
http://www.oup.com

Library of Congress Cataloging-in-Publication Data
A Guide to Composition Pedagogies / Gary Tate, Texas Christian University, Amy Rupiper-Taggart,
North Dakota State University, Kurt Schick, James Madison University, Brooke Hessler, Oklahoma
City University. -- Second Edition.
     pages cm
   Includes index.
   ISBN 978-0-19-992216-1 (acid-free paper) 1. English language--Rhetoric--Study and teaching.
2. Report writing--Study and teaching (Higher) I. Tate, Gary.
   PE1404.G85   2014
   808'.042071--dc23
                                                                                2013037168

Printing number: 9 8 7 6 5 4 3 2

Printed in the United States of America
on acid-free paper

CONTENTS

ACKNOWLEDGMENTS   vii

✓What Is Composition Pedagogy? ①
An Introduction   1
Amy Rupiper Taggart, H. Brooke Hessler, and Kurt Schick

PEDAGOGIES

Basic Writing   20
Deborah Mutnick and Steve Lamos

Collaborative Writing   37
Krista Kennedy and Rebecca Moore Howard

Community-Engaged   55
Laura Julier, Kathleen Livingston, and Eli Goldblatt

Critical   77 (maybe)
Ann George

Cultural Studies   94 (maybe)
Diana George, Tim Lockridge, and John Trimbur

✓Expressive   111 ③
Chris Burnham and Rebecca Powell

✓Feminist   128
Laura R. Micciche

v

Genre 146
Amy J. Devitt

Literature and Composition 163
Christine Farris

New Media 177
Collin Gifford Brooke

Online and Hybrid 194
Beth L. Hewett

Process 212
Chris M. Anson

Researched Writing 231
Rebecca Moore Howard and Sandra Jamieson

Rhetoric and Argumentation 248
David Fleming

Second Language Writing 266
Paul Kei Matsuda and Matthew J. Hammill

**Writing in the Disciplines
and Across the Curriculum** 283
Chris Thaiss and Susan McLeod

Writing Center 301
Neal Lerner

CONTRIBUTORS 317

AUTHOR INDEX 323

SUBJECT INDEX 335

ACKNOWLEDGMENTS

W e dedicate this collection to our mentor, Gary Tate, who conceived of the first edition as a way to introduce newcomers to a discipline that he helped create. Writing Studies was substantially shaped and enriched by three decades of Gary's contributions, many of which were published by Oxford University Press.

We wish to thank the editorial staff at Oxford University Press, especially Frederick Speers and Talia Benamy. We appreciate the help of many outside reviewers for their thoughtful feedback, including Robert Cummings, University of Mississippi; Amy Pawl, Washington University in St. Louis; Lynee Lewis Gaillet, Georgia State University; Joanne Leibman Matson, University of Arkansas at Little Rock; Brian Fehler, Tarleton State University; Sue Whatley, Stephen F. Austin State University; Annette March, California State University–Monterey Bay; Chris Anson, North Carolina State University; Richard Bower, Cayuga Community College; Karen Keaton Jackson, North Carolina Central University; Cynthia Vigliotti, Youngstown State University; Bret Kofford, San Diego State University; Morgan Gresham, University of South Florida St. Petersburg; Jennifer Camden, University of Indianapolis; Nancy DeJoy, Michigan State University; Octavio Pimentel, Texas State University–San Marcos; Susan Garza, Texas A&M University–Corpus Christi; Georgia Rhoades, Appalachian State University; Paul Dahlgren, Georgia Southwestern State University; Amy Vetter, University of North Carolina–Greensboro; Deborah Miller, University of Georgia; Kimberli Lee, Northeastern State University; Clinton Gardner, Salt Lake Community College; Carol Zitzer-Comfort, California State University–Long Beach; and Michelle Sidler, Auburn University. For her candid readings of many of the early drafts, reading as a member of the primary target audience, and for her hard work on citation copyediting and indexing, we must thank North Dakota State University PhD student MK Laughlin. NDSU Masters student David Lemke also served as a reviewer of early drafts. And for its institutional commitment of Amy's developmental leave, we are grateful to NDSU's administration.

Most significantly, we are indebted to the contributions of our authors and the many scholars whose work they have synthesized. That so much has been thought and said about composition pedagogy is a testament to our field's commitment to teaching and learning.

What Is Composition Pedagogy?
An Introduction

Amy Rupiper Taggart
H. Brooke Hessler
Kurt Schick

"Pedagogy"

1. A place of instruction; a school, a college; a university. Also *fig*. Now *hist.* and *rare*.
2. Instruction, discipline, training; a system of introductory training; a means of guidance. *Obs.*
3. The art, occupation, or practice of teaching. Also: the theory or principles of education; a method of teaching based on such a theory.

—Oxford English Dictionary

We came to this subject, years ago, as graduate students sitting in a circle with Gary Tate at Texas Christian University, questioning composition pedagogy—what it is, how many ways there are to do it, and to what extent our talking about it matches our doing it. Tate pushed us, as relatively new writing teachers, to play "doubting and believing games" with each pedagogical theory we encountered (Elbow), encouraging us to consider our personal investments and how those intersected with the theories. As we explored a variety of approaches, each of us had moments of spark and moments of panic. For example, like Ann George in this collection, each of us at one time or another discovered that critical pedagogy is deeply important—but also deeply challenging to implement. Over time, we made tentative allegiances and found focus and direction in approaches that suited our understanding of writing and its role. Kurt leaned toward teaching argument and aligning with writing centers while Amy started with community-engagement and genres and Brooke gravitated toward community-engagement and new media. As we reflect on Tate's course over fifteen years later (now ourselves teachers of composition pedagogy), what we value most is the way its combination of mentorship, focused reading, and critical self-reflection helped us understand the complexity and wisdom of each pedagogical area. It helped us become more comfortable with the fact that there is no single correct way to teach writing, nor even one unified set of goals all writing teachers need to help students achieve.

1

It also helped us to see how pedagogical theories and approaches blend and interact. We became more self-aware about our pedagogical choices.

It is that rich, exploratory, sometimes disorienting, but more often illuminating experience we hope to bring to readers of this collection. Each chapter presents a different argument and body of knowledge for how and why teachers should draw from that particular pedagogy (often in combination with others) as they teach. While readers will find diverse approaches in the collection, they will also find common touchstones and resonances across the chapters. To navigate the variations, we first think some discussion of the overarching concept, *composition pedagogy*, is warranted.

DEFINITIONS

Many of us come to understand the term *pedagogy* inductively. We remember the teaching that impressed us as students and use those memories to visualize the theories and methods discussed by peers and scholars. Over time, we develop a general sense of what pedagogy means in the field of writing instruction. But that inductive learning takes significant time that busy writing teachers may not afford and that newcomers may find frustrating. We have become somewhat dissatisfied with our field's definitions of this term because they are either too indirect or too brief, particularly when compared to other terms such as *rhetoric*, *discourse*, and *literacy*, whose definitions have been the subject of rich discussion and debate (see, for instance, James Gee's "Literacy, Discourse, and Linguistics: Introduction").

The first edition of *A Guide to Composition Pedagogies* was no exception. We began the book with the following: "*Pedagogy* is among the most commonly used, yet least defined, terms in composition studies. In our professional discussions, the term variously refers to the practices of teaching, the theories underlying those practices, and perhaps most often, as some combination of the two—as praxis" (vi). We then promised newcomers to the field that "by surveying its many forms," our collection would provide enough information about the history, theory, and practices of twelve diverse pedagogies that newcomers could somehow build their own definitions.

Previous scholars take similar approaches, often defining pedagogy indirectly by building systems for classifying and contrasting pedagogical approaches. James Berlin's important overview in "Contemporary Composition: The Major Pedagogical Theories" categorizes various pedagogies by their epistemological assumptions— their view of how language relates to and represents reality. He suggests that what differentiates pedagogies from each other is their vision of the world, and specifically the vision of the writing process that each pedagogy advances. The entry on *pedagogy* in the brief *Keywords in Composition Studies* mirrors Berlin's classifying and historical scheme as it traces three major movements: current-traditional, process, and critical pedagogies (Fitts 168).

Another reference, the *Encyclopedia of Rhetoric and Composition*, provides a more rhetorical orientation but also largely allows readers to understand rhetorical pedagogy through its history. That entry, by Linda Ferreira-Buckley, provides this insight into the way pedagogy fits into a study of rhetoric: "Central to the study of rhetoric, especially at the secondary and postsecondary level; concerned with teaching both the production and analysis of discourse" (495). We should note that while composition pedagogy, too, deals with production and analysis of discourse, and for many the line between rhetorical and writing instruction is a fine one, this entry is focused enough on the history of rhetoric that some composition pedagogies may not be captured by its discussion.

One of the more satisfying definitions we encountered comes from Nancy Myers, in her article, "The Slave of Pedagogy":

> Pedagogy suggests to me an ethical philosophy of teaching that accounts for the complex matrix of people, knowledge, and practice within the immediacy of each class period, each assignment, each conference, each grade. For me that is pedagogy—the *art* of teaching—the regular, connected, and articulated choices made from within a realm of possibilities and then acted on. Historically, it accounts for the goals of the institution and to some extent society; it manifests the goals of the individual teacher, which may include an agenda to help students learn to critique both the institution and society; and it makes room for the goals of the individual students. (166)

Part of what makes Myers' definition seem more complete than the others is its acknowledgment of the rhetorical situation of teaching—the people, the class, and the institution that shape pedagogy, even as teachers try to play their roles in that situation as agents attentive to teaching's goals and practices and student needs.

In this introductory chapter, we build on these definitions to help newcomers understand the *concept* of composition pedagogy more completely before they hear about varied permutations of it, and to highlight some of the roles pedagogical knowledge plays in composition studies. So we provide a working definition, but we also complicate and extend that definition with the discussion that follows.

Drawing on the research cited in this collection, we offer the following definition: Composition pedagogy is a body of knowledge consisting of theories of and research on teaching, learning, literacy, writing, and rhetoric, and the related practices that emerge. It is the deliberate integration of theory, research, personal philosophy, and rhetorical praxis into composition instruction at all levels from the daily lesson plan to the writing program and the communities it serves. *Composition pedagogy* is an umbrella term like *theory*, *rhetoric*, or *literacy*; it contains much that is worthy of extensive scholarly and practitioner attention, and the more deeply we engage it, the more complex and diverse it becomes—which is why *composition pedagogy* morphs into *composition pedagogies* just as *literacy* becomes *literacies*. The same holds true for the pedagogical subcategories discussed in this collection: While each chapter title denotes a body of knowledge, its variations are infinite.

PEDAGOGY IS THEORETICAL

Writing pedagogy is a body of knowledge that typically links writing theories to teaching theories and practices. Each writing pedagogy provides a theory of teaching and learning informed by a particular set of writing principles and knowledge. The distinction between writing *theory* and writing *pedagogy* can be confusing, in part because the difference is not simply that one is theoretical and one practical. Writing theory deals with text production, circulation, and reception, while writing pedagogy explains the teaching and learning of writing. Pedagogy draws attention to the underlying philosophies, theories, and goals of teaching practices. Further, there is a difference between *teaching* and *pedagogy* as functioning terms. Teaching is the practice while pedagogy almost always also draws attention to its underlying philosophies. As James Berlin explains:

> To teach writing is to argue for a version of reality, and the best way of knowing and communicating it—to deal, as Paul Kameen has pointed out, in the metarhetorical realm of epistemology and linguistics. And all composition teachers are ineluctably operating in this realm, whether or not they consciously choose to do so. ("Contemporary Composition" 234)

It is in the conscious attention to worldview and goals that teaching becomes pedagogy. Teachers ask themselves: *What goals and principles inform my teaching decisions each day and across the course, program, and curriculum?*

To illustrate the relationship between theory and pedagogy, consider how genre theory, a production and reception theory, suggests that types of writing emerge out of social conditions to meet communicative needs (see, e.g., Miller). Those genres are then circulated by people who need to solve some communication problem, broadly conceived, and received by those who might participate in solving the problem. So when a teacher needs to create a frame for her course and communicate it to students, the teacher develops a syllabus. Genre theory helps us to understand why and how such documents exist, as well as how to challenge and question existing patterns and practices in textual use. If patterns and practices around a genre have become orthodoxy, a genre theorist might identify the control exerted over users and provide insights into changing social practices for the better. What genre theory *does not do* is explain how to help students or novice writers understand and write genres better. It is genre pedagogy that must fill in that gap, drawing together the twin strands of learning theory and genre theory and bringing them to inform classroom and extracurricular practice. Given the close relationship between writing theories and the pedagogies that draw on them, it is perhaps unsurprising that pedagogical categories wax and wane in response to theoretical (and other research) trends in the field. Theory, research, and pedagogy push and pull each other.

Though both writing theory and writing pedagogy have theoretical dimensions, and though both are brought to practical applications, theory or "pure" theory has historically been valued over the teaching and learning arm in higher education generally and in English departments in particular (this belief is advanced by writing specialists at times, as well). We join Ernest Boyer in arguing that theory, research, and pedagogy are complementary, not hierarchical, ways of knowing. The chapters in this volume exemplify that complementarity.

PEDAGOGY IS RESEARCH BASED

Theories shape our thought and give it direction. Our research tests those theories. To differentiate the relative values of theories and practices, it is important to draw on the data and tested knowledge of the field, and by tested knowledge we mean a range of things, including the accumulation of classroom practice and teacher research but also including more social-scientific approaches. In a 2008 article, Chris Anson issued a clarion call explaining the deep importance of research to good pedagogy:

> My point is this: if we continue to rely on belief in our pedagogies and adminis-
> trative decisions, whether theorized or not, whether argued from logic or anecdote,
> experience or conviction, we do no better to support a case for those decisions than
> what most detractors do to support cases against them. Instead, we need a more
> robust plan for building on the strong base of existing research into our assump-
> tions about how students best learn to write. In the process, we may discover that
> some of our own beliefs fail to stand the test of inquiry, prompting further re-
> search into the foundations of success in student learning and development and
> further modifications of our dominant pedagogies. (11–12)

Anson pushes against our tendency as humanists to rely on narratives of experience and theoretical formulations, important knowledge to be sure, but incomplete if we do not seek other kinds of data.

The cognitivists provided an early model of this kind of data-driven research with their think-aloud protocols regarding writers' processes (Flower and Hayes, among others). Current researchers, such as the members of the Consortium for the Study of Writing in College (2008–present), draw on large bodies of National Survey of Student Engagement (NSSE) data to better understand how writing instruction impacts students over the course of their undergraduate careers. To-gether with myriad classroom studies and theoretical analyses, we build significant pedagogical knowledge.

PEDAGOGY IS RHETORICAL

When teachers first attempt to teach two sections of the same course or to teach the same course twice across semesters, they quickly discover that no two in-stances of a class are the same. The lesson on analyzing advertisements that seems to activate and enhance students' knowledge of the rhetorical appeals so well at 11:00 a.m. falls like a rock at 1:00 p.m., not because the lesson has changed but because the situation has. Such shifts happen at all levels, from class period to class period, instructor to instructor, room to room, institution to institution, region to region. Like other communicative situations, teaching is *rhetorical*, meaning that it inevitably depends on the particulars of specific audiences, purposes, occasions, and constraints.

As expert communicators, teachers detect patterns and ways to draw on pre-vious experience in particular situations, but teachers need a range of theories, methods, and tools to use somewhat flexibly as they work. Hence, the evolution of a wide range of pedagogies. Pedagogies are analogous to genres; they emerge out of practice and need but also sometimes drive practice (take on a life of their own). With a nod to Carolyn Miller, we observe that pedagogy is a kind of *social action*. Hence, pedagogy never looks the same way twice, though we can recognize patterns we cluster and name as such things as critical pedagogy, Writing Across the Curriculum (WAC) pedagogy, and so on.

To say that pedagogies are varied and address differing goals and situations is not to suggest that nothing at all is shared. To be a writing pedagogy, the instructional emphasis should be more heavily on text production, as compared with, for instance, literature pedagogies, which typically emphasize text reception. Both may teach reading and writing, but as complementary curricula, writing classes provide more guidance in creating texts while literature courses provide more support for reading and critiquing texts (there is some contention in the field about whether writing classes always retain that emphasis). As we discuss later in this chapter, we also believe most writing pedagogy now allows for process and research as useful components of instruction, representing further shared territory among diverse writing pedagogies.

PEDAGOGY IS PERSONAL

When choosing a pedagogy, instructional goals should be foremost. And goals are partly set by programs, by departments, by student populations, and by institutions in the form of expected learning outcomes such as general education requirements. Yet teachers typically have much flexibility to interpret those externally defined goals. It is in that layer of decision making that instructors engage their personal philosophies: *How can I teach this material in a way that aligns with my view of what's important in education and the world?*

An individual's pedagogical choices also often link up with her scholarly path. Someone asking questions about the relationship between storytelling and social activism in her research will likely bring some of that knowledge and expertise to the writing classroom. The genres she assigns, the readings or models she selects, will likely come from her pool of textual experience. That scholar might be primarily a critical, feminist, or community-engagement pedagogue. A scholar of digital literacies may gravitate toward online teaching and learning (OTL) or new media pedagogies. While we often align with one (or two) more strongly than others, rare is the teacher who does not blend the practices of many pedagogical philosophies.

PEDAGOGY'S PURPOSES

We hope this collection will help readers to cultivate a nuanced understanding of how pedagogy functions beyond the teaching of a specific lesson or class. For that reason, in this section we briefly discuss additional ways pedagogy influences the teaching and learning experience. We suggest that pedagogy principally works to meet student needs, drives practice (as a heuristic for generating new practices), refines practice (as an evaluative lens to test the validity of a practice), and ensures that practice is not arbitrary or unexamined. Because of its reflexive nature, pedagogy also encourages the development of new theories and new pedagogies. Thus, it refines not just practice but thought. Finally, we want to acknowledge the ways in which pedagogy can either push against or reinforce norms.

David Kolb's learning cycle can help illustrate the role of pedagogies and their relationship to practice. Kolb suggests that experience is not useful for building new knowledge and understanding unless combined with cycles of reflection. In fact, that experience could "miseducate," in John Dewey's terms. Each teaching experience (practice) may be examined and refined and each future practice planned with an abstract conceptualization (pedagogical theory) in mind. Theory and practice complement and refine each other. Like many cyclical representations, learning is not as tidy and linear as this discussion suggests, but these components happen in many good learning situations.

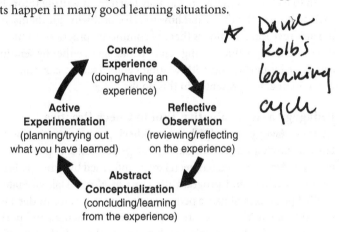

Pedagogy as a Response to Student Needs

At its core, pedagogy exists to respond to student writers' needs. Composition classes are typically smaller than those of other subjects—in part because of the grading load, but mostly because smaller classes help us to differentiate instruction according to the needs of heterogeneous writers.

Student writers are a diverse lot. They arrive at college with thirteen years of formal education, including literacy instruction that spans English, Social Studies, Math, Science, and other courses. A high school graduate may have received instruction from dozens of teachers who employed disparate and sometimes divergent strategies for teaching reading, writing, and critical and creative thinking. Moreover, many of our students read and write constantly online, while others may not have access to technology or print materials in their homes. Their life experiences and future goals differentiate their instructional needs.

Ultimately, composition programs and instructors must choose a blend of pedagogies that they believe will meet the needs of their particular students within their particular contexts. Each pedagogy enacts specific motives for teaching and embodies specific ways that we construct students—for example, as communica-tors, as scholars, as disenfranchised citizens, or as future professionals (Tate).

Pedagogy as a Heuristic to Create New Practice

In our own classrooms, we have used pedagogical theory to create new practices, often in those moments when something just didn't seem to be working well enough. For example, Kurt's overlapping experiences as a composition teacher and as a writing center consultant helped him begin to address a common teaching challenge: engaging students earnestly and productively in peer review.

Students often hesitate to participate in classroom peer review because they lack confidence to solicit and use constructive feedback and because, subsequently, they don't trust their peers' advice. As Neal Lerner discusses in this volume, writ-ing center pedagogy can help by emphasizing social writing skills. Tutors model how to engage productively in the give and take of collaboration. Students can begin to feel more empowered as they learn from writing tutors how to talk about their writing with others, and how to solve problems for themselves by using edit-ing and revision techniques that are commonly practiced in tutorials. As Kurt has discovered, importing writing center pedagogies, either by sending students to the center or by partnering with writing center faculty, can complement any of the other approaches presented in this book.

Pedagogy as an Evaluative Tool to Check Practice

Genre pedagogy has helped Amy to check practice, reminding her of the impor-tance of moving students through genre performance to genre critique. The writing program Amy directed has been largely informed by genre pedagogy. For almost a decade, teachers and program directors at North Dakota State University have applied principles of genre pedagogy: using models for understanding and analy-sis, exploring a range of genres with differing audiences and purposes, and so on. Simultaneously, they examine their practices through the lens of genre pedagogy.

Even upon reading Amy Devitt's contribution to this edition, Amy was re-minded of the importance of getting students to critique genres, a challenge in the first-year classroom. Reading the pedagogy chapter allowed her to think again about the role the vertical writing program (general education courses at both the first and third year) played at her institution and the ways she and the other pro-gram director could think about explicitly emphasizing aspects of genre pedagogy in the courses at the first-year and third-year levels. Emphasizing understanding and analysis of genres in the first-year program, Amy and her colleagues feel they should find ways to get students in the third-year courses to critique genres. Even further, reflection on genre pedagogy and its goals can help shape lower- and upper-division assessments. When NDSU instructors read portfolios for a "Com-municating effectively in a variety of genres for a range of audiences, purposes, and situations" goal, they might need to add a layer to the rubric for upper-division assessment that more directly looks for evidence of genre critique. Thus, pedagogy helps us to check practice at all levels: daily plans, units or assignments, courses, and programs.

Pedagogy as Critically Reflective Practice

Browsing composition scholarship, new teachers quickly find that reflection is part of our culture; it's a component of writing and learning activities, assessments, and research and teaching narratives. Much of this work exhibits the characteristics of *critically reflective practice*, as described by Stephen Brookfield:

> [R]eflection becomes critical when it has two distinctive purposes. The first is to understand how considerations of power undergird, frame and distort so many educational processes and interactions. The second is to question assumptions and practices that seem to make our teaching lives easier but that actually end up working against our own best long term interests . . . (8)

Community-engagement pedagogies typically emphasize the use of critically reflective writing to help students contextualize and personalize their learning experiences. This commitment to critical reflection extends to the instructor as well.

For over a decade, much of Brooke's teaching has centered on museum-based service-learning projects involving the digital preservation of artifacts and oral history. As Laura Julier, Kathleen Livingston, and Eli Goldblatt explain in their chapter, sustainability is a key challenge for community-engaged writing pedagogies. So in the early years Brooke drew upon the insights of community literacy pioneers such as Linda Flower to pursue a handful of long-term, mutually beneficial relationships. As these partnerships deepened over time, some unexpected challenges emerged. For example, at one museum her partners are so personally committed to the project that they sometimes sacrifice too much of their own time, streamlining work to accommodate the students in ways that protect students from potentially frustrating but pedagogically valuable pitfalls. In a similar vein, the students—and at times Brooke herself—are so deeply invested in the partnership and in the museum's mission that extra scaffolding is needed (such as weekly debriefings, orally and in writing) to help them maintain a critical perspective on the museum's complex role(s) in the community and on their own complex roles as they both narrate and critique the museum's stories (Hessler, "Identification"). Brooke and her students tap into the lore and scholarship of other community-engaged writers to get a sense of how their experiences connect to larger issues of civic identity and discourse.

Pedagogy as a Heuristic to Create New Writing Theory

Just as writing pedagogy is informed and complemented by writing theories, discussions of and experiments with pedagogy can influence our understanding of how writing gets done, by whom, why, with which tools, and so on. Thinking about how writing is learned can shed light into corners of our theories that are not sufficiently explanatory. For example, in the 1960s, as Composition Studies was emerging as a field of study in the United States, we came to acknowledge that writers had processes that were more complicated than our previous, broadly labeled current-traditional pedagogies had made apparent. For about two decades, as they used process approaches in the classroom, scholars sought something like an ideal process that could be taught and would ensure success. Think-aloud protocols and other research conducted with student writers revealed that processes are multiple, flexible, and recursive (e.g., Flower and Hayes). In part because of the field's process pedagogy orientation at the time, our scholarship evolved to suggest that writing is more social than we were even acknowledging, leading to the "social turn" of thought in the field. The cross-pollination of theory and pedagogy is mutually influential.

Pedagogy as a Normalizing and/or Revolutionary Social Force

Pedagogy is also enmeshed in social situations and is a medium (or set of media) for delivering instruction and thereby is on some level the message (*a la* Marshall McLuhan's notion that "the medium is the message"). McLuhan suggests that media are extensions of people that change the "scale or pace or pattern" of human life (24). Pedagogy informs the scale, pace, and pattern of education, which means pedagogy can disrupt or reinforce normative socialization. For example, institutionalized grading of individuals reinforces the prominence of ideas of originality and individual success, which may undermine efforts to train people to work together collaboratively to solve large-scale problems (Rupiper Taggart). Therein lies the dark side of pedagogy that we acknowledge, ways in which pedagogy is defined and even co-opted by institutions, or at the very least ways in which there are unintended consequences of pedagogy put into practice. Karen Fitts suggests that "[P]edagogy is sometimes defined as vigilance against the coercion of pedagogy itself" (170).

USING THE BOOK

With this examination of the term *composition pedagogy* and its uses in mind, the chapters that follow introduce the most important work in the field on each pedagogy, while attempting to offer readers a sense of the spirit of the approach, often through personal teaching narratives. Each chapter is a bibliographic guide written primarily for newcomers to the field, especially graduate students, but also for scholars looking for an overview of pedagogical scholarship in key areas. The pedagogies themselves are categories commonly recognized in the disciplinary scholarship. We envision teacher preparation, composition pedagogy, and even composition theory courses, as well as professional development reading groups, as locations for exploring these chapters.

Each pedagogy is separated out as a category largely in terms of its emphasis and often in terms of how it evolved historically. Choosing from among the approaches can seem daunting upon first glance. In wading through the many good but sometimes conflicting choices among composition pedagogies, Gary Tate provides a simple approach: The pedagogy or pedagogies we choose must respond to the goals we want to achieve in our courses, and those goals depend primarily on "how we construct our students" and their needs.

> If we see students as mute or semiliterate, then we help them find their "voices" so that they can speak out. If we view them as unthinking repositories of largely conservative beliefs, then we might decide to help them learn to critique those beliefs. If we see them as college students who need to be successful in their

majors, then we will probably help them learn to write academic discourse. And so on. (2)

Often an instructor will benefit from reading about and employing pedagogies in combination. For instance, instructors employing a genres-based approach may emphasize rhetorical genres as the key frame for their instruction, but the insights of the researched writing chapter become important partners for teaching about genres informed by research. Many feminist teacher-scholars employ collaborative approaches, as Micciche suggests in her chapter; community-engaged teachers frequently find philosophical grounding in critical pedagogy. Wendy Bishop describes her impulse to combine and test varied pedagogies in this way:

> I do not believe I can have a smorgasbord pedagogy, but I do feel entitled to range widely, as a teaching generalist, as a writing specialist. Then I'm obliged to think systematically about my practice . . . I am obliged to define, refine, name, and explain my practice and to build new knowledge from which to set out again. . . . Writing teachers who get up each day and do their work are doing their work; they do not have to apologize for having values and beliefs, for coming from one section of a field and for moving—perhaps—to another section—from one understanding of instruction to another understanding of it—as long as they are willing to talk, to share, to travel on in company. (75–76)

Readers of this book will start to see affinities among pedagogies and ways that elements of more than one might be productively combined.

SELECTIONS: WHAT'S NEW TO THIS EDITION

As Kenneth Burke said, "[People] seek for vocabularies that will be faithful *reflections* of reality. To this end, they must develop vocabularies that are *selections* of reality. And any selection of reality must, in certain circumstances, function as a *deflection* of reality" (*Grammar* 59). Any list of pedagogies will be necessarily limited and limiting; in bibliographic work, the best we can hope for is a reflection of categories that have come to prominence in this moment in our field. The original *Guide* contained twelve chapters reflecting what we felt were the most prominent clusters of pedagogical thought in Writing Studies at the time; this edition presents seventeen. The proliferation of thought regarding possible approaches to the teaching of writing might seem to signal a lack of agreement. However, we suggest that a range of thought and approach allows us as a field to respond to a range of student and contextual needs and to draw on a range of instructor strengths. Yet we encourage readers to think as they read and conduct pedagogical research about what points of agreement there are underlying these conversations.

Beyond updating the bibliographies to represent the last decade's developments, there were several areas we felt were either missing or underexplored in that first edition. Perhaps most important, we took seriously a reviewer's suggestion that issues related to diversity were not well enough represented. Because each of the pedagogies might be used to teach diverse students or to address issues related to diversity in our culture, we asked all of the authors to consider diversity's presence in the pedagogical literature. We also added a chapter on second language writing, since non-native writers represent a relatively large population in writing classes, with needs and strengths different from those of native writers.

As we rethought the chapter formerly titled "Technology and the Teaching of Writing," we concluded that in 2014 all pedagogies would likely be augmented and enhanced by technologies other than just the computer, from online and database research to content management course shells to new media delivery to collaborative authoring tools. So, while we created a New Media Pedagogies chapter to highlight the exciting work done by the technological specialists in our field and a chapter on Fully Online and Hybrid Writing Instruction to address the particular issues of going more fully online with courses, we also encouraged the authors to consider any discussions scholars were having about the roles of technologies in accomplishing the particular goals of the pedagogy.

A final new area of emphasis in this edition that crosscuts the chapters is the question of assessment. While the assessment research is less connected to pedagogical subfields, the chapter authors were tasked with considering the particulars of assessing writing in these pedagogical areas. If each pedagogy has at least a segment of unique goals, surely there would be implications for assessment. It seems that there is more work to be done in this area.

While all chapters have been significantly updated, several chapters remain the same in terms of title and general focus: Expressive Pedagogy, Collaborative Writing, Cultural Studies and Composition, Critical Pedagogies, Feminist Pedagogies, Writing Across the Curriculum, Writing Center Pedagogy, and Basic Writing. Most of these areas have vibrantly evolved in the ensuing ten-year period.

In his response to the *Guide*'s Rhetorical Pedagogy chapter in the first edition, Richard Fulkerson suggested expanding the presentation of rhetoric from one chapter to three—covering argument, genre, and procedural rhetoric ("Composition in the Twenty-first Century"). Rhetoric informs most chapters in this collection, but we reimagined the original chapter as Rhetoric and Argumentation and added a new chapter on Genre Pedagogies. In his essay on Rhetoric and Argumentation, David Fleming surveys theories and practices of argumentation from classical times through the modern era, introducing major rhetorical frameworks from Aristotle and Isocrates to Kenneth Burke, Stephen Toulmin, and Chaim Perelman. Fleming's chapter culminates with practical suggestions for integrating rhetoric into writing instruction. Amy Devitt's chapter on Genre Pedagogies takes as its leaping-off point the types of writing in the world and how they are used to get things done—genres as windows into the rhetorical situation. Genre-based pedagogy is deeply rhetorical in nature and used increasingly in textbooks and classrooms nationwide, as well as figuring prominently in the discourse of the discipline, connected as it is to scholarship on discourse communities, activity systems, and genre theory.

In the first edition, we included one chapter addressing students with unique needs. In their chapter on Basic Writing Pedagogy, Deborah Mutnick and Steve Lamos situate developmental writing instruction in its historical and social context. They describe how pedagogical goals define the major approaches ("error-centered," "academic initiation," and "critical literacy"), then discuss exemplary programs and address future concerns for teaching basic writers in higher education. Paul Kei Matsuda and Matthew J. Hammill's new chapter on Second Language Writing Pedagogy adds a much needed discussion of the linguistic and cultural challenges that second language writers face, with particular attention to issues of mechanics and source-based writing. The authors provide both strategies for differentiating instruction and additional resources for learning more about how to support language development in the writing classroom.

Expressive Pedagogy and Literature and Composition Pedagogy are noteworthy because they are closely tied to ways many of us originally came to the profession of composition—as passionate writers and readers—and yet both pedagogies have, over time, been contested in our field, as the chapters in this collection indicate. Our professional scholarship distanced itself from expressivism and from the teaching of literature in composition classrooms. That underlying tension was manifested in Burnham's bibliographic essay on expressivist pedagogy in the first edition of our book, where he both explains and defends that pedagogical heritage. Indeed, literature pedagogy was deliberately omitted from the first edition because a too-common practice in the preceding decades was to teach composition classes *as* literature classes, rather than using literature to teach composition; further, there was little scholarly literature that really spoke to using literature in the writing classroom. Even now, this focus is less robust than we might expect given the long relationship between literature and writing rooted in English departments. Both pedagogical approaches continued to be employed widely within composition classrooms despite these debates.

Several chapters in the previous and current edition share a vision for the classroom as a site for social action and change: critical pedagogy, cultural studies approaches, community-engagement, feminist, and even at times basic writing pedagogies. The sociopolitical pedagogies tend to envision writing and language use as always socially enmeshed; therefore, according to many of these thinkers, teaching writing without helping students understand the implications of what the writing does for and to people, how it does it, and how to craft language for social purposes (wide-ranging, not just activist) is central to teaching writing. Laura Micchiche suggests this hopeful, social-change-oriented outlook might be the primary factor uniting feminist pedagogies. Feminist approaches, not just "women's issues" themed approaches, involve questioning, challenging, and seeing the world differently; a feminist teacher may find himself or herself exploring intersections of power, norm, and privilege. Linked originally to social class oppression, critical pedagogies value questioning and even a decentering of authority, and Ann George suggests that the tools of critique so powerful in a critical classroom may even be turned on the teaching itself so it never becomes unquestioned or unquestioning. Community-engagement approaches often seek change or awareness, typically through direct, local action. Laura Julier, Kathleen Livingston, and Eli Goldblatt discuss ways university and community partners are working together, as well as issues that affect the sustainability of those partnerships, such as institutional and individual power relationships, material resources, the physical (and metaphorical) spaces for this work, as well as diverse perspectives on the purposes of community service writing.

At first blush the New Media Pedagogy and Fully Online and Hybrid Writing Instruction chapters are both about the use of technology to teach writing. In the time between the first and second editions, technology has permeated composition pedagogy to such an extent that a chapter *about* the use of technology has become too instrumentalist, too reductive. These new chapters are about the expanded contexts of writing brought about through technology, and also about our expanded sense of what is possible, of what constitutes writing itself. We commissioned Collin Brooke's New Media chapter because we recognized that writing teachers employing new media were not only experimenting with digital tools but also reconceiving the range of media and modalities needed for twenty-first-century writers. To understand how we arrived at this pedagogical frontier, Beth Hewett traces the technologizing of the word from Socratic skepticism to today's networked world in which online writing instruction (OWI) is a natural extension of how we live and learn. Drawing upon her work with the Conference on College Composition and Communication's (CCCC) Committee for Effective Practices in Online Writing Instruction, Hewett explains the building blocks of OWI and offers heuristics to help instructors determine how to begin assembling an OWI pedagogy for their unique context, priorities, and students.

Process has become one of the unspoken foundations of teaching writing. Even when one espouses a feminist or argumentation approach, for instance, it is typical to assign drafts, build in response, structure activities leading up to and beyond a first draft, even engage peers. Thus, the Process Pedagogy and Its Legacy chapter serves a kind of anchoring function for this collection. Process presents familiar, shared territory that we do not want to take for granted and newcomers need to understand; it is the rare teacher today who teaches process without some other operating theory or goal. Chris M. Anson's account of the revolutionary, transformative effect of the process movement provides readers with an idea of just how much process has shaped our disciplinary world.

Because the processes envisioned at the beginnings of Composition Studies largely were individual except for the feedback provided in writing groups, different processes and even theories inform collaboration. As culture shifts, even collaborative processes are moving targets. The shift Krista Kennedy and Rebecca Moore Howard account for in their chapter on collaborative writing pedagogies is the one brought on by new technologies and new media. They suggest collaboration is, to writing studies specialists, the norm for writing, from invention to team writing to peer response, and that the pervasiveness of digital collaboration demands that teachers consider collaborative pedagogies.

Like the writing process, research writing is nearly ubiquitous across composition pedagogies. Rebecca Moore Howard and Sandra Jamieson review scholarship that makes the traditional library research paper seem as antiquated as the five-paragraph essay. Synthesizing information literacy scholarship with what we know about how students *really* use sources, Howard and Jamieson enable us to begin considering how inquiry-based writing can and should be taught in the information age.

Two chapters address writing instruction that happens outside the composition classroom. Writing centers and Writing Across the Curriculum programs often work in tandem as a kind of writing co-curriculum to support writers and teachers of writing in all disciplines. Neal Lerner (Writing Center Pedagogy) explains how writing centers provide a unique, facilitative learning space for students to develop as writers with the guidance of peer tutors and professional consultants. Lerner describes tutoring pedagogy and explains how the writing center can be a site for classroom faculty to learn more about how students really write and how to help them one-on-one. In their chapter on Writing Across the Curriculum, Chris Thaiss and Susan McLeod explain how "writing to learn" and "writing to communicate" pedagogies can support literacy development in writing classes across the disciplines. Of special importance to composition teachers, Thaiss and McLeod examine intersections between first-year writing (FYW) and trends in technology, internationalization, advanced writing courses, and writing beyond college.

DEFLECTIONS: WHAT'S NOT INCLUDED (YET)

What, then, got deflected in this edition? While there are likely many other things that have fallen through the cracks of our schema in this edition, there are two chapters we carefully considered, debated including, and asked reviewers to weigh as possibilities that did not make the final cut in this edition: Writing about Writing (WaW) and multimodal pedagogies. We feel strongly about the importance of discussion in both of these areas but ultimately decided not to devote whole chapters to them in this edition.

Writing about Writing, advocated in Downs and Wardle's *CCC* article and follow-on textbook (Wardle and Downs), reconstitutes FYW as an "introduction to writing studies." Writing about Writing is less a pedagogy than a curriculum that employs scholarship about writing as the subject matter of the course and the research methods of the field as ways to help issue students into the work of Writing Studies. Proponents argue that course readings prompt student metacognition about writing, with the added bonus of providing a means of professional development for grad students or faculty with less background in Composition Studies. Though popular enough to prompt a CCCC Special Interest Group, WaW is still so fresh that we lack enough scholarship on its success to devote a full bibliographic chapter. Potentially, though, WaW offers one promising answer to post-process critiques, as Anson indicates in the Process Pedagogy and Its Legacy chapter, and may also provide a good model for core courses in a writing major. We anticipate that if this book has a third edition, WaW will likely be a chapter.

Likewise, we foresee a future stand-alone chapter on multimodal pedagogies. Multimodal composition, in some regards, has existed as long as visual rhetoric itself as a subject of rhetorical instruction; however, as an identifiable composition pedagogy around which scholarship clusters it is comparatively recent. Multimodal pedagogies take as central to their purpose teaching students to produce "texts that exceed the alphabetic and may include still and moving images, animations, color, words, music and sound" (Takayoshi and Selfe 1). Although the use of digital media is not essential for the production of multimodal texts, many teachers experimenting with multimodality gravitate to digitally generated end products, such as audiovisual essays and the various social media projects (e.g., blogs, YouTube videos, digital activism) increasingly appearing in composition textbooks. The popularity and visibility of such projects are perhaps why the terms *multimodal* and *multimedia* are sometimes conflated. Recent scholarship is working to clarify multimodal composition as a matter of process (and cognition) as well as product, of pedagogical perspective as well as praxis, and of media that are physical as well as digital (see, e.g., Fleckenstein; Lutkewitte; National Council of Teachers of English; Palmeri). In the present edition, several authors discuss the evolving presence of multimodal composition in our field—in particular, Collin Brooke ("New Media Pedagogy") and Diana George, Tim Lockridge, and John Trimbur ("Cultural Studies and Composition"). Readers will observe multimodal principles and practices in many of the pedagogies featured in this collection.

CONCLUSIONS

Composition Studies distinctly emphasizes pedagogy, perhaps more than any discipline outside of colleges of education. We publish about pedagogy, build careers around the pursuit of pedagogical knowledge, host conferences focused in large part on issues of teaching and learning, and take up the work of training future generations of teacher-scholars in our graduate curricula. We have even made arguments, through such organizations as the Council of Writing Program Administrators, that program administration, curriculum reform, and assessment should be considered as "intellectual labor" akin if not equivalent to conventional scholarship. The hard sciences, social sciences, humanities, arts—even applied disciplines such as engineering and business—focus on producing specialized knowledge first, then teaching that knowledge to students. Though we all have colleagues across the disciplines who are exceptional teachers, and though faculty conduct scholarship of teaching and learning (SoTL) in other departments, we have noted in our interactions with colleagues across campus and at SoTL conferences that our pedagogical expertise is somewhat unusual and that knowledge about teaching and learning we virtually take for granted seems very new to others.

Our attention to pedagogy seems to come from a number of sources, the first of which is history. Worldwide, the teaching of writing and the scholarly specialization in Writing Studies remains concentrated in English-speaking countries, mostly heavily in the United States. The process movement and the emergence of the Conference on College Composition and Communication as a place for people to talk about teaching shaped a distinctive historical trajectory. Further, the field's desire to become a legitimate scholarly field like others in higher education led to the development of serious pedagogical scholarship involving theoretical and qualitative methods and even empirical research. The goals of our courses have also influenced this unusual focus on pedagogy. While many fields convey their subject matter first *before* asking students to generate new knowledge, composition classes typically aim for young scholars to create new understandings for themselves by practicing writing and critical thinking—not simply as a means for them to do well in their majors (though that's certainly part of what happens) but as complex modes of making sense of the world and communicating that sense to others. Thus, though Writing Studies clearly teaches a body of knowledge, many of us agree that much learning about writing must come through experience, practice, and something that looks more like apprenticeship.

So, yes, we value pedagogy and give it a kind of attention one might expect only from educational specialists, because we believe it must be learned at least in part through practice and because we learn so much about writing from studying developing writers in action. We are not certain that pedagogy always makes us better teachers. But it helps us become more self-aware teachers, able to situate our practices and understand what else exists, and why. We share Berlin's commitment to continuous improvement, because "Not doing so can have disastrous consequences, ranging from momentarily confusing students to sending them away with faulty and even harmful information" (234–235). Teaching is hard enough with good role models and operating principles to inform practice. We hope the chapters that follow will guide readers to rhetorically sensitive, philosophically grounded, experientially (and experimentally) tested practices.

SUMMARY OF CHANGES TO THE SECOND EDITION

- The new introduction to the collection defines the central term *composition pedagogy* in depth to provide a disciplinary frame for the rest of the chapters and for readers new to the field of Composition Studies.
- Throughout the collection, contributing authors have given increased attention to issues of diversity in the classroom and to the assessment of teaching and learning.
- All of the original chapters retained in the collection (Basic Writing Pedagogy, Critical Pedagogies, Collaborative Writing, Community-engaged Pedagogies, Cultural Studies and Composition, Expressive Pedagogy, Feminist Pedagogies, Process Pedagogy and Its Legacy, Writing Across the Curriculum, and Writing Center Pedagogy) have been revised and their bibliographies updated.
- Three of those chapters (Feminist Pedagogies, Process Pedagogy and Its Legacy, and Writing Center Pedagogy) have been completely rewritten by new authors.
- The original chapter on Technology and the Teaching of Writing has been removed, and that subject has been distributed across all chapters, with more in-depth coverage in the chapters on New Media Pedagogy and Fully Online and Hybrid Writing Instruction.

- The original chapter on Rhetorical Pedagogy has been split into two new chapters, written by new authors: Genre Pedagogies and Rhetoric and Argumentation.
- New chapters on Literature and Composition, New Media Pedagogy, Fully Online and Hybrid Writing Instruction, Researched Writing, and Second Language Writing Pedagogy have been added.

BIBLIOGRAPHY

Anson, Chris M. "The Intelligent Design of Writing Programs: Reliance on Belief or a Future of Evidence." *WPA: Writing Program Administration* 32.1 (2008): 11–36. Print.

Berlin, James A. "Contemporary Composition: The Major Pedagogical Theories." *College English* 44.8 (1982): 765–77. Rpt. in *Cross-talk in Comp Theory*. Ed. Victor Villanueva. Urbana: National Council of Teachers of English, 1997. 233–48. Print.

Bishop, Wendy. "Teaching Composition Is (Still) Mostly about Teaching Composition." *Composition Studies in the New Millennium: Rereading the Past, Rewriting the Future.* Ed. Lynn Z. Bloom, Donald A. Daiker, and Edward M. White. Carbondale: Southern Illinois UP, 2003. 65–77. Print.

Boyer, Ernest. *Scholarship Reconsidered: Priorities of the Professoriate.* Princeton: Carnegie Foundation for the Advancement of Teaching. 1990. Print.

Brookfield, Stephen D. *Becoming a Critically Reflective Practitioner.* San Francisco: Jossey-Bass, 1995. Print.

Burke, Kenneth. *Grammar of Motives.* 1945. Berkeley: U of California P, 1969. Print.

Council of Writing Program Administrators. *Evaluating the Intellectual Work of Writing Administrators.* WPA, 1998. Web. 23 May 2013.

Dewey, John. *Experience and Education.* 1938. New York: Collier MacMillan, 1963. Print.

Downs, Doug, and Elizabeth Wardle. "Teaching about Writing, Righting Misconceptions: (Re)Envisioning 'First-Year Composition' as 'Introduction to Writing Studies.'" *College Composition and Communication* 58.4 (2007): 552–84. Print.

Elbow, Peter. "The Doubting Game and the Believing Game: An Analysis of the Intellectual Process." *Writing without Teachers.* New York: Oxford UP, 1973. 147–91. Print.

Ferreira-Buckley, Linda. "Pedagogy." *The Encyclopedia of Rhetoric and Composition: Communication from Ancient Times to the Information Age.* Ed. Theresa Enos. New York: Garland, 1996. 495–96. Print.

Fitts, Karen. "Pedagogy." *Keywords in Composition Studies.* Ed. Paul Heilker and Peter Vandenberg. Portsmouth: Boynton/Cook Heinemann. 1996. 168–72. Print.

Fleckenstein, Kristie S. *Vision, Rhetoric, and Social Action in the Composition Classroom.* Carbondale: Southern Illinois UP, 2009. Print.

Flower, Linda. "Intercultural Inquiry and the Transformation of Service." *College English* 65.2 (Nov. 2002): 181–201. Print.

———— and John Hayes. "A Cognitive Process Theory of Writing." *College Composition and Communication* 32.4 (1981): 365–87. Print.

Fulkerson, Richard. "Composition at the Turn of the Twenty-First Century." *College Composition and Communication* 56.4 (June 2005): 654–87. Print.

Gee, James. "Literacy, Discourse, and Linguistics: Introduction." *Journal of Education* 171.1 (1989): 5–17. Print.

Hessler, H. Brooke. "Identification as Civic Literacy in Digital Museum Projects." *Community Literacy Journal* 6.1 (Fall 2011): 23–37. Print.

Kameen, Paul. "Rewording the Rhetoric of Composition." *Pre/Text* 1-2 (1980): 73-92. Print.

Kolb, David A. *Experiential Learning: Experience as a Source of Learning and Development.* Englewood Cliffs: Prentice Hall, 1984. Print.

Lutkewitte, Claire, ed. *Multimodal Composition: A Critical Sourcebook.* Boston: Bedford/ St. Martin's, 2013. Print.

McLuhan, Marshall. "The Medium Is the Message." *Understanding Media: The Extensions of Man.* New York: Signet. 1964. Print.

Miller, Carolyn R. "Genre as Social Action." *Quarterly Journal of Speech* 70.2 (1984): 151–76. Print.

Myers, Nancy. "The Slave of Pedagogy: Composition Studies and the Art of Teaching." *Teaching Writing: Landmarks and Horizons.* Ed. Christina Russell McDonald and Robert L. McDonald. Carbondale: Southern Illinois UP, 2002. 155–70. Print.

National Council of Teachers of English. *NCTE Position Statement on Multimodal Literacies.* National Council of Teachers of English, 2005. Web. 1 May 2013.

Palmeri, Jason. *Remixing Composition: A History of Multimodal Writing Pedagogy.* Carbondale: Southern Illinois UP, 2012. Print.

"pedagogy." *The Oxford English Dictionary.* Oxford UP, 2012. Web. 23 May 2013.

Rupiper Taggart, Amy. "One or Many? Tensions with Authorship and Evaluation in Community Engagement Writing." *Michigan Journal of Community Service Learning.* 13.2 (2007): 54–65.

Takayoshi, Pamela, and Cynthia L. Selfe. "Thinking about Multimodality." *Multimodal Composition: Resources for Teachers.* Hampton, 2007. 1–12. Web. 23 May 2013.

Tate, Gary. "The Primary Site of Contention in Teaching Composition" *Teaching Composition in the 90s: Sites of Contention.* Ed. Christina G. Russell & Robert L. McDonald. New York: Harper Collins, 1994. 1–7. Print.

_____, Amy Rupiper, and Kurt Schick, eds. *A Guide to Composition Pedagogies.* New York: Oxford UP, 2001. Print.

Wardle, Elizabeth, and Doug Downs. *Writing about Writing: A College Reader.* Boston: Bedford/St. Martin's, 2011. Print.

✒

Basic Writing Pedagogy
Shifting Academic Margins in Hard Times

Deborah Mutnick
Steve Lamos

More than a decade ago, the pressures on four-year colleges to jettison basic writing (BW) courses and programs were clearly evident. In 1999, the City University of New York ended its historic open admissions policy and raised admissions standards. In 2001, the U.S. Congress passed the No Child Left Behind Act, ushering in a new era of federal K-12 regulations tied to standardized testing, a phenomenon that has affected a generation of college students and haunted higher education's assessment practices ever since. In October 2008, the economic crash and recession that followed resulted in slashed budgets in higher education, especially remedial programs. Meanwhile, the student debt bubble threatens to burst, tuition costs soar, and nearly half of recent college graduates are jobless or underemployed (Weissman).

Though part of a longer history of remedial writing instruction for students considered unprepared for college (Berlin; Stanley; Ritter), BW *per se* emerged in the 1970s in response to militant student demands for equal access to higher education. Like the Morrill Land Grant Acts in the late nineteenth century and the G.I. Bill after World War II, open admissions significantly expanded access to colleges and universities; and like those earlier chapters in American higher education, open admissions was driven by economic as well as social exigencies. As Deborah Brandt contends, such policies reflect the economic sponsorship of literacy in response to rising needs for an educated managerial class and workforce in a rapidly industrializing (and de-industrializing) society. In addition to seeing BW as a democratizing force, we understand it as a particular form of remedial education institutionalized in response to economic interests at the end of the postwar economic boom, just as its current contraction comes in the midst of a global recession precipitated by a neoliberal agenda of privatization, deregulation, and austerity.

Throughout the relatively brief history of BW, many teachers—ourselves included—have felt inspired by its capacity to foster literacy learning through what Paulo Freire called "critical consciousness," and we have positioned ourselves with our students on the academic margins. That task is harder now because the margins have shifted and, increasingly, students who might have been placed into BW prior to 1999 are denied access to four-year and even some community colleges. Others who gain admission but have shaky literacy skills may not be identified and supported due to cutbacks affecting programs and services such as writing centers (Greene and McAlexander). Complicating these shifting margins is the impact of persistent racial discrimination and class inequalities on the demographics of higher education (Fox; Lamos; Mutnick, *Writing*). By situating this guide to teaching basic writing in a historical context, we aim to provide a compass for the pedagogical approaches outlined herein. As we move from one approach to another, it will help to bear in mind our final destination, a pedagogy that imbues in students the ability "1) *to understand* first of all, 2) *to interpret* that understanding, and 3) *to apply* the knowledge gained in the act of reflexivity . . . to the subject matter under investigation and to life experiences" (Salvatori 139).

As a teacher of BW students, you are likely to encounter tremendous diversity in terms of race, ethnicity, class, nationality, language, age, and degree of preparation; you will grapple not only with student error but also with perennial questions about "why Johnny can't write"; and you will work amid loudly buzzing media and political complaints about the ineffectiveness of the whole enterprise. Along with these likely scenarios, we want to foreground several key principles and practices that we think cut across various approaches to teaching BW:

1. Assume students can learn and deserve to be engaged in serious intellectual activities and curricula, not skill-and-drill-based "remediation."
2. Engage in "extra" student-centered work—whether in the form of time, conferences, feedback, or other related scaffolding techniques.
3. Address "higher-order" issues of argumentation, evidence, and analysis alongside "lower-order" issues of grammar, style, syntax, and punctuation.
4. Integrate academic writing *and* reading instruction.
5. Value the inevitable tension between acknowledging what students "*already* know" and trying to "move them to what they *need* to know." (Smitherman 219)

KEY APPROACHES TO TEACHING BW

We suggest there are four major BW pedagogical approaches that correspond with some of the field's most important theoretical shifts since its emergence: (1) error-centered approaches, (2) academic initiation approaches, (3) critical literacy approaches, and (4) and spatial approaches that rearrange the locus of instruction. Throughout, we wish to emphasize that these approaches operate on uneven, circular tracks rather than linearly or unilaterally, leaving individual programs and practitioners to sort out the contradictions and develop local responses that meet students' needs in specific institutional contexts. For example, BW faculty—ourselves included—may agree with critiques of dominant cultural discourses and honor the multiple literacies students bring to college yet still insist that they compose relatively error-free, Standard Written English for particular purposes and audiences.

"The Logic of Error": Error-Centered Approaches

What we will be calling "error-centered" approaches to BW, largely influenced by pioneering BW scholar Mina Shaughnessy's theory of "the logic of error" (*Errors*), became especially common throughout the 1970s and early 1980s. These approaches arose from concerns that universities needed to serve "new" students from different racial, cultural, linguistic, and/or class backgrounds, enrolling in record numbers through programs like Open Admissions (Shaughnessy, "Open Admissions"). They also arose in reaction to the argument advanced in mainstream media that these students' poor literacy skills deemed them uneducable and undeserving of a college education. In this respect, error-focused approaches had egalitarian origins: All students *could* be and *should* be taught to write Standard Written English, viewed as normative and neutral rather than ideological and culturally biased—at least, once teachers and scholars came to understand the logic of writers' errors.

Error-focused approaches tend to define the BW student as someone who lacks familiarity with the linguistic and/or cognitive processes necessary for successful academic writing: From this perspective, the BW student is a "novice" or "beginner." For Shaughnessy and those influenced by her (Bartholomae, "Study"; Hull; Lunsford, "What" and "Cognitive"; Perl; Sommers), this beginner's status was a function of linguistic inexperience in adult learners whose errors resulted from a mixture of "[v]ariant and standard forms as if [they] had half-learned two inflectional systems" (*Errors* 10), indicating not dialect interference or vernacular speech but hybrid codes in the writer's attempt to appear literate. This same insight led subsequent theorists to view such hybridity as an "interlanguage" in the appropriation of academic discourse (Bartholomae, "Study"; Horning). Shaughnessy asserts, "BW students write the way that they do, not because they are slow or nonverbal, indifferent to or incapable of academic excellence, but because they are beginners and must, like all beginners, learn by making mistakes" (*Errors* 5).

Error-centered approaches further assume that BW is best defined by "errors" that underprepared adult students typically make as they acquire academic discourse. For Shaughnessy, these errors are best imagined as "unintentional and unprofitable intrusions upon the consciousness of the reader . . . [that] demand energy without giving any return in meaning; they shift the reader's attention away from where he is going (meaning) to how he is getting there (code)" (*Errors* 12). Here Shaughnessy argues that errors represent the writer's attempt to systematize language, to approximate the standard written code in the absence of adequate instruction and practice—thereby revealing error to be logical, a sign of intention and intelligence as the writer gropes for conventional forms. Also notable is Shaughnessy's focus on errors at the surface level of discourse—manifest in unclear sentence boundaries (for example, run-ons), garbled syntax, and incoherent paragraphs—rather than on invention, argumentation, and/or the larger writing processes of drafting and revising.

Finally, error-centered pedagogical approaches are rooted in "error analysis" (Bartholomae, "Study"; Hull), which posits that the BW teacher should focus on students' actual prose rather than "skill-and-drill" exercises (Hull 220). Succinctly summing up this approach, Glynda Hull asserts first that teachers should help students identify patterns of error by making them "as salient as possible by grouping all errors of a general kind together in order to represent them as instances of the same problem" (219). Second, teachers should work closely with students, especially through one-on-one or small group conferencing, to identify and practice correcting these patterns (219–20). Third, teachers should encourage students to engage in extensive analysis of their own writing in order to gain practice in error correction (220).

Error-centered approaches thus clearly advocate responding to students' actual writing to promote critical thinking and self-sufficiency. And these approaches continue to influence some contemporary methods aimed at helping students learn grammatical conventions (Blaauw-Hara; Dawkins; Robinson; Wichman). But they have also rightly been criticized in the decades since their ascendancy for reproducing dominant cultural discourses that take a reductive, uncritical, acontextual, arhetorical, and/or apolitical approach to notions of error (Gay; Lu, "Conflict"; Rose, "Narrowing"; Rouse), and thus must be complemented by the contextual and political awareness embedded in other, more critical approaches.

"Inventing the University": Academic Initiation Approaches

Academic initiation approaches to BW arose as the academy underwent a "social turn" in the mid-1980s and remained popular through the 1990s. Generally speaking, these approaches postulate that BW ought to be less defined by linguistic or cognitive views of error, and more by discourse theories. Central to academic-initiation approaches is the idea that BW students ought to be held to the same rigorous expectations and standards as "regular" students in the work they are asked to produce so that BW can "easily be imagined as an honors course and not a remedial or developmental one" (Bartholomae and Petrosky 1). These approaches typically integrate writing *and* reading, which are seen as interrelated, mutually reinforcing processes (Bartholomae and Petrosky; Horning; Jolliffe and Harl).

In general, academic-initiation theorists view BW students as unfamiliar with the conventions and expectations of academic discourse. David Bartholomae makes this point in his 1985 essay "Inventing the University" when he argues that the BW student

> has to appropriate (or be appropriated by) a specialized discourse, and he has to do this as though he were easily and comfortably one with his audience, as though he were a member of the academy or an historian or an anthropologist or an economist; he has to invent the university by assembling or mimicking its language while finding some compromise between idiosyncrasy, a personal history, on the one hand, and the requirements of convention, the history of a discipline, on the other. He must learn to speak our language. . . . And this, understandably, causes problems. (135)

For Bartholomae, the BW student has not yet "invented" herself as a student in ways recognizable to the larger academy. Her sentence-level "errors"—less a function of linguistic or cognitive immaturity than of a lack of academic socialization—are thus likely to fade once she comprehends the expectations of an academic audience.

Initiation theorists thus define BW by its unfamiliarity with academic expectations and conventions rather than the presence of sentence-level errors. While error still matters to advocates of this approach, the main concern is with sophisticated critical thinking and argumentation. One clear example appears in Bartholomae's discussion of the "White Shoes" essay in "Inventing the University." Commenting on a student football player's placement essay on the nature of "creativity," Bartholomae suggests that, on first glance, the essay's argument seems "seamless [and] tidy" while its prose seems both "natural [and] smooth" (150). But this tidiness is also why Bartholomae ultimately characterizes the essay as "basic": It remains content merely to rehearse cultural commonplaces about creativity—that is, to "'place' an example within a standard system of belief" (150)—rather than engage substantively with academic questions or present critical academic viewpoints. In this sense, Bartholomae declares that BW can seem "correct" at the level of the sentence yet still fail to demonstrate academic ways of knowing effectively.

Finally, academic initiation approaches tend to promote pedagogies that lead students through three overlapping stages: first, writing about issues more familiar to them (for example, personal experience); second, engaging in summary, analysis, and critique of scholarly or literary texts related to these familiar issues; and third, synthesizing personal and academic perspectives into novel academic arguments. One especially well-known version of this pedagogy is presented in David Bartholomae and Anthony Petrosky's *Facts, Artifacts, and Counterfacts*. During the course of a semester focused on the theme "Growth and Change in Adolescence" (48), the authors assign a series of early essays based on students' own understandings of and experience with adolescence. They ask students to engage in substantive reading and writing about the topic and then, through a series of tasks, to synthesize personal and academic understandings into a research project (8). In so doing, Bartholomae and Petrosky ask students to transform the "facts" of the "materials we put before them, the terms and imaginative structures that could make that material available . . . [and] the institutional context in which they are required to speak and to write" into "artifacts—student papers and performances," all the while stressing "'counterfactuality,' the motive to alter those artifacts, to reject their apparent inevitability" (8). This transformation, they insist, helps students "reimagine themselves as readers and writers" in the academy (8).

These various processes of comprehension, interpretation, and application are seen as fundamental to academic-initiation approaches in BW: They help students work from experience through academic analysis toward synthesis, thereby affording greater access to academic ways of knowing. Certainly, the basic thrust of these approaches continues to influence contemporary pedagogies that, for instance, engage students in sustained and systematic work with academic writing and reading activities of increasing difficulty during the course of a semester

(Horning; Jolliffe and Harl). But it is also true that these approaches have been critiqued, both by later critical scholars (Lu, "Conflict" and "Professing") and by some initiation advocates themselves (Bartholomae, "Tidy") for viewing academic communities and discourses as fixed, static entities to which the student must adapt rather than questioning how the institution itself is produced by asymmetrical power relations that regulate writing and literacy instruction and reinforce oppressive or stereotypical attitudes and ideologies. Contemporary versions of these pedagogies must therefore take issues of context and politics into greater account than earlier versions did.

Critical Approaches to BW Instruction

Critical approaches to BW instruction—here we mean "critical" in the sense of being grounded in sociocultural critique and invested in understanding and re-forming unjust relations of power and privilege—became especially prominent in the late 1980s and early 1990s. Many such approaches draw on theories of border crossing and "contact zone" pedagogies to conceptualize BW pedagogy at the intersection of cultures that "meet, clash, and grapple with each other, often in contexts of highly asymmetrical relations of power" (Pratt 34). Others highlight New Literacy Studies' focus on the relationship between literacy and power (e.g., Carter). What unites these approaches is a belief that the discipline has paid inadequate attention to the social and political contexts of BW, the "conflict and struggle" that Min-Zhan Lu associates with BW ("Conflict" 887), and the "psychic woe" (904) it routinely causes for students.

In general, critical approaches conceive of the BW student as having been marginalized by mainstream societal exclusions and inequalities with respect to race, class, gender, sexuality, language, and culture. Lu argues, for example, that basic writers are likely to be defined as "'beginners' or 'outsiders'" ("Professing Multiculturalism" 448) as a function of "sources well beyond the classroom—coming from unequal power relationships pervading the history, culture, and society [that] students live in" (448). Shannon Carter similarly contends that BW students are often labeled by problematic testing regimes requiring little more than "responses to a generic writing prompt and multiple-choice questions about grammar and usage" (3). Historically, she argues, these tests have "indicated little more than the darker color of our students' skin and the lower socioeconomic status of their caretakers" (4).

Relatedly, proponents of these approaches look beyond "errors" in BW texts to examine social contexts and dynamics involved in all communication. Bruce Horner, for example, argues that BW is often judged by a culture that views error "not as social but as individual, evidence of an individual writer's cognitive or perceptual difficulties" (139). He suggests that BW instruction should redefine error(s) as "flawed social transactions, instances of a failure on the part of *both* the writer and reader to negotiate an agreement . . . as to the kind of significance to be attributed to the written notations offered" (141). Tom Fox similarly notes that the writing generated by his BW students, especially those of color, tends to be judged in terms of its purported "linguistic or academic deficit" (63). However, while acknowledging that his students' "basic" texts can feature misspellings and "idiosyncratic punctuation" (68), he insists that they also frequently reveal their authors' abilities to "use literacy to reflect on and gain wisdom from complex experiences" (68).

Lastly, the pedagogies associated with critical approaches tend to redefine BW by recasting students' extant skills and abilities as critical strengths rather than deficits to be overcome. One important example of this appears in Lu's essay "Professing Multiculturalism" with her story of a Malaysian student whose use of the verb phrase "can able to" demonstrates the semantic intention—the Chinese translation of "can" and "able" is the same—underlying what appears to be a simple ESL error. Lu leads her class through a careful explication of this purported error, touching on various definitions of the words in English and Chinese, cultural concepts of ability and agency, and the student's intentions in writing this particular phrase. Lu concludes that, although the student ultimately chose to rewrite the phrase in "standard" English, this pedagogical exercise "broadens students' sense of the range of options and choices facing a writer" (457).

Centrally important to critical approaches to BW, then, is the idea that students' "outsider" status in the academy can be used as a source of strength in the classroom. These approaches resonate with the work of New Literacy Studies (NLS) theorists like James Paul Gee and Brian Street, who assert that literacy is always ideological, local, and inflected by specific historical and social circumstances as opposed to being universal, natural, and normative. Gee makes a useful distinction between primary discourse—the discourse we all get "free" into which we are born—and secondary discourses which we acquire mainly through practice in natural settings and which include languages of the street, church, and gangs as well as professions and academic disciplines (22). According to NLS, basic writing instructors should recognize students' intellectual capacity and existing knowledge of secondary discourses, encourage the application of this knowledge to the acquisition of new discourses, including academic literacies, and foster the ability to stand outside a discourse and critique it.

Importantly, however, these critical approaches have been subject to the charge that they are overly concerned with politics and not enough with day-to-day writing instruction. Maxine Hairston famously characterized this tendency as putting "dogma before diversity, politics before craft, ideology before critical thinking, and the social goals of the teacher before the educational goals of the student" (180). Others have argued that critical approaches can, at times, ignore students' need to acquire status discourses and their related goods and privileges (Delpit; Gilyard). Those who adopt contemporary critical pedagogies should thus be prepared to explain how their approach allows students to engage with political issues free of constraints imposed by their teachers' particular beliefs and values as well as to acquire, albeit critically, certain types of mainstream-sanctioned secondary discourses (see also George, Lockridge, and Trimbur, this volume).

Spatial Approaches to BW Instruction
A final set of approaches, which we call "spatial," focuses most directly on where the work of BW should or can take place and what that location's impact would be.

In this sense, these spatial approaches combine some of the interests of the aforementioned critical approaches to BW with an explicit focus on the dynamics through which pedagogical and institutional spaces are constructed and operate, both literally and metaphorically. An understanding of these spaces is often inflected by work in critical geography (Grego and Thompson; Reynolds).

Bartholomae helped to initiate spatial approaches to BW through his controversial keynote speech, "The Tidy House: Basic Writing in the American Curriculum," at the 1992 Conference on Basic Writing, and these approaches continued to gain prominence in BW scholarship during the "mainstreaming" debates of the early 1990s (McNenny). Bartholomae declared that, by the early 1990s, the traditional spaces of BW had begun to reify rather than contest "a tidy distinction between basic and mainstream" (8); hence, BW was marginalizing the very students it purported to help. Bartholomae further asserted that traditional BW programs should be carefully replaced with new programs that require all students, "basic" or "mainstream," to attend to the dynamics of the contact zone, thereby connecting the critical and the spatial contexts of teaching and learning. Bartholomae's initial comments met with resistance from critics like Karen Greenberg, who worried that support offered by BW—already under attack by university boards of trustees and elected officials for entirely different reasons, namely, to raise standards and deny access to underprepared students—would be lost if programs were dismantled. But Bartholomae's critiques were echoed and extended by other "abolitionists" like Ira Shor, who called for the immediate dissolution of BW, arguing that it was a clear tool of oppression—indeed, a type of "academic apartheid" (91).

In general, proponents of spatial approaches stress that both BW students and their writing have been constructed in negative ways by power structures of traditional BW courses and institutional configurations. For example, Bartholomae argues that BW students have been directly "produced by" the BW traditional classroom and its attendant desire to "enforce a commonness among our students by making the differences [between them] superficial, surface-level, and by designing a curriculum to both insure them and erase them in 14 weeks" ("Tidy" 12). Rhonda Grego and Nancy Thompson agree, positing that BW students have been frequently been marginalized by problematic practices within traditional BW spaces, including standardized testing regimes, placement mechanisms, and educational histories; for these authors, basic writers are defined by "institutional politics, preferences, and power relations" (5).

Proponents of spatial approaches stress, consequently, that we need to imagine and implement new forms of BW space. For Bartholomae, this move would replace traditional BW courses with new courses in which the contact zone is simultaneously a theory and a method for instruction. His ideal reformulated BW space offers "classes with a variety of supports for those who need them . . . [in which] the difference in students' writing becomes the subject of the course," producing "a course in 'multiculturalism' that work[s] with the various cultures represented in the practice of its students" (14). For Grego and Thompson, the ideal reformulated BW space is a studio environment in which students meet weekly in small groups to discuss assignments in "regular" first-year courses, offer peer review of one another's work, and otherwise address the demands of

academia. Rather than provide a curriculum of its own, the studio makes supporting students' work in other classes its primary goal, ensuring that the "students and
their work, not any course instructor's plan, provide the 'curriculum' of the studio
sessions" (10). Grego and Thompson thus invite students to engage in metacognitive reflection on assignments from others' classes, critically highlighting the
larger institutional contexts in which such work is done: this encourages "third-
space" analysis of writing and writing instruction designed to cultivate a "height-
ened awareness of the institutional power relations that define not only 'BW' but
also 'student writing'" (Grego and Thompson 5).

Since the early 1990s, spatial approaches have yielded several important new
forms of BW instruction: "Studio" (Grego and Thompson; Tassoni and Lewiecki-
Wilson), "Stretch" (Glau); "Supplemental Writing Workshop" (Rigolino and
Freel); "Accelerated Learning Program" (Adams, Gearhart, Miller, and Roberts);
service-learning models (Davi); and others (Gleason; Lalicker; Soliday). One
especially intriguing, recent spatial innovation is the Accelerated Learning
Program (ALP), spearheaded by Peter Adams at the Community College of
Baltimore County. Through ALP, students who place into upper-level developmental writing enroll in English 101 sections with a slightly higher proportion of
mainstream learners. To receive additional support, ALP learners also take a
smaller, companion workshop taught by the same instructor. The ALP model is
important for several reasons: First, preliminary findings indicate that it reduces
attrition by half and improves timely graduation rates (Adams et al. 64); second,
it reduces cost-per-successful-student (64), crucially important in combating
perceptions about the high cost of BW in a period of increasingly scarce resources;
and third, it is gaining traction nationwide with more than eighty schools imple-
menting some form of it (Adams, personal communication). Given these significant gains, and in light of its growing popularity, we see ALP as signaling a new,
promising direction for BW.

Overall, spatial approaches to BW display a profound concern with the
"wheres" and "hows" of literacy instruction. Teachers who share this concern aim
in some cases to alter the conditions in which BW students learn by shifting the
physical and/or curricular location of instruction and in others to focus on
metaphorical spaces of unjust, institutionalized power relations that marginalize
these students as an explicit topic of instruction and critical analysis. But we
also stress that these approaches have been critiqued for, at times, threatening to
eliminate long-standing BW spaces without regard for the potential impact on
students (Greenberg; Mutnick, "Strategic"). Contemporary proponents of spatial
approaches, then, must take care to balance attention to critical spatial theories
with attention to the historical role of BW programs and the potential impact of
their loss on the students they serve.

CURRENT AND FUTURE ISSUES IN BW PEDAGOGY

We conclude this chapter by noting several contemporary issues and trends
(Bernstein; Glau and Duttagupta; Stahl and Boylan) that we believe are most likely

to affect BW pedagogy in the foreseeable future. Three trends strike us as particularly important to follow: the need for BW assessment, both of programs and of students; the adoption of "translanguaging" pedagogies in response to increasing cultural and linguistic diversity in the classroom; and the impact of digital technology on BW instruction.

Issue 1: The Need for BW Assessment

As previously mentioned, BW spaces are currently disappearing at a rapid rate: College and university budgets are being cut, the public is clamoring for more "accountability" and "standards," the winds of anti-remediation are blowing at gale force, and the future not only of BW but (far more important) of the students it has served very much seems in jeopardy. We feel strongly that these pressures prompt all of us, whether BW newbies or veterans, to engage in careful assessment and documentation of the crucially important contemporary work of BW in ways administrators and other stakeholders can understand and support.

A first important strain of assessment in BW involves our efforts to measure and characterize students' growth and development as writers. Such measurement and characterization should reflect our five aforementioned principles and practices: challenging students with serious work, providing them with enough support to accomplish this work successfully, helping them attend to both higher-order and lower-order issues, engaging them in both academic writing and reading, and enabling them to cultivate their extant skills while fostering new ones. Assessing individual students will also depend on which approaches or combinations thereof we adopt: error-centered approaches will likely emphasize (or, if we aren't careful, overemphasize) grammatical "correctness"; academic initiation approaches may attend to form or genre; critical approaches may stress promoting awareness of power relationships; and so on. Whatever approach one adopts, we think it wise to follow Paul Kei Matsuda and Matthew J. Hammill's advice in this volume—namely, that assessment of students' writing ought "to be proportional to the amount of attention" we pay to those same issues in our courses. In other words, our assessment practices ought to reflect what we explicitly attempt to teach rather than some mythical "standard" that we assume students should meet.

A second important strain of BW assessment attempts to integrate course- and program-level measures of student success with increasingly ubiquitous institutional and governmental calls for accountability in higher education. This shift in how accrediting bodies evaluate institutions focuses on learning outcomes and teaching effectiveness. Fortunately, the critical work already done on assessment in composition and rhetoric situates us to respond to these calls productively, having gone from objective tests to holistically scored essays, portfolios, and most recently, what Elizabeth Wardle and Kevin Roozen term "an 'ecological' model of writing assessment" (107) combining portfolio grading with ethnographic and longitudinal studies across various locations and moments of writing (see also Huot; White; Yancey). These trends are important for basic writing instructors at all levels because they will likely be called on to participate in yearly institutional assessments of programmatic effectiveness. Moreover, such assessment, done well, can help BW students—and us as their instructors—construct an increasingly robust understanding of how writing ability develops and how this knowledge can best be leveraged.

Finally, a third important strain of BW assessment work uses institutional data to understand relationships between efficacious BW programs and retention and graduation rates. Greg Glau, for instance, has documented retention and graduation rates in the Stretch program at Arizona State University, especially for students of color, and found significant gains among students who complete the program (37). Matthew McCurrie has performed similar research on the Summer Bridge program at Columbia College, noting improved retention gains for students of color along with modest cost savings (45). Also, by smartly using data to report the success of the Integrated Reading/Writing Program at San Francisco State University, Sugie Goen-Salter criticizes the California State University's efforts since the 1980s to end remediation, arguing that "basic writing sits not at the point of exit from high school, but at the *entry* point to higher education" (98). Further, as noted previously, Adams and his colleagues have been usefully tracking course completion, retention, and graduation rates of students in the Accelerated Learning Program at the Community College of Baltimore County.

Issue 2: Growing Diversity and Translanguaging Pedagogy in BW

A second notable trend regarding the future of BW involves its growing diversity and the notion of "translanguaging" as an intellectual and linguistic asset. As Matsuda has usefully noted, BW needs to take a more expansive view of its students by recognizing "the increasing diversity of students who come to basic writing classrooms" (84). It thus seems clear to us that BW instruction should focus more even explicitly on issues of language diversity with respect to U.S.-born students of color, foreign-born students who speak one or more versions of "global English," and students who immigrate to the United States in their teens (Canagarajah, "Place"; diGennaro; Matsuda and Hammill, this volume).

Because BW serves increasingly diverse students, we encourage teachers and scholars to pay particular attention to very recent pedagogical work on translanguaging—especially how this work posits multilingualism and multidialecticalism as communicative and intellectual assets rather than deficits to be overcome (Canagarajah, "Place"; Horner, Lu, Royster, and Trimbur; Young and Martinez). Suresh Canagarajah asserts that translanguaging is best understood as "the ability of multilingual speakers to shuttle between diverse languages, treating the diverse languages that form their repertoire as an integrated system" ("Codemeshing" 401). Furthermore, he notes, this approach ultimately demands "more, not less, from minority students. They have to not only master the dominant varieties of English, but also know how to bring in their preferred varieties in rhetorically strategic ways" ("Place" 598–99). Finally, Canagarajah points out, translanguaging requires a positive ethical and emotional orientation on the part of both students and teachers that assumes "speakers don't have to be experts in another variety of English in order to speak to other communities. They simply need the metalinguistic, sociolinguistic, and attitudinal preparedness to negotiate differences even as they use their own dialects" (594).

We feel that translanguaging is highly relevant to BW, serving as a critical approach to BW instruction that takes into account error-focused and academic initiation perspectives. It assumes that all students, especially multilingual students, can and should use their existing skills and talents to meet the demands of wider, more varied rhetorical situations. It also highlights the need for "patience, tolerance, and humility" (593) on the part of teachers and students, thereby stressing that *how* we engage with multilingual and multidialectical situations within the context of BW may easily be as important as *what* gets explicitly taught and learned. Both points seem fundamental to effective BW instruction as we move forward.

Issue 3: BW and the Responsible Uses of Technologies and Modalities

The issue of responsible technology use is, finally, critically important to contemporary BW instruction. On the one hand, we believe that those who teach primarily online need to know and be prepared to negotiate aspects of each of the major approaches to BW. But we also realize that the online environment will mediate an individual teacher's use of these approaches given how radically society's relationship to literacy practices is changing in response to technology, a point stressed by Cheryl Smith: "Students today write more, but in less conventionally academic ways, than new students only a decade ago, and they arrive on our campuses with entirely new skill sets and a new relationship to composition and expression" (35–36). Acknowledging this "new relationship" is central to future work in BW.

Along with the prevalence of social media and its embedded literacy practices, we see three particular issues arising in a growing body of literature on teaching BW with technology. First, BW students are far more likely to succeed in hybrid or blended courses than ones that are exclusively online insofar as they tend to have more limited access to technology and to benefit as relative academic outsiders from a stronger sense of community gained through face-to-face contact (Merriam; Stine). Second, the stress of having to learn a new technology on top of academic rules, practices, and behaviors can cause "academic overload." And third, weak academic skills, particularly writing, serve to make online BW instruction a particularly "complicated and messy place, one that few researchers have studied" (Stine 141).

A key to providing BW students with multiple access points across multiple modalities is to apply the principles of universal design—universal accessibility—to course design and teaching with technology. As Patricia A. Dunn and Kathleen Dun de Mers observe, "the difference between assistive technology and Universal Design is that the former focuses on an individual adapting to a rigid curriculum, while the latter focuses on curriculum designed from its inception to be flexible and inclusive." Arising as it does from disability studies, universal design "examines and critiques not individuals, but disabling environments and the assumptions behind them" (Dunn and Dun de Mers; see also Hewett, this volume).

A MICROCOSM OF U.S. DEMOCRACY

We end as we began, by emphasizing our belief that BW has from its inception been a response to political and economic pressures, changing demographics, and local conditions. At its best, BW provides access to higher education for masses of people who would otherwise never go to college; at its worst, it perpetuates "academic apartheid," a reification of racial, cultural, and linguistic stereotypes that is buttressed by the uncritical usage of placement mechanisms and standardized test scores. Throughout this chapter, we have tried to make clear that the pedagogical approaches we have outlined represent the best efforts of teachers, scholars, and researchers—all of whom are always responding to specific historical and cultural conditions—to address a thorny and complex set of issues related to teaching and learning writing. While we think some theories are better than others, we emphasize that BW contributors have, on the whole, sought to inflect their work with a deeply democratic and humanistic ethos. And we also emphasize that, as we theorize the future of BW in venues ranging from the *Journal of Basic Writing* and *Teaching English in the Two-Year College* to *College Composition and Communication* and *College English*, as well as in conferences including the yearly Conference on Basic Writing (CBW) at the Conference on College Composition and Communication and various meetings of the Two-Year College English Association (TYCA), we should attempt to preserve this emphasis on democracy and humanism.

In this spirit, we encourage BW teachers and scholars to recognize some of the dissonances and contradictions between and among these approaches—and to prepare to negotiate them in practice. For instance, error-centered approaches typically assume that error is best addressed by focusing on individual students and their actions, while critical approaches assume that error and other deviations from academic conventions are produced more by social than individual factors, and thus require a focus on larger social structures. Similarly, academic-initiation approaches to BW assume that students need to be taught the "rules of the academic game" and provided with opportunities to learn and practice them; in contrast, spatial approaches posit that these rules, the game itself, and the terms of such practice all depend centrally on where and how each is imagined, and posit as well that members of any given discourse community may contest those rules. Understanding the nuances and historical contexts of these approaches is important as we engage in day-to-day instruction, deciding for ourselves how best to shuttle between individual and societal dimensions of error or autonomous and ideological models of literacy. Complementing such practices, we view theories of teaching writing as collective, dynamic, unfinished explanations of complex phenomena that we all struggle to understand.

As Susan Griffin says in "Red Shoes," an essay about the relationship between theory and experience, "Theory pales when faced with the complex world of experience" but "the realm of experience longs for more than knowledge" (10). The complex world of the BW class (and other contexts) in which we encounter students labeled "basic writer," students who struggle with their writing, or students whose writing perplexes us, is embedded in histories of individuals, communities, and the discipline itself. Really, the most useful parting words we can leave with a new teacher encountering these issues for the first time are to see yourself as a researcher and theorist of your own students. We also suggest that you take the theories we outline in this chapter as invitations to grasp the relationship between the words on the page and the student who authored them. To do so can help dissolve the abstractions of basic writing and reveal the concrete, material production of meaning occurring in that moment and with that person struggling (as we all do) to make sense of experience. For it is ultimately such reflective practice that offers us a sense of hope—including a belief that BW, when done well, can be "a key mechanism in a democratic model of human development" (Rose, "Colleges").

BIBLIOGRAPHY

Adams, Peter. Message to the authors. 15 May 2012. E-mail.

Adams, Peter, Sarah Gearhart, Robert Miller, and Anne Roberts. "The Accelerated Learning Program: Throwing Open the Gates." *Journal of Basic Writing* 28.2 (2009): 50–69. Print.

Bartholomae, David. "The Study of Error." *College Composition and Communication* 31.3 (1980): 253–77. Print.

_____. "The Tidy House: Basic Writing in the American Curriculum." *Journal of Basic Writing* 12.1 (1993): 4–21. Print.

_____. "Inventing the University." *When a Writer Can't Write: Studies in Writers' Block and Other Composing Process Problems.* Ed. Mike Rose. New York: Guilford, 1985. 134–65. Print.

Bartholomae, David, and Anthony Petrosky. *Facts, Artifacts, and Counterfacts: Theory and Method for a Reading and Writing Course.* Portsmouth: Boynton/Cook, 1986. Print.

Berlin, James. *Rhetoric and Reality: Writing Instruction in American Colleges, 1900–1985.* Carbondale: Southern Illinois UP, 1987. Print.

Bernstein, Susan Naomi, ed. *Teaching Developmental Writing: Background Readings.* 3rd ed. Boston: Bedford/St. Martin's, 2007. Print.

Blaauw-Hara, Mark. "Mapping the Frontier: A Survey of Twenty Years of Grammar Articles in *TETYC.*" *Teaching English in the Two Year College* 35.1 (2007): 30–40. Print.

Brandt, Deborah. *Literacy in American Lives.* Cambridge: Cambridge UP, 2001. Print.

Canagarajah, Suresh. "Codemeshing in Academic Writing: Identifying Teachable Strategies of Translanguaging." *The Modern Language Journal* 95.3 (2011): 401–417. Print.

_____. "The Place of World Englishes in Composition: Pluralization Continued." *College Composition and Communication* 57.4 (2006): 586–619. Print.

Carter, Shannon. *The Way Literacy Lives: Rhetorical Dexterity and Basic Writing Instruction.* Albany: SUNY P, 2008. Print.

Dawkins, John. "Teaching Meaning-Based Punctuation." *Teaching English in the Two Year College* 31.2 (2003): 154–62. Print.

Davi, Angelique. "In the Service of Writing and Race." *Journal of Basic Writing* 25.1 (2006): 73–95. Print.

diGennaro, Kristen. "Assessment of Generation 1.5 Learners for Placement into College Writing Courses." *Journal of Basic Writing* 27.1 (2008): 61–79. Print.

Delpit, Lisa. "The Silenced Dialogue: Power and Pedagogy in Educating Other Peoples' Children." *Harvard Educational Review* 58.3 (1988): 280–98. Print.

Dunn, Patricia A., and Kathleen Dunn DeMers. "Reversing Notions of Disability and Accommodation: Embracing Universal Design in Writing Pedagogy and Web Space." *Kairos* 7.1 (2002). Web. 2 January 2013.

Fox, Tom. *Defending Access: A Critique of Standards in Higher Education*. Portsmouth: Boynton/Cook, 1999. Print.

Freire, Paulo. 1968. *Pedagogy of the Oppressed*. 30th anniv. ed. New York: Continuum, 2000. Print.

Gay, Pamela. "Rereading Shaughnessy from a Postcolonial Perspective." *Journal of Basic Writing* 12.2 (1993): 29–40. Print.

Gee, James Paul. "What Is Literacy?" *Journal of Education* 171.1 (1989) 18–25. Print.

Gilyard, Keith. *Voices of the Self: A Study of Language Competence*. Detroit: Wayne State UP, 1997. Print.

Glau, Greg. "*Stretch* at 10: A Progress Report on Arizona State University's *Stretch* Program." *Journal of Basic Writing* 26.2 (2007): 30–48. Print.

Glau, Greg, and Chitralekha Duttagupta, eds. *The Bedford Bibliography for Teachers of Basic Writing*. 3rd ed. Boston: Bedford / St. Martin's, 2009. Print.

Gleason, Barbara. "Evaluating Writing Programs in Real Time: The Politics of Remediation." *College Composition and Communication* 51.4 (2000): 560–88. Print.

Goen-Salter, Sugie. "Critiquing the Need to Eliminate Remediation: Lessons from San Francisco State." *Journal of Basic Writing* 27.2 (2008): 81–105. Print.

Greenberg, Karen. "The Politics of Basic Writing." *Journal of Basic Writing* 12.1 (1993): 64–71. Print.

Greene, Nicole Pipenster, and Patricia J. McAlexander. *Basic Writing in America: The History of Nine College Programs*. Cresskill: Hampton, 2008. Print.

Grego, Rhonda, and Nancy Thompson. *Teaching / Writing in Thirdspaces: The Studio Approach*. Carbondale: Southern Illinois UP, 2008. Print.

Griffin, Susan. "Red Shoes." *The Politics of the Essay: Feminist Perspectives*. Ed. R. B. Joeres and E. Mittman. Bloomington: Indiana UP, 1993. 1–11. Print.

Hairston, Maxine. "Diversity, Ideology, and the Teaching of Writing." *CCC* 43.2 (1992): 179–93. Print.

Horner, Bruce. "Rethinking the 'Sociality' of Error: Teaching Editing as Negotiation." *Representing the Other: Basic Writers and the Teaching of Basic Writing*. Eds. Bruce Horner and Min-Zhan Lu. Urbana: National Council of Teachers of English, 1999. 139–65. Print.

Horner, Bruce, Min-Zhan Lu, Jacqueline Jones Royster, and John Trimbur. "Language Difference in Writing: Toward a Translingual Approach." *College English* 73.3 (2011): 303–21. Print.

Horning, Alice S. *Teaching Writing as a Second Language*. Carbondale: Southern Illinois UP, 1987. Print.

Hull, Glynda. "Acts of Wonderment: Fixing Mistakes and Correcting Errors." *Facts, Artifacts, and Counterfacts: Theory and Method for a Reading and Writing Course*. Ed. David Bartholomae and Anthony Petrosky. Portsmouth: Boynton/Cook, 1986. 199–226. Print.

Huot, Brian. *(Re)Articulating Writing Assessment for Teaching and Learning*. Logan: Utah State UP, 2002. Print.

Jolliffe, David A., and Allison Harl. "Texts and Our Institutional Lives: Studying the 'Reading Transition' from High School to College: What Are Our Students Reading and Why?" *College English* 70.6 (July 2008): 599–617. Print.

Lalicker, William. "A Basic Introduction to Basic Writing Program Structures: A Baseline and Five Alternatives." *Teaching Developmental Writing: Background Readings*. 3rd ed. Ed. Susan Naomi Bernstein. Boston: Bedford St. Martins, 2007. 15–25. Print.

Lamos, Steve. *Interests and Opportunities: Race, Racism, and University Writing Instruction in the Post-Civil Rights Era*. Pittsburgh: U of Pittsburgh P, 2011. Print.

Lu, Min-Zhan. "Conflict and Struggle: The Enemies or Preconditions of Basic Writing?" *College English* 54 (1992): 887–913. Print.

———. "Professing Multiculturalism: The Politics of Style in the Contact Zone." *College Composition and Communication* 45.4 (1994): 442–58. Print.

Lunsford, Andrea. "Cognitive Development and the Basic Writer." *College English* 41.1 (1979): 38–46. Print.

———. "What We Know—and Don't Know—about Remedial Writing." *College Composition and Communication* 29.1 (1978): 47–52. Print.

Matsuda, Paul Kei. "Basic Writing and Second Language Writers: Toward an Inclusive Definition." *Journal of Basic Writing* 22.2 (2003): 67–89. Print.

McCurrie, Matthew Killian. "Measuring Success in Summer Bridge Programs: Retention Efforts and Basic Writing." *Journal of Basic Writing* 28.2 (2009): 28–49. Print.

McNenny, Gerri. "Writing Instruction and the Post-Remedial University: Setting the Scene for the Mainstreaming Debate in Basic Writing." In *Mainstreaming Basic Writers: Politics and Pedagogies of Access*. Ed Gerri McNenny. Mahwah: Erlbaum, 2001. 1–18. Print.

Merriam, Sharan B. *Third Update on Adult Learning Theory: New Directions for Adult and Continuing Education*. New York: Jossey-Bass, 2008. Print.

Mutnick, Deborah. "The Strategic Value of Basic Writing." *Journal of Basic Writing* 19.1 (2000): 69–83. Print.

———. *Writing in an Alien World: Basic Writing and the Struggle for Equality in Higher Education*. Portsmouth: Boynton/Cook, 1996. Print.

Perl, Sondra. "The Composing Processes of Unskilled College Writers." *Research in the Teaching of English* 13.4 (1979): 317–36. Print.

Pratt, Mary Louise. "Arts of the Contact Zone." *Profession* 9 (1991): 33–40. Print.

Reynolds, Nedra. *Geographies of Writing: Inhabiting Places and Encountering Difference*. Carbondale: Southern Illinois UP, 2004. Print.

Rigolino, Rachel, and Penny Freel. "Re-Modeling Basic Writing." *Journal of Basic Writing* 26.2 (2007): 51–74. Print.

Ritter, Kelly. *Before Shaughnessy: Basic Writing at Yale and Harvard, 1920–1960*. Carbondale: Southern Illinois UP, 2009. Print.

Robinson, William S. "Sentence Focus, Cohesion, and the Active and Passive Voices." *Teaching English in the Two Year College* 27.4 (2000): 440–45. Print.

Rose, Mike. "Colleges Need to Re-Mediate Remediation." *The Chronicle of Higher Education* 3 August 2009. Web. 5 June 2012.

———. "Narrowing the Mind and the Page: Remedial Writers and Cognitive Reductionism." *College Composition and Communication* 39.3 (1988): 267–98. Print.

Rouse, John. "The Politics of Composition." *College English* 41.1 (1979): 1–12. Print.

Salvatori, Mariolina. "The Dialogical Nature of Basic Reading and Writing." *Facts, Artifacts, and Counterfacts: Theory and Method for a Reading and Writing Course*. Ed. David Bartholomae and Anthony Petrosky. Portsmouth: Boynton/Cook, 1986. 137–66. Print.

Shaughnessy, Mina. *Errors and Expectations*. New York: Oxford UP, 1977. Print.

_____. "Open Admissions and the Disadvantaged Teacher." *College Composition and Communication* 24.5 (1973): 401–04. Print.

Shor, Ira. "Our Apartheid: Writing Instruction and Inequality." *Journal of Basic Writing* 16.1 (1997): 91–104. Print.

Smith, Cheryl C. "Technologies for Transcending a Focus on Error: Blogs and Aspirations in First-Year Composition. *Journal of Basic Writing* 27.1 (2008): 35–60. Print.

Smitherman, Geneva. *Talkin' and Testifyin': The Language of Black America*. Boston: Houghton Mifflin, 1977. Print.

Soliday, Mary. *The Politics of Remediation: Institutional and Student Needs in Higher Education*. Pittsburgh: U of Pittsburgh P, 2002. Print.

Sommers, Nancy. "Revision Strategies of Student Writers and Experienced Adult Writers." *College Composition and Communication* 31.4 (1980): 378–88. Print.

Stahl, Norman A., and Hunter Boylan, eds. *Teaching Developmental Reading: Historical, Theoretical, and Practical Backgrounds Readings*. Boston: Bedford/St. Martin's, 2003. Print.

Stanley, Jane. *The Rhetoric of Remediation: Negotiating Entitlement and Access to Higher Education*. Pittsburgh: U of Pittsburgh P, 2009. Print.

Stine, Linda. "Basically Unheard: Developmental Writers and the Conversation on Online Learning." *Teaching English in the Two-Year College* 38.2 (2010): 132–48. Print.

Street, Brian V. *Literacy in Theory and Practice* (Cambridge Studies in Oral and Literate Culture). Cambridge: Cambridge UP, 1985. Print.

Tassoni, John Paul, and Cynthia Lewiecki-Wilson. "Not Just Anywhere, Anywhen: Mapping Change through Studio Work." *Journal of Basic Writing* 24.1 (2005): 68–92. Print.

Wardle, Elizabeth, and Kevin Roozen. "Addressing the Complexity of Writing Development: Toward an Ecological Model of Assessment." *Assessing Writing* 17 (2012): 106–119. Web. 25 December 2012.

Weissman, Jordan. "53% of Recent College Grads Are Jobless or Underemployed—How?" *The Atlantic* 23 April 2012. Web. 4 June 2012.

White, Edward M. "The Misuses of Writing Assessment for Political Purposes." *Journal of Writing Assessment* 2.1 (2005): 21–36. Web. 2 January 2013.

Wichman, Nanette. "Speaking of Sentences: Chunking." *Teaching English in the Two Year College* 36.3 (2009): 281–90. Print.

Yancey, Kathleen Blake. "Looking Back as We Look Forward: Historicizing Writing Assessment." *College Composition and Communication* 50.3 (1999): 483–503. Print.

Young, Vershawn Ashanti, and Aja Y. Martinez. *Code-Meshing as World English: Pedagogy, Policy, Performance*. Urbana: National Council of Teachers of English, 2011. Print.

Collaborative Writing, Print to Digital

Krista Kennedy

Rebecca Moore Howard

The model of solitary authorship advanced in Romantic literary theory was in wide circulation when composition began to be taught in late nineteenth-century U.S. colleges. Despite the fact that collaboration is inherent in most workplace writing, the influence of the Romantic model on humanistic thought, including writing instruction, persisted until Foucault's and Barthes' poststructuralist challenges to the very possibility of solitary authorship.

In 1984 Kenneth A. Bruffee, working from a social constructionist perspective (which is not incommensurate with poststructuralism but is much more focused on interpersonal than textual relations), published influential arguments for collaborative learning. Working from a mix of social constructionist and poststructuralist theories of authorship, the scholarly work on collaboration (collaborative learning, peer review, and collaboratively authored texts) in the latter half of the twentieth century challenged that model and built pedagogies to counter it. Bruffee's three principles of collaborative learning moved quickly to canonical status in writing curricula:[1]

1. [B]ecause thought is internalized conversation, thought and conversation tend to work largely in the same way (639).
2. If thought is internalized public and social talk, then writing of all kinds is internalized talk made public and social again. If thought is internalized conversation, then writing is internalized conversation re-externalized (641).
3. To learn is to work collaboratively to establish and maintain knowledge among a community of knowledgeable peers through the process that Richard Rorty calls "socially justifying belief" (qtd. in Bruffee 646).

For Bruffee, collaborative learning is "a way of engaging students more deeply with the text" (635), and collaborative pedagogy provides "a social context in which students can experience and practice the kinds of conversation valued by college teachers" (642).

---

[1] From the period in which these ideas were entering Writing Studies, Crowley offers a solid overview of poststructuralism, and Rafoth and Rubin of social construction.

Subsequent writing scholars attended to collaborative contributions to individually authored texts (Elbow, *Writing without*; Gere), collaboratively authored texts (Lunsford and Ede), and peer review—collaborative contributions to individually authored work. Although Gere locates its origins in nineteenth-century pedagogy, peer review has been a staple of writing pedagogy for nearly a half century.[2] Elbow's 1973 *Writing without Teachers* describes pedagogical techniques in which writers not only work in small groups without teachers but also do not themselves model traditional teacherly methods. Instead of judging whether a text is "good" or "bad" (what Elbow calls the "doubting game"), group members respond to a text by standing in the position of author rather than critic and considering reasons for what the text undertakes and possibilities for its accomplishing those goals—the "believing game" (*Writing without* 147–91, also Special Issue).

For guiding students through peer review, Spear offers an overview of principles developed in the 1980s and still in use today. Ching adds a history of peer review pedagogy. Even though peer review remains a widely accepted pedagogy among experienced instructors, it may not sit well with students, including graduate teaching assistants (TAs). Spigelman offers an excellent exploration of the ways in which student writers' assumptions of solitary authorship and individual "ownership" of text can complicate peer review. Patchan, Charney, and Schunn conduct research to allay TAs' concerns that undergraduate peers might provide bad advice to each other. Bedore and O'Sullivan detail a variety of reasons for the ambivalence that teaching assistants may have to peer review and urge TA trainers to engage actively with the TAs' reasons for hesitating and even to maintain a flexible stance toward the very definition of the term *peer review* (31).

Karen Burke LeFevre, moreover, critiques the assumption embedded in peer review practices that the work under review is already in draft before anyone else sees it. Describing four models of invention, LeFevre argues that not just revision but also invention is a collaborative act. If writing instructors take seriously her claim that invention is social, even when apparently conducted by an individual (44), they must consider pedagogy that includes not only peer review of drafts in progress but also collaborative invention.

By the beginning of the twenty-first century, in Writing Studies that debate had been settled in favor of collaboration as the natural, unavoidable basis of all textual production (even though in writing courses, students continue to be assessed individually). Writing scholarship about individual-versus-collaborative writing has largely subsided. In its place has arisen a lively scholarly discussion about the ways in which digital media are challenging and changing how writers and instructors experience authorship, pedagogy, and literacy itself. This scholarship has significantly expanded the pedagogical possibilities for collaboratively authored texts. It has also made the digital an essential part of any discussion

---

[2]Peer review is taking on a new life in Writing MOOCs (massive open online courses) being launched at the time of this writing—a phenomenon beyond the purview of this chapter but illustrated by Comer.

about collaboration. When the first edition of this book was published in 2000, it was entirely plausible to write a chapter about collaboration that did not address collaborative writing in digital environments (Howard, "Collaborative"). Today, that would be ridiculous.

STRATEGIES FOR COLLABORATIVE WRITING, PRINT AND DIGITAL

Of all the collaborative pedagogies, the one that has proven most challenging to teach is collaboratively authored texts, usually signaled by the term *collaborative writing* or *team writing*. While the available technologies and possibilities have changed over the decades, the basic principles of sound collaborative pedagogy have not (see Wolfe; Fontaine and Hunter). The following principles may help ensure success in both print and digital collaborative writing projects. These derive from a combination of published scholarship and our own classroom practices.

Delay Students' Collaborative Writing

Although the collaborative writing assignment may be announced and distributed on the very first day of class, it should not be begun until a substantial portion of the term has elapsed. In the interim, pedagogy should be sufficiently collaborative (e.g., collaborative class discussion, small-group work, collaborative invention, collaborative revision) that the students get to know each other, resolve some of the small interpersonal tensions that inevitably arise, and anticipate each other's collaborative assets and shortcomings.

Design the Assignment for a Group, Rather Than Redesigning an Individual Task

The collaborative writing assignment should be one best accomplished by a group rather than by an individual; otherwise, the task is artificial, leading to students' frustration and irritation. Lunsford and Ede describe

> . . . three types of tasks which invite . . . collaboration: "labor-intensive" tasks that need to be divided into smaller subtasks in order to be accomplished effectively and efficiently; "specialization" tasks that call for multiple areas of expertise; and "synthesis" tasks that demand that divergent perspectives be brought together into a solution acceptable to the whole group or an outside group. (123)

Provide for Student-Initiated Collaboration

While planning the course, consider whether any of the assignments designated for individual authorship lend themselves to collaborative authorship. Alert the class to these possibilities and introduce them to methods and rationales for collaboration. If some of the students opt to write collaboratively, work with the groups to ensure that they are accomplishing something other than dividing an individual text among several writers.

Discuss Methods and Problems of Collaborative Writing before the Project Begins

If the collaboration is to be online, explore available methods (Breuch; Forbes; Selfe). Alert students to the ways in which stereotyped role expectations (based on factors such as gender and race) can affect the distribution of power within the group. Encourage them to pay close attention to each other's ideas and to delegate responsibility according to the actual characteristics of the individuals in the group, rather than stereotyped role expectations (Fox; Morgan; Villanueva). Discuss technology aspects and issues, and outline your expectations for acceptable milestones and excuses.

Choose the Type of Collaboration

Lunsford and Ede describe *dialogic* and *hierarchical* collaboration: In dialogic collaboration, the group works together on all aspects of the project, whereas in hierarchical collaboration, the group divides the task into component parts and assigns certain components to each group member. Dialogic collaboration offers the benefit of discovery: Students learn more by working together. Hierarchical collaboration offers the benefit of efficiency: Work done by individuals is stitched together and reviewed by the group. Many collaborative writing projects involve both types of collaboration (133–34).

Anticipate Problems

Some students are better prepared to accomplish their tasks than are others— hence a variation in quality. Writing groups must be ready to exert critical judgment, and the members must be braced for the sobering prospect of having their work changed or eliminated. The group must dedicate itself to the best possible written product, and its members must be ready to help each other through potentially ego-deflating moments.

Anticipate and Prepare for Student Resistance

Some students may be uncertain as to whether their classmates will accept them as coauthors, or have a much higher opinion of their own writing "ability" than do their classmates. Usually these students will nevertheless benefit if they understand how prevalent collaboration is in workplace writing, how much their "individual" writing will improve from having worked in a group and having seen firsthand how others articulate and solve writing problems, and how much more they can accomplish than if they were working alone—what Hughes and Lund call "a union that is greater than the . . . parts that composed it" (49; see also Rogers and Horton). But some students are implacably opposed to collaboration, and the instructor must decide whether to require them to participate or to offer the option of individual writing. If the pedagogical motivation for assigning collaboration is to improve the students' skill in writing collaboratively, they must all participate. If, however, the class is designed to enhance individual writing skills (as is the case in most required introductory writing classes), the instructor may want to allow solitary writing, reasoning that the student's writing skills will not benefit from an activity that he or she so stoutly resists.

Let the Class Decide How the Groups Will Be Constituted and Discuss the Pros and Cons of Each Possibility

Both of us tell our classes that choosing their own groups would allow them maximum comfort but would leave some students feeling unloved, and we also tell them the comfort of self-chosen groups can sometimes result in poor decision making, with too much consideration for established relations and not enough for the project at hand. An alternative is teacher-designated groups, trying to fix each group with a range of writing skills (e.g., a good researcher, a good editor, etc.), in each group. We recommend against too-small groups (in which one person's absence might be devastating) or too-large groups (in which leadership issues could too easily arise and in which one person could too easily disappear). For us, the most effective number is typically no more than five.

When Considering Group Makeup and Size, Take into Account Students with Disabilities

Collaborative assignments may present difficulties that are unforeseen by able-bodied or neurotypical teachers, and there are no blanket solutions for individual bodies or minds. Advance consideration, private discussion with disabled students, and consultation with the campus Office of Disability Services can help instructors negotiate accommodations that address individual needs. (Accommodation is itself a collaborative process.)

Not all disabled students require the use of more obvious accommodations such as sign language interpreters or Braille readers. For instance, students with varying levels of deafness may not sign and may generally not need accommodation, but they may then experience challenges when working in larger groups because of the difficulty of following the conversation between multiple speakers while filtering out the normal background noise of any classroom or computer lab. Students with moderate sight difficulties may need to be able to sit directly in front of a monitor rather than peering from the side as the group crowds around a single screen. Those with joint diseases or who are recovering from recent surgeries or managing permanent but invisible injuries (which are not uncommon for returning veterans) may need to stand or sit in particular ways in order to manage pain, and so the group's workspace should accommodate them.

Collaborative pedagogies may pose particular challenges to non-neurotypical students. Writers with diagnoses on the autism spectrum will face challenges with reading their peers' social cues, which may in turn mean that the neurotypical students in the group will need to learn to accommodate miscues or misreadings. These writers may encounter particular difficulties with collaborative assignments that assume that all participants not only can read general social cues but also can feel empathy toward other writers and feel comfortable while engaging deeply with others while editing their work (see Gerstle and Walsh; Wyatt). It may be necessary to accommodate these students with individual work opportunities or through helping groups develop distinct, linear roles for each member that can be accomplished with some independence.

While most disabled students will have registered with Disability Services prior to entering the classroom, some may not identify as disabled or may not understand themselves as "disabled enough" for disability accommodation. The instructor's discussions with them should respect these self-identifications. A low-pressure way to check in is to casually arrange to speak with the student privately and simply ask, "How are things going for you? Is there anything you need?" If disabled students say that things are fine, the instructor should respect their response and create space for them to find their own way through the collaboration process. Disabled students are typically very accustomed to living in their bodies; what may look difficult or altered to an able-bodied person is often mundane and normal for them. (For specific information on disability and accessibility in digital contexts, see "New Media Pedagogy," this volume.)

Give the Groups Autonomy in Deciding Their Methods and Timetables

But also require that they actively engage in project management and commit their timetable and milestones to writing. Devote class time to these planning discussions, and give students maximum guidance to help them make sound decisions.

Prepare for Dissent within the Groups and Prepare to Manage It in Two Dimensions: The Instructor and the Students

Neither should attempt to suppress dissent or enforce consensus (see Clark and Ede; Janangelo; Trimbur). Successful collaboration, say Lunsford and Ede, allows not only for "group cohesion" but also for "creative conflict" and the protection of "minority views" (123). Linda Flower recommends that the instructor welcome rather than dread dissent. From conflict can emerge "a joint inquiry into thorny problems, opening up live options that let us construct a language of possibility and a more complicated ground for action" (Lunsford and Ede 50–52). It is important for students to anticipate in advance that dissent and conflict will arise and to be ready to respond to it productively rather than wasting time trying to suppress, reform, or eject dissenters. Two textual methods of accommodating dissent are *counterevidence* and *minority opinions*. The presentation of counterevidence draws on established models of academic persuasion, in which a thesis (the opinion of the majority) is advanced but in which counterevidence as well as evidence is presented. In employing this option, students must avoid the approach to counterevidence that traditional argument offers. Rogerian models of argument apply here: Counterevidence must not be discounted or "refuted"; rather, it should serve to enrich the thesis, showing its complexities and ambiguities. The presentation of minority opinions draws on Supreme Court practice. Collaborative writing groups employing this tactic present a final text, to which is attached one or more statements of dissenting opinion. Nor are these statements individually authored;

the entire group works dialogically not only on the majority text but also on the minority opinion(s).

Explain in Advance How the Project Will Be Graded,
Preferably Involving the Students in the Decision
Before work on the project begins, the instructor or the groups should determine whether a student who does not carry his or her load will nevertheless receive the group's grade, whether the shirking member will receive a lesser grade than the others, or whether a shirker will be ejected from the group and either given a zero or required to write his or her own text. Both of us tell our classes that each collaborative group will receive a single grade but that the groups would decide in advance how a shirker would be graded. We also provide our criteria for grading, telling them that we expect a better product than we would of a single individual. Some instructors try to assign individual grades for a collaborative project—a method that we cannot recommend, since it undermines the purposes of collaboration. The urge to individualize grades arises from the gatekeeping responsibility for judging and ranking individuals that is endemic to many writing programs (see Holdstein). Before assigning collaborative writing projects, the instructor should ascertain that the institutional purposes for the course and the instructor's own purposes in assigning collaboration are sufficiently harmonious that the institutional agenda will not undermine the collaborative pedagogy—or vice versa.

DIGITAL COLLABORATION

Virtual networks have facilitated collaboration since ARPANET, the first operational packet switching network, was launched in 1969 as a means of transferring information on collaborative projects between Department of Defense research laboratories. This limited network later became the core infrastructure of the Internet. While Rhetoric and Composition's adoption of both stand-alone and networked digital writing technologies has been incremental, it began early (Burns). Stand-alone word processing technologies occupied the field's attention at first, and networked digital technologies have seen progressive adoption in collaborative writing instruction since the 1980s (Barker and Kemp; Bump; Kemp). Similarly, classes in the early 1990s used MUDs (Multi-User Dungeons) and MOOs (MUD Object-Oriented), text-based digital environments in which multiple users connected synchronously, for collaborative learning and peer review. These efforts included not just local classes but cross-university collaborations (Zappen, Gurak, and Doheny-Farina).

With the introduction of the proprietary WebCT and Blackboard platforms in the mid-1990s and their subsequent wide adoption across U.S. campuses, more instructors gained access to a centrally supported, stable course management system (CMS) / learning management system (LMS) with a growing portfolio of tools. Writing instructors began to make use of its built-in discussion boards for activities that were formerly handled via e-mail and other text-based environments. Other proprietary CMS vendors (including but not limited to Angel,

Desire2Learn, Sakai, Canvas, and Pearson Learning Suite) have also seen significant adoption of their platforms. Today, most academic institutions in North America provide some form of secure, closed CMS access to their students. At the same time, the toolbox of digital environments has grown to include other prevalent tools that function in the more open environment of the Web. Google Suite now provides universities with campus-specific, centralized access that consolidates classroom access to Google applications like Google Drive and Google Sites. Moodle offers an open source CMS environment that is supported by some campuses and is also available for server installation, and other open-source content management systems such as WordPress and Drupal can be modified for the same purposes. Social media applications such as individual and class blogs, wikis, photo sharing platforms such as Flickr, and social media platforms devoted to community such as Facebook and Twitter also see frequent pedagogical use.

Each of these changes made digital collaboration more ubiquitous in the field of Writing Studies. Early edited collections on digital writing included dedicated essays on collaboration (see Cyganowski; Duin and Hansen; Forman), but as the Web became increasingly social, digital interaction and collaboration became naturalized within the Writing Studies literature. Digital collaboration certainly continues to merit critical consideration, but it is rarely a fixed scholarly topic. The field was well positioned to navigate and incorporate the ambiguity of networked spaces partly because of our established comfort with postmodern authorship (Porter). The complications of open-ended texts and ambiguous authorship are further compounded in digital environments, which lend themselves to anonymously written texts that are open to interactive collaboration and discussion and can be distributed across the globe in within a few keystrokes (Gurak).

The need to create assignments that reflect the reality of contemporary writing environments remains a pressing pedagogical concern, along with the need to prepare students for workplaces that are increasingly reliant on digital, global communication and collaborative labor. While this is true in any writing classroom, it is particularly so for teachers of technical and professional writing. Effective digital collaboration is an essential skill for students who will likely engage in *symbolic-analytical work* after graduation. (This term, drawn from the work of labor theorist Robert Reich and adopted by professional and technical writing scholars, refers to workers from industries whose primary labor focuses on manipulating symbols: writers, researchers, managers, bankers, architects, etc.) Johndan Johnson-Eilola reminds us how ubiquitous this skill set has become:

> Collaboration helps symbolic analysts work together to solve problems while crossing complex disciplinary domains. Software projects, for example, typically require not only programmers, but user interface designers, marketing experts, usability testers, technical communicators, and graphic artists. Team members brainstorm ideas and solutions, critique each other's work, and provide support and feedback to the teammates. (29–30)

Further, students must learn to collaborate in digital environments that necessarily obscure social cues such as facial expression and vocal tone. (Video conferencing is an exception to this rule.) The simple fact that digital spaces do not require human bodies to be present in the same place at the same time opens up additional possibilities for all collaboration types, particularly in online classes. It also opens up different possibilities for using classroom time in traditional classrooms, since students who are exploring the collaborative uses of digital applications do not necessarily need to use class time or schedule face-to-face meetings in order to complete the assignment. Learning to work with people in other time zones or on other continents is a crucial skill for students entering the global marketplace; digital collaboration in the writing classroom offers a lower-stakes place to learn these skills.

Central pedagogical challenges brought about by the emergence of digital collaboration include the potential for public, multimodal end products; the negotiation of privacy; and the need for instructors to develop sufficient digital literacies to select the best tool for the form of collaboration that is most suited to their classroom goals. (For more on multimodality, see the chapter on "New Media Pedagogy.") The possibility of distributed, large-scale collaboration has also changed the possibilities for group sizes, which range from small groups to whole-class assignments to multiclass assignments spread over multiple semesters or years.

The Internet's inherent aspects of speed and reach have also enhanced the potential for reader-text collaboration, since students have a nearly infinite range of media at their fingertips that can easily be downloaded or captured for recomposition (Howard, *Standing*; Gurak; Lessig). The term *remix*, which loosely refers to repurposing multimodal artifacts into new texts, permeated U.S. culture after Apple's 2001 "Rip, Mix, Burn" campaign and was a subject of much scholarly discussion in the first decade of the twenty-first century (see Davis, Webb, Lackey, and DeVoss; Lessig; Logie, among others). Scholars have recently turned to consideration of more specialized types of collaboration afforded by digital technologies such as the human-machine collaboration found in database-created texts (Brooke) and robot-written texts (Kennedy). Specific rhetorical aspects of collaboration through recomposition and recirculation in social media include rhetorical velocity (Ridolfo and DeVoss; Sheridan, Ridolfo, and Michel), rhetorical uptake (Warnick and Heineman), and rhizomatic travel (Kephart and Rafferty). There is also continued discussion of Yochai Benkler's concept of commons-based peer production (CBPP), "collaboration among large groups of individuals, sometimes in the order of tens or even hundreds of thousands, who cooperate effectively to provide information, knowledge or cultural goods without relying on either market pricing or managerial hierarchies to coordinate their common enterprise" (Benkler and Nissenbaum; see also Benkler). CBPP is the sort of radically distributed collaborative writing that drives the production of large-scale projects such as Wikipedia or the LINUX operating system. This form of collaboration can be successfully incorporated into the writing classroom in both full-scale and small-scale ways; the most common CBPP-based assignments ask students to contribute to Wikipedia through composing or editing articles or to participate in developing a wiki-based project built by multiple classes. We discuss wiki-based assignments and issues in greater detail later in the chapter.

Digital Literacies

Incorporating technology into the collaborative composition classroom is not a matter of using technology for technology's sake—that is, in order to simply meet technology-based outcomes or in hopes of sparking student interest with a shiny tool. As Kittle and Hicks point out, it's the difference "between a world that is simply full of more technology and a mindset that encourages participation and collaboration in many new ways" (526). While it is frequently worthwhile to explore and play with digital tools in more general writing assignments, the stakes are often higher in collaborative assignments, which include pressure for the instructor to ensure that the required technologies will provide more benefits than obstacles. One need not understand the nuts and bolts of a given platform before incorporating it in assignments, since it is always possible for instructors as well as students to continue learning over the course of the semester. However, it is beneficial to understand the basic uses and focus of a tool and the specific features that make it the best tool for the job at hand and its processes. (For more on this aspect of digital writing, see the chapter on "New Media Pedagogy.")

When incorporating public, Web-based tools into assignments, it is essential to understand the full range of privacy options and discuss them with students while introducing the assignment. Social media applications provide many levels of privacy and, correspondingly, publicness for student writing. These are separate elements to be considered and balanced, and it is not uncommon to find that one stage of a project requires more privacy than others. One of the most crucial early steps of designing a digital collaborative assignment is deciding what level of privacy is most sensible for the tasks and goals at hand. For early discussions and drafting stages, the safety of a closed environment may be beneficial. Later drafts may be made available to the entire class itself for peer-review and usability testing before fully opening up the final product to the public, as with some of the examples of large, public projects listed previously. (For more on usability testing, see "New Media Pedagogy.") More traditional essay assignments may require group privacy at first before being made available to peers and the instructor; the final products may be available only to the class or showcased in a virtual gallery. Using a campus-approved course management system will always enable privacy for students, since such course shells are typically accessible only to the instructor, students, any guests approved by the instructor, and technology support personnel. Instructors need to consider their own beliefs concerning student privacy as well as FERPA (Family Education Rights and Privacy Act) interpretations and CMS requirements at their individual campuses. However, we would caution against automatically choosing complete privacy because it seems simpler or safer. There are a number of excellent pedagogical reasons to choose more public environments, not least of which is that students often report a higher level of engagement when they know that they are writing for a public audience that may make real use of their work. They also report being "more aware of writing within a rhetorical community in which their readers have a lot of power" (Beech, Anson, Breuch, and Swiss, 9). Other reasons for strategically choosing more public environments is encouraging the personal responsibility that comes with public writing as well as the public exchange of ideas, contributing to community-engagement, or exploring other aspects of public communication. (For more on public writing and pedagogy, see Isaacs and Jackson; Sheridan et al.)

STRATEGIES AND APPLICATIONS FOR DIGITAL COLLABORATION PEDAGOGY

While enterprising instructors can, with careful consideration, make a collaborative application or platform work for almost any size group, the fact remains that technologies are typically developed for specific uses and with individual features that facilitate particular kinds of interaction. With that in mind, we offer basic recommendations based on group size. We refer to technologies by type (blog, wiki, photo-sharing application) rather than by brand name because the individual platforms will change over time, whereas the central uses of the technologies remain relatively stable.

Small Groups

Often, students take the initiative to include technology in small-group work through everyday technologies they are accustomed to using: **texting and instant messaging** (IM). Ask them; they'll most likely report that they've already used these short forms of writing to set up meetings, assign tasks on the fly, conduct casual status reviews, and ask questions of each other. Formally incorporating these technologies in collaborative assignments is worthwhile, especially with IM and its cousin, **video conferencing**, which many corporations rely on.

Simple peer review and collaboration are frequently achieved by using discussion boards and forums within campus-supported CMSs. **Document sharing applications** are an excellent way to begin incorporating external technology into these same tasks. Rather than commenting on and uploading multiple versions of documents to a CMS, both students and instructors can develop a more streamlined workflow that includes composing and commenting on a centrally hosted, shared, dynamically updated document. While up to fifty writers can typically be given access to the file, these applications are especially suited for smaller groups or even partners. They also provide a full record of contributions and changes that is useful for assessment purposes. Since changes and comments are reflected in real time on the screens of anyone who has opened the document in their browser, classes may choose to incorporate synchronous editing and discussion in either face-to-face or online collaborative situations. (For more on synchronous and asynchronous learning environments, see "Fully Online and Hybrid Writing Instruction," this volume.) Privacy levels are granular; instructors may elect to keep groups set to student-only in early drafting stages or to include themselves from the beginning, and all parties can rest assured that no one who has not been given access to the file will view or change it. (See also Evans and Bunting.)

Weblogs, or blogs, provide a different set of features and possibilities for writing assignments. Blogging platforms typically facilitate creation of posts, or short written pieces that may include audio, video, or still images, that are time stamped and presented in reverse chronological order. They commonly include a comments function that permits visitors to the site to leave responses as well as an email address or link to their own site. These basic features can be customized through the use of templates and plug-ins, and now blogs are often used not just as journals, as they were in the early days, but as customizable content management systems that support portfolios, magazines, community-based sites, business sites, and many other genres. Most campus-approved CMSs, such as Blackboard, also include a private blogging function; major blogging platforms, such as WordPress, are typically installed on individual domains, department servers, or campus-supported blogging systems, such as the University of Minnesota's UThink project, and are public unless password protection is enabled.

Blogs can be used in a wide variety of collaborative assignments: peer review of single-authored writing, group project logs, group-produced online magazines, individual portfolios that undergo peer review, collaboratively produced websites for campus organizations or local businesses, and more. They also scale easily to large-group assignments.

Large Groups

Photo sharing applications enable students to upload photos to a central location for use in their own projects. They also commonly enable license-based searches for images created by others who have licensed their work through Creative Commons to indicate that they approve of re-use by others. These images can be embedded in central group projects, such as magazines or websites, or can serve as a central database of example images.

Social tagging applications are useful in a wide variety of collaborative activities and can be part of a stand-alone assignment or incorporated into much larger project development phases. Their use is scalable from individual to full-class to public; we list them here as a "large-group" application because that is the way we have primarily used them in the classroom. During the initial research stages of group or full-class collaborative projects, we often ask students to tag a set number of resources each week. Classes collaboratively develop a central vocabulary for common terms and then begin tagging not just for their own individual topics but also for the topics of others in the class.

The inventor of **wikis**, Ward Cunningham, describes a wiki as "a freely expandable collection of interlinked Web pages, a *hypertext system* for storing and modifying information—a *database*, where each page is easily editable by any user with a . . . Web browser client" (Leuf and Cunningham, 14, emphases original). This rather involved definition may mask the simplicity of wikis, which are simple content management systems that permit any user with access to edit pages. Contributors need not know how to code, but instead use wiki syntax that is primarily handled via a toolbar with icons similar to those found in common word processing applications. Each wiki page has four tabbed, easily-navigable layers: the primary article, the article's editing screen, the relevant edit history, and a full transcript of discussions concerning that article. Central page text can be as simple or fully multimodal as is appropriate for the class, since wikis can host anything from straight written text to still and moving images as well as audio. Multiple collaborators can work simultaneously, and the resulting edit history is useful for assessment purposes. Wiki platforms have become increasingly robust and stable; consequently, they can support not only small-group and full-class collaboration projects but also projects with collaborators from multiple institutions or public contributions.

The nature of wiki collaboration means that writers move frequently between being writers and being readers. The blurring of these roles demonstrates the complications of digital authorship, and further incorporating CBPP (which we think of as wide collaboration) extends these complications. However, asking students to participate in real-world, radically collaborative projects that stretch beyond the classroom has the potential to add immense value by purposefully introducing real-world problems, as Cummings notes: "locating relevant and interesting projects that need their talents, developing expertise rapidly, negotiating feedback, and delivering only the most valuable information to readers" (23).

Wikis also demand more flexibility, training, and support from both the instructor(s) and the students. Krista usually devotes a least a full class period to discussion of wikis and demonstration of the basic interface. (Helpful introductory case studies on wikis include selections from Tapscott and Williams.) Students begin with full-class collaboration on the site architecture before breaking into small groups based on subject-area interests. They begin page composition by outlining pages with plain text, and the skills for incorporating multimodal text objects like images, video, or dynamic maps are introduced on a need-to-know basis later in the semester. Early stages of the project are best focused on extensive planning and research; despite these preparations, the writing and development process will likely feel very messy at the midpoint milestones. Wikis facilitate the messiness of the writing process, but they also render it transparent and obvious. This is why it is crucial to build in time later in the semester not just for peer review but also for usability testing and revision. (For more on practical aspects of usability testing and collaboration, see Krug.)

Wikis present additional privacy issues that require management. The platform was developed for openness on multiple levels: to exist on the open Web, to be editable by any user, and to share information publicly in alignment with open-access philosophies. Each of these levels is negotiable for classroom use. Instructors may choose to password-protect the site so that it is only available to or editable by class members. Maintaining an open wiki can have benefits, but it also requires that the administrator develop a management plan for unwanted collaborations in the form of wiki vandalism. Vandalism most often involves specious page edits that include insertion of misinformation and spam as well as deletion or alteration of approved content. A number of plug-ins and barriers have been developed to help automatically manage vandalism, but at some point in the wiki's life span human management will be needed either in the form of site clean-up or to tighten basic security measures.

Krista uses wikis frequently as a platform for teaching digital instructions sets in technical writing classes as well as the central platform for place-based guides on topics such as the 35W Bridge Collapse in Minneapolis, the 2008 RNC Protests in St. Paul, and points of interest in the greater Syracuse area. There are many other potential uses as well: wikibooks (Barton), resource compendiums, presentations, simulations, and annotation wikis that are devoted to close reading of texts (Phillipson). Robert Cummings and Matt Barton's edited collection *Wiki Writing: Collaborative Learning in the College Classroom* provides an extensive overview of issues associated with wiki-based pedagogies; Cummings' *Lazy Virtues: Teaching Writing in the Age of Wikipedia* addresses the nuances of including Wikipedia-based work in the composition classroom.

Collaboration after the Fact

In much the same way that collaborators can contribute to wiki pages long after the original writers have moved on, Twitter presents possibilities for collaboration after the fact. This free application invites account holders to post updates of 140 characters or less from their desktops or mobile devices. Tweets can fulfill a number of functions in the synchronous collaborative classroom, from students asking and answering each others' questions to bringing linked resources to the class's attention to publicizing their finished projects. This last aspect may lead to collaboration after the fact and may indeed be part of a Twitter-based assignment. Tweets have become a common method for organizations and individuals to distribute announcements and other information by including descriptive wording and a link to additional Web resources, which may include websites and press releases. Goals for this sort of tweeting include not just the initial distribution of information to the initial account's followers but persuading other users to "retweet" the information to their followers, who may in turn re-distribute it further (Ridolfo and DeVoss). In the case of Twitter, such strategies for inviting later collaboration include not only composing for interest but also working with the length constraints imposed by the system. Using all 140 characters is not strategic for a tweet designed for redistribution; users must compose even shorter tweets that leave room for the retweeting user's name. One space-saving strategy is using URL shortening services that reduce lengthy web addresses to just a few characters. (Sagolla provides thorough discussion of style and audience-focused composition of tweets.)

Added to all that we have already described, collaboration after the fact highlights the vast array of approaches to, reasons for, and technologies for collaborative pedagogy today. We recommend that instructors not allow themselves the overwhelming—and misguided—feeling that they must master all those possibilities before launching into collaborative pedagogy or its digital possibilities. As Collin Gifford Brooke points out elsewhere in this volume, "new media replace expertise with exploration and engagement"; the same is true for digital collaborative pedagogies. It is better, we believe, to reflect on this chapter's overview, to explore any interesting sources it suggests, to think about one's own pedagogical goals, to choose one plausible-looking option, and to try it out in the classroom. With pedagogies this rich, instructor mastery is a lifetime's task, whereas a rhetorically thoughtful buffet-style approach is exciting, challenging, and doable.

BIBLIOGRAPHY

Barker, Thomas T., and Fred O. Kemp. "Network Theory: A Postmodern Pedagogy for the Writing Classroom." *Computers and Community: Teaching Composition in the Twenty-First Century*. Ed. Carolyn Handa. Portsmouth: Boynton/Cook, 1990. 1–27. Print.

Barthes, Roland. "The Death of the Author." *Aspen: The Magazine in a Box*. 5+6 (1967). As presented at UbuWeb: http://www.ubu.com/aspen/aspen5and6/index.html. Web. 12 Sept. 2012.

Barton, Matt. "Is There a Wiki in This Class? Wikibooks and the Future of Higher Education." *Wiki Writing: Collaborative Learning in the College Classroom*. Ed. Robert E. Cummings and Matt Barton. Ann Arbor: U of Michigan P, 2008. 177–93. Print.

Bedore, Pamela, and Brian O'Sullivan. "Addressing Instructor Ambivalence about Peer Review and Self-Assessment." *WPA: Writing Program Administration* 34.2 (Spring 2011): 11–36. Print.

Beech, Richard, Chris Anson, Lee-Ann Kastman Breuch, and Thom Swiss. *Teaching Writing Using Blogs, Wikis, and Other Digital Tools*. Norwood: Christopher-Gordon, 2008. Print.

Benkler, Yochai. *The Wealth of Networks: How Social Production Transforms Markets and Freedom*. New Haven: Yale UP, 2007. Print.

Benkler, Yochai, and Helen Nissenbaum. "Commons-based Peer Production and Virtue." *The Journal of Political Philosophy* 14.4 (2006): 394–419. Print.

Breuch, Lee-Ann Kastman. *Virtual Peer Review: Teaching and Learning about Writing in Online Environments*. Albany: SUNY P, 2004. Print.

Brooke, Collin Gifford. *Lingua Fracta: Towards a Rhetoric of New Media*. Cresskill: Hampton, 2009. Print.

Bruffee, Kenneth A. "Collaborative Learning and the 'Conversation of Mankind.'" *College English* 46.7 (November 1984): 635–52. Print.

Bump, Jerome. "Collaborative Learning in the Postmodern Classroom." *Situating College English: Lessons from an American University*. Ed. Evan Carton and Alan W. Friedman. Westport: Bergin & Garvey, 1996. 111–20. Print.

Burns, Hugh Lee, Jr. "Stimulating Rhetorical Invention in English Composition through Computer-Assisted Instruction." Diss., U of Texas, 1979. Print.

Ching, Kory Lawson. "Peer Response in the Composition Classroom: An Alternative Genealogy." *Rhetoric Review* 26.3 (2007): 303–19.

Clark, Suzanne, and Lisa Ede. "Collaboration, Resistance, and the Teaching of Writing." *The Right to Literacy*. Ed. Andrea A. Lunsford, Helene Moglen, and James Slevin. New York: Modern Language Association, 1990. 276–85.

Comer, Denise. "English Composition I: Achieving Expertise." Duke UP. n.d. Web. 5 Jan. 2013.

Crowley, Sharon. *A Teacher's Introduction to Deconstruction*. Urbana: National Council of Teachers of English, 1989. Print.

Cummings, Robert E. *Lazy Virtues: Teaching Writing in the Age of Wikipedia*. Nashville: Vanderbilt UP, 2009. Print.

Cummings, Robert E., and Matt Barton, eds. *Wiki Writing: Collaborative Learning in the College Classroom*. Ann Arbor: U of Michigan P, 2008. Print.

Cyganowski, Carol Klimick. "The Computer Classroom and Collaborative Learning: The Impact on Student Writers." *Computers and Community: Teaching Composition in the Twenty-First Century*. Ed. Carolyn Handa. Portsmouth: Boynton/Cook, 1990. 68–88. Print.

Davis, Andréa, Suzanne Webb, Dundee Lackey, and Dànielle Nicole DeVoss. "Remix, Play, and Remediation: Undertheorized Composing Practices." *Writing (and) the Digital Generation.* Ed. Heather Urbanski. Jefferson: McFarland, 2010. 186–97. Print.

Duin, Ann Hill, and Craig Hansen. "Reading and Writing on Computer Networks as Social Construction and Social Interaction." *Literacy and Computers: The Complications of Teaching and Learning with Technology.* Ed. Cynthia L. Selfe and Susan Hilligoss. New York: Modern Language Association, 1994. 89–112. Print.

Elbow, Peter. *The Journal of the Assembly for Expanded Perspectives on Learning.* Special Issue: "Pictures of the Believing Game." 15 (Winter 2009-2010)

_____. *Writing without Teachers.* New York: Oxford UP, 1973. Print.

Evans, Donna J., and Ben S. Bunting, Jr. "Cooperative and Collaborative Writing with Google Docs." *Collaborative Learning and Writing: Essays on Using Small Groups in Teaching English and Composition.* Ed. Kathleen M. Hunzer. Jefferson: McFarland and Company, 2012. 109–129. Print.

Flower, Linda. "Negotiating the Meaning of Difference." *Written Communication* 13.1 (January 1996): 44–92.

Fontaine, Sheryl I., and Susan M. Hunter. *Collaborative Writing in Composition Studies.* Boston: Wadsworth, 2006. Print.

Forbes, Cheryl. "Cowriting, Overwriting, and Overriding in Portfolio Land Online." *Computers and Composition* 13.2 (1996): 195–205. Print.

Forman, Janis. "Literacy, Collaboration, and Technology: New Connections and Challenges." *Literacy and Computers: The Complications of Teaching and Learning with Technology.* Ed. Cynthia L. Selfe and Susan Hilligoss. New York: Modern Language Association, 1994. 130–43. Print.

Foucault, Michel. "What Is an Author?" *Bulletin de la Société française de Philosophie* 63.3 (1969): 73–104. Rpt. *Language, Countermemory, Practice: Selected Essays and Interviews.* Ed. Donald F. Bouchard. Trans. Donald F. Bouchard and Sherry Simon. Ithaca: Cornell UP, 1977. 113–38.

Fox, Thomas. "Race and Gender in Collaborative Learning." *Writing With: New Directions in Collaborative Teaching, Learning, and Research.* Ed. Sally Barr Reagan, Thomas Fox, and David Bleich. Albany: SUNY P, 1994. 111–22.

Gere, Anne Ruggles. *Writing Groups: History, Theory, and Implications.* Carbondale: Southern Illinois UP, 1987. Print.

Gerstle, Val, and Lynda Walsh. *Autism Spectrum Disorders in the College Composition Classroom.* Milwaukee: Marquette UP. 2011. Print.

Gurak, Laura J. *Cyberliteracy: Navigating the Internet with Awareness.* New Haven: Yale UP, 2003. Print.

Holdstein, Deborah H. "The Institutional Agenda, Collaboration, and Writing Assessment." *Writing With: New Directions in Collaborative Teaching, Learning, and Research.* Ed. Sally Barr Reagan, Thomas Fox, and David Bleich. Albany: SUNY P, 1994. 77-88. Print.

Howard, Rebecca Moore. "Collaborative Pedagogy." *A Guide to Composition Pedagogies.* 1st ed. Ed. Gary Tate, Amy Rupiper, and Kurt Schick. New York: Oxford UP, 2001. 54–71. Print.

_____. *Standing in the Shadow of Giants: Plagiarists, Authors, Collaborators.* Stamford: Ablex, 1999. Kindle e-book file.

Hughes, Linda K., and Michael Lund. "Union and Reunion: Collaborative Authorship." *Authority and Textuality: Current Views of Collaborative Writing.* Ed. James S. Leonard,

Christine E. Wharton, Robert Murray Davis, and Jeanette Harris. West Cornwall: Locust Hill, 1994. 41–60.

Isaacs, Emily, and Phoebe Jackson, eds. *Public Works: Student Writing as Public Text.* Portsmouth: Heinemann, 2001.

Janangelo, Joseph. "Intricate Inscriptions: Negotiating Conflict between Collaborative Writers." *Journal of Teaching Writing* 15.1 (1996): 91–105.

Johnson-Eilola, Johndan. *Datacloud: Toward a New Theory of Online Work.* Cresskill: Hampton, 2005. Print.

Kemp, Fred. "The Origins of ENFI, Network Theory, and Computer-Based Collaborative Writing Instruction at the University of Texas." *Network-Based Classrooms: Promises and Realities.* Ed. Bertram Bruce, Joy Kreeft Peyton, and Trent Batson. Cambridge: Cambridge UP, 1993. 161–80. Print.

Kennedy, Krista. "Textual Machinery: Authorial Agency and Bot-Written Texts in Wikipedia." *The Responsibilities of Rhetoric.* Ed. Michelle Smith and Barbara Warnick. Long Grove: Waveland, 2010. 303–309. Print.

Kephart III, John M., and Steven F. Rafferty. "'Yes We Can': Rhizomatic Rhetorical Agency in Hyper-modern Campaign Ecologies." *Argumentation and Advocacy* 46.1 (Summer 2009): 6–20. Print.

Kittle, Peter, and Troy Hicks. "Transforming the Group Paper with Collaborative On-line Writing." *Pedagogy: Critical Approaches to Teaching Literature, Language, Composition, and Culture* 9.3 (2009): 525–38. Print.

Krug, Steve. *Don't Make Me Think: A Common Sense Approach to Web Usability.* 2nd ed. San Francisco: New Riders. 2005. Print.

LeFevre, Karen Burke. *Invention as a Social Act.* Carbondale: Southern Illinois UP, 1987. Print.

Lessig, Lawrence. *Remix: Making Art and Commerce Thrive in the Hybrid Economy.* New York: Penguin, 2008. Print.

Leuf, Bo, and Ward Cunningham. *The Wiki Way: Quick Collaboration on the Web.* Boston: Addison-Wesley, 2001. Print.

Logie, John. "Cut and Paste: Remixing Composition Pedagogy for Online Workspaces." *Internet-Based Workplace Communication: Industry and Academic Perspectives.* Ed. Kirk St. Amant and Pavel Zemliansky. Hershey: Information Science-Idea Group, 2005. 299–316. Print.

Lunsford, Andrea A., and Lisa Ede. *Singular Texts/Plural Authors: Perspectives on Collaborative Writing.* Carbondale: Southern Illinois UP, 1990. Print.

Morgan, Meg. "Women as Emergent Leaders in Student Collaborative Writing Groups." *Journal of Advanced Composition* 14.1 (Winter 1994): 203–19. Print.

Patchan, Melissa M., Davida Charney, and Christian D. Schunn. "A Validation Study of Students' End Comments: Comparing Comments by Students, a Writing Instructor, and a Content Instructor." *Journal of Writing Research* 1.2 (2009): 124–52. Print.

Phillipson, Mark. "Wikis in the Classroom: A Taxonomy." *Wiki Writing: Collaborative Learning in the College Classroom.* Ed. Robert E. Cummings and Matt Barton. Ann Arbor: U of Michigan P, 2008. 19–43. Print.

Porter, James E. *Rhetorical Ethics and Internetworked Writing.* Greenwich: Ablex, 1998.

Rafoth, Bennett A., and Donald L. Rubin. *The Social Construction of Written Communication.* Norwood: Ablex, 1988. Print.

Reagan, Sally Barr, Thomas Fox, and David Bleich, eds. *Writing With: New Directions in Collaborative Teaching, Learning, and Research.* Albany: SUNY P, 1994. Print.

Ridolfo, Jim, and Danielle Nicole DeVoss. "In the (Re)mix: Rhetorical Velocity and Delivery." *Kairos: A Journal of Rhetoric, Technology, and Pedagogy* 13.2 (2009). Web.

Rogers, Priscilla S., and Marjorie S. Horton. "Exploring the Value of Face-to-Face Collaborative Writing." *New Visions of Collaborative Writing*. Ed. Janis Forman. Portsmouth: Boynton/Cook, 1992. 120–46. Print.

Sagolla, Dom. *140 Characters: A Style Guide for the Short Form*. Hoboken, NJ: Wiley, 2009.

Selfe, Cynthia L. "Computer-based Conversations and the Changing Nature of Collaboration." *New Visions of Collaborative Writing*. Ed. Janis Forman. Portsmouth: Boynton/Cook, 1992. 147–69. Print.

Sheridan, David M., Jim Ridolfo, and Anthony J. Michel. *The Available Means of Persuasion: Mapping a Theory and Pedagogy of Multimodal Public Rhetoric*. Anderson: Parlor, 2012. Print.

Spear, Karen. *Sharing Writing: Peer Response Groups in English Classes*. Portsmouth: Boynton/Cook, 1988. Print.

Spigelman, Candace. *Across Property Lines: Textual Ownership in Writing Groups*. Carbondale: Southern Illinois UP, 2000. Print.

Tapscott, Don, and Anthony D. Williams. *Wikinomics: How Mass Collaboration Changes Everything*. New York: Portfolio Trade, 2010. Print.

Trimbur, John. "Consensus and Difference in Collaborative Learning." *College English* 51.6 (Oct. 1989): 602–616. Print.

Villanueva, Victor. "On Writing Groups, Class, and Culture: Studying Oral and Literate Language Features in Writing." *Writing With: New Directions in Collaborative Teaching, Learning, and Research*. Ed. Sally Barr Reagan, Thomas Fox, and David Bleich. Albany: SUNY P, 1994. 123-40. Print.

Warnick, Barbara, and David S. Heineman. *Rhetoric Online: The Politics of New Media*. 2nd ed. New York: Peter Lang, 2012. Print.

Wolfe, Joanna. *Team Writing: A Guide to Working in Groups*. New York: Bedford St. Martin's, 2010. Print.

Wyatt, Christopher Scott. *Online Pedagogy: Designing Writing Courses for Students with Autism Spectrum Disorders*. Diss., U of Minnesota, 2010. Web.

Zappen, James P., Laura J. Gurak, and Stephen Doheny-Farina. "Rhetoric, Community, and Cyberspace." *Rhetoric Review* 15.2 (1997): 400–419. Print.

Community-Engaged Pedagogies

Laura Julier
Kathleen Livingston
Eli Goldblatt

> Information severed from thoughtful action is dead, a mind-
> crushing load.
>
> John Dewey, *Democracy and Education*, 153

The three of us come to the work of community-engaged pedagogy by distinctly different paths. When Laura stumbled into collaboration with her colleague David Cooper in 1994, it was from the study of composition theories and pedagogies and years of teaching in both first-year writing and advanced undergraduate nonfiction writing programs. From the standpoint of social constructivist and critical-activist theories of the teaching of writing, an arrangement whereby students engaged with groups outside of the classroom to write (at whatever level of production and toward whatever purposes) just made good sense. That the engagement might also be on behalf of organizations focused on social justice issues created for her a perfect confluence of method and matter. Katie came to community-engagement work in the Youth Empowerment Program at an LGBT community center in metro-Detroit, where youth-driven initiatives are common practice. Beginning with the service-learning writing courses created by her mentor, Laura Julier, through teaching a number of other courses grounded in community-engagement, and studying theories of community-based and civic pedagogies with Terese Guinsatao Monberg, she has come to recognize and value community work for the ways it can teach us about integrity and consent. Eli began his first community-based writing course in the early 1990s, when he was teaching at a small Catholic university with a history of offering courses at a nearby maximum-security prison. At first he was just looking for a way to step off the well-kept suburban campus into a place with a very different atmosphere of political and social urgencies, but he found that the students responded with a redoubled commitment to their own educations even as the incarcerated men welcomed the attention and the intellectual challenge each week. For all three of us, community-engaged pedagogies have enlivened our teaching practices and forced us to reflect on our own goals as citizens and humans on the planet.

Certainly service learning, or what we call here "community-engaged pedagogies," and writing instruction began to move toward one another long before the early composition-rhetoric publications on the subject from 1994 to 1997 (see Adler-Kassner, Crooks, and Watters; Goldblatt, "Van Rides"; Herzberg; Peck, Flower, and Higgins). The spirit of hands-on learning that permeates the work of John Dewey and connects with the liberating attitudes toward student-centered instruction of Paulo Freire and bell hooks has long been influential in the field of Writing Studies. As American college populations expanded while political consciousnesses rose in the late 1960s, writing teachers looked for ways to make school assignments relevant to their students. Early expressivists like Ken Macrorie and Peter Elbow asked beginning writers to compose from their own feelings and responses, and they linked the power of what people wrote to a sense of honesty and truth in the world they knew. In *Telling Writing*, for example, Macrorie says: "But it's truthtelling that does the most to release language powers. We ask for truth to the world out there, which can be verified; and the truth to the world inside, the writer's feelings, which no one can verify. A double obligation, but one that miraculously frees our seminar writers" (7). Expressivists have long been criticized for seeming to encourage self-involved personal discourse, but Macrorie's emphasis on truthtelling indicates another legacy of sixties pedagogy: the desire to connect personal commitments to social and political realities, the hope that writing could address problems the writer recognizes in the world. Thus, even before faculty began arranging for their students to work in prisons and soup kitchens, senior centers and clinics for undocumented immigrants, composition theorists were linking the strength and flow of their students' essays to a felt sense of internal and external reality students encountered outside the classroom.

There are no easy formulas about how to teach reading and writing in the context of community-based courses. We point readers to a wealth of books and articles on the subject of service learning (see Butin; Eyler and Giles; Rhoads; Stanton, Giles, and Cruz; Waterman) and a growing list of publications on the subject within composition and rhetoric (see Ackerman and Coogan; Cella and Restaino; Cushman; Deans; Deans, Roswell, and Wurr; Flower; Grabill; Long; Mathieu; Rose and Weiser). We have chosen here to answer as directly as we can five questions we think will be most likely on the minds of people either starting out with community-engaged pedagogies or well on the way but seeking supportive allies. Each answer comes from one of us, framed in our own voices and variously representing our personal experiences with such pedagogical challenges. Work among neighborhoods and across institutional barriers requires honoring personal differences while combining individual contributions into a collective understanding and direction.

1) WHAT IS COMMUNITY-ENGAGED PEDAGOGY, AND HOW WILL IT HELP STUDENTS IN A WRITING COURSE? (LAURA)

Community-engaged pedagogy is a kind of experiential learning grounded in the understanding of writing as a situated, social act. Although in practice a writing course defined by community-engagement may take many forms, fundamentally what all have in common is that students work in relationship with a community-based organization or initiative, to write for purposes that are shaped or defined by the public sphere.

In designing a community-engaged writing course, there are reams of decisions to make about the structure and goals of such classes, as well as questions to negotiate—such as the role of the instructor, the evaluation of student work, and relationships between instructor and community partners. Campus service-learning centers often regulate or facilitate (to varying degrees) matters pertaining to relationships, liability, and partnerships.

Community-engaged writing courses differ widely in the purposes and audiences for which students write, the forms of writing they produce, the way that the community-engagement serves the goals of the writing program, the understanding of "community," and the means of assessing learning in the course. The community partnership, for instance, might serve to further mastery of learning outcomes or to motivate students to value writing. It might provide authentic purposes and audiences for student writing, or engage students in meaningful action to effect social change, or serve larger institutional goals such as connecting the work of universities with local needs—the range of experiences is wide and all are possibilities for basing the design of a writing course around this kind of pedagogy.

In some versions of a community-engaged writing course, students might research, draft, revise, and edit documents that serve an organization's needs: Students interview residents of a nursing home to record personal histories, tutor underserved school kids in after-school reading and writing programs, help elementary students write and illustrate school newspapers or zines, or produce media that does work on behalf of nonprofit organizations. In others, students partner with an organization or community group to learn about and advocate on behalf of particular civic and social issues in that community. In any of these arrangements, when students engage with audiences, projects, and purposes outside of the classroom, they are able to wrestle with, analyze, revise, and produce variations of discourse in ways sometimes presumed not possible in a classroom.

In designing community-engaged writing courses, it's useful to consider a couple of different frames. In her 1994 article on service learning, Nora Bacon describes a binary for the functions of the writing students do (and consequently the ways students may be positioned in relationship to the community organizations) as either writing *as* service or writing *about* service ("Community Service and Writing Instruction"). Thomas Deans later describes a distinction between writing for, writing about, and writing with community partners (*Writing Partnerships*), which has the effect of shifting attention from the function of the texts to the relationships of texts to community agency in the course design.

Students often find the purposes for writing by engaging with agents outside the classroom and must discover those purposes in context, rather than having them defined by instructors. Matters of form, genre, voice—and even process— emerge from exigencies in the social situation, and students are often themselves charged with discovering or inventing appropriate solutions to these writing questions with or on behalf of a community organization. It results in, as Bacon has said, "writing instruction . . . reconceived to accommodate the fact of rhetorical variation" ("Building" 591).

Choices about community partners rest often in the instructor's understanding of what constitutes "community." Cheryl Hofstetter Duffy, for example, describes an early service-learning course in which her first-year writing students partnered with international students at the university, then from those interactions "honed their interviewing and note-taking skills as they worked one-on-one with the international students," and later wrote academic papers using material from their interactions (3). Or the community partner might be part of the university, such as the Safe Walk project at Michigan State University, for which my students one semester developed a suite of advertising materials to raise awareness about the service among other students on campus and to recruit more volunteers.

With the social turn in Composition Studies, many scholars and teachers have designed courses that engage one of a variety of forms of literacy instruction. Looking to Dewey and Freire, some see literacy as enabling learners to become active, critical, responsible participants in democratic processes. With Henry Giroux and Peter McLaren, building on Freire's work, some also see literacy as critical reading of cultural texts and practices. Literacy projects represent a variety of discourses within and without the university and thus also suggest the necessity of engaging and valuing multiple literacies and discourses. In programs such as the Dayton Literacy Project (see Conniff and Youngkin), Bruce Herzberg's course at Bentley, the tutoring project at the Ellis School in Pittsburgh that Norma Greco describes, and Eli's work with New City Writing in Philadelphia (Luetzow, Macaluso, and Goldblatt), literacy itself is both the service and the subject of investigation. As students engage in literacy tutoring, they develop a new expertise: Their experience becomes a position from which they are invited to re-compose themselves and their knowledge. They reflect upon and investigate discursive practices in order to better understand how these practices shape the nature of social issues.

In any of these designs, the instructor may orchestrate an experience limited to that class and that semester, or participate in a project that has its genesis and life outside of the limits of a course's needs and timetable. For example, in Herzberg's class, work in the community functioned as a complement to a structured set of readings and writing assignments that allowed him to raise issues and push students to a deeper consideration of the complex forces at work in social situations begging for change, thereby developing their skills in critical analysis. Linda Flower's students at Carnegie Mellon serve as student mentors to urban teens and adults at the Community Literacy Center (an ongoing collaboration between Carnegie Mellon University and Pittsburgh's Community House), using writing and public dialogue to take action in response to the problems of the urban neighborhoods it serves.

Most instructors who embrace community-engaged pedagogies understand that the movement back and forth between action and reflection is essential to these kinds of learning experiences. It's a commitment that may be found in community-engaged pedagogy's roots, part of which are in activist and liberatory pedagogies such as Freire's (see *Pedagogy* and *Education*, among others). The Wingspread Report's "Principles of Good Practice for Combining Service and Learning" were developed (under the aegis of the National Society for Internships and Experiential Education) in order to make clear that the connections between service and "reflective learning" must be integral not secondary to any educational experience that engages students in work in the community (Honnet and Poulsen).

Designing a writing course around community partnerships initially grabbed hold of me because it seemed to offer the possibility of grounding writing instruction in purposes that emerge from the public sphere rather than to serve academic purposes only. In the first-year writing curricula in which I'd previously taught, motivating students to see the course and assignments as anything other than a pesky requirement was a persistent challenge. More important, providing students with experiences for which what they said and wrote had consequences—often unsettling or ambiguous ones—spoke to the values of critical pedagogy and experiential learning in which I had always sought to ground any class I taught. My experience, however, raised more questions than I had anticipated and forced me back upon the same questions which any writing program must answer: What educational goals are served when we choose to teach writing by creating opportunities to engage and partner with various communities in different ways?

For some, community-engagement encourages critical thinking by asking students to examine and reflect upon experiences in which they're currently engaged. As students interact with others outside their classroom around issues of social justice, economic disparity, or identity, for instance, they are building a knowledge base that allows them to "join the academic conversation from a position of authority" (Bacon, "Community Service and Writing Instruction" 14). The most obvious advantage of community-engaged writing courses is the way in which student writers can explore and negotiate the complexities of rhetorical exigencies: the ways in which audiences differ, words work, and meanings multiply in various social settings. Engaging students in writing in community settings, Nora Bacon argues, "demonstrates the enormous variety in written discourse and the degree to which the forms, processes, and purposes of writing are embedded in particular contexts" and consequently "points us toward a curriculum of textual studies based on inquiry into variation in discourse" ("Community Service Writing" 53).

The self-evident contradiction between one of the central tenets of Composition Studies—to attend to audience—and one of the most fundamental assumptions enacted in most composition classrooms—that students write for one audience in one type of context—seems to make the case for moving the work of writing classes into more varied contexts, including non-academic ones. One caution many of us who do this work would offer has to do with how little writing instructors often know about the requirements and expectations of writing in non-academic contexts. In a carefully narrated and analyzed case study of San Francisco State University's Community Service Writing program, Bacon notes, "All of us found that community-based writing assignments fit awkwardly into our courses. Many of us re-examined our assumptions about what writers need to know, and many of us formulated a vision of writing instruction grounded in rhetorical theory" ("Building" 605). If, Bacon argues, instructors make rhetorical instruction central to their courses and use varieties of genres and contexts, then there is a much higher chance that learning in composition classrooms will indeed transfer to other contexts, both academic and non-academic: "If students write in more than one genre, in more than one rhetorical context, they have access to a *comparative* view of discourse—which is an essential step toward a *critical* view" (606).

Without thoughtful consideration about the meaning, the mutuality, or the purposes of the work with community partners, community-engaged writing courses may also (as Arca; Herzberg; Adler-Kassner; and Cleary, among others, argue) unwittingly raise issues of class distinctions and risk replicating the kinds of divisions between service provider and service recipient with which some students—such as many underprepared writers or nontraditional or community college students—have had too much personal experience. The rhetoric of sending students "out" into "the" community may, in some settings and course designs, confirm for students an insider-outsider understanding of academic purposes and replicate condescending models of charity and missionary work, which do more to undermine than to advance the goals of multicultural education and social transformation. Issues of social class, race, gender, identity, and expression play out variously when we ask students to engage in service of any kind to local communities. Tracy Hamler Carrick, Margaret Himley, and Tobi Jacobi offer stories about using these kinds of disjunctions as moments for reflective analysis and resistance to "the master narratives of service learning, reciprocity, happy endings, and the public discourse of activisms" (311).

These issues can suggest further differences in the goals and configurations of community-engaged writing courses. Adler-Kassner, in responding to Herzberg, raises the question, "Should issues about social structures, ideology, and social justice be focuses for community service course [sic] for underprepared students?" and answers, "The primary difference between Herzberg's course and [mine] is that the primary emphasis in my courses was not on raising critical consciousness, but in helping students articulate whatever consciousness they had in a way that was acceptable in the academy" ("Digging" 55). What characterizes these conversations on community-engaged pedagogies in writing instruction are, more than anything, the philosophical and ideological differences among instructors' commitments. The tensions arising from those differences can and ought to be both disruptive and generative.

2) HOW DO I FIND COMMUNITY PARTNERSHIPS FOR MY STUDENTS? (KATHLEEN)

There are many versions of community-engaged pedagogy in writing instruction, many curricular configurations, grounded in sometimes conflicting assumptions about everything from the goals of writing instruction in public, personal, and

academic settings, to the kinds of literacies that (should) count in academic enterprises, to the relationships between academics and community members/spaces,
and the obligations of higher education to participate in social justice and reform
initiatives, among a host of other matters. No matter which version of community-
engagement an instructor uses, Ellen Cushman's foundational work on reciprocity
has made negotiating mutually beneficial relationships among students, instructors,
and community members common practice ("Rhetorician" 16). Community-based
literacy work requires listening carefully to community needs and negotiating
relationships, which can lead to a deeper understanding of the work and needs of
community organizations (Goldblatt, "Story" 65).

Finding community sites for students to do community-engagement projects
might begin with the instructor examining existing commitments in communities.
In moving to Lansing in 2008, I ran into one of the common problems in community-
engagement work: Though well-connected in Detroit and the metro area, I barely
knew anyone in mid-Michigan. Missing home, missing the concrete and store-
fronts of 9 Mile, the familiar faces at the LGBT community center, and the routines
we'd built together around the center's rhythms, I longed for the casual conversations, familiarity, and extravagance of gay life. In talking openly with my mentor
Laura about missing home and my community, I decided to teach the first-year
writing course, *Writing Public Life in America,* designed around community-
engagement. Through the slow process of making LGBTQ and feminist community
relationships in Lansing, I've become more involved with community organizations and work here, broadened my sense of community, reconnected with people
from home, and begun to stitch together a sense of myself as a local (Michigander)
in a new place (mid-Michigan).

The process of getting involved with local communities can be modeled
for community-engaged students, who may or may not feel like they belong, and
students' prior commitments can serve as inspiration as well. As Eric Ball and Alice
Lai remind us in an article on student investment in community-engagement
work, students are not always deeply invested in the university and in local communities (268). At large, research institutions like Michigan State—which draw
local students, those from across the country, and growing communities of international students—students in community-engaged courses may be literally and
metaphorically far from home, looking for a sense of local community. As Ball and
Lai suggest, foregrounding the local by inviting local community art, literature,
and activism to guide course design can lead to a greater sense of student investment
in the university and surrounding communities (261) and encourage instructors
and educational institutions to remain accountable in their community-engagement
work by being aware of what is going on locally (271).

Encouraging local students to guide conversations on local community issues,
if they choose, can be a way to foster a sense of pride in their position in their
communities and deepen their investment in community work. In community-
based courses I've taught, students from communities where we work—LGBTQ
and feminist communities, for example—often act as peer mentors, sharing
community-based understandings, languages, and resources. This can be tiring

work, so it is an important practice to foster some sense of self-care, boundaries, and limits in students who are also community members.

No matter the level of commitment or investment involved (from students, instructors, community members) in the intended community-engagement work, negotiating relationships takes time (see Monberg 22). And time may sit in tension with institutional interests, such as the necessity of having a curriculum design and course projects in place before the semester starts; or the impossibility of imagining students' community affiliations ahead of time; or the attempt to balance community, student, and instructor needs and desires. Laura Julier's chapter in the previous edition of this book, "Community-Service Pedagogy," addresses important differences between service learning and national service, community service, voluntarism, and academic internship or field placement (134). As work on community-engagement pedagogies indicates, projects must both have an educational benefit (Waterman 3) and be reciprocal or mutually beneficial to students and communities (see Cushman, *Rhetorician*; Goldblatt, *Because*).

At Affirmations LGBT community center, where I grew up as a youth, volunteer, and staff member, visitors from local universities and community groups often asked to use the community center as a site for community projects involving varying levels of commitment and investment. Students fulfilling a diversity requirement would walk through the community center space, look around, and ask well-intentioned questions. The job of volunteers and staff members when tours came was to dispel any myths about LGBTQ communities and teach the students that we are not monstrous after all. While touring a community space may be part of a community-engagement experience, this activity alone requires little time commitment on the part of students. Distanced projects also run the risk of positioning community members as what Margaret Himley has described as "the stranger," or the other, a figure Himley suggests "reveals the power asymmetries, social antagonisms, and historical determinants that are all too often concealed by discourses of volunteerism or civic literacy or active citizenship or experiential learning or rhetorical training—or, now, patriotism" (417).

At Affirmations, AmeriCorps volunteers would come in large groups and do small projects for center staff—pruning the community bulletin board; cataloguing books in the lending library; organizing the clothes closet; filling a bowl with condoms, dental dams, and lube; painting a chipped wall. Small projects were useful and soothing to overwhelmed staff members, community members who worked at the center for more than 40 hours a week. Project help meant staff members' time could be put to use working directly with center users—being a friendly person to talk to, providing access to resources (such as the Internet or a phone), organizing discussion and support groups, or planning large-scale special events. Practical as such short-term projects were, however, community-engagement courses require a longer-term commitment and push for a deeper investment on the part of students, instructors, and community members.

Ongoing university-community partnerships can provide an existing framework for instructors trying to design new courses around community-engaged pedagogies. In addition to identifying community relationships that instructors may already have and negotiating with community members how they might translate into mutually beneficial community projects, instructors also need to carefully design course projects to fit their objectives. Each of the potential project configurations mentioned earlier (writing for, with, about) has pros and cons. In community-engaged courses I've taught, projects that ran the smoothest were often those in which the instructor and/or students were also community members or allies. Terese Guinsatao Monberg's 2009 article calls this version of community-engagement work "writing *as* the community," re-framing community-engagement to open spaces for historically marginalized communities, specifically students of color, inviting them to deepen their existing community commitments (24). Acknowledging students' prior commitments, even if they don't yet have connections locally, can be a way to honor the power that community members have in mediating access to communities.

When working with historically marginalized communities, relationships among students, instructors, and community members require prior education and training. Community partnerships with American Indian nations, for instance, require respect for tribal customs and sovereignty issues. I am thinking here of Ellen Cushman's article on doing ethical work with and for Cherokee communities ("SSY Gadugi" 58). Cushman explains why it is important to begin with certain cultural understandings, and how she learned to do so through the Cherokee concept of gadugi: "an ethic that weds praxis and belief. This civic action taken for social justice enacts a spiritual connection to community and people, to legacies of social action" (58).

Within LGBTQ communities, cultural competency includes using the common courtesy of calling people by their requested pronouns, the carefulness not to "out" people in situations that might be dangerous, and a working understanding of racism, classism, sexism, ableism, homo- and transphobia. The center filled this need by holding community-based workshops and trainings—LGBT 101, Trans 101, sex education, white privilege, etc.—and being in the space was often a crash course. SAFE Space Ally programs are an example of community-based education that relies on community volunteers and allies to do cultural competency work (see Poynter and Tubbs). Prepping students with cultural competency training relieves community members of having to spend a lot of time educating people in spaces that should be safe. Peggy McIntosh's essay "Unpacking the Invisible Knapsack" is widely used to teach students about power and privilege. I have used the blogs *Autostraddle, Crunk Feminist Collective,* and *Racism School,* inviting students to do the research on relevant community issues. Community-engaged courses might also create and facilitate cultural competency workshops or teach-ins as part of their community-engagement.

Developing an effective community-engaged curriculum requires explicitly negotiating roles through significant planning and communication throughout. For example, while course instructors might take responsibility for prior education, community members may want to take on providing students with historical background and cultural context about the places and spaces where they work. How participants negotiate roles and the terms of relationships depends on the specific context and participants. Partly because of a need to give students more time to understand community issues and negotiate relationships, and partly because of ongoing efforts to sustain community-engagement work institutionally, ongoing conversations in the literature on community-engaged teaching about sustainability provide examples of effective single-semester, multisemester, and ongoing community projects, and although there are advantages in having more time to develop relationships with communities and to get work done, not every institutional situation affords that time.

The onus is on collaborations between instructors and community members to set up the conditions for ethical and mutually beneficial relationships between students and communities. Goldblatt's work reveals the complexities involved in community-engaged teaching that involves multiple institutions, schools, community colleges, universities, and community literacy centers, using Saul Alinsky's concept of self-interest to suggest how partners develop projects to their mutual benefit (Goldblatt, *Because*). Cushman makes a persuasive case for the benefits—to both student learning and project longevity—of creating community partnerships built on a faculty member's research agenda, "long term, well resourced, stable collaborations in inquiry that connect the university with the community" ("Sustainable" 41). Sustainable partnerships make it more likely that there will be institutional support for the partnership and create the conditions for more extended periods of reflection around relevant issues. Paula Mathieu's work in *Tactics of Hope* urges community-engaged writing courses to adopt a "project orientation" rather than a "problem orientation," developing tactical projects that "tap into existing debates or campaigns and define small interventions into that debate" rather than attempting to fix a large-scale problem (76). Tania Mitchell describes The Citizen Scholars Program, a four-semester program designed to teach students "to think more deeply about and develop commitments to act for social justice" (101) and "to be aware of root causes that lead to the flaws and problems they now recognize in the community" (102). Vanessa Marr's work reminds community-engagement scholars to listen to the stories of community members, in her case black women community gardeners involved with service-learning projects in Detroit, as they transform communities from the grassroots.

In all these varieties of community work, instructors need to be thinking about how community-engagement initiatives will be sustained once the course is over and whether they should be sustained (see Mathieu; Cella and Restaino). If students are positioned as skillful writers, and community members as the recipients of their writing products, then it may make sense to negotiate a semester-long project that lives on in an effective piece of writing. If the instructor's goal is working toward social change or social justice, then community-engagement may be spread out over the course of several semesters or years, where institutional conditions allow. Having an answer to the sustainability question will help those who need to make a case for community-engagement work at an institutional level talk about the benefits and risks of various versions of institutional-community partnerships (see Cella and Restaino).

3) WHAT KINDS OF WRITING ASSIGNMENTS WORK BEST FOR SUCH COURSES? (KATHLEEN)

One of the challenges in imagining a community-engaged course is developing writing assignments that balance various people's needs. Plenty of community organizations are glad for assistance with marketing and communications. Students involved in such projects work in groups, negotiating with each other and community partners to produce media—videos, newsletters, blogs, writing for the Web. Students doing professional writing projects may gain a sense of themselves as working writers whose work will be public, as well as an understanding of professional communication and negotiation skills. In such an arrangement, significant time is spent on reviewing drafts and considering how to sensitively take community partners' feedback into account while honoring students' voices as writers.

As Jonathan Alexander, Janell Haynes, and Jacqueline Rhodes suggest, community-engagement "fulfills multiple fantasies in composition studies": "the necessity of teaching literacy strategies so students can survive as thoughtful writers beyond the first year of college *and* the desire to prepare students for literate participation in complex public spheres and multicultural democracies" ("Public/ Sex" 2). Alexander's project worked with a year-long sequence of first-year writing classes to research issues related to HIV/AIDS. Using a peer education model common in LGBTQ communities, Alexander's course used community-based practices, inviting young students to engage with "youth culture" by making various media with an audience of college-aged youth (6–7). Knowing their writing would be published, Alexander suggests, gave students a sense of "rhetorical efficacy" and "a sense of how to 'talk' to one another about sexuality and sexual health issues" (7). In a similar writing course, Tobi Jacobi created collaborations between writing students and adolescent zinesters to examine assumptions about how youth literacies work.

The research and end-of-semester-project version of this kind of course front-loads self-education about community issues before students work directly with community members or make their messages "public." For example, because Gwendolyn Pough positions the Black Studies classroom as a public sphere, it's possible to understand her course as a model of community-engaged pedagogy. Bringing radical texts (e.g., Black Panther Party autobiographies and documents) into the classroom offered students a framework with which to analyze their own experiences, allowing students to use what Pough calls critical reading and writing pedagogies "to take social action" (468). The course involved heavy reading, weekly responses, a research paper, and a proposal for change, resulting in several students publishing diversity-related writings and, drawing on Black Panther Party rhetoric, starting a student group that led to ongoing conversations about diversity at their university (469).

Another way of conceptualizing writing assignments in community-engaged courses is by beginning with the community work and activism students are already doing, such as in Haivon Hoang's case study of a student group called the

Vietnamese American Coalition (VAC), where student leaders used liberal democratic rhetoric to discuss interracial conflict and to advocate for their mentoring
program's funding (387). Hoang proposes that community-engaged pedagogies
might learn from the VAC student leaders and their peers who were "acculturated
into and, at times, actively sought historical understandings of their university
communities" (405). Students in VAC began, Hoang writes, "to reconsider racial
differentiation historically and, through this lens, re-examine the possibilities and
limitations of mentoring younger students into their university community" (405).
Writing assignments that invite students to theorize and historicize the conflicts
they experience doing community-engagement work may teach how to use these
lenses as part of social justice work.

Each configuration for writing assignments has benefits and risks. Reflective
writing, especially journals, are commonly used in community-engaged pedagogies
as a practice of critical reflection (see Anson; Cooper, "Reading"). However,
Herzberg cautions that students may "regard social problems as chiefly or only
personal, [and] they will not search beyond the personal for a systemic explanation" (58, qtd. in Julier 141). There are a number of ways to resolve the difficulty
of dealing with large-scale social issues, such as prompting journal entries and
involving readings that ask students to investigate systemic and historical issues.
Angelique Davi, Mark Frydenberg, and Girish Gulati claim that because students
are already familiar with blogs, they may facilitate a more engaged classroom (1).
Blogging can function as a tool for aggregating research and reflections on
community-engagement work in a more public way, inviting students to join
online communities of bloggers writing on similar topics, and bringing up issues
of representation that are significant in community work and activism.

When designing writing courses around community-based work, I try to
imagine the students at the large, research institution where I teach. What are
some of the issues these students face in their everyday lives, and how can community work give them ways of analyzing these issues and understanding them in
social, cultural, and historical contexts? What theories and practices will they need
to work through practical problems? What community affiliations and relationships might serve as teaching-learning partners? It is not enough to include content and projects involving historically marginalized communities; we might also
consider the ways in which community-based practices, such as peer mentoring in
LGBTQ communities, can set a framework for the course. Working locally on
global issues may involve participating in local community literary, arts, and activist projects, whether through literacy centers, community organizations, schools,
or grassroots groups.

4) HOW DO I KNOW MY STUDENTS LEARNED
ANYTHING? (LAURA)

Researchers have sought to assess community-engaged writing courses, but
assessment is challenging in the light of the array of stakeholders involved in
community-university projects. Studies about the efficacy of service-learning or

community-engaged writing courses have typically measured the value added to student learning when community-engaged activities are combined in some way with academic coursework by gathering data about matters such as perceptions of social problems, concern about social justice issues, empathy for different points of view, ability to view social problems as systemic, citizenship skills, willingness to volunteer, sense of social responsibility, and willingness to work on behalf of social justice (Eyler and Giles; Eyler, Giles, and Braxton). They have also assessed attitudes towards learning and classroom work, factors having to do with student retention and satisfaction with courses and instructors (Kendrick and Suarez). It's not surprising these studies find that involvement in service-learning courses improves these measures, and has a positive effect on student learning as well.

Studies such as that by Kendrick and Suarez point to the difficulty of assessing the relative effectiveness of using this pedagogy, in part because students enrolling in community-engaged writing courses usually have made a choice to take the "different" course. They compared students' writing in a service-learning writing course with the writing of students in traditional classrooms, but their study, using a Campus Compact protocol, focuses more on the "value added" parts of service learning, which is to say "those outcomes for which service learning is uniquely suited: improving attitudes toward citizenship and community service and developing a greater sense of personal efficacy" (36). Seeking (and finding) evidence of a positive effect on improving student writing, Wurr conducted a study using text-based measures of writing quality, but even he acknowledges some limitations of using such a method to learn about the development of writing abilities ("Text-based"). While he and other community-engaged applied linguists continue to pursue empirical assessment methods, much of this work has emphasized broader literacy-acquisition benefits of service-learning pedagogy, particularly for non-native speakers of English (Wurr, "Composing"; Wurr and Hellebrandt).

Less research or surveying has been done to consider the community partner's assessment of the work of the community-engagement project or the university's contribution to the partnership, as Cruz and Giles indicate in their 2000 review of the literature. However, since their review, interdisciplinary service-learning research has gradually worked to address that gap, indicating a range of ways that community-based organizations report that they benefit from such partnerships, including a common interest in student learning, labor power, direct positive contributions to organizational mission, and access to the resources of higher education (see, among others, Clarke; Sandy and Holland; Worrall). Using case studies of community-engaged writing classes, Bacon ("Building") examined the assessment of written products by the classroom writing teacher and by the community agency, and offers a cautionary tale that focuses, in the end, on the teacher: Instructors need to understand their own limitations and knowledge about the textual practices and rhetoric of the sites with which they partner.

Rather than asking about the effect of community-engagement on individual student learning over the course of a single semester—a problematic, some would say flawed, question to begin with—more useful research has been undertaken about the larger structures, partnerships, and practices of community-engagement.

Composition-rhetoric literature has turned to investigate local institutions and tactical methods through which particular oral and literate strategies might be fostered (Cushman, *The Struggle*), power mapped and redistributed (Grabill, *Community Literacy Programs*), or practices expanded into effective advocacy (Mathieu). Goldblatt's study, *Because We Live Here*, suggests a way that partners develop projects to their mutual benefit. Many have used Deborah Brandt's concept of literacy sponsorship as a crucial lens to analyze any specific instance of interaction between learner and teacher. Brandt defines sponsors of literacy as "any agents, local or distant, concrete or abstract, who enable, support, teach and model as well as recruit, regulate, suppress, or withhold literacy—and gain advantage by it in some way" (19), a definition that directs the gaze of researchers in schools, unions, workplaces, or community centers to the benefits and losses that both the learners and the organizers accrue. Yet, as Elenore Long points out in *Community Literacy and the Rhetoric of Local Publics*, Brandt's influential definition may not fully exhaust the possible relationships that culturally sanctioned institutions have with groups wishing to express and explore their needs and desires through reading and writing. Long's overview of multiple community-literacy projects represents "a complex (and no doubt incomplete) set of relationships between local publics and formal institutions that shape and constrain how ordinary people go public" (7), and some of those "local publics" simply resist having anything to do with institutions wishing to form partnerships with them.

5) HOW DOES THIS WORK BENEFIT THE COMMUNITIES WE WORK IN? (ELI)

When I think about the courses I have taught over the years where students worked in off-campus neighborhoods, I think first about the agencies where the students have worked. Whether the setting is a Cambodian Buddhist temple in South Philadelphia where elder immigrants prepare for the citizenship test, or Open Borders where Puerto Rican and Andean people learn technology skills for job and home projects, if the students from my classes aren't forwarding the mission of the community organization, then the effort is a Disney fantasy at best and an exploitive trap for everyone at worst. Whether I have developed the partnership or another agency or office works with the site, as the teacher I must feel confident that there are regular checks to make sure the learners and their sponsor organization are getting what they want from the relationship. This may mean I visit at least once or twice in the semester—more if it is a partnership I am myself responsible for—and I should always be looking for ways to assess the outcomes for the partner as well as for my own students.

Among the composition-rhetoric scholars and activists who identify their work with the terms "community literacy" (Peck, Flower, and Higgins) and "the public turn" (Mathieu), interest in pedagogy became linked with the need to develop partnerships between higher education and community groups. Tom Deans' influential book *Writing Partnerships* emphasizes that the kind of writing and the nature of the engagement students experience in a course depend significantly on the structural relationship between their school and the agency or center they are writing for, about, or with. At the same time, scholar-practitioners such as Ellen Cushman, Jeff Grabill, Tiffany Rousculp, and Kirk Branch were scrutinizing the institutional settings of the programs they studied and taught in; this led them to raise questions about power relations, historical oppression, and the role of the teacher within dominant culture. It is no longer a matter of how college professors should teach their undergraduates to tutor or act within underserved communities. Branch puts the increasingly complex question in fittingly awkward language: "What role will what I teach have to do in working toward a world in which we need to live?" (12). Such a question places the teacher's desire for social change within the larger social theater of economic demands and players' conflicting motivations.

So what assessment tools can a teacher use to judge if the community partner is benefitting adequately? No off-the-shelf software package or standardized questionnaire will serve this purpose, but of course this is a major concern for any successful partnership (see the bibliography compiled by Eyler, Giles, Stenson, and Gray, which includes a section on outcomes for communities, 10). Working through an agency or service-learning office may mean that an instructor will not come directly in contact with a partner organization without taking strong initiative to reach out to it. It's certainly possible to ask many questions of the intermediate agency; they will probably appreciate a teacher who actually cares about how his or her students are doing at the site. Even though it adds extra work, I recommend doing the homework to know the story of a community partner. I'm most comfortable if I've at least met the executive director and toured the facilities, maybe talked to clients with whom my students will be working or teachers for whom students will act as aids or tutors. In most situations, the teacher can observe students at work during the semester. The closer the communications, the more a teacher will get a sense of how students are or are not fitting into the culture of the place. Indeed, some of the best experiences I've had are with organizations with which I've become deeply involved, serving on boards, working with staff on grants or clients on a project. If students see their teacher working with their placement agency, too, they more readily accept that the places where people live and colleges where people study can interact productively. Even if students are working with an agency with which the instructor is less familiar, the fact that the instructor demonstrates a commitment to similar community groups makes the discussion in class that much more grounded in the realities of the outside rather than projections from within the classroom.

Of course, things can go terribly wrong, as when a director I'm working with is fired, takes another job elsewhere, or does something with which I deeply disagree. But this is the challenge of developing relationships with people I don't know. Stepping outside the campus is a chance we take, and working in an environment for which academic credentials aren't the main currency can be unfamiliar, but the rewards of connection and added perspective are great. In those cases I simply have to learn to trust my ability to tell if things are going wrong for the partner. Asking directly about how the partnership is going may not always work, but in my experience the dialogue is always worth pursuing. The more the work with an off-campus agency achieves a sense of mutual benefit and equal exchange, the more the dialogue is likely to be rich and meaningful. For this reason, some projects such as the Inside/Out Prison Exchange Program emphasize college students studying alongside incarcerated students rather than having the students tutor those in the prisons (Pompa). The relationships must be live and active to reach anything approaching mutuality: That is both the commitment and the pleasure of community-engaged pedagogies.

BIBLIOGRAPHY

Ackerman, John, and David Coogan, eds. *The Public Work of Rhetoric: Citizen-Scholars and Civic Engagement.* Columbia: U of South Carolina P, 2010. Print.

Adler-Kassner, Linda. "Digging a Groundwork for Writing: Underprepared Students and Community Service Courses." *CCC* 46.4 (Dec. 1995): 552–55. Print.

Adler-Kassner, Linda, Robert Crooks, and Ann Watters, eds. *Writing the Community: Concepts and Models for Service-Learning in Composition.* Washington: American Aassociation for Higher Education/National Council of Teachers of English, 1997. Print.

Alexander, Jonathan, Janell Haynes, and Jacqueline Rhodes. "Public/Sex: Connecting Sexuality and Service Learning." *Reflections: A Journal of Public Rhetoric, Civic Writing, and Service Learning* 9.2 (Spring 2010): 1–19. Print.

Anson, Chris M. "On Reflection: The Role of Logs and Journals in Service-Learning Courses." Adler-Kassner, Crooks, and Watters 167–80. Print.

Arca, Rosemary L. "Systems Thinking, Symbiosis, and Service: The Road to Authority for Basic Writers." Adler-Kassner, Crooks, and Watters 167–80. Print.

Autostraddle: News, Entertainment, Opinion and Girl-on-Girl Culture. Web. 31 May 2013.

Bacon, Nora. "Building a Swan's Nest for Instruction in Rhetoric." *CCC* 51:4 (June 2000): 589–609. Print.

———. "Community Service and Writing Instruction." *National Society for Experiential Education Quarterly* 14 (Spring 1994): 14–27. Print.

———. "Community Service Writing: Problems, Challenges, Questions." Adler-Kassner, Crooks, and Watters 39–55. Print.

———. "The Trouble with Transfer: Lessons from a Study of Community Service Writing." *Michigan Journal of Community Service Learning* 6.1 (Fall 1999): 53–62. Print.

Ball, Eric L., and Alice Lai. "Place-Based Pedagogies for the Arts and Humanities." *Pedagogy* 6.2 (2006): 261–87. Print.

Bickford, Donna, and Nedra Reynolds. "Activism and Service-Learning: Reframing Volunteerism and Acts of Dissent." *Pedagogy* 2.2 (2002): 229–52. Print.

Bowdon, Melody, and J. Blake Scott. *Service Learning in Technical and Professional Communication.* New York: Longman, 2002. Print.

Branch, Kirk. *Eyes on the Ought to Be: What We Teach When We Teach about Literacy.* Cresskill: Hampton, 2007. Print.

Brandt, Deborah. *Literacy in American Lives.* New York: Cambridge UP, 2001. Print.

Butin, Dan. *Service-Learning in Theory and Practice: The Future of Community Engagement in Higher Education.* New York: Palgrave Macmillan, 2010. Print.

Campus Compact. "Presidents' Statement of Principles." 1996. Web. 20 Dec. 2012.

Carrick, Tracy Hamler, Margaret Himley, and Tobi Jacobi. "Ruptura: Acknowledging the Lost Subjects of the Service Learning Story." *Language and Learning across the Disciplines* 4.3 (October 2000): 56–75. Rpt. in Deans, Roswell, and Wurr 298–313. Print.

Cella, Laurie, and Jessica Restaino, eds. *Unsustainable: Re-imagining Community Literacy, Public Writing, Service-Learning, and the University.* New York: Lexington Books, 2012. Print.

Clarke, Melinda. "Finding the Community in Service Learning Research: The 3-'I' Model." Ed. Shelley H. Billig and Janet Eyler. *Deconstructing Service-Learning: Research Exploring Context, Participation and Impacts.* Greenwich: Information Age, 2003. 125–46. Print.

Cleary, Michelle Navarre. "Keep It Real: A Maxim for Service-Learning in Community Colleges." *Reflections: A Journal of Public Rhetoric, Civic Writing, and Service Learning* 3.1 (Winter 2003): 55–63. Print.

Conniff, Brian, and Betty Rodgers Youngkin. "The Literacy Paradox: Service-Learning and the Traditional English Department." *Michigan Journal of Community Service-Learning* 2.1 (Fall 1995): 86–94. Print.

Cooper, David D. "Can Civic Engagement Rescue the Humanities?" *Community-Based Learning and the Work of Literature.* Ed. Susan Danielson and Ann Marie Fallon. Bolton: Anker, 2007. Print.

———. "Reading, Writing, and Reflection." Rhoads and Howard. 47–56. Print.

Cooper, David D., and Laura Julier. *Writing in the Public Interest: Service Learning and the Writing Classroom.* East Lansing: The Writing Center of Michigan State University, 1995. Print.

———. "Writing the Ties that Bind: Service Learning in the Writing Classroom." *Michigan Journal of Community Service Learning* 2.1 (Fall 1995): 72–85. Print.

Crunk Feminist Collective. http://www.crunkfeministcollective.com/. Web 31 May 2013.

Cruz, Nadinne I., and Dwight E. Giles, Jr. "Where's the Community in Service Learning Research? *Michigan Journal of Community Service Learning,* Special Issue 1 (2000): 28–34. Print.

Cushman, Ellen. "The Rhetorician as Agent of Social Change." *CCC* 47.1 (Feb. 1996): 7–28. Print.

———. *The Struggle and the Tools: Oral and Literate Strategies in an Inner City Community.* Albany: SUNY P, 1998. Print.

———. "Sustainable Service Learning Programs." *CCC* 64.1 (2002): 40–65. Print.

———. "SSY Gadugi: Where the Fire Burns." *Rhetorical Activists.* Ed. Seth Kahn. London: Routledge, 2010. 56–61. Print.

Cushman, Ellen and Erik Green. "Knowledge Work with the Cherokee Nation: The Pedagogy of Engaging Publics in a Praxis of New Media." Ackerman and Coogan 175–92. Print.

Davi, Angelique, Mark Frydenberg, and Girish Gulati. "Blogging across the Disciplines: Integrating Technology to Enhance Liberal Learning." *Journal of Online Learning and Teaching* 3.3 (2007). Web.

de Acosta, Martha. "Journal Writing in Service-Learning: Lessons from a Mentoring Project." *Michigan Journal of Community Service Learning* 2.1 (Fall 1995): 141–49. Print.

Deans, Thomas. "Community Service and Critical Teaching: A Retrospective Conversation with Bruce Herzberg." *Reflections: A Journal of Public Rhetoric, Civic Writing, and Service Learning* 7.9 (Winter 2003): 71–76. Print.

———. "English Studies and Public Service." Deans, Roswell, and Wurr. 97–116. Print.

_____. "Shifting Locations, Genres, and Motives: An Activity Theory Analysis of Service-Learning Writing Pedagogies." *The Locations of Composition.* Ed. Christopher Keller and Christian Weisser. Albany: SUNY P, 2007. 289–306. Rpt. in Deans, Roswell, and Wurr. 451–64. Print.

_____. *Writing and Community Action: A Service-Learning Rhetoric and Reader.* New York: Longman, 2002. Print.

_____. *Writing Partnerships: Service-Learning in Composition.* Urbana: National Council of Teachers of English, 2000. Print.

Deans, Thomas, Barbara Roswell, and Adrian Wurr. "Teaching and Writing across Communities: Developing Partnerships, Publics, and Programs." Deans, Roswell, and Wurr. 1–12. Print.

_____, eds. *Writing and Community Engagement: A Critical Sourcebook.* Boston: Bedford/ St. Martin's, 2010. Print.

Dewey, John. *Democracy and Education.* 1916. New York: Free P, 1944. Print.

Duffy, Cheryl Hofstetter. *Teaching Civic Literacy: Prentice Hall Resources for Writing.* Upper Saddle River: Pearson Prentice Hall, 2006. Print.

Elbow, Peter. *Writing without Teachers.* New York: Oxford UP, 1973; 1998. Print.

Eyler, Janet, and Dwight Giles, Jr. *Where's the Learning in Service-Learning?* San Francisco: Jossey-Bass, 1999. Print.

Eyler, Janet, Dwight Giles, Jr., and John Braxton. "The Impact of Service Learning on College Students." *Michigan Journal of Community Service Learning* 4.1 (1997): 5–15. Print.

Eyler, Janet, Dwight E. Giles, Jr., Christine M. Stenson, and Charlene J. Gray. "At a Glance: What We Know about the Effects of Service-Learning on College Students, Faculty, Institutions and Communities, 1993–2000." *Campus Compact.* 3rd ed. Learn and Serve America National Service Learning Clearinghouse, 31 August 2001. Web. May 2013.

Ferrari, Joseph R., and Laurie Worrall. "Assessments by Community Agencies: How 'the Other Side' Sees Service-Learning." *Michigan Journal of Community Service Learning* 7.1 (2000): 35–40. Print.

Flower, Linda. *Community Literacy and the Rhetoric of Public Engagement.* Carbondale: Southern Illinois UP, 2008. Print.

_____. "Partners in Inquiry: A Logic for Community Outreach." *Writing the Community.* Adler-Kassner, Crooks, and Watters 95–117. Print.

_____. "Talking across Difference: Intercultural Rhetoric and the Search for Situated Knowledge." *CCC* 55.1 (Sept. 2003): 38–68. Print.

Flower, Linda, and Shirley Brice Heath. "Drawing on the Local: Collaboration and Community Expertise." *Language and Learning across the Disciplines* 4.3 (Oct. 2000): 43–55. Print.

Freire, Paulo. *Education for Critical Consciousness.* New York: Continuum, 1982. Print.

_____. *Pedagogy of the Oppressed.* New York: Continuum, 1993. Print.

Giroux, Henry A., and Peter McLaren. "Teacher Education and the Politics of Engagement: The Case for Democratic Schooling." *Harvard Educational Review* 56.3 (1986): 213–38. Print.

Goldblatt, Eli. *Because We Live Here: Sponsoring Literacy beyond the College Curriculum.* Creskill: Hampton, 2007. Print.

_____. "Van Rides in the Dark: Literacy as Involvement in a College Literacy Practicum." *Journal for Peace and Justice Studies* 6.1 (1995): 77–94. Print.

_____. "Who Serves Whom? Institutional Commitments in Community-Based Learning?" *Conference on College Composition and Communication.* Chicago. 22 Mar. 2002. Address.

Goldblatt, Eli, with Manuel Portillo and Mark Lyons. "Story to Action: A Conversation about Literacy and Organizing." *Community Literacy Journal* 2.2 (Summer 2008): 45–66. Print.

Grabill, Jeffrey. *Community Literacy Programs and the Politics of Change.* Albany: SUNY P, 2001. Print.

———. *Writing Community Change: Designing Technologies for Citizen Action.* Creskill: Hampton, 2007. Print.

Greco, Norma. "Critical Literacy and Community Service: Reading and Writing the World." *English Journal* 81.5 (1992): 83–84. Print.

Herzberg, Bruce. "Community Service and Critical Teaching." *CCC* 45.3 (Oct. 1994): 307–319. Rpt. in Adler-Kassner, Crooks, and Watters. 57–69. Print.

Hessler, H. Brooke. "Composing an Institutional Identity: The Terms of Community Service in Higher Education." *Language and Learning across the Disciplines* 4.3 (Oct. 2000): 27–42. Print.

Higgins, Lorraine, Elenore Long, and Linda Flower. "Community Literacy: A Rhetorical Model for Personal and Public Inquiry." *Community Literacy Journal* 1.1 (2006): 9–43. Rpt. in Deans, Roswell, and Wurr 167–201. Print.

Himley, Margaret. "Facing (Up to) 'The Stranger' in Community Service Learning." *CCC* 53.3 (Feb. 2004): 416–37. Print.

Hoang, Haivon. "Campus Racial Politics and a Rhetoric of Injury." *CCC* 61.1 (Nov. 2009): 385–408. Print.

Honnet, Ellen Porter, and Susan J. Poulsen, eds. *Wingspread Special Report: Principles of Good Practice for Combining Service and Learning.* Racine: The Johnson Foundation, 1989. Print.

hooks, bell. *Teaching Community: A Pedagogy of Hope.* New York: Routledge, 2003. Print.

———. *Teaching to Transgress: Education as the Practice of Freedom.* New York: Routledge, 1994. Print.

———. "Toward a Revolutionary Feminist Pedagogy." *Talking Back: Thinking Feminist, Thinking Black.* Boston: South End, 1989. 49–54. Print.

Jacobi, Tobi. "The Zine Project: Innovation or Oxymoron." *English Journal* 96.4 (2007): 43–49. Print.

Julier, Laura. "Community-Service Pedagogy." *A Guide to Composition Pedagogies.* Ed. Gary Tate, Amy Rupiper, and Kurt Schick. New York: Oxford UP, 2001. 132–48. Print.

Kells, Michelle Hall. "Writing Across Communities: Diversity, Deliberation, and the Discursive Possibilities of WAC." Deans, Roswell, and Wurr 369–85. Print.

Kendrick, J. Richard, and John Suarez. "Service-Learning Outcomes in English Composition Courses: An Application of the Campus Compact Assessment Protocol." *Reflections: A Journal of Public Rhetoric, Civic Writing, and Service Learning* 3.1 (Winter 2003): 36–54. Print.

Lathan, Rhea Estelle. "Crusader: Ethel Azalea Johnson's Use of the Written Word as a Weapon of Liberation." *Women and Literacy: Inquiries for a New Century.* Ed. Beth Daniell and Peter Mortensen. Urbana: National Council of Teachers of English, 2007. 59–70. Print.

Logan, Shirley Wilson. "Free-floating Literacy: Early African American Rhetorical Traditions." *Liberating Language: Sites of Rhetorical Education in Nineteenth-century Black America.* Carbondale: Southern Illinois UP, 2008. 10–28. Print.

Long, Elenore. *Community Literacy and the Rhetoric of Local Publics.* West Lafayette: Parlor, 2008. Print.

Luetzow, Darcy, Lauren Macaluso, and Eli Goldblatt."Garden in a Vacant Lot: Growing Thinkers at Tree House Books." Ed. Valerie Kinloch and Peter Smagorinsky. *Service-Learning in Literacy Education: Possibilities for Teaching and Learning.* Charlotte: Information Age Publishing, 2014.

Macrorie, Ken. *Telling Writing.* 4th ed. Portsmouth: Boynton/Cook, 1985. Print.

Marr, Vanessa. "Ditchin' the Master's Gardening Tools for Our Own: Growing a Womanist Service-Learning Methodology from the Grassroots." 2013. MS forthcoming in *Feminist Teacher* (Spring 2014).

Mathieu, Paula. *Tactics of Hope: The Public Turn in English Composition.* Portsmouth: Boynton, 2005. Print.

Mathieu, Paula, Steve Parks, and Tiffany Rousculp. *Circulating Communities: The Tactics and Strategies of Community Publishing.* New York: Lexington Books, 2011. Print. Excerpted in Deans, Roswell, and Wurr 277–97. Print.

McGuiness, Ilona M. "Educating for Participation and Democracy: Service-Learning in the Writing Classroom." *The Scholarship of Teaching* 1.2 (1995): 3–12. Print.

McIntosh, Peggy. "Unpacking the Invisible Knapsack." *Independent School* (Winter 1990). Amptoons.com. Web. 31 May 2013.

Mitchell, Tania D. "Critical Service-Learning as Social Justice Education: A Case Study of the Citizen Scholars Program." *Equity & Excellence in Education* 40.2 (2007): 101–12. Print.

Monberg, Terese Guinsatao. "Writing Home or Writing as the Community: Toward a Theory of Recursive Spatial Movement for Students of Color in Service-Learning Courses." *Reflections: A Journal of Public Rhetoric, Civic Writing, and Service Learning* 8.3 (2009): 21–51. Print.

Morton, Keith. "The Irony of Service: Charity, Project, and Social Change in Service-Learning." *Michigan Journal of Community Service Learning* 2.1 (1995): 19–32. Rpt. in Deans, Roswell, and Wurr 117–37. Print.

Parks, Stephen. *Gravyland: Writing Beyond the Curriculum in the City of Brotherly Love.* Syracuse: Syracuse UP, 2010. Print.

Parks, Steve, and Nick Pollard. "Emergent Strategies for an Established Field: The Role of Worker-Writer Collectives in Composition & Rhetoric." *CCC* 61.3 (Feb. 2010): 476–509. Print.

Peck, Wayne C., Linda Flower, and Lorraine Higgins. "Community Literacy." *CCC* 46.2 (1995): 199–222. Print.

Pompa, Lori. "Disturbing Where We Are Comfortable: Notes from Behind the Walls." Deans, Roswell, and Wurr. 509–520. Print.

Pough, Gwendolyn D. "Empowering Rhetoric: Black Students Writing Black Panthers." *CCC* 53.3 (2002): 466–86. Print.

Poynter, Kerry John, and Nancy Jean Tubbs. "Safe Zones: Creating LGBT Safe Space Ally Programs." *Journal of LGBT Youth* 5.1 (2008): 121–32. Print.

Racism School. http://racismschool.tumblr.com/. Web. 31 May 2013.

Reynolds, Nedra. *Geographies of Writing: Inhabiting Spaces and Encountering Difference.* Carbondale: Southern Illinois UP, 2007. Print.

Rhoads, Robert A. *Community Service and Higher Education.* Albany: SUNY P, 1997. Print.

Rhoads, Robert A., and Jeffrey P. F. Howard, eds. *Academic Service Learning: A Pedagogy of Action and Reflection.* San Francisco: Jossey-Bass, 1998. Print.

Rose, Shirley, and Irwin Weiser. *Going Public: The WPA as Advocate for Engagement.* Logan: Utah State UP, 2010. Print.

Rousculp, Tiffany. "When the Community Writes: Re-envisioning the SLCC DiverseCity Writing Series." Deans, Roswell, and Wurr. 386–400. Print.

Royster, Jacqueline Jones. *Traces of a Stream: Literacy and Social Change among African American Women.* Pittsburgh: U of Pittsburgh P, 2000. Print.

Royster, Jacqueline Jones, and Jean Williams. "History in the Spaces Left: African American Presence and Narratives of Composition Studies." *CCC* 50.4 (June 1999): 563–84. Print.

Sandy, Marie, and Barbara Holland. "Different Worlds and Common Ground: Community Partner Perspectives on Campus-Community Partnerships." *Michigan Journal of Community Service Learning* 13.1 (Fall 2006): 30–43. Print.

Schmidt, Adeny, and Matthew A. Robby. "What's the Value of Service-Learning to the Community?" *Michigan Journal of Community Service Learning* 9.1 (Fall 2002): 27–33. Web. 20 Dec. 2012.

Stanton, Timothy K., Dwight E. Giles, and Nadinne I. Cruz. *Service-Learning: A Movement's Pioneers Reflect on Its Origins, Practice, and Future.* San Francisco: Jossey-Bass, 1999. Print.

Vernon, Andrea, and Kelly Ward. "Campus and Community Partnerships: Assessing Impacts and Strengthening Connections." *Michigan Journal of Community Service Learning* 6.1 (1999): 30–37. Web. 20 Dec. 2012. Print.

Waterman, Alan S. ed. *Service-Learning: Applications from the Research.* Mahwah: Erlbaum, 1997. Print.

Welch, Nancy. "'And Now That I Know Them': Composing Mutuality in a Service Learning Course." *CCC* 54.2 (Dec. 2002): 243–63. Print.

Worrall, Laurie. "Discovering the Community Voice: The Community Perspective of the Service-Learning Program at DePaul University (Illinois)." Diss., U of Pennsylvania, 2005. Print.

Wurr, Adrian J. "Composing Cultural Diversity and Civic Literacy: English Language Learners as Service Providers." *Reflections: A Journal of Public Rhetoric, Civic Writing, and Service Learning* 9.1 (Fall 2009): 162–90. Print.

———. "Text-based Measures of Service-Learning Writing Quality." *Reflections: A Journal of Public Rhetoric, Civic Writing, and Service Learning* 2.2 (Spring 2002): 41–56. Print.

Wurr, Adrian J., and Josef Hellebrandt, eds. *Learning the Language of Global Citizenship: Service-Learning in Applied Linguistics.* Bolton: Anker, 2007.

Young, Morris. *Minor Re/visions: Asian American Literacy Narratives as a Rhetoric of Citizenship.* Carbondale: Southern Illinois UP, 2004. Print.

JOURNALS, PRESSES, AND CENTERS

Campus Compact
www.compact.org

Community Literacy Center
http://english.cmu.edu/research/clc/default.html

Community Literacy Journal
http://www.communityliteracy.org/index.php/clj

Literacy in Composition Studies Journal
http://www.licsjournal.org

Michigan Journal of Community Service Learning
http://ginsberg.umich.edu/mjcsl/

New City Community Press
http://www.newcitycommunitypress.com/

Reflections: A Journal of Public Rhetoric, Civic Writing, and Service Learning
http://reflectionsjournal.net/

Undergraduate Journal of Service Learning and Community-Based Research
http://www.bk.psu.edu/academics/journal.htm

⤚

Critical Pedagogies
Dreaming of Democracy
Ann George

> Nothing less than the very thorough training in the discounting
> of rhetorical persuasiveness can make a citizenry truly free.
> —Kenneth Burke, "Linguistic Approach to Problems of Education"

I remember the scene well: It's 1998, two weeks before classes begin at the small, private Texas university where I teach. The tapes of vigorous, radical class discussions that I've played in my head all summer begin to fade as I struggle with the syllabus for my first-year writing course. Like many compositionists, I'm attracted to student-centered pedagogies and themes of social justice. I want to empower students, to engage them in cultural critique, to make a change. But as Ira Shor observes, the start of a new semester is both "rich in possibilities and cluttered with disabling routines" (*Empowering Education* 200), and as I plan my class, I am reminded that, despite my subversive intentions and the liberatory rhetoric of my course description, my teaching often retreats to the level of sporadic creativity or, worse, to predictable English-teacher experimentation and circling of chairs. I fear that I am, in Peter Elbow's phrase, "bamboozled"—that is, I "call things by the wrong name. . . . [I] preach freedom, but [I] don't really practice it" (92, 98). I wrote this essay then—and return to it now—in hopes of reducing the bamboozlement of compositionists everywhere (including myself)—if that is, indeed, what we suffer from—by examining the goals, practices, realities, and controversies of critical pedagogies.

Traditionally, critical pedagogies (a.k.a. liberatory pedagogy, empowering pedagogy, radical pedagogy, progressive pedagogy, or pedagogy of possibility or hope or love) envision a society not simply pledged to, but successfully enacting, the principles of freedom and social justice. "Dedicated to the emancipatory imperatives of *self-empowerment and social transformation*," traditional critical pedagogies engage students in analyses of the unequal power relations that produce and are produced by cultural practices and institutions (including schools), and they hope to enable students to challenge this inequality (McLaren 163). In this, critical pedagogies closely resemble and often overlap with cultural studies and feminist pedagogies (see essays by D. George, Lockridge, and Trimbur and by Micciche in this volume). However, critical pedagogies are distinctive in their usually explicit commitment to education for citizenship. Henry Giroux, arguably the foremost American theorist of radical education, claims that the task of critical pedagogies is nothing short of "reconstructing democratic public life" ("Liberal Arts Education" 120). To do so, critical pedagogies attempt to reinvent the roles of teachers and students in the classroom and the kind of activities they engage in. As bell hooks insists, "To educate for freedom . . . we have to challenge and change the way everyone thinks about pedagogical process" (*Teaching to Transgress* 144).

The urtext for most critical pedagogies is Paulo Freire's *Pedagogy of the Oppressed* (1970). A Brazilian educator, Freire was exiled in 1964 for his work in the national literacy campaign, teaching peasants to read both the word and the world of oppressive economic and political domination. *Pedagogy of the Oppressed* introduces many of the terms, assumptions, and methods that still define some critical pedagogies today. In it, Freire presents his well-known critique of the "banking" model of education, in which students are seen as "receptacles" waiting to be filled with the teacher's official knowledge; education thus becomes little more than information transfer, "an act of depositing" (58). Instead, Freire practices "problem-posing education," dialogue designed to help students develop conscientização (critical consciousness)—the ability to define, analyze, and problematize the economic, political, and cultural forces that shape their lives. Hence, classroom dialogue revolves around "generative themes"—domination, marriage, work—drawn from students' experience (accounts of which come from extensive ethnographic research). Freire's Marxist agenda is explicitly revolutionary: "This pedagogy makes oppression and its causes objects of reflection by the oppressed, and from that reflection will come their necessary engagement in the struggle for their liberation" (48). This relationship between reflection and action, which Freire labels "praxis," is crucial for him: Neither critical consciousness nor unreflective action alone will enable people to transform the world.

Critical educators have found Freire attractive for many reasons, not least of which are his analysis of schooling as an instrument of domination and his understanding of the situatedness of all theory and practice. Ira Shor's volumes, *Freire for the Classroom* and *Empowering Education,* illustrate the interdisciplinary applicability of Freirean pedagogy, even to fields we might not expect, such as life sciences and mathematics. However, as James Berlin suggests, compositionists are especially interested in Freire's insistence that knowledge is a socially constructed, linguistic product: "[L]anguage—in its mediation between the world and the individual . . .—contains within its shaping force the power of creating humans as agents of action" (170). Because language and thought are inextricably linked, language instruction becomes a key site where dominant ideology is reproduced—or disrupted.

For several decades, at the center of critical pedagogy scholarship, ironically (though not too surprisingly, given gender and racial configurations within the academy), was a group of mostly white, middle-class men: the "Big Three"—Freire,

Giroux, and Shor—and Stanley Aronowitz, Donaldo Macedo, Peter McLaren, and Roger Simon. They were steeped in Marxist theory and, with the exception of Shor, were scholars in education. So, although critical pedagogies have found a home in Composition, we're relative latecomers to the conversation, still dominated by education professors, who understandably have their own discipline-specific concerns.

American critical pedagogies have roots in the turn-of-the-century progressive educational reform movement (see, for instance, discussion of John Dewey later in the chapter), but the 1980s marks the contemporary rebirth of the project as radical educators responded to conservative reports on education, particularly *A Nation at Risk* and *Action for Excellence*. These reports announced a crisis in American education, a system wallowing in mediocrity that crippled America's ability to compete in the global economy. Giroux argues that the 1980s signaled a turning point in public education as conservatives worked to undo reforms of the 1960s and to redefine schools as "company stores" in which good citizenship is equated with economic productivity (*Schooling* 18). The success of conservatives' authoritarian, back-to-basics curriculum suggested to radical educators that the country was experiencing not just a crisis in education but, as Giroux and McLaren argue, "a crisis in American democracy itself" (216).

Three important early studies by Giroux—*Theory and Resistance in Education* (1983), *Education Under Siege* (with Aronowitz; 1985), and *Schooling and the Struggle for Public Life* (1988)—advanced the radical critique of public education. Giroux explores "the hidden curriculum," the subtle but powerful ways schools construct students' and teachers' knowledge and behavior, validating positivism and competitiveness over other forms of knowing and behaving. For Giroux, it is crucial that radical educators contest conservative definitions of education and citizenship not only to give voice to the poor and marginalized but also to reach countless middle-class Americans who have "withdrawn from public life into a world of sweeping privatization, pessimism, and greed" ("Literacy" 63).

Other leftist critics echoed Giroux's concerns. Jonathan Kozol (*Illiterate America*), whose study found that one-third of adult Americans are illiterate, argues that public education was designed to "perpetuat[e] ... disparities in power and ... inequities in every form of day-to-day existence" (93). Schools, that is, function as "sorting mechanisms" (McLaren 160) to inculcate and maintain passive acceptance of inequality. In *Critical Teaching and Everyday Life*, Shor presents a blistering Marxist critique of the community college system, developed during the late 1950s and bulging by the late 1970s, as a warehouse for surplus workers. Community colleges, he argues, simultaneously feed off and short-circuit the American Dream by building a large pool of skilled workers for a shrinking number of increasingly deskilled jobs.

Not surprisingly, twenty-first-century radical educators argue that the stakes for the future of democracy have risen dramatically, and, consequently, they increasingly shift their attention to a cultural-studies-style critique of what Giroux calls "public pedagogy" ("Public Pedagogy" 14) distributed by, in bell hooks's terms, the "imperialist white-supremacist capitalist patriarchal mass media" (*Teaching*

Community 8). In the post-9/11 era, hooks sees "the seeds of fascist ideology . . . bearing fruit everywhere" (10). Giroux similarly condemns "[t]he breathless rhetoric of the global victory of free market rationality" ("Public Pedagogy" 8) as well as "the ever-expanding armies of well-paid anti-public intellectuals who fill the air waves with poisonous lies, stupidity, ignorance, all in the name of so-called 'common sense' and a pathological notion of freedom" ("Memories" 115). The aim, then, of mainstream critical pedagogies is to revitalize students' conceptions of freedom and inspire them to collectively recreate a society built on democratic values and respect for difference.

It's a compelling mission, to be sure. But questions arose almost from the get-go, and they have much to do with contemporary critical pedagogies' roots in Brazilian literacy campaigns; with the race, class, gender, and disciplinary home of its early advocates and their highly theoretical, revolutionary discourse. Thus, critical teachers and skeptics, alike, wrestle with five central questions:

- What does a critical writing classroom look like?
- Can we create democratic classrooms within traditional institutions?
- Is the goal to produce radical student activists? How?
- Is Freirean pedagogy applicable to American schools?
- How might we understand student resistance to leftist critiques?

Criticizing critical pedagogy has become something of a growth industry in Composition Studies. But this chapter is not the story of a pedagogy under siege; it is of one whose proponents continually reflect upon and refine their work, thereby producing a tremendous body of new scholarship that redefines the field—a CP 2.0. A next generation of poststructuralist, feminist, critical race, composition, and rhetoric scholars brings powerful new lenses to already rich critical pedagogy enterprises. One thing becomes immediately obvious: Critical pedagogy is not one-size-fits-all (good thing, too—my Ira Shor impersonation was rarely convincing, even to me); instead, as Patti Lather says, it's "an ensemble of practices and discourses with competing claims" put in service of social justice (184). Hence, this is also a story about my own coming of age as a critical teacher. What follows is an explanation of how scholars understand central questions within critical pedagogies (and sometimes give answers) and how recent work opens up space for the not-yet radical or differently radical teachers like me.

SHOW ME THE (WRITING!) CLASSROOM

Giroux and others' early analyses of institutional power effectively laid some theoretical groundwork and recruited scores of sympathetic teachers. But their often-abstract theory frustrated many critical teachers, who bemoaned their inattention to classroom practice. The notable exception has been Ira Shor, the best-known American translator of Freirean pedagogy, who helped a generation of critical teachers imagine what a critical classroom might look like or do. Shor's accounts of his teaching experiences, *Empowering Education* (1992) and *When Students Have Power* (1996), are funny, provocative, and full of classroom conversations and activities. *Empowering Education* is quite simply one of the most compelling books on education I've read. As a new critical teacher, I looked to Shor for concrete examples of decentered classrooms. From the first day of class, Shor foregrounds student writing and voices, asking students to critically examine course material and institutional power—everything from "What is good writing?" and "How do you become a good writer?" to "Why are you taking this course?" and "Why is it required?" (37). That is, he "poses the subject matter [of the course] itself as a problem" (37). Students in Shor's classes co-create the syllabus by contributing readings and voting on unit themes, write classroom bylaws, and negotiate grading contracts right down to the attendance policies.

In *When Students Have Power*, he talks at length about the after-class group during which he and a small group of students met to evaluate the day's session and to plan classes and projects. Shor's students offered up scathing criticism of his chosen texts and time management; the result was a remarkable redistribution of power and responsibility. Shor's knowledge and authority had not been erased; instead, another avenue of power had been constructed—it became, Shor says, a two-way street: "I found myself *immediately and continually accountable to students*" (125). Perhaps more than any other aspect of Shor's pedagogy, the after-class group undercuts complaints that critical teachers merely impose radical agendas on students, for within this space, students take responsibility for the means and ends of the course. My own after-class group, though less assertive than Shor's, pushed me and their classmates to raise the level of discussion and expand their options for writing and learning—and convinced me that an after-class group creates the opportunity for students and instructors to tackle *together* the difficulties inherent in classrooms. Behind Shor's power-sharing practices lies his belief that "*both teachers and students start out at less than zero and more than zero simultaneously. . . .* Both bring resources and obstacles to class" (*Empowering Education* 201). I find Shor's more-than- and less-than-zero approach particularly productive, for then teachers are not the standard against which students' knowledge and power are measured. In addition, to the extent that Shor's line of thinking encourages teachers to recognize their own (and not just their students') multiple and contradictory positions in relation to dominant culture, it creates a place in critical education for not-quite-radical teachers like me. That is, a lack of "political clarity" or radical commitment that might seem like a minus may actually be a plus in the critical classroom because it means one less barrier between teacher and student; simultaneous criticism of and entanglement in dominant culture can become a problem that instructor and students sort through together.

But accounts of critical classrooms, including those by compositionists, typically emphasize the "critical" rather than the "writing" part of critical writing pedagogies. Happily, that's changing as more compositionists adopt ethnographic research methods. Two impressive book-length classroom studies, one by David Seitz (more on which later; here, note Seitz's provocative discussions of students' work memoirs and other ethnographic writing) and one by Amy Lee, are especially welcome remedies for critical pedagogies' inattentiveness to *writing* instruction. In *Composing Critical Pedagogies*, Lee highlights goals, assignments, and assessment (a woefully neglected topic) for a critical composition course. In a nutshell, she suggests writing courses "make visible the cultural and political work of our reading and writing practices" (10). That includes helping students become better writers but also examining academic notions of authorship and authority as well as how students might navigate—and rhetorically intervene in—networks of power that authorize some voices and silence others. Lee also provides a wonderfully detailed account of co-developing grading criteria with students, who, interestingly, prioritize process (contributions to peer review, collaborative projects, discussion) over the merits of written products.

Carol Winkelmann's ethnography of a technology-themed writing course ("Electronic Literacy, Critical Pedagogy, and Collaboration") also foregrounds critical *composing*. Winkelmann assigned sixteen students to write one "corporate text" on any topic addressing the relationship between computers and culture. The students picked a topic and genre; shared the research, writing, and editing; and chose grading criteria and an outside evaluation team. The campus's lack of a computer classroom and large labs dispersed students' physical workspaces, increasing the fluidity of the process and product. The result, she claims, was "heteroglossic and hypertextual, cooperative and conflicted, fused and fragmentary, totally irreverent and thoroughly intertextual" (444). Importantly, the class project revealed that "the 'text' was a corporate process in which social relations were reaffirmed, reproduced, realigned, and refabricated" (445). The student learning and the work of the course lay in the composing process rather than the product. Like Lee, then, Winkelmann suggests that critical composition pedagogy challenges not just how but what we grade.

CAN CLASSROOMS BE DEMOCRATIC?

Giroux and McLaren argue that critical teachers should conceive of schools as democratic public spheres where "students are given the opportunity to learn the discourse of public association and civic responsibility" by doing—that is, by participating in democratic dialogue about lived experience, including the content and conduct of their own education (224). In calling for schools constituted as public spheres, Giroux and others seek to recover the nearly forgotten American tradition of radical education found in the work of John Dewey, whom Shor dubs "the patron saint of American education" (*When Students Have Power* x). Dewey pioneered experiential, student-centered learning aimed at integrating education with public life and developing the "free and equitable intercourse," and hence the shared interests, essential for communal life (*Democracy and Education* 98). Often dismissed as merely liberal, Dewey is making a long-overdue comeback as critical teachers such as Kate Ronald and Hephzibah Roskelly seek homegrown traditions of critical pedagogy. Readers today may find Dewey's texts surprisingly in tune with current understandings of the relationships among ideology, cultural practice, and language. Dewey further offers critical teachers a robust understanding of democracy as "a mode of associated living, of joint communicated experience" in which citizens "refer [their] own action[s] to that of others, and . . . consider the action of others to give point and direction to [their] own" (87).

It's this vision of democratic public practice that attracts me to critical pedagogy. It's why I teach writing—an occupation that has always been for me a high-stakes enterprise with implications not only for students' academic and professional success (important as those are) but also for the health of our democratic culture. I admire those who struggle to enact a pedagogy that would itself be the practice of democracy. But as Shor observes, "It's a tricky business to organize an untraditional class in a traditional school" (*Freire for the Classroom* 106).

Early in his career, for instance, Shor envisions not just a student-centered, dialogic classroom, but one in which the teacher essentially disappears. Such too-easy equations of dialogue and democracy have created a tangled, potentially paralyzing debate about teachers' classroom authority. "How," Paul Lynch asks, "can a teacher who embraces critical pedagogy raise questions about authority without imposing authority in order to raise those very questions?" (728). Oversimplifications and misrepresentations of critical pedagogy forced Freire to issue repeated disclaimers: "The dialogical relationship," he insists, "does not have the power to create such an impossible equality" between teachers and students (Shor and Freire 92). Dialogue is a *directed* means toward an end; hence, Freire argues, "I have to be radically democratic and responsible and directive. *Not* directive of the *students*, but directive of the *process*" (Shor and Freire 46). Transformation depends on different, unequal voices interacting, and the primary source of that authoritative voice, Shor suggests, is the more analytical, more politically committed teacher. Freire says there is no getting around that fact: "[W]ithout authority it is very difficult for the liberties of the students to be shaped. Freedom needs authority to become free. It is a paradox but it is true" (Shor and Freire 91).

Patricia Bizzell shows how hard it often is to work within this paradox. *Academic Discourse and Critical Consciousness* traces her search for means by which compositionists can foster democratic exchange. Initially, Bizzell taught academic discourse, believing that its "critical detachment" would "more or less automatically" spark recognition of injustice and a desire to intervene (20). Later she realizes that no analytical method, in and of itself, creates enlightened political commitment. Arguments have to be made for it. But, she asks, "[w]hat is the legitimate authority of teachers" to make those arguments (273)? She determines, following Isocrates, that authority must be "established rhetorically" (283)—by building her case on students' existing values. Arguments against sexism, for example, might appeal to the American ideal of equality embedded in our founding documents and communal discourse. Bizzell's commitment to social justice prompts her to make two other crucial moves: help students develop their own rhetorical authority and use course materials that highlight shared American values, not by glossing over difference but by emphasizing that Americans are "united by a common experiment in negotiating difference"—and that, historically, some movements toward greater equality have succeeded (293).

Amy Lee bluntly declares, "[d]emocracy is not, finally, possible in a classroom" (131), but she seeks to shift both scholarly discourse and classroom practice to "foreground students as active participants in and cocreators of our pedagogies" (12). She bypasses unproductive debates about what authority teachers should/do have, focusing instead on positive ways to give students more authority. For instance, by providing substantial introductions of the students in her ethnography and by featuring their texts and voices, Lee demonstrates ways to increase students' presence and acknowledge them as authors in our writing about pedagogy.

Perhaps an even knottier (and much less discussed) issue critical teachers face is students' relationships to each other. In what can only be a utopian vision, Giroux describes a classroom in which "all voices in their differences become unified both in their efforts to identify and recall moments of human suffering and in their attempts to overcome the conditions that perpetuate such suffering" ("Literacy" 72). Poststucturalist, feminist educator Elizabeth Ellsworth challenges this idealistic rhetoric in her controversial article, "Why Doesn't This Feel Empowering? Working Through the Repressive Myths of Critical Pedagogy," which analyzes her experience teaching a graduate education course on media and race. Like Ellsworth, the students—a diverse group of American and international men and women—were committed to combating campus racism. Nevertheless, the group soon fractured into smaller "affinity groups," each with its own agenda. She argues, in short, that notions of unfettered expression and emancipatory authority in critical pedagogy theory were inadequate for dealing with the class's dynamics and ultimately undermined its egalitarian agenda: "As long as the literature on critical pedagogy fails to come to grips with issues of trust, risk, and the operations of fear and desire around such issues of identity and politics in the classroom, their rationalistic tools will continue to fail to loosen deep-seated, self-interested investments in unjust relations" (313). Shor's right: Democracy is tricky business.

(THE MEANS OF) PRODUCING STUDENT ACTIVISTS

Many high-profile critics flatly reject attempts to radicalize or liberate students. Maxine Hairston scorns teachers who put "dogma before diversity, politics before craft" (180), and Stanley Fish's recent book title shouts, "*Save the World on Your Own Time.*" Hairston and Fish would have instructors enter classrooms displaying academic expertise but no ideology—what Bizzell dismissively calls "brain[s] in a jar" ("Composition Studies Saves the World!" 178).

Other educators sympathetic to critical pedagogy's goals nevertheless argue that the means are flawed or downright counterproductive. Thus, in "*Who Owns School?*" Kelly Ritter provocatively suggests that, via the Internet, students are already writing and reading without teachers and that we should have the good sense to get out of the way. She argues that PinkMonkey.com's readers' forum and Ratemyprofessor.com show students performing the very work we try (and fail) to achieve in critical classrooms: They become "wholly *independent* learners who are capable of enacting the principles of civic discourse in internet spaces, for socioeducational ends" (169). (Ritter, Barbara Duffelmeyer, and Donna LeCourt further deplore critical teachers' inattention to cyberliteracy issues, including the panopticon effect of classrooms designed with computers against the walls; shifting definitions of authorship and authority, composing and text; and negotiating power online.)

And in "Considerations of American Freireistas," although Victor Villanueva shares Freireans' revolutionary goals, he finds their strategy of making the classroom a "political arena" precisely the wrong means for the end. Villanueva presents an ethnographic study of Floyd, a Freirean-trained teacher working in a Writer's Project for low-income, primarily black youths. By Freirean standards, Floyd seems perfect for the job. A talented black teacher who grew up in the neighborhood served by the project, he has participated in literacy campaigns in Nicaragua and Grenada. He taught the Writing Project students about black history and culture, ideology and oppression. He encouraged them to become radical intellectuals: They wrote; they participated in antiracism demonstrations. Yet, in the end, Villanueva argues, Floyd's message reached only those predisposed to accept his revolutionary agenda. Why would such a talented teacher fail? Because, Villanueva says, "Floyd's students . . . were in school to fulfill . . . a longtime American dream of success through education. They were not in school to have their dreams destroyed. They would naturally resist any such attempt" (256). In fact, Floyd's success actually fed their dreams: "In the students' eyes, Floyd made a better model of the bootstrap mentality than he made a model of the revolution" (256).

Similarly, in *Who Can Afford Critical Consciousness? Practicing a Pedagogy of Humility*, David Seitz argues compellingly that critical pedagogies fail when instructors proceed deductively. Seitz's ethnographic studies of critical classrooms, including his own, convinced him of two things: (1) Theorists of critical pedagogy often misjudge the motives behind students' instrumental goals and resistance; and (2) students remain unmoved by theoretical critiques imposed from above/outside—as when an instructor hands students a ready-made critical theory with which to deconstruct their experience. Seitz asserts that the key to effective critical pedagogy is teachers' and students' inductive, richly descriptive ethnographic practice. Seitz finds that instructors' ethnographic study of students can help them "remain continually attentive to the local situations, motives, and understanding of the students" and "constrain the possible theoretical arrogance of the critical pedagogue" (xi). And when students *begin* by examining their own lived experience and the concrete power relationships embodied in their communities, Seitz argues, they make knowledge and construct cultural theory from the ground up; then the very materiality of this work enables students to form "[their] own internally persuasive critiques"—the only kind likely to stick (229).

Other challenges to critical pedagogy focus on ends rather than means, and one of these in particular gives me pause: Jeff Smith's "Students' Goals, Gatekeeping, and Some Questions of Ethics." Smith argues that radical teachers often willfully confuse means and ends, most obviously by not acknowledging that they function primarily as means to students' ends. If writing teachers are serious about being democratic, about letting students set the agenda for their education, then they should honor students' desires for the credentials needed to secure professional-managerial jobs. "To do otherwise," Smith claims, "is undemocratic at best, if not infantilizing and frankly oppressive" (317). My sympathies for Smith's argument stem partly from a similar uneasiness with some critical pedagogy discourse. In *Composition and Resistance*, for instance, Mark Hurlbert and Michael Blitz celebrate a student who "resisted composure" by ignoring the conventions of an assigned research paper and turning in, instead, a series of quotations followed by reflective paragraphs. The authors suggest that compositionists can help subvert dominant ideology by not "teaching students to underwrite the university . . . [or] demanding written material which can be easily *gathered* and *assessed*" (7). I am not a great fan of wrapped-in-a-tidy-package-with-a-bow papers, but such proclamations make me nervous, for while students benefit from developing the desire and rhetorical wherewithal to "resist composure," some work in the world (the kind that pays the rent but also forms of political activism) requires them to be proficiently, even eloquently composed. Yet, even as I am moved by Smith's plea to respect students' goals, Tony Scott's *Dangerous Writing* pointedly reminds me that those goals come from somewhere—that they are not "private, autonomous motivations" but part and parcel of the "consumerist conceptions of democracy" (31) and individual choice that permeate capitalist culture.

Even within the ranks of critical teachers, questions about pedagogical ends are more unsettled than ever, particularly the political intervention seemingly mandated by Freirean pedagogy. Hence, Lee shares a manuscript reviewer's complaint that she doesn't really do (Freirean) critical pedagogy, which requires "actual political action" outside class (144). Lee wonders, "[W]hat constitutes 'actual political action?'" and questions any definitive boundary between inside and outside, between language and action (144). She challenges critical pedagogy's outcome-based agenda: "'[c]ritical consciousness,' 'liberation,' and 'radical social transformation,'" she argues, "are presented as the ideal *products*, which an effective radical political pedagogue will somehow produce in her classroom or will teach her students to produce" (47). Lee's pedagogy, informed by poststructuralist theory and process pedagogy, emphasizes textual and self "revisioning" in the form of a "critical self-inventory" (182). "The *aim*," Lee insists, "is not a definitive end (actual action, political or otherwise), so much as the development of a critical *process*" that shows students the constructed nature of their worlds (153). Even Shor argues that not all students or teachers or institutions can accommodate an activist agenda, that "[c]ritical learning is by itself a form of social action because of its transforming potential" (*Empowering* 195). Scott agrees: "When we articulate, we do; we act upon ourselves and our environments" (30). In other words, how we name things "matters"—has material consequences. To speak of *climate change* rather than *global warming* is to see a different problem, a different reality, a different course of action.

FREIREAN PEDAGOGY IN THE UNITED STATES: "WHO IS TO BE LIBERATED FROM WHAT?"

Working among Brazilian peasants, Freire presumably could easily identify the oppressed students needing liberation. But when American compositionists today step into the classroom—or look into the mirror—identifying the oppressed and the oppressors can become a fraught task. C. H. Knoblauch and Lil Brannon wonder whether the traditional goal of critical pedagogies to empower "outsiders" fits American society, leaving all sorts of bewildering questions: "Who is to be liberated from what? Who gets to do the liberating? Is the U.S. government an oppressor in the same sense that [South Africa's apartheid] government is? Are middle-class black persons as 'outside' as underclass Hispanic? . . . Is the goal to make the outsider into an insider?" (60). And for writing instructors like me, who walk into classrooms populated primarily with white, middle-class students, it can be hard to see their work as liberating the oppressed. Indeed, radical American teachers often seem to assume the opposite—that students are the oppressors. What can liberation possibly mean under these circumstances? Given the self-interest that might render students' critical examination of their status counterproductive, Knoblauch wonders, "Is critical teaching anything more than an intellectual game in such circumstances?" (Knoblauch and Brannon 64).

Additionally, some educators question how closely critical teachers actually align themselves with "the oppressed." Knoblauch and Brannon ask, "What is the meaning of 'radical teacher' for faculty in . . . privileged institutions—paid by the capitalist state?" (60). Questions such as these cause Stephen North to refuse the language of critical pedagogy, although he admires many of its advocates. One sticking point for North is the mismatch he sees between the revolutionary pedagogy he'd advocate inside the classroom and the time spent outside class "on a life that I would characterize as a system-supporting, system-supported, pro-capitalist, American mainstream life" (132). It's a point that should worry more radical teachers than it does. Freire quips about this inconsistency, noting how many American Marxists "have never drunk coffee in the house of a worker!" and how many American teachers (I am one) come to critical pedagogy because of something they've read in a book (Shor and Freire 136).

It's at this point in the conversation that poststructuralist and feminist educators make invaluable contributions to critical pedagogies by complicating conventional understandings both of knowledge and power and of representations of students' and teachers' identities. These educators reject traditional critical pedagogies' "master discourses of 'liberation'" that posit a universal, disinterested way to free another (Lather 185). So, Jennifer Gore argues that instead of broadcasting "what we can do for you!" or debating "what *should* we do for you?," critical educators must reexamine "what *can* 'we' do for 'you'?" Gore brilliantly analyzes the troubling ethical and theoretical assumptions grounding their decidedly *uncritical* use of empowerment rhetoric. First, *empowerment* suggests an agent who does the empowering and an object whom receives power from another. Here, power travels in one direction only, from the "powerful" teacher to the "powerless" student, replicating the very hierarchies that critical pedagogies hope to dismantle. Second, empowerment rhetoric assumes that power is a property (56) or, as Bruce Horner puts it, a commodity that you either have or don't have and that can be handed off like a football (123). Like Gore, Horner insists that power is "relational" (123), situation-specific, and (á la Foucault) "exercised," not owned (Gore 59). In a sense, then, power is more verb than noun, distributed within specific, shifting networks among people and institutions. In this view, critical pedagogues are simply *incapable* of liberating or empowering students.

The scare quotes in Gore's question "what *can* 'we' do for 'you'?" also emphasize poststructuralists' rejection of traditional constructions of teacher ("we") and students ("you"). In the discourse of critical pedagogy, "the teacher" is the "transformative intellectual," who liberates, inspires, saves; "the student" is a deficit, who lacks agency, voice, knowledge, and, ultimately, humanity. As Min-Zhan Lu and Bruce Horner observe, it's the student's experience that is subject "to critical analysis and alteration. . . . [The teacher's] theoretical knowledge remains . . . unimpeachable" (267). Poststructuralists argue, however, that static, generic categories—"the teacher," "the student," "the classroom"—do not exist.

Poststructuralist and feminist analyses, thus, move beyond untenable class-based binaries of oppressor and oppressed and academic binaries of teacher and student to account for power dynamics based on gender, race, religion, sexual orientation, age, body type, etc., which do not play out, Horner argues, in predictable ways—nor, according to the theory of intersectionality, independently. Rather, identities form (and reform) at the intersection of multiple axes of difference and power. Does a female, Asian, tenure-track professor at a public research institution have more or less agency than a white, male adjunct at a community college, who may be freer from monitoring? Poststructuralists argue that there's no simple or stable reading of individuals and social relations; difference and oppression come in many forms, not all of which are visible—as I was forcefully reminded recently when a bubbly, wealthy, white female student (marked "oppressor" in Marxist terms) wrote a harrowing tale of abuse by her father. In short, students occupy multiple, often contradictory positions in relation to dominant culture. As do teachers. Thus, Lather insists upon the impossibility "of a universalizing discourse of truth telling and correct readings" (188). (It follows that critical pedagogies are insistently tied to local, material circumstances, which may make curricula difficult, perhaps impossible, to transfer from teacher to teacher and institution to institution.)

Pedagogies of difference, then, so fundamental to critical education, are nonetheless complicated to theorize and practice. Educators generally agree that differences are assigned rather than fixed, biological categories (e.g., biologically, there's only one human race) that erect specific but shifting socio-economic/political hierarchies. But which differences teachers should address or stress (if any) and how to move toward greater equality are open questions. Antiracist pedagogies are a prime example. Antonio Darder and Rodolfo D. Torres ("After Race: An Introduction") advocate a post-race discourse, arguing that the "specious concept" of race clouds cultural analyses and essentializes race as a marker of identity (157). Instead, Darder and Torres speak of *racism(s)* or *racialization*, claiming that to talk and act as if race were real fuels rather than challenges white supremacy; for them, class remains the critical factor. However, most educators of color seek more, not less, race consciousness and draw upon critical race theory (CRT)—and subdivisions such as Latino, Asian American, and Native American critical race studies (LatCrit, AsianCrit, TribalCrit)—to create critical race pedagogies. CRT posits race as the key factor in producing inequality. Marvin Lynn ("Inserting the 'Race' into Critical Pedagogy") and Gloria Ladson-Billings and William Tate ("Toward a Critical Race Theory of Education") explain the centrality, in CRT, of personal voice, experiential knowledge, and story as means for people of color to understand their oppression and to make that reality felt by others. As Ladson-Billings and Tate observe, "Without authentic voices of people of color"—in scholarship and in pedagogy—"it is doubtful that we can say or know anything useful about education in their communities" or about injustice in America (175). (See also Parker and Stovall; Trifonas.)

RHETORICAL ANSWERS TO STUDENT RESISTANCE

How to understand and deal with student resistance to leftist politics is another tricky question facing critical teachers. In early scholarship, student resistance is presented as, at worst, something that comes with the territory and, at best, a sign that students may be shedding their passive roles. Thus, Berlin jokes that when his students resisted cultural critique, he "decided that was a victory because it would've been easy for them to play along with me" (qtd. in Hurlbert and Blitz 9). Critical teachers today, however, find that student resistance accomplishes little except to confirm media portrayals of radical academics indoctrinating students or, worse, push "students already hunkered down in the 'everybody-has-a-right-to-an-opinion' foxhole [to] dig even deeper" (Anderson 198).

I find especially persuasive arguments by rhetorically minded critical educators that understand student resistance primarily as a rhetorical problem—one that might be lessened by employing rhetorical theory or smarter rhetorical strategies. Attempting to foreground discussions of difference in the face of a conservative backlash, critical pedagogues, they argue, have forgotten that classrooms are rhetorical spaces, that teachers are rhetors and students a resistant audience partly of their own making. (See brilliant studies by Goodburn on religious fundamentalist students and Trainor on white students' resistance to discussions of race.) As Virginia Anderson notes, critical teachers often "align themselves with those the students hope never to become, and they depict themselves as enemies of what many students are" (203). Why, then, are they surprised that some students resist? Anderson advocates using questions from classical *stasis* theory (What is it? What causes it? How do we evaluate it?) to drive critical analyses. The beauty of Anderson's strategy is that the probing questions "are supplied by the theory itself, which can be taught as theory, and not by the teacher as his or her politics" (210).

Karen Kopelson similarly asks, "*How* might we speak, *as whom* might we speak, *so that students listen*?" (142). Her intriguing answer is that critical teachers "may simply need to be sneakier" (121)—or, more precisely, cunning in the sense of the classical *metis*. Metis "willingly operates through reversal, deception, and disguise when necessary" (131). The particular disguise Kopelson has in mind is, paradoxically, a performance of exactly what students expect—authoritative, academic neutrality, a "deliberate, reflective, self-conscious masquerade ... [done] in the service of other—disturbing and disruptive—goals" (123). If students perceive instructors as having no *personal* political agenda, they may be more willing to engage in political discussions. (See also excellent ethnographies by Gorzelsky; Wallace and Ewald.)

Finally, Jessica Enoch encourages critical compositionists to look to the rhetorical theorist Kenneth Burke as a source of pedagogical guidance. According to Enoch, Burke's essay "Linguistic Approach to Problems of Education" (LAPE) outlines a "pedagogy of critical reflection" (273). In LAPE, Burke explains an approach designed to help students track how language forms identifications and divisions, an "us" vs. "them," that lead to competition, ambition, and, ultimately, violence. Burke teaches students how "to question the many symbolically-stimulated goads that are now accepted too often without question" (26) and to short-circuit the rush to judgment: He "offers a technique for stopping to analyze an exhortation precisely at the moment when the exhortation would otherwise set us to swinging violently" (24).

CONCLUSION

Lather says that "[i]mplementing critical pedagogy in the field of schooling [is] impossible" (189). Some instructors seize this as a reason to reject critical pedagogies; for others, impossibility is simply the necessary condition of the work we do. "Theorizing out of problems of practice," Lather continues, "interrupts the mysticism that often attends critical pedagogy and its inflated promises" (190). In an odd way, impossibility might even be "liberating" for compositionists, freeing them to reimagine pedagogical praxes. If critical pedagogies are burdened with bamboozlement or ambiguity, I'd suggest that's not entirely due to inadequate theory or methods. Rather, some complications result from having to live and teach with the knowledge that "human action can move in several directions at once, that something can contain itself and also its opposite" (Shor and Freire 69). These paradoxes are neither solvable nor necessarily debilitating. They keep teachers honest and inventive and, well, critical. In an interview with Gary Olson, Freire notes the complicated position of the radical writing instructor who stands with one foot in the system, today's reality, and the other foot outside the system, in a future utopia: "This is why it's so difficult . . . for us to walk: we have to walk like this. [With a playful smile, Freire begins to waddle across the room.] Life is like this. This is reality and history" (Olson and Gale 163).

As for me, I've found my own way of walking that walk, but it's Burke, not Freire, I waddle beside. I've admired and taught Burke's work for years, but I'm just beginning to understand that his theorizing was meant for practical—i.e., pedagogical—use. Burke was, at heart, a teacher of critical methods for citizens in everyday life. And only in the writing of this essay have I understood him to be the critical pedagogue par excellence—for me, in this time and place. In a scene distressingly like ours—growing inequality and suffering, "war now always threatening" (LAPE 14)—Burke constructed a methodology to expose language's ideological nature and capitalism's voracious appetite and to warn Americans of the "danger[ous] . . . personal aggrandizement [that] beset[s] us . . . as citizens identified with a nation of almost terrifyingly vast and expansive political and economic power" ("Responsibilities" 46). Burke's work is now the centerpiece of my critical pedagogy as I teach student writers that "[a] way of seeing is also a way of not seeing" (*Permanence and Change* 49), that we see the world through the lens of symbols so natural, so unremarkable (*war on terror, illegal alien, No Child Left Behind*) that we often don't see how they persuade us to think and act in certain ways and not others. In my critical pedagogy, we write together about the invisible.

BIBLIOGRAPHY

Anderson, Virginia. "Confrontational Teaching and Rhetorical Practice." *CCC* 48.2 (1997): 197–214. Print.

Aronowitz, Stanley, and Henry Giroux. *Education under Siege: The Conservative, Liberal, and Radical Debate over Schooling*. London: Routledge and Kegan Paul, 1985. Print.

Berlin, James A. "Freirean Pedagogy in the U.S.: A Response." *(Inter)views: Cross-Disciplinary Perspectives on Rhetoric and Literacy*. Eds. Gary A. Olson and Irene Gale. Carbondale: Southern Illinois UP, 1991. 169–76. Print.

Bizzell, Patricia. *Academic Discourse and Critical Consciousness*. Pittsburgh: U of Pittsburgh P, 1992. Print.

_____. "Composition Studies Saves the World!" *College English* 72.2 (2009): 174–87. Print.

Burke, Kenneth. "Linguistic Approach to Problems of Education." 1955. Rpt. in *Humanistic Critique of Education: Teaching and Learning as Symbolic Action*. Ed. Peter M. Smudde. West Lafayette: Parlor P, 2010. 3–41. Print.

_____. *Permanence and Change: An Anatomy of Purpose*. 3rd ed. Berkeley: U of California P, 1984. Print.

_____. "Responsibilities of National Greatness." *Nation* 17 July 1967, 46–50. Print.

Darder, Antonia, and Rodolfo D. Torres. "After Race: An Introduction." *The Critical Pedagogy Reader*. 2nd ed. Ed. Antonia Darder, Marta P. Baltodano, and Rodolfo D. Torres. New York: Routledge, 2009. 150–66. Print.

Dewey, John. *Democracy and Education: An Introduction to the Philosophy of Education*. New York: Macmillan, 1916. Print.

Duffelmeyer, Barbara B. "Critical Work in First-Year Composition: Computers, Pedagogy, and Research." *Pedagogy* 2.3 (2002): 357–74. Print.

Elbow, Peter. *Embracing Contraries: Explorations in Learning and Teaching*. New York: Oxford UP, 1986. Print.

Ellsworth, Elizabeth. "Why Doesn't This Feel Empowering? Working through the Repressive Myths of Critical Pedagogy." *Harvard Educational Review* 59.3 (1989): 297–324. Print.

Enoch, Jessica. "Becoming Symbol-Wise: Kenneth Burke's Pedagogy of Critical Reflection." *CCC* 56.2 (2004): 272–96. Print.

Fish, Stanley. *Save the World on Your Own Time*. New York: Oxford UP, 2008. Print.

Freire, Paulo. *Pedagogy of the Oppressed*. 1970. New York: Continuum, 2005. Print.

Giroux, Henry, A. "Liberal Arts Education and the Struggle for Public Life: Dreaming About Democracy." *South Atlantic Quarterly* 89.1 (1990): 113–38. Print.

_____. "Literacy and the Pedagogy of Voice and Political Empowerment." *Educational Theory* 38.1 (1988): 61–75. Print.

_____. "Memories of Hope in the Age of Disposability." *JAC* 31.1–2 (2011): 103–21. Print.

_____. "Public Pedagogy and the Politics of Resistance: Notes on a Critical Theory of Educational Struggle." *Educational Philosophy and Theory* 35.1 (2003): 5–16. Print.

_____. *Schooling and the Struggle for Public Life: Critical Pedagogy in the Modern Age.* Minneapolis: U of Minnesota P, 1988. Print.

_____. *Theory and Resistance in Education: A Pedagogy for the Opposition.* Westport: Greenwood: Bergin-Garvey, 1983. Print.

Giroux, Henry, and Peter McLaren. "Teacher Education and the Politics of Engagement: The Case for Democratic Schooling." *Harvard Educational Review* 56.3 (1986): 213–38. Print.

Goodburn, Amy. "It's a Question of Faith: Discourse of Fundamentalism and Critical Pedagogy in the Writing Classroom." *JAC: A Journal of Advanced Composition Theory* 18.2 (1998): 333–54. Print.

Gore, Jennifer. "What We Can Do for You! What *Can* 'We' Do for 'You'? Struggling over Empowerment in Critical and Feminist Pedagogy." *Feminisms and Critical Pedagogy.* Ed. Carmen Luke and Jennifer Gore. New York: Routledge, 1992. Print.

Gorzelsky, Gwen. "Working Boundaries: From Student Resistance to Student Agency." *CCC* 61.1 (2009): 64–84. Print.

Hairston, Maxine. "Diversity, Ideology, and Teaching Writing." *CCC* 43.2 (1992): 179–93. Print.

hooks, bell. *Teaching Community: A Pedagogy of Hope.* New York: Routledge, 2003. Print.

_____. *Teaching to Transgress: Education as the Practice of Freedom.* New York: Routledge, 1994. Print.

Horner, Bruce. "Politics, Pedagogy, and the Profession of Composition: Confronting the Commodification and the Contingencies of Power." *JAC* 20.1 (2000): 121–52. Print.

Hurlbert, Mark, and Michael Blitz, eds. *Composition and Resistance.* Portsmouth: Boynton/ Cook, 1991. Print.

Knoblauch, C. H., and Lil Brannon. *Critical Teaching and the Idea of Literacy.* Portsmouth: Boynton/Cook, 1993. Print.

Kopelson, Karen. "Rhetoric on the Edge of Cunning; Or, The Performance of Neutrality (Re)Considered as a Composition Pedagogy for Student Resistance." *CCC* 55.1 (2003): 115–46. Print.

Kozol, Jonathan. *Illiterate America.* New York: Anchor/Doubleday, 1985. Print.

Ladson-Billings, Gloria, and William F. Tate IV. "Toward a Critical Race Theory of Education." Darder, Baltodano, and Torres 167–82. Print.

Lather, Patti. "Ten Years Later, Yet Again: Critical Pedagogy and Its Complicities." *Feminist Engagements: Reading, Resisting, and Revisioning Male Theorists in Education and Cultural Studies.* Ed. Kathleen Weiler. New York: Routledge, 2001. 183–95. Print.

LeCourt, Donna. "Critical Pedagogy in the Computer Classroom: Politicizing the Writing Space." *Computers and Composition* 15.3 (1998): 275–95. Print.

Lee, Amy. *Composing Critical Pedagogies: Teaching Writing as Revision.* Urbana: National Council of Teachers of English, 2000. Print.

Lu, Min-Zhan, and Bruce Horner. "The Problematic of Experience: Redefining Critical Work in Ethnography and Pedagogy." *College English* 60.3 (1998): 257–77. Print.

Lynch, Paul. "Composition as a Thermostatic Activity." *CCC* 60.4 (2009): 728–45. Print.

Lynn, Marvin. "Inserting the 'Race' into Critical Pedagogy: An Analysis of 'Race-based Epistemologies.'" *Educational Philosophy and Theory* 36.2 (2004): 153–65. Print.

Macedo, Donaldo. *Literacies of Power: What Americans Are Not Allowed to Know.* Boulder: Westview P, 1994. Print.

McLaren, Peter. *Life in Schools: An Introduction to Critical Pedagogy in the Foundations of Education.* New York: Longman, 1989. Print.

North, Stephen M. "Rhetoric, Responsibility, and the 'Language of the Left.'" Hurlbert and Blitz 127–36. Print.

Olson, Gary A., and Irene Gale, eds. *(Inter)views: Cross-disciplinary Perspectives on Rhetoric and Literacy.* Carbondale: Southern Illinois UP, 1991. Print.

Parker, Laurence, and David O. Stovall. "Actions Following Words: Critical Race Theory Connects to Critical Pedagogy." *Educational Philosophy and Theory* 36.2 (2004): 167–82. Print.

Ritter, Kelly. *Who Owns School? Authority, Students, and Online Discourse.* Cresskill: Hampton, 2010. Print.

Ronald, Kate, and Hephzibah Roskelly. "Untested Feasibility: Imagining the Pragmatic Possibility of Paulo Freire." *College English* 63.5 (2001): 612–32. Print.

Scott, Tony. *Dangerous Writing: Understanding the Political Economy of Composition.* Logan: Utah State UP, 2009. Print.

Seitz, David. *Who Can Afford Critical Consciousness? Practicing a Pedagogy of Humility.* Cresskill: Hampton, 2004. Print.

Shor, Ira. *Critical Teaching and Everyday Life.* 1980. Chicago: U of Chicago P, 1987. Print.

———. *Empowering Education: Critical Teaching for Social Change.* Chicago: U of Chicago P, 1992. Print.

———, ed. *Freire for the Classroom: A Sourcebook for Liberatory Teaching.* Portsmouth: Heinemann, 1987. Print.

———. *When Students Have Power: Negotiating Authority in a Critical Pedagogy.* Chicago: U of Chicago P, 1996. Print.

Shor, Ira, and Paulo Freire. *A Pedagogy for Liberation: Dialogues on Transforming Education.* South Hadley: Bergin and Garvey, 1987. Print.

Simon, Roger. "Empowerment as a Pedagogy of Possibility." *Language Arts* 64 (1987): 370–82. Print.

Smith, Jeff. "Students' Goals, Gatekeeping, and Some Questions of Ethics." *College English* 59.3 (1997): 299–320. Print.

Trainor, Jennifer Seibel. "Critical Pedagogy's 'Other': Constructions of Whiteness in Education for Social Change." *CCC* 53.4 (2002): 631–50. Print.

Trifonas, Peter Pericles, ed. *Pedagogies of Difference: Rethinking Education for Social Change.* New York: RoutledgeFalmer, 2003. Print.

Villanueva, Victor, Jr. "Considerations of American Freireistas." *The Politics of Writing Instruction: Postsecondary.* Ed. Richard Bullock and John Trimbur. Portsmouth: Boynton/Cook, 1991. Print.

Wallace, David L., and Helen Rothschild Ewald. *Mutuality in the Rhetoric and Composition Classroom.* Carbondale: Southern Illinois UP, 2000. Print.

Winkelmann, Carol L. "Electronic Literacy, Critical Pedagogy, and Collaboration: A Case for Cyborg Writing." *Computers and the Humanities* 29.6 (1995): 431–48. Print.

Cultural Studies and Composition

Diana George
Tim Lockridge
John Trimbur

I t has been more than a dozen years since the original version of this chapter was written and first appeared in print. At that time, our task was both to answer Richard Johnson's question—What is cultural studies, anyway?—and to explore the uses of and possibilities for cultural studies in the teaching of writing. Cultural studies, it appeared then, had established a firm foothold in composition—in our journals, monographs, textbooks, and conferences. Today, however, the very designation "Cultural Studies and Composition" reads more like a piece of the field's past than a promise for its future. It is fair to say, at least, that our task here has shifted considerably. Rather than detail a cultural studies approach to the teaching of writing, we pose a different question altogether: Whatever happened to "cultural studies and composition," anyway?

That is not to dismiss the influence of cultural studies on the study and teaching of writing. Since the first version of this chapter went to press, works that explore cultural studies have continued to appear, often ones that link cultural studies to a related field, such as the collections *At the Intersection: Cultural Studies and Rhetorical Studies* (Rosteck) and *Critical Power Tools: Technical Communication and Cultural Studies* (Scott, Longo, and Wills). We acknowledge at the outset, however, that the questions at one time raised by composition's cultural studies moment—What is it? What is its history? What arguments have been made for bringing cultural studies into the writing classroom?—feel less urgent today. Instead, we would argue that "the cultural studies approach to teaching writing" has been so thoroughly incorporated into much composition theory and pedagogy that today there is little need for the kind of scrutiny we originally gave this area. At the same time, its own pressures and limits transformed the cultural studies project within composition in at least three important ways: (1) the rapid development of Web technologies, gaming communities, and social networking has meant a shift in the study of digital media and theories of multimodality from a focus on the semiotic to a social semiotic approach, as well as an increase in ethnographic investigations of how people use technology or interact in digital spaces; (2) what Paula Mathieu first identified as a "public turn" in composition and writing studies (*Tactics*, 2005) acknowledged what had become a growing emphasis on public rhetoric, civic writing, community publishing, and the like as both legitimate areas of study and one basis for classroom practice; and (3) a recognition of the limits of national borders in cultural studies has demanded a new attention to globalization, transnational perspectives, and the pluralization of English.

Our purpose here is to follow the trajectory cultural studies and composition has taken since the first edition of this collection—to explain how cultural studies has informed or been absorbed by writing pedagogy and scholarship even as the designation itself has disappeared from our journals and conferences. To do that, we begin by revisiting briefly some conceptual terrain—the various histories, definitions, and traditions that have characterized cultural studies as a distinct political and intellectual project.

CULTURAL STUDIES:
HISTORIES, DEFINITIONS, TRADITIONS

The most influential history of cultural studies traces how a cluster of works published within a few years of each other in the late 1950s and early 1960s—Richard Hoggart's *The Uses of Literacy* (1957), Raymond Williams' *Culture and Society* (1958) and *The Long Revolution* (1961), and E. P. Thompson's *The Making of the English Working Class* (1963)—marked a decisive break with established ways of thinking about culture, literature, and history, thereby constituting what Stuart Hall calls "the *caesura* out of which . . . 'Cultural Studies' emerged" ("Cultural Studies: Two Paradigms" 34). In this account of the founding of cultural studies, Hoggart, Williams, and Thompson are joined in a common project of articulating a notion of culture to replace the cultivation of sensibility implied in the high/low binaries of literary studies and mass culture critiques, on the one hand, and the reductionist sense of culture as an epiphenomenal superstructure of the economic base in mechanical Marxism, on the other. All three figures wanted to think of culture as a way of life, a set of ordinary, everyday practices linked in creative and consequential fashion to the social order and the formation of class consciousness. Most of all, they wanted to recover the culture of the common people, to reclaim culture from its monopoly by antidemocratic and elitist forces both inside and outside the academy.

This history establishes a cultural studies tradition of politically engaged and theoretically eclectic critique and intervention into the "history of the contemporary." It also points to the historical and political moment the Centre for Contemporary Cultural Studies (CCCS) was established at the University of Birmingham in 1964 with Hoggart (later Stuart Hall, then Richard Johnson) as director. Beginning (at least symbolically) in 1956, with the Suez crisis, the Soviet invasion of Hungary, and the Khruschev relations about Stalinist terror, as well as the formation the following year of the Campaign for Nuclear Disarmament, a New Left was forming in the United Kingdom, activated by the crisis in traditional Marxism and the growing sense that the Old Left was unable to engage the realities of postwar capitalism, the persistence of racism and imperialism, the role of ideology in maintaining class society, and the growing influence of consumer culture and "Americanization" among the British working classes. Against the historical backdrop and with the upheavals of the 1960s about to take place, the CCCS sought to develop an open Marxism and socialist humanism distinct from the doctrinaire Marxism of the Stalinized Communist parties of the Third International and the postwar welfare-state settlement engineered by the reformist British Labor Party.

From those New Left origins in the late 1950s and early 1960s, cultural studies in the United Kingdom took up the leading political and intellectual questions of its time. Unlike the traditional established disciplines, however, the version of cultural studies that spread from Birmingham relied not so much on systemic research programs and questions that define the field as on what Johnson has called "a kind of alchemy for producing useful knowledge" (38). This alchemy typically involved collaborative and interdisciplinary—in some cases nondisciplinary and even antidisciplinary—work, such as *Resistance Through Rituals: Youth Subcultures in Post War Britain* (Hall and Jefferson, 1976), *Policing the Crisis: Mugging, the State, and Law and Order* (Hall, Cricther, Jefferson, Clarke, and Roberts, 1979), *Working Class Culture: Studies in History and Theory* (Clarke et al., 1979), *Unpopular Education: Schooling and Social Democracy in England since 1944* (CCCS, 1981), *Making Histories: History-Writing and Politics* (CCCS, 1982), and *Education Limited: Schooling and Training and the New Right since 1979* (CCCS, 1991). Linked to moments of engagement and analysis—whether of Thatcherism, the Falklands crisis, the New Times initiative, or the Sony Walkman—British cultural studies insisted on seeing itself as an open project that is politically committed but nondoctrinaire, one that resists reductive conceptions of culture.

From another angle, however, it should be noted that this account does not fully represent the struggles within cultural studies. Of these, perhaps the most telling are the interventions of feminism and antiracism. The appearance in 1978 of *Women Take Issue: Aspects of Women's Subordination* from the Women's Studies Group at CCCS challenged the masculinist tradition in cultural studies and its focus on class cultures to the exclusion of race and gender, and Angela McRobbie's "Settling Accounts with Subcultures: A Feminist Critique" pointed out that the category "youth" in Paul Willis' *Learning to Labor: How Working-Class Kids Get Working-Class Jobs* and Dick Hebdige's *Subculture: The Meaning of Style* is coded as male. Along similar lines, the Race and Politics Group at CCCS published *The Empire Strikes Back: Race and Racism in 70s Britain* in 1982, with contributions by Hazel V. Carby, Paul Gilroy, Errol Lawrence, and Pratibha Parmar, as a "corrective to the narrowness of the English left whose version of the 'national-popular' continues to deny the role of blacks and black struggles in the making and remaking of the working class" (Gilroy, "Preface"). Gilroy developed further this line of inquiry into the ethnocentric biases in British cultural studies' fixation on "Englishness" and the nation as the natural unit of class struggle in *There Ain't No Black in the Union Jack*, published in 1987.

These groundbreaking books and all the work that preceded them from its founding in 1964 mark the heyday of collaborative and individual work in British cultural studies at CCCS in Birmingham. In the 1980s, the Centre was folded into a department of cultural studies and sociology. This institutional change meant for the first time an attention to undergraduate as well as graduate education, but it also foreshadowed an end to the relatively autonomous status of CCCS as a research center and think tank on the left. In 2002, the department was dismantled by University of Birmingham administration, with only four of its fourteen cultural studies faculty assigned to other departments, in a highly controversial "restructuring" move, ostensibly for its scoring just below the highest marks on the Research Assessment Exercise, despite the fact that cultural studies had come out with top scores in teaching year after year. It is hard not to think this amounted to retribution for CCCS's legacy of political radicalism and, at the same time, registered in a backhanded way the fact, as university officials argued, that cultural studies was now being taught in many departments across the curriculum.

BRINGING CULTURAL STUDIES INTO COMPOSITION

When cultural studies entered composition, the first task was to explain what it was doing there, and early discussions were typically arguments for the place of cultural studies in the writing classroom. The most prominent voices in those introductions to cultural studies and composition—Trimbur, James A. Berlin, John Schilb, and Lester Faigley—offered somewhat different accounts of how cultural studies fit into composition.

Trimbur's 1988 article "Cultural Studies and the Teaching of Writing" was the first to make explicit connections between cultural studies and composition pedagogy. In this and later discussions ("Articulation Theory"; "The Politics of Radical Pedagogy") Trimbur drew upon cultural studies to emphasize the concerns of popular education, especially the ties of writing instruction to the democratization of higher education through the land grant universities, the GI bill, and open admissions. For Trimbur, contemporary composition emerges in the late 1960s and early 1970s as a part of a larger struggle to re-represent students and adult learners stigmatized as uneducable because of cognitive deficiencies, the culture of poverty, or the restricted codes of oral culture.

James A. Berlin, the figure most readily associated with cultural studies and composition, on the other hand, focused on the role of cultural studies in the English department, especially as it brings to the surface what he called "the invidious distinction between poetics and rhetoric . . . that has valorized poetics while considering rhetorical texts and their production as not worth serious study" ("Composition" 48). In a series of articles and chapters ("Poststructuralism"; "Composition Studies"; "Rhetoric, Poetic"), and culminating in the posthumous *Rhetorics, Poetics, and Cultures,* Berlin elaborated the goal of rhetoric as enabling students to "master the operations of signification in the distribution of power" and thus "to become better writers and readers as citizens, workers, and critics of their cultures" (*Rhetorics* 145).

For John Schilb and Lester Faigley, cultural studies had to be understood in its problematic relations to postmodernism. As Schilb notes in "Cultural Studies, Postmodernism, and Composition," the term *postmodernism* contains a range of meanings: "a critique of traditional epistemology, a set of artistic practices, and an ensemble of larger social conditions" (174). The question, for Schilb, is whether "we should link or oppose cultural studies and postmodernism" (174). Faigley sees postmodernism not just as a theoretical problem but as a sensibility that increasingly pervades contemporary social life. In *Fragments of Rationality: Postmodernity and the Subject of Composition*, Faigley links postmodernism to the transition from a Fordist world of mass production and consumption to a post-Fordist order of flexible and mobile production and the fragmentation of national markets into specialized niches. The result, Faigley says, is the "breakup of mass culture as it was constituted in the United States throughout much of this century into a pluralization of tastes, styles, and practices," with a consuming subject whose unstable and unfulfillable desires are shaped by "not so much objects but images of objects" (12).

Challenges to these accounts of the history of composition and cultural studies pointed to the fact that they tended to be male and monocultural. Nedra Reynolds, for example, charged Trimbur, Berlin, and Faigley with having written a male narrative of cultural studies and composition, missing "radical changes wrought by feminism's intervention into cultural studies" following, she argues, "the rhetorical pattern of so many cultural studies narratives, which walk neatly through the 'seminal' texts of the all-male trinity of Hoggart, Williams, and Thompson" ("Interrupting" 68). Reynolds likens this omission in composition studies to the omissions of gender in Birmingham noted previously. Much the same could be said about the ways race and ethnicity had been omitted in composition, subsumed, as Catherine Prendergast argued in 1998, "into the powerful tropes of 'basic writer,' 'stranger' in the academy, or the trope of the generalized, marginalized 'other'" (36).

NEW MEDIA ENTERS THE MIX

Perhaps one of the most notable shifts to occur since this chapter's initial publication is the growth of new media studies as an area of inquiry and a site of pedagogical practice. Many theoretical explorations of new media extend, to varying degrees, from a cultural studies tradition: for example, Donna Haraway's critiques of technology and her metaphor of the cyborg as a means reconsidering social dualisms ("A Manifesto for Cyborgs"); Sherry Turkle's examination of digital connectedness and "the robotic moment" (*Alone Together*); and Jay David Bolter and Richard Grusin's concept of "remediation" as a kind of dialectic between new and old media (*Remediation*). In this section, we identify two major threads of cultural studies inquiry within current composition and new media scholarship: first, the influence of social semiotic thought on the study of multimodality, and second, the ethnographic turn toward amateur and vernacular texts published in digital spaces. Ours is not a comprehensive look at digital rhetoric or computers and writing (for that, see Brooke, this volume); instead, we wish to point to the arm of new media studies that has taken up the spirit (if not the charge) of composition and cultural studies.

While much initial cultural studies work in composition drew from semiotic and structuralist thought, the study of new media and multimodality has pushed those investigations in new directions. This early thread of semiotic inquiry, heavily influenced by Roland Barthes, focused on the examination of visual texts (advertising, television, etc.) as well as common objects and popular activities of all sorts as cues for interpreting cultural codes (e.g., Barthes, "Toys," "Wine and Milk," "The World of Wrestling"). In British cultural studies, this line of investigation might be best evidenced by Dick Hebdige's (1979) *Subculture: The Meaning of Style* in which Hebdige examines how a 1970s punk style, through the repurposing of everyday objects such as clothespins and leather jackets, functions as a signifying practice. The earliest appearance of cultural studies in composition pedagogy drew heavily on this work, especially bringing a more deliberate use of popular culture and media studies into the composition course.

By the end of the twentieth century, however, the emergence of new media, with its multiple forms and modalities, had prompted scholars like Gunther Kress and Theo Van Leeuwen to develop theories of multimodality based on social semiotics, shifting the focus away from the structural semiotics-oriented practice of interpreting signs in terms of signifiers and signifieds and toward the affordances of semiotic resources in specific social contexts (*Reading Images*; *Multimodal Discourse*; Kress, *Multimodality*). Multimodality is itself not a function of new media but rather a means of analyzing how linguistic and nonlinguistic modalities (e.g., images, color, sound, motion, page design, etc.) combine in scribal, print, and electronic compositions. Kress has been particularly interested in how changing ratios of writing and images create textual meanings as the locus of literacy expands from page to screen (*Literacy*).

Yet another body of scholarship linking composition, cultural studies, and new media comes through Henry Jenkins and the study of consumer practices. Jenkins' (1992) *Textual Poachers* is an ethnographic study of fan practices in pre-Web contexts (such as print fanzines and conventions), extending Michel de Certeau's understanding of the reader as a type of poacher. Drawing on Bourdieu, Jenkins argued that media fans disrupt traditional cultural hierarchies, "treating popular texts as if they merited the same degree of attention and appreciation as canonical texts" (17). Jenkins challenged the then-typical conceptions of media consumption as a mindless or antisocial activity (e.g., Postman), instead presenting media fans as engaged in acts of creation and activism—"as spectators who transform the experience of watching television into a rich and complex participatory culture" (23). For Jenkins, television consumption was a productive activity, one in which viewers study, rewrite, and advocate for programming.

In recent years, connections between popular culture and literacy practices have offered a frame for the study of online identity (B. T. Williams; Banks; Nakamura); plagiarism and intellectual property (DeVoss; Rife); gaming communities and practices (Gee; Selfe and Hawisher); and digital authorship and collaboration

(Brooke; Laquintano), among others, signaling a shift toward vernacular texts and practices. This movement, however, has also coincided with a post-Napster culture of digital file-sharing and remix, often placing the work of vernacular texts in direct tension with print-driven intellectual property laws and commercial ownership. Where de Certeau and Hoggart offered a cultural studies project centered in everyday practice, the tensions of digital distribution have found those practices mired in courts and conflicts. Jenkins has referred to this tension as "convergence culture"—"where the power of the media producer and the power of the media consumer interact in unpredictable ways" (*Convergence Culture* 2)—and the work of legal and media studies scholars (Lessig; Vaidhyanathan; Wu) has offered composition scholars an important frame for thinking through the clash between digital practices and commercial interests.

Studies of the digital have also shifted due to the growth of Web technologies and their influence on social change and activism. Liz Losh's work ("Hacktivism and the Humanities"), for example, sits in the space between composition's public turn and its study of the everyday, considering how public practice and political policy function in digital spaces. Likewise, texts such as John Scenters-Zapico's *Generaciones' Narratives* have used digital narrative and video ethnography to explore the role of digital and media literacies in marginalized publics. The prevalence of the digital narrative in composition studies might offer one of the strongest connections between composition and cultural studies, as evidenced by Berry, Hawisher, and Selfe's *Transnational Literate Lives* and the *Digital Archive of Literacy Narratives*, which is curated by Cynthia Selfe. These projects, though situated in new technologies, offer a notable extension of composition's cultural studies moment—extending the field's long-standing exploration of the personal and vernacular work of writing into digital and transnational spaces.

THE PUBLIC TURN

In 2005 Paula Mathieu argued that composition had taken a "public turn," an increased interest in public rhetoric, community-engagement, and the kinds of communication practices characteristic of public debate and action. In her account of composition's roots for this public turn, Mathieu points especially to the continuing influence of cultural studies and the Birmingham School; Berlin's critiques of the persistence of current-traditional pedagogy; Anne Gere's 1993 CCCC's address in which she identified an "extracurriculum" for composition; Trimbur's call for attention to the materiality of writing (e.g., "Composition and the Circulation of Writing"; "Delivering the Message"); Diana George's work on alternative and street press writing ("Word on the Street"); and to writers whose work called attention to questions of the public sphere (e.g., Susan Wells, "Rogue Cops"; Rosa Eberly, "From *Writers, Audiences,* and *Communities* to *Publics*").

As might be imagined from this brief listing, the notion of a "public turn" enters composition and writing studies in a number of different ways. At least three areas of investigation have emerged: a series of historical and contemporary studies of the literacy practices of marginalized or previously ignored groups; a demand for and emphasis on school-community partnerships and service-learning projects connected to writing programs; and a growing body of literature that engages with activist rhetorics and public sphere theory.

Accompanying these trends we see a move away from a sole focus on the first-year writing course *per se* (composition studies) to the more recent emphasis on the kinds of scholarship that might more accurately come under the domain of writing studies. Gere's call ("Kitchen Tables") for research on the self-sponsored writing of individuals outside of the academy—that "extracurriculum" of composition—laid the groundwork for a number of important literacy studies, including her own of the literacy practices of women's clubs between 1880 and 1920 (*Intimate Practices*, 1997); Jacqueline Jones Royster's *Traces of a Stream: Literacy and Social Change Among African American Women* (2000), Deborah Brandt's *Literacy in American Lives* (2001); Janet Eldred and Peter Mortensen's history of women's writing practices between the American Revolution and the Civil War (*Imagining Rhetoric*, 2002); Elaine Richardson's *African American Literacies* (2003) and *Hiphop Literacies* (2006); and Shirley Wilson Logan's *Liberating Language: Sites of Rhetorical Education in Nineteenth Century Black America* (2008).

For others, the public turn has meant community literacy programs and service-learning projects (e.g., Goldblatt; Flower; Joliffe). As Shirley K. Rose and Irwin Weiser explain in their introduction to the edited collection *Going Public: What Writing Programs Learn from Engagement* (2010), the recent call for writing programs to "go public" springs from demands for accountability to a broader public, a demand that has implications for curriculum development, service-learning and community literacy projects, and historical as well as contemporary scholarship in public discourse (1). Readers will find a more thorough account of community-engagement and service-learning in this volume's chapter on Community-engaged Pedagogies.

Discussions of activist rhetorics appear in works such as Rachel Riedner and Kevin Mahoney's *Democracies to Come: Rhetorical Action, Neoliberalism, and Communities of Resistance* (2008); John Ackerman and David Coogan's collection *The Public Work of Rhetoric: Citizen-Scholars and Civic Engagement* (2010); and Phyllis Ryder's *Rhetorics for Community Action: Public Writing and Writing Publics* (2011). These books clearly extend the discussion beyond service-learning to address larger questions of public rhetoric and civic action. For others, this public turn has led to the streets and the world of street papers, activist publications, prison writing, and community press work (e.g., George and Mathieu; Goldblatt; Jacobi).

Much of the work that has emerged from the public turn in composition engages the notion of public sphere as Jürgen Habermas defined it in *The Structural Transformation of the Public Sphere* and his critics, such as Oskar Negt and Alexander Kluge (*Public Sphere and Experience*), Nancy Fraser ("Rethinking the Public Sphere"), and Michael Warner (*Publics and Counterpublics*), who charge Habermas with limiting public sphere activity to the bourgeois, male, white, straight, and moneyed. Negt and Kluge, Fraser, Warner, and others (e.g., The Black Public Sphere Collective 1995) open public sphere theory to possibilities for the formation of alternative or counterpublics. As Mathieu, Parks, and Rousculp note, "public-sphere theory can help students and scholars gain an understanding of the tricky asymmetries and politics of circulation taking place in today's world" (*Circulating Communities* 14). This emphasis on publics and counterpublics is evident in articles such as Susan Jarratt's, "Classics and Counterpublics"; David Coogan's, "Counterpublics in Public Housing"; Mathieu and George's, "*Not* Going It Alone"; and Nancy Welch's, "We're Here and We're Not Going Anywhere," as well as Gwendolyn D. Pough's *Check It While I Wreck It: Black Womanhood, Hip-Hop Culture, and the Public Sphere.*

TOWARD A TRANSNATIONAL PERSPECTIVE

By the early 1990s, postcolonial theorists (Bhabha; Said; Spivak; Robert Young) and their critics (Ahmad; Dirlik; McClintock) were raising fundamental questions about the scope of cultural studies and intellectual work on the left. Stuart Hall addressed some of these concerns in a series of articles and chapters, including "New Ethnicities" and "When Was 'the Post-Colonial'? Thinking at the Limit," where he argues that postcolonialism is not a matter of periodization so much as a re-reading of "colonisation as part of an essentially transnational and transcultural 'global' process" in order to produce a "decentred, diasporic or 'global' rewriting of earlier nation-centred imperial grand narratives" (247). Paul Gilroy likewise proposed a transnational perspective to replace static First World–Third World, core–periphery binaries with the diasporic movement of people and the circulation of hybrid identities throughout the "black Atlantic" (*Black Atlantic*).

Given the ready availability of writing on postcolonialism by prominent cultural studies figures, not to mention Spivak's well-known call in 1993 for a "transnational cultural studies," it may seem odd that composition did not pick up these themes immediately. There were, to be sure, efforts to link composition and post-colonialism, such as the 1998 *JAC* special issue, titled "Exploring Borderlands: Postcolonial and Composition Studies," and the book that followed in 2004, with a somewhat different roster of writers, *Crossing Borderlands: Postcolonial and Composition Studies* (Lunsford and Ouzgane). And there is Victor Villanueva's essential corpus of works on rhetoric, writing, colonialism, and racism (*Bootstraps*; "On the Rhetoric and Precedents of Racism"; "*Memoria* Is a Friend of Ours").

But there were also obstacles in the structure of U.S. college composition, and perhaps the most imposing were the institutional and conceptual separation of students marked as "international" or "English as a second language learner" and the taken-for-granted status of English as the medium of teaching and learning, writing and knowledge in the university. Min-Zhan Lu was among the first to recognize this set of tensions in her 1994 article "Professing Multiculturalism: The Politics of Style in the Contact Zone," where she uses the soon-to-be-replaced language of "multiculturalism" and "contact zone" to describe, in a remarkably prescient way, how non-native speakers do not so much acquire English as they work in and against it to make meaning.

Under the pressure of globalization and the diasporic movement and inter-minglings of people, culture, and language, a transnational perspective begins to emerge in composition in the early 2000s, influenced by postcolonial theory and transnational feminism but more eclectic and wide-ranging in its intellectual affiliations. Notions of World Englishes (Kachru), linguistic imperialism (Phillipson), and the hybridization of English (Rampton) have led to a re-examination of the status of language in college composition and what Paul Kei Matsuda calls "the myth of linguistic homogeneity." This development is marked, at least symboli-cally, by Bruce Horner and John Trimbur's "English Only and U.S. College Com-position," where they argue that composition has historically been a particular national-cultural formation based on a "unidirectional monolingualism" or tacit English-only policy dedicated to eradicating language differences and is (and has always been) out of touch with the linguistic realities of a multilingual world. Lu's "An Essay on the Work of Composition: Composing English against the Order of Fast Capitalism" examines the image of English as the language of mobility in a world dominated by global capitalism, arguing for a view of English not as a stable entity and means to success in the global marketplace but as the ever-changing result of the linguistic inventiveness of its users. A. Suresh Canagarajah extends this line of inquiry in "The Place of World Englishes in Composition" by redefin-ing language differences as linguistic and rhetorical resources rather than prob-lems and by examining the code-shuttling, code-meshing practices of multilingual writers.

Language and the politics of English involve an important reengagement with fields of linguistic study, such as the critical applied linguistics of Alastair Pennycook and Jan Blommaert's "sociolinguistics of globalization." In addition, as Wendy Hesford notes, a transnational cultural studies poses a challenge to "disciplinary methods and identities that take for granted the nation-state and citizen-subject as units of analysis and ignore global forces shaping individual lives and literate prac-tices" ("Global Turns" 788). Hesford's *Spectacular Rhetorics: Human Rights Visions, Recognitions, Feminisms* and the collection she coedited with Wendy Kozol, *Just Advocacy? Women's Human Rights, Transnational Feminisms, and the Politics of Representation*, offer good examples of work at the intersection of rhetoric, trans-national feminism, and critical globalization theory, as do Rebecca Dingo's *Networking Arguments: Rhetoric, Transnational Feminism, and Public Policy Writing* and the collection *The Megarhetorics of Global Development*, which Dingo coedited with J. Blake Scott.

From another angle, scholars have developed what might be called a transna-tional perspective to re-read and rewrite traditional narratives of immigration and assimilation—the Ellis Island story of foreigners becoming Americans—seeing border crossings instead as an unfinished and open-ended process. In *Minor Re/Visions: Asian-American Literacy Narratives as a Rhetoric of Citizenship*, Morris Young explores how race and literacy have shaped the terms of citizenship in the United States. LuMing Mao's *Reading Chinese Fortune Cookies: The Making of Chinese-American Rhetoric* further problematizes conventional understandings of citizenship and participation in civic life, identifying the complex rhetorical strategies of Chinese-Americans. In *Mestiz@ Scripts, Digital Migrations, and the Territories of Writing*, Damian Baca challenges the history of rhetoric and the alphabetic literacy narrative by revealing the fusion of Mesoamerican pictography with European writing that has produced "mestiz@" rhetoric, expressive cultural practices in which "the available means of identification . . . are mediated at the intersection of knowledge constructed by the dominance of Western colonialism on the one hand, and on the other hand, knowledge emerging from anticolonial perspectives in the borderlands" (83).

CULTURAL STUDIES AND THE COMPOSITION CLASSROOM

At the time cultural studies was taking shape in the late 1980s, it seemed to offer an answer to a persistent question that had troubled composition over the years— namely, does composition have a subject matter? Does it have its own content? One of cultural studies' contributions to the teaching of writing was designating an object of inquiry for the composition classroom by turning popular media and culture into "texts" to be studied and by providing a repertoire of methods to analyze and interpret contemporary culture that included semiotic, rhetorical, ethnographic, and historical perspectives. The influence of cultural studies in composition can be traced by examining three typical cultural-studies-inspired writing assignments.

The first cultural studies writing assignment was modeled on the rhetoric of denaturalization found in Roland Barthes' essays in *Mythologies*, John Berger's *Ways of Seeing*, and elsewhere, with the emphasis on the critical work of exposing a culture's underlying codes and systems of meaning. This approach was elaborated most notably in Berlin's *Rhetorics, Poetics, and Cultures* and is evident as well in the earliest cultural studies textbooks such as *Rereading America* (which is organized by national "myths"; Colombo, Cullen, and Lisle), *Signs of Life* (Maasik and Solomon), and *Reading Culture* (George and Trimbur). In turn, Joseph Harris pointed out the limits of emulating the critic by arguing that such writing assignments relied on a subject position that made ordinary people into dupes of the culture and reserved for the critic alone the required resistance to brainwashing by popular culture and media ("The Other Reader").

The limits of the essay of cultural critique led to a second-generation cultural-studies-based assignment, the microethnography, which positioned students not so much as expert critics but rather as participant-observers studying their own engagement in culture as shoppers, consumers, fans, gamers, spectators, workers, and so on. This turn to a fieldwork approach can be found in Lester Faigley's *Fragments of Rationality*. Fieldwork assignments such as participant-observation, interviews, surveys, and oral histories are developed in Bonnie Stone Sunstein and Elizabeth Chiseri-Strater's *Fieldworking: Reading and Writing Research*, a textbook staple now in its fourth edition, and included in the third (1999) and subsequent editions of *Reading Culture*.

The third type of writing assignment locates the student writer as not just an analyst but also a producer of culture. As Diana George notes, there is a long history in composition of analyzing visual artifacts of all sorts—whether movies, television, ads, artworks, or buildings—but little on producing forms of visual communication ("From Analysis to Design"). With the emergence of new media, production becomes increasingly possible, and composition teachers are now able to design assignments in media that were once unthinkable—video, audio, comics, websites, blogs, tweets, posters, public exhibits, and so on. This new accessibility of the means of production, moreover, overlaps with the public turn in composition and has led to a range of assignments, such as public service announcements, informational flyers and brochures, and social advocacy campaigns.

The questions first raised by that original cultural studies moment in composition have shifted, become more complex, perhaps even farther reaching. For the cultural-studies-influenced writing class today, that shift is especially evident any time a teacher asks students to move their investigations out of the classroom—physically or virtually—to map spaces, record oral histories, examine the uses of language in a given community, create political blogs, and pay serious attention to the world as lived experience both local and transnational.

BIBLIOGRAPHY

Ackerman, John M., and David Coogan. *The Public Work of Rhetoric: Citizen-Scholars and Civic Engagement*. Columbia: U of South Carolina P, 2010. Print.

Ahmad, Aijaz. *In Theory: Nations, Classes, Literatures*. London: Verso, 2008. Print.

Baca, Damián. *Mestiz@ Scripts, Digital Migrations, and the Territories of Writing*. New York: Palgrave Macmillan, 2008. Print.

Banks, Adam J. *Race, Rhetoric, and Technology: Searching for Higher Ground*. Mahwah: Lawrence Erlbaum, 2006. Print.

Barthes, Roland. *Mythologies*. New York: Hill and Wang, 1972. Print.

Berger, John. *Ways of Seeing*. New York: Viking, 1973. Print.

Berlin, James A. "Composition and Cultural Studies." *Composition and Resistance*. Ed. C. Mark Hurlbert and Michael Blitz. Portsmouth: Boynton/Cook, 1991. 47–55. Print.

———. "Composition Studies and Cultural Studies: Collapsing Boundaries." *Into the Field: Sites of Composition Studies*. Ed. Anne Ruggles Gere. New York: Modern Language Association, 1993. 99–116. Print.

———. "Poststructuralism, Cultural Studies, and the Composition Classroom: Postmodern Theory in Practice." *Rhetoric Review* 11.1 (1992): 16–33. Print.

———. "Rhetoric, Poetic, and Culture: Contested Boundaries in English Studies." *The Politics of Writing Instruction: Postsecondary*. Eds. Richard Bullock, John Trimbur, and Charles Schuster. Portsmouth: Heinemann, Boynton/Cook, 1991. 23–38. Print.

———. *Rhetorics, Poetics, and Cultures: Refiguring English Studies*. Urbana: National Council of Teachers of English, 1996. Print.

Berry, Patrick W., Gail E. Hawisher, and Cynthia L. Selfe. *Transnational Literate Lives in Digital Times*. Logan: Computers and Composition Digital P/Utah State UP, 2012. Web.

Bhabha, Homi K. *The Location of Culture*. New York: Routledge, 1994. Print.

The Black Public Sphere Collective, ed. *The Black Public Sphere: A Public Culture Book*. Chicago: U of Chicago P, 1995. Print.

Blommaert, Jan. *The Sociolinguistics of Globalization*. Cambridge: Cambridge UP, 2010. Print.

Bolter, Jay David, and Richard Grusin. *Remediation: Understanding New Media*. Cambridge: MIT P, 1999. Print.

Brandt, Deborah. *Literacy in American Lives*. Cambridge: Cambridge UP, 2001. Print.

Brooke, Collin Gifford. "Authorship and Technology." *Authorship in Composition Studies*. Ed. Tracy Hamler Carrick and Rebecca Moore Howard. Boston: Wadsworth, 2006. 89–100. Print.

Canagarajah, A. Suresh. "The Place of World Englishes in Composition: Pluralization Continued." *CCC* 57.4 (2006): 586–619. Print.

Centre for Contemporary Cultural Studies. *The Empire Strikes Back: Race and Racism in 70s Britain*. London: Hutchinson, 1982. Print.

_____. *Making Histories: History-Writing and Politics*. London: Hutchinson, 1982. Print.

Centre for Contemporary Cultural Studies Education Group. *Education Limited: Schooling, Training, and the New Right since 1979*. London: Unwin Hyman, 1991. Print.

_____. *Unpopular Education: Schooling and Social Democracy in England since 1944*. London: Hutchinson, 1981. Print.

Clarke, John, Chas Critcher, and Richard Johnson, eds. *Working-Class Culture: Studies in History and Theory*. New York: St. Martin's, 1979. Print.

Colombo, Gary, Robert Cullen, and Bonnie Lisle. *Rereading America: Cultural Contexts for Critical Thinking and Writing*. Boston: Bedford/St. Martin's, 2010. Print.

Coogan, David. "Counterpublics in Public Housing: Reframing the Politics of Service-Learning." *College English* 67.5 (2005): 461–82. Print.

de Certeau, Michel. *The Practice of Everyday Life*. Berkeley: U of California P, 1984. Print.

DeVoss, Dànielle, and Suzanne Web. "Media Convergence: *Grand Theft Audio:* Negotiating Copyright as Composers." *Computers and Composition* 25.1 (2008): 79–103. Print.

Dingo, Rebecca A. *Networking Arguments: Rhetoric, Transnational Feminism, and Public Policy Writing*. Pittsburgh: U of Pittsburgh P, 2012. Print.

Dingo, Rebecca, and J. Blake Scott, eds. *The Megarhetorics of Global Development*. Pittsburgh: U of Pittsburgh P, 2012. Print.

Dirlik, Arif. "The Postcolonial Aura: Third World Criticism in the Age of Global Capitalism." *Critical Inquiry* 20.2 (Winter, 1994): 328–56. Print.

Eberly, Rosa A. "From *Writers, Audiences,* and *Communities* to *Publics*: Writing Classrooms as Protopublic Spaces." *Rhetoric Review* 18.1 (1999): 165–78. Print.

Eldred, Janet C., and Peter Mortensen. *Imagining Rhetoric: Composing Women of the Early United States*. Pittsburgh: U of Pittsburgh P, 2002. Print.

Faigley, Lester. *Fragments of Rationality: Postmodernity and the Subject of Composition*. Pittsburgh: U of Pittsburgh P, 1992. Print.

Flower, Linda. *Community Literacy and the Rhetoric of Public Engagement*. Carbondale: Southern Illinois UP, 2008. Print.

Fraser, Nancy. "Rethinking the Public Sphere: A Contribution to the Critique of Actually Existing Democracy." *Social Text* 25/26 (1990): 56–80. Print.

Gee, James Paul. *What Video Games Have to Teach Us about Learning and Literacy*. Basingstoke: Palgrave Macmillan, 2008. Print.

George, Diana. "From Analysis to Design: Visual Communication in the Teaching of Writing." *CCC* 54.1 (2002): 11–39. Print.

_____. "The Word on the Street: Public Discourse in a Culture of Disconnect." *Reflections: A Journal of Writing, Service-Learning, and Community Literacy* 2.2 (Spring 2002): 6–18. Print.

George, Diana, and Paula Mathieu. "A Place for the Dissident Press in a Rhetorical Education: 'Sending Up a Signal Flare in the Darkness.'" Ackerman and Coogan 247–66. Print.

George, Diana, and John Trimbur. *Reading Culture: Contexts for Critical Reading and Writing.* 8th ed. New York: Longman, 2012. Print.

Gere, Anne Ruggles. "Kitchen Tables and Rented Rooms: The Extracurricular of Composition." *College Composition and Communication* 45.1 (1994): 75–92. Print.

_____. *Intimate Practices: Literary and Cultural Work in U.S. Women's Clubs, 1880–1920.* Urbana: U of Illinois P, 1997. Print.

Gilroy, Paul. *"There Ain't No Black in the Union Jack": The Cultural Politics of Race and Nation.* London: Hutchinson, 1987. Print.

_____. *Black Atlantic: Modernity and Double Consciousness.* Cambridge: Harvard UP, 1993. Print.

Goldblatt, Eli. "Alinsky's Reveille: A Community-Organizing Model for Neighborhood-Based Literacy Projects." *College English* 67.3 (Jan. 2005): 274–95. Print.

Habermas, Jürgen. *The Structural Transformation of the Public Sphere: An Inquiry into a Category of Bourgeois Society.* Cambridge: MIT P, 1989. Print.

Hall, Stuart. "Cultural Studies: Two Paradigms." *Media, Culture, and Society: A Critical Reader.* Ed. Richard Collins et al. London: Sage, 1986. 33–48. Print.

_____. "New Ethnicities." *Critical Dialogues in Cultural Studies.* Ed. David Morely and Kuan-Hsing Chen. New York: Routledge, 1996. Print.

_____. "When Was 'the Post-Colonial'? Thinking at the Limit." *The Post-Colonial Question: Common Skies, Divided Horizons.* Ed. Iain Chambers and Lidia Curti. New York: Routledge, 1996. Print.

Hall, Stuart, Chas Cricther, Tony Jefferson, John N. Clarke, and Brian Roberts, eds. *Policing the Crisis: Mugging, the State, and Law and Order.* London: Macmillan, 1979. Print.

Hall, Stuart, and Tony Jefferson, eds. *Resistance through Rituals: Youth Subcultures in Post-War Britain.* London: Hutchinson, 1976. Print.

Haraway, Donna. "A Manifesto for Cyborgs: Science, Technology, and Socialist Feminism in the 1980s." *Socialist Review* 80 (1985): 65–108. Print.

Harris, Joseph. "The Other Reader." *Journal of Advanced Composition* 12.1 (1993): 27–37. Print.

Hebdige, Dick. *Subculture: The Meaning of Style.* New York: Routledge, 1979. Print.

Hesford, Wendy S. "Global Turns and Cautions in Rhetoric and Composition Studies." *PMLA* 121.3 (2006): 787–801. Print.

_____. *Spectacular Rhetorics: Human Rights Visions, Recognitions, Feminisms.* Durham: Duke UP, 2011. Print.

Hesford, Wendy S., and Wendy Kozol, eds. *Just Advocacy? Women's Human Rights, Transnational Feminisms, and the Politics of Representation.* New Brunswick: Rutgers UP, 2005. Print.

Hoggart, Richard. *The Uses of Literacy.* London: Essential Books, 1957. Print.

Horner, Bruce, and John Trimbur. "English Only and U.S. College Composition." *College Composition and Communication* 53.4 (2002): 594–630. Print.

Jacobi, Tobi. "Writers Speaking Out: The Challenges of Community Publishing from Spaces of Confinement." Mathieu et al. 173–200. Print.

Jarratt, Susan C. "Classics and Counterpublics in Nineteenth-Century Historically Black Colleges." *College English* 72.2 (2009): 134–59. Print.

Jenkins, Henry. *Textual Poachers: Television Fans and Participatory Culture.* New York: Routledge, 1992. Print.

_____. *Convergence Culture: Where Old and New Media Collide.* New York: New York UP, 2006. Print.

Johnson, Richard. "What Is Cultural Studies Anyway?" *Social Text* 16.1 (1986-87): 38–80. Print.

Jolliffe, David. "The Community Literacy Advocacy Project: Civic Revival through Rhetorical Activity in Rural Arkansas." Ackerman and Coogan. 266–82. Print.

Kachru, Braj B. *The Alchemy of English: The Spread, Functions, and Models of Non-Native Englishes*. Oxford: Pergamon, 1986. Print.

Kress, Gunther R. *Literacy in the New Media Age*. London: Routledge, 2003. Print.

_____. *Multimodality: A Social Semiotic Approach to Contemporary Communication*. London: Routledge, 2010. Print.

Kress, Gunther R., and Theo Van Leeuwen. *Multimodal Discourse: The Modes and Media of Contemporary Communication*. London: Arnold, 2001. Print.

_____. *Reading Images: The Grammar of Visual Design*. London: Routledge, 1996. Print.

Laquintano, Tim. "Sustained Authorship: Digital Writing, Self-Publishing, and the Ebook." *Written Communication* 27.4 (2010): 469–93. Print.

Lessig, Lawrence. *Remix: Making Art and Commerce Thrive in the Hybrid Economy*. New York: Penguin Books, 2009. Print.

Logan, Shirley W. *Liberating Language: Sites of Rhetorical Education in Nineteenth Century Black America*. Carbondale: Southern Illinois UP, 2008. Print.

Losh, Elizabeth. "Hactivism and the Humanities." *Debates in the Digital Humanities*. Ed. Matthew K. Gold. Minneapolis: U of Minnesota P, 2012. 161–86. Print.

Lu, Min-Zhan. "Professing Multiculturalism: The Politics of Style in the Contact Zone." *College Composition and Communication* 45.4 (Dec. 1994): 442–58. Print.

_____. "An Essay on the Work of Composition: Composing English against the Order of Fast Capitalism." *College Composition and Communication* 56.1 (2004): 16–50. Print.

Lunsford, Andrea A., and Lahoucine Ouzgane. *Crossing Borderlands: Composition and Post-colonial Studies*. Pittsburgh: U of Pittsburgh P, 2004. Print.

_____. *Exploring Borderlands: Postcolonial and Composition Studies*. Spec. issue of *JAC: A Journal of Composition Theory* 18.1 (1998). Print.

Maasik, Sonia, and Jack Solomon, eds. *Signs of Life in the USA: Readings on Popular Culture for Writers*. Boston: Bedford/St. Martins, 2012. Print.

Mao, LuMing. *Reading Chinese Fortune Cookie: The Making of Chinese American Rhetoric*. Logan: Utah State UP, 2006. Print.

Mathieu, Paula. *Tactics of Hope: The Public Turn in English Composition*. Portsmouth: Boynton/Cook, 2005. Print.

Mathieu, Paula, and Diana George. "*Not* Going It Alone: Public Writing, Independent Media, and the Circulation of Homeless Advocacy." *College Composition and Communication*. 61.1 (2009): 130–49. Print.

Mathieu, Paula, Steve Parks, and Tiffany Rousculp. *Circulating Communities: The Tactics and Strategies of Community Publishing*. Lanham: Lexington Books, 2012. Print.

Matsuda, Paul Kei. "The Myth of Linguistic Homogeneity in U.S. College Composition." *College English* 68.6 (Jul. 2006): 637–51. Print.

McClintock, Anne. *Imperial Leather: Race, Gender, and Sexuality in the Colonial Contest*. New York: Routledge, 1995. Print.

McRobbie, Angela. "Settling Accounts with Subcultures: A Feminist Critique." *Screen Education* 34.1 (1980): 37–49. Print.

Nakamura, Lisa. *Digitizing Race: Visual Cultures of the Internet*. Minneapolis: U of Minnesota P, 2008. Print.

Negt, Oskar, and Alexander Kluge. *Public Sphere and Experience: Toward an Analysis of the Bourgeois and Proletarian Public Sphere*. Minneapolis: U of Minnesota P, 1993. Print.

Pennycook, Alastair. *Global Englishes and Transcultural Flows*. London: Routledge, 2007. Print.

Phillipson, Robert. *Linguistic Imperialism*. New York: Oxford UP, 1992. Print.

Postman, Neil. *Amusing Ourselves to Death: Public Discourse in the Age of Show Business*. New York: Penguin Books, 1985. Print.

Pough, Gwendolyn D. *Check It While I Wreck It: Black Womanhood, Hip-Hop Culture, and the Public Sphere*. Boston: Northeastern UP, 2004. Print.

Prendergast, Catherine. "Race: The Absent Presence in Composition Studies." *College Composition and Communication* 50.1 (1998): 36–53. Print.

Rampton, Ben. *Crossing: Language and Ethnicity among Adolescents*. London: Longman, 1995. Print.

Reynolds, Nedra. "Interrupting Our Way to Agency: Feminist Cultural Studies and Composition." *Feminism and Composition Studies: In Other Words*. Ed. Susan C. Jarratt and Lynn Worsham. New York: Modern Language Association, 1998. 58–73. Print.

Richardson, Elaine B. *African American Literacies*. London: Routledge, 2003. Print.

_____. *Hiphop Literacies*. London: Routledge, 2006. Print.

Riedner, Rachel, and Kevin Mahoney. *Democracies to Come: Rhetorical Action, Neoliberalism, and Communities of Resistance*. Lanham: Lexington Books, 2008. Print.

Rife, Martine Courant. "The Fair Use Doctrine: History, Application, and Implications for (New Media) Writing Teachers." *Computers and Composition* 24 (2007): 154–78. Print.

Rose, Shirley K., and Irwin Weiser. "Introduction: The WPA as Citizen-Educator." *Going Public: What Writing Programs Learn from Engagement*. Ed. Shirley K. Rose and Irwin Weiser. Logan: Utah State UP, 2010. 1–14. Print.

Rosteck, Thomas, ed. *At the Intersection: Cultural Studies and Rhetorical Studies*. New York: Guilford, 1999. Print.

Royster, Jacqueline Jones. *Traces of a Stream: Literacy and Social Change among African American Women*. Pittsburgh: U of Pittsburgh P, 2000. Print.

Ryder, Phyllis M. *Rhetorics for Community Action: Public Writing and Writing Publics*. Lanham: Lexington Books, 2011. Print.

Said, Edward W. *Culture and Imperialism*. New York: Knopf, 1993. Print.

Scenters-Zapico, John. *Generaciones' Narratives*. Logan: Computers and Composition Digital P/Utah State UP, 2012. Web.

Schilb, John. "Cultural Studies, Postmodernism, and Composition." *Contending with Words: Composition and Rhetoric in a Postmodern Age*. Ed. Patricia Harkin and John Schilb. New York: Modern Language Association, 1991. 173–88. Print.

Scott, J. Blake, Bernadette Longo, and Katherine V. Wills, eds. *Critical Power Tools: Technical Communication and Cultural Studies*. Albany: SUNY P, 2006. Print.

Selfe, Cynthia L., and Gail E. Hawisher. *Gaming Lives in the Twenty-First Century: Literate Connections*. New York: Palgrave Macmillan, 2007. Print.

Spivak, Gayatri C. *Outside in the Teaching Machine*. New York: Routledge, 1993. Print.

Sunstein, Bonnie Stone, and Elizabeth Chiseri-Strater. *Fieldworking: Reading and Writing Research*. Boston: Bedford/St. Martins, 2012. Print.

Thompson, E. P. *The Making of the English Working Class*. New York: Vintage, 1963. Print.

Trimbur, John. "Articulation Theory and the Problem of Determination: A Reading of *Lives on the Boundary*." *Journal of Advanced Composition* 13.1 (1993): 33–50. Print.

_____. "Composition and the Circulation of Writing." *College Composition and Communication* 52.2 (Dec. 2000): 188–219. Print.

_____. "Cultural Studies and the Teaching of Writing." *Focuses* 1.2 (1988): 5–18. Print.

_____. "Delivering the Message: Typography and the Materiality of Writing." *Rhetoric and Composition as Intellectual Work*. Ed. Gary Olson. Carbondale: Southern Illinois UP, 2002. 188–202. Print.

_____. "The Politics of Radical Pedagogy: A Plea for 'A Dose of Vulgar Marxism.'" *College English* 56.2 (1994): 194–206. Print.

Turkle, Sherry. *Alone Together: Why We Expect More from Technology and Less from Each Other*. New York: Basic Books, 2011. Print.

Vaidhyanathan, Siva. *Copyrights and Copywrongs: The Rise of Intellectual Property and How It Threatens Creativity*. New York: New York UP, 2001. Print.

Villanueva, Victor. *Bootstraps: From an American Academic of Color*. Urbana: National Council of Teachers of English, 1993. Print.

_____. "*Memoria* Is a Friend of Ours: On the Discourse of Color." *College English* 67.1 (Sep 2004): 9–19. Print.

_____. "On the Rhetoric and Precedents of Racism." *College Composition and Communication* 50.4 (June 1999): 645–661. Print.

Warner, Michael. *Publics and Counterpublics*. New York: Zone Books, 2002. Print.

Welch, Nancy. "'We're Here, and We're Not Going Anywhere'": Why Working-Class Rhetorical Traditions Still Matter." *College English* 73.3 (Jan. 2011): 221–42. Print.

Wells, Susan. "Rogue Cops and Health Care: What Do We Want from Public Writing?" *College Composition and Communication* 47.3 (1996): 325–41. Print.

Williams, Bronwyn T. "Which *South Park* Character Are You? Popular Culture, Literacy, and Online Performances of Identity." *Computers and Composition* 25.1 (2008): 24–39. Print.

Williams, Raymond. *Culture and Society: 1780–1950*. London: Chatto and Windus, 1958. Print.

_____. *The Long Revolution*. London: Chatto and Windus, 1961. Print.

Willis, Paul. *Learning to Labor: How Working-Class Kids Get Working-Class Jobs*. New York: Columbia UP, 1977. Print.

Women's Study Group, Centre for Contemporary Cultural Studies. *Women Take Issue: Aspects of Women's Subordination*. London: Hutchinson, 1978. Print.

Wu, Tim. *The Master Switch: The Rise and Fall of Information Empires*. New York: Alfred A. Knopf, 2010. Print.

Young, Morris. *Minor Re/visions: Asian American Literacy Narratives as a Rhetoric of Citizenship*. Carbondale: Southern Illinois UP, 2004. Print.

Young, Robert. *Colonial Desire: Hybridity in Theory, Culture, and Race*. London: Routledge, 1995. Print.

Expressive Pedagogy
Practice/Theory, Theory/Practice

Chris Burnham
Rebecca Powell

INTRODUCTION

Rebecca: I was afraid I had made a mistake, a move-your-family-across-the-country-spend-a-few-thousand-dollars-on-graduate-school-tuition kind of mistake. After five years of teaching high school English and freelance writing, I returned to graduate school clutching Peter Elbow's *Writing Without Teachers* in one hand and Neil Postman's and Charles Weingartner's *Teaching as a Subversive Activity* in the other. This was the type of teaching that had taught me to write, that I had used to teach other people to write. Yet, in my first semester toward a master's degree I read scholars who dismissed expressivism, and, when we stumbled on an essay by Wendy Bishop, a self-proclaimed expressivist, my classmates claimed it was not scholarly enough.

I became a writer in an expressivist classroom. In Kevin Davis's advanced composition course, I gave muddled first drafts to peers who responded to my autobiographical writing using Peter Elbow's movies of the mind. Alternately thrilled, shocked, or bored by their feedback, I revised and waited for the professor's response, a one- to one-and-a-half-page letter, detailing his reading of my words. His readings were gifts. He asked questions, made connections, responded to my writing as if it mattered. Because he acted as if my writing mattered, I started to treat it as if it did. I would revise again, this time writing not to fulfill an assignment, but to find and express myself with flesh-and-blood people, my classmates and professor. Writing became expression and communication, a people-filled endeavor, in which I let the acts of writing, workshopping, and revising help me discover what I had to say and what I meant to say.

When I had a classroom of my own, I relied on those practices to teach high school students. We wrote about our lives, journaling, freewriting, looking for centers of gravity, drafting, workshopping, revising. Moreover, I lived by Davis's advice, "Love the little buggers." To love them, I had to respond to them as writers, as individuals. As a teacher and a writer, I could not have named the theoretical underpinnings of expressivism. I did not even know what I was doing was called "expressivism," but I knew the practices, and those practices led me back to graduate school, intent on studying writing, on becoming a better teacher.

I knocked on Chris Burnham's door sure I had made a mistake, willing to rethink the whole teach writing, research writing PhD plan. With no introduction, I blurted: "Is expressivism dead?" He turned from his computer to face me. "Why do you ask?" I recounted my readings, complete with full citations. He replied, "You need to read more." So, I did. I read more. Many, many pages later, I see expressivism as the source for, and target of, many of the developments in the field. Expressivism is not dead; it grew up.

Chris: When Rebecca knocked on my door, I had been teaching writing for thirty years. Though trained as a literary critic in my doctoral studies, I nurtured a long-term interest in writing and composition and was thought an oddity among my grad program peers. At least until I landed my first full-time job as a writing specialist in 1975. I taught writing with more enthusiasm than expertise, without a theoretical framework. Call it serendipity, *kairos*, or blind luck; I had the opportunity to take an National Endowment for the Humanities summer seminar, Writing and Learning in Humanities, in 1977 at Rutgers University. With colleagues like Toby Fulwiler, and with Bob Parker, Dixie Goswami, and Janet Emig all becoming leaders in the field, providing direction, I read and wrote and discovered, just as I advised Rebecca many years later, that expressivism lived in the work of James Kinneavy and James Britton. Just as lucky, we worked in a room next to where Emig was directing one of the first New Jersey Writing Project Summer Institutes. Expressivism was in the air. It found me. A true believer in the expressivist mission, over time my research led me to thinkers like bell hooks, the African-American feminist and liberatory teacher, who presents an arguably expressivist pedagogy in *Sisters of the Yam: Black Women and Self-Recovery* (1993) and *Teaching to Transgress: Education as the Practice of Freedom* (1994). She assigns great value and responsibility to the teacher, as well as to the writer as a person, insisting that education at every level and in every context should attend to ethical formation. She invokes Thomas Merton, Trappist monk and peace and justice activist, to challenge teachers to accept the ethical responsibility of "professing." Confronted with students "desperately yearning to be touched by knowledge," many professors fail to rekindle the passion they once felt and reject the challenge and opportunity their students offer. Her answer destabilizes the contemporary, academic sense of the term *profess*, recalling its original sense of passionate commitment as in professing a vow. She raises the stakes for university teachers:

> If, as Thomas Merton suggests in his essay on pedagogy "Learning to Live," the purpose of education is to show students how to define themselves "authentically and spontaneously in relation" to the world, then professors can best teach if we are self-actualized. (*Teaching to Transgress* 199, emphasis added)

Like Merton, hooks accepts the responsibility to be passionate and to develop socially and morally aware citizens whose actions begin in mutual respect. Over the years, I, and Rebecca's Kevin Davis, and many others, have met that responsibility, working to help students become morally aware citizens through self-reflective, expressivist writing.

However, our classrooms are not solely expressivist classrooms, if such a classroom should exist. Chris incorporates the classical rhetorical tradition and critical pedagogy, and Rebecca employs process and critical pedagogy, but it is expressivism's commitment to individual expression that we believe makes our pedagogies work. Expressivism places the writer at the center of its theory and pedagogy, assigning highest value to the writer's imaginative, psychological, social, and spiritual development and how that development influences individual consciousness and social behavior. Expressivist pedagogy employs freewriting, journal keeping, reflective writing, and small-group dialogic collaborative response to foster a writer's aesthetic, cognitive, and moral development. Expressivist pedagogy encourages, even insists upon, a sense of writer presence even in research-based writing. This presence—"voice" or ethos—whether explicit, implicit, or absent, functions as a key evaluation criterion when expressivists examine writing. For expressivist teachers, the education of the writer is the central problem. This concern cuts across subdisciplinary boundaries and methodologies.

Fittingly for a pedagogy concerned with the development of the whole person, expressivist pedagogy and theory weaves together several sources: nontraditional textbooks, in a sense, anti-textbooks, offering innovative practices for teaching writing; commentaries by early expressivists who began to articulate theory to counter scholarly and ideological attacks; and, recently, syntheses that integrate expressivism with social and liberatory rhetorics and with postmodern thinking. In this chapter, we trace the contributions of these sources to the theory and practices of expressivism.

ANTI-TEXTBOOKS:
STATEMENTS OF VALUE AND METHOD

Expressivism's first coherent statements of value and method occur in alternative textbooks, really anti-textbooks. Donald Murray, Ken Macrorie, Peter Elbow, and William Coles all offered counterapproaches to current-traditional pedagogy. They wrote to teachers as much as to students. Though radical in their time, many of these methods now constitute mainstream writing instruction.

Current-traditional teaching, the dominant paradigm between the ends of World War II and the Vietnam War, emphasized academic writing in standard forms and "correct" grammar. In "Contemporary Composition: The Major Pedagogical Theories," Berlin critiques current-traditional rhetoric for its static, empirically based epistemology that holds that all knowledge can be found in concrete reality through close observation, that language is an uncomplicated medium for communicating already existing knowledge, and that the work of teaching writing is limited to getting students to use grammar correctly, to conform to formal and stylistic conventions, and to argue exclusively from existing authority available through research in proper sources. Berlin's critique, along with another strong critique of current-traditional rhetoric offered by Sharon Crowley in *The Methodical Memory* (1990), are significant to expressivists because the relations among the individual, language, and epistemology, and the nature of rhetoric, not accounted for in current-traditional thinking, became the unarticulated originating force for the original expressivists, as well as the central focus for the more recent syntheses of expressivism and social rhetoric.

In anti-textbooks like Murray's *A Writer Teaches Writing* (1968), Macrorie's *Telling Writing* (1970), and Elbow's *Writing without Teachers* (1973), these teacher/writers offered an alternative to current-traditional teaching, a different kind of pedagogy. This pedagogy used nondirective feedback to return the responsibility for writing back to the student (Murray, Elbow). It encouraged students to use their own language and to reject "Engfish," the academic language of schools (Macrorie). It saw writing as more than the product of communication, as a means for making meaning and creating identity. Thus, this pedagogy attended to invention, the discovery of ideas, and encouraged students and teachers to keep journals as a reflective exercise for documenting individual experience and personal development (Elbow, Macrorie).

In their attention to invention and student responsibility, expressivists developed writing and thinking exercises now common in composition classrooms: freewriting, peer response, and revision. Freewriting helps students discover ideas and their significance, center of gravity exercises develop and focus these ideas, and peer response groups allow writers to test their writing on an actual audience and revise on the basis of that response. In an appendix essay, "The Doubting Game and the Believing Game—An Analysis of the Intellectual Enterprise," Elbow critiques conventional Western skepticism, encouraging writers to engage a dialectic of perspectives—self and others, the familiar and the strange—to make themselves better writers, thinkers, and citizens.

During the 1980s, expressivism became more rhetorical, exemplified in Elbow's *Writing with Power* (1981). The writing context is social and active; the writer is concerned with having an impact on an actual audience. Elbow instructs writers to maintain a productive paradoxical tension between individual and group. Equipped with well-developed personal identities, individuals can function effectively in groups or culture. Interdependence is both the source and the locus of power. Voice, a concern of the original anti-textbooks, becomes central in *Writing with Power*. Elbow and the expressivists, anticipating feminist pedagogy, work to subvert teaching practices and institutional structures that oppress, appropriate, or silence an individual's voice (see also Micciche's chapter in this volume).

A THEORY OF THE PERSONAL: EXPRESSIVIST COMMENTARIES AND THEORY

In "A Method for Teaching Writing" (1968), Elbow recounts his experience counseling applicants for conscientious objector (CO) draft status during the Vietnam conflict. Elbow's reflections exemplify how early expressivists theorized. He argues from his personal experience as a teacher and a CO that voice empowers individuals to act in the world. He sees writing as political action. He teaches those he counsels that they must do more than just make sense when writing applications for CO status; they must communicate intense belief through voice. Writing thus becomes a form of political or social activism. The essay establishes voice as a central concern for expressivists and demonstrates how personal experience works in theory building.

Expressivist theory includes two major sources: Britton's expressive function in language and Kinneavy's expressive discourse. The combination creates something of an ambiguity. Expressivists do not distinguish between the expressive function of language and expressive discourse, a type of text. This eventually causes a problem for some critics, especially Jeanette Harris. She condemns the indiscriminate use of the term *expressive*, suggesting rather four separate labels for textual phenomena in order to describe more precisely the various forms of discourse considered expressive. However, expressivists reject dichotomous thinking, viewing ambiguity and paradox as sources of productive dialectic. In "Expressive Rhetoric: A Source Study," Chris examines Britton, Kinneavy, and commentary by Murray, Coles, and Elbow to construct an expressivist theory of language and epistemology.

Expressivists share some theoretical grounding with process pedagogy (see Anson's chapter in this volume). For example, in "Writing as Process: How Writing Finds Its Own Meaning," Murray proposes an instrumental relation between composing and meaning-making (3). He examines three related activities: rehearsing, drafting, and revising. These involve complex interactions between contrary impulses: exploring and clarifying; collecting and combining; and writing and reading. Through these interactions, meaning evolves: "The writer is constantly learning from the writing what it intends to say. The writer listens for evolving meaning. . . . The writing itself helps the writer see the subject" (7). Murray includes a social element in the process, insisting that his students work within a writing community. Meaning results from the interaction of teacher and students, writers and readers, process and product—all accomplished through language.

Although expressivist theory often begins with the personal, it relies on the relations between language, meaning-making, and self-development. In "Toward a Phenomenology of Freewriting," Elbow notes that the initial "experimental form of freewriting" evolved in his journaling (190). He describes a process similar to the generating/structuring/evaluating movement in Murray's model of the writing process. Elbow posits an analytic urge based in writing that results in understanding leading to action. Through the process the writer gains control of the subject, either the writer per se or an intellectual concept.

Elbow's perspective on the relations between language, meaning-making, and self-development suggests the relations between writer, language, and the world that Kinneavy articulates in *A Theory of Discourse* (1971). He argues that the expressive aim is psychologically prior to all others. Using Sartre and the phenomenologists, Kinneavy claims that through expressive discourse the self moves from private meaning to shared meaning that results ultimately in some action. Rather than a "primal whine," expressive discourse traces a path away from solipsism toward accommodation with the world and thus accomplishes purposeful action.

But expressive discourse is not the exclusive province of the individual; it also has a social function. Kinneavy's analysis of the *Declaration of Independence* makes this clear. Contesting the claim that the purpose of the *Declaration* is persuasive, Kinneavy traces its evolution through several drafts to prove that its primary aim is expressive: to establish an American group identity (410). Kinneavy's analysis suggests that rather than being individualistic and otherworldly, or naïve and narcissistic, expressive discourse can be ideologically empowering.

BORROWING FROM SOCIAL LINGUISTICS: BRITTON'S EXPRESSIVE FUNCTION

Although expressivism borrows freely from a wide variety of sources, Britton's expressive function contains its theoretical center and so demands attention. Britton offered a developmental taxonomy of writing derived from close observation of the process through which children learn language. With origins in linguistics and cognitive and developmental psychology, the taxonomy emphasizes the expressive function of language, providing a wealth of linguistic and pedagogical insights that can be developed for a variety of purposes, from theorizing expressivist rhetoric to justifying the study of literature to providing a write-to-learn methodology for writing across the curriculum (see McLeod and Thaiss, this volume). Britton's expressivism has, in a sense, become part of the tacit tradition in contemporary teaching of writing; it is at the center of the National Writing Project movement.

Language and Learning (1970) presents Britton in the role of theorist. He blends narrative based on his experiences as teacher, writer, and parent with then-cutting-edge literary criticism, linguistics, philosophy, and psychology. Invoking Sapir's distinction between the referential and expressive functions of language, Britton emphasizes the expressive function. It opposes the referential, whose purpose is to represent and transcribe material reality. For Britton, the expressive function makes language personal and idiosyncratic. It provides a means for individuals to connect abstract concepts with personal experience and to negotiate the boundaries between public and private knowledge. The result is concrete understanding and learning.

The Development of Writing Abilities (11–18) (1978) presents Britton as a researcher validating the theoretical insights offered in the earlier book. It offers an observational and empirical analysis of the writing students do in school. Britton and his colleagues focus on the two primary roles writers can play when producing language: the participant role, in which writers use language to get things done, and the spectator role, in which writers use language to relive the past. As participants, writers shape reality to an end. As spectators, writers recreate reality.

Locating participant and spectator roles at either end of a continuum, Britton introduces a third mediating role, the expressive, in which the writer functions as both participant and spectator. From each role he derives a category of writing. In the participant role, writers produce *transactional* writing, through which language accomplishes the business of the world. On the other end of the continuum, writers acting in the spectator role produce *poetic* writing. Poetic writing is language whose purpose is to be an object that pleases or satisfies the writer. The reader's response is to share that satisfaction. In traditional terms poetic writing is literary discourse, language that "exists for *its own sake* and not as a means of achieving something else" (Britton et al. 91).

With transactional and poetic writing constituting boundaries on the participant/spectator continuum, Britton establishes a third category, *expressive* writing, that mediates the two. As a functional category, expressive writing represents a mode rather than a form. More important than its existence as a text, expressive writing achieves its purpose through allowing the text to come to existence. Examples include notes and drafts intended for the personal and private use of writers and their collaborators, journal writing, and personal letters (89).

In the expressive mode, writers shuttle back and forth between participant and spectator roles, generating ideas, then shaping them into language that can stand on its own. The interaction mirrors Elbow's free writing and Murray's process writing. With its generative function, expressive writing plays an obvious role in learning to write: "Thus, in developmental terms, the expressive is a kind of matrix from which differentiated forms of mature writing are developed" (83). In addition, as a link between the private and personal and the public and social, as the language of association and connection, expressive language is the language of learning.

From its inception, Britton's taxonomy has influenced process-based approaches to teaching writing. In "Expressivist Rhetoric," Chris argues that Britton's taxonomy creates common space that contains the seeming oppositions among expressive, cognitive, and social approaches to rhetoric, providing a coherent model for understanding writing as the result of interactions among individually and culturally defined forces.

RECEPTION, IDEOLOGICAL CRITIQUES, AND THEORETICAL DEFENSES

The most aggressive critiques of expressivism originate in social epistemic rhetoric, specifically from Berlin. Berlin offers an extended ideological critique in "Contemporary Composition: The Major Pedagogical Theories," where he portrays "expressionist theory" as an untheorized and ideologically debased form of neo-Platonism (774). Elsewhere he links expressivism to "Emersonian romantic" rhetoric and subsequently to the "rhetoric of liberal culture" and to Dewey and the progressive education movement ("Rhetoric and Ideology in the Writing Class" 484). He locates expressivist rhetoric among "subjective" theories of rhetoric (*Rhetoric and Reality* 11). His critique is rich, attending in considerable detail to expressivist practices and theory despite his claim that expressivism has none. His self-admitted allegiance to social epistemic rhetoric, however, results in readings that are not verified by close analysis of expressivist work. Berlin and the other social rhetoricians view expressivism's primary flaw as a false and otherworldy epistemology of the self that privileges individualism and rejects the material world.

In a more recent assessment, "Composition at the Turn of the Twenty-First Century," Richard Fulkerson does not critique expressivism per se but the implementation of expressivism in the classroom. In "Composition in the Eighties" he declared that the field had achieved "axiological consensus" but "pedagogical diversity." At the turn of the twenty-first century, however, he finds that the field has again diverged in terms of goals and is dominated by three major pedagogical schools: critical/cultural studies, expressivism, and procedural rhetorics. Of these, he observes, expressivism, "despite numerous poundings by the canons of post-modernism and resulting eulogies, is, in fact, quietly expanding its region of command" (655).

Multicultural consciousness motivates critiques from teachers working with students of color and multilingual students. In *Other People's Children: Cultural Conflict in the Classroom* (1995), Lisa Delpit, a noted educator and scholar, out-lines the dissonance between black educators' experience with students and the claims of an expressivist pedagogy advanced by the National Writing Project. According to Delpit, the National Writing Project's emphasis on fluency ignores black educators' perception of their black students as fluent with language but un-familiar with the forms and skills of academic discourse. Delpit does not com-pletely dismiss expressivism; instead, she advises black and white educators to discuss their differences. Similarly, multilingual educators Vai Ramanthan and Dwight Atkinson charge that the individualism of expressivist teaching practices (voice, peer reviewing, critical thinking, and textual ownership) demand that students from collective cultures "create a new self," a process which Ramanthan and Atkinson view as negative (56).

CONTINUING SYNTHESES: FROM SOCIAL EXPRESSIVISM TO NEO-EXPRESSIVISM

Attacks by expressivism's critics resulted in several syntheses that challenge the presumption that expressivism is atheoretical by exploring the latent theoretical framework of expressivism. Sherrie Gradin's purpose in *Romancing Rhetorics: Social Expressivist Perspectives on the Teaching of Writing* (1995) is to politicize expressivism and "establish a pedagogy of equity" in which all can contribute to be heard (121). She explores a commonly overlooked connection between romanticism and expressivism. Pointing to German romanticism's concern for social justice and political action, she counters the claim that expressivism values individualism to the exclusion of social concerns. Rather, expressivists value autonomy as sig-naled in their concern to empower people through voice, and they believe in agency and resistance. Individuals can use personal awareness to act against op-pressive material and psychological conditions. She also connects expressivism with feminism, noting that Elbow and his pedagogy are referenced in Mary Belenky et al. (Belenky, Clinchy, Goldberger, and Tarule, 1986). Similarly, Carolyn Erickson Hill (1990) considers Elbow and other expressivists to be models for building a new pedagogy of awareness and equity. Another book connecting ex-pressivist theory, feminism, and the teaching of writing is Cynthia Gannett's *Gender and the Journal: Diaries and Academic Discourse* (1992), a work of teacher-research that offers historical as well as ideological analyses of journal use in personal and pedagogical contexts.

Elbow offers more theoretical framing, examines his application, and provides an extended defense of voice in *Landmark Essays: On Voice and Writing* (1994), a collection of sixteen essays by various theorists, both allies and critics of expressivism, including bell hooks. In an introductory essay, "Introduction: About Voice and Writing," Elbow traces the voice controversy as far back as Aristotle and Plato. He equates voice and ethos. "Resonant" voice, one of five empirically verifiable instances of voice, is Elbow's primary concern. Sensitive to critiques of the expressivist view of self, Elbow walks a careful line. Resonant voice manages to get a great deal of the self "behind the words." Discourse can never "articulate a whole person," but at times we can "find words that seem to capture the rich complexity of the unconscious . . . that somehow seem to *resonate with* or *have behind them* the unconscious as well as the conscious [his italics]. . . . [W]ords of this sort . . . we experience as resonant—and through them we have a sense of presence with the writer" (xxxiv). As with voice, Elbow relates "presence" to ethos in classical rhetoric. Connecting resonant voice with self-identity, and both with ethos, he argues that voice in writing is a locus for power. From a pragmatic perspective, he argues against a binary view that opposes sentimental (expressivist) and sophisticated (postmodern) views of the self; writers need to use both. The sentimental self (the believer) functions best in exploratory writing. The sophisticated self (the doubter) works well when revising with a pragmatic end in mind.

Recent discussions of "neo-expressivism" are reenergizing expressivism. Byron Hawk's *A Counter-History of Composition: Toward Methodologies of Complexity* (2007) reframes Berlin's critique of expressivism, claiming that Berlin's categories were based on disciplinary politics and his need to politicize writer subjectivity (58). Moreover, in later work in an implicit reference to Berlin's categories, Hawk writes that "For better or worse, our maps of the discipline encouraged us to think that, if we agreed with the social, we must dismiss the alternatives" ("Foreword: NeoExpressivisms" para. 2). *A Counter-History of Composition: Toward Methodologies of Complexity* works to reclaim vitalism, an element dismissed within Berlin's theories of romanticism. Hawk asserts that a return to vitalism will reinstate invention as the central canon of rhetoric. In a vitalist framework, invention allows for possibilities beyond the experience of a single self. Writers use personal experience in conjunction with social, historical, material reality, even time, when inventing. The self invents and is invented by many influences.

Hawk's work draws attention to Paul Kameen, a proponent of neoexpressivisms ("Meditation"). Kameen's *Writing/Teaching: Essays toward a Rhetoric of Pedagogy* (2000) imagines the classroom as place of becoming for both teachers and students, where teachers and students respond to ideologically loaded texts on race, class, and gender through their personal experiences. We hear an echo of hooks's challenge to the professorate in Kameen. For Kameen and many neoexpressivists, the personal is rhetorical, a site of invention and a catalyst for change. In this way, neoexpressivm incorporates the social and the personal, encompassing the context, embodiment, and material circumstances of the writer. Although they work from different theoretical frameworks of the subject (Deleuze, Coleridge), neoexpressivists seek to maintain expressivism's commitment to voice and connectedness as they complicate the ideas of authenticity and self (Hilst).

OTHER RECENT WORK

As new pedagogies compete for classroom, journal, and textbook space, the practices of expressivism color each innovation, making freewriting, journal keeping, reflective writing, and dialogic groupwork commonplaces of composition practice. Additionally, expressivism's concern for the individual writer's development has matured into a concern for the writer's relationships with audience, context, and subject. Thus, although expressivism began as a reaction against current-traditionalism, its principles are integral to many pedagogies, including feminist, critical, community service, and multimodal. Nevertheless, recent scholars invoking expressivist values and practices illustrate the field's uneasy relationship with the personal. They position themselves in relation to existing theory and debate in one of four ways: (1) synthesizing, revising, and extending; (2) adopting practices but not the theory; (3) refusing the expressivism label but citing expressivist theory/practice to justify an argument; and (4) fully engaging the debates about expressivism.

Synthesis, Revisions, and Extensions

As neoexpressivism and feminist scholars synthesize and revise expressivism, others extend the theory by explicating its nuances and complexity. In an ethnographic study of two expressivist writing instructors, Karen Surman Paley's *I-Writing* (2001) seeks to correct misreadings of expressivism. She notes the complexity of the expressivist classroom, illustrating how students and teachers are firmly embedded in political and social dimensions as they write in personal genres. Paley's research excuses expressivism from charges of naiveté and solipsism, and at the same time she exemplifies the blending of personal and academic discourse. Throughout the book, Paley examines her biases, history, and location as a researcher, sharing her frustrations, hopes, and disappointments. Extending Elbow's theoretical work on voice to empirical case studies, Lizbeth Bryant uses the same blending of the scholarly and personal voice in *Voice as Process*. This blend of personal and academic discourse reflects a curious dissonance in the field; although many noteworthy scholars employ the personal to make sophisticated theoretical arguments (Richard Miller, Julie Jung, Malea Powell), that same rhetorical choice, the use of the personal to build ethos, is often denied to students. Two monographs, Anne Herrington and Marcia Curtis's *Persons in Process: Four Stories of Writing and Personal Development in College* and Nick Tingle's *Self Development in College Writing*, contend that students may not only need that rhetorical choice, but may have a "psychological need to believe in personal agency" (Herrington and Curtis 359). Working from psychology and psychoanalysis, both books emphasize the relationship between personal development and writing.

In an exemplar of embodied, expressivist, writing, Jane Hindman's "Making Writing Matter: Using 'the Personal' to Recover[y] an Essential[ist] Tension in

Academic Discourse" recounts her experience recovering from alcoholism to explore what she sees as the productive tension between the expressivist self who makes meaning out of experience and the socially constructed self "who is always already constrained by the conventions of discourse" (89). Drawing on the work of Richard Miller, Hindman claims that complementing personal writing with self-reflection can illuminate the field's work, creating an academic discourse that "matters":

> A composing process which requires me to evoke my beliefs at their most invisible embodied place, to scrutinize relentlessly the stakes in maintaining those individual beliefs and to confront the privileges they afford me, and to stage self-consciously my methods for persuading you of the authority of those beliefs—that kind of composing produces writing that matters. (105)

Expressivism continues to receive attention in the field's major journals. In 2001 and 2003, *College English* published special issues on the personal. In these issues, scholars engage expressivism from varying stances and viewpoints. To contend that the personal narrative is legitimate scholarly argument, Candace Spigelman traces the use of the personal in argumentation from Aristotle to the present day. Drawing on the work of expressivist teacher and scholar Wendy Bishop, in another piece, Will Banks asks the field to revalue the personal, writing that

> For all the failings James Berlin and Lester Faigley have usefully suggested about a certain kind of expressivism, such a pedagogy reminds us of something important about teaching and learning: [. . .] when we ignore the "embodied" in discourse, we miss the ways in which liberation is always both social and individual, a truly symbiotic relationship. (22)

The binary tension between the personal/professional and the personal/social has inspired extensions and revisions of expressivism that produce ethically, politically, and socially aware personal writing.

Current thinking about self-assessment also employs expressivist principles. In *Self-Assessment and Development in Writing: A Collaborative Inquiry* (2000), Smith and Yancey confront questions about the legitimacy of expressive writing. In "Reflections on Self-Assessment," their final summary and implications chapter, they "conclude that self-assessment seems to be one of the best kept secrets of the field" (169). Why? They reason, "For some, self-assessment seems little more than a kind of expressive absorption with the self" (173).

While self-assessment might simply ask students to think about what they do when they write, such reflection fosters growth. They invoke Donald Schön's work on reflection and reflective practice. Schön labels such thinking "'reflection in action' and argues that the awareness of, and inquiry into, one's intellectual processes will make the learning more felicitous" (Smith and Yancey 170). Self-assessment can also refer to general procedures that employ heuristics aimed at helping the student "to establish a habit of critical inquiry that is active, rather than passive, to integrate the learning into what is already known and to project what more can or should be learned" (171). Chris's Learning Outcomes Log, a classroom-based student self-assessment technique, uses reflective writing, focusing on the published learning outcomes of a course to foster deeper learning and involve teachers and students in continuing dialogue (see www.borderlandswritingproject.com). In another example, Sam Watson's "Confessions from Our Reflective Classroom" has self-assessment at its heart. Watson demonstrates that reflection and self-assessment are means through which students can construct identity, not only identities as writers per se, but more important, identity in general. This sense of identity is deemed crucial to developing as a writer.

This brings Smith and Yancey to the controversy surrounding the nature of the self. "Of course, the notion of self, [...] the heart of any self-assessment enterprise, is itself problematic" (171). Yet they argue that "It is through diverse contexts and communities that the self is defined" (172). Based on the richness and complexity of the self-assessment context, they claim that using self-assessment is "a highly ideological act" (173), a means through which students can resist and claim agency. Ideally, they hope self-assessment enables the student to "go beyond our standards to his or hers, talk back to us and begin to negotiate the terms that will govern a text. . . ." and "these behaviors—about developing criteria and talking back and negotiating them—. . . [are] behaviors that cut across assignments, that cut across classes, that we hope begin to help students develop what is often called a habit of mind, a disciplined way of seeing the world and engaging in it" (172). It is this reflective, action-oriented habit of mind that so much expressivist pedagogy hopes to encourage.

Adopting the Practices, Not the Theory

Although digital and multimodal pedagogy may not mention the word *expressivism*, the practices of expressivism have experienced a revival and revision in digital spaces. Traditional expressivist practices, like groupwork and journal writing, have digital counterparts in wikiwriting and blogging. Additionally, new media and multimodality encourage self-expression through a variety of mediums (see Brooke's chapter in this volume). Specifically, Bronwyn Williams's *Shimmering Literacies: Popular Culture and Reading and Writing Online* (2009) finds students using their writings on popular culture as an outlet for self-expression and identity construction. Although Williams never mentions expressivism, his last chapter insists on honoring student experiences with popular culture, particularly the literacies they have gained by being immersed in participatory, multimodal forums. This insistence on honoring, and building on, student experience echoes expressivist tenets.

Refusing the Label, Citing the Theory and Practitioners

Reflecting back on this review of the scholarship highlights the discipline's problematic attitude toward the personal. Given the controversy, some scholars choose to distance their work from the expressivist label but still draw on the theories, principles, and primary practitioners. For example, Jane Danielwicz makes an important contribution to the field's understanding of the relationship between the personal and the public and voice and audience in "Personal Genres, Public Voices." She recounts her experiences teaching a first-year composition course themed around personal genres of writing. In writing their own stories, students gained a public voice, which allowed them to develop a sophisticated rhetorical awareness of audience. Clearly, students moved between Britton's participant and spectator roles. Although Danielwicz cites Elbow's work with voice, she chooses not to engage the debates surrounding expressivism.

Full Engagements

Others, like longtime collaborators Fishman and McCarthy, fully engage attacks on expressivism. Using discourse community theory in "Is Expressivism Dead?" they tackle the social-constructionist versus expressivism debate encapsulated in a CCC's colloquy between David Bartholomae and Peter Elbow. Bartholomae represents the social constructionist position, arguing that all writing is situated and that as representatives of the academy, teachers must focus on the academic. Elbow represents the expressivist position, defending personal writing, self-expression, and creativity. Fishman and McCarthy argue that expressivism does not endorse the concept of the isolated, autonomous individual. Echoing Gradin's socially concerned German romanticism, and implicitly invoking Deweyan progressivism, they contend that expressivist techniques can be used to achieve social-constructivist goals in a writing-across-the-curriculum context. In "Community in the Expressivist Classroom," they explore the tension between conventional authoritarian and expressivist liberal and communitarian classroom values. Fishman, a philosophy professor, claims some success in promoting student voice while teaching his discipline's conventions. However, his experience underscores the complexity of the expressivist classroom where students function as experts and teachers as learners. They conclude that this complexity, rather than the reductive either/or positions generally presented in the scholarly literature, offers significant opportunities for progress.

The next essay, "Teaching for Student Change: A Deweyan Alternative to Radical Pedagogy," defends the safe cooperative classroom championed by the expressivists against the recent charges by feminist and critical teachers that expressivist pedagogy protects the status quo by encouraging politeness that camouflages inherent conflicts in the classroom and society at large. Fishman and McCarthy offer an alternative that privileges diversity and encourages transformation for teachers who "find certain types of conflict unattractive but who seek student critique and change" (344). In *John Dewey and the Challenge of Classroom Practice* (1998), Fishman and McCarthy propose an approach that integrates the curricular interests and needs of teachers and the needs and experiences of students. The approach is writing-intensive, employing dialogical, written commentaries where students pose and answer each other's questions, with Fishman providing additional written commentary as a mentor and co-inquirer. Fishman's question-and-answer approach merges class topics with student experience and exigencies, allowing Fishman to accomplish his goal of having students learn substantive intellectual content through personalizing and applying philosophical concepts in their own lives.

Their latest collaboration, *John Dewey and the Philosophy and Practice of Hope* (2007), continues enacting Dewey's theories of continuous learning to improve the lives of both the individual and the collective. Through the course Fishman invites his students to become "co-inquirers" with him as they work to construct both a theory and a practice of hope derived from the whole of Dewey's work. The course is built around reading and exploratory and analytical writing to understand and apply learning in everyday living. Fishman and McCarthy's work exemplifies expressivist pedagogy in which meaning is constructed through dialogue between persons passionately investigating how to use philosophy. The pedagogy helps students understand and enact Dewey's philosophy and to achieve Plato's grand philosophical goal, to live a good and thoughtful life.

CODA: PRACTICE/THEORY, THEORY/PRACTICE

Writing helps us pursue the "good and thoughtful life," and expressivist practices help us give our students space to reflect, make meaning, communicate, and take action. Early expressivists found themselves defending their practice by disputing criticism. The disputation allowed seeing and theorizing the relations among language, the self, meaning-making, and the social in ways that help writers write. These theories and practices have evolved to incorporate growing understandings of the self, the social, the material, digital environments and tools, and the complexity of the classroom. The process has been challenging and rewarding. Rebecca has it just right; expressivism grew up.

Back to bell hooks. *Teaching to Transgress* centers itself squarely on the problem of dichotomizing theory and practice. A student of Paulo Freire, she views praxis, the convergence of theory and practice, as the primary concern of liberatory pedagogy. She recalls her childhood, a time of alienation in which she felt the oppressive power of her family shaping her into a proper black girlchild. It was then that she developed a habit of theorizing. She calls that experience her introduction to critical thinking:

> Living a childhood without a sense of home, I found a place of sanctuary in "theorizing," in making sense out of what was happening. I found a place where I could imagine possible futures, a place where life could be lived differently. This "lived" experience of critical thinking, of reflection and analysis, because [sic, became] a place where I worked at explaining the hurt and making it go away. Fundamentally, I learned from this experience that theory could be a healing place. (61)

Praxis is the means and locus for building critical consciousness. With Elbow she shares a goal; the aim of her pedagogy is to create a place for voices. The voices in the classroom include the voice of the teacher as well as those of the students. Her expectations of the teachers are extremely high: to bring students to voice, teachers must have, and understand, voice. And voice is related to self-actualization. She calls this kind of teaching "engaged pedagogy":

> Progressive, holistic education, *engaged pedagogy*, is more demanding than conventional critical or feminist pedagogy. For unlike these two teaching practices, it emphasizes well-being. That means that teachers much be actively committed to a process of self-actualization that promotes their own well-being if they are to teach in a manner that empowers students. (15)

Tilly Warnock sheds light on what it might mean to be a self-actualized teacher of writing. Reflecting on the work of Jim Corder, Warnock defends teacher-writers like Wendy Bishop, Lad Tobin, and Kathleen Yancey, who "demonstrate the rich possibilities of expressivist rhetorics" and "affirm the practice of using such ideological arguments to create identification across differences that doesn't deny differences" (215). To ignore expressivist rhetorics and practice only conventional academic discourse is just one more way, says Warnock, echoing hooks' comment about being taught proper manners, to "'Hush your mouth. Mind your manners, do what you're supposed to do, and don't cause trouble,'" the lessons taught her as a girl growing up in the just de-segregating South (215). Self-actualized teachers of writing do not hush.

Engaged pedagogy involves a holism that repairs the habitual dichotomizing of conventional thinking, repairing splits between body and mind, intellect and spirit, teaching and learning, and theory and practice. hooks describes a set of dialectical relationships that echoes Elbow's theme in "A Method for Teaching Writing": "Any classroom that employs a holistic model of learning will also be a place where teachers grow, and are empowered by the process. That empowerment cannot happen if we refuse to be vulnerable while encouraging students to take risks" (21). Engaged pedagogy, holistic teaching, and self-reflective writers: these are the expressivist project.

FURTHER RESOURCES

This chapter traces the uneasy relations between expressivist and mainstream English Studies and Rhetoric and Composition theory and practice. Important as it is to continue to track the dialogue in the occasional but rare mainstream professional journal article dealing with expressivism, alternate venues listed here have evolved that attend to these concerns. To engage with the expressivist project, consult the following organizations and journals:

- The National Writing Project provides K-16 professional development for teachers of writing. (http://nwp.org)
- Assembly for Expanded Perspectives on Learning is a National Council of Teachers of English (NCTE) assembly for scholars and teachers interested in reflective teaching and untraditional learning and teaching. (https://www.sworps.tennessee.edu/aepl/index.html)
- *Writing on the Edge* publishes pedagogical and personal essays on writing and the teaching of writing. (http://woe.ucdavis.edu/)
- *Teacher's College Record* is a leader in teacher inquiry, a mode of reflective practice and engaged pedagogy. (https://www.tcrecord.org/)

BIBLIOGRAPHY

Banks, William P. "Written through the Body: Disruptions and 'Personal' Writing." *The Personal in Academic Writing.* Special issue of *College English* 66.1 (2003): 21–40. Print.

Bartholomae, David. "Writing with Teachers: A Conversation with Peter Elbow." *College Composition and Communication* 46.1 (1995): 62–71. Print.

Belenky, Mary, Blythe M. Clinchy, Nancy Goldberger, and Jill Tarule. *Women's Ways of Knowing: The Development of Self, Voice, and Mind.* New York: Basic Books, 1986. Print.

Berlin, James A. "Contemporary Composition: The Major Pedagogical Theories." *College English* 44.8 (1982): 765–77. Print.

_____. *Rhetoric and Reality: Writing Instruction in American Colleges, 1900–1985.* Carbondale: Southern Illinois UP, 1987. Print.

_____. "Rhetoric and Ideology in the Writing Class." *College English* 50.5 (1988): 477–94. Print.

Britton, James. *Language and Learning.* New York: Penguin, 1970. Print.

Britton, James, Tony Burgess, Nancy Martin, Alex McLeod, and Harold Rosen. *The Development of Writing Abilities (11-18).* Urbana: National Council of Teachers of English, 1978. Print.

Bryant, Lizbeth A. *Voice as Process.* Portsmouth: Boynton/Cook, 2005. Print.

Burnham, Christopher C. "Expressive Rhetoric: A Source Study." *Defining the New Rhetorics.* Ed. Theresa Enos and Stuart C. Brown. Newbury Park: Sage, 1993. 154–70. Print.

Crowley, Sharon. *The Methodical Memory: Invention in Current-Traditional Rhetoric.* Carbondale: Southern Illinois UP, 1990. Print.

Danielewicz, Jane. "Personal Genres, Public Voices." *College Composition and Communication* 59.3 (2008): 420–51. Print.

Delpit, Lisa. *Other People's Children: Cultural Conflict in the Classroom.* New York: New P, 1995. Print.

Elbow, Peter. "Introduction: About Voice in Writing." *Landmark Essays on Voice and Writing.* Ed. Peter Elbow. Davis: Hermagoras P, 1994. xi–xlvii. Print.

_____. "A Method for Teaching Writing." *College English* 30.2 (1968): 115–25. Print.

_____. "Toward a Phenomenology of Freewriting." *Nothing Begins with N: New Investigations of Freewriting.* Ed. Pat Belanoff, Peter Elbow, and Sheryl I. Fontaine. Carbondale: Southern Illinois UP, 1991. 189–213. Print.

_____. *Writing with Power: Techniques for Mastering the Writing Process.* New York: Oxford UP, 1981. Print.

_____. *Writing without Teachers.* New York: Oxford UP, 1973. Print.

Fishman, Stephen M., and Lucille P. McCarthy. "Is Expressivism Dead? Reconsidering Its Romantic Roots and Its Relation to Social Constructionism." *College English* 54.6 (1992): 647–61. Print.

_____. "Community in the Expressivist Classroom: Juggling Liberal and Communitarian Visions." *College English* 57.1 (1995): 62–81. Print.

_____. *John Dewey and the Challenge of Classroom Practice.* New York: Teachers College P, 1998. Print.

_____. *John Dewey and the Philosophy and Practice of Hope.* Urbana and Chicago: U of Illinois P, 2007. Print.

_____. "Teaching for Student Change: A Deweyan Alternative to Radical Pedagogy." *College Composition and Communication* 47.3 (1996): 342–66. Print.

Fulkerson, Richard. "Composition at the Turn of the Twenty-First Century." *College Composition and Communication* 56.4 (2005): 654-87.

Gannett, Cinthia. *Gender and the Journal: Diaries and Academic Discourse.* Albany: SUNY P, 1992. Print.

Gradin, Sherrie L. *Romancing Rhetorics: Social Expressivist Perspectives on the Teaching of Writing.* Portsmouth: Boynton/Cook, 1995. Print.

Harris, Jeanette. *Expressive Discourse.* Dallas: Southern Methodist UP, 1990. Print.

Hawk, Byron. *A Counter-History of Composition: Toward Methodologies of Complexity.* Pittsburg: U of Pittsburg P, 2007. Print.

_____. "Foreword: Neo-Expressivisms." *Enculturation* 13 (2012): n.p. Web. 16 May 2012.

Herrington, Anne, and Marcia Curtis. *Persons in Process: Four Stories of Writing and Personal Development in College.* Refiguring English Studies. Urbana: National Council of Teachers of English, 2000. Print.

Hill, Carolyn Erikson. *Writing from the Margins: Power and Pedagogy for Teachers of Composition*. New York: Oxford UP, 1990. Print.

Hilst, Joshua. "Deleuze: (Neo)Expressivism in Composition." *Enculturation* 13 (2012): n pag. Web. 16 May 2012.

Hindman, Jane. "Making Writing Matter: Using 'the Personal' to Recover[y] an Essential[ist] Tension in Academic Discourse." *Personal Writing*. Special issue of *College English* 64.1 (2001): 88–108. Print.

hooks, bell. *Sisters of the Yam: Black Women and Self-Recovery*. Boston: South End P, 1993. Print.

_____. *Teaching to Transgress: Education as the Practice of Freedom*. New York: Routledge, 1994. Print.

Kameen, Paul. *Writing/Teaching: Essays toward a Rhetoric of Pedagogy*. Pittsburgh: U of Pittsburgh P, 2000. Print.

_____. "Meditation and Method: Reflections on the Relationship between Discourse and Time." *Enculturation*.13 (2012).np. Web. 30 January. 2012.

Kinneavy, James. *A Theory of Discourse*. Englewood Cliffs: Prentice Hall, 1971. Print.

Macrorie, Ken. *A Vulnerable Teacher*. Rochelle Park: Hayden, 1974. Print.

_____. *Telling Writing*. Rochelle Park: Hayden, 1970. Print.

_____. *Uptaught*. New York: Hayden, 1970. Print.

Merton, Thomas. "Learning to Live." *Thomas Merton: Spiritual Master*. Ed. Lawrence Cunningham. New York: Paulist P, 1992. Print.

Miller, Richard E. *Writing at the End of the World*. Pittsburg: U of Pittsburg P, 2005. Print.

Murray, Donald. "Writing as Process: How Writing Finds Its Own Meaning." *Eight Approaches to Teaching Composition*. Ed. Timothy R. Donovan and Ben McClelland. Urbana: National Council of Teachers of English, 1980. 3–20. Print.

_____. *A Writer Teaches Writing*. New York: Holt, 1968. Print.

Paley, Karen Surman. *I-Writing: The Politics and Practice of Teaching First-Person Writing*. Carbondale: Southern Illinois UP, 2001. Print.

The Personal in Academic Writing. Special issue of *College English* 66.1 (2003). Print.

Personal Writing. Special issue of *College English* 64.1 (2001). Print.

Postman, Neil, and Charles Weingartner. *Teaching as a Subversive Activity*. New York: Delacorte P, 1969. Print.

Ramanathan, Vai, and Dwight Atkinson. "Individualism, Academic Writing, and ESL Writers." *Journal of Second Language Writing* 8.1 (1999): 45–57. Print.

Smith, Jane Bowman, and Kathleen Blake Yancey, eds. *Self-Assessment and Development in Writing: A Collaborative Inquiry*. Cresskill: Hampton P, 2000. Print.

Spigelman, Candace. "Argument and Evidence in the Case of the Personal." *Personal Writing*. Special issue of *College English* 64.1 (2001): 63–87. Print.

Tingle, Nick. *Self-Development and College Writing*. Carbondale: Southern Illinois UP, 2004. Print.

Warnock, Tilly. "Bringing over Yonder over Here: A Personal Look at Expressivist Rhetoric as Ideological Action." *Beyond Postprocess and Postmodernism: Essays on the Spaciousness of Rhetoric*. Ed. Theresa Enos, Keith Miller, and Jill McCracken. Mahwah: Erlbaum, 2003. 203–16. Print.

Watson, Sam. "Confessions from Our Reflective Classroom." Smith and Yancey, 75–96. Print.

Williams, Bronwyn. *Shimmering Literacies: Popular Culture and Reading and Writing Online*. New York: Peter Lang, 2009. Print.

⚘

Feminist Pedagogies

Laura R. Micciche

When I was a junior in college, my writing teacher's pedagogy included collaborative projects, writing journals, cultural critiques, and lots of in-class drafting sessions. The reading material focused on marginalized subjects: sexual abuse, women's poverty and illness, and lesbian identity. Later, in graduate school, another teacher valued collaboration in and outside the classroom, often creating opportunities for students to join her in reading groups and writing projects. She contextualized rhetorical theory within feminist scholarship; she presented herself as both an active scholar and a caring mentor for female students. Another set very high expectations because she felt women students needed to toughen up to survive patriarchal academic culture. She unschooled our deferential curtsies and gender-appropriate hedging, and she delivered devastating feedback on our papers, notably short on sugarcoating.

All were feminist teachers. Their combined approaches valued

- the personal and political
- theoretical, political, intellectual, and emotional understandings of inter-sectional identities
- systemic analyses of inequality aimed at uncovering the production of knowledge, meaning, power, and belief in particular contexts
- writing as a tool for self-revelation, critique, and transformation
- distributed agency through collaborative practices and alternative classroom arrangements
- content focused on women's experiences and contributions to knowledge-making
- teaching and mentoring as forms of professional activism

Feminist pedagogies, regardless of differences, share a common goal of actualizing social justice through teaching and learning methods. And while "social justice" has, within first- and second-wave feminism, largely concerned itself with gender, sexuality, class, and race, contemporary feminisms, including third- and fourth-wave manifestations, increasingly address a much wider spectrum and entangled set of interests. These interests emerge from the material, political, corporeal, and emotional effects of living in a globalized economy characterized by a spectacular disparity between wealthy and impoverished people, corporate interests and workers.

Feminist pedagogies in Composition Studies emerge from this wider context and orbit around the idea that pedagogy has the potential, even the responsibility, to interrogate and transform social relations (see Jarratt, "Feminist Pedagogy," for a fuller account). Feminist pedagogies connect local, personal experiences to larger contexts of world-making, harkening back to the familiar second-wave feminist maxim, "The personal is political." Within Writing Studies, activist pedagogical functions are linked to writing and literacy practices broadly conceived, making clear that there is no bracketing the world or politics from the classroom.

The evolution of feminist pedagogies that I sketch herein begins with efforts to develop feminist teaching methods, followed by critical reassessments of those efforts alongside new directions for research and teaching. Feminist pedagogy is a hopeful practice that envisions learning spaces as sites where more just social relations can begin to take root. Increasingly, as will be evident in what follows, feminist pedagogy is not a discrete set of practices but, much like feminism generally, a flexible basis from which to launch intersectional pedagogical projects—projects focused on a dialectic of multiple identity categories rather than, for instance, on gender or sex alone. Feminism's distribution and infusion across areas of study and across pedagogical models (i.e., expressivist, collaborative, and critical pedagogies) make for a rewardingly difficult bibliographic task.

GENDER DIFFERENCES AND EXPERIENCE

In the nineteenth century, first-wave feminists coalesced around women's suffrage and the abolition of slavery. Second wavers, politicized in the United States by antiwar and civil rights movements of the 1960s, struggled for women's economic, political, educational, and sexual liberties. Fractures within feminism itself led to the proliferation of activism and scholarship by feminists of color as well as lesbian feminists, often excluded from mainstream feminist movement. More recently, third-wave feminism (1988–2010) rejects prescriptive feminist ideology, posits an individualist agenda, and, like sex-positive movements, views sexual freedom as fundamental to women's freedom. Fourth-wave feminism (2010–present) is associated with the strategic use of new media to wage politically motivated campaigns for human rights (Baumgardner). We can see traces of these popular, rather than academic, movements in research described in this chapter, but on the whole I refer to post-second-wave feminisms through the less definitive "contemporary feminisms," seeking to avoid an overly taxonomic plotting. Whatever terms we use, it's clear that since the 1960s feminists have continued to expand struggles for equality as well as objects of analysis and critique; while second-wave feminism began with a focus on gender equity in a variety of contexts (family, workplace, education, religion), feminism has grown to address race, class, age, disability, queer, linguistic, immigrant, global, and other categories of identification that include and exceed women's issues.

Early feminist pedagogical models in the 1970s focused largely on women students, addressing, for instance, the consequences of gendered differences in various contexts and the effects of glaring inequities within higher education. This focus reflected the influx of female students at U.S. universities that ushered in widespread political and ideological changes in the culture. The ripple effects of this wider movement did not reach Composition Studies until the mid-1980s, trailing feminism's migration to the academy by at least fifteen years. Influenced especially by the feminist movement, feminist literary studies, and developmental psychology, work published during this early phase tended to focus on experience as a legitimate form of knowledge, inherent gender differences and effects on writing, and alternative classroom assignments aimed at encouraging women students to write from positions of power.

Feminists continually return to experience as fraught but powerful territory for female students. In the 1970s Florence Howe expressed concern about female students' "passivity and dependency" (864), and Joan Bolker developed assignments to combat the "good girl" complex. She recommended experimental assignments— "fictional letters to enemies" and "free writing, involving poetry, or playing with words, or even, God help us, with obscenities"—and essays that begin with the personal, "even the selfish" (908; see Pigott for the opposite argument). Pamela Annas, writing in 1985, advocates a pedagogy that values personal experience to "ground [students'] writing in their lives rather than to surmount their lives before they write" (362). To achieve this, Annas assigns process papers in which students examine the material conditions of their own writing (influenced, most notably, by their reading of Virginia Woolf), position papers that ask women to risk a public stance, and an argument essay in which students blend their personal experience with source material. Her goal is to help students discover their own voices while paying attention to the ways in which women's voices have been historically muted by inequitable cultural conditions (see Gannett).

Validating women's experiences is central to Elizabeth Flynn's "Composing as a Woman." Flynn's essay suggests a possible way forward for feminist researchers of pedagogy, helping to encourage a view of pedagogy as practice and object of scholarly inquiry. An examination of four student narrative essays through a gendered lens, Flynn's study suggests that the women's narratives emphasize relational connections and identifications, and the men's accentuate individual achievement. Like others during this early wave of feminist composition, Flynn adopts feminist theories of psychological and social development by Gilligan, Chodorow, and Belenky et al. Based on the gendered patterns she finds in student writing, Flynn advocates for empowering women students "to write from the power of [their] experience" (434). Later research included both efforts to identify gender difference at the level of writing and challenges to the essentialism inherent in this approach (e.g., Brody; Graves; Lamb; Looser; Ratcliffe "Re-Considering"; Ritchie; Zawacki).

Contributors to *Gender Issues in the Teaching of English* (McCracken and Appleby) call for "gender sensitive" teaching keyed to gender differences, awareness of how listening and interruption are gendered, attention to the gendered nature of reading and responding to literature, consideration of prefab essay forms that fore-stall women's voices, the importance of adding gender to curricula, and more. Like-wise, Karyn Hollis supports "woman-friendly" classrooms in which teachers call on women students more often and "use non-competitive and student-centered activities" like sequencing small- and large-group discussions to help female stu-dents move from "private discourse to public pronouncements" (341; see Peterson). Donnalee Rubin's *Gender Influences* features an empirical study, influenced by reader-response theory, of how gender differences shape teachers' responses to stu-dent writing. Rubin finds that nondirective conference and process-based pedago-gies are the best means for overcoming and suppressing gender bias (96).

Since at least the publication of Flynn's essay, feminists have sought to create a more complex understanding of experience that recognizes the role of narrative, context, and myriad other factors toward producing "experience." Illustrating this point, Min-Zhan Lu develops sequenced, reiterative assignments that offer different ways of seeing and analyzing experience over time (239). Likewise, Candace Spigelman argues for personal academic writing that treats experience as a construct rather than as evidence of an authentic self, clarifying that experience remains valuable to feminist teaching but should be approached critically.

Later feminist work also raised questions about the feminist teacher as facili-tator of a cooperative, student-centered learning environment (see Eichhorn et al.). Eileen Schell ("Costs"), for example, argues that this ethic of care obscures a central problem in the field: the preponderance of women in "contingent (part-time and non-tenure-track) writing instructorships" (75). Indeed, images of non-authoritative female teachers have informed characterizations of composition's feminized labor force. Among the vivid descriptors dramatizing the subordinate positions women have occupied throughout composition's history are gypsies, wives, whores, handmaids, daughters, mothers, and "sad women in the basement" (i.e., Miller; Reichert; Schell, *Gypsy*; Tuell).

DIVERSE DISCOURSES AND PRACTICES

As poststructuralist and postmodernist notions of agency, selfhood, subjectivity, and power have interacted with feminist theory, pedagogical models began to reflect these ideas. One result was a turn to experimental writing and the value of diverse discourses, a natural outgrowth of the emphasis on discursive play and experimentation characteristic especially of French poststructuralist writing, in-fluencing much feminist work in the 1980s and 1990s (i.e., Irigaray; Marks and de Courtivron). In addressing the flexibility of language to render alternative realities and values, feminist pedagogues aimed their sights at a staple of composition classes: the argument essay and its tendency to be taught as a thesis-driven pursuit to legitimize a single viewpoint.

Adopting different modes of argumentation, Catherine Lamb describes a multi-step pedagogy for mediation and negotiation. The mediation assignment sequence asks students to discuss in small groups problems they want to write about, then to write individually, and finally to take on roles of disputants and mediators in response to one another's written work. The feminist outcomes of this and the negotiation assignment include an awareness of knowledge "as cooperatively and collaboratively constructed" (21), though not without contestation. Sheree Meyer challenges the "confidence game" based on "an illusion of mastery" central to academic discourse (52; see Tompkins). She advocates an alternative model in which students sustain complex positions that permit gaps and confusions rather than propagating writing as "acts of aggression" aimed at annihilating other views and encouraging what she calls the "Imposter Phenomenon" (48, 50). Meyer, borrowing from Ann Berthoff's dialectical notebook, develops an assignment she calls Double Trouble. Students fold a piece of paper in half; on one side, they write one or two sentences culled from a class reading followed by an explanation of what they think is being said, and on the other, they begin with "But something bothers me . . ." and are encouraged to show hesitancies, to question claims on the other side, to think about contradictions, and so forth (60). This model resonates with Nedra Reynolds's reclamation of interruption as a feminist writing strategy counter to agonistic forms of academic discourse.

In another effort to circumvent the constraints of academic prose, Terry Myers Zawacki envisions writing as a "means of creating a self," emphasizing the constructive, rather than exclusively reflective or expressive, quality of writing (37). Lillian Bridwell-Bowles finds traditional academic forms inflexible, and so adopts what she calls "alternative," "feminist," or "diverse" discourse options in her writing classes (350). Her essay includes samples in which student writers try out a personal voice, express anxiety about writing that does not strive for objectivity, reveal estrangement from dominant texts, and write from an interrogatory rather than argumentative stance.

More recently, Julie Jung has developed a model of feminist revision "as a process of delayed connection" (*Revisionary* 13). She offers an alternative to well-circulated theories of revision that aim for "clarity and connection," arguing that this approach fails to account for real differences and the "inevitable disconnections that permeate [readers' and writers'] experiences with texts" (11). Rhetorical listening, discussed in this chapter's "Emotion" section, is central to Jung's model, and multigenre texts—"experimental scholarly essays that are marked by the conscious juxtaposition of the academic essay with other genres" (33)—provide spaces where writers can practice rhetorical listening and delayed revision (for more on feminist experimental writing, see Micciche, "Writing"). Spotlighting the value of alternative feminist genres, Jacqueline Rhodes resuscitates the manifesto, offering a passionate history of its use by second-wave radical feminists and contemporary feminists writing online. The manifesto, a form of radical feminist textuality, creates opportunities for "composition studies to retheorize student writers as active producers of the strategic discourses of resistance" (3).

Technologically mediated genres also create productive opportunities for feminist teachers. Sibylle Gruber's study of Alba, a Latina student from inner-city Chicago enrolled in a basic writing course with an online component, provides a localized view of how one student's written work in electronic forums intersects with her identity as a nontraditional student. Alba uses the electronic forum to reveal "her 'otherness'" and to "define her position as a nontraditional student" (117). Laura Sullivan describes a class in which she asked students to produce "feminist activist autobiographical hypertexts" designed to create alternative narratives about female subjectivity. In creating these texts, students use hypertext strategies of collage, montage, reappropriation, and recasting of images available in the mass media for subversive purposes. Also highlighting the unique affordances of hypertext, Donna LeCourt and Luann Barnes argue that multivocal hypertexts present students with opportunities to disrupt "textual elements— reader considerations, genre assumptions, and the ideology of a unified 'I'—that feminists indict as the primary mechanisms by which . . . gendered ideology is produced" (59). While such texts are no guarantee that students will discover multiple subject positions unavailable through more traditional forms, their potentiality, particularly in light of long-standing feminist goals to create spaces for marginalized voices and resist the constraints of academic discourse, is cause for cautious optimism.

Feminists have also intervened in classroom arrangements and writing practices, particularly by investigating the value of collaboration. A rich body of rhetorical scholarship (Gere; Logan, *We Are Coming*; Lunsford and Ede, "Collaborative," *Writing Together*; Royster), has convincingly unearthed and argued for the value of collaborative writing and links to feminist practices: sharing linguistic ownership and questioning the idea that anyone can "own" language; distributing agency and authorship, and thereby casting doubt on writing models that enshrine the individual; and connecting writing practices to activism. In feminist pedagogical models, collaboration has been valued for the emphasis it places on interactive learning, writing, and meaning-making as social acts, and self–other relations (Lunsford and Ede, "Collaborative").

Collaboration has also been the basis for critical assessment, however. Evelyn Ashton-Jones, for instance, questions collaborative pedagogies that purport to eliminate hierarchy and create more equitable classroom relations. The politics of gender is alive and well in groups; thus, to forward collaborative pedagogies as inherently feminist is to "perpetuate and collude in the silence that helps to conceal the reproduction of gender ideology" (17; see Stygall). Research on collaboration has recently expanded to account for human and nonhuman interactions—environmental factors, technology, animals, etc.—affecting scenes of composing (i.e., Cooper; *Special Issue*), a topic that will likely get more attention in the coming years.

CONFLICT AND DIFFERENCE

Increasingly, teacher-scholars in Composition Studies have not only applied feminist principles to pedagogical practices but also to critical stances that affect every aspect of learning environments. Feminist pedagogy, in other words, is more than a set of practices; it is an orientation to learning and knowing charged by social justice commitments. This section describes embracing conflict as a reoccurring orientation for feminist compositionists.

Susan Jarratt's "Feminism and Composition: The Case for Conflict" is an excellent example of the disruptive power of pedagogy. She responds to feminist rejections of argument and renunciations of teacher-authority influenced by student-centered pedagogies, especially expressivism. Drawing from critical pedagogy and Sophistic rhetoric, Jarratt argues that teachers should engage in conflict in order to "negotiate the oppressive discourses of racism, sexism, and classism surfacing in the composition classroom" (106). Dale Bauer, too, supports confrontation and discomfort as central to feminist classrooms: "Political commitment—especially feminist commitment—is a legitimate classroom strategy and rhetorical imperative" (389). Bauer insists on both teacher authority and student agency in her dialogic model of teaching, implicitly identifying limitations of student-centered class-rooms that require renunciation of teacher authority. In the same vein, Andrea Greenbaum urges female teachers to practice "bitch pedagogy," an assertive, confident, argumentative stance aimed at modeling how female students can occupy positions of power.

For bell hooks, conflict in the feminist classroom should be viewed "as a catalyst for new thinking, for growth" (113); hooks's pedagogy is informed by the knowledge that, in predominantly white institutions, "the majority of students who enter our classrooms have never been taught by black women professors. . . . I know from experience that this unfamiliarity can overdetermine what takes place in the classroom" (86; see Logan, "When"; Middleton). Cheryl Johnson, an African-American literary critic, comes to a similar conclusion in her study of how students read her body to deauthorize her status in the classroom. She argues that student responses to texts are troubled by their readings of teachers' racial/gendered bodies, in turn inflected by dominant sociopolitical beliefs. In her view, teachers "have no other choice but to allow space in the classroom for such encounters with our students and to confront, finally, the persistent distortions, lies, and mythologies surrounding race, gender, and other kinds of difference" (418).

Indeed, students will always embody homegrown knowledge and experience; thus, feminist teachers must confront rather than overcome this reality. Donna Qualley does so through sustained collaborative research and writing projects based on María Lugones's concept of "world"-traveling, which describes the divided positions that immigrants and outsiders experience as they shift between spaces of foreignness and familiarity. Through ongoing collaborative work, Qualley hopes students will find that "travelling to someone's 'world' is a way of identifying with them . . . we can understand *what it is to be them and what it is to be ourselves in their eyes*" (Lugones, qtd. in Qualley 39; emphasis in original).

Achieving this kind of double vision is slow work because what's required is revised thinking that evolves through talk, reflection, and writing. Emphasizing the rewards of working slowly, Gwendolyn Pough describes how she responds to student resistance produced by her use of black feminist pedagogy and womanist rhetoric coupled with her identity as an African-American woman. While teaching Alice Walker's poem, "Each One, Pull One: Thinking of Lorraine Hansberry," and working with her students' resulting silences, Pough poses questions that interrogate the students' readings of the poem as offensive. When that fails, she turns to textual analysis, and then continually returns to their resistances through a series of assignments, readings, and class discussions, demonstrating that confrontations with difference are never easy, one-shot deals.

Shifting focus from classrooms to the wider academic system that circumscribes them, Wendy Hesford ("Ye") encourages students to engage in institutional critique through what she calls "a pedagogy of witnessing" aimed at "develop[ing] students' abilities to interrogate those neutral legal principles and conceptualizations of the academy that are based on the imperatives of the white, Anglo, male world" (151). Feminist treatments of technology have similarly questioned neutral and/or egalitarian representations of online spaces. Since the mid-1990s, feminists have been careful to point out that values, political realities, ideologies, social customs and beliefs, and other cultural organizing structures travel into spaces that humans create; thus, there is no purely democratic, utopian space available to us in face-to-face or virtual realities (see Blair and Takayoshi). Indeed, feminist studies of online pedagogies are keenly sensitive to this issue. Donna LeCourt's study of student participation in an online discussion board, for instance, focuses on whether the scene of writing can provide her "female students with any alternatives to culturally available subject positions" ("Writing" 156). And Christine Boese concludes that when electronic forums "illustrat[e] the subtle effects of sexist, racist, and homophobic language," as they will most assuredly do, the formerly "underground" discriminatory beliefs will "serve as proof to counter those who claim that the war is over, that the battle already has been won" (221–22).

Feminist engagements with conflict represent decisive moves to insert dominant ideologies and tools into the arena of critique (see also Hesford, "Documenting"). Critique, however, runs both ways. Feminist awareness of self-critique and its value to the continuation of any social justice project is unmistakably clear, as is self-consciousness about the dangers of occupying positions of mastery (see Desmet; LaDuc; Luke and Gore). Given feminism's critique of patriarchy, heterosexism, whiteness, capitalism, and other systemic forms of oppression, it's no wonder feminists cyclically reexamine their own motives so as to combat self-righteous tendencies to view themselves as already transformed, and others in need of transformation (see Gil-Gomez).

EMOTION

As the preceding section indicates, the political and social turn that began in the 1980s in Composition Studies called attention to cultural difference specifically, and the politics of literacy generally, as significant elements in teaching and learning. It also made possible an interventionist view of pedagogy as that which produces critical examinations of culture extending far beyond the confines of a classroom, writing assignment, or university setting. In this context, and influenced by interdisciplinary feminist research, compositionists began in the late 1990s to address emotion in teaching environments. They did so not by employing feminized emotions to signal irrationality, an association that has stuck for centuries, but by locating emotion in the realm of the social and political.

Describing emotion as "our primary education," Lynn Worsham argues that "our most urgent political and pedagogical task remains the fundamental reeducation of emotion" (216). Understood this way, emotion is bound up with judgment, belief, ideology, and social life broadly conceived; it is the grounds of self–other relations and an inescapable element of all cultural institutions. Inculcating ways of feeling, then, is tightly woven into the fabric of all literacies. This embeddedness has become important to feminist pedagogues who seek to transform pedagogy into a site for questioning links between power/control and emotion/embodiment. "Emotions are not simply located in an individual or a personality," writes Megan Boler, "but in a subject who is shaped by dominant discourses and ideologies and who also resists those ideologies through emotional knowledge and critical inquiry" (20).

Michelle Payne's *Bodily Discourses* puts these ideas into practice through an examination of unsolicited student writing about sexual abuse and eating disorders. She argues that personal writing will emerge whether we ask for it or not, so teachers need thoughtful response strategies. "Students writing about sexual abuse," she notes, "are often constructed as both vulnerable and in need of protection (especially from professors) and yet threatening to the ideological purposes a writing class should support" (11). As she notes, social construction has tended to exclude emotions, reproducing beliefs that emotions emanate from within individuals and are privately experienced. In contrast, Payne asks, "Why shouldn't a student bring her battered body into her written text and learn how her experience is socially constructed, historically situated, and woven through with cultural values and power relations?" (30). She goes on to suggest that students can write critically about their experiences by examining them alongside historical narratives of abuse or eating disorders, thereby locating experience "within a historical, cultural, and ideological context" that wards against pathologizing (58).

Both Boler and Payne address the importance of listening, a guiding ethos for many feminist pedagogies, particularly when investigating power differentials. Listening has received sustained treatment by Krista Ratcliffe (*Rhetorical Listening*; see also Glenn and Ratcliffe; Ronald and Roskelly). She defines rhetorical listening as "a code of cross-cultural conduct" guided by a "stance of openness" (1; see Wallace and Ewald on mutuality, close cognate to rhetorical listening). She is particularly interested in employing rhetorical listening to "hear some of our troubled identifications with gender and whiteness" and to resist narratives of blame and guilt these issues tend to generate among white students and teachers (16). To that end, Ratcliffe asks students to write a nonfiction essay on whiteness as it functions in the culture and in their own lives, an assignment designed to resist dominant efforts to make whiteness invisible and to ground writing in pedagogical listening, which requires students to "recognize resistance, analyze it, and when necessary, resist it" (133; see also Hinshaw).

This approach dovetails with Amy Winans' study of whiteness as learned affect ("Local Pedagogies"). At her predominantly white university in rural Pennsylvania, Winans practices a stance of openness both by acknowledging the embodied experiences that have shaped her students' views and misperceptions of racial differences and by teaching students to "question their own narratives, the stand-points from which they craft those narratives, and the consequences of those narratives" (258). Writing and self-analysis are the primary tools Winans uses to move students toward examining the "strong, often unstated emotions" bound up with race (263). As such, she foregrounds ideologies of whiteness and the emotions that both sustain and threaten to unhinge associated belief systems.

Winans' pedagogical approach is consistent with the view that emotions are relational and social rather than exclusively interiorized and private. Julie Lindquist begins "Class Affects, Classroom Affectations" from this premise. She focuses on the emotional dissonance that working-class students frequently experience in college classrooms, and the tendency of theorists to treat class as a largely rational experience. Drawing on Ratcliffe's theory of rhetorical listening, Lindquist writes that teachers can listen to students for help in figuring out "not only how, but who to be with them" (200). Like shape-shifter extraordinaire Frank Abnegale, Lindquist recommends that teachers "stag[e] empathy" to "enable students to locate their own affectively structured experiences of class within more integrated understandings of social structures and identity formation" (201, 188; see also Bean; Micciche, *Doing Emotion*).

CORPOREALITIES

Because feminist pedagogies have been vital to pedagogical models that fore-ground bodies, their representations and embodiments, I turn now to a discussion of two important pedagogical projects that attach primacy to bodies: queer and disability studies pedagogy. In addition to positioning bodies as a locus from which to develop praxis, both also address creating safe institutional spaces for students and teachers and for considering the value of "coming out" in the class-room. Brenda Jo Brueggemann and Debra Moddelmog note that while coming out has typically referred to "the act of making visible an identity that has been largely invisible, discredited, or actively ignored in the academy" and linked to LGBT people, it has also become important to those interested in "how and why to claim a disability identity rather than remaining silent about one's body and ability in the classroom" (210). Brueggemann and Moddelmog argue that, by revealing an "abject identity," the two fields have effectively "questioned the traditional expectations for the kind of knowledge that can be shared with students, thereby redrawing the lines between the intellectual and the personal, the sanctioned and the taboo, and the academic and the experiential" (210). Feminist, queer, and dis-ability studies pedagogies are interconnected and increasingly engaged with embodiment and performance (rather than identity-based views of the self), personal and political issues, social justice, pedagogy as a site for critical investigation of dominant ideology, and writing as a tool for exploring non-normative beliefs and practices.

Queer pedagogy has expanded feminist pedagogy by creating opportunities to (re)think gender and sexuality through robust frameworks and by emphasizing the value of doing so for *all* teachers and students. Jonathan Alexander (*Literacy*), for example, calls out the tendency among feminists to exclude sexuality from studies of difference. He notes that queer theory offers social justice advocates a framework for studying not just marginalized sexualities and identities but *"all sexualities in our culture as sites of identity, knowledge, and power"* (14, emphasis in original). Emphasis on the inclusive reach of queer pedagogy is a distinctive refrain in the literature. Amy Winans ("Queering") puts it like this: "Queer pedagogy challenges all students regardless of their sexual identities because it calls into question the process of normalizing dominant assumptions and beliefs, as it challenges instructors to question and to continue to test their own pedagogy" (106). While feminist pedagogy arguably has a similar effect, practitioners have not made this point as often or with as much shared commitment.

Performativity, particularly as articulated by feminist queer theorist Judith Butler, plays a significant role in queer pedagogies (see Gonçalves). For Butler, gender and sexuality are unstable categories that do not signify identity, which "is performatively constituted by the very 'expressions' that are said to be its results" (25). Gender and sexuality performances have the potential to both reproduce, through repetitious instantiations that solidify over time, *and* subvert dominant cultural norms. Reflecting some of this ambivalence is Harriet Malinowitz's groundbreaking study of gay and lesbian students' learning processes and interactions within discourse communities. She outlines a pedagogy that acknowledges both the alienating marginality gay students frequently occupy in college classrooms as well as the creative, desirable standpoints marginality makes possible, what Malinowitz calls "sharp vision that comes from living with friction and contradiction" (252). The differences these students embody, in other words, can be assets for the writing classroom, because they expose "modes of making meaning" and "systems of signification" that might otherwise go unchecked (43). Malinowitz argues convincingly that the implications of her study, which focuses on the conditions that affect gay and lesbian student writers' composing processes, are far-reaching. After all, writing and learning in a homophobic culture affects *all* students (xviii).

More recently, "queering" the writing classroom has received substantial treatment. Jennifer DiGrazia and Michel Boucher, for instance, introduce queer theory in an experimental writing course to help students reimagine identity categories. Others have expressed frustration with identity-based approaches to queering the classroom. Barclay Barrios finds such approaches limiting, offering instead a model of queer pedagogy in which students come to see themselves as agents in the public sphere able to contextualize identity "within a project of critical thinking about rights and responsibilities that benefits all students" (342). This "action horizon" pedagogy informs an assignment for which students explore online pride flags to understand how they function in sociopolitical contexts. Students were able to connect pride to nationalism, differential power relations in American culture, and other wide-spectrum issues not specifically focused on identity or queerness. Noting that one might wonder what's queer about this pedagogy, Barrio writes that an action horizon pedagogy is deliberately not "inherently queer." Rather than foregrounding queer *content*, Barrios harnesses for his teaching *methods* the complex ways of seeing and thinking that queer theory enables.

Offering another way to complicate identity-based pedagogy, Jonathan Alexander ("Transgender") strives for material, embodied understandings of gender and sexuality through the use of trans theories. To facilitate this, Alexander designs a "paired fiction writing" assignment for which students collaboratively write narratives in response to teacher prompts (59). Working with partners of the same gender, students compose "stories from what they perceived to be the experiences and assumptions of someone of a different gender," and then share their stories with the larger group and discuss their representations of gender (59). Alexander finds that the student narratives transcribe gender onto characters' bodies, creating "embodiments . . . slightly beyond the 'performative'; they seem more 'transsexual'—the literal crafting of the body to meet certain 'ideal types' of gender 'performance'" (69). The exercise puts into relief the multiple ways to be gendered and the construction of embodiments as political acts of "scrutiny, sculpting, and legibility" (70).

Viewing embodiments as social constructions is central to (some versions of) disability studies, a movement informed by feminist and queer theories of the body. In a description that shares principles with both feminism and queer theory, Cynthia Lewiecki-Wilson and Jay Dolmage contend that disability studies "decenters ableist and normative assumptions: it examines the history and subjugating power of 'the norm,' critiques the medicalization and objectification of bodies with differences, makes visible the invisible structuring power of ableism, and resists the standardization of learning that fits only a narrow range of people" (315). By noting that disability studies offers teachers and students opportunities for creating "inclusive and diverse" classrooms, Lewieki-Wilson and Dolmage put their project in conversation with feminists, queer theorists, multiculturalists, critical and community-engagement advocates, and, more recently, proponents of world Englishes, multiliteracies, and translingualism (i.e., Horner, NeCamp, and Donahue; Young and Martinez). Striving toward equity and inclusiveness, they note, will require changes to curriculum and pedagogy that foreground learning differences (317). This differs from what Julie Jung ("Textual") terms an accommodationist stance. Her analysis of composition readers that mainstream disability narratives leads her to conclude that such narratives "locat[e] the responsibility for adaptation within the 'abnormal' body rather than within the institutions and ideologies that construct it as such" (161).

James Wilson and Lewiecki-Wilson locate the responsibility for adaptation of classrooms with teachers and institutions rather than with students. Drawing from the architectural concept of universal design (UD), they contend that learning spaces should be configured both spatially and pedagogically for the widest possible access. Dolmage and Lewiecki-Wilson also address UD principles in teacher-training and faculty-development workshops "so that hopefully fewer and fewer teachers will proceed from exclusionary normative assumptions" (26). This is particularly important because, as Dolmage points out elsewhere ("Mapping"), "disability is always present. There is no perfect body or mind. And there is no normal body or mind" (17).

In an argument that echoes the expansive importance of queer pedagogy, Lewiecki-Wilson and Brenda Brueggemann contend that including disability content in classes is warranted because students with disabilities are in our classes and a focus on disability improves critical thinking for everyone (4). Pedagogical choices that acknowledge students with disabilities are those typical of a process-based writing classroom (small group workshops, student-teacher conferences, drafting, etc.) as well as audio response methods and Web-based access to class information (Lewiecki-Wilson and Brueggemann 7–8). In addition, teachers can address learning differences with their students and accommodate students' needs "by providing large-print lecture notes, sending notes by e-mail, or allowing students to audiotape classes" (Wilson and Lewiecki-Wilson 301). Teachers can also "adapt or codesign assignments" as needed and revise goals and strategies to help ensure student success (301). When it comes to physical accommodations, Wilson and Lewiecki-Wilson "offer to meet with students in alternate and more accessible . . . locations," particularly when university conditions like broken elevators create barriers to access (301). By acknowledging diverse learning styles and developing strategies for success based on students' differences, disability studies pedagogy suggests that teachers can practice a more inclusive social justice pedagogy (see Dunn).

✦✦✦✦

As a student in feminist classrooms, I felt excitement, fear, discomfort, anguish, utter confusion, and worry. I learned how to question much of what I took for granted, to see the world and my role in it freshly, and to read and write with renewed purpose. As a teacher, those classrooms taught me how to be patient, to risk a variety of standpoints, to approach learning holistically as a body/mind pursuit, and to model interrogatory, sometimes combative, modes of delivery. These classrooms also taught me that engaging with intersectional identity could be a portal through which to visualize, encourage, and act meaningfully toward more just social relations in and beyond classrooms. Feminist pedagogies do not strive for "quick, simple, and agreeable" student learning outcomes (Broad 4); depending on their slant, they might solicit active questioning; applied curiosity; rigorous critique of cultural, political, and emotional norms; collaborative knowledge-making activities; innovative forms of intellectual work; analyses and challenges to dominant culture; creative approaches to representing identity and embodiment; new media studies of intersectional identities; and so forth. Learning in feminist classrooms, as I can attest, is frequently emergent, less measurable than is perhaps fashionable in assessment talk. In a way, this inchoateness is its most powerful effect: These classrooms can make you feel differently about the world, creating alternative alignments with others and investments in wild, imaginative, hopeful, unorthodox futures.

BIBLIOGRAPHY

Alexander, Jonathan. *Literacy, Sexuality, Pedagogy: Theory and Practice for Composition Studies*. Logan: Utah State UP, 2008. Print.

_____. "Transgender Rhetorics: (Re)Composing Narratives of the Gendered Body." *CCC* 57.1 (2005): 45–82. Print.

Annas, Pamela J. "Style as Politics: A Feminist Approach to the Teaching of Writing." *College English* 47.4 (1985): 360–71. Print.

Ashton-Jones, Evelyn. "Collaboration, Conversation, and the Politics of Gender." *Feminine Principles and Women's Experience in American Composition and Rhetoric.* Ed. Louise Wetherbee Phelps and Janet Emig. Pittsburgh: U of Pittsburgh P, 1995. 5–26. Print.

Barrios, Barclay. "Of Flags: Online Queer Identities, Writing Classrooms, and Action Horizons." *Computers and Composition* 21.3 (2004): 341–61. Print.

Bauer, Dale M. "The Other 'F' Word: The Feminist in the Classroom." *College English* 52.4 (1990): 385–96. Print.

Baumgardner, Jennifer. *F'em: Goo Goo, Gaga, and Some Thoughts on Balls.* New York: Seal, 2011. Print.

Bean, Janet. "Manufacturing Emotions: Tactical Resistance in the Narratives of Working-Class Students." *A Way to Move: Rhetorics of Emotion and Composition Studies.* Ed. Dale Jacobs and Laura R. Micciche. Portsmouth: Boynton/Cook, 2003. 101–12. Print.

Belenky, Mary Field, Blythe McVicker Clinchy, Nancy Rule Goldberger, and Jill Mattuck Tarule, eds. *Women's Ways of Knowing: The Development of Self, Voice, and Mind.* New York: Basic Books, 1986. Print.

Berthoff, Ann. "Dialectical Notebooks and the Audit of Meaning." *The Journal Book.* Ed. Toby Fulwiler. Portsmouth: Boynton/Cook, 1987. 11–18. Print.

Blair, Kristine, and Pamela Takayoshi, eds. *Feminist Cyberscapes: Mapping Gendered Academic Spaces.* Stamford: Ablex Publishing, 1999. Print.

Boese, Christine. "A Virtual Locker Room in Classroom Chat Spaces: The Politics of Men as 'Other.'" Blair and Takayoshi 195–25. Print.

Boler, Megan. *Feeling Power: Emotions and Education.* New York: Routledge, 1999. Print.

Bolker, Joan. "Teaching Griselda to Write." *College English* 40.8 (1979): 906–908. Print.

Bridwell-Bowles, Lillian. "Discourse and Diversity: Experimental Writing within the Academy." *CCC* 43.3 (1992): 349–68. Print.

Broad, Bob. *What We Really Value: Beyond Rubrics in Teaching and Assessing Writing.* Logan: Utah State UP, 2003. Print.

Brody, Miriam. *Manly Writing: Gender, Rhetoric, and the Rise of Composition.* Carbondale: Southern Illinois UP, 1993. Print.

Brueggemann, Brenda Jo, and Debra A. Moddelmog. "Coming Out Pedagogy: Risking Identity in Language and Literature Classrooms." *The Teacher's Body: Embodiment, Authority, and Identity in the Academy.* Ed. Diane P. Freedman and Martha Stoddard Holmes. Albany: SUNY P, 2003. 209–233. Print.

Butler, Judith. *Gender Trouble: Feminism and the Subversion of Identity.* New York: Routledge, 1990. Print.

Chodorow, Nancy. *The Reproduction of Mothering: Psychoanalysis and the Sociology of Gender.* Berkeley: U of California P, 1978. Print.

Cooper, Marilyn M. "Rhetorical Agency as Emergent and Enacted." *CCC* 62.3 (2011): 420–49. Print.

Desmet, Christy. "Equivalent Students, Equitable Classrooms." Jarratt and Worsham 153–71. Print.

DiGrazia, Jennifer, and Michel Boucher. "Writing InQueeries: Bodies, Queer Theory, and an Experimental Writing Class." *Composition Studies* 33.2 (2005): 25–44. Print.

Dolmage, Jay. "Mapping Composition: Inviting Disability in the Front Door." Lewiecki-Wilson and Brueggemann 14–27. Print.

Dolmage, Jay, and Cynthia Lewiecki-Wilson. "Refiguring Rhetorica: Linking Feminist Rhetoric and Disability Studies." *Rhetorica in Motion: Feminist Rhetorical Methods and Methodologies.* Ed. Eileen E. Schell and K. J. Rawson. Pittsburgh: U of Pittsburgh P, 2010. 23–38. Print.

Dunn, Patricia A. *Talking, Sketching, Moving: Multiple Literacies in the Teaching of Writing.* Portsmouth: Boynton/Cook, 2001. Print.

Eichhorn, Jill, Sara Farris, Karen Hayes, Adriana Hernandez, Susan Jarratt, Karen Powers-Stubbs, and Marian Sciachitano. "A Symposium on Feminist Experiences in the Composition Classroom." *CCC* 43.3 (1992): 297–321. Print.

Flynn, Elizabeth A. "Composing as a Woman." *CCC* 39.4 (1988): 423–35. Print.

Gannett, Cinthia. *Gender and the Journal: Diaries and Academic Discourse.* Albany: SUNY P, 1992. Print.

Gere, Anne Ruggles. *Intimate Practices: Literacy and Cultural Work in U.S. Women's Clubs, 1880–1920.* Urbana: U of Illinois P, 1997.

Gil-Gomez, Ellen M. "The Practice of Piece-Making: Subject Positions in the Classroom." Jarratt and Worsham 198–205. Print.

Gilligan, Carol. *In a Different Voice: Psychological Theory and Women's Development.* Cambridge: Harvard UP, 1982. Print.

Glenn, Cheryl, and Krista Ratcliffe, eds. *Silence and Listening as Rhetorical Arts.* Carbondale: Southern Illinois UP, 2011. Print.

Gonçalves, Zan Meyer. *Sexuality and the Politics of Ethos in the Writing Classroom.* Carbondale: Southern Illinois UP, 2005. Print.

Graves, Heather Brodie. "Regrinding the Lens of Gender: Problematizing 'Writing as a Woman.'" *Written Communication* 10.2 (1993): 139–63. Print.

Greenbaum, Andrea. "'Bitch' Pedagogy: Agonistic Discourse and the Politics of Resistance." *Insurrections: Approaches to Resistance in Composition Studies.* Ed. Andrea Greenbaum. Albany: SUNY P, 2001. 151–68. Print.

Gruber, Sibylle. "'I, a Mestiza, Continually Walk out of One Culture into Another': Alba's Story." Blair and Takayoshi 105–32. Print.

Hesford, Wendy S. "Documenting Violations: Rhetorical Witnessing and the Spectacle of Distant Suffering as Pedagogy." Ronald and Ritchie 93–113. Print.

———. "'Ye Are Witnesses': Pedagogy and the Politics of Identity." Jarratt and Worsham 132–52. Print.

Hinshaw, Wendy Wolters. "Making Ourselves Vulnerable: A Feminist Pedagogy of Listening." Glenn and Ratcliffe 264–77. Print.

Hollis, Karyn L. "Feminism in Writing Workshops: A New Pedagogy." *CCC* 43.3 (1992): 340–48. Print.

hooks, bell. *Teaching to Transgress: Education as the Practice of Freedom.* New York: Routledge, 1994. Print.

Horner, Bruce, Samantha NeCamp, and Christiane Donahue. "Toward a Multilingual Composition Scholarship: From English Only to a Translingual Norm." *CCC* 63.2 (2011): 269–300. Print.

Howe, Florence. "Identity and Expression: A Writing Course for Women." *College English* 32.8 (1971): 863–71.

Irigaray, Luce. *This Sex Which Is Not One.* Trans. Catherine Porter. Ithaca: Cornell UP, 1985. Print.

Jarratt, Susan C. "Feminism and Composition: The Case for Conflict." *Contending with Words: Composition and Rhetoric in a Postmodern Age.* Ed. Patricia Harkin and John Schilb. New York: Modern Language Association, 1991. 105–23. Print.

_____. "Feminist Pedagogy." *A Guide to Composition Pedagogies*. Ed. Gary Tate, Amy Rupiper, and Kurt Schick. New York: Oxford UP, 2001. 113–31. Print.

Jarratt, Susan C, and Lynn Worsham, eds. *Feminism and Composition Studies: In Other Words*. New York: Modern Language Association, 1998. Print.

Johnson, Cheryl L. "Participatory Rhetoric and the Teacher as Racial/Gendered Subject." *College English* 56.4 (1994): 409–19. Print.

Jung, Julie. *Revisionary Rhetoric, Feminist Pedagogy, and Multigenre Texts*. Carbondale: Southern Illinois UP, 2005. Print.

_____. "Textual Mainstreaming and Rhetorics of Accommodation." *Rhetoric Review* 26.2 (2007): 160–78. Print.

LaDuc, Linda M. "Feminism and Power: The Pedagogical Implications of (Acknowledging) Plural Feminist Perspectives." *Pedagogy in the Age of Politics: Writing and Reading (in) the Academy*. Ed. Patricia A. Sullivan and Donna J. Qualley. Urbana: National Council of Teachers of English, 1994. 153–65. Print.

Lamb, Catherine E. "Beyond Argument in Feminist Composition." *CCC* 42.1 (1991): 11–24. Print.

LeCourt, Donna. "Writing (without) the Body: Gender and Power in Networked Discussion Groups." Blair and Takayoshi 153–75. Print.

LeCourt, Donna, and Luann Barnes. "Writing Multiplicity: Hypertext and Feminist Textual Politics." *Computers and Composition* 16.1 (1999): 55–71. Print.

Lewiecki-Wilson, Cynthia, and Brenda Jo Brueggemann, eds. *Disability and the Teaching of Writing: A Critical Sourcebook*. Boston: Bedford/St. Martin's, 2008. Print.

Lewiecki-Wilson, Cynthia, and Jay Dolmage. "Comment/Response: Neurodiversity." *College English* 70.3 (Jan 2008): 314–18. Print.

Lindquist, Julie. "Class Affects, Classroom Affectations: Working through the Paradoxes of Strategic Empathy." *College English* 67.2 (2004): 187–209. Print.

Logan, Shirley Wilson. *"We Are Coming": The Persuasive Discourse of Nineteenth-Century Black Women*. Carbondale: Southern Illinois UP, 1999. Print.

_____. "'When and Where I Enter': Race, Gender, and Composition Studies." Jarratt and Worsham 45–57. Print.

Looser, Devoney. "Composing as an 'Essentialist'?: New Directions for Feminist Composition Theories." *Rhetoric Review* 12.1 (1993): 54–69. Print.

Lugones, María. "Playfulness, 'World'-Traveling, and Loving Perception." *Women, Knowledge, and Reality: Explorations in Feminist Philosophy*. Ed. Ann Garry and Marilyn Pearsall. Boston: Unwin Hyman, 1989. 275–90.

Luke, Carmen, and Jennifer Gore, eds. *Feminisms and Critical Pedagogies*. New York: Routledge, 1992. Print.

Lu, Min-Zhan. "Reading and Writing Differences: The Problematic of Experience." Jarratt and Worsham 239–51. Print.

Lunsford, Andrea A., and Lisa Ede. "Collaborative Authorship and the Teaching of Writing." *Cardozo Arts & Entertainment Law Journal* 10.2 (1992): 681–702. Print.

_____. *Writing Together: Collaboration in Theory and Practice*. Boston: Bedford/St. Martin's, 2012. Print.

Malinowitz, Harriet. *Textual Orientations: Lesbian and Gay Students and the Making of Discourse Communities*. Portsmouth: Boynton/Cook, 1995. Print.

Marks, Elaine, and Isabelle de Courtivron, eds. *New French Feminisms*. New York: Schocken, 1981. Print.

McCracken, Nancy Mellin, and Bruce C. Appleby, eds. *Gender Issues in the Teaching of English*. Portsmouth: Boynton/Cook, 1992. Print.

Meyer, Sheree L. "Refusing to Play the Confidence Game: The Illusion of Mastery in the Reading/Writing of Texts." *College English* 55.1 (1993): 46–63. Print.

Micciche, Laura R. *Doing Emotion: Rhetoric, Writing, Teaching.* Portsmouth: Boynton/ Cook, 2007. Print.

_____. "Writing as Feminist Rhetorical Theory." *Rhetorica in Motion: Feminist Rhetorical Methods and Methodologies.* Ed. Eileen E. Schell and K. J. Rawson. Pittsburgh: U of Pittsburgh P, 2010. 173–88. Print.

Middleton, Joyce Irene. "Back to Basics; or, The Three R's: Race, Rhythm, and Rhetoric." *Teaching English in the Two-Year College* 21.2 (1994): 104–113. Print.

Miller, Susan. *Textual Carnivals: The Politics of Composition.* Carbondale: Southern Illinois UP, 1991.

Payne, Michelle. *Bodily Discourses: When Students Write about Abuse and Eating Disorders.* Portsmouth: Boynton/Cook, 2000. Print.

Peterson, Linda H. "Gender and the Autobiographical Essay: Research Perspectives, Pedagogical Practices." *CCC* 42.2 (1991): 170–83. Print.

Pigott, Margaret B. "Sexist Roadblocks in Inventing, Focusing, and Writing." *College English* 40.8 (1979): 922–27. Print.

Pough, Gwendolyn D. "Each One, Pull One": Womanist Rhetoric and Black Feminist Pedagogy in the Writing Classroom." *Teaching Rhetorica: Theory, Pedagogy, Practice.* Ed. Kate Ronald and Joy Ritchie. Portsmouth: Boynton/Cook, 2006. 66–81. Print.

Qualley, Donna J. "Being Two Places at Once: Feminism and the Development of 'Both/And' Perspectives." *Pedagogy in the Age of Politics: Writing and Reading (in) the Academy.* Eds. Patricia A. Sullivan and Donna J. Qualley. Urbana: National Council of Teachers of English, 1994. 25–42. Print.

Ratcliffe, Krista. "Re-Considering Essentialism for Feminist Composition Pedagogy: Adrienne Rich's 'Politics of Location' as a Theory of Writerly Agency." *The Writing Instructor* 13.2 (1994): 55–66. Print.

_____. *Rhetorical Listening: Identification, Gender, Whiteness.* Carbondale: Southern Illinois UP, 2005. Print.

Reichert, Pegeen. "A Contributing Listener and Other Composition Wives: Reading and Writing the Feminine Metaphors in Composition Studies." *JAC* 16.1 (1996): 141–57. Print.

Reynolds, Nedra. "Interrupting Our Way to Agency: Feminist Cultural Studies and Composition." Jarratt and Worsham 58–73.

Rhodes, Jacqueline. *Radical Feminism, Writing, and Critical Agency: From Manifesto to Modern.* Albany: SUNY P, 2005. Print.

Ritchie, Joy S. "Confronting the 'Essential' Problem: Reconnecting Feminist Theory and Pedagogy." *JAC* 10.2 (1990): 249–74. Print.

Ronald, Katharine, and Hephzibah Roskelly. "Listening as an Act of Composing." *Journal of Basic Writing* 5.2 (1986): 28–40. Print.

Royster, Jaqueline Jones. *Traces of a Stream: Literacy and Social Change among African American Women.* Pittburgh: U of Pittsburgh P, 2000. Print.

Rubin, Donnalee. *Gender Influences: Reading Student Texts.* Carbondale: Southern Illinois UP, 1993. Print.

Schell, Eileen E. "The Costs of Caring: 'Femininsm' and Contingent Women Workers in Composition Studies." Jarratt and Worsham 74–93. 1998. Print.

_____. *Gypsy Academics and Mother-Teachers: Gender, Contingent Labor, and Writing Instruction.* Portsmouth: Boynton/Cook, 1998. Print.

Special Issue of JAC. "The Human–Animal Encounter." 30.3–4 (2010): 405–869.

Spigelman, Candace. *Personally Speaking: Experience as Evidence in Academic Discourse.* Carbondale: Southern Illinois UP, 2004. Print.

Stygall, Gail. "Women and Language in the Collaborative Writing Classroom." Jarratt and Worsham 252–75. Print.

Sullivan, Laura L. "Wired Women Writing: Towards a Feminist Theorization of Hypertext." *Computers and Composition* 16.1 (1999): 25–54. Print.

Tompkins, Jane. "Fighting Words: Unlearning to Write the Critical Essay." *Georgia Review* 42.3 (1988): 585–90. Print.

Tuell, Cynthia. "Composition Teaching as 'Women's Work': Daughters, Handmaids, Whores, and Mothers." *Writing Ourselves into the Story: Unheard Voices from Composition Studies.* Ed. Sheryl I. Fontaine and Susan Hunter. Carbondale: Southern Illinois UP, 1993. 123–39. Print.

Wallace, David L., and Helen Rothschild Ewald. *Mutuality in the Rhetoric and Composition Classroom.* Carbondale: Southern Illinois UP, 2000. Print.

Wilson, James C., and Cynthia Lewiecki-Wilson. "Constructing a Third Space: Disability Studies, the Teaching of English, and Institutional Transformation." *Disability Studies: Enabling the Humanities.* Ed. Sharon L. Snyder, Brenda Jo Brueggemann, and Rosemarie Garland-Thomson. New York: Modern Language Association, 2002. 296–307. Print.

Winans, Amy E. "Local Pedagogies and Race: Interrogating White Safety in the Rural College Classroom." *College English* 67.3 (2005): 253–73. Print.

_____. "Queering Pedagogy in the English Classroom: Engaging with the Places Where Thinking Stops." *Pedagogy* 6.1 (2006): 103–122. Print.

Worsham, Lynn. "Going Postal: Pedagogic Violence and the Schooling of Emotion." *JAC* 18.2 (1998): 213–45. Print.

Young, Vershawn Ashanti, and Aja Y. Martinez, eds. *Code-Meshing as World English: Pedagogy, Policy, Performance.* Urbana: National Council of Teachers of English, 2011. Print.

Zawacki, Terry Myers. "Recomposing as a Woman—An Essay in Different Voices." *CCC* 43.1 (1992): 32–38. Print.

RESOURCES

For more on feminism broadly, see http://www.datehookup.com/content-feminism-resources.htm.

For information within the discipline, see http://www.ncte.org/college/briefs/feminism and http://www.ncte.org/cccc/committees/statusofwomen/bibliography.

Genre Pedagogies

Amy J. Devitt

Although every writing course uses genres—whether literary or academic, digital or hybrid, personal or public—courses based in genre pedagogy go well beyond asking students to write particular types of texts. Contemporary understandings see genres as rhetorical acts rather than textual conventions. In addition to romances, mysteries, or Petrarchan sonnets, genres encompass grocery lists, literacy narratives, and creative hypertexts. Since the 1980s, Composition Studies, and particularly Rhetorical Genre Studies (see Bazerman or Devitt, "Generalizing" for overviews), has redefined genre rhetorically, stemming primarily from Carolyn Miller's 1984 article "Genre as Social Action." Miller defines genres as "typified rhetorical actions based in recurrent situations" (159). In simple terms, genres become what they are because writers faced with similar writing tasks ("recurrent situations") make similar strategic choices ("rhetorical actions"); readers come to expect those similarities and come to recognize the rhetorical situation when they see its rhetorical traces ("typified"). When teachers make students aware of genres as rhetorical, they give access to strategies and choices as well as cultural expectations. Genres make rhetoric visible. Since all writing courses use genres—at least through the traditional, hybrid, or mediated genres that students write—all teachers should understand the rhetorical nature of genres and their potential to help students enact their goals. With genres understood as actions rather than forms, and as rhetorically meaningful rather than just conventional, writing teachers can use genre-based pedagogies to do much more than teach students the conventions of a few genres. If genres are rhetorical actions, then genre pedagogies can help students learn to act rhetorically; and if genres are based in situations, then genre pedagogies can use genres to help students perceive, understand, and even change situations.

COMBINING THREE APPROACHES TO TEACHING WRITING THROUGH GENRES

Ann M. Johns, in the Preface to her edited collection *Genre in the Classroom: Multiple Perspectives*, notes that there is no "one 'true way' to approach genre theory or practice" (i). Hence, this chapter is entitled "Genre Pedagogies," plural. Since the 1980s, genre theories relevant to composition have developed from multiple traditions distinct in theory and institutional practice (see Bawarshi and Reiff's *Genre: An Introduction to History, Theory, Research, and Pedagogy* for a full introduction to these bodies of scholarship). Because of their different student populations and cultural and institutional contexts, those traditions have emphasized different ways of teaching writing through genres. For our purposes in Composition Studies, though, we can draw relevant practices from each.

Drawing from and crossing multiple scholarly traditions, I define in this chapter three broad pedagogical approaches:

- teaching particular genres
- teaching genre awareness
- teaching genre critique

Rather than being mutually exclusive, these three approaches combine in effective college writing instruction. Their methods emphasize complementary goals:

- to give students access to and control of particular genres
- to help students learn how to learn any unfamiliar genres they might encounter, whatever the medium and context
- to help students see the cultural and ideological nature of genres in order to make their own choices and gain critical understanding

Each of these pedagogies has value and limitations for different students and settings. Although I begin here with teaching particular genres, most college composition courses would likely teach particular genres in order to lead students to genre awareness and critique. With the best of all three combined, as Richard Coe described in 1994, "we [teachers and students] are empowered by our increased control of each genre, by our increased ability to master unfamiliar genres, and by our increased understanding of how we can sublate the constraints of genre" ("Arousing" 186–187). Combining all three approaches creates a pedagogy that goes well beyond genre and supports lofty goals for our composition courses: to help students act rhetorically and consciously within and beyond the situations they will encounter throughout their lives.

TEACHING PARTICULAR GENRES

Perhaps the most obvious type of genre pedagogy, and the one with longest standing, is teaching students the particular genres they have to write. Sunny Hyon captures the essential rationale for teaching particular genres, especially as defined by Systemic Functional Linguistics (see Martin and Rose): "[Teach] students the formal, staged qualities of genres so that they can recognize these features in the texts that they read and use them in the texts that they write" ("Genre" 701).

The primary rationale for teaching particular genres is to let everyone play the game, to give everyone access to the rules and tricks. Whether Lisa Delpit arguing for African-American students in writing courses or Mary Macken-Horarik for aboriginal populations in Australian primary schools, the belief holds that "students at risk of school failure fare better within a visible curriculum" (Macken-Horarik 17). Australian scholars J. R. Martin and David Rose state the case even more strongly: "[A]ccess to the discursive resources of power is the democratic right of all citizens, and . . . it is our responsibility to make these resources available to all" (229). That rationale has been a long-standing one for teachers in many contexts who teach particular genres (though too often teaching only formal conventions), including new media and multimodal genres: You will need to write this research paper/argument/lab report/Web page; I will teach it to you and then you can write one of your own.

With genres redefined as powerful perceptual and embodied approaches to the world, though, choosing which genres to include in a writing course matters. Writing to secondary teachers, Deborah Dean notes some of the distinct stances and goals of popularly taught genres: "the genres we select favor and develop certain perspectives more than others. Repeatedly selecting five-paragraph essays promotes logic and distance. Repeatedly selecting personal narratives promotes individual and chronological perspectives. Consistently choosing work-related genres shows a valuing of one worldview, while consistently choosing poetry shows another" (39). Add in digital genres and electronic spaces, and deciding which genres to teach to students becomes even more fraught with epistemological as well as academic significance.

Because genre no longer means a simple classification of textual forms, too, teaching a particular genre no longer means teaching a static set of formal rules. One metaphor that I have found useful is Anne Freadman's metaphor of a game, especially, for this pedagogy, the rules of the game. Freadman suggests thinking of genre rules as "rules for play" (46, original emphasis) so that "knowing the rules is knowing how much play the rules allow and how to play with them" (47). Teaching the etiquette of a particular genre (57) involves teaching the context, time and place, audience's expectations, and strategies for working within the genre. Students writing blog posts, for example, investigate where blogs appear, who reads and writes them, what subjects and styles are usual, and how to attract readers. Later in this chapter, I include a critical view of working within the game, as Freadman and Medway in "Locating"; Luke; and others note that we shouldn't teach students to accept the rules of games as given, inflexible, and not open to critical action. As Freadman concludes, "Learning to write . . . is learning to appropriate and occupy a place in relation to other texts, learning to ensure that the other chap will play the appropriate game with you, and learning to secure a useful uptake: the rules for playing, the rules of play, and the tricks of the trade" (63–64).

Teaching the rules for playing particular genre games often leads to methods referred to as "explicit teaching," wherein the features and rules of the genre are taught directly. The most fully detailed and rationalized method is the "teaching-learning cycle" (see Feez for the historical development of this pedagogy). Although college writing teachers in North America generally have not adopted this specific method, it has been widely used in the Australian schools for which it was designed, may be more widely adopted in second-language pedagogies, and illustrates how one might make the textual regularities of a particular genre more fully transparent to students whose backgrounds require such explicit instruction. The teaching-learning cycle usually consists of three components, typically depicted in a wheel to indicate that the cycle repeats: modeling, joint negotiation of text, and independent construction of text (see Macken et al.'s diagram in Cope and Kalantzis 11). This method of explicit instruction begins with the teacher giving students model texts of the genre being learned. In a process simplified from Macken et al.'s wheel, the teacher leads students in analyzing these models for their social function, organizational structure, and linguistic features, drawing from Systemic Functional Linguistics discourse analysis. The class then works (with teacher as note-taker) to compose collaboratively a new text that conforms to the features of the genre being learned. In the third phase, each student individually drafts a new text within the genre. Ideally, the third phase includes "creative exploitation of genre and its possibilities," with students, for example, writing the genre in a different context.

While not always as fully specified as the teaching-learning cycle, other methods also analyze discourse to describe particular genres explicitly, especially for teachers of advanced second-language students within English for Specific Purposes (ESP, see Swales, *Genre*). In John Swales' analysis of rhetorical moves, for example, he describes introductions to research articles (which he later divided into theoretical and experimental articles [*Research* 208]) and their characteristic three moves: establishing a territory, establishing a niche, and occupying the niche (*Genre* 141), a set of moves that Brian Sutton has adapted to teaching the research paper genre in composition courses. In teaching such genres as the research article, dissertation, and research presentation, Swales teaches students to discover those rhetorical structures themselves, for effective instruction requires more than simple description. In her observation of two composition students, Elizabeth Wardle found that learning the conventions of a new genre required that the teacher have students "write the new genre, be told the conventions, and reaffirm those conventions among themselves [in peer workshops], hearing the conventions again, and revising" ("Understanding" 111). Some teachers follow ESP scholar Johns (*Text* 105–113) in having students conduct ethnographic research, including interviews and observations, to understand more fully the disciplinary-specific contexts of the genres within which they are learning to write. Teaching needed genres in discipline-specific courses, rather than college composition courses, can embed instruction in context more deeply so that, as Mary Soliday concludes from studying a Writing across the Curriculum program, "Giving skills flesh and bone . . . turns 'conventions' into meaningful rhetorical craft and opens up one pathway to a genre" (103). In all these methods of teaching particular genres, the goal is, in Aviva Freedman and Peter Medway's terms, "demystifying" genres (*Learning* 12). Freedman is perhaps the scholar most critical of explicit teaching, however, arguing that teachers cannot explicate any genre fully or out of the genre's authentic context, as I describe later in this chapter. She argues instead for situated learning of genres in their authentic settings.

Although teachers of college composition likely find the other two emphases—genre awareness and critique—more compatible with contemporary educational goals, all teachers confront students' questions about the genres they are writing. And, in all courses, teaching particular genres explicitly might well benefit students, especially those who are first-generation and second language writers (see Matsuda and Hammill's chapter, "Second Language Writing Pedagogy," in this volume). As is true of so much instructional practice, what serves well one student with particular needs would serve all students well. Ken Hyland argues that the advantages of such explicit genre-based instruction for second language writing teachers are that it is explicit, systematic, needs-based, supportive, empowering, critical, and consciousness-raising (10–11).

Many of the better practices for teaching a particular genre apply to all composition instruction: embedding the writing in meaningful tasks, not just classroom exercises; sequencing the activities and scaffolding learning; and not dominating during modeling and collaborative composing. Other issues arise more dramatically for this genre-based pedagogy. For second language teachers, Brian Paltridge notes several difficulties: identifying relevant contextual information, gathering authentic texts to serve as examples, minimizing the repressive effects of generic models, encouraging students' "individual voices" within a generic pattern, and recognizing that genres change, are embedded within another, and mix (122–124). Tony Dudley-Evans cautions against "teaching of a set of generalized moves" without confronting the particularities that a writer encounters in actual situations (235). Some reservations have in fact led to the development of the two other pedagogies I describe in this chapter, genre awareness and genre critique, including reservations that Hyland counters: that "genres are too complex and varied to be removed from their original contexts and taught in the artificial environment of the classroom" (16), that teaching genres reproduces "the dominant discourses of the powerful and the social relations that they construct and maintain" (18), and that genre teaching "inhibits writers' creativity and self-expression" (19). Although these methods of teaching particular genres may include awareness of context, critique, and creativity, in the end they emphasize textual production following explicitly learned formal features. Learning to write a credible text within a particular genre remains the primary goal.

Even teachers with different primary goals will need at times to address particular genres and will encounter some of the same benefits and difficulties. Though their motives and methods differ, all genre pedagogies use particular genres. Teachers whose goals are to teach genre awareness and genre critique, for example, use particular genres as examples to analyze, practice, critique, parody, and change. In the textbook I wrote with Mary Jo Reiff and Anis Bawarshi, *Scenes of Writing: Strategies for Composing with Genres,* which follows largely a pedagogy of critical genre awareness, we lead students through analyzing, critiquing, and writing academic analysis papers. We chose that particular genre not only because it matters to college writing but also because it can serve as an "antecedent genre," a genre that, once learned, can serve as a grounding for writing new genres with some similar elements (see Devitt, "Proposal"). To avoid prescription and formula, we included samples from student papers rather than ideal models; began with the academic cultural context rather than the features; interpreted all textual features for their rhetorical meaning; and used those features to reveal and question academic values and assumptions. For some who teach genre awareness and critique, assigning any particular genre is troubling. Kevin Brooks encourages critical genre awareness, including the "remediation" of existing genres, through a hypertext autobiography assignment in his advanced courses, but worries that "assigning a single genre, particularly in a class that has no explicit goal of teaching certain genres, may send students the message of rigid, formal requirements to be met, even if I try to emphasize the looseness of genre conventions" (349). In fact, Byron Hawk criticizes Brooks' use of creative hypertext as being focused on product and form (247), but he does so by assuming that genres equal form and that some compositions might be devoid of genre, two assumptions challenged by contemporary genre theory. Any view of genre as inhibiting creativity ignores that all creativity works within constraints (see Devitt, "Creative Boundaries: An Argument for Genre as Standard, Genre as Muse"). Better for students to see the constraints within which everyone works than to pretend that one can compose free of existing culture. Even in the media-rich environment of digital technology, and even with hybridity becoming a marker of digital composition, writers still create texts— alphabetic, visual, and digital—within a genre-rich environment of their existing genre repertoires. Hybrids combine, merge, or invent new genres not in a communicative void but out of previous as well as new rhetorical actions.

The challenge for all writing teachers is to use existing genres without reinforcing a rigid—or worse yet, inaccurate—formula for writing. Swales observes, "While there can be no doubt that a fair amount of poor explicit teaching takes place, that does not imply that all such teaching is necessarily poor" (*Research* 243). All teachers who use particular genres—and especially the teacher who wishes to give students access to particular genres through explicit instruction— can attend to the cautions of others and resist teaching formulaic models:

- Keep the genre contextualized, and remind students continually that their unique writing situations are more complicated than the situation described for a genre.
- Provide a wide range of models and demonstrate the variation within that genre, including perhaps across time or culture.
- Encourage students to vary from the models in their individual texts for rhetorical purposes.
- Require students to reflect on their practice using the abstract concepts and principles of genre to aid transfer to other genres.
- Critique the genre to be aware of its limitations and discourage mindless conformity.

TEACHING GENRE AWARENESS

Another genre pedagogy aims to give students access not to particular genres but to strategies for learning any genre in the future. As Anne Beaufort argues, we should be producing "students who are expert at learning writing skills in multiple social contexts, rather than expert writers in a single context" (8).

Bawarshi and Reiff, in their comprehensive *Genre: An Introduction to History, Theory, Research, and Pedagogy*, frame the problem as how to "teach genres in ways that maintain their complexity and their status as more than just typified rhetorical features" (189). Teaching genre awareness rather than genres is one answer to the problem, as I argued more fully in "A Proposal for Teaching Genre Awareness and Antecedent Genres" in my book *Writing Genres*. Genre awareness pedagogy treats genres as meaningful social actions, with formal features as the visible traces of shared perceptions. Analyzing the contexts and features of a new genre provides an inroad to understanding all genres. In an advanced writing course, for example, Coe sequences assignments so students write a brochure, a description of how to write an unfamiliar genre, and a political brief, with the result, he states, that "most students also come to understand generic structures as rhetorical strategies and genres as social processes" ("New" 207).

In the textbook I co-authored with Reiff and Bawarshi, we try to enact a genre awareness pedagogy that is also critical. For genre awareness, we teach students a process for understanding contextually any genre they might encounter:

- Collect samples of the genre.
- Identify the larger context and the rhetorical situation in which the genre is used (including setting, subject, participants, and purposes).
- Identify and describe patterns in the genre's features (including its content, rhetorical appeals, structure, format, and sentence and word style).
- Analyze what these patterns reveal about the situation and larger context (*Scenes* 93–94).

Simplified, the process helps students see what genres people read and write, where, in what forms, and why. Students apply this process to any genre that interests them. My students have used this basic process to analyze birth announcements, college viewbooks, nutrition labels, legal briefs, syllabi, scouting reports, children's picture books, movie reviews, lesson plans, an online meme, how-to websites, and dozens more. Coe, in "Teaching Genre as a Process," describes assigning students to analyze any genre and then write a "mini-manual" for others on how to write that genre (164). Irene Clark argues that students can be taught to analyze writing prompts so they may better understand their roles and respond to the prompts more effectively. For K-12 teachers, Sarah Andrew-Vaughan and Cathy Fleischer describe their Unfamiliar Genre Project, in which students select a genre they find challenging, collect and cull samples of the genre, keep a research journal, write their own version of the genre, write a reflective letter, and solicit response to their version from a parent or guardian (38). Like the teaching of particular genres, this teaching of genre awareness begins with samples of a genre and describes specific textual patterns, but the goal is understanding the context and rhetorical meaning of those patterns, rather than producing a similar text, and, as I've stated before, "the ends make all the difference" ("Proposal" 198). The goal is not to learn to write a better birth announcement or lesson plan, though that might be a result.

The goal is to learn to write any genre better through tackling it not as a neutral set of required conventions but as meaningful social action.

Genre awareness must highlight not just rhetorical and textual features but also social and ideological contexts. Like Johns, Reiff recommends having students do mini-ethnographies to "[cultivate] a consciousness of the rhetorical strategies used to carry out the social actions of a community, thus making that community more tangible and accessible" (46). In *Scenes of Writing* (Devitt, Reiff, and Bawarshi), we offer students Guidelines for Observing and Describing Scenes, including gaining access, taking observation notes, observing specific situations more closely, and only then identifying the genres within the scene by interviewing participants and noticing patterns and repeated actions. Text and context must interact in this genre pedagogy. The goal of the entire process is for students to write, to write with a fuller understanding of how, why, and for whom, and as they write to make deliberate decisions about their own purposes, motives, and strategies.

The benefits and limitations of a genre awareness approach to teaching writing differ from those of teaching particular genres, though the same general strictures of good practices apply. Because it uses genre samples for strategic analysis rather than models for mastery, this pedagogy teaches metacognitive reflection and explicitly discourages formulaic writing. Because students often gather the samples, though, teachers have less control over their quality and range; they must ensure that samples include sufficient variation, demonstrating the possibilities within a single genre. Since context is so important to understanding the meaning of the textual features, teachers generally have to spend time teaching students how to observe, interview, or otherwise gather contextual information. Still, teachers and students both must recognize that the context that anyone can describe is necessarily limited and can't capture the full complexity of writing situations. The move from analysis to writing requires particular attention, as it does in any writing course that emphasizes rhetorical analysis. Especially tricky can be deciding what genres students should write. If writing the genre being analyzed, students might retreat to seeing the samples as models; so additional writing should call special attention to their unique situations and choices. Students can write improved or resituated versions of that genre, parodies, hybrids, or, perhaps most common, rhetorical analyses of the genre (which require applying their genre awareness skills to the rhetorical analysis genre they need to write). Coe emphasizes letting students "appreciate genre as choice" ("New" 205), so students can choose their situations and genres. Teachers must emphasize that students are learning strategies to apply later when they are immersed in contexts other than the writing classroom. Essential to the argument for teaching genre awareness rather than particular genres is the notion that genre awareness can help students transfer their knowledge to other writing tasks and contexts (a topic I address more fully later), so teachers must assign frequent reflective writing to encourage metacognitive awareness.

I argue in "Proposal" that genre awareness may "[arm] students against rigid prescriptivism as well as against hidden ideologies" (212). For students in college writing courses, a successful genre awareness pedagogy that understands how to help students transfer their knowledge can create lifelong learners who can write strategically and knowingly in any context they might encounter.

TEACHING GENRE CRITIQUE

Rather than teaching students particular genres or strategies for learning new genres, genre critique teaches students to think critically about existing genres and their cultures. In the introductions to their two 1994 collections, *Learning and Teaching Genre* and *Genre and the New Rhetoric*, Aviva Freedman and Peter Medway tell us in their section headings of "The Need to Criticize Genres" and head us "Toward More Critical Genre Studies" that would enfranchise students not just by giving them access to genres but by enabling them to subvert, legitimize, or revise genres ("Locating" 15). Sixteen years later, Bawarshi and Reiff review the work on teaching critical awareness of genre and conclude that "genre analysis can move beyond teaching academic forms to teaching purposeful rhetorical uptakes for social action and can enable students to engage more critically in situated action" (*Genre* 202).

Although teaching particular genres gives students knowledge of a genre and its contexts that they could critique, two of that pedagogy's major proponents, J. R. Martin and David Rose, define their practice as "interventionist rather than critical" (20). They seek to address inequalities of access to those genres of power, not to critique the genres themselves. Another proponent, Feez, asserts that "Through making the literacy practices and literacy demands of different types of texts in English-speaking cultures more visible, genre pedagogy also makes more visible the values and worldviews embodied in those texts" (57). For most genre critics, visibility is not enough. Commenting on early versions of explicit genre teaching, Bill Green and Allison Lee argue that students need to "acquire a critical dimension to literacy, one which allows them to adopt various authoritative positions within a discourse or subject area field, yet not to assume 'identity' with these positions" (221).

Those advocating genre awareness typically support genre critique as well, and genre awareness might be necessary for genre critique. "[W]e need to teach them the process of genre analysis," Coe argues, "so they can think critically about genres" ("Teaching" 163). Some argue that raising students' rhetorical awareness of genres alone enhances their critical awareness: Swales comments, "We are never free of our institutional roles, but becoming more aware of their constraints somehow loosens their grip" (*Research* 252). Coe asserts that understanding the rationale for generic structures is a means for overthrowing the "tyranny of genre" ("Teaching" 161). Viewing genres as social actions, not formal rules, already reframes genre "as a social strategy historically located in a network of power relations in particular institutional sites and cultural fields," as Allan Luke details in his critique of the notion of "genres of power" (333). In their collection on *The Rhetoric and Ideology of Genre*, Coe, Lorelei Lingard, and Tatiana Teslenko include Coe and Freedman's list of "critical, meta-rhetorical questions" to help students discern the ideological import of genres:

- What sorts of communication does the genre encourage, what sorts does it constrain against?

- Who can—and who cannot—use this genre? Does it empower some people while silencing others?
- Are its effects dysfunctional beyond their immediate context?
- What values and beliefs are instantiated within this set of practices?
- What are the political and ethical implications of the rhetorical situation constructed, persona embodied, audience invoked and context of situation assumed by a particular genre? ("Introduction" 6–7).

Whether teaching particular genres or genre awareness, instructors need, as Bawarshi and Reiff write, "to be critical in their uses of genre and to teach this critical awareness to students" (*Genre* 197).

Teaching strategies for genre critique include, from Coe, having students "reinvent a genre" by tackling a task with purposes, audiences, and contexts of situation similar to an existing genre; and teaching students multiple genres with similar functions so they see generic choices ("Teaching" 163–165). Such practices lead students "to notice genres, to make sense of genres, even to renovate genres" ("Teaching" 165). Within *Scenes of Writing*, too, we (Devitt, Reiff, and Bawarshi) worked to incorporate critique alongside analysis, though less successfully than we might achieve today. In one activity, for example, my co-authors and I ask students to analyze the course syllabi they received at the start of the semester, looking for expectations and roles, and then to critique the syllabus genre for what it enables and limits, for both teachers and students. Another activity asks students to rewrite the genre, to work in groups to create a new syllabus that violates those expectations in some ways, perhaps by reconceiving the appropriate roles for students or creating it in a wiki. Seeing that the syllabus could be different opens students' eyes to ways that the current syllabus genre defines and constrains their behavior and actions as they take up the expected role of student.

The very choice of what we assign students to write can promote or discourage genre critique, of course. Brad Peters argues that teachers should allow students to write antigenres, when the urge arises, "helping them rather than resisting their experiments" (214). Peters also teaches what he calls the genres of autobiography, cultural critique, and biography in critical ways, saying that he wants to help students "to acquire—rather than acquiesce to—the grammar of a genre" (202). Genres from times and cultures not their own, like war posters, remove students from familiar settings and make them more capable of critique, Heather Bastian argues. Calling students' attention to hybrid, blurred, or emerging genres can help students gain a critical stance toward genres more fully normalized. Brooks argues that his pedagogy for creative hypertexts applies to "whatever blurred or evolving genres students are inspired by and see fit to explore" (338). Brooks's three-stage genre-based pedagogy for creative hypertexts (and presumably for other blurred or evolving genres) involves

- Having students understand that all texts, including hypertexts, are rooted in one or more genres.
- Having students choose a genre that will meet their communicative needs.

- Encouraging students to reinvent genres, to play with conventions, and to play with one or two specific texts as a way of engaging a genre (343–344).

Genre is especially helpful for Web-based and hypertext instruction, he argues, because it enables teachers to talk about more than form and structure and "provides a succinct, useful way of talking about the interplay of looseness and structure, the combination of the familiar and new" (341).

A critical perspective on genres can be used to critique not just the genre but also the society or culture within which the genre is embedded. Viewing genres as "cultural artefacts" (Miller, "Rhetorical" 69) lets genres offer insight into cultures, as scholars have demonstrated by examining our own academic culture through the lens of its genres. Summer Smith analyzed "The Genre of the End Comment," delineating the habitual moves that teachers make (for example, positive comment, then negative evaluation) and arguing that this genre's stability constrains teachers' ability to comment on student papers effectively. Bawarshi analyzed the common classroom genres of syllabus, writing prompt, and student essay for their roles as sites of invention in which students and teachers position themselves. These and other critiques demonstrate that genre can, as Luke prescribes, focus attention on the "social identities and power relations" in particular sites as their "primary objects of analysis, critique, and study" (333).

Simply explicating the "social identities and power relations" underlying a genre is not sufficient for Luke and others who wish to transform genres and their institutions. Pedagogies of genre critique may, then, ask students to rewrite genres to enable differences (as the assignment to rewrite the syllabus might exemplify), parody the genres (Swales' student writes a parody of a Research Article introduction, *Research* 251), or write for social action. Bawarshi and Reiff view Bruce McComiskey's paired assignments as critical genre pedagogy because the assignment leads students, after analyzing and critiquing "the cultural and social values encoded in the genre," to "produce new genres or genres that encode alternative values for the purpose of intervening" (Bawarshi and Reiff, *Genre* 201). A similar assignment common to my classes after students analyze and critique a genre is to write something that might effect change in that genre. Students have written letters to advertisers asking them to change their form of advertising, to newspapers asking them to allow more variation in wedding announcements, and to university officials asking them to change the depiction of their majors in brochures. None of these actions, of course, addresses the complexity or reality of power in our worlds. Luke would certainly not find these adequate ways of subverting and critiquing institutional sites. Rather, they merely create an opening for students to realize that what has always been is not what must always be.

Carolyn Miller notes that "what we learn when we learn a genre is not just a pattern of forms or even a method of achieving our own ends. We learn, more importantly, what ends we may have" ("Genre" 165). Helping students perceive the significance of—even challenge and resist—those ends is a primary goal of a pedagogy of genre critique, with benefits and limitations comparable to those of all critical pedagogies, addressed well by Ann George's chapter in this volume. Learning to become aware of and critique genres may be especially powerful. As routinized and typified actions, genres may be especially difficult—and especially important—ideological nuts to crack.

HOW TO MAKE GENRE PEDAGOGIES WORK

If a teacher wishes to know only whether students have developed competency in producing a text of a particular genre in a classroom setting, then genre pedagogies all have the advantages of making formal criteria explicit and hence easily assessable. Such assessment might be sufficient for those teaching student populations who lack the background knowledge needed to acquire particular genres in context or through the more abstract approach of genre awareness (see Hyland for a fuller discussion of such classroom-based assessment for second-language writing). The question of whether those students go on to have access not just to genres but also to higher education, higher paying jobs, or other markers of longer term success is a question open to research.

For most teachers within contemporary Composition Studies, the assessment question is not whether students can demonstrate that they learned the conventions of a genre or how to produce texts like the models they have seen. The goal is not to enable students to produce competent literacy narratives, rhetorical analyses, or creative hypertexts. Rather, studying and producing those genres serve other ends, whether increasing rhetorical flexibility, writing more effectively within unfamiliar writing situations or within new technologies, or developing critical thinking and effecting change. As is true for virtually all writing pedagogies, the assessment question instead becomes whether students can use their knowledge and skills in other contexts. Students in our courses may successfully write in multiple genres, analyze unfamiliar genres, and explicate the link between textual and contextual features, but does that knowledge transfer to other writing situations? And how can teachers help students make those connections and transfer their genre knowledge?

Even if teachers can successfully teach students a genre that might be useful in the future, what they can teach will differ from what students need to learn. Freedman has presented an elaborated argument against the effectiveness of explicitly teaching particular genres. Based on research into language acquisition, Freedman argues that teaching a particular genre in order to acquire that genre "is unnecessary, for the most part not even possible, and where possible not useful (except during editing, for a limited number of transparent features)" (202). Instead, she advocates situated learning, acquiring a genre from expert insiders in the context and at the time it is needed. Most important for teachers to note, perhaps, is Freedman's warning that "explicit teaching may be dangerous, if the instructor is an outsider or alternatively is an insider with inaccurate representations of the genre," or if the students are ones who overgeneralize or focus too heavily on form (206). To my earlier list of cautions for teachers teaching particular genres, I need to add two more: know your stuff, and know your students.

Direct research into the effectiveness of genre pedagogies is still somewhat limited (see Christine M. Tardy for a comprehensive review of both first- and second-language genre learning). Studying the effectiveness of explicit genre instruction for second-language students' reading of texts, Hyon found that "a short genre-based course" was most effective for raising students' awareness of "rhetorical elements that correspond to readily identifiable linguistic cues" but less effective for more variable and discipline-specific features ("Genre and ESL Reading" 136). Hyon concludes, "knowledge gained about specific genres develops rhetorical sensitivity that students can apply to processing various texts" (137). Catherine McDonald conducted an ethnographic study of students in a writing course using a genre awareness pedagogy and concludes that students could "translate [their genre awareness] into an accelerated ability to discern new rhetorical expectations and to learn how to approximate effective writing" (227–228), even reportedly years after taking the course. The students who made best use of their genre knowledge to handle new writing tasks were the ones, McDonald states, who understood the ideological nature of genres, supporting a pedagogy of genre critique along with genre awareness.

Not all research has found such smooth transfer of genre knowledge, so much so that Elizabeth Wardle argues that first-year writing courses should be redesigned either to teach students to transfer such knowledge or to teach students *about* writing, giving up on teaching students *to* write ("Mutt Genres"). Reiff and Bawarshi conducted cross-institutional research to investigate what prior genre knowledge students carried with them into first-year composition and how they were able to transfer that knowledge into new writing contexts. They found that students sometimes acted as "boundary crossers" who "repurposed and reimagined their prior genre knowledge for use in new contexts," but other students acted as "boundary guarders" who kept genres in distinct domains and tended to import whole genres rather than strategies when faced with new writing tasks (325). Natasha Artemeva and Janna Fox studied engineering students in engineering communication courses and found general inability to transfer their prior genre knowledge. Students largely knew the features of the assigned genre but did not recall or use that knowledge when producing their own texts. The authors discovered that students needed to have experience writing the expected genre, not just to know it analytically; that even prior writing experience might not be recalled without first raising students' genre awareness; and that teachers needed to alert students to the need to transfer their knowledge. Elizabeth Wardle's longitudinal study, following seven students from an honors first-year composition course, found that the one skill that the students did use consistently was meta-awareness of writing, language, and rhetorical strategies ("Understanding").

These researchers and others have suggested ways teachers can help students transfer their prior and newly acquired genre knowledge. Many suggestions involve developing students' metacognition. Artemeva and Fox recommend using a diagnostic assessment at the beginning of the course both to learn of students' competencies and to start them thinking about the need to use antecedent genre knowledge. To encourage students to cross boundaries and use their prior genre knowledge in new situations, Reiff and Bawarshi recommend that teachers, when giving an assignment, ask students to reflect: "first ask students to tell us what they think the task is asking them to do, what it is reminding them of, and what prior resources they feel inclined to draw on in completing the task" to cue their prior knowledge (332). They also advise that teachers give assignments that "invite students to use a wider range of their discursive resources" and "reflect afterward on the experience of crossing between genres and domains" (332). Rebecca S. Nowacek, in her extensive study of transfer as a rhetorical act, emphasizes the need to "[get] students to question how the genre knowledge they already possess might apply or need to be reconstructed in order to provide an optimal framework for their work in other classes" (133). She recommends "a series of reflective assignments" for first-year composition courses that would help students see genre knowledge "as a flexible construct that might be applied but might also be reconstructed" (133). Her assignments include having students create taxonomies of their own types of writing and compare theirs to those of other students at the beginning of the semester; articulate aloud in conference the connections between what they've written in one paper and what they've written in other contexts; and end the semester by placing the writing done that semester into the taxonomy they created at the beginning, noting especially the writing that doesn't fit in neatly (133–135).

In her own research into transfer and her case study of a student "Tim" as he traverses first-year writing, history courses, engineering courses, and the engineering workplace, Beaufort concludes that teachers should follow three principles to help students acquire and transfer multiple knowledges, including genre awareness:

1. Teach learners to frame specific problems and learnings into more abstract principles that can be applied to new situations (177).
2. Give students numerous opportunities to apply abstract concepts in different social contexts (180).
3. Teach the practice of mindfulness, or metacognition, to facilitate positive transfer of learning (182).

Whatever genres they assign, whichever genre pedagogy they emphasize, teachers should consider their end goals and help students move their knowledge beyond the writing classroom.

CONCLUSION

All genre-based pedagogies for composition courses should incorporate all three approaches—particular genres, genre awareness, and genre critique. To avoid formulaic writing and enable transfer, teachers of particular genres must bring a larger metacognitive awareness and a critical stance on existing, dominant discourses. To make abstractions concrete and avoid accommodation, teachers of genre awareness must analyze particular genres and move to critique the values and assumptions discovered. To provide alternative genres and establish the basis for genres as ideological, teachers of genre critique must help students discover particular hybrids, parodies, and antigenres and raise awareness of genres' social nature. How any given genre-based pedagogy incorporates the three, though, depends on the teachers' larger goals and the institutional setting, including especially the nature of the student body and their prior genre knowledge.

Understood as social acts within dynamic worlds, genres make rhetoric and culture visible. Helping students create their own unique meanings in the midst of shared social understanding is the heart of all genre pedagogies.

BIBLIOGRAPHY

Andrew-Vaughan, Sarah, and Cathy Fleischer. "Researching Writing: The Unfamiliar-Genre Research Project." *The English Journal* 95.4 (2006): 36–42. Print.

Artemeva, Natasha, and Janna Fox. "Awareness Versus Production: Probing Students' Antecedent Genre Knowledge." *Journal of Business and Technical Communication* 24.4 (2010): 476–515. Web. 8 July 2012.

Bastian, Heather. "The Genre Effect: Exploring the Unfamiliar." *Composition Studies* 38.1 (Spring 2010): 27–49. Print.

Bawarshi, Anis. *Genre and the Invention of the Writer: Reconsidering the Place of Invention in Composition.* 1st ed. Logan: Utah State UP, 2003. Print.

Bawarshi, Anis S., and Mary Jo Reiff. *Genre: An Introduction to History, Theory, Research, and Pedagogy.* West Lafayette: Parlor P/Fort Collins: WAC Clearinghouse, 2010. Print. Reference Guides to Rhetoric and Composition.

Bazerman, Charles. "The Life of Genre, the Life in the Classroom." *Genre and Writing: Issues, Arguments, Alternatives.* Ed. Wendy Bishop and Hans Ostrom. Portsmouth: Boynton/Cook, 1997. 19–26. Print.

Beaufort, Anne. *College Writing and Beyond: A New Framework for University Writing Instruction.* Logan: Utah State UP, 2007. Print.

Brooks, Kevin. "Reading, Writing, and Teaching Creative Hypertext: A Genre-Based Pedagogy." *Pedagogy* 2.3 (2002): 337–56. Web. 17 May 2012.

Clark, Irene. "A Genre Approach to Writing Assignments." *Composition Forum* 14.2 (2005): n.p. Web. 18 June 2012.

Coe, Richard M. "'An Arousing and Fulfilment of Desires': The Rhetoric of Genre in the Process Era—and Beyond." Freedman and Medway, *Genre* 181–90.

———. "The New Rhetoric of Genre: Writing Political Briefs." *Genre in the Classroom: Multiple Perspectives.* Mahwah: L. Erlbaum, 2002. 197–210. Print.

———. "Teaching Genre as a Process." Freedman and Medway, *Learning* 157–69.

Coe, Richard M., Lorelei Lingard, and Tatiana Teslenko, eds. *The Rhetoric and Ideology of Genre: Strategies for Stability and Change.* Cresskill: Hampton P, 2002. Print.

Cope, Bill, and Mary Kalantzis. "Introduction: How a Genre Approach to Literacy Can Transform the Way Writing Is Taught." *The Powers of Literacy: A Genre Approach to Teaching Writing.* Ed. Bill Cope and Mary Kalantzis. Pittsburgh: U of Pittsburgh P, 1993. 1–21. Print.

Dean, Deborah. *Genre Theory: Teaching, Writing, and Being.* Urbana: National Council of Teachers of English, 2008. Print.

Delpit, Lisa. *Other People's Children: Cultural Conflict in the Classroom.* 1st ed. New York: New P, 1995. Print.

Devitt, Amy J. "Creative Boundaries: An Argument for Genre as Standard, Genre as Muse." Devitt, *Writing Genres* 137–62.

_____. "Generalizing about Genre: New Conceptions of an Old Concept." *College Composition and Communication* 44.4 (1993): 573–86. Print.

_____. "A Proposal for Teaching Genre Awareness and Antecedent Genres." Devitt, *Writing Genres* 191–213.

_____. *Writing Genres.* Carbondale: Southern Illinois UP, 2004. Print.

Devitt, Amy, Mary Jo Reiff, and Anis Bawarshi. *Scenes of Writing: Strategies for Composing with Genres.* New York: Longman, 2004. Print.

Dudley-Evans, Tony. "The Teaching of the Academic Essay: Is a Genre Approach Possible?" Johns, *Genre in the Classroom* 225–35.

Feez, Susan. "Heritage and Innovation in Second Language Education." Johns, *Genre* 43–69.

Freadman, Anne. "Anyone for Tennis?" Freedman and Medway, *Genre* 43–66.

Freedman, Aviva. "'Do as I Say': The Relationship between Teaching and Learning New Genres." Freedman and Medway, *Genre* 191–210.

Freedman, Aviva, and Peter Medway. "Locating Genre Studies: Antecedents and Prospects." Freedman and Medway, *Genre* 1–20.

Freedman, Aviva, and Peter Medway, eds. *Genre and the New Rhetoric.* London: Taylor & Francis, 1994. Print.

_____. *Learning and Teaching Genre.* Portsmouth: Boynton/Cook, 1994. Print.

Green, Bill, and Alison Lee. "Writing Geography: Literacy, Identity, and Schooling." Freedman and Medway, *Learning* 207–224.

Hawk, Byron. *A Counter-History of Composition: Toward Methodologies of Complexity.* Pittsburgh: U of Pittsburgh P, 2007.

Hyland, Ken. *Genre and Second Language Writing.* Ann Arbor: U of Michigan P, 2004. Print.

Hyon, Sunny. "Genre in Three Traditions: Implications for ESL." *TESOL Quarterly* 30.4 (1996): 693–722. Print.

_____. "Genre and ESL Reading: A Classroom Study." Johns, *Genre* 121–41.

Johns, Ann M. *Genre in the Classroom: Multiple Perspectives.* Mahwah: Erlbaum, 2002. Print.

_____. "Preface." Johns, *Genre.*

_____. *Text, Role and Context: Developing Academic Literacies.* New York: Cambridge UP, 1997. Print.

Luke, Allan. "Genres of Power? Literacy Education and the Production of Capital." *Literacy in Society.* Ed. Ruqaiya Hasan and Geoffrey Williams. London: Longman, 1996. 308–338. Print.

Macken-Horarik, Mary. "'Something to Shoot For'": A Systemic Functional Approach to Teaching Genre in Secondary School Science." Johns, *Genre* 17–42.

Martin, J. R., and David Rose. *Genre Relations: Mapping Culture.* London: Equinox Publishing, 2008. Print.

McDonald, Catherine. "The Question of Transferability: What Students Take Away from Writing Instruction." Diss., U of Washington, 2006. Web.

Miller, Carolyn. "Genre as Social Action." *Quarterly Journal of Speech* 70.2 (1984): 151–67. Print.

_____. "Rhetorical Community: The Cultural Basis of Genre." Freedman and Medway, *Genre* 67–78.

Nowacek, Rebecca S. *Agents of Integration: Understanding Transfer as a Rhetorical Act.* Carbondale: Southern Illinois UP, 2011. Print.

Paltridge, Brian. *Genre and the Language Learning Classroom.* Ann Arbor: U of Michigan P, 2001. Print.

Peters, Brad. "Genre, Antigenre, and Reinventing the Forms of Conceptualization." *Genre and Writing: Issues, Arguments, Alternatives.* Ed. Wendy Bishop and Hans Ostrom. Portsmouth: Boynton/Cook, 1997. 199–214. Print.

Reiff, Mary Jo. "Mediating Materiality and Discursivity: Critical Ethnography as Meta-Generic Learning." *Ethnography Unbound: From Theory Shock to Critical Praxis.* Ed. Stephen G. Brown and Sidney I. Dobrin. New York: SUNY P, 2004. 35–51. Print.

Reiff, Mary Jo, and Anis Bawarshi. "Tracing Discursive Resources: How Students Use Prior Genre Knowledge to Negotiate New Writing Contexts in First-Year Composition." *Written Communication* 28.3 (2011): 312–37. Web. 8 July 2012.

Smith, Summer. "The Genre of the End Comment: Conventions in Teacher Responses to Student Writing." *College Composition and Communication* 48.2 (1997): 249–68. Web. 8 July 2012.

Soliday, Mary. *Everyday Genres: Writing Assignments across the Disciplines.* SIU P, 2011. Print.

Sutton, Brian. "Swales's 'Moves' and the Research Paper Assignment." *Teaching English in the Two-Year College* 27.4 (2000): 446–51. Print.

Swales, John M. *Genre Analysis: English in Academic and Research Settings.* New York: Cambridge UP, 1990. Print. The Cambridge Applied Linguistics Series.

_____. *Research Genres: Explorations and Applications.* New York: Cambridge UP, 2004. Print. The Cambridge Applied Linguistics Series.

Tardy, Christine M. "Researching First and Second Language Genre Learning: A Comparative Review and a Look Ahead." *Journal of Second Language Writing* 15.2 (2006): 79–101. Print.

Wardle, Elizabeth. "Understanding 'Transfer' from FYC: Preliminary Results from a Longitudinal Study." *WPA: Writing Program Administration* 31.1–2 (2007): 65–85. Print.

_____. "'Mutt Genres' and the Goal of FYC: Can We Help Students Write the Genres of the University?" *College Composition and Communication* 60.4 (2009): 765–89. *JSTOR.* Web. 22 Feb. 2013.

Literature and Composition Pedagogy

Christine Farris

In 1998, Sharon Crowley in *Composition in the University* summed up the view of most English disciplinary historians: that "composition gives literary studies something to define itself against" (2). The other side of the coin, of course, is that literature (or not-literature) has been, for over a century, the key factor shaping the identity and practices of Composition Studies. The relation of literature to composition is central to pedagogical and political issues in English Studies.

Boundary disputes between literature and composition can be traced as far back as the revision of the classical trivium (grammar, rhetoric, and logic), study intended to develop intellectual rather than occupational abilities. The tension between literary knowledge and literacy skills figures prominently in the rise of English as a discipline and in perpetual reconsiderations of the purpose of a college education. Binaries abound and continue to shape what is at stake in the lit/comp relationship: (1) the centrality of writing over reading in first-year English courses; (2) hierarchy and labor in departments where composition instruction makes large-scale literary specialization possible; and (3) a growing fear that down-sized English departments will be reduced to service courses as a consequence of a competitive education marketplace that pits vocationalism against a liberal arts life of the mind. Nevertheless, what literature and composition specialists share in their understanding of reading and writing as complex cultural practices can reshape introductory English courses and their purpose in the college curriculum, provided we do not lose sight of our students in attending to our professional and disciplinary needs.

Institutional and economic shifts that pose new challenges to the relationship between composition and literature were just coming over the horizon six years ago, when my literature colleague Judith Anderson and I edited *Integrating Literature and Writing Instruction*, a collection that examines successful pairings of literature and composition in courses centered on textual analysis and production applicable to students' work across the curriculum. After MLA published our book, a friend from another university, who had not yet read it, inquired as to its content and the gist of our argument. A literature colleague of his had mentioned that apparently it was okay to teach literature again in composition. For a minute, I felt like Fredo in *The Godfather* when his brother, Michael Corleone, tells him not to ever take sides with anyone against the Family. What in the history and tradition of composition explains my friend's incredulity and the necessity of my defense? While the new generation of English MAs and PhDs in the current job market may be striking a balance in their attention to literature and writing, it is important to know something of the history of that separation. When we choose to use literature in a writing course, we need to attend to what purpose it serves, and why others might applaud or contest its use.

Composition's one-hundred-year association with a required set of adisciplinary skills has made it something literary specialists try to move up and out of as soon as possible. Historically, in a course thought to have no "content," originally designed to address gaps in secondary education, ideas in literary works served as prompts, models, and jumping-off points for the writing of daily or weekly "themes." Traces of this tradition remain, most often where there is a second required course focused on writing about literature. The rise of Composition Studies as a discipline concerned with the ways in which literacy is context-dependent, has, thankfully, resulted in a more complex use of texts in first-year courses of all types. Nevertheless, rhetoric and composition specialists in many English departments have fought an uphill battle in arguing for the legitimacy of their field, despite a body of work linking composition studies and literary studies. Winifred Horner's edited collection, *Composition and Literature: Bridging the Gap* in 1983, includes essays by J. Hillis Miller, Wayne Booth, and E. D. Hirsch, variously making the case for reading and writing as mutual acts of interpretation.

John Clifford and John Schilb, in *Writing Theory and Critical Theory,* a 1994 follow-up to their 1985 essay "Composition Theory and Literary Theory," also attempt to bridge the lit/comp gap, in a collection of essays utilizing philosophical schools of thought that transcend literary theory and inform the study of situated discourse more broadly. Rhetoric, most often, provides that bridge. Schilb and Clifford's textbook, *Making Literature Matter*, is both a literary anthology and a practical enactment of their earlier work—a writing text that helps students use rhetorical strategies to develop their positions. Literary texts make arguments, as do we, when we interpret them. Schilb and Clifford offer students strategies for constructing arguments that often begin with interesting questions they find in a poem or narrative. Similarly, Faye Halpern sees herself as teaching argument when she encourages students to make the case for one reading of a literary text over another, as opposed to acknowledging and producing "endless close readings" that don't "need much proving" (146).

Claims for rhetoric, textuality, and genre studies as common intellectual bases for reconfiguring departments and curricula, however, have not been all that successful on the ground. Typically, English departments just add new faculty lines and courses, expanding into new subfields, which struggle for power, resources, and students (Graff, *Beyond the Culture Wars* 10; Seitz 155). Literature scholars, while boundary-crossers in work with gender, race, and postcolonial studies, may still defend the turf associated with periodization and the pleasure and creativity of language—as Robert Scholes, Nancy Comley, and Gregory Ulmer say, "those things that make literature literary" (*Text Book* iii). For composition scholars, who may themselves cross disciplinary borders, literature in composition courses may signal the return of literary interpretation at the expense of attention to students' writing processes and production of texts, which are central to what composition does. In short, there is political and pedagogical ground to be won and lost for both sides.

While tied to larger disciplinary and institutional issues, the stakes in the composition/literature relationship have focused primarily on what first-year composition is *for*, more than on whether or not faculty in both fields study and teach the same thing. The purpose of the course was the key question posed by Erika Lindemann, first in her historic debate on the role of literature in composition with Gary Tate at the 1992 Conference on College Composition and Communication (CCCC), and then in follow-up essays published in 1993 and 1995 in *College English*. By the time these debates took place in the early 1990s there was consensus, for the most part, that first-year composition students should master a process of written communication in preparation for future writing in college and beyond. Informed by a revived attention to the canons of rhetoric, especially invention, and, later, in the 1980s, by the "social turn," instruction emphasized writing as a rhetorical act and a means of discovery. Concerns in the 1960s and 1970s with the personal growth and cognitive development of student writers coalesced into the "process movement," displacing literary texts as models and sources of writing ideas. While entire literary texts were seldom included in early twentieth-century courses, as Robert Connors (323) and Sharon Crowley (97–98) point out in their respective histories of composition in American colleges, their employment was designed to maintain standards of usage and taste. No longer charged with preparation for public rhetoric, college courses replaced the classics with imaginative literature, the appreciation of which presumably was shared by educated persons. English departments grew larger, however, primarily because of a series of "crises" in basic literacy skills of incoming students, even as literature specialists distanced themselves from the more utilitarian composition courses intended to address these deficiencies. College courses were concerned first, as Connors points out, with belletristic and, later, modal classification of the features of finished products codified in textbooks (224). Driven by grammar rules and prescriptive modes (narration, description, exposition, persuasion), curricula settled into what would later be called "current-traditional" composition for half a century.

In the 1960s, reform efforts to align and redefine K-16 English and find antidotes to top-down canon mastery and form-and-correctness resulted, as Joseph Harris points out, not in a reintegration of literature and composition, but in new pedagogies emphasizing subjectivity in interpretation and strategies of the writing process: prewriting, drafting, and peer group work, key tenets of composition to this day (*Subject* 13–14).

The composing process of student writers became the concern of both student-centered compositionists like Peter Elbow and Donald Murray and quasi-empiricists like Janet Emig, James Britton, and Sondra Perl, whose findings from case studies of writers in the 1970s and 1980s were central to composition's search for a disciplinary identity grounded in research, the findings of which produced a generalizable model of "good writing." In both approaches, school-based writing that imposed structure and restricted expression was the primary foe. Literature in a writing course was also considered an obstacle to the delivery of direct composition instruction, which had shifted emphasis from the features of finished products to the recursive and collaborative process of writing and revision. In the last twenty-five years, challenges to a monolithic model of composition have come from various directions, some of which are linked to historical, textual, genre, and cultural inquiry in the rest of English Studies; they all offer possibilities for a revitalized use of literary texts in writing courses.

One challenge has also come from the Writing Across the Curriculum movement, which, beginning in the 1980s, called into question the extent to which one first-year writing course could adequately prepare students for the rhetorical practices and genres in "discourse communities" beyond English, but for which English, nevertheless, felt responsible (Crowley 27). Lindemann's rejection of literature is tied to this responsibility of composition to offer "guided practice in reading and writing the discourses of the academy and the professions. That is what our colleagues across the campus want it to do; that is what it should do if we are going to drag every first-year student through the requirement" (Lindemann 1993, 312; cited in Crowley 28). Use of imaginative literature, as opposed to texts from a variety of disciplines, risks shifting the emphasis in writing courses from students' composing processes to their teacher-centered reception of texts. Crowley finds this rationale for a requirement—that composition instructors can "anticipate every discursive exigency" in disciplines and professions other than their own— no more satisfactory than the notion that first-year composition students should read literary works for their inspirational value to their lives and craft, the position advanced by Gary Tate and other participants in the *College English* exchanges. Anticipating "the increasing professionalization of undergraduate education in this country," Tate laments the extent to which, by replacing literature with rhetoric, composition has been turned into the "ultimate 'service course' for all the other disciplines in the academy" ("Place" 319). He would use literature to help students join "conversations . . . *outside the academy*" (320), a traditional humanist position as objectionable to Crowley as Lindemann's service ethic, but one that does resurface in the pedagogy of critical literacy and cultural studies.

LITERATURE AND WRITING ACROSS THE CURRICULUM

Writing Across the Curriculum (WAC) doctrine, however, has also been used to turn composition back toward the teaching of literature, most notably in Art Young and Toby Fulwiler's collection, *When Writing Teachers Teach Literature: Bringing Writing to Reading*. Most of the contributors, who identify with composition, emphasize the ways in which attention to students' writing processes can disrupt the transmission-of-knowledge model long associated with literature instruction and help students connect personal experience to the works they encounter. Published in 1995, Young and Fulwiler's volume is faithful to the tenets of both the writing process and writing-to-learn movements, regarding literature courses, for the most part, as sites for the same sort of pedagogical intervention WAC makes into other disciplines.

In keeping with what Crowley calls composition's "legitimating claim" to prepare students for future discursive work (262), literary scholar Gerald Graff, in *Clueless in Academe* (and in his textbook *They Say/I Say*, written with Cathy Birkenstein), stakes such a claim for literature and composition alike: We can fill literacy gaps by clarifying for students the "culture of ideas and arguments" we take for granted and by demystifying the common moves of argument and analysis that constitute the reading and writing "game" in the academy (*Clueless* 3). Graff, who for years advocated sharing with undergraduates "the conflicts" among scholars in literary studies, is not alone in tackling how students become acclimated to interpretive communities and academic habits of mind through reading. Reading (what "*they say*"), not literature per se, is key.

READING AND TEXTUALITY

David Bartholomae, in his landmark essay, "Inventing the University" and in his textbook authored with Anthony Petrosky, *Ways of Reading*, similarly argues that what students "need" to learn is how to do interesting and increasingly complicated things in their writing with the ideas in what they read. While Bartholomae and Petrosky are pioneers in exposing even basic writers to complex, mostly nonliterary readings from a variety of disciplines, their approach to the connection between close and critical reading and successful writing has implications for the use of literary texts. *Ways of Reading* argues that what student writers need most is to locate themselves within academic, not just literary, discourse. They employ a method of rereading and sequenced assignments that invite student writers to use the ideas of one author to complicate those of another as they evolve their own increasingly complex interpretations. Bartholomae and Petrosky believe strongly in providing students with difficult but "readable" texts, as opposed to short and tidy readings that would serve as models or that "solve all the problems they raise" (viii).

Their notion of using texts that "leave some work for readers to do" in their papers has made all the difference in my own use of literature in a writing course. Rather than choosing works that would elicit only emotional or ideological responses for writing, I go for those texts that present interesting and vexing problems. There is analytical and rhetorical "work to do," for instance, when I teach Tim O'Brien's *In the Lake of the Woods* and ask students to make an argument for whether one of the main characters has deliberately disappeared or has been murdered by her Vietnam-veteran-turned-politician husband. Students have to contend with O'Brien's construction of a hybrid (detective, historical, and psychological) text and with their own genre expectations. O'Brien provides no definitive answer but rather chapters from multiple perspectives and extensive intertextual footnotes regarding the My

Lai massacre trial and post-traumatic stress disorder, all of which may or may not function as evidence. Similarly, Paul Auster's intertextual meta-detective novel, *City of Glass*, is not just a "whodunit" but an opportunity for students to investigate the relationship between language and reality as they try to distinguish Paul Auster, the character, from Paul Auster, the book's author, and determine, finally, who is narrating the story and whether or not Auster is "playing" them as readers. Students who say they hate novels but love puzzles have written papers on *City of Glass* that make convincing, if not brilliant, arguments. I bring difficult or enigmatic texts to the composition course in the context of what I hope are compelling topics (Private and Public Identities, in this case) that generate questions that will drive the writing, rather than as texts to master or simply appreciate. The argument for putting literature in a composition course, as Clyde Moneyhun points out, should not be "that since a text is a text, we might as well use literature" (230). Literature has to be more than just a test object for amassing details that support arguments with which no one would disagree. As Faye Halpern discovered in her work with the Harvard Study of Undergraduate Writing, some students may even excel at exegesis, but then hit a dead end with what becomes a formulaic claim that, on closer reading, a text is more complex than we first thought—what the Harvard Study called the "complexity thesis" (127). What's often missing, she says, is what the complexity signifies about the work or the topic as a whole, why it matters. Students' ability to move to the "So what?" in their writing depends, I think, on how we have framed the course. Is there a topic for sustained inquiry? Do some readings provide "lenses" for reading more critically or analyzing one work in terms of another? Have we included a variety of texts, both literary and nonliterary, that generate questions worth writing about?

Robert Scholes has long been the main advocate for intertextuality as the way to reunite literature and composition in compelling multigenre courses. Coming from literary studies back to rhetoric, he proposes in *The Rise and Fall of English* and in *Text Book: Writing Through Literature* (written with Nancy Comley and Gregory Ulmer for students), a modern trivium that would shift the focus of English from canonical literature to intertextuality as the core of a curriculum "organized around a canon of concepts, precepts, and practices" to be understood through the analysis of works from a range of media (*Rise* 120). His goal, like Bartholomae and Petrosky's, is to have students *work* with literature—to teach reading (narrative, metaphor), along with writing, as a "craft."

Both Scholes and Graff ("Afterword") argue for uniting the concerns of literature and composition around textuality, recommending that students in introductory courses analyze rhetorical language in both literary and nonliterary works. Scholes takes issue with the exclusion of literature as advocated by Lindemann and the WAC mandate, claiming that what faculty in other disciplines respect about our expertise in English is not so much "that we will teach them to write like social scientists or engineers . . ." as that "what we can teach about writing involves mainly those elements of it that are literary or rhetorical" (*Rise* 34).

Joseph Harris, a former colleague of Bartholomae's at Pittsburgh, also believes that students learn to write intertextually, focusing on a method for writing in terms of the ideas of others. In his innovative book, also written for students, *Rewriting: How to Do Things with Texts,* Harris complicates the process approach, echoing Bartholomae and Petrosky's re-reading assignment sequences and Scholes' new canonical practices in his sequential method for introducing students to the "moves" of the critical essay: Coming to Terms; Forwarding; Countering; Taking an Approach, and Revising. What matters in his pedagogy is not which texts are taught, or even what genre, but what you teach students to do with them in their writing. In several writing courses I have taught with literature, I have followed Harris's suggestion (*Rewriting* 131) and constructed a digital class forum to encourage deeper and more complex collaborative readings of texts. In taking turns as first and follow-up responders to one another's entries, students cannot merely repeat or agree/disagree. They must pick up a thread in the first responder's post and build on an idea, taking it somewhere new. Class discussion, then, following the online discussion, can proceed right to specific passages in a text that particular students have already investigated and to issues they have raised.

LITERATURE AND LANGUAGE

Taking some cues from Scholes, Comley, and Ulmer's focus on literary language and form, my colleague Judith Anderson and a group of graduate instructors designed a course combining composition and literature, Language, Metaphor, and Thought: The Way We Think in Words, described in detail in our volume. Early in the course, the lectures, discussion, and writing assignments focused on the dictionary, etymologies, the function of words, naming, and categorizing. Readings included excerpts from the autobiographies of Malcolm X and Helen Keller, Addie's chapter in Faulkner's *As I Lay Dying,* and the chapter on the language reformers in Swift's *Gulliver's Travels.* As the course built in complexity, they took on the colonization of language, cultural metaphors, and word play, examining works by Anzaldua, Friel, Lewis Carroll, Borges, Auster, and excerpts from Morrison's *Playing in the Dark.* Students' writing, in both short exercises and longer comparative analyses, reflected new awareness of how language shapes their thinking and the ways in which metaphor is fundamental to culture and common ground across genres and disciplines (Anderson and Farris 281–305).

In their commitment to courses that demystify academic discourse, Graff, Bartholomae, Scholes, and Harris would seem to agree on the importance of the transferability of academic writing skills to other courses in the college curriculum. While they consider their methods applicable to all of English Studies, they also help make an argument that writing in terms of literary texts can be part of something transferable as well as disciplinary.

LITERATURE AND CULTURE

However, the reintroduction of literature to composition, along with nonliterary and visual texts, has the potential to change what English is exporting. Any work with texts—reading, writing, and interpretation—is context-dependent, with significance in the world beyond the university. James Berlin, in his final book, *Rhetorics, Poetics, and Cultures*, points to the importance of "textuality in all its manifestations" in the redesign of a profession responsive to changes, not just in the university, but in the world (176). He calls for literary and cultural studies scholars to collaborate with specialists in rhetoric and composition, who focus on production as well as reception of a wide range of print and visual texts that persuade in ways that are not merely aesthetic. In short, English Studies can heal the rhetoric/poetics split through analysis of all forms of signifying practices that reproduce power dynamics and shape our responses to issues. In doing so, we equip students not just for the writing that is to come in college but for lifelong critical awareness and civic participation.

What has been termed *post-process theory*, in questioning both the notion of a unified writing process and that of a monolithic academic discourse into which students are acculturated, assumes that writing is a situated, public, noncodifiable act (Kent 1–2). Composition's shift in attention to writing as situated and affected by larger forces has resulted in courses that include literary and nonliterary texts and artifacts that address historical and social issues, so as to raise students' awareness of how literature and other texts intervene in culture (Robison and Wolfe 209) in ways that can still introduce them to lines of cultural inquiry typical of other disciplines.

Genre theory also has the potential to unite literature and composition around the mutual understanding, as Amy Devitt maintains, that "text and textual meaning, whether literary or rhetorical, are not objective and static, but rather dynamic and created through interaction of writer, reader, and context" (699). It might be helpful for students in writing courses to think not just of rhetorical texts as responsive to purpose and audience but also of literary texts as social actions that respond to particular moments and needs, "requiring," as Devitt, says, "both conformity with and variation from expectations" (715).

Lori Robison and Eric Wolfe frame their literature and composition course in terms of Stephen Greenblatt's notion of literature as "working at the 'boundaries' of culture, against the 'limits within which social behavior must be contained'" (Greenblatt 226, 225; quoted in Anderson and Farris 197). Students read Greenblatt's essay "Culture" and write essays analyzing the arguments that works of fiction, like Shirley Jackson's "The Lottery" and Charlotte Perkins Gilman's "The Yellow Wallpaper," make against "dominant beliefs and social structures" (Greenblatt 231; quoted in Robinson and Wolfe 197). Writing—that of authors and students—becomes part of larger ideological conversations both in and out of school (Robison and Wolfe 209).

WHY LITERATURE IN COMPOSITION?

Both textuality and the notion of literacy as social action, as emphasized in first-year courses, have the potential to curtail the endless demarcation of the iconic Lindemann–Tate literature/composition boundaries. If we cannot narrow the gap between humanists and utilitarians—literacy for life vs. literacy for other disciplines and professions—we can at least offer new terms and foci as we reconsider the purpose of English, writing, and a college education. The question of whether a first-year course, including literature, focused more broadly on language as a social phenomenon could still deliver writing instruction is what brought me into collaboration with my colleague Judith Anderson, a Renaissance scholar—first in the design of first-year courses and the graduate proseminars that preceded them, and then in the volume we put together for MLA, *Integrating Literature and Writing Instruction*. We benefited from a department that is less bifurcated than some. A long-time PhD concentration in what was originally named Language, Literacy, and Literature and a two-semester version of composition, Introduction to the Study of Literature and Writing, meant that, unlike some English departments, first-year pedagogy was the business of more than just the rhetoric-composition faculty, and graduate instructors came to the teaching of composition-with-literature only after teaching a version of composition with nonliterary print and visual texts. I believe that our instructors have been successful at integrating literature into writing courses because they first teach composition without it. As the director of composition, I deliberately designed a common curriculum emphasizing strategies for rhetorical and ideological analysis that instructors and their students can apply to a variety of cultural texts—critical essays, photographs, newspapers, advertisements, and films—not just literature. Our graduate instructors teach first with a common syllabus and sequence of moves: summary, critique, comparative analysis, and research-based analysis, tied to readings (Nietzsche, Foucault, Du Bois, Geertz, Berger) that provide broader frameworks and theoretical and methodological lenses for understanding representation. In addition, we assign Rosenwasser and Stephen's *Writing Analytically*, which offers strategies for analyzing patterns in the language and images in any text and for evolving a complex thesis in terms of confirming and complicating evidence.

The two-semester thematic literature and composition course which both Judith Anderson and I taught numerous times no longer exists, but after one or more years teaching composition, our graduate instructors are encouraged to design their own one-semester writing courses, called Projects in Reading and Writing, which focus on sustained inquiry into an issue or problem, often combining classic, theoretical, and popular works from a variety of fields in the investigation of cultural phenomena, concepts, myths, and stereotypes. For instance, an instructor might design a course on monsters that traces their hold on us—from Shelley's *Frankenstein* to AMC's *The Walking Dead,* or a course on the single woman in American culture that includes Dreiser's *Sister Carrie* as well as *Sex in the City*'s Carrie Bradshaw. Instructors already have experience making visible to students, a la Graff and Harris, the moves of academic analysis and argument. They have experience teaching students to be active, critical subjects, aware of how language and visual representations invite them to occupy various and sometimes conflicting positions as readers and writers. We trust that instructors will be able to connect, not "separate the writing done by students from the texts they write about" (Scholes et al., *Text Book* iii).

Other English departments and programs have also successfully integrated literature and writing instruction. Judith and I found numerous other instances and collaborations in a variety of private colleges and public universities. Instructors, many of them well aware of the history and stakes in the comp/lit debates, found ways to move beyond the composition/literature divide in the design of composition, first-year seminar, and humanities core courses. In keeping with their institutional contexts, our contributors describe courses that do more than merely balance literature and composition. We were struck, as we say in our Introduction, by how much we all encouraged students "to work with binaries, tensions, and contradictions in both their reading and writing: for example, between their own voices and interpretive frames and those typical of literary discourse, between historical and fictional narratives, between contemporary and earlier treatments, between and within generic conventions and between these and social change, between and within representations of gender and race, between their own readings and those of their peers" (Anderson and Farris 14). These tensions, between the literary and nonliterary and between academic and student discourse can, in fact, become, as Graff says, the textualized "object of study" in courses that brings the concerns of literature and composition together ("Afterword" 333). The three groupings of essays in our book, some of which I have alluded to in this chapter, include core humanities courses with literature and writing; courses with literature as a source of discovery; literature as a means of engaging with culture; and then the final chapter, in which we outline our cross-disciplinary faculty/graduate student collaboration and the course I described earlier that focuses on language and metaphor as the basis of reading, writing, and conceptual thinking.

Another collection, *Composition and/or Literature: The End(s) of Education*, edited by Linda S. Bergmann and Edith M. Baker and published by the National Council of Teachers of English (NCTE) in 2006, also revisits debate over the teaching of literature in composition courses, but it is somewhat less optimistic about collaboration and unification. Essays by its eleven contributors review the historical bases for the split between composition and literature, discuss departmental and institutional conditions surrounding it, and examine several classroom applications, which, as in our volume, redefine "literature" to include a wide range of texts and contexts for writing. The main thrust of this volume is reexamination of the divisions between the two specialties and what should reconstitute the teaching of rhetoric, reading, and writing in the "postuniversity," as contributor Eve Wiederhold, invoking Bill Readings, terms it (88). Patricia Harkin, in her "Afterword," acknowledges the institutional and disciplinary "roadblocks" to rebuilding described by several contributors, but she points to the ways in which even those who oppose the use of literature in composition "approve of critical attention to reading" as a dialectical process. What's important, she says, "regardless of departmental or disciplinary affiliation," is that we are *teaching* reading, not merely assigning it (217).

I would echo Harkin's charge in my question to any instructor incorporating literature in a writing course: Why include literature? Ask to what extent you are teaching reading and textual work that informs writing—as opposed to an introduction for English majors or your specialty adapted for the freshman level. In turning to the concerns of those who have debated the use of literature and of those who more recently scrutinize and seek to streamline postsecondary general education, we must ask what is the purpose of the course? Will it permit students to work with and write about texts in ways that are different from high school English?

In thematic first-year experience or humanities core courses, for instance, which are often team-taught, instructors typically do not emphasize a literary canon or traditional aesthetics, but rather practices of textual and hypertextual analysis across genres and disciplines that students will transfer into upper division courses. In the Anderson and Farris volume, Clark and Losh describe UC Irvine's Humanities Core, in which literary texts foreground language, unlike the other genres colleagues bring to an interdisciplinary investigation of a topic like Exploration and Discovery. As Clyde Moneyhun, also in our volume, points out in his defense of transferability, juxtaposition with other genres makes students aware of what literature and literary criticism are not (217). Moneyhun describes a course he designed that includes three "Assignment Games" (Authorial Intent, Reader Response, and Text in Context) that point to "the artificial and constructed nature of the interpretive frames" (219–226). Moneyhun's chief reason for using short stories and novels is that they make it easier for students to understand that meaning is "highly constructed, shaped by a writer with intentions (the first assignment), created by an active reader (the second assignment), and understood in a critical context (the third assignment)." That understanding, he says, "can be sharpened into a disciplined habit of mind and then transferred to the interpretation of any text, including the nonliterary texts students encounter in other classes and beyond the classroom" (230).

Courses that successfully integrate literature and writing can give students new "work to do" in calling attention to genres across disciplines, sometimes by pairing accounts of the same event, as Tamara Goeglein does in her first-year seminar course on historical fiction, so that students will grapple with "what constitutes truth in historical fiction writing and fiction in history writing" (150). In analyzing point of view, characterization, narrative sequencing, and cinematography in multiple genres, including the Ken Burns' documentary, *The Civil War*, her students "learn how figurative modes of language operate in nonliterary texts." Figurative language, Goeglein says, "calls forth our imagination to apprehend and to comprehend the relations among the real, the true, and the past" (172). Certainly, one goal of humanities general education that shapes composition courses with literature, and which we hope to retain, concerns the ways in which figurative language is, as Goeglein suggests, "an analytic habit of mind . . . a way of knowing" (172).

Laura Brady points to the importance of "contingent local practices" as the most effective means of redrawing the boundaries between composition and literature (80). I agree that collaboration with our colleagues across the department and across our institutions—actually teaching reading and writing together in new ways, not just talking about what we mean by reading, writing, texts, and genres—is our best hope for changing the literature/composition relationship and the best evidence of progress, not just in our theory but in our practice.

BIBLIOGRAPHY

Anderson, Judith H., and Christine R. Farris, eds. *Integrating Literature and Writing Instruction: First-Year English, Humanities Core Courses, Seminars*. New York: Modern Language Association, 2007. Print.

Auster, Paul. *City of Glass*. New York: Penguin, 1985. Print.

Bartholomae, David. "Inventing the University." *When a Writer Can't Write: Studies in Writer's Block and Other Composing Problems*. Ed. Mike Rose. New York: Guilford, 1985. 134–65. Print.

Bartholomae, David, and Anthony Petrosky. *Ways of Reading: An Anthology for Writers*. 8th ed. Boston: Bedford/St. Martin's, 2008. Print

Bergmann, Linda S., and Edith M. Baker, eds. *Composition and/or Literature: The End(s) of Education*. Urbana: National Council of Teachers of English, 2006. Print.

Berlin, James A. *Rhetorics, Poetics, and Cultures: Refiguring College English Studies*. Urbana: National Council of Teachers of English, 1996. Print.

Brady, Laura. "Retelling the Composition-Literature Story." *College English* 71.1 (2008): 70–81. Print.

Britton, James, et al. *The Development of Writing Abilities (11–18)*. London: Macmillan 1975. Print.

The Civil War. Dir. Ken Burns. PBS, 1990. 2002. DVD.

Clark, Michael P. and Elizabeth Losh. "Intellectual Community and Integrated Curricula in the First-Year Experience: The Humanities Core Course at the University of California, Irvine." Anderson and Farris, 31-62. Print.

Clifford, John, and John Schilb. "Composition Theory and Literary Theory." *Perspectives on Research and Scholarship in Composition*. Ed. Ben W. McClelland and Timothy R. Donovan. New York: Modern Language Association, 1985. 45–67. Print.

_____.*Writing Theory and Critical Theory*. New York: Modern Language Association, 1994. Print.

Connors, Robert J. *Composition-Rhetoric: Backgrounds, Theory, and Pedagogy*. Pittsburgh: U of Pittsburgh P, 1997. Print.

Crowley, Sharon. *Composition in the University: Historical and Polemical Essays*. Pittsburgh: U of Pittsburgh P, 1998. Print.

Devitt, Amy J. "Integrating Rhetorical and Literary Theories of Genre." *College English* 62 (2000): 696–718. Print.

Dreiser, Theodore. *Sister Carrie*. Ed. Donald Pizer. New York: Norton, 1991. Print.

Elbow, Peter. *Writing without Teachers*. New York: Oxford UP, 1973. Print.

Emig, Janet. *The Composing Processes of Twelfth Graders*. Urbana: National Council of Teachers of English, 1971. Print.

Farris, Christine R. and Judith H. Anderson. "Introduction." Anderson and Farris, 1–27. Print.

Faulkner, William. *As I Lay Dying*. New York: Random. 1964. Print.

Friel, Brian. *Translations*. London: Faber, 1981. Print.

Gilman, Charlotte Perkins. *The Yellow Wallpaper*. Ed. Dale M. Bauer. Boston: Bedford, 1998. Print.

The Godfather. Dir. Francis Ford Coppola. Paramount, 1972. Film.

Goeglein, Tamara. "'You May Find It a Different Story from the One You Learned in School': Teaching Writing in a First-Year Seminar on Historical Fiction." Anderson and Farris 150–73. Print.

Graff, Gerald, "Afterword." *When Writing Teachers Teach Literature: Bringing Writing to Reading*. Ed. Art Young and Toby Fulwiler. Portsmouth: Boynton/Cook, 1995, 324–33. Print.

_____. *Beyond the Culture Wars: How Teaching the Conflicts Can Revitalize American Education*. New York: Norton, 1992. Print.

_____. *Clueless in Academe: How Schooling Obscures the Life of the Mind*. New Haven: Yale UP, 2003. Print.

Graff, Gerald, and Cathy Birkenstein. *They Say/I Say: The Moves That Matter in Persuasive Writing*. 2nd ed. New York: Norton, 2009. Print.

Greenblatt, Stephen. "Culture." *Critical Terms for Literary Study*. Ed. Frank Lentricchia and Thomas McLaughlin. Chicago: U of Chicago P, 1990. 225–32. Print.

Halpern, Faye. "The Detail versus the Debate: Literature, Argument, and First-Year Writing." Anderson and Farris, 135-149. Print.

Harkin, Patricia. "Afterword: A Complex Affirmation of Reading and Writing." Bergmann and Baker, 205–219. Print.

Harris, Joseph. *A Teaching Subject: Composition Since 1966*. Upper Saddle River: Prentice-Hall, 1997. Print.

_____. *Rewriting: How to Do Things with Texts*. Logan: Utah State UP, 2006. Print.

Horner, Winifred, ed. *Composition and Literature: Bridging the Gap*. Chicago: U of Chicago P, 1983. Print.

Jackson, Shirley. "The Lottery." *The Lottery and Other Stories*. New York: Farrar, 1949. Print.

Keller, Helen. *The Story of My Life*. New York: Grosset, 1905. Print.

Kent, Thomas. "Introduction." *Post-Process Theory: Beyond the Writing-Process Paradigm*. Ed. Thomas Kent. Carbondale: Southern Illinois UP, 1999, 1–6. Print.

Lindemann, Erika. "Freshman Composition: No Place for Literature." *College English* 55.3 (1993): 311–16. Print.

_____. "Three Views of English 101." *College English* 57.3 (1995): 287–302. Print.

Malcolm X and Alex Haley. *The Autobiography of Malcolm X*. New York: Ballantine, 1992. Print.

Moneyhun, Clyde. "Literary Texts as Primers in Meaning Making." Anderson and Farris 211–30. Print.

Morrison, Toni. *Playing in the Dark: Whiteness and the Literary Imagination*. Cambridge: Harvard UP, 1992. Print.

Murray, Donald M. "Writing as Process: How Writing Finds Its Own Meaning." *Eight Approaches to Teaching Composition*. Ed. Timothy R. Donovan and Ben W. McClelland. Urbana: National Council of Teachers of English, 1980, 17–31. Print.

O'Brien, Tim. *In the Lake of the Woods*. New York: Penguin, 1994.

Perl, Sondra. "Understanding Composing." *College Composition and Communication* 31 (1980): 363–69. Print.

Readings, Bill. *The University in Ruins*. Cambridge: Harvard UP, 1996. Print.

Robison, Lori, and Eric A. Wolfe. "Writing on Boundaries: A Cultural Studies Approach to Literature and Writing Instruction." Anderson and Farris 195–210. Print.

Rosenwasser, David and Jill Stephen. *Writing Analytically*. 6th ed. Wadsworth/Cengage, 2012. Print.

Schilb, John, and John Clifford. *Making Literature Matter*. 5th ed. Boston: Bedford/St. Martin's, 2012. Print.

Scholes, Robert. *The Rise and Fall of English*. New Haven: Yale UP, 1998. Print.

Scholes, Robert, Nancy R. Comley, and Gregory L. Ulmer, eds. *Text Book: Writing through Literature*. 3rd ed. Boston: Bedford/St. Martin's, 2002. Print.

Seitz, James. "Changing the Program(s): English Department Curricula in the Contemporary Research University." *Beyond English. Inc.: Curricular Reform in a Global Economy*. Ed. David B. Downing, Claude Mark Hurlbert, and Paula Mathieu. Portsmouth: Boynton, 2002, 151–163. Print.

Sex and the City. Television drama. HBO. 1998–2004.

Shelley, Mary. *Frankenstein*. Ed. Johanna M. Smith. Boston: Bedford/St. Martin's, 1992. Print.

Swift, Jonathan. *Gulliver's Travels and Selected Writings in Prose and Verse*. Ed. John Hayward. Bloomsbury: Nonesuch, 1934. Print.

Tate, Gary. "A Place for Literature in Composition." *College English* 55.3 (1993): 317–21. Print.

——. "Notes on the Dying of a Conversation." *College English* 57.3 (1995): 303–309. Print.

The Walking Dead. Television drama, AMC Studios, 2010-present.

Wiederhold, Eve. "Rhetoric, Literature, and the Ruined University." Bergmann and Baker 73–90. Print.

Young, Art, and Toby Fulwiler, eds. *When Writing Teachers Teach Literature: Bringing Writing to Reading*. Portsmouth: Boynton/Cook, 1995. Print.

New Media Pedagogy

Collin Gifford Brooke

> Humanities 2.0 is a humanities of engagement that addresses
> our collective histories and concern for history. To be valued
> by one's time requires making oneself responsible and respon-
> sive to one's time. For academics, this engagement entails a
> willingness to reconsider the most cherished assumptions and
> structures of their discipline.
>
> —Cathy Davidson, "Humanities 2.0: Promise, Perils,
> Predictions." *PMLA* 123.3 (2008): 707–717

In the ten-plus years that have elapsed since the first edition of this volume was published, there has been no larger "growth industry" in the field of composition (and perhaps in pedagogy more broadly) than the study and adoption of new media in our lives, classrooms, and institutions. Charles Moran's chapter in that volume, on "Technology and the Teaching of Writing," has not aged well, through no fault of his own. In the late 1990s, applications like "electronic mail," online discussion platforms, the Web, and hypertext/media were (with some exceptions) the province of a small subset of the field, a community comprised mostly of grad-uate students and assistant professors. Online journals in the field were in their infancy,[1] which explains what would now be a startling absence of electronic re-sources in the bibliography of Moran's chapter. The various (economic, cultural, social) barriers to access and adoption, while not insurmountable for most, were nonetheless significant.

Moran closes his chapter with an "envoi" that presages Cathy Davidson's re-marks in my epigraph. He explains that, if our students have access to contemporary information and communication technology, "they will be using it" (220). It is our responsibility as writing teachers, he says, to understand the scenes where our stu-dents write, the tools they will be using to write, and the often uneven attitudes (and access) that our students may have with respect to these technologies. To put it in Davidson's terms, Moran's conclusion can be read as a promise (or threat!) that our

---

[1] *Kairos*, for example, published its first issue in 1996.

students will be responsive to their technological moment, and as teachers we had best be prepared to join them in that moment. This perspective has not aged at all; if anything, the challenges posed by technology have increased. Many institutions have bought into corporate course management systems (CMS) and automated plagiarism detection software, the proliferation of mobile devices has transformed the ways we interact with each other and with knowledge, and those industries and professions that have been unwilling to "reconsider [their] most cherished assumptions and structures" have in some cases been swept aside. The writing classroom is not somehow separate from the changes wrought by new media; it may be possible to resist those changes to a degree, but we can no longer ignore them.

WHY NEW MEDIA?

Where should we begin as writing teachers when it comes to understanding and engaging with new media? Unfortunately, the terminology we have used to describe technology seems to change as rapidly as the technologies themselves, and different communities adopt and adapt vocabulary at different times and rates.[2] This can make it a challenge to locate resources, to collaborate with other teachers, and to find a place to begin. "New media" is one among many possible terms; it may strike some in our field as quaint at best and misleading at worst. At what point, one might ask, does a given medium cease being "new"? Is there a statute of limitations past which blogging, for example, simply assumes a place among a more general understanding of media? Or is it that, as Lisa Gitelman observes in *Always Already New*, "This overdetermined sense of reaching the end of media history is probably what accounts for the oddly perennial newness of today's new media" (3)? Books like Bolter's *Writing Space* (1991), Handa's *Computers and Community: Teaching Composition in the Twenty-First Century* (1990), or even Lanham's *The Electronic Word* (1993)—texts that arguably signal the start of our field's engagement with new media—are older than the vast majority of students entering our first-year classrooms. What do we gain by insisting on this particular terminology?

There are certainly alternatives to this particular nomenclature. In the field of rhetoric and composition, there has been a great deal of interest in recent years in what has come to be known as "multimodal pedagogy," a phrase that layers together not only multimedia but the multiliteracies advocated by the New London Group, who call for teaching a broader range of meaning-making "modalities," including visual, audio, spatial, and gestural literacies alongside more traditional textual/linguistic practices. In their opening chapter to the 2007 collection *Multimodal Composition*, Pamela Takayoshi and Cynthia Selfe invoke the challenges of "digital composing environments" and suggest that multimodal composition provides the means of meeting those challenges. What several authors in that collection note, however, is that multimodality and a focus on contemporary technologies are not necessarily coterminous, a distinction that has been reinforced more recently.

---

[2]See, for example, Claire Lauer's "What's in a Name? The Anatomy of Defining New/Multi/Modal/Digital/Media Texts."

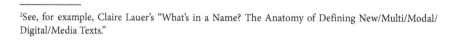

In *Remixing Composition*, Jason Palmeri suggests, among other things, that composition history holds a wealth of forgotten work on multimodality that predates new media. He contends that our emphasis on the "new" has "inadvertently deleted from view many of the vivid multimodal scenes that flourished in our field's past" (5). In *Toward a Composition Made Whole*, Jody Shipka echoes this admonition, urging "that we not limit our attention to a consideration of new media texts or to what the newest computer technologies make possible—or even make problematic—but attend to the highly distributed, complexly mediated, multimodal dimensions of all communicative practice" (29).

While "multimodal pedagogy" turns to the histories of literacy and composition to guide our adoption of new media, terms like *digital pedagogy* and *hybrid pedagogy* have emerged in recent years to approach it from the direction of technologies themselves. These discussions occur in the context of the recent turn across various disciplines to the digital humanities (DH), a loose confederation of academics devoted to exploring how new media are transforming our disciplines and institutions. While the initial emphasis of DH has been to revitalize research methods and practices across humanities disciplines (see Brier), digital pedagogy has emerged as a complementary focus. Matthew Gold's *Debates in the Digital Humanities*, for example, emphasizes "Teaching the Digital Humanities" (alongside defining, theorizing, critiquing, and practicing them). Dan Cohen and Tom Scheinfeldt's *Hacking the Academy* attends equally to scholarship, pedagogy, and institutions. And a number of new journals and conferences (see "Resources" later in the chapter) have sprung up with the express purpose of bringing together teachers from across disciplines interested in exploring the pedagogical potential of new media.

Despite these various developments and terminological shifts, there is still some value in the idea of "new media pedagogy." One of the challenges facing any technology-oriented activity is the shifting terminological ground it occupies, and teaching is no exception in this regard. Gitelman explains that "When media are new, they offer a look into the different ways that their jobs get constructed as such" (6), and it is this attitude that recommends a phrase like "new media pedagogy" to us. Gitelman's point is that the "newness" of media highlights the transitional context in which they appear; they call attention to "the contested relations of force that determine the pathways by which new media may eventually become old hat" (6). In this sense, then, new media pedagogy marks (for me) a site where the long history of multiple modalities intersects with recent developments in technology, but it also includes important shifts in audience, institutions, and context. There is no single, proper way to draw the Venn diagram that includes these various terms and accounts for their overlap, but they provide the new teacher with a broad range of starting points from which to begin thinking about technology and pedagogy.

NEW MEDIA PRINCIPLES AND ATTITUDES

New media pedagogy involves more than simply moving one's writing class to a computer lab, posting short, formal essays to a weblog, or using library databases. Part of the challenge of adopting new media in the classroom is avoiding the instrumentalist attitude that technology should be deployed as a supplement to traditional, print-based writing. What follows are some of the principles I've developed for my own courses that draw on new media.

1.   New media pedagogy is more than "teaching to the text."

In *Lingua Fracta*, one of my broader themes is that we should think about writing less in terms of products and/or objects, and more in terms of practices, and this is one of the ways that individual teachers can mitigate potential conflicts between adopting new media and mandated course outcomes. In other words, it is worth our time to consider what new media *do* apart from the end products themselves, to consider their affordances. For example, one of the canonical assignments that many teachers use as part of the process for extended research writing is the annotated bibliography. We ask our students to gather together a number of sources for their project, to read and describe them, with the goal of synthesizing them for their own contribution for a given discussion. The end-product itself, the actual bibliography, can be monotonous both to read and to write. Ryan Hoover writes about requiring his students to compose annotated bibliographies using the presentation software Prezi:

> Annotations stayed pretty much identical to what they'd be if done in Word. . . .
> But then those paragraphs had to be copied into Prezi text boxes. And the students had to design the Prezi in a way that communicated how the sources relate to each other and to the research question. (n.p.)

Prezi is typically considered as an alternative to PowerPoint or Keynote; that is, most people understand it as a piece of software whose primary function is delivery. What Prezi *does*, however, is to allow a user to arrange spatially information that would be delivered sequentially; Hoover ties this affordance to the goal of synthesis for his students, asking them to communicate visually relationships that remain largely implicit in an alphabetized list of annotated sources. Just as "teaching to the test" can keep a teacher from pushing students beyond a set amount of information, "teaching to the text" may focus our students' attention on end-products rather than the practices and skills those products were originally meant to develop.

2.   New media function as a writer's laboratory, a site of experimentation.

Taking an incremental approach to new media, one that ties specific affordances to established outcomes, is a frequent point of advice from experienced new media pedagogues. It is possible to take such an approach too far, however, to assume that only those platforms with bounded, specific, and recognizable products should be adopted in the writing classroom or to assume that documented outcomes provide the only context for our students' writing. "Add technology and stir" is perhaps a poor way to improve education in general, but on the smaller scale of the writing classroom, it can be a positive source of experimentation and innovation. For example, a couple of semesters ago, I came across graphic designer Kyle Tezak's "Four Icon Challenge." As the name suggests, the challenge is to summarize visually a book or a movie using only four icons (such as those available at

Blogs
Twitter
Storify

The Noun Project).[3] Typically, I try to intersperse larger projects with smaller, less directed assignments, and one week, I asked my students to complete a four icon challenge. Weeks later, when my students were working on designing infograph-ics, the practice of generalizing and compressing ideas in the form of graphic icons ended up being a skill that many of them drew upon in their designs. Not every assignment will dovetail with another as well as those two did, but my openness in adopting the former ended up improving the later assignment and giving students additional context for the work they were doing.

We can court this kind of serendipity by encouraging invention and experi-mentation from our students as well. In the late spring of 2012, Quinn Warnick shared an example of a long-form essay that a student of his had composed using Storify[4]; it was jayarr's "Video Game Communities on Kickstarter." Jayarr's "essay" draws on activity theory to understand the recent use of Kickstarter in video game development, examining questions of credibility, agency, audience, and commu-nity, among other things. It is an interesting essay in its own right, but it also raises questions about how our students negotiate questions of citation and source use, as well as the relationship between argumentation and curation. While such ques-tions can certainly arise in response to an explicit Storify assignment, it can be more productive (and engender more energy) when they emerge through students' own innovation. Our responsibility in this regard involves creating the classroom spaces that can encourage our students to experiment.

3.   **New media often operate on "Internet time" (and so must we).**

I often think of the carefully plotted stages of the traditional classroom's writing process as the *chronos* to new media's *kairos*. Often, in our handbooks, the writing process is a series of well-articulated, logical steps that begins with invention and ends in an essay. The measured writing process of the traditional handbook bears little resemblance to the bursts and spikes of activity that typically occur online. For example, shortly after the opening ceremonies of the 2012 Summer Olympics, when criticisms of NBC's coverage of the event were peaking (and the Twitter hashtag #nbcfail was trending), Brandon Ballenger, a freelance writer and gradu-ate student at Florida Atlantic University, published a Storify that aggregated many of those criticisms.[5] Within a month of its publication, Ballenger's essay had been viewed more than 50,000 times, retweeted frequently on Twitter, shared on Face-book, and linked on a variety of websites.

Ballenger's "essay" is a perfect example of the kind of impact that any writer can have online; the composition classroom, however, with its slow and steady ap-proach to writing, may not prepare students to seize upon those kinds of moments and achieve that kind of impact. While our students need to know how to conduct academic research, they should also learn how to follow trending topics, gather

---

[3] Four Icon Challenge: http://kyletezak.com/portfolio/the-four-icon-challenge/ The Noun Project: http://thenounproject.com/
[4] Storify is one of a new genre of online applications that allow users to curate stories by allowing them to embed a range of online sources from social media like Facebook, Twitter, Instagram, YouTube, etc.
[5] http://storify.com/btballenger/nbcfail-x-ways-nbc-blew-olympics-coverage (July 30, 2012).

information, filter through it, and curate it. Sometimes, we are so accustomed to treating Kenneth Burke's famous "conversation parlor" as an allegory for academic writing (with its conversations that span months if not years) that we overlook the dynamic conversations that are taking place online. Some of what our students learn as they participate in those conversations may scale to the more sedate pace of the academic essay (e.g., linking as a variation on academic citation practice) and some of it may seem to us a case study in "how not to write," but we should be having these conversations with students rather than pretending they're not relevant to the writing classroom. Making space in our classrooms for this kind of work requires us to negotiate among the different paces implied by our institutions and our technologies, and this can mean preparing our students to move with ease from "class time" to "Internet time."

4.   New media replace expertise with exploration and engagement.

A frequent concern in technology-oriented courses is the uneven levels of expertise and experience among our students (and ourselves). Teachers must abandon the notion that all expertise must flow from the front of the classroom, particularly when it comes to technology. Even those who are considered experts or "power users" cannot expect to master every single program or application, and many of the platforms associated with new media lend themselves to (and indeed encourage) collaboration, as Basic Writing Pedagogy in this volume discusses.

One assignment that I often use, particularly in courses with a wide range of expertise, is what I call the "T + 1" assignment, a variation on the "literacy autobiography." I ask students to reflect upon and account for the various media they use during their writing processes (T stands for their current level of engagement with information technologies), and then to commit to adding one element for the semester. Some students elect to start a blog, Tumblr, or Twitter account. Others may adopt a social bookmarking platform such as Delicious or Diigo, or note-taking applications like Evernote or Zotero. The output for the assignment can vary, from end-of-semester reflections to Screenr tutorials to in-class presentations, as does the ultimate "success" of the adoption. Some students will abandon their applications as soon as the assignment is complete, some change their minds during the semester, and some will integrate their chosen platforms into their activity permanently. But they all learn a great deal about a range of new media options, acquiring and sharing their new expertise with each other and with me. The value of this kind of assignment is that it proves no less useful for the "power user" than it does for the beginner; rather than holding them all to a single standard of expertise, students at every level of experience receive credit for the exploration that they do.

Assessment is considered in more depth later in the chapter, but it is worth mentioning here as well for its formative value. One of the core elements of my "T + 1" assignment is reflection; at its outset, I ask students to reflect upon their habits of media usage, both curricular and extracurricular, and they conclude their projects with reflection as well. Metacognition like this is a common feature of much new media pedagogy; teachers who adapt new media to their classrooms consider carefully the value, appropriateness, and effectiveness of both their own pedagogy and the affordances that new media provide. There is no single right way to accomplish this kind of reflection, but heuristics like those provided by Stuart Selber in *Multiliteracies for a Digital Age* can be a useful place to start. Selber suggests that we think of computer literacy as multilayered, comprised of functional, critical, and rhetorical dimensions. Selber describes these dimensions in detail, articulating several parameters for each that can provide guidance in designing assignments, reflecting on practice, and articulating potential outcomes for the writing teacher. Depending upon the particular application, student access, and pedagogical infrastructure, different platforms require different ratios of emphasis, but Selber's framework is a valuable one for thinking about new media pedagogy.

Working with new media in the writing classroom can often be as simple as adopting these attitudes and approaches, and they are quite compatible with the student-centered, peer-directed focus of many composition courses. When we focus on the processes and practices of writing, downplaying more product-oriented outcomes without abandoning them, it becomes much easier to invite our students to investigate and experiment with new media. The pace at which this happens in our classrooms can vary considerably; while this can mean ceding some of the control we normally exercise in our courses, the corresponding energy that we gain is often worth the trade. And the responsibility for this experimentation can be shared with students, an invitation to research collaboratively the discursive potentials of new media. And heuristics such as Selber's can help us guide that research, ensuring that our students use new media not only effectively but critically and rhetorically.

NEW CHALLENGES

Integrating contemporary technologies into our teaching does require more than a simple change of attitude. There are a number of potential obstacles to the successful integration of new media into the classroom, concerns that we need to address if that integration is to be both mindful and effective. (See New Media Pedagogy in this volume for additional discussion of many of the following issues.)

Access

In addition to their potential pedagogical impact, new media carry with them social, cultural, and economic implications. At the turn of the century, questions of access and the "digital divide" dominated discussions of technology. Moran, for instance, relates a story from *Scientific American* about the substantial advantage that computer ownership bestows upon more affluent students. Cynthia Selfe's CCCC Chair's Address, later published as *Technology and Literacy in the 21st Century: The Importance of Paying Attention*, called upon our entire field to attend to questions of economy and privilege alongside those of technology and literacy. In the past decade, however, a number of factors have intervened: the consolidation of Internet Service Providers, financial advantages accruing to public wifi, the proliferation of mobile devices, the availability of cloud storage and applications, the shifting metaphors with which access is described (e.g., from privilege to utility), and so forth. According to a 2012 Pew Report, "88% of American adults have a cell phone, 57% have a laptop, 19% own an e-book reader, and 19% have a tablet computer; about six in ten adults (63%) go online wirelessly with one of those devices." The report continues to explain that mobile devices have "chang[ed] the story" of the digital divide, making access much more than a question of yes, no, or sometimes.

It would be naive to imagine that the divide has somehow been solved (see, e.g., Bessette), but the picture is much more complicated than it was even a few years ago. There is discussion of a secondary digital divide between those who have access to high-speed Internet service and those who do not. There are still important divides among specific populations; "significant differences in use remain, generally related to age, household income, and educational attainment" (Pew). Culturally, there is also a constantly shifting divide between those who produce content online and those who consume it. When the iPad was first released, for instance, many reviewers were critical of the relative lack of applications that could be used for creation rather than consumption. Whether or not we wish to retain the notion of a digital divide, there remain a number of important dimensions that separate certain groups of users from others, and these differences can enter our classrooms in unpredictable ways.

Infrastructure

There are a number of divides that operate on most campuses that can have a more direct effect on our classrooms as well. While many institutions have committed to providing wifi access, there are often marked differences among colleges and departments with respect to equipment, maintenance, resources, and support, and these can all have an impact on individual classroom adoptions of technology. The presence of computer (and/or smart) classrooms, facilities for faculty, equipment maintenance, and specialized software often varies widely on a single campus. As DeVoss, Cushman, and Grabill explain in "Infrastructure and Composing: The When of New Media Writing,"

> in order to teach and understand new media composing, some understanding of new media infrastructure is necessary. Without such an understanding, writing teachers and students will fail to anticipate and actively participate in the emergence of such infrastructures, thereby limiting—rhetorically, technically, and institutionally—what is possible for our students to write and learn. (37)

DeVoss et al. offer important advice about taking an activist stance toward that infrastructure, encouraging us not to treat it as inevitable, invisible, or immutable. This may mean something as seemingly small as thinking about where students will store files of their works in progress, to making sure that necessary software is installed on computers, to laying the groundwork with administration for new or expanded departmental facilities.

DeVoss et al. also explain that infrastructure is not a strictly material proposition. There are cultural and organizational structures that may encourage or impede the adoption of new media in one's courses; "Infrastructure also entails decision-making processes and the values and power relationships enacted by those processes, and infrastructure is thoroughly penetrated by issues of culture and identity . . ." (22). It can be important for new teachers to understand both the material and the cultural landscapes of their institutions as they consider integrating technology into their courses, and scale can be a relevant consideration in this regard. Spending extra class time on online search strategies or the proper citation style for digital resources, for example, is a different matter from replacing a departmentally mandated research essay with infographics. As with any significant change to one's pedagogy, it is important to know whether such changes will be supported and/or encouraged.

Accessibility

As new media have shifted from largely text-based genres (first-generation websites, e-mail, etc.) to increasingly multimodal experiences, and as the types of devices used to go online have diversified, questions of design as they relate to both accessibility and usability are important to consider. Sean Zdenek observes that "Too often, our excitement about new media, even when that excitement is tempered by sober reflection, leaves intact a set of normative assumptions about students' bodies, minds, and abilities" (n.p.) Online accessibility draws on principles for universal design, the idea that products and environments should be as inclusive as possible with respect to potential users. As Patricia Dunn and Kathleen Dunn De Mers explain in their *Kairos* essay on universal design and online writing pedagogy, "In a way, universal design helps us see text-only pedagogies as 'disabled,' not those individuals who don't happen to use writing-as-a-mode-of-learning in the same way their English teachers do" (n.p.). Accessibility is a pedagogical responsibility that needs to take place both in the planning stages of a course and during the course itself, as something that students account for as they produce new media content.

Usability is another distinctive quality that technologically oriented writing should account for; much like accessibility, usability is a part of credibility in online environments. The relative technological stability of the printed page makes us forget that it, too, was once a site of usability innovations (spaces between words, paragraph indentations, punctuation, etc.). While usability is still associated primarily in our field with technical communication, the recent publication of texts such as Susan Miller-Cochran and Rochelle Rodrigo's *Rhetorically Rethinking Usability* suggests that the broader field of rhetoric and composition is beginning to recognize its importance. Usability can be an important way to prompt our students to avoid simply taking technologies at face value, and it is vital when we ask our students to produce their own content. As Michael Salvo and Paula Rosinski explain, ". . . proficiency in information design has become a key component of literacy in work contexts. It is now essential to include information design in any discussion of digital literacy" (103). They emphasize a range of features—including navigability, findability, signposting, and metadata—that contribute toward creating the "virtual space" entailed by information design.

Assessment

One of the persistent challenges in teaching with technology is the question of actually incorporating new media into the writing classroom, particularly when it comes to course outcomes. How does a three- to five-page paper translate to blog entries or Twitter updates? Many programs find themselves in the complicated position of maintaining certain kinds of requirements (perhaps university-mandated) on the one hand while wanting to encourage pedagogical innovation on the other, and these goals may come into conflict. New teachers, justifiably, may not want to play out such conflicts in their own classrooms. But just as our institutions are slowly shifting to recognize and reward scholarship produced across a range of media, rhetoric and composition is beginning to articulate common goals and standards for the kinds of work that our students can create using new media. Without careful reflection, however, the writing teacher may fall back onto tried and true assessment criteria and strategies that were designed for evaluating the printed page; worse still, there is the temptation to treat new media compositions as "excellent" simply because they take novel forms. Think, for example, about posting to Twitter. It's not unusual to see Twitter-based assignments that simply require students to post a certain number of times over a fixed duration (day, week, semester). Tweeting in 140 characters or less, however, is not the same as typing a sentence in an essay. Even in the compressed space of a tweet, there are rhetorical considerations (citation, hashtags, etc.). David Silver writes about having his students use Twitter, with the expectation that they compose what he terms "thick tweets" (as opposed to the "thin" status updates that sometimes dominate the medium):

> thick tweets convey two or more layers of information. They often, but not always, include a hyperlink that takes readers from twitter to another source of information—a newspaper article, a blog post, a flickr set, a video. I encourage my students to use 140 characters or less to compose a thick tweet that is so compelling that no reader in his or her right mind can avoid clicking the link. (n.p.)

There is value in setting expectations for quantity (it can encourage experimentation, for example), but without some corresponding attention to quality, teachers run the risk of either rewarding banality or holding students accountable to a hidden standard. Silver goes on to offer several examples of student work that fulfill those expectations (and advice for a couple that could be improved).

Silver's approach to Twitter provides an excellent example of what Madeline Sorapure describes as her "broadly rhetorical approach" to assessing new media, "an assessment strategy that focuses on the effectiveness with which modes such as image, text, and sound are brought together or, literally, composed" (n.p.). Sorapure acknowledges that such a strategy needs to be combined with specific criteria geared toward the modalities of the assignment; no single strategy, regardless of how broad it might seem, can be equally effective for every assignment. In Silver's case, he makes explicit the broader rhetorical point of Twitter (compelling tweets/links) while articulating criteria (density, constraint) distinctive to that particular platform. Such a strategy does not have to be invented anew for each possible modality or application, though. In "The New Work of Assessment: Evaluating Multimodal Compositions," Elizabeth Murray, Hailey Sheets, and Nicole Williams write of their experience as teaching assistants in a program that requires them to teach multimodal composition. They offer concrete examples of their efforts to translate departmental outcomes into terms specific to these kinds of projects, translating print-based outcomes into goals that can be accomplished in multiple ways, depending on the modalities of the project. The National Writing Project's Multimodal Assessment Project has also begun the process of developing criteria and best practices that can be brought to bear on a broad range of new media writing. They name five criteria—context, artifact, process management, substance/content, and habits of mind—that they identify as "domains that many felt were critical for assessing and improving our work as creators of multimodal texts" ("Cross-Walking").

One of the strategies emerging in discussions of new media and/or multimodal assessment is the importance of reflection on the parts of both students and teachers, and it is easy to see how such strategies work across several of the domains noted previously. For example, Sonya Burton and Brian Huot advocate for the use of in-progress, formative assessment (studio sessions, progress journals, collaborative rubrics, etc.). "Such an approach," they explain, "also keeps teachers and students appropriately focused on rhetorical matters, whether they are composing multimodal essays or essays that are primarily alphabetic-only" (101). It is not unusual to see teachers assigning short, print-based reflections at the conclusion of new media projects, asking students to reflect upon their compositions' effectiveness and the strategies and choices deployed to achieve those goals. Approaches like these invite students to engage in the same sorts of reflective practices that we do as teachers when we ask them to work with new media, a fact that underscores the importance of many of the attitudes described earlier. New media pedagogy is not simply a matter of trading out one set of products for newer models; they change the dynamics of the classroom itself in addition to what it means to write and to write well.

NEW POSSIBILITIES

At some point, new media will simply become an accepted part of the definition of what it means to write well. Assuming that such a moment arrives, the idea of a "new media pedagogy" as something that can be separated conceptually from "pedagogy" will become an historical curiosity. For the present, we are still deeply embedded in a transitional phase, caught between the relatively stable habits and practices of literacy and the chaos of what Gregory Ulmer has termed "electracy." It can be easy to feel as though this transition is inevitable; while it may be irreversible, however, it is by no means certain what electracy will ultimately look like. Ten years ago, there were no Facebook pages, no Twitter feeds, no YouTube, no Instagram, no iPhones/iPads, no Androids, and very few weblogs; social software, the precursor to social media, was coined as a term after the first edition of this book was published. While the shape of our new media landscape has shifted dramatically in that time, what hasn't changed is Moran's reminder that we should be joining our students where, when, and how they write. As the WIDE Research Center Collective puts it, "if we want to teach writing or help students learn how to write more effectively, then we have to be with them where they write" (n.p.).

But there is more to new media pedagogy than simply surrendering to the demands of the present moment or accommodating our given audience. Taking an active role in contemporary discussions of pedagogy, and working with technology ourselves in mindful, reflective ways, can put us in the position to shape that landscape ourselves. Think about the #hashtag, which in a few short years developed from an emergent generic practice on a once-obscure social media platform (Twitter) to a marketing strategy employed across media to promote television shows, movies, events, and the like. Only a few short years ago, online credibility was widely understood as an extension of "real world" *ethos*; we've moved quickly to the point where we can investigate *ethos* on sites like Facebook and Twitter without treating them as imperfect reflections.[6] We can see where new media match up with our practices, goals, and outcomes, and where they prompt us to rethink those structures and assumptions. Perhaps most important, they provide us with the means for sharing and aggregating this exploration and experimentation with an audience broader than the people with whom we share an office, hallway, or department.

I have spent a disproportionate amount of time in this chapter on the challenges facing us as writing teachers with the advent of new media, but that shouldn't be taken as a sign that the barriers for entry or the obstacles somehow outweigh the benefits. The WIDE Collective explains that "These needs complicate and extend the pressures we already feel and that we already exert—perils and possibilities related to teaching and working spaces, evaluation, class size, access to computer labs, access to wireless teaching spaces, design of curricula, staffing and labor, and more. Many more" (n.p.). Those pressures and challenges, we must remember, occur in the broader context of our relevancy as writing teachers. As with any change to our courses, philosophies, and classrooms, there will be perils and possibilities both; this is what it means to teach in a time where the media are "new."

RESOURCES

The following is a collection of resources about new media for the interested teacher, one that is by no means exhaustive. I have also extended the bibliography beyond those texts cited herein.

Resources/Organizations/Conferences

Alliance of Digital Humanities Organizations: http://digitalhumanities.org/
Association of Internet Researchers: http://aoir.org/

---

[6] See, for example, Cate Blouke's "Analyzing Ethos Using Twitter and Storify" (http://lessonplans.dwrl. utexas.edu/content/analyzing-ethos-using-twitter-and-storify).

Computers and Writing Conference (website rotates): http://www.ncte.org/
cccc/committees/7cs
Digital Humanities Summer Institute: http://dhsi.org/
Digital Is (National Writing Project): http://digitalis.nwp.org/
DWRL Lesson Plans (University of Texas): http://lessonplans.dwrl.utexas.edu/
Educause: http://www.educause.edu/
Humanities, Arts, Sciences, and Technology Advanced Collaboratory: http://
hastac.org/
International Society for Technology in Education: http://www.iste.org/
welcome.aspx
National Institute for Technology in Liberal Education: http://www.nitle.org/
The Humanities and Technology Camp (THATCamp): http://thatcamp.org/

Journals

Computers and Composition (print): http://computersandcomposition
.candcblog.org/
Computers and Composition Online: http://www.bgsu.edu/departments/
english/cconline/
Contemporary Issue in Technology and Teacher Education: http://www
.citejournal.org/
Hybrid Pedagogy: http://www.hybridpedagogy.com/
Journal of Interactive Technology and Pedagogy: http://jitp.commons.gc
.cuny.edu/
Kairos: A Journal of Rhetoric, Technology, and Pedagogy: http://www
.technorhetoric.net/
Technology, Pedagogy, and Education: http://www.tandfonline.com/loi/rtpe20

BIBLIOGRAPHY

Alexander, Jonathan. "Out of the Closet and into the Network: Sexual Orientation and the Computerized Classroom." *Computers and Composition* 14.2 (1997): 207–216. Print.
Alexander, Jonathan, and William P. Banks. "Sexualities, Technologies, and the Teaching of Writing: A Critical Overview." *Computers and Composition* 21.3 (2004): 271–397. Print.
Allen, Christopher. "Tracing the Evolution of Social Software." *Life with Alacrity*. 13 October 2004. Web. 1 July 2012.
Anderson, Daniel. "Prosumer Approaches to New Media Composition: Production and Consumption in Continuum." *Kairos: A Journal of Rhetoric, Technology, and Pedagogy* 8.1 (2003). Web. 1 July 2012.
Anson, Chris. "Distant Voices: Teaching and Writing in a Culture of Technology." *College English* 61.3 (1999): 261–80. Print.
Banks, Adam J. *Race, Rhetoric, and Technology: Searching for Higher Ground*. Mahwah: Erlbaum, 2006. Print.
Baron, Dennis. "From Pencils to Pixels: The Stages of Literacy Technologies." *Passions, Pedagogies and 21st Century Technologies*. Ed. Gail E. Hawisher and Cynthia L. Selfe. Urbana: National Council of Teachers of English, 1999. 15–33. Print.

Bessette, Lee Skallerup. "It's About Class: Interrogating the Digital Divide." *Hybrid Pedagogy*. 2 July 2012. Web. 8 July 2012.

Bolter, Jay David. *Writing Space: The Computer, Hypertext, and the History of Writing*. Hillsdale: Erlbaum, 1991. Print.

Borton, Sonya C., and Brian Huot. "Responding and Assessing." *Multimodal Composition: Resources for Teachers*. Ed. Cynthia L Selfe. Cresskill: Hampton P, 2007. 99–112. Print.

Boyd, Stowe. "Social Media Blur: Blogs, Networks, Streams." *Stowe Boyd*. 20 May 2010. Web. 1 July 2012.

Brier, Stephen. "Where's the Pedagogy? The Role of Teaching and Learning in the Digital Humanities." *Debates in the Digital Humanities*. Ed. Matthew K. Gold. Minneapolis: U of Minnesota P, 2012. Print.

Brooke, Collin Gifford. *Lingua Fracta: Toward a Rhetoric of New Media*. Cresskill: Hampton P, 2009. Print.

Burton, Sonya C. and Brian Huot. "Responding and Assessing." *Multimodal Composition: Resources for Teachers*. Ed. Cynthia L. Selfe. Cresskill: Hampton P, 2007. Print.

Cohen, Dan, and Tom Scheinfeldt, eds. *Hacking the Academy: A Book Crowdsourced in One Week*. Ann Arbor: U of Michigan P, 2012. Web. 1 July 2012.

Davidson, Cathy. "Humanities 2.0: Promise, Perils, Predictions." *PMLA* 123.3 (2008): 707–717. Print.

DeVoss, Dànielle. *Understanding and Creating Multimodal Projects*. Boston: Bedford/ St. Martins, 2012. Print.

DeVoss, Dànielle, Ellen Cushman, and Jeff T. Grabill. "Infrastructure and Composing: The When of New Media Writing." *College Composition and Communication* 57.1: 14–44. Print.

Dewitt, Scott Lloyd. *Writing Inventions: Identities, Technologies, Pedagogies*. Albany: SUNY P, 2001. Print.

digirhet. "Old + Old + Old = New." *Kairos: A Journal of Rhetoric, Technology, and Pedagogy* 12.3 (2008). Web. 1 July 2012.

Dolmage, Jay. "Disability, Usability, and Universal Design." *Rhetorically Rethinking Usability*. Eds. Susan Miller-Cochran and Rochelle Rodrigo. Cresskill: Hampton P, 2009. Print.

Dubisar, Abby M., and Jason Palmeri. "Palin/Pathos/Peter Griffin: Political Video Remix and Composition Pedagogy." *Computers and Composition* 27.2 (2010): 77–93. Print.

Dunn, Patricia, and Kathleen Dunn De Mers. "Reversing Notions of Disability and Accommodation: Embracing Universal Design in Writing Pedagogy and Web Space." *Kairos: A Journal of Rhetoric, Technology, and Pedagogy* 7.1 (2002). Web. 1 July 2012.

Fleckenstein, Kristie S. "Faceless Students, Virtual Places: Emergence and Communal Accountability in Online Classrooms." *Computers and Composition* 22.2 (2005): 149–76. Print.

Gitelman, Lisa. *Always Already New: Media, History, and the Data of Culture*. Cambridge: MIT P, 2006. Print.

Gold, Matthew K., ed. *Debates in the Digital Humanities*. Minneapolis: U of Minnesota P, 2012. Print.

Grabill, Jeffrey T. "On Divides and Interfaces: Access, Class, and Computers." *Computers and Composition* 20.4 (2003): 455–72. Print.

Handa, Carolyn, ed. *Computers and Community: Teaching Composition in the Twenty-First Century*. Portsmouth: Boynton/Cook, 1990. Print.

Hawisher, Gail E., and Cynthia L. Selfe, eds. *Passions, Pedagogies and 21st Century Technologies*. Urbana: National Council of Teachers of English, 1999. Print.

Hawisher, Gail E., Cynthia L. Selfe, Brittney Moraski, and Melissa Pearson. "Becoming Literate in the Information Age: Cultural Ecologies and the Literacies of Technology." *College Composition and Communication* 55.4 (June 2004): 642–92. Print.

Hea, Amy Kimme, ed. *Going Wireless: A Critical Exploration of Wireless and Mobile Technologies for Composition Teachers and Researchers*. Cresskill: Hampton P, 2009. Print.

Hocks, Mary E. "Understanding Visual Rhetoric in Digital Writing Environments." *College Composition and Communication* 54.4 (2003): 629–656. Print.

Hoover, Ryan. "Prezi for Annotated Bibliographies." *The Power of Persuasion*. 15 May 2012. Web. 1 July 2012.

Inman, James. *Computers and Writing: The Cyborg Era*. Mahwah: Erlbaum, 2004. Print.

Inman, James, and Beth L. Hewett, eds. *Technology and English Studies: Innovative Professional Paths*. Mahwah: Erlbaum, 2006. Print.

Inman, James A., and Donna N. Sewell, eds. *Taking Flight with OWLs: Examining Electronic Writing Center Work*. Mahwah: Erlbaum, 2000. Print.

jayarr. "Video Game Communities on Quickstarter." *Storify*. Web. 1 July 2012.

Johnson-Eilola, Johndan, and Stuart Selber. "Plagiarism, Originality, Assemblage." *Computers and Composition* 24.4 (2007): 375–403. Print.

Kress, Gunther. "Gains and Losses: New Forms of Texts, Knowledge, and Learning." *Computers and Composition* 22.1 (2005): 5–22. Print.

Lanham, Richard. *The Electronic Word: Democracy, Technology, and the Arts*. Chicago: U of Chicago P, 1993. Print.

Lauer, Claire. "What's in a Name? The Anatomy of Defining New/Multi/Modal/Digital/Media Texts." *Kairos: A Journal of Rhetoric, Technology, and Pedagogy* 17.2 (Fall 2012). Web. 25 August 2012.

Lee, Carmen K.-M. "Affordances and Text-Making Practices in Online Instant Messaging." *Written Communication* 24.3 (July 2007): 223–49. Print.

Lowe, Charles, and Terra Williams. "Moving to the Public: Weblogs in the Writing Classroom." *Into the Blogosphere*. Ed. Laura Gurak, Smiljana Antonijevic, Laurie Johnson, Clancy Ratliff, and Jessica Reyman. U of Minnesota, 2004. Web. 1 July 2012.

Manovich, Lev. *The Language of New Media*. Cambridge: MIT P, 2002. Print.

Miller-Cochran, Susan, and Rochelle Rodrigo, eds. *Rhetorically Rethinking Usability: Theories, Practices, and Methodologies*. Cresskill: Hampton P, 2009. Print.

Monroe, Barbara. *Crossing the Digital Divide: Race, Writing, and Technology in the Classroom*. New York: Teachers College P, 2004. Print.

Moran, Charles. "Access: The 'A' Word in Technology Studies." *Passions, Pedagogies and 21st Century Technologies*. Ed. Gail E. Hawisher and Cynthia L. Selfe. Urbana: National Council of Teachers of English, 1999. 205–220. Print.

———. "Technology and the Teaching of Writing." *A Guide to Composition Pedagogies*. Eds. Gary Tate, Amy Rupiper, and Kurt Schick. New York: Oxford UP, 2001. 203–224. Print.

Murray, Elizabeth A., Hailey A. Sheets, and Nicole A. Williams. "The New Work of Assessment: Evaluating Multimodal Compositions." *Computers and Composition Online* (Spring 2010). Web.

National Writing Project. "Cross-walking between Frameworks and Student Work." *Digital Is* (September 22, 2011). Web.

Nelson, Mark Evan, Glynda A. Hull, and Jeeva Roche-Smith. "Challenges of Multimedia Self-Presentation: Taking, and Mistaking, the Show on the Road." *Written Communication* 25.4 (October 2008): 415–40. Print.

Palmeri, Jason. *Remixing Composition: A History of Multimodal Writing Pedagogy*. Carbondale: Southern Illinois UP, 2012. Print.

Penrod, Diane. *Composition in Convergence: The Impact of New Media on Writing Assessment*. Mahwah: Erlbaum, 2005. Print.

Peterson, Patricia Webb. "The Debate about Online Learning: Key Issues for Writing Teachers." *Computers and Composition* 18 (2001): 359–70. Print.

Pew Research Center. "Digital Difference." *Pew Internet and American Life Project.* 13 April 2012. Web. 1 July 2012.

Rhodes, Jacqueline. "'Substantive and Feminist Girlie Action': Women Online." *College Composition and Communication* 54.1 (September 2002): 116–42. Print.

Rice, Jeff. "Networks and New Media." *College English* 69.2 (Nov. 2006): 127–33. Print.

Rice, Jeff, and Marcel O'Gorman, eds. *New Media/New Methods: The Academic Turn from Literacy to Electracy.* West Lafayette: Parlor P, 2008. Print.

Ridolfo, Jim, and Dànielle Nicole DeVoss. "Composing for Recomposition: Rhetorical Velocity and Delivery." *Kairos: A Journal of Rhetoric, Technology, and Pedagogy* 13.2 (2009). Web.

Salvo, Michael J., and Paula Rosinski. "Information Design: From Authoring Text to Architecting Virtual Space." *Digital Literacy for Technical Communication: 21st Century Theory and Practice.* Ed. Rachel Spilka. New York: Routledge, 2010. 103–127. Print.

Samuels, Robert. "The Future Threat to Computers and Composition: Nontenured Instructors, Intellectual Property, and Distance Education." *Computers and Composition* 21.1 (2004): 63–71. Print.

Selber, Stewart A. *Multiliteracies for a Digital Age.* Carbondale: Southern Illinois UP, 2004. Print.

_____. "Reimagining the Functional Side of Computer Literacy." *College Composition and Communication* 55.3 (February 2004): 470–503. Print.

Selfe, Cynthia. *Technology and Literacy in the 21st Century: The Importance of Paying Attention.* Carbondale: Southern Illinois UP, 1999. Print.

Selfe, Cynthia L., ed. *Multimodal Composition: Resources for Teachers.* Cresskill: Hampton P, 2007. Print.

Sheridan, David, Jim Ridolfo, and Anthony Michel. *The Available Means of Persuasion: Mapping a Theory and Pedagogy of Multimodal Public Rhetoric.* Anderson: Parlor P, 2012. Print.

Shipka, Jody. *Toward a Composition Made Whole.* Pittsburgh: U of Pittsburgh P, 2011. Print.

Sidler, Michelle, Richard Morris, and Elizabeth Overman Smith, eds. *Computers in the Composition Classroom: A Critical Sourcebook.* Boston: Bedford/St. Martins, 2008. Print.

Silver, David. "The Difference between Thin and Thick Tweets." *Silver in SF.* 25 February 2009. Web. 1 July 2012.

Sorapure, Madeleine. "Between Modes: Assessing Student New Media Compositions." *Kairos* 10.2 (Winter 2006). Web.

Stroupe, Craig. "Visualizing English: Recognizing the Hybrid Literacy of Visual and Verbal Authorship on the Web." *College English* 62.5 (May 2000): 607–632. Print.

Takayoski, Pamela, and Brian A. Huot, eds. *Teaching Writing with Computers: An Introduction.* Boston: Houghton Mifflin, 2003. Print.

Takayoshi, Pamela, and Cynthia L. Selfe. "Thinking about Multimodality." *Multimodal Composition: Resources for Teachers.* Ed. Cynthia L. Selfe. Cresskill: Hampton P, 2007. 1–12. Print.

Taylor, Todd W., and Irene Ward, eds. *Literacy Theory in the Age of the Internet.* New York: Columbia UP, 1998. Print.

Turnley, Melinda. "Contextualized Design: Teaching Critical Approaches to Web Authoring through Redesign Projects." *Computers and Composition* 22.2 (2005): 131–48. Print.

Ulmer, Gregory L. *Internet Invention: From Literacy to Electracy*. New York: Longman, 2003. Print.

Vie, Stephanie. "Digital Divide 2.0: 'Generation M' and Online Social Network Sites in the Composition Classroom." *Computers and Composition* 25.1 (2008): 9–23. Print.

Whithaus, Carl. *Teaching and Evaluating Writing in the Age of Computers and High-Stakes Testing*. Mahwah: Erlbaum, 2005. Print.

Writing in Digital Environments (WIDE) Research Center Collective. "Why Teach Digital Writing?" *Kairos: A Journal of Rhetoric, Technology, and Pedagogy* 10.1 (2005). Web. 1 July 2012.

Wysocki, Anne Frances. "Seeing the Screen: Research into Visual and Digital Writing Practices." *Handbook of Research on Writing*. Ed. Charles Bazerman. Mahwah: Erlbaum, 2008, 599–612. Print.

_____. "Awaywithwords: On the Possibilities in Unavailable Designs." *Computers and Composition* 22.1 (2005): 55–62. Print.

Wysocki, Anne Frances, Johndan Johnson-Eilola, Cynthia L. Selfe, and Geoffrey Sirc. *Writing New Media: Theory and Applications for Expanding the Teaching of Composition*. Logan: Utah State UP, 2004. Print.

Yancey, Kathleen Blake. "Made Not Only in Words: Composition in a New Key." *College Composition and Communication* 56.2 (2004): 297–328. Print.

Zdenek, Sean. "College Students on the Margins in the New Media Classroom." *Accessible Podcasting*. 26 May 2008. Web. 1 July 2012.

Fully Online and Hybrid
Writing Instruction

Beth L. Hewett

Through online writing instruction (OWI), rhetoric and composition instruction has developed a new discipline and body of knowledge, as well as new questions of efficacy, human (dis)connection, and effective practices. Teaching through OWI is no longer a choice in many institutions, which is reasonable given that contemporary academic and workplace writing tends to occur in digital settings. This chapter outlines some primary considerations for effective OWI.

HISTORICAL VIEW OF LITERACY EDUCATION

When we write with cutting-edge tools, it is easy to forget that whether it consists of energized particles on a screen or ink embedded in paper or lines gouged into clay tablets, writing itself is always first and foremost a technology, a way of engineering materials in order to accomplish an end. . . . we often lose sight of writing as technology, until . . . we try it on, try it out, reject it, and then adapt it to our lives—and of course, adapt our lives to it. (Baron 16)

In ancient Greece and Rome, knowledge of dialectics and rhetoric was passed orally from teacher to student. Philosophers like Socrates expressed faith in this face-to-face teaching process. Oral communication required memory and enabled dialectical analysis. Written communication—whether as a recorded speech to be shared widely or as a means for teaching speech—was not considered as trustworthy. Socrates would wonder: *Could the written word ever convey the integrity of the spoken one and engender critical thinking?* Plato, Socrates' scribe in *Phaedrus*, delicately balances the questionable primacy of orality against an untrusted new literacy. Written instruction, seen to deplete the memory's powers, cannot be questioned or yield answers other than what it already presents (Plato; Ong; Baron).

Nonetheless, such rhetoricians as Aristotle, Isocrates, Cicero, and Quintilian used the written medium as an adjunct to oral instruction for teaching rhetorical communication and for remembering and transmitting information. As Dennis Baron acknowledges, writing itself is a technology, once highly innovative, that inspired the development of writing tools (18). As such tools developed from the stylus to pencils, sustainable ink, varied paper materials, and the printing press, the primary rhetorical educational goal gradually shifted to instruction about writing rather than orality and speech. In nineteenth-century America, oral speech for citizenship purposes met the belletristic stress on written poetry, fiction, drama, and the essay; therefore, both social interactions and college curricula changed (Halloran 162).

Access to textbooks and writing technologies enabled a rising middle class of North Americans to acquire these literacy skills (Halloran) and admittance to privileges once extended only to the elite. People adopted new technologies like mass-produced notebooks, textbooks, refillable/reusable pens and pencils, and typewriters. As particular technologies became ubiquitous, access broadened. People adjusted, as Baron suggests they will. Educators employed new communication-conveying tools by requiring typed essays, for example, over handwritten ones.

Distance Education as Precursor to OWI

In the mid-nineteenth century and throughout the twentieth, correspondence teaching used writing technologies to engage distance education (Declair). Educators used written materials and mail to teach far-flung students who otherwise had no access to traditional oral, onsite instructional settings. Beyond text, distance-based educational technologies included the twentieth-century lantern slide, motion pictures, instructional radio programs, and educational television stations. Advanced technologies infused textual correspondence courses with new life over time: cable and satellite television, recorded cassette tapes between teacher and student, and videotapes. While extended-stay, on-campus workshops supplemented some educational programs, technology returned voice and facial expressions to text-based instruction.

In the 1980s, microcomputers that mediated the communication among teachers and students were adapted for both writing and writing instruction. Digital technologies quickly became "pedagogical tools" (Gouge 357) and learning environments that worked in the classroom and, through the Internet, in distance-based settings. OWI revived and extended distance writing education while simultaneously filling a classroom-based need.

Concerns about OWI

Any new technology introduced to education leads to differing views about its appropriateness for teaching and learning (Peterson). Praised for the potential to level teacher-to-student power (Faigley, *Fragments* and "Subverting") and feared for the potential to restrict empathetic contact within a faceless, body-less environment (Gouge 338; DePew and Lettner-Rust; Ehmann Powers in Hewett, *The Online* 168), computer technology promised to change how writing was taught. Key scholars of the late twentieth century, whose early texts explore both optimistic and apprehensive views, include Cynthia Selfe, Gail Hawisher, and Carolyn Handa.

Catherine Gouge expresses that a great divide exists between the so-called "tech savvy" and "non-tech-savvy, onsite instructors," who no longer can share the same perspectives about teaching writing (339; see also Prensky's *digital natives* and *digital immigrants*). These concerns need to be balanced against the reality that those not born to using digital environments also use such technologies for writing. Similarly, one cannot assume that students who would call themselves digital natives gravitate educationally to OWI; many choose OWI for expedience (e.g., distance-taught soldiers and other working students) rather than as educational preference. It is the unfamiliarity with technology in an educational setting— particularly instruction about writing—that seems most at issue. Nonetheless, while worries about OWI have increased, technological developments have outpaced the rate at which they can be researched and discussed in scholarship.

Although Socrates would be most displeased, and some educators remain dissatisfied with this turn of events, other teachers, scholars, and rhetoricians ("technorhetoricians") express excitement: "Myopic, Luddite fantasies of returning to pencil and paper, the disavowal of the role of technology in the classroom, and the supposition that technology is a passing fad are tired arguments now giving way to a new era of digital rhetoric . . ." (Clark 27). Clearly, OWI is both a distinctive pedagogical approach and one whose benefits remain too little understood from empirical and theoretical research (Hewett, "Generating New Theory").

THE BUILDING BLOCKS OF OWI

Teaching writing with online technologies holds vast, yet complex, potential. OWI cannot be equated with only one way of teaching writing, because it is comprised of building blocks that, once understood, can be moved around to create various computer-mediated environments and scenarios. Minimally, these building blocks consist of course setting, pedagogical purpose, digital modality, medium, and student audience. Each component is addressed in this section.

Course Setting

The Conference on College Composition and Communication (CCCC) Committee for Effective Practices in Online Writing Instruction ("OWI Committee") perceives that institutions recognize different nuances in their definitions of course settings. Therefore, the OWI Committee currently defines course settings (explained next) as either *fully online* or *hybrid* (CCCC, "State-of-the-Art" 5).

Fully online classes are those with no face-to-face components. All of the interactions among teachers and students occur online and at-a-distance through the Internet or an intranet; there are no scheduled onsite interactions. Students can be geographically located from short (i.e., campus-based) or long (i.e., across state/international borders) distance. Either is a distributed setting where the computer technology mediates most interactions, although other communication technologies like the phone can be used. Fully online OWI students and teachers may mistake the course for an old-fashioned correspondence course where the only interactions are about the papers written. Indeed, some teachers treat OWI as if content delivery is the primary focus, not realizing they can create an interactive online writing course.

Hybrid classes meet in either distance-based or computer-mediated settings and in traditional onsite classrooms; they sometimes are called "blended" or "mixed mode" (Snart; Gouge; Hewett, *The Online*). At times, hybrid courses are *both* computer-mediated *and* face-to-face in that all classes are conducted in a networked computer or laptop classroom. Some scholars consider hybrid courses to be superior to fully online ones in terms of efficiency, flexibility, and the opportunity for face time (Gouge; Sapp and Simon). David Sapp and James Simon believe that fully online courses have a measurably higher dropout rate than traditional courses and that hybrid courses provide a remedy (480; CCCC, "State-of-the-Art" 7, 10). In preferring hybridity over fully online settings, teachers may demonstrate partiality for face-to-face interactions.

Pedagogical Purpose

In most cases where traditional views of college composition hold sway, OWI's primary *pedagogical purpose* is to *teach and learn writing*. Such instruction can occur using a number of ideological perspectives and pedagogies. For example, expressivism, social construction, critical pedagogies, and rhetorical argument lend themselves to OWI. One of OWI's benefits is the opportunities it provides for teaching writing interactively (Warnock; Hewett, *The Online*; Reinheimer). Wherever technology enables peer response and discussion groups, decentered classrooms and collaboration are possible (see Kennedy and Howard's chapter in this volume; Breuch). Kristie Fleckenstein sees group interaction as a primary way to bring "communal accountability" to the facelessness of most OWI settings, where hurtful or educationally inappropriate communication can occur. An eclectic theoretical approach to OWI seems best because online writing teachers "need to use any and all effective strategies from any and all epistemologies" (Hewett, *The Online* 79).

While pedagogical purposes for OWI vary, any genre that can be taught onsite can be taught online. OWI courses, especially first-year writing (FYW), typically address more traditional essay and argument forms, which, according to J. Elizabeth Clark, should "be replaced by an intentional pedagogy of digital rhetoric" (28; see also Lundin). Certainly, digitally conceived genres like Web pages, blogs, and wiki pages are best taught in their native online setting. Nonetheless, while OWI could upend the contemporary essay-based writing program, divergent writing forms simply may require additional and differently focused courses (see Brooke's chapter in this volume).

At base, OWI is about writing, and learning writing means practicing writing of various genres and receiving feedback. As Socrates might say, particularly for writing courses, reading alone is insufficiently instructive—student writers need appropriate and comprehensible instruction and feedback. I believe that teachers and tutors need new strategies for teaching students through written responses, particularly language that has semantic integrity. The concept of semantic integrity stems from an incongruence between the fundamentally textual nature of

OWI and the simple migration of traditional communication/instructional strategies. Written instruction has semantic integrity when it addresses the students' own writing in a problem-centered and straightforward manner; enables teachers/tutors to own, but not abuse, their earned authority as educators; and "uses instructional language that provides sufficient information to students, offers clear guidance about potential next steps . . . , and works to prompt new thinking . . ." (*The Online* xviii). An appropriate teaching strategy for OWI provides sufficient information to enact revision—recognizing that a face-to-face or synchronous meeting likely will not occur as intervention. This strategy:

- Uses linguistically direct, rather than indirect, language to explain problems in student writing: "You have one long paragraph that addresses two different issues."
- Explains why it is a problem: "Readers need clear signals (transitions) when the topic changes."
- Teaches how to make changes: "Read the paragraph. Highlight where the shift in ideas occurs. Make a paragraph break there. Use our lesson on transitions to write an appropriate transitional sentence in the new paragraph." (Hewett "Instructor's")

Contemporary, onsite writing courses are focused highly on producing multiple drafts of an essay and on interactions among students and teachers (e.g., one-to-one, one-to-group, and group-to-group). While OWI can employ these pedagogical strategies, it requires a different type of student work than occurs in other, content-based online courses (e.g., history or math). The disciplinary purpose of teaching writing drastically affects online strategy choices because significant amounts of interactive writing and reading are needed to teach writing as skill, process, product, and content. Both students and teachers must be aware of these goals and of the critical importance of reading—students so that they are prepared to meet the challenges of learning to write better or differently through the online setting and teachers so that they develop the right kinds of assignments and assessments for the online environment.

Pedagogical purpose should account for feedback and interactivity processes. Recent research supports a commonly held belief that OWI is more time-intensive than traditional writing instruction. David Reinheimer convincingly argues from a study of one onsite class and three online sections that the online instruction required almost twice as much of the teacher's time. In a study of "literacy load" (the quantity of text to be read and written), June Griffin and Debbie Minter find that teachers read two to three times as much student writing in laptop-based and fully online courses than in a similar onsite course. As teachers consider the pedagogical purposes of their OWI, time and work load factor in, particularly when stakeholders argue that online writing education is more efficient or effective than its onsite counterpart and uncritically use these arguments to raise course caps. On the contrary, retention may be aided by teaching fewer students per course. Arguing for efficiency and cost effectiveness when making decisions about composition ignores "the tensions that exist between what is most efficient and what is most instructionally robust" (DePew, Fishman, Romberger, and Ruetenik 64).

Another factor in achieving OWI's pedagogical purpose is writing support. Because fully online students do not meet their teachers in physical spaces, where facial and body cues convey otherwise unexpressed meaning, the opportunity to share their writing with a trained, capable tutor is critical. However, while helpful tutoring generally can occur either onsite or online, OWI students need an accessible online writing lab (OWL) for supplemental learning (see Lerner's chapter in this volume). As with OWI, online tutoring often happens textually, requiring a language of semantic integrity. Clarity of intention and problem-based teaching remain important whether the tutoring occurs through text or through audio and/or video chat. Most of the available technological options for teaching an online course, including an institution's learning management software (LMS), are potential components of an OWL. Online writing support typically involves a teaching or coaching approach, which can occur along a range of directive to nondirective assistance (Batt; Cooper, Bui, and Riker; Corbett; Hewett, *The Online*; Thonus). OWL support also represents a focused teaching and learning opportunity for students who otherwise experience less teacher-to-student interaction than needed in their traditional setting.

Digital Modality

Particular technologies and software will come and go. More will be developed, and others will be scrapped. Modality, however, has been stable for more than thirty years. The third building block of OWI, modality, shapes interactions among teachers and students, and the desired goals determine the best modality choices. An online writing course can occur in two primary modalities or a blend of the two: *asynchronous* or *synchronous*. Understanding modality helps one to learn and use technology affordances effectively.

The asynchronous modality has a significant time lag (non-real time) between and among interactions. This means that interactions with students likely will occur at different times over the course of a week, for example. "Attendance" is measured not by time or day but by having completed and posted assigned work within given time frames. When people prefer the asynchronous modality, they often like the time flexibility for thinking and writing rather than responding automatically and quickly. Teachers need to go online frequently to interact with various students.

Typically, asynchronous interactions occur through text, although one-way recorded voice and video communications are possible, as with earlier distance education. This modality often is used for text-based peer discussions about ideas and student writing. It also is used to submit drafts and completed assignments for teacher response. Entire courses can be asynchronous with both textual and audio/video components: syllabus, assignments, content delivery, instructions, peer/teacher discussions, conferencing, and responses to student writing.

Asynchronous online writing courses are relatively inexpensive to launch and maintain given that much asynchronous material is text-based and easily reused.

They are not so inexpensive to develop, however, as many professional hours go into shaping such a course with both the students and the modality in mind. When taught with the student's writing growth foremost, such courses are highly time-intensive for teachers (especially at the front end of the process and with written response) and, from this perspective, resource-costly.

Some believe that asynchronous courses are less interpersonal than synchronous ones. Indeed, Sapp and Simon find a higher dropout rate and lower grades in asynchronous courses (475), possibly because some students believe it "will be easier and less demanding" than it is (476). Student persistence in any online course is problematic, with a common drop rate of 50 percent. The OWI Committee's "State-of-the-Art" report, derived from two national surveys in 2011, finds that attrition is high in OWI, but survey respondents made no clear distinction regarding modality. Others find that the simplicity in asynchronous interactions can be inclusive and helpful to student writers (Warnock). To some degree, the nature of fully online and hybrid course settings may be more crucial to persistence than modality, as the "State-of-the-Art" report notes (8). Guided self-selection and adequate student preparation for these courses can assist with retention.

Doubtless, asynchronous teachers must engage their students interactively often and thoughtfully. The difficulty for many online teachers is that they have learned their craft in traditional classroom settings where they can talk to their students about assignments and content, looking to facial and body cues for interest and comprehension. In the purely asynchronous setting, however: "Though many writing teachers may have the skills to communicate content and assignment instructions to students online, few have the sophisticated communication skills necessary to connect with students interpersonally, to build trust and rapport in unfamiliar virtual environments" (Sapp and Simon 478). While they may be unfamiliar to many teachers, there are strategies that help to mitigate losses of facial and bodily cues, such as using instant messaging (IM) and phone calls (Hewett, *The Online*; Warnock).

Conversely, the synchronous modality provides an immediate (real-time) or nearly immediate (near-real-time) time frame during which participants can communicate. Therefore, individual students or student groups must be available at a particular time to meet each other or the teacher, mimicking a more traditional instructional framework. Some of the asynchronous flexibility is lost, but it is balanced by the potential for real-time talk where miscommunication can be addressed immediately. When people prefer synchronous interactions, they most often look forward to the opportunity to talk in real time.

Whereas real-time online interactions occur through two-way voice or voice and video, near-real-time synchronous interactions most often occur textually in chat-based (e.g., IM) or other textual (e.g., whiteboard software) settings. Some LMSs offer synchronous text writing and editing tools. Synchronous technology is less often used for entire OWI courses because of the relative costs of the software and the need for students to have access to microphones, speakers, and video cameras to engage fully (Grabill). However, existing free technology (e.g., Skype and Oovoo) can enable synchronous portions of the course to accomplish tasks:

discussions, interactive class lectures, and one-to-one and one-to-group chats. A blend of the two modalities most often is used because essays typically are written asynchronously, and the teacher's response—even if it is audio or video taped—typically is provided asynchronously.

Medium

The fourth component of OWI is the medium in which it is taught. Media differ from modality, although these definitions may be blended in New Media scholarship. Much of the teaching and learning in an online writing course will occur textually, making *text* the most common medium. *Voice/audio* is a medium some scholars dearly miss in the heavily text-based OWI setting (Sapp and Simon). To offset what can seem to be a quietly sterile environment, some teachers add elements of voice/audio and *video*—at times through asynchronous recordings and other times using free synchronous software.

Anecdotally, some students prefer text-based response to their essays because they can reread it and digest it over time. Others like to hear the teacher's voice recording about their writing, although they may find digitally rewinding to review the advice both exacting and frustrating. Also anecdotally, some students do not access the instructional recordings they are provided.

The following technologies use voice/audio, recorded or live text (see Silva), and/or video: Web pages (Alexander), blogs (Snart), wikis (Lundin; Snart), social networking spaces (DeVoss, Eidman-Aadahl, and Hicks; Maranto and Barton; Vie), gaming software (Hawisher and Selfe), as well as collaborative whiteboards/pages and Internet-based, synchronous meeting spaces. Usually, near-real-time text-based chat is available in these spaces.

Student Audience

When OWI settings, purposes, modalities, and media are selected consciously, then powerful online teaching and learning can occur. However, one also must consider student audience, OWI's fifth building block. The various student audiences and their writing raise issues.

When rhetoric and composition scholars write about OWI students, they typically mean first-year writing students; advanced undergraduates and graduate students with different courses and purposes for learning online sometimes are considered. Although one would hope such students would correctly self-select into their courses, many who choose OWI are ill-prepared for the experience. The OWI Committee's research indicates that student preparedness is critical to ability to succeed; characteristics of preparedness include self-motivation, understanding how an OWI course differs from other online courses, time management skills, and reading and writing skills (CCCC, "State-of-the-Art"10). If their institution does not have a quantifiable method for determining student preparedness, students can search the Internet for learning-readiness tools that measure online study readiness in life factors, individual attributes, learning styles, reading rate and recall, technical competency, technical knowledge, and typing speed/accuracy.

Indicator tests also exist for determining readiness to teach online. However, OWI-specific indicator tests are open to research and development.

Such readiness indicators do not of themselves ensure success because there always are the elements of course design, teacher skill, and unpredictable or un-manageable elements, as well as students' writing abilities and desire/ability to learn. Indeed, students can struggle with maintaining the characteristics that suggest success over the semester's long haul:

> Students . . . reported least liking the need to remain motivated, keeping up with the class, and technological problems (especially in the hybrid setting where a technology glitch could offset an entire class session's work). Many indicated that online class discussions, while interesting, are inefficient and take longer because of typing the remarks and its typically asynchronous nature. (CCCC, "State of the Art" 10)

Various studies suggest that students need much preparation to succeed in an online writing course (CCCC, "State of the Art" 8; Gouge; Sapp and Simon), and a need exists for student and teacher training, particularly for developing "productive discussions" (Gouge 7–8). However, students also need preparation in how to access each other (and why) and the teacher (why and when), how to read the course syllabus and content efficiently and well, and how to understand and use individual conferences and teacher/tutor responses to their writing (Hewett, *Reading* and *The Online*; Warnock). Surprisingly, nationwide survey participants rated students' ability to read and write lower in importance for being "adequately oriented for OWI courses," ironically suggesting that these skills are considered less critical than technology orientation and time-management skills in a text-heavy environment (CCCC, "State-of-the-Art" 10). This inattention to reading is particularly remarkable because OWI is a reading-intensive prospect in both asynchronous and synchronous settings, and it is an issue for both the student and the teacher who must write instructional text that matches the student audiences' abilities (Hawisher and Selfe; Hewett, *Reading*; Wolf).

This section has considered a "traditional" (ages 17–24) student audience thus far. These typically would be compared against so-called nontraditional students (ages 25 and up), who may demonstrate greater timidity in the online classroom than one might expect (Blair and Hoy). However, the era of the digital-age "native" and "immigrant" (Prensky) upends such age-based categories and suggests that all current students are somewhat nontraditional in that they present educators with attitudes, skills, and needs that differ drastically from previous ones (Hewett, *Reading*).

Additionally, some student audiences are less straightforwardly accommodated in OWI than others (Kerschbaum; *Open Words*). Their challenges signal a need for technology usability testing (Miller-Cochran and Rodrigo; Salvo, Ren, Brizzee, and Conard-Salvo). For example, blind students require all text to be readable by text readers; hence, any visual (i.e., video, pictures, and graphs) materials must be captioned, and the technology must enable such captioning. Typically disenfranchised students include those with more basic English reading and writing skills, like developmental and multilingual writers (Chang; Hewett and Lynn; Jin and Zhu; Miller-Cochran and Rodrigo; Tuzi). They also include students with learning differences like dyslexia and those with physical limitations that hinder their senses or typing speed (Burgstahler and Doe; CCCC, "State-of-the-Art"; Meloncon; Oswal and Hewett). Furthermore, students from rural and urban areas and those with impoverished backgrounds may not have had home or school computer and Internet access. Indeed, for any of these students, technology access alone may be insufficient because fluency with online gaming and social networking do not equal education-based computing and interpretive skills.

Difficulties in an online writing course can be exacerbated for marginalized students or those with special needs. For example, most online writing courses will be highly, if not totally, text-based even when synchronous technologies are used. Therefore, while a student with an audio processing disorder might thrive in a quieter, text-centered setting, a student with a reading processing disorder may flounder. Similarly, students with particular writing disabilities may be challenged because they not only must complete the course's expected formal writing, but also must communicate regularly through informal written discussions and messages to the teacher and peers (Hewett, "Characteristics of"). OWI requires students to read not only the syllabus and course materials, but also the teacher's updates and comments, as well as peer writing and content/idea-focused discussions. As Griffin and Minter suggest, this reading/writing load is higher than in a traditional course setting. Therefore, students who are challenged by written English may spend even more time with the reading load *if they choose to complete it*. As discussed, motivation can wane to the student's detriment.

Technology Availability

This list of OWI components does not include technology availability, although some might argue that availability is primary. From the building blocks perspective, however, examining availability first would eliminate a number of choices by virtue of which software, LMS, or other technologies are available through the institution. While the selection process might move faster, the programmatic or individual teacher's power to choose the OWI strategies to meet the students' needs would be muffled. Such choices would be made for expediency rather than for instructional strengths. As written, this list forces examination of teaching preferences, ideologies, and biases. It also requires understanding the basics of OWI—what makes a writing course or writing center "online." With this knowledge, one is prepared to make a broader range of informed decisions. Every online Writing Program Administrator (WPA) and writing teacher/tutor needs this range.

OWI teachers sometimes do not have many choices about the available technology; often, it is selected by technology administrators with no knowledge of writing instruction (Pope). When any particular software or LMS is available institutionally to the OWI program, knowing OWI components means that one can align affordances to instructional goals. A match of affordances to goals means deciding how to bend them to meet the goals set by desired (and required) course setting, pedagogical purpose, digital modality, medium, and student audience. Alternatively, to bend the goals to the affordances is to abandon instructional authority to the technology—to let the technology drive the educational experience. Although sometimes that decision is necessary, it may be avoided by choosing and using the most beneficial affordances of the available technology in the service of predetermined education goals.

A Synthesis of OWI Components

These five components, when considered both programmatically and per individual teacher, will assist in developing a strong OWI program. Even when WPAs and teacher/tutors have no choice in their given assignments and technological tools, these five components empower them to make educationally favorable adaptations. Use the following heuristic to fit the OWI building blocks together:

1. What is the *course setting* in which I will be teaching? Fully online or hybrid? Do I have any choice? If so, what is my choice, and why? If not, do I have any concerns about the setting in which I am being asked to teach? What are they? How can I adapt my teaching to the setting?

2. What is the *pedagogical purpose* of the OWI? Am I providing a teaching/learning experience to writing students? Am I providing learning support through an OWL? Do I have any choice? Although many of the approaches can be similar because online tutoring should have some teaching elements, the students and I would have different goals for the sessions.

   How does the purpose influence whether I want to work fully online or in a hybrid setting? Do I have any choice? If so, this is an opportunity to identify and examine my own biases around OWI. In the case of a teaching/learning scenario, why is the course going online? Does the institution need more seats, which suggests a hybrid setting, or is it trying to appeal to a different student demographic like adults who are geographically distributed, which suggests a fully online setting? If, on the other hand, I am providing OWL support and want a hybrid setting for face-to-face interactions, will all of the online students who need such support be able to travel to campus for the tutoring? How would a fully online tutoring setting differently meet their needs?

3. *Digital modality* is the next component. If my online writing offering is going to be fully online and teaching/learning based, then I need to decide whether it is best taught asynchronously or synchronously or in some blend of the two modalities. Do I have any choice? Do I favor the time flexibility and text-based interactions of asynchronous work or the time sensitivity and more speaker-focused interaction of synchronous work? Why? Do I have the opportunity to combine the two? If so, why or how would I prefer to do that? What goals will doing so meet?

4. Thinking about *medium* naturally follows modality preference. Do I have any choice? How do I want to talk with the students, and how do I want them to respond to me? Text, voice/audio, and even video can be provided to students in asynchronous settings. They are more time-flexible this way

for individual (and repeatable) use. How will these help my students? What are the advantages for me? With the general exception of text—where only a few technologies enable real-time writing and viewing of the writing—voice/audio and video can be provided synchronously, taking advantage of a more spontaneous interaction. Do I want that in my online writing setting? If so, why? What are the advantages for students? For me? How will I support student preferences through the chosen media?

5. The *student audience* is crucial for OWI. Do I have any choice? I may or may not have a choice of whether to teach FYW or advanced undergraduates or graduate students through OWI. In these cases, I should apply the audience factor to the decisions I have made regarding course setting, pedagogical purpose, digital modality, and medium. In doing so, what do I learn about my personal communicative and teaching preferences? How do I think the particular student audience fits those preferences? How should I adjust my preferences to benefit my students?

More challenging, however, are the less fully understood student populations of developmental writers, multilingual writers, students with learning or physical differences, and adult students—as well as the nature of new digital-age native/immigrant categories. If, for example, my writing course is specifically for developmental writers or multilingual writers, do I want to meet them in a hybrid or fully online setting? Why? Do I think that an asynchronous or synchronous or blended setting is best for them? Why? Does my decision change if I learn later that these students are mainstreamed into my FYW course? If I have made a general decision based on questions provided in this list and later learn that I have a dyslexic student or one with a writing disability, how is my planning affected? What if the student is deaf? What accommodations must I make for this student, or should I change my choice of modality or medium in any way? Why? If the class has primarily adult students, should I revise my choices? If so, how and why?

Only at this point, I believe, is it appropriate to consider technology availability, because course plans can be changed to accommodate what is available once one understands OWI's building blocks. For example, if I have been assigned an FYW class and have made the choice to teach it as a hybrid in a computer classroom, what must I adjust when I learn that my section has been moved last minute to a fully online setting with an LMS that has no synchronous tools beyond a one-to-one IM chat feature? Why did I want the hybrid setting to begin with? What did I want to accomplish there? If I wanted to meet the entire class at one time and my LMS will not allow me such synchronicity, what will I lose without those meetings? What can asynchronicity afford me that I did not think of originally? If the loss seems too great, how can an asynchronously made video substitute? If it cannot, should I introduce my students to free software and ask them to join me in a synchronous meeting? If I do that, will it be fully accessible and non-frustrating to all my students? Will my WPA approve the choice given that my OWI program currently is configured for the LMS? In this scenario, note that teaching decisions must be made around available technology, but the teaching goals and accessibility drive the decisions and not the technology. Most important, the understanding of *teaching writing online*— not just generic online instruction—focuses educational decisions.

RESOURCES FOR OWI

Far too little is known about the efficacy of any OWI in either modality using any particular media. Technology is being used and studied, but the technologies— many of which students adapt easily to their social lives—are coming at educators fast and often are being used without sufficient reflection educationally. While a trial-and-error approach is understandable in a fast-paced digital world, uncritical experimentation can be useless at best and harmful at worst for students. For example, a critically responsible use of Massive Open Online Courses (MOOCs) for writing instruction—currently, a hot experimental educational platform—must provide ways to respond to student writing meaningfully. To this end, before adopting new technology, it is crucial to understand the building blocks presented in this chapter and the OWI Committee's recommended OWI Principles (discussed in the next section). From them, technology can be understood, considered, and selected thoughtfully for its potentially most helpful qualities.

Studies of writing and revision based on online modalities are relatively scarce, primarily because empirical and textual analysis studies require deeply time-intensive labor—often for little pay. For example, in the 1990s, Michael Palmquist argued passionately for the benefits of peer collaboration in such settings, but too few studies have provided textual proof of writing change and development. Using student perceptions, Patricia Webb Boyd explains that written, threaded discussions allow students to envision an otherwise invisible audience, making them "co-constructors of knowledge"; however, they still preferred their teacher's feedback as "most important to their learning" (239). She cautions teachers that their presence, therefore, remains crucial to the teaching and learning process even though students can be included in the construction of their courses by making use of this "transitional point" between completely traditional and online settings (240–41). Similarly, limited general studies of asynchronous and synchronous conferences and revision suggest that students can learn how to develop their writing through instructional responses in both modalities (Hewett, "Asynchronous," "Synchronous"). Additional research is crucial.

Despite incomplete understanding of OWI from nascent studies, there are excellent compendium resources:

- Charles Moran's "Technology and the Teaching of Writing" and bibliography in the first edition of this volume
- The CCCC OWI Committee's "Annotated Bibliography" covering (1) OWI pedagogy; (2) OWI technology; (3) e-learning; and (4) online writing centers from early inception through 2008
- CompPile, a comprehensive inventory of composition- and rhetoric-focused publications

A few contemporary essays or essay collections consider issues that globally affect OWI teachers and programs rather than local institutional-level issues. Kelli Cargile Cook and Keith Grant-Davie's *Online Education 2.0: Evolving, Adapting, and Reinventing Online Technical Communication* and *Online Education: Global Questions, Local Answers* satisfy this need. Similarly, relatively few monographs examine OWI comprehensively or theoretically. Among the most important are Selfe's *Technology and Literacy in the Twenty-First Century*; Beth L. Hewett and Christa Ehmann's *Preparing Educators for Online Writing Instruction: Principles and Processes*; Hewett's *The Online Writing Conference: A Guide for Teachers and Tutors,* and Scott Warnock's *Teaching Writing Online: How and Why*. Each attempts to theorize major OWI themes.

Even though educators are wading through new technologies—weekly, it seems—a concerted effort is needed to distill what is known about OWI into theories that can move them to the next level of understanding, practical application, and expertise. The OWI Committee is preparing a book regarding some of these needs: *Foundational Practices in Online Writing Instruction* (Parlor Press, forthcoming 2014). Another book in process is Hewett's *Reading to Learn and Writing to Teach: Literacy Strategies for OWI* (Bedford/St. Martins, forthcoming 2014).

THE FUTURE OF OWI

The OWI Committee has been tasked by the CCCC with conducting necessary research. For seven years it has reviewed the literature; interviewed OWI teachers, WPAs, and other stakeholders; fielded two nationwide surveys; and engaged in intensive meetings with expert teachers and stakeholders. The National Council of Teachers of English (NCTE), through the OWI Committee, recently has released a position statement defining the fundamental principles and illustrating effective strategies that it understands to ground strong OWI. This document is available through the CCCC Web page. Additionally, the OWI Committee is developing the "OWI Open Resource," available on its Web page and open to the educational community for sharing and discussing example effective practices.

Among the position statement's key points, the OWI Committee believes that the most fundamental principle for OWI is one of maximum access. Accessibility in OWI (and higher education generally) has long been ignored, spurring necessary study into usability testing and how to include students who have been excluded from both onsite and online settings. The OWI Committee formed its fundamental principles around accessibility instead of making it an adjunct to a predetermined program because OWI students require proactivity rather than retroactivity; this stance is grounded morally, ethically, and legally through the Americans with Disabilities Act of 1990. When teachers fail to provide reasonable and fair access, students may fail, too.

Another main principle is that an OWL's online writing support is critical and should be provided using the same modality and technologies used in the online course setting. Thus, the OWL is considered a necessary online support system and not an optional adjunct to the traditional writing center. Coupled with the decreased face time and access to physical communication cues, the reading and writing stresses of OWI require that a solid online writing support structure should be in place, and teachers and students should learn how to use it advantageously.

Similarly, the OWI Committee believes that online writing teachers/tutors should receive two types of training for which they are compensated. First, they need technology-focused, instructional training using the same online modalities that they will use in the classroom. They should be afforded the benefits of immersion and individualization as educational principles that help them learn to teach in the digital setting—first by being students in that setting and then by receiving individual attention that supports their strengths and mentors their weaknesses. Second, OWI teachers/tutors need discipline-focused training regarding how to teach *writing* online because, however transferable some traditional writing instruction strategies are to online settings, there are unique qualities to teaching writing online that training should address (see also Hewett and Ehmann; McGrath).

CONCLUSION

Technologies for writing—and, therefore, for the teaching and learning of writing—will continue to develop and likely will outpace educators' slow, careful investigation and any principled adoption of them. Indeed, new technologies can prompt us to challenge long-held assumptions about composition—what it is and how it is taught. It is not to the profession's benefit to adopt for teaching purposes *every* new technological wonder; however, it is important to engage OWI and learn how to teach writing well online. Soon, all students and more teachers will be digital-age natives. As Danielle DeVoss et al. say about the tools that enable the writing and the writing that the tools enable: "Digital writing matters because we live in a networked world, and there's no going back. Because, quite simply, *digital is*" (ix). Indeed, digital technologies are our newest writing technologies, and OWI is their natural offshoot.

BIBLIOGRAPHY

Alexander, Jonathan. *Digital Youth: Emerging Literacies on the World Wide Web*. Cresskill: Hampton P, 2006. Print.

Baron, Dennis. "From Pencils to Pixels: The Stages of Literacy Technologies." *Passions, Pedagogies, and 21st Century Technologies*. Ed. Gail E. Hawisher and Cynthia L. Selfe. Logan: Utah State UP, 1999. 15–33. Print.

Batt, Thomas A. "The Rhetoric of the End Comment." *Rhetoric Review* 24.2 (2005): 207–23. Print.

Blair, Kristine, and Cheryl Hoy. "Paying Attention to Adult Learners Online: The Pedagogy and Politics of Community." *Computers and Composition* 23.1 (2006): 32–48. Print.

Boyd, Patricia Webb. "Analyzing Students' Perceptions of Their Learning in Online and Hybrid First-Year Composition Courses." *Computers and Composition* 25.2 (2008): 224–43. Print.

Breuch, Lee-Ann Kastman. "Enhancing Online Collaboration: Virtual Peer Review in the Writing Classroom." Cargile Cook and Grant-Davie 141–56. Print.

Burgstahler, Sheryl, and Tannis Doe. "Improving Postsecondary Outcomes for Students with Disabilities: Designing Professional Development for Faculty." *Journal of Postsecondary Education and Disability* 18.2 (2006): 135–47. Print.

Cargile Cook, Kellie, and Keith Grant-Davie, eds. *Online Education: Global Questions, Local Answers.* New York: Baywood, 2005. Print.

_____. *Online Education 2.0: Evolving, Adapting, and Reinventing Online Technical Communication.* New York: Baywood, 2013. Print.

Chang, Ching-Fen. "Peer Review via Three Modes in an EFL Writing Course." *Computers and Composition* 29.1 (2012): 63–78. Print.

Clark, J. Elizabeth. "The Digital Imperative: Making the Case for a 21st-Century Pedagogy." *Computers and Composition* 27.1 (2010): 27–35. Print.

CompPile: 1939–Present. Accessed July 6, 2012. http://comppile.org/search/comppile_main_search.php

Conference on College Composition and Communication, Committee for Effective Practices in Online Writing Instruction. "Annotated Bibliography." Keith Gibson and Beth Hewett, Eds. Web. 6 July 2012.

_____. *Foundational Practices in Online Writing Instruction.* Parlor P, forthcoming 2014.

_____. "The State-of-the-Art of OWI: April 12, 2011." Web. 6 July 2012.

Cooper, George, Kara Bui, and Linda Riker. "Protocols and Process in Online Tutoring." *A Tutor's Guide: Helping Writers One to One.* Ed. Ben Rafoth. Portsmouth: Boynton/ Cook, 2000. 91–101. Print.

Corbett, Stephen. "Using Case Study Multi-Methods to Investigate Close(r) Collaboration: Course-Based Tutoring and the Directive/Nondirective Instructional Continuum." *The Writing Center Journal* 31.1 (2011): 55–81. Print.

Declair, D. P. "History." Web. 4 July 2012 http://iml.jou.ufl.edu/projects/spring01/declair/ history.html

DePew, Kevin Eric, T. A. Fishman, Julia E. Romberger, and Bridget Fahey Ruetenik. "Designing Efficiencies: The Parallel Narratives of Distance Education and Composition Studies." *Computers and Composition* 23.1 (2006): 49–67. Print.

DePew, Kevin Eric, and Heather Lettner-Rust. "Mediating Power: Distance Learning Interfaces, Classroom Epistemology, and the Gaze." *Computers and Composition* 26.3 (2009): 174–89. Print.

DeVoss, Danielle Nicole, Elyse Eidman-Aadahl, and Troy Hicks. *Because Digital Writing Matters: Improving Student Writing in Online and Multimedia Environments.* San Francisco: Jossey-Bass, 2010. Print.

Dolmage, Jay, ed. Open Words: Access and English Studies 5.1 (2011). Web.

Faigley, Lester. *Fragments of Rationality: Postmodernity and the Subject of Composition.* Pittsburgh: U of Pittsburgh P, 1992. Print.

_____. "Subverting the Electronic Workbook: Teaching Writing Using Networked Computers." *The Writing Teacher as Researcher: Essays in the Theory and Practice of Class-Based Research.* Ed. Donald A. Daiker and Max Morenberg. Portsmouth: Boynton/ Cook, 1990. 290–311. Print.

Fleckenstein, Kristie S. "Faceless Students, Virtual Places: Emergence and Communal Accountability in Online Classrooms." *Computers and Composition* 22.2 (2005): 149–76. Print.

Gouge, Catherine. "Conversation at a Crucial Moment: Hybrid Courses and the Future of Writing Programs." *College English* 71.4 (2009): 338–62. Print.

Grabill, Jeffrey T. "On Divides and Interfaces: Access, Class, and Computers." *Computers and Composition* 20.4 (2003): 455–72. Print.

Griffin, June, and Debbie Minter. "Expert Views from Student Voices Regarding Fully Online & Hybrid OWI." Conference on College Composition and Communication, St. Louis, MO, March 2012. Address.

Halloran, S. Michael. "From Rhetoric to Composition: The Teaching of Writing in America to 1900." *A Short History of Writing Instruction: From Ancient Greece to Twentieth-Century America.* Ed. James J. Murphy. Davis: Hermagoras P, 1990. 151–82. Print.

Handa, Carolyn, ed. *Computers and Community: Teaching Composition in the Twenty-First Century.* Portsmouth: Boynton/Cook Publishers, 1990. Print.

Hawisher, Gail. *Computers and the Teaching of Writing in American Higher Education.* Norwood: Ablex, 1996. Print.

Hawisher, Gail, and Cynthia Selfe. *Passions, Pedagogies, and 21st Century Technologies.* Logan: Utah State UP, 1999. Print.

Hewett, Beth L. "Asynchronous Online Instructional Commentary: A Study of Student Revision." *Readerly/Writerly Texts: Essays in Literary, Composition, and Pedagogical Theory.* (Double Issue) 11 & 12.1 & 2 (2004–2005): 47–67. Print.

_____. "Characteristics of Interactive Oral and Computer-Mediated Peer Group Talk and Its Influence on Revision." *Computers & Composition* 17.3 (December 2000): 265–88. Print.

_____."Generating New Theory for Online Writing Instruction." *Kairos: Rhetoric, Technology, and Pedagogy* 6.2 (Fall 2001). Web.

_____. "Instructor's Study Guide for *The Online Writing Conference: A Guide for Teachers and Tutors.*" Portsmouth: Heinemann, 2012. Print.

_____. *Reading to Learn and Writing to Teach: Literacy Strategies for OWI.* Bedford/St. Martins, forthcoming 2014. Print.

_____. "Synchronous Online Conference-Based Instruction: A Study of Whiteboard Interactions and Student Writing." *Computers and Composition,* 23.1 (2006), 4–31. Print.

_____. *The Online Writing Conference: A Guide for Teachers and Tutors.* Portsmouth: Heinemann, 2010. Print.

Hewett, Beth L., and Christa Ehmann. *Preparing Educators for Online Writing Instruction: Principles and Processes.* Urbana: National Council of Teachers of English, 2004. Print.

Hewett, Beth L., and Robert Lynn. "Training ESOL Instructors for Online Conferencing." *The Writing Instructor* (September 2007). Web.

Jin, Li, and Wei Zhu. "Dynamic Motives in ESL Computer-Mediated Peer Response." *Computers and Composition* 27.4 (2010): 284–303. Print.

Kerschbaum, Stephanie L. "Avoiding the Difference Fixation: Identity Categories, Markers of Difference, and the Teaching of Writing." *CCC* 63.4 (2012): 616–44. Print.

Lundin, Rebecca Wilson. "Teaching with Wikis: Toward a Networked Pedagogy." *Computers and Composition* 25.4 (2008): 432–88. Print.

Maranto, Gina, and Matt Barton. "Paradox and Promise: MySpace, Facebook, and the Sociopolitics of Social Networking in the Writing Classroom." *Computers and Composition* 27.1 (2010): 36–47. Print.

McGrath, Laura. "In Their Own Voices: Online Writing Instructors Speak Out on Issues of Preparation, Development, & Support." *Computers and Composition Online,* Spring 2008. Web. 23 August 2012.

Meloncon, Lisa. Ed. *Rhetorical Access-ability: At the Intersection of Technical Communication and Disability Studies.* Amityville: Baywood, Forthcoming 2013. Print.

Miller-Cochran, Susan, and Rochelle L. Rodrigo. "Determining Effective Distance Learning Designs through Usability Testing." *Computers and Composition* 23.1 (2006): 91–107. Print.

Moran, Charles. "Technology and the Teaching of Writing." *A Guide to Composition Pedagogies.* Ed. Gary Tate, Amy Rupiper, and Kurt Schick. New York: Oxford UP, 2001. 203–223. Print.

Ong, Walter J. *Orality and Literacy: The Technologizing of the Word.* 2nd ed. New York: Routledge, 2002. Print.

Oswal, Sushil K., and Beth L. Hewett. "Accessibility Challenges for Visually Impaired Students and Their Online Writing Instructors." Meloncon. 134-56. Print.

Palmquist, Michael E. "Network-Supported Interaction in Two Writing Classrooms." *Computers and Composition* 10.4 (1993): 25–57. Print.

Peterson, Patricia Webb. "The Debate about Online Learning: Key Issues for Writing Teachers." *Computers in the Composition Classroom: A Critical Sourcebook.* Ed. Michelle Sidler, Richard Morris, and Elizabeth Overman Smith. New York: Bedford/St. Martin's, 2008. 373–84. Print.

Plato, *Phaedrus.* Trans. B. Jowett. From *The Works of Plato: Four Volumes in One.* New York: J. J. Little & Ives Co.. n.d. Volume 3, 359-449. Print.

Pope, Adam R. "The Ethics of Adopting a Course Management System." *Computers and Composition Online* (Fall 2011). Web. 23 August 2012.

Prensky, Marc. "Digital Natives, Digital Immigrants." *On the Horizon.* MCB UP, 9.5 (October 2001). Web. 29 May 2007.

Reinheimer, David A. "Teaching Composition Online: Whose Side Is Time On?" *Computers and Composition* 22.4 (2005): 459–70. Print.

Salvo, Michael J., Jingfang Ren, H. Allen Brizzee, and Tammy S. Conard-Salvo. "Usability Research in the Writing Lab: Sustaining Discourse and Pedagogy." *Computers and Composition* 26.2 (2009): 107–21. Print.

Sapp, David Alan, and James Simon. "Comparing Grades in Online and Face-to-face Writing Courses: Interpersonal Accountability and Institutional Commitment." *Computers and Composition* 22.4 (2005): 471–89. Print.

Selfe, Cynthia L. *Technology and Literacy in the Twenty-First Century: The Importance of Paying Attention.* Carbondale: Southern Illinois UP, 1999. Print.

Silva, Mary Lourdes. "Camtasia in the Classroom: Student Attitudes and Preferences for Video Commentary or Microsoft Word Comments during the Revision Process." *Computers and Composition* 29.1 (2012): 1–22. Print.

Snart, Jason Allen. *Hybrid Learning: The Perils and Promises of Blending Online and Face-to-face Instruction in Higher Education.* Santa Barbara: Praeger, 2010. Print.

Thonus, Therese. "Triangulating the Key Players: Tutor, Tutee, and Instructor Perceptions of the Tutor's Role." *Writing Center Journal* 22.1 (2001): 59–82. Print.

Tuzi, Frank. "The Impact of E-Feedback on the Revisions of L2 Writers in an Academic Writing Course." *Computers and Composition* 21.2 (2004): 217–35. Print.

Vie, Stephanie. "Digital Divide 2.0: 'Generation M' and the Online Social Networking Sites in the Composition Classroom." *Computers and Composition* 25.1 (2008): 9–23. Print.

Warnock, Scott. *Teaching Writing Online: How and Why.* Champaign: National Council of Teachers of English, 2009. Print.

Wolf, Maryanne. *Proust and the Squid: The Story and Science of the Reading Brain.* New York: Harper, 2007. Print.

Process Pedagogy and Its Legacy

Chris M. Anson

THE PROCESS REVOLUTION: A PERSONAL ACCOUNT

I taught my first course—Freshman English—as a graduate student pursuing an MA in creative writing. It was 1978. At that time, the nascent field of Composition Studies was developing its own disciplinarity, marked especially by the creation of the earliest doctoral programs in Composition Studies. But the course that the well-meaning administrators asked us TAs to teach was, like most such courses across the United States, based on principles that had developed much earlier, in the 1950s. And methodologically, it had evolved from some of the earliest expository writing programs, which had their genesis at Harvard at the end of the nineteenth century (see Brereton).

I was both thrilled and terrified. My students were just a few years behind me, and although I struggled to convince myself of my own authority, they still saw me as someone credentialed enough to assign them papers, tell them about various elements of prose, and grade them fairly, based on my undergraduate major in English and the several years of academic writing and reading experience I had on them. If the students passed the first-semester composition course, they would then enroll in a series of instructor-designed minicourses that focused on some topically relevant stories and short novels. Toward the end of the fall semester, my peers looked forward gleefully to creating and teaching their spring minicourses, as if they were being released from calisthenics to go play outside.

The required book in the first-semester course was Sheridan Baker's *The Complete Stylist*, first published in 1972. In this bestselling text, students learned how to create essays based on a keyhole structure: an introduction that funneled into a thesis statement, three paragraphs supporting the thesis, each with a topic sentence, and a conclusion that recapitulated the thesis. Typically, I lectured for about forty-five minutes using the board and handouts (which helped to take the twenty-five pairs of indifferent eyes off me) and saved a few minutes at the end to explain what the students were supposed to do next. My "assign-and-collect" approach yielded the dreaded semi-weekly burden of covering piles of typewritten "current—tradition"

papers with corrections and explanations—yes, in red ink (Anson, "Beginnings"). In spite of this retrograde pedagogy, many of my students accepted their fate in my course with dignity and even came to think I was doing a good job. They were newly in college, uncritically surrendering to its rites of passage and happy to be away from home. And just as they learned how to survive, so did I—by creating some of my own handouts (on a ditto machine), grading faster, and gaining a little more confidence lecturing to the class about various principles of good writing, including a regular focus on style and grammar.

Around this time, some young faculty I'd come to know invited me to their monthly reading group. They'd been taking up various books and articles in an emerging research area, "Composition," that they predicted would blossom into a major field of inquiry. When I shared this news with my friends in the creative writing program, they cried foul. To them, "researching" writing was like carving up a beautiful creature to see how it worked. Writing was a mystery, a talent to be honed but, if you didn't already have the creative mojo, not really learned or taught. Even so, I was curious, and I signed on.

The next reading selection was Janet Emig's *The Composing Processes of Twelfth Graders*, a slim monograph published by the National Council of Teachers of English, an organization I'd barely heard of. As soon as I dug into its pages, I was intrigued. Here was a scholar who showed how little we really knew about what people *do* when they write. Then, through interviews and an innovative "composing aloud" method, she painstakingly mined the experiences of a few developing writers to figure out what really happened as they used, and tried to improve, this astonishingly complex and miraculous technology of communicating through little marks on a page.

As our group progressed, I was exposed to a couple of other early writing researchers and theorists. But because I was closing in on the MA, my introduction to this emerging scholarship was really just a passing glance. Meanwhile, without anything to guide my teaching beyond *The Complete Stylist* and chit-chat with fellow TAs, I saw little connection between this new work and my classroom. I was also realizing that no matter how well I lectured about thesis statements and the passive voice or marked up students' papers, the method itself was intellectually bankrupt. My students didn't improve much, and I saw almost no signs of creativity or engagement in the work I asked them to do. In some ways, I wasn't cultivating their interest in writing but killing it.

But I was already hooked, and was soon accepted into a PhD program in Composition Studies at Indiana University, where I was awarded a TAship and assigned to teach first-year writing. The program's director, Michael Flanigan, invited each new TA to meet with him before the orientation program to discuss what sort of course they imagined they would teach. I showed up with a textbook I'd found on the shelves of the reading room—a collection of essays grouped into various modes (narration, exposition, argument) and patterns (cause/effect, description, comparison/contrast). Surely this would be an improvement over *The Complete Stylist*; after all, it had lively readings that I (naively) thought would engage my students, like E. B. White's "Once More to the Lake" and Bruce Catton's "A Study in Contrasts," a comparison of Robert E. Lee and Ulysses S. Grant.

Flanigan patiently listened to my plan, and then gently pushed me to elaborate. What would the students do in class, he asked. Well, we would discuss the essays and look for ways the students could use the patterns in their own writing. Would the students work on their essays in class? Probably not, because there wouldn't be time. What would they write about? Oh, they could do essays like those we would read—a comparison/contrast of two grandparents, a description of a favorite place. Would they revise their drafts? Well, if they were smart, yes, at home. What would I do to get them started thinking about their topics? I hesitated. I could assign an outline. Would they talk to each other about their plans? Probably not, so they wouldn't take each other's ideas. How would I know what they were really doing as writers? I hesitated again, wondering why that mattered. And then suddenly Emig's monograph came to mind: how her student subjects composed, the strategies they used or didn't use or had mis-learned.

Not long after the meeting, I had rethought the models-and-patterns approach. In fact, I'd junked it. Then followed a couple of days of TA orientation when we all wrote—a lot—and spent time discussing, revising, and presenting our writing, and reading articles and book chapters on the teaching of writing. The experience was stimulating, but by design it also made us feel vulnerable. The leaders asked us to reflect on the relationship between our experiences and those of our soon-to-be-enrolled undergraduates. Writing was hard, especially knowing it would be shared. Peer response, at first uncomfortable, offered raw feedback that unraveled our certainty and led to lots of new thinking and copious revision. "Skill" and prior experience seemed to fail us as we struggled to find the right words, organize our ideas, and produce something that other readers would find interesting, amusing, or informative. We realized that if we were wrestling this much with relatively simple narratives, our students would need far more than lectures on the thesis, practice recognizing cause/effect, or corrections in the margins of their papers if they were to become more self-aware, competent, and confident writers.

Something was happening to me. As I read more of the literature and designed my course, I came to realize that I was being transformed by the *process movement*. Much later, I would encounter the stories of writing teachers across the country, from the grade school to college, who had similar experiences. They wrote or spoke about how the process movement was liberating, even *revolutionary* (Tobin, "Introduction" 4; Knoeller), utterly upending what they had been doing. Some even confessed to feeling guilty about "ruining" generations of previous students. Even as a young, relatively inexperienced teacher, I too was going through a kind of metamorphosis. My approach to teaching and learning—not just of writing, but everything—would never be the same.

THE PARADIGM SHIFT

I chronicle these early experiences to show how writing pedagogy at the time was evolving but also conflicted—about the content, focus, and goals of composition courses, and about the best methods for teaching, mentoring, and evaluating students.

Those and many other concerns continue to drive the field to this day. In this respect, it is important to recognize the dangers of essentializing the development of the process movement or creating what Nelms calls a "heroes and villains" narrative. Much previous commentary dichotomizes pre-process and process as if the latter suddenly appeared as a new item on the shelf with no traces of what it replaced. But those who implemented it often did so erratically or without fully understanding its principles, and many others remained uninformed about it and went on with business as usual—sometimes with continued success.

In practice, process pedagogy admits to considerable diversity. From a theoretical perspective, however, we can identify assumptions that intentionally contrasted with, and replaced, the generalized pedagogy that was prevalent at the time and had at least some consistent history across higher education (but see Gold). What preceded process has come to be known as the "current-traditional paradigm" (a term coined by Young, "Paradigms"; see also Adams and Adams; Berlin, "Writing" 58)—*traditional* because it was based on a long history of product-focused instruction; *current* because that focus still persists among those who have ignored the field or deliberately resisted what it has said about the acquisition of writing ability; *paradigmatic* because it was based on a worldview of writing against which process pedagogy represented a seismic shift (Hairston). Descriptions of the current-traditional paradigm mirror what I had been doing in my first teaching assignment, including

> an emphasis on the written product rather than the composing process; a reduction of discourse to "the modes" . . . ; formulaic notions of arrangement (e.g., the five-paragraph theme); an inflated concern with usage and style; the assignment of topics for compositions; no discussion of drafting and little, if any, of revision; the assignment of weekly or even daily "themes"; and a focus on grammatical and mechanical correctness—and often even neatness—during evaluation of written products. (Nelms 359)

Drawing on these characteristics, Figure 1 offers a generalized set of distinctions between the assumptions of process pedagogy and what it supplanted. Of course, the very dichotomies in Figure 1, presented as generalized features and not instantiations in specific classrooms, provided the intellectual space for further debate and scholarship (see Connors, *Composition-Rhetoric*).

Perhaps the most common defining characteristic of the new paradigm was a shift from a focus on the *product* of writing to its *process*. Traditionally, teaching assumed that students need rules of discourse based on the qualities of final, polished (and often professional) texts. Good writing is correct, well organized, and stylistically appealing. Because students' writing usually falls short of these attributes, instruction aimed to provide the "missing information." Lectures on grammar, punctuation, usage, and style filled the gaps. Students were supposed to apply these principles to their own writing of essays whose subjects were usually prescribed by the teacher. Learning took place mostly by trial and error; marginal and end comments, accompanied by a grade, were the main (or only) form of individualized instruction. What students did to get from essay prompt to final text happened on

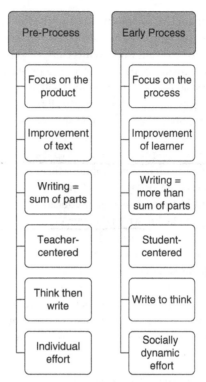

Figure 13.1 Key Distinctions

their own time, usually without support. Because most faculty who taught composition were trained as literary scholars, first-year composition was often a course in writing about literature—that is, finished, artfully written texts (see Lindemann, "Freshman Composition," and New Media Pedagogy in this volume). Teachers also might take apart nonfiction readings to reveal certain features of common modes such as narration, exposition, and argumentation (see Connors, "Rise"). The concept of genre that would later play an important role in composition scholarship remained the province of literary theorists. Professional essays, which came to be called "models," were supposed to show students how to write by example (Flanigan).

Nothing more clearly articulates this first distinction than Donald Murray's 1972 article "Teach Writing as a Process, Not Product." An award-winning journalist before joining the professoriate, Murray became one of the most ardent and influential advocates of the early process movement:

> What is the process we should teach? It is the process of discovery through language. It is the process of exploration of what we know and what we feel about what we know through language. It is the process of using language to learn about our world, to evaluate what we learn about our world, to communicate what we learn about our world. (2)

For Murray, the writing process can be divided into three distinct stages, *prewriting*, *writing*, and *rewriting*. The most time (85%) is spent in prewriting, which yields a first draft (see also Rohman). Then, rewriting reconsiders the draft through the lenses of subject, form, and audience—"it is researching, rethinking, redesigning, rewriting—and finally, line-by-line editing, the demanding, satisfying process of making each word right" (3).

Focusing on these stages leads naturally, Murray argued, to several principles: The text of the course should be the student's own text; the student finds his or her own subject and language; multiple drafts are allowed to encourage the act of discovery; mechanics are relegated to the end of the process; students need plenty of time to refine their papers; and there are no rules or absolutes. In its historical context, process resisted the imposition of norms, regulations, and conventions; it was "decidedly antiestablishment, antiauthoritarian, anti-inauthenticity" (Tobin, "Process" 4; Marshall; Newkirk). For some process scholars, conventional teaching led to dull, uninspired academic writing, which Ken Macrorie called "Engfish," while process teaching focused on creativity, imagination, and the development of an authentic voice (*Telling*). Elbow's *Writing with Power* was all about "letting go," freeing oneself from the constraints that lead to lifeless, voiceless prose. Personal journal writing spread quickly across composition curricula and into the K-12 context (Platt; Progoff). Macrorie's book *Uptaught* almost bitterly critiqued the conventional composition classroom for its academic "enslavement," rejecting, as one reviewer put it, cycles of "prescriptions and proscriptions," "inevitable exercises," and "assignments on impersonal subjects" (Baron 9).

Perhaps because it could be seen as a set of neutral procedures for all writing, process pedagogy broadened beyond the emphasis on expression and authentic voice, and soon it was applied to other purposes, genres, and writers' relationships to their texts. Eventually, scholars contested expressivism itself as a major goal of the introductory writing course, and lively debates ensued, especially between Peter Elbow and David Bartholomae (see Bartholomae, "Writing," and Elbow, "Being," and a series of interchanges in the same issue; see also Feminist Pedagogies in this volume).

An obvious consequence of a new focus on students' processes was to shift the orientation of learning away from expectations for a final text and toward developing the knowledge and abilities needed to produce it. Articles such as Richard Larson's "Process or Product: The Evaluation of Teaching or the Evaluation of Learning?" asked about the locus of instructional attention. Muriel Harris's work helped to make evaluation "formative"—as a tool to be used during the process and not just at its end, a hallmark of the "independent writer" ("Evaluation" 83). Instructional guides introduced teachers to methods of analyzing students' learning and mapping their progress by considering more than the final texts they produced (Murray, *Writer*; Lindeman, *Rhetoric*). It was no longer sufficient to identify error in students' writing but to figure out what caused it (Kroll and Schafer). In *Errors and Expectations,* a book historically central to the development of basic writing programs (see Basic Writing Pedagogy in this volume), Mina Shaughnessy shared the struggles of underprepared students who were entering newly open-admissions universities. Meeting this instructional challenge required the teacher to stop "guarding the tower" and "dive in," becoming "a student of new disciplines and of . . . students themselves in order to perceive both their difficulties and their incipient excellence" ("Diving In" 238). The struggles associated with composing, such as writer's block, now became fertile ground for analysis and support (Rose). As scholarship eventually broadened into the realm of writing centers, Stephen North famously quipped that "our job is to produce better writers, not better writing" ("Idea" 438). It would take many more years for the standardized assessment of writing to catch up to this principle, however, and even today, "testing" students' writing abilities usually means evaluating a timed essay written in a controlled setting, in one draft, based on a prompt the writer has not yet thought about (see Anson, "Closed," and Yancey). The current SAT writing test, taken in twenty-five minutes, now offers the most universally recognized example, while new methods such as portfolio assessment provide more authentic contexts for gauging student achievement.

A corollary of the product/process distinction was a movement away from viewing writing as the sum of its linguistic parts (words, syntax, semantics), an orientation that had affinities with New Critical literary theory and structural linguistics. Instead, writing was to be seen as the "manifestation of complex and interpenetrating cognitive, social, and cultural processes reflecting the literate meaning making of writers" (Sperling 243). Instructionally, this resulted in a shift from the teacher as giver of knowledge to the student as active participant in the creation of knowledge (and writing). Lectures were replaced with individual writing, small-group "workshopping," and discussion. Because instruction now focused on students as writers, the teacher took on the persona of facilitator or "coach." Peter Elbow's highly influential book, *Writing without Teachers*, came to be associated with the "student-centered classroom," a concept paralleled in the more general literature on teaching and learning.

No history of process pedagogy is complete without an acknowledgment of the major contributions of classical and contemporary rhetoric to its development. And no aspect of the process movement opened the door wider to the principles of classical rhetoric than the focus on prewriting—that is, on "invention" or the discovery of ideas (see Lauer, *Invention in Rhetoric*, for a full account). This focus owes strongly to the remnants of the classical five-part rhetorical canons of invention, arrangement, style, memory, and delivery. As process was developing its own momentum, a number of scholars trained in classical rhetoric (re)introduced concepts such as *topoi*, or categories of relationships among ideas, that could help students to discover what to write. Richard Larson ("Discovery" and "Invention") and Richard Young showed how classical questioning techniques could lead to new ideas. Ross Winterowd, among others, helped to popularize the "New Rhetoric" by creating instructional methods from heuristic schemes such as Kenneth Burke's pentad. Several doctoral theses by scholars who would become household names in the emerging field (e.g., Lauer, *Contemporary*; Odell) focused on the process of invention. Other principles from classical rhetoric helped students to create effective arguments (see Lunsford, "Aristotelian Rhetoric" and "Aristotelian vs. Rogerian"), and textbooks quickly followed. For its part, Elbow's *Writing without Teachers* reinforced a principle at the heart of the process movement and ripe for the use of invention strategies: Writers don't figure out what they want to say and then write it; they write in order to figure out what they want to say, and "end up somewhere different from where [they] started" (15). Soon teachers everywhere were creating invention strategies to help students explore and expand their ideas—trees, bubble maps, cluster diagrams, spider webs, sets of questions, and "freewriting"—writing quickly without stopping.

If writers and readers participate in a socially rich "transaction" through texts (Purves and Beach), then facilitating that transaction would help novice writers and their readers to negotiate their understandings and develop proficiency. To build audience awareness into the process, teachers introduced peer-group conferencing sessions (Bruffee, "Brooklyn," "Practical," and "Conversation"; Flanigan and Menendez; Hardaway; Hawkins), which also advanced one of the most important elements of the writing process: *revision* (see Horning and Becker for a full account). Process classrooms took on the characteristics of busy workshops, with students often working in pairs and small groups to brainstorm ideas together or provide feedback on drafts. Soon peer response for individual writers' papers extended into pedagogies involving papers collaboratively written by several students (see Collaborative Writing, Print to Digital in this volume). A new and eventually intense focus on the nature of teacher commentary on students' papers encouraged response to students' drafts in progress (Anson, "What Good Is It?").

As this brief sketch has shown, the assumptions guiding the teaching of composition within the process approach represented an important shift in priorities, attitudes, and the use of class time. But, like any complex movement involving the relationship of theory and practice in socially dynamic situations, process pedagogy didn't develop from a single source of knowledge or among a single group of actors. Instead, it thrived in an environment that cultivated the growth of diverse ideas and approaches from various sources.

DIGGING DEEPER

The process movement was founded on theories about the way people write and should learn to write. But those theories didn't show up ready-made. They were formulated, shaped, and reshaped by constant classroom and curricular experimentation, various kinds of empirical research (see North, *Making*; Massey and Gebhardt), popular textbook authors, and organizational influences.

The Influence of Research
The shift toward process pedagogy is often associated with the development of composition studies as a discipline (see Nystrand, Greene, and Wiemelt for a brief history). For some scholars, Braddock, Lloyd-Jones, and Shoers' *Research in Written Composition* (1963) launched the field by synthesizing existing studies and claiming that there were at least twenty-seven important writing issues about which there was little or no research, a point reinforced by West in 1967, who wrote that "research in written composition remains in a kind of pre-scientific era" (159). For others, the field has its roots in a famous conference at Dartmouth in

1966 that brought together literacy experts from the United States and the United Kingdom to ask serious questions about the development of writing abilities. In addition to Emig's study, a substantial British research project by James Britton and colleagues, *The Development of Writing Abilities (11–18),* is also given credit for inspiring further thinking and investigation, especially across the span of students' development. Much of this activity came in the wake of increasing public concerns about students' writing.

Whatever its driving source, the process movement soon generated intense interest in the empirical investigation of writing.[1] Curiosity about the composing process fit well with the cognitivist orientation that was also dominating work in educational psychology. Many early studies focused on the behaviors of novice writers. Important studies by Perl, Matsuhashi, Daiute, and other researchers meticulously taxonomized writers' composing processes and examined their pauses and planning behaviors. Nancy Sommers compared the revision strategies of students and more accomplished adult writers. Sommers' work also prefigured other comparative research, including a series of studies by Linda Flower, with co-author and cognitive psychologist John Hayes, that led to the creation of a highly influential cognitive-process model of writing. Using composing-aloud protocols, Flower and Hayes's studies provided evidence of a more constructivist view of writing: a complex series of strategic rhetorical and linguistic processes involving planning, monitoring, and reconsidering text while it's being produced. Although the model was critiqued and refined, it became emblematic of process-based research in its sophisticated scientific representation of what goes into composing.

As this kind of writer-focused research mushroomed, other areas of inquiry also thrived—the assessment of writing, writers' awareness of their audiences, the nature of peer response in small revision groups, the effects of certain experimental interventions, how teachers responded to students' essays, and what happened when students wrote with (early) word processors. By the mid-1980s, so much research had accumulated that a meta-analysis was possible, namely Hillocks' *Research on Written Composition,* which focused mostly on different instructional methods. Eventually, cognitively based and traditionally empirical research gave way to many more contextually sensitive studies, a focus on diverse student populations (and then academic and professional contexts), a more strongly social and cultural orientation, and an interest in richly descriptive and ethnographic explorations (see Smagorinsky for a synthesis).

The Influence of Organizations and Curricular and Instructional Development

As research on individual writers provided a clearer picture of composing, classroom-based studies tested their findings or revealed hidden complexities that looped

---

[1]"Scholarship" in composition encompasses a wide range of approaches and methodologies: historiography, text analysis, case studies, descriptive and ethnographic studies, interpretive studies, controlled experiments, and the like. I am focusing here primarily on investigations of writers and what they do when they write, which are often most strongly associated with the process movement.

back to modify theory and raise new questions for investigation. But most teachers of composition were not leaning heavily on the results of empirical research; instead, they were informed by practitioner-based advocacy if and when it came to them.

Entire programs, organizations, and curricula, on the other hand, wielded the power to create broader change. The Conference on College Composition and Communication, founded in 1949 under the umbrella of the older National Council of Teachers of English, became the clearinghouse for the exchange of research, theory, and pedagogy as the process movement developed in higher education. Established in 1976, the Council of Writing Program Administrators grew out of a grassroots effort to help colleges and universities improve their curricula (see McLeod). Now a substantial national organization with a journal and an annual conference, the CWPA clearly influenced the spread of process pedagogy and its implementation in institutions across the country, where millions of students enroll in first-year composition courses. At the campus level, the influence of preparation programs for graduate teaching assistants and other newly hired instructors was, as my personal history suggests, significant. As the TAs finished their degrees and took faculty positions elsewhere, they exported their pedagogies (see Anson and Rutz). Graduate programs in Composition Studies produced future administrators eagerly sought by institutions that had no experts in the field and wanted fresh approaches to their undergraduate curricula. The National Writing Project, which eventually focused predominantly on teachers in the K-12 environment, played a central role through many rich, localized experiences in reorienting classroom teachers to new ideas about fostering written literacy in young people. Faculty in colleges of education became fast friends with those directing or teaching in first-year composition programs, resulting in many productive collaborations. Meanwhile, other allied organizations, such as the American Educational Research Association, the Rhetoric Society of America, and the American Association for Higher Education, also provided support.

The Influence of Scholar-Practitioners

Also informing the development of the process movement were "scholar-practitioners." These were individuals who expressed a deep interest in how they wrote and spent time reflecting on their own experiences as well as what they observed in others, particularly their students. Most held academic positions, but some also had experience as professional writers.

In addition to the work of Elbow, Murray, and Macrorie, William Coles's influential *The Plural I: The Teaching of Writing* took readers on a journey through an alternative composition pedagogy based on the author's own classroom experiences (see Keith, "Plural," for a contemporaneous review). James Moffett's wide-ranging work, but most influentially his *Teaching the Universe of Discourse*, advocated for "noisy," student-centered writing classrooms. In addition, scholars such as James Kinneavy (*A Theory of Discourse*) and Frank D'Angelo ("Generative" and *Conceptual*) contributed new perspectives that encouraged further classroom adaptation. In most cases, the work of scholar-practitioners was not based on empirical research. For example, when Peter Elbow described his now-famous "freewriting" strategy by arguing that "trying to write well for most people means constantly stopping, pondering, and searching for better words," and that to write well one should stop trying to write well (*Writing without Teachers* 25), he was relying on intuition and a lot of experience, not on any sort of systematic investigation of whether such a method led to positive results. Of course, a career teaching writing brings its own "evidence," but as powerful as it may be from the lips or pens of charismatic and believable experts, testimony alone is insufficient for universal and sustained acceptance.

A substantial part of the published scholarship on process pedagogy, then, explained and theoretically justified classroom techniques and ways of working with students or offered theoretical perspectives amenable to application. This literature, sometimes dismissed as lacking the rigor of formal research, nevertheless helped to build the foundation of the discipline of Composition Studies, especially in the way it stimulated empirical investigation to answer critics' doubts about the effectiveness of specific practices.

The Influence of Textbooks

Motivated by profit, the textbook industry contributes to both the stasis and the advancement of the field's pedagogy. If a publisher knows there is a market for an existing approach, it will continue to develop books advocating that approach or market older books in new, minimally revised editions—creating stagnation. If more progressive educators want newer approaches, the publisher will sign authors to create books that support those approaches. Put into the hands of other administrators and teachers who may be unfamiliar with their innovations, these books begin dropping the seeds of change. Because publishing is based on demand, the array of books available for composition courses always reflects the wide diversity of the field itself, from its oldest and most conservative approaches all the way to its cutting edge.

Before the process movement, composition textbooks were rather limited. Handbooks, the purveyors of information about grammar and style, could be counted on one hand (see Connors, "Handbooks"). The most popular was the *Harbrace College Handbook*, written by John C. Hodges and adopted extensively across the United States. (It is now in its 18th edition and barely recognizable next to its progenitor.) Without much competition, Hodges was able to endow the library building at the University of Tennessee in the 1960s with a bequest of three-fourths of all the future royalties from sales of the book (Clark and Gervin). Today, every publisher in the college English and composition market has at least one handbook, and most publishers have several in multiple forms, all competing against each other.

As the process movement evolved, the textbook market began differentiating itself into categories: *handbooks* continued to provide conventional information about grammar and style; *rhetorics* offered practical strategies for writing, usually supported by particular theories; and *readers* provided compilations of essays for students to use as models or as ideas for their own writing. Although the publication of new books in all three categories continued to expand and diversify, the rhetorics saw the greatest innovation throughout the 1980s and 1990s. Meanwhile, as theory and research exploded, the expanding textbook market continued to distill and translate that scholarship, influencing later adopters of the new material.

A review of those many contributions is far beyond the scope of this chapter, but a few references will illustrate their diversity. Peter Elbow's influential books have already been mentioned, their focus on authenticity and freedom from constraint contrasting dramatically with formulaic approaches. In the vein of Elbow, Macrorie's *Telling Writing* strongly critiqued the kind of prose that students often produced in traditional expository writing classes—prose that was lifeless, disingenuous, artificial, pretentious, flabby, or generalized. William Coles's *Composing: Writing as a Self-Creating Process*, attacked clichéd writing and emphasized students' self-expression. Donald Murray, who for years resisted assigning or writing textbooks for students (preferring to focus on their own writing), eventually published *Write to Learn* in the early 1980s. This popular text epitomized process pedagogy by leading students through stages of writing (invention, drafting, revising, editing), illustrated by Murray's own process of writing an autobiographical essay about his grandmother. Anne Berthoff's text, *Forming, Thinking, Writing*, drew on the work of I. A. Richards, Paulo Friere, Kenneth Burke, and other theorists in an eclectic, phenomenological approach that characterized writing as dialectical, imaginative, and transformational. In the midst of the emphasis on process, Berthoff critiqued all approaches that turned students into discursive robots and stripped writing of its deeply symbolic, critical, and discovery-based nature (see Keith, "Berthoff," for a contemporaneous review). Edward P. J. Corbett's *Classical Rhetoric for the Modern Student*, first published in 1965, enjoyed continued success as process-minded teachers adopted its methods. Linguistically based approaches to invention such as tagmemics were the focus of Young, Becker, and Pike's *Rhetoric: Discovery and Change*, a textbook so conceptually sophisticated that it became more popular in graduate courses in composition theory than first-year writing courses (see Brent for a further analysis). These were among dozens of new books flooding the market, some of them by noted scholars and others by unknown classroom teachers who were actively experimenting with new ideas and strategies.

PUSH-BACK: POST-PROCESS

Early critiques of process pedagogy did not aim to replace the theory but to enhance and refine it. After all, it's hard to argue against the idea that to develop stronger writers we should intervene in and support the activity of writing itself, any more than we could argue against coaches' work with their athletes or violin makers' tutelage of their apprentices. Rather, concerns arose about the essentialized nature of the writing process as a generalized set of complex cognitive, linguistic, ideational, and interpersonal activities relying on prior experience with print literacy—what Kent calls the "Big Theory" (1).

A clear example of process pedagogy's limitations can be seen in the way theory and research lost their complexity on the way to the classroom. Eager to translate process theory into workable classroom strategies, many teachers created easily digestible schemes that helped to structure their syllabi. Among the most ubiquitous was the "process wheel," a visual representation of the stages discussed earlier (with arrows connecting "prewriting," "writing," "revising," and "presenting"). The model suggested that writers pass through the stages of writing in a relatively lockstep way. Challenged by researchers such as Nancy Sommers and Sondra Perl, the linear or "one-directional wheel" model soon gave way to a more sophisticated version that included arrows pointing both forward and backward or between the stages, which made the circle _recursive_: a writer can, for example, go back to brainstorming after realizing there's a serious problem with a draft during the revision process. Or, as the writer drafts, she can find herself inventing and revising at the same time. But the convenience of the discrete stages for structuring classroom instruction and activities held great sway, trickling down into grade school. A day or two could be spent on invention as students worked in groups to create tree diagrams or bubble charts of ideas, and then the next few days could be spent working on drafting, such as writing introductory paragraphs, and then on revising. Many scholars consequently objected to the mindless translation of what the field was learning.

Perhaps more important, scholars began contesting already entrenched assumptions about composing, especially in the context of different populations of learners. For example, research had established that novice writers don't revise effectively and that good writing requires copious revision. In "Composing Processes of One-Draft and Multi-Draft Writers," Muriel Harris showed that writers behave differently depending on a host of factors and that these differences are not necessarily tied to the quality of performance. Harris's study is a good example of the way that the field itself was progressing, as researchers contested existing assumptions, complicated established views of composing, and conducted studies that contradicted earlier findings. Broader ideological changes were also under way, especially in the context of what scholars have called the "social turn": a new emphasis on social and cultural issues that had been dormant in the strongly cognitivist, even laboratory-like early process research.

For Trimbur, the social turn was synonymous with a movement toward a "post-process" stage in the field's development. As Matsuda describes it, "the use of the term 'post-process' to denote the social view of writing reduced process to expressive and cognitive theories and pedagogies, while the social theories of composition became a separate category. This rhetorical move made the process movement even more vulnerable in the already shifting landscape of composition studies" (73). Several scholars, including Matsuda, have pointed out that post-process was not really another paradigm shift but a loose, undifferentiated set of assumptions and theories that pushed back, sometimes gently, sometimes more strongly, against the process movement—suggesting not so much a rift in the field as a period of major development. The clearest distinctions are based on what process was lacking up to the start of the 1990s: sensitivity to the cultural, social, ideological, public, situated, and interactive dimensions of writing. Noting how little was written about post-process in almost fifteen years since Trimbur had coined the term in 1994, Heard suggested that the term *post-process* had "become muddled and insignificant—confused with general classification signaling merely a next phase in composition history" (285). At the core of post-process, he continued, is the assumption that "communication is paralogic—unpredictable and uncodifiable—and that composition must find ways to reflect this idea in theory and practice" (285). Coming at a time when even process research was still highly unsettled and inconclusive, it is easy to see how such critiques could threaten the pedagogical foundations of strongly process-based classrooms (for fuller accounts of the post-process movement, see Matsuda; Heard; and Kent). But without a clearly theorized *replacement* for attention to students' writing processes, that part of instruction remained constant even while the focus and content of courses delved into cultural, political, and civic realms (see Ede).

One recent development that appears to reconcile process and post-process theories is a pedagogy called "writing about writing" (Downs and Wardle, "Teaching"). A WaW course "explicitly recognizes the impossibility of teaching a universal academic discourse and rejects that as a goal for first-year composition. It seeks instead to improve students' understanding of writing, rhetoric, language, and literacy in a course that is topically oriented to reading and writing as scholarly inquiry and that encourages more realistic conceptions of writing" (552). Instead of introducing students to particular methods, the course engages them in an interrogation of writing and literacy that helps to bring to the surface tacitly held beliefs and unexamined practices. Rather than "translating" scholarship in the field, it brings it into the classroom for discussion and application—so that "learning about writing [can] change students' conceptions of, approaches to, and processes of writing by putting content, form, and process in harmony rather than constant tension" (Downs and Wardle, "Reimagining").

THE LEGACY OF PROCESS

It is important for anyone not fully acquainted with the history of the process movement to realize that we've just finished the quick tour—the one that gives a few brief photo ops of the most recognizable intellectual monuments. A complete account would take at least a book-length journey, and even then it would have to bypass many interesting studies, debates, and other artifacts that more accurately show the complexities and nuances of the movement. And even then, much other information is buried deep in the annals of the field's development and is the stuff of historiography—or, as Nelms points out, was primarily oral and therefore dissipated into the ether of its moment. Readers interested in a slower experience with more stops along the way are well advised to put the process movement into a broader perspective and read histories of the entire field of Composition Studies (e.g., Berlin, "Rhetoric," Crowley, or Murphy), or work through all the chapters in the present volume.

In spite of extensive development and refinement, process pedagogy was bound to be challenged by new generations of scholars who represent emerging ideologies of education and inquiry. Monikers like "post-process" suggest a rejection of an existing system, which is replaced with a new set of assumptions and methods in much the same way that process displaced its own predecessor. But the core of process pedagogy remains. Hardly a well-informed composition program exists whose curriculum, teacher-development program, and daily routines do not engage students in the activities of writing and help them to become more conscious of themselves as writers and the strategies they use to produce text. *Framework for Success in Postsecondary Writing*, a document recently developed by three major writing and literacy organizations, describes the "rhetorical and twenty-first century skills as well as habits of mind and experiences that are critical for college success" (1). Among these are "writing processes—multiple strategies to approach and undertake writing and research" (1). A random scan of almost any composition program's Web presence quickly shows the centrality of process in the curriculum. Technologically rich writing courses in which students create multimedia productions are at least as dependent on process pedagogy as conventional paper-driven courses, adding elements of design, choice of medium, and the skills of technological manipulation.

At base, process pedagogy is designed to help students *engage* in their writing, to develop self-efficacy, confidence, and strategies for meeting the challenges of multiple writing situations. These goals, like the methods that help to achieve them, are now deep in the discipline's bones, and are the lifeblood of its praxis.

BIBLIOGRAPHY

Adams, Katherine H., and John L. Adams. "The Paradox Within: Origins of the Current-Traditional Paradigm." *Rhetoric Society Quarterly* 17.4 (1987): 421–31. Print.

Anson, Chris M. "Beginnings." *Narration as Knowledge*. Ed. Joseph Trimmer. Portsmouth: Heinemann, 1998. 61–70. Print.

———. "Closed Systems and Standardized Writing Tests."*College Composition and Communication* 60.1 (2008): 113–28. Print.

———. "What Good Is It? The Effects of Teacher Response on Students' Development." *Writing Assessment in the 21st Century: Essays in Honor of Edward M. White*. Ed. Norbert Elliot and Les Perelman. New York: Hampton, 2012. 187–202. Print.

———. and Carol Rutz. "Graduate Students, Writing Programs, and Consensus-Based Management: Collaboration in the Face of Disciplinary Ideology." *WPA: Writing Program Administration* 21.2/3 (1998): 106–120. Print.

Baker, Sheridan. *The Complete Stylist*. New York: Crowell, 1972. Print.

Baron, Henry. "In the Library." *Fforum* 1.1 (1979): 8–11. Web. 15 May 2013. http://comppile .org/archives/fforum/fforum1(1).htm.

Bartholomae, David. "Writing with Teachers: A Conversation with Peter Elbow." *College Composition and Communication* 46.1 (1995): 62–71. Print.

Berlin, James A. *Writing Instruction in Nineteenth-Century American Colleges*. Carbondale: Southern Illinois UP, 1984. Print.

———. *Rhetoric and Reality: Writing Instruction in American Colleges, 1900–1985*. Carbondale: Southern Illinois UP, 1987. Print.

Berthoff, Ann. *Forming, Thinking, Writing: The Composing Imagination*. Rochelle Park: Hayden, 1978. Print.

Braddock, Richard, Richard Lloyd-Jones, and Lowell Schoer. *Research in Written Composition*. Urbana: National Council of Teachers of English, 1963. Print.

Brent, Doug. "Young, Becker and Pike's 'Rogerian' Rhetoric: A Twenty-Year Reassessment." *College English* 53.4 (1991): 452–66. Print.

Brereton, John C. *The Origins of Composition Studies in the American College, 1875–1925: A Documentary History*. Pittsburgh: U of Pittsburgh P, 1995. Print.

Britton, James, Tony Burgess, Nancy Martin, Alex McLeod, and Harold Rosen. *The Development of Writing Abilities (11-18)*. Urbana: National Council of Teachers of English, 1979. Print.

Bruffee, Kenneth. "The Brooklyn Plan: Attaining Intellectual Growth through Peer-Group Tutoring." *Liberal Education* 64.4 (1978): 447–68. Print.

_____. "Collaborative Learning and the 'Conversation of Mankind.'" *College English* 46.7 (1984): 635–52. Print.

_____. "Collaborative Learning: Some Practical Models." *College English* 34.5 (1973): 634–43. Print.

Clark, Brooks, and Cari Wade Gervin. "How the 'Harbrace Handbook of English' Changed the Way Americans Learn about Writing." *Metro Pulse*. 15 June 2011. Web. 16 May 2013.

Coles, William. *Composing: Writing as a Self-Creating Process*. Rochelle Park: Hayden, 1974. Print.

_____. *The Plural I: The Teaching of Writing*. New York: Holt, Rinehart and Winston, 1978. Print.

Connors, Robert J. *Composition-Rhetoric: Backgrounds, Theory, and Pedagogy*. Pittsburgh: U of Pittsburgh P, 1997. Print.

_____. "Handbooks: History of a Genre." *Rhetoric Society Quarterly* 13.2 (1983): 87–98. Print.

_____. "The Rise and Fall of the Modes of Discourse." *College Composition and Communication* 32.4 (1981): 444–55. Print.

Corbett, Edward P. J. *Classical Rhetoric for the Modern Student*. New York: Oxford UP, 1965. Print.

Crowley, Sharon. *Composition in the University: Historical and Polemical Essays*. Pittsburgh: U of Pittsburgh P, 1998. Print.

Daiute, Colleen. "Psycholinguistic Foundations of the Writing Process." *Research in the Teaching of English* 15 (1981): 5–22. Print.

D'Angelo, Frank J. *A Conceptual Theory of Rhetoric*. Cambridge: Winthrop, 1975. Print.

_____. "A Generative Rhetoric of the Essay." *College Composition and Communication* 25.5 (1974): 388–96. Print.

Downs, Doug, and Elizabeth Wardle. "Reimagining the Nature of FYC: Trends in Writing-about-Writing Pedagogies." *Exploring Composition Studies: Sites, Issues, and Perspectives*. Ed. Kelly Ritter and Paul Kei Matsuda. Logan: Utah State UP, 2012. 123–44. Print.

_____. "Teaching about Writing, Righting Misconceptions: (Re)Envisioning 'First-Year Composition' as 'Introduction to Writing Studies.'" *College Composition and Communication* 58.4 (2007): 552–84. Print.

Ede, Lisa. "Reading the Writing Process." Tobin and Newkirk, 31–43. Print.

Elbow, Peter. "Being a Writer vs. Being an Academic: A Conflict in Goals." *College Composition and Communication* 46.1 (1995): 72–83. Print.

_____. *Writing with Power*. New York: Oxford UP, 1981. Print.

_____. *Writing without Teachers*. New York: Oxford UP, 1973. Print.

Emig, Janet. *The Composing Processes of Twelfth-Graders*. Urbana: National Council of Teachers of English, 1971. Print.

Flanigan, Michael C. "Composition Models: Dynamic and Static Imitations." *Theory into Practice* 19 (1980): 211–19. Print.

_____. and Diane S. Menendez. "Perception and Change: Teaching Revision." *College English* 42.3 (1980): 256–66. Print.

Flower, Linda S., and John R. Hayes. "Problem Solving Strategies and the Writing Process. *College English* 39 (1977): 449–61. Print.

Framework for Success in Postsecondary Writing. Council of Writing Program Administrators, National Council of Teachers of English, and the National Writing Project. Creative Commons. Print.

Gold, David. *Rhetoric at the Margins: Revising the History of Writing Instruction in American Colleges, 1873–1947*. Carbondale: Southern Illinois UP, 2008. Print.

Hairston, Maxine. "The Winds of Change: Thomas Kuhn and the Revolution in the Teaching of Writing." *College Composition and Communication* 33.1 (1982): 76–88. Print.

Hardaway, Francine. "What Students Can Do to Take the Burden Off You." *College English* 36.5 (1975): 577–80. Print.

Harris, Muriel. "Composing Behaviors of One- and Multi-Draft Writers." *College English* 51.2 (1989): 174–91. Print.

_____. "Evaluation: The Process for Revision." *Journal of Basic Writing* 1.4 (1978): 82–90. Print.

Hawkins, Thom. "Group Inquiry Techniques for Teaching Writing." *College English* 37.7 (1976): 637–45. Print.

Heard, Matthew. "What Should We Do with Postprocess Theory?" *Pedagogy: Critical Approaches to Teaching Literature, Language, Composition, and Culture* 8.2 (2008): 283–304. Web 10 Jan. 2013.

Hillocks, George, Jr. *Research on Written Composition: New Directions for Teaching*. Urbana: ERIC Clearinghouse on Reading and Communication Skills and National Conference on Research in English, 1986. Print.

Hodges, John Cunyus. *Harbrace College Handbook*. New York: Harcourt, Brace, 1946. Print.

Horning, Alice, and Anne Becker. *Revision: History, Theory, and Practice*. Anderson: Parlor P and the WAC Clearinghouse, 2006. Print.

Keith, Philip M. "Ann Berthoff and the Problem of Method in Writing: A Review Essay." *Rhetoric Society Quarterly* 10.2 (1980): 98–103. Print.

_____. Rev. of "The Plural I: The Teaching of Writing by William E. Coles." *Rhetoric Society Quarterly* 8.1 (1978): 16–19. Web 14 Nov. 2012.

Kent, Thomas, ed. *Post-Process Theory: Beyond the Writing-Process Paradigm*. Carbondale: Southern Illinois UP, 1999. Print.

Kinneavy, James. *A Theory of Discourse: The Aims of Discourse*. Englewood Cliffs: Prentice-Hall, 1971. Print.

Knoeller, Christian. "Book Review: *Within and Beyond the Writing Process . . .* , by Dornan, Rosen & Wilson." *The Quarterly of the National Writing Project* 25.4 (2005): n.p. Web.

Kroll, Barry M., and John C. Schafer. "Error-Analysis and the Teaching of Composition." *College Composition and Communication* 29.3 (1978): 242–48. Print.

Larson, Richard L. "Discovery through Questioning: A Plan for Teaching Rhetoric Invention." *College English* 30.2 (1968): 126–34. Print.

_____. "Invention Once More: A Role for Rhetorical Analysis." *College English* 32.6 (1971): 665–72. Print.

_____. "Process or Product: The Evaluation of Teaching or the Evaluation of Learning?" *ADE Bulletin* 35 (1972): 53–58. Print.

Lauer, Janice. *Invention in Contemporary Rhetoric: Heuristic Procedures.* Doctoral diss., U of Michigan, 1967. Print.

_____. *Invention in Rhetoric and Composition.* Anderson: Parlor P and the WAC Clearing house, 2004. Print.

Lindemann, Erika. "Freshman Composition: No Place for Literature." *College English* 55.3 (1993): 311–16. Print.

_____. *A Rhetoric for Writing Teachers.* New York: Oxford UP, 1982. Print.

Lunsford, Andrea A. "Aristotelian vs. Rogerian Argument: A Reassessment." *College Composition and Communication* 30.2 (1979): 146–51. Print.

_____. "Aristotelian Rhetoric: Let's Get Back to the Classics." *Journal of Basic Writing* 2.1 (1978): 2–12. Print.

Macrorie, Ken. *Telling Writing.* Rochelle Park: Hayden, 1970. Print.

_____. *Uptaught.* Rochelle Park: Hayden, 1970. Print.

Marshall, James. "Of What Does Skill in Writing Really Consist? The Political Life of the Writing Process Movement. Tobin and Newkirk, 45–55. Print.

Massey, Lance, and Richard C. Gebhardt. *The Changing of Knowledge in Composition: Contemporary Perspectives.* Logan: Utah State UP, 2011. Print.

Matsuda, Paul Kei. "Process and Post-Process: A Discursive History." *Journal of Second Language Writing* 12 (2003): 65–83. Print.

Matsuhashi, Ann. "Pausing and Planning: The Tempo of Written Discourse Production." *Research in the Teaching of English* 15.2 (1981): 113–34. Print.

McLeod, Susan. "A History of Writing Program Administration." *Writing Program Administration.* Ed. Susan H. McLeod. Anderson: Parlor P and the WAC Clearinghouse. 23–79. Print.

Moffett, James. *Teaching the Universe of Discourse.* Boston: Houghton-Mifflin, 1968. Print.

Murphy, James J., ed. *A Short History of Writing Instruction from Ancient Greece to Contemporary America.* 3rd ed. New York: Routledge, 2012. Print.

Murray, Donald. "Teach Writing as a Process, Not Product." *Leaflet* (November 1972): 11–14. Rpt. in *The Essential Don Murray: Lessons from America's Greatest Writing Teacher.* Ed. Thomas Newkirk and Lisa C. Miller. Portsmouth: Boynton/Cook, 2008. 1–5. Print.

_____. *Write to Learn.* New York: Holt, Rinehart, and Winston, 1984. Print.

_____. *A Writer Teaches Writing: A Practical Method for Teaching Composition.* Boston: Houghton Mifflin, 1968. Print.

Nelms, Gerald. "The Case for Oral Evidence in Composition Historiography." *Written Communication* 9.3 (1992): 356–84. Print.

Newkirk, Thomas. "The Writing Process—Visions and Revisions." *To Compose: Teaching Writing in High School and College.* Ed. Thomas Newkirk. Portsmouth: Heinemann, 1990. Print.

North, Stephen M. "The Idea of a Writing Center." *College English* 46.5 (1984): 433–46. Print.

_____. *The Making of Knowledge in Composition: Portrait of an Emerging Field.* Portsmouth: Boynton-Cook, 1987. Print.

Nystrand, Martin, Stuart Greene, and Jeffrey Wiemelt. "Where Did Composition Studies Come From? An Intellectual History." *Written Communication* 10.3 (1993): 267–333. Print.

Odell, Lee. *Discovery Procedures for Contemporary Rhetoric: A Study of the Usefulness of the Tagmemic Heuristic Model in Teaching Composition.* Doctoral diss., U of Michigan, 1970. Print.

Perl, Sondra. "The Composing Processes of Unskilled College Writers." *Research in the Teaching of English* 13.4 (1979): 317–36. Print.

Platt, Michael D. "Writing Journals in Courses." *College English* 37.4 (1975): 408–11. Print.

Progoff, Ira. *At a Journal Workshop: The Basic Text and Guide for Using the Intensive Journal Process*. New York: Dialogue House Library, 1975. Print.

Purves, Alan, and Richard Beach. *Literature and the Reader: Research in Response to Literature, Reading Interests, and the Teaching of Literature*. Urbana: National Council of Teachers of English, 1972. Print.

Rohman, D. Gordon. "Pre-Writing: The Stage of Discovery in the Writing Process." *College Composition and Communication* 16.2 (1965): 106–12. Print.

Rose, Mike. *Writer's Block: The Cognitive Dimension*. Carbondale: Southern Illinois UP, 1984. Print.

Shaughnessy, Mina. *Errors and Expectations: A Guide for the Teacher of Basic Writing*. New York: Oxford UP, 1977. Print.

Smagorinsky, Peter, ed. *Research on Composition: Multiple Perspectives on Two Decades of Change*. New York: Teachers College P, 2006. Print.

Sommers, Nancy. "Revision Strategies of Student Writers and Experienced Adult Writers." *College Composition and Communication* 31.4 (1980): 378–88. Print.

Sperling, Melanie. "Process Theory of Writing." *Theorizing Composition: A Critical Sourcebook of Theory and Scholarship in Contemporary Composition Studies*. Ed. Mary Lynch Kennedy. Westport: Greenwood, 1998. 243–49. Print.

Tobin, Lad. "Introduction: How the Writing Process Was Born—and Other Conversion Narratives." *Taking Stock: The Writing Process Movement in the '90's*. Ed. Lad Tobin and Thomas Newkirk. Portsmouth: Heinemann-Boynton/Cook, 1994. 1–14. Print.

_____. "Process Pedagogy." *A Guide to Composition Pedagogies*. Ed. Gary Tate, Amy Rupiper, and Kurt Schick. New York: Oxford UP, 2001. 1–18. Print.

_____. and Thomas Newkirk, eds. *Taking Stock: The Writing Process Movement in the '90s*. Portsmouth: Boynton/Cook, 1994. Print.

Trimbur, John. "Consensus and Difference in Collaborative Learning." *College English* 51 (1989): 602–16. Print.

West, William W. "Written Composition." *Review of Educational Research* 37.2 (1967): 159–67. Print.

Winterowd, Ross W. "'Topics' and Levels in the Composing Process." *College English* 34.5 (1973): 701–709. Print.

Yancey, Kathleen Blake. "Looking Back as We Look Forward: Historicizing Writing Assessment." *College Composition and Communication* 50.3 (1999): 483–503. Print.

Young, Richard. "Invention: A Topographical Survey." *Teaching Composition: 10 Bibliographic Essays*. Ed. Gary Tate. Fort Worth: Texas Christian UP, 1976. Print.

_____. "Paradigms and Problems: Needed Research in Rhetorical Invention." *Research on Composing: Points of Departure*. Ed. Charles Raymond Cooper and Lee Odell. Urbana: National Council of Teachers of English, 1978. 29–48. Print.

_____. Alton Becker, and Kenneth Pike. *Rhetoric: Discovery and Change*. Fort Worth: Harcourt Brace Jovanovich, 1970. Print.

Researched Writing

Rebecca Moore Howard
Sandra Jamieson

> Even at a time when the traditional "research" essay (e.g., write
> ten pages on censorship using ten sources) is fizzling out—
> thank goodness—those of us who teach composition still
> acknowledge that research skills are important.
>
> —Jackie Grutsch McKinney

In 2007, the website *StudentHacks.org* published "How to Write a Great Term Paper in One Evening," a stunning (yet sincere) parody of process theory. The purpose of this Web page is to teach students to construct a quick simulacrum of research. The unidentified writer declares procrastination to be his or her norm and then reorders the usual research process so that fellow procrastinators can start the paper the night before deadline and finish it in just over ten hours. To do this, one *begins* the research process with a thesis statement, followed by drafting a "killer introduction" and then "defend[ing] your thesis"—all in ninety minutes. *Then* procrastinators are urged to conduct their research—for no more than two hours. The writer's rationale? "This is the part that most people wast [sic] time. . . ."

From this student's perspective, researched writing is a meaningless activity, simply a hoop through which students must jump. The writer of "How to Write a Great Term Paper in One Evening" endeavors to protect peers from wasting time in the jump.

We begin our chapter with this anecdote as a way of highlighting the powerful conflicts in assigning and mentoring researched writing. These conflicts are evident in Ford's 1995 edited collection: Many of the contributors identify the research paper as a troubled genre, and then proceed to offer solutions to the problem. Our own research—we are the principal researchers in the Citation Project, a multi-institution research project responding to educators' concerns about plagiarism and the teaching of writing—contributes to the critiques. It is hard to look at the results of Citation Project research and imagine that the assigning of traditional research papers can be sustained in first-year writing (FYW) courses.

Even though the research paper itself is in question, the reasons for assigning it are more compelling than ever. The question is whether writing instructors will continue to assign this problematic genre or whether they will find other, better ways of teaching research *practices*. Toward that end, scholars and practitioners of Writing Studies have developed a variety of sound pedagogical moves that involve students in authentic research and research writing. To those we add our own recommendations, derived from our research and our combined fifty years of experience as writing instructors.

RATIONALES AND GOALS FOR ASSIGNING RESEARCHED WRITING

Late nineteenth-century U.S. higher education was powerfully influenced by the German model of "rigorous 'scientific' philology and historical criticism," and Russell explains that this influence caused research papers to become part of FYW instruction in the 1860s and 1870s (79–80). In a 1955 study, 33 percent of 1,309 courses surveyed assigned "documented papers" ranging from one thousand to five thousand words. The majority of these 433 courses were junior- and senior-level writing courses (CCCC, "Writing").

That rate subsequently increased, and the research paper increasingly became a staple of FYW, not just advanced courses. Of the 171 colleges surveyed in 1961, 83 percent required a research paper in the first year (Manning), and that rate held steady thereafter. Of 397 institutions surveyed in 1982, 84 percent included a first-year research paper, and 78 percent required it (Ford, Rees, and Ward). Of 166 respondents to a 2010 survey on the listserv *WPA-L*, 86 percent reported giving some sort of researched assignment in FYW (Hood).

The research paper was originally assigned to help students learn research skills and practice incorporating sources in an extended, often argument-driven, paper. More recently those research skills have connected with the larger imperative to teach information literacy skills, and the "paper" has expanded to include multimedia. Despite concern over the form of the paper itself, over the model of research it represents, and over the transferability of the skills taught in the process, the research paper is still the major assignment in many FYW curricula.

The research paper as an academic genre endures, too, as a function of academic inertia: What has been done for so long cannot be undone without a revolution of Kuhnian proportions. Its durability also derives from the ideals held by many educators and articulated by Leverenz and by Davis and Shadle ("Building," *Teaching*): teaching students how to inquire, evaluate, sift, sort, choose, argue, explain.

Instructors who assign the research paper in FYW are almost unanimous about what they want the paper to accomplish, and have been so since the first study of the paper by the Conference on College Composition and Communication (CCCC) in 1955 ("Objectives"). Yet Head and Eisenberg's analysis of research handouts and assignments reveals that most faculty tend to issue open-ended invitations to research a question or topic of interest, with little or no discussion of purpose of larger questions of why we conduct research ("Assigning Inquiry").

When asked, proponents of the assignment argue that it familiarizes students with the library and with online databases and research; engages them in the development of an extended paper (usually an argument) written in conversation with the voices and research of others; provides a vehicle for instruction in correct citation and preparation of works cited lists and bibliographies; and includes an emphasis on integration of the voices of others through summary, paraphrase, quotation, and synthesis. These benefits are articulated in textbooks, guides, and course descriptions nationwide, and were most recently endorsed in 2008 by the Council of Writing Program Administrators as part of their list of recommended outcomes for FYW ("Outcomes").

PROBLEMS WITH AND CRITIQUES OF "THE RESEARCH PAPER"

Despite its popularity, the problems with the genre are widely acknowledged, inescapable. Too often the word that comes to mind when people say "research paper" is "plagiarism." The research paper is at the center of contemporary plagiarism hysteria, fanned by inflammatory discourse from the media and from corporations poised to accrue economic capital from that hysteria. In an undated Web page accessed in 2003, the iParadigms corporation, in its *Turnitin.com* iteration, declares,

> Perhaps the greatest resources for would-be plagiarists are the hundreds of online paper-mills, or "cheatsites," that exist solely for the purpose of providing students with quick-fix homework and term-paper solutions. Many of these services contain hundreds of thousands of papers on a wide variety of topics, and some even offer customized papers for an additional fee.

Turnitin.com says nothing in this statement that has not been voiced by many college instructors, some of whom are reluctant to assign research for fear of having to deal with plagiarists (see Adler-Kassner and Estrem 119–20; Schmidt).

Questions about patchwriting, which some consider to be a misuse of sources and others plagiarism (Council, "Defining"; Howard, "Plagiarism"), led to the Citation Project and its study of the ways students use sources in researched writing. Pilot research at one institution found that students did not use summary to report the ideas in their sources, instead working from sentences in ways that did not suggest engagement with or sometimes even comprehension of source material. The findings "raise questions about problems students may have with source-based writing . . . that are both prior to and foundational to their correct citation of sources" (Howard, Rodrigue, and Serviss 188).

The subsequent Citation Project study of FYW students' researched papers from sixteen colleges across twelve states supports many of the initial findings of the pilot. Of the 1,911 citations analyzed in eight hundred pages of students' researched writing, only 6 percent were to summarized material, while 16 percent were to *patchwriting*, defined as "restating a phrase, clause, or one or more sentences while staying close to the language or syntax of the source" ("What Is Plagiarism?"). This small percentage hides a more complex problem. Of the 174 papers studied, 52 percent included at least one incidence of cited patchwriting within the five pages examined within each paper; however, 78 percent of them included at least one incidence of cited paraphrase, and almost all of the students who patchwrote also paraphrased at least once (Jamieson and Howard). The high incidence of patchwriting co-occurring with paraphrase suggests that the students' patchwriting is not plagiarism but attempted, unsuccessful paraphrase: These students are still in the process of mastering the art of paraphrase.

Even more compelling is the finding that 46 percent of the 1,911 citations were to material from the first page of the source—and a total of 77 percent of the citations were to material no deeper than page 3 of the source. Of the 930 sources cited, 56 percent were cited only once, and 76 percent only twice. The research papers produced at the end of the FYW at sixteen institutions of higher education (including state universities, community colleges, religious colleges, Ivy League institutions, liberal arts colleges, and research universities in twelve states from around the country) paint a picture of students who are in the process of mastering the skills of paraphrase and summary and who are not yet able to reproduce the arguments and ideas of their sources in their own words. Those students do not seem to be engaging with the entire text, and they frequently simplify or partially misrepresent the source to make it fit their arguments. In ways too complex to explain here, the Citation Project student papers provide a convincing array of evidence that the student writers are earnestly striving to enact what they had been taught in FYW. We must assume that their instruction had not addressed practices of textual *engagement*; or that such instruction, if it was offered, did not suffice to give the students facility in understanding and engaging with entire texts, and successfully talking about them in paraphrase or summary; or that, despite such effective instruction, the students, when assigned The Research Paper, defaulted to vacuous genre practices.

Others' concerns about research papers precede our study. Scholars object to research papers for philosophical (McCormick) or ideological (Davis and Shadle, "Building") reasons. As they build their argument for inquiry-based research, Davis and Shadle describe traditional undergraduate research assignments as grounded in modernist ideology that values "expertise, detachment, and certainty" ("Building" 5–6). Marsh also associates the research paper with modernist ideals of students as conduits of information that others have developed—not as themselves originators (64). Anson, too, raises the question of students' relationship with new ideas or information, advocating constant interrogation of the purpose served by each citation (213).

Students and instructors hold different ideals for the research paper, and pedagogy may not resonate with instructors' goals for the assignment. Whereas students interviewed by Schwegler and Shamoon reported that the research paper is "an exercise in information gathering" that demonstrates their skills using the library and documenting sources (819), faculty they interviewed described their own research process as one of discovery that leads to exploratory, analytical, and interpretative writing. Alvarez and Dimmock's surveys of faculty two decades later reveal that although "professors implicitly wish that students imitated their own research and writing styles" (4), they do not adopt pedagogies designed to accomplish this. Schwegler and Shamoon add that faculty expectations for the research paper reproduce the students' version of research as "close-ended, informative, skills-oriented" (820), as do the textbooks and pedagogies they select. Other studies have found a similar disjuncture between faculty and student expectations of, and commitment to, research (Leckie; Valentine, "Legitimate Effort").

Those who call for the abolition of the research paper from FYW frequently cite this disjuncture between what most academics consider to be "research" and the version taught in preparation for the first-year research paper. As far back as 1945, Farrison described those papers as simply "digests" (484) that do not involve research as any disciplines define it, and as such both misrepresent real research and confuse students. Forty years later, in 1982 Larson also condemned the assignment for reducing research to "looking up books in the library and taking down information from those books" (813). Today, Citation Project data suggest that, regardless of the assignment, undergraduates regard research papers as an inauthentic genre fit only for the sort of empty performance that Blum identifies as undergraduate students' objective throughout their academic work (61).

BEST PRACTICES IN TEACHING STUDENT RESEARCH

The alternative is not to cease teaching research but to teach it differently. We writing instructors need to focus students' attention on the purposes of research more than on its mechanics. We need to teach students how to find relevant, reliable sources from the vast array of information available to them. We need to teach students how to understand and work with the ideas in the sources they find. We also need to teach them how to recognize the ways audience, purpose, perspective, and context shape the content of those sources and in turn invite readers to ask questions as they read. And we need to devise assignments that do not impel students to default to the vacuous exercise described by *StudentHacks.org.*

The fundamental difficulty, we believe, is that a single Writing course, or especially a single unit *in* a Writing course, is insufficient to teach first-year students how to produce an authentic academic research paper. All it can do is teach them how to produce a simulacrum of such a paper, while expending syllabus time that might better be focused on component research practices such as finding, evaluating, reading, comprehending, synthesizing, and talking about (not just quoting from) complex, lengthy sources.

With very few exceptions, that characterizes the papers analyzed in the Citation Project: They are simulacrums of research. We are confident that a great deal of good pedagogy preceded the students' production of these papers, yet when those papers were produced, the students seemed to be doing little more than what *StudentHacks.org* describes. They appear to have defaulted to an empty genre, regardless of what instruction they may have received.

The best answer we can offer is to remove The Research Paper from FYW, to make space for more extensive and intensive mentoring of research *practices*, in the hope that students who have become comfortable with these practices will more readily be able to put them to work when they produce research papers in their other classes. Toward that end, we offer a variety of recommendations for writing instructors' consideration.

Devise Alternatives to the Research Paper

There are many ways to teach research and source-based writing without assigning "The Research Paper" of old. Rooted in a print-only universe, the very concept of "research paper" has now become an anachronism. Dirk, for example, now assigns small research texts, but never The Research Paper. Head and Eisenberg, however, find that the majority of instructors in other disciplines do still assign the traditional paper ("Assigning Inquiry"), which may explain why many also hold firm to the belief that it should be taught in FYW—even though every discipline has different research conventions and expectations (to the extent that, as Bizup observes, what constitutes a "primary" source in one discipline may count as "secondary" in another). Some instructors within Writing Studies do, too, but the majority of Hood's survey respondents have turned to what might be called research *projects*. Built into this terminological shift is the idea that genres and media might felicitously mix when undergraduates conduct research.

Foster's argument for scaled-back research assignments would seem an appropriate consideration. She calls on instructors to "focus on the skills the students really need to know by a process of scaffolding in which experts and novices collaborate" through what she calls an "information retrieval scaffold" (IRS) that both "foregrounds the importance" of information retrieval and reveals the "multiple embedded tasks" within the process. In her model, the instructor selects a topic or topic area based on course content, professorial expertise, and/or availability of resources, and then selects appropriate sources and designs activities around them. She suggests creating an "appropriate research domain" from library databases; "an instructor-prepared webliography of reputable links"; or one of the commercially prepared research databases made available by publishers (174). Classroom activities allow students to practice the skills embedded within the IRS, including the development of keywords and decisions about which sources are appropriate (172).

While the Citation Project findings do not necessarily suggest that FYW should cease to assign formal, multisource researched papers, both of our institutions have chosen to do so as a result of this research. At Syracuse University, Rebecca teaches a required fourth-semester Writing course dedicated to research. In direct response to the Citation Project findings, she and many of her colleagues no longer assign The Research Paper in the course, instead focusing on component practices. Indeed, The Research Paper is no longer among the learning outcomes identified for that research writing course at Syracuse.

Focus on Engagement Rather Than Mechanics

Leading the way in the refocusing of research instruction are two key books: Ballenger's *Beyond Notecards: Rethinking the Freshman Research Paper* and Davis and Shadle's *Teaching Multiwriting*. Though dated by occasional assumptions of print-dominated literacy—Ballenger speaks, for example, of the "mail-order term paper business" (6)—*Beyond Notecards* remains an important touchstone in the discipline-wide search for research assignments that foster authentic, engaged learning. Ballenger argues for replacing a research paper with a researched essay that positions students as meaning-making inquirers (75). Writing eight years later, Davis and Shadle also advocate research assignments that are based in inquiry, but they urge "an open method of composing—where different genres, media, disciplines, and cultures may be useful or essential, depending on rhetorical situations . . ." (3). At the heart of Davis and Shadle's recommended pedagogy is the practice of asking questions (45), an openness to multiple discourses (56), reading as a form of inquiry (67), and a rhetorical foundation for that inquiry (103). Implicitly or explicitly endorsing Davis and Shadle's agenda, instructors have answered this call in an inventive variety of ways, including mixed-genre research; archival research; multimedia research; field research; a critical engagement with secondary sources; and a revived interest in information literacy.

As digital products expand and complicate print-based notions of research, writing instructors may struggle to stay abreast and thus find themselves making quantified assignments: "Your paper must include references to at least two books"; "You may not cite websites"; "You may not cite *Wikipedia*"; "All of your sources must be scholarly"; and so forth. For students, many of whom have never produced a research project before, lost in such an approach is any reason for *doing* research, beyond demonstrating the researcher's obedience to seemingly arbitrary instructors' demands.

The response of many vanguard writing instructors is to focus on students' engagement with their sources. Writing before the Internet became part of our cultural fabric, Chappell, Hensley, and O'Neill worried about students' information overload and recommended Evaluating Sources workshops as an antidote. Austin starts from the student's voice, asking her class to highlight places in their drafts where they are themselves speaking, in order not only to encourage that voice but also to illuminate the passages in which citations and clear integration are needed. Kennedy's research suggests that fluent writers engage fully with their sources before writing, whereas the "not-so-fluent" do so as they write (450)— perhaps somewhat in the spirit of *StudentHacks*'s recommended limitations on time spent with sources. Responding to Citation Project data, Kleinfeld positions the writing center tutorial as an ideal place for "excessive research: helping students see the initial sources they're drawn to as starting points and resisting the urge to immediately narrow and focus on the first few sources located."

Collaborate with Librarians

Research described by Kolowich shows how little students understand libraries and how little they consult librarians. Those findings can apply not just to students but to their instructors as well. With information retrieval and evaluation more complex than ever, responsible researched writing instruction in FYW must be offered in collaboration with information specialists—librarians.

There are significant theoretical, pedagogical, and ideological differences between the fields of Information Science and Writing Studies, some of which reveal themselves in the use of the term "information literacy" itself. The emphasis on finding and evaluating *information* at the heart of the work of the library definition can sometimes overshadow the *literacy* aspect for writing instructors, who tend to perceive finding and evaluating as only the first step in a process of inquiry. Fister observes that "the portion of library instruction that deals with finding materials tends to emphasize a sequential, tool-oriented search technique," which differs significantly from "the processes scholars go through when they do research" (163). Eadie complains that such instruction "provides the answer before the question has arisen" (45). Syllabi for FYW should be crafted to surmount these limitations and to create *dialogic* collaboration (see Kennedy and Howard, this volume).

Many of the established practices in writing instructors' pedagogical collaborations with librarians are dismal, indeed. Norgaard explains that libraries "evoke, for composition instructors and their students, images of the quick field trip, the scavenger hunt, the generic stand-alone tutorial, or the dreary research paper" (124). Such arrangements may be partnerships, but they are hardly collaborative. They also fail to help students overcome their resistance or indifference to academic research. Mellon describes students who are intimidated by the complexities of college libraries but afraid to reveal their "ignorance" by asking questions (75). When they are confused, they report themselves more likely to consult family members (Foster and Gibbons 81) or friends (Valentine, "Undergraduate" 302). The FYW instructor can alleviate this fear and help students feel comfortable using library resources by presenting reference librarians as an essential part of the research and writing process. By familiarizing themselves with the Association of College and Research Libraries' "Information Literacy Competency Standards," instructors may discover new collaborative possibilities and bridge some of the terminology gaps. Instead of focusing on writing and researching as discrete skills that are a "means to an end," FYW instructors should present both as part of the "practice of making knowledge and inseparably integrated with the intellectual project undertaken by the student" (Corbett 266).

Real collaboration of the sort advocated by Norgaard and others is less a physical exchange of time and skills than an intellectual one. His argument is that the fields of Writing Studies and Information Studies should actively inform each other, because "information literacy informed by work in rhetoric and composition would help yield a more situated, process-oriented literacy relevant to a broad range of rhetorical and intellectual activities" (125). It is this "situated, process-oriented" version of information literacy that we need to develop if the research paper is to be a useful part of FYW.

Writing instructors and librarians might undertake some form of team teaching, with each responsible for her or his own area of expertise. Or they might undertake what Kesselman and Watstein call "embedded librarians" working within writing classes to foster students' information literacy (388). The team-teaching model is relatively common, and embedded librarians are increasingly popular in Writing Across the Curriculum (WAC) programs. A third option, a cross-training model in which librarians and writing instructors gain expertise in each other's areas, is very rare (see Alvarez and Dimmock; Deitering and Jameson). An examination of successful collaborations may reveal other models or suggest adaptations appropriate for different institutions (see Jacobs and Jacobs; Jacobson and Mackey).

Teach the Rhetoric of Finding and Evaluating Sources

Today's students seem no wiser about how to find or use information than were their pre-Internet predecessors. Head and Eisenberg's multi-institutional study of student information-seeking practices "suggest[s] that students conceptualize research, especially tasks associated with seeking information, as a competency learned by rote, rather than as an opportunity to learn, develop, or expand upon an information-gathering strategy" ("Lessons Learned" 1).

Gavin describes a sequence of five collaboratively designed research lab sessions taught by librarians collaborating with writing instructors. Each session incorporates "inquiry, problem solving and critical thinking skills" along with research skills that parallel the writing being completed in the writing courses (231). Other programs integrate a sequence of information literacy lessons into FYW (Holliday and Fagerheim). According to Gavin, detailed, context-specific library research instruction that is reinforced in the writing course challenges students to "re-think their assumptions about research"; to realize that it is not acceptable to "haphazardly pick a few sources and simply rephrase facts and ideas of others and fit the data into a term paper"; and instead to "examine points of view as well as verify facts and statistics from a variety of sources" (232).

As a result of Drew University's participation in the Citation Project, a revised FYW sequence was designed that includes instruction on finding relevant sources that can be used to create a dialogue with assigned readings, in a version of the controlled model of scaled-back research assignments that Foster advocates. Sandra and her colleagues at Drew assign specific texts, which they teach their students to assess, paraphrase, summarize, and correctly cite. Working with the works cited lists of those articles, they then invite students to explore the broader conversations revealed by the sources that are cited. Whose voice seems important to the author? With whom does the author disagree? Selecting sources from the works cited list, students then repeat the process of assessment, paraphrase, summary, and correct citation. As they enter deeper into the network of sources, the students begin to understand citations as a trail writers lay out for others who might wish to find and read the same sources and thereby join the conversation. In other words, Drew students achieve the goals of the information literacy component of the program without going near a "research paper."

Teach Engaged and Critical Reading

Despite the importance of teaching information literacy, too much of contemporary pedagogy is focused on finding and citing sources, and the result is evident in the Citation Project statistics described previously. When 75 percent of students' citations come from the first three pages of the source, it seems obvious that the students are often not reading the entire source, but instead mining it for good quotations. When the "killer quote" has been located, the student quits reading, leading to only 44 percent of the sources being cited more than once.

The search for the perfect quotation is not new; most of us probably remember it from our own undergraduate days. However, the transition to digital sources makes it easier, which requires instructors to understand how students read. Research suggests that reading habits are changing as we spend more time online, and Carr is one of the leading voices arguing that thinking patterns are changing as well, becoming more "staccato" as we skim and scroll through pages. His claims gain credence in a study of users of the British Library's digital collection; readers "from undergraduates to professors" tend to read in a "shallow, horizontal, 'flicking'" way (300), reading only a few pages from each text on scholarly sites and "power browsing" without doing "any real reading" (Rowlands, Nicholas, Williams, Huntington, and Fieldhouse 306). As part of the rhetoric of research, FYW instruction must include attention to *how* sources should be read: not just for a quotation or thesis but also for the evidence for the thesis; the ways in which the source makes its argument; whether the source itself cites other sources; whether it argues only one point of view or explores all the possibilities; what kinds of evidence it uses; and so forth.

To accomplish such an objective, FYW instructors need to slow the reading process down and teach students how to read for content rather than quotations. Even this may be insufficient. Kantz describes sophomores struggling to overcome a naive understanding of "truth" and "facts" in sources, leading them to unquestioningly reproduce chunks of information without comment or explanation. She argues that students must be taught to read rhetorically, using heuristic questions to explore texts and "discover what is worth writing about" (85).

For first-year students to absorb such instruction and be able to enact it, a good deal of the course will necessarily be devoted to what has traditionally been called *critical reading*, which we propose might better be reframed as *engaged reading*. Engaged reading will of course incorporate the critical stance but also Elbow's "believing game" (see Kennedy and Howard, this volume). It will *explore* a source, looking at it from a variety of angles and perspectives, considering what arguments it makes and what arguments might be made from it, uncovering its assumptions. This, we argue, is necessarily the center of researched writing instruction in FYW. Without practice in engaged reading, students can do *nothing more than* find killer quotes, stitch them together, cite them accurately, insert a thesis, and call it a day.

Teach Summary and Paraphrase

Paraphrase, summary, and rhetorical analysis of sources are essential components of teaching engaged reading. In Rebecca's FYW course, analysis comes first, and the instruction begins with students finding claims and identifying evidence in shared sources (Howard, "Comp 1"). Simple techniques of rhetorical analysis come next, as the class explores elements of *logos, ethos,* and *pathos* in the sources; weighs the balance between evidence and counterevidence; and considers how (and how well) the author commands readers' adherence. They then begin picking out key sentences and paraphrasing them, working deliberately to avoid patchwriting.

Next comes summary of the sources, figuring out how to capture the main claims in the source while including but backgrounding the evidence. Then synthesis. *Then* students begin searching for additional sources to expand an argument that they wish to make from the shared sources. This includes intensive evaluation of sources, looking both at intrinsic issues such as the validity of the source's evidence and at extrinsic issues such as the quality of the publisher or the qualifications of the author. The class pauses for a day or two on citation of sources—not just the mechanics, but how to blend in quotation, paraphrase, and summary in ways that highlight the student's own voice and put it *in conversation with* the source. In the written argument that concludes the semester, the culminating assignment in the course, students are *limited to* three sources. When Rebecca teaches the course again next fall, she intends to choose the shared sources not just according to the common topic they address but also according to the range of rhetorical strategies they illustrate.

In a number of ways, such a syllabus departs from traditional research instruction. Its components, nevertheless, are available in established pedagogical scholarship and textbook publishing. The first edition of Behrens and Rosen's textbook *Writing and Reading across the Curriculum*, published in 1982, offered summary-writing as one of three keys, and subsequent texts have duplicated that emphasis. In her scholarship Rebecca has described summary as an essential skill for text comprehension (Howard, "Plagiarism"). Shi's research demonstrates how challenging summary-writing is for multilingual writers. Summary-writing is a learned skill, and as Bean concludes, "Writing summaries or précis of articles or lectures is a superb way to develop reading and listening skills, to practice decentering, and to develop the skills of precision, clarity, and succinctness" (128). It is not a "simple" skill that should have been learned in secondary school; it is an advanced practice that academic writers are always developing. Instructors interested in including summary-writing in FYW might consult Bean, as well as other entries in the "Summary and Paraphrase" bibliography at Rebecca's website (Howard, "Bibliographies").

The same is true of paraphrase. Roig demonstrates that even professors have a difficult time avoiding patchwriting when they summarize texts on an unfamiliar topic. Writing instructors wishing to consider possibilities for paraphrase instruction might begin with Shirley's "The Art of Paraphrase" and then explore other entries in the "Summary and Paraphrase" bibliography.

Pedagogies of rhetorical analysis, though hardly a dominant force, are more familiar in Writing Studies. D'Angelo offers an overview of rhetorical criticism, and Rebecca's website provides a "Rhetorical Analysis" bibliography (Howard, "Bibliographies").

Explore Multimedia Genres

Multiple media are becoming increasingly common in researched assignments. Instructors may ask students to publish their research in two media, making the necessary adaptations for medium and audience. Perry, for example, describes *PowerPoint* presentations as a staple of his inquiry-based research instruction. Pegram asks his students to write a proposal for solving a local problem.

Other instructors may ask for the research to be published in any medium *except* writing. They may ask for multiple media to be integrated in a single project—embedding sound files in an online text or inserting visuals into a print text, for example. Or they may begin the researched assignment with a response to a visual text. Such assignments challenge the notion of FYW researched assignments as procedural exercises in knowledge-reporting, and they also open up opportunities for discussing ethical and legal issues in using visual and audio texts produced by others.

The theoretical foundations for multimedia research vary; Jones, for example, draws on performance studies and multimodal discourse studies to explain why she asks her students to develop researched podcasts. Although Jones' students are taking an advanced writing course, her principles are readily applicable in FYW as well.

ASSESSING RESEARCHED WRITING

Just as the relationship between information selection, assessment, and retrieval needs to be wrapped into the process of reading, writing, and thinking, so assessment should treat all parts of the research and writing process as equal. Effective assessment recognizes that information literacy and research writing are intrinsically linked and cannot be assessed by a series of separate rubrics or criteria. Students who select sources they do not understand will be unable to use them meaningfully in their papers. Students who select sources that are themselves summaries of other sources will find themselves unable to further summarize or paraphrase those sources, leaving them at risk of unintentional misuse of sources. Students who select sources based on the title of the article will be less likely to be able to create a dialogue between those sources than those who develop a list of sources from works cited lists and in consultation with instructors who have some familiarity with the topic. In contrast, students who select sources intentionally rather than by rote can write more effective papers. Because failures to retrieve appropriate sources lead to weaker papers, assessing each set of skills separately penalizes students twice.

Reducing the research component of the course to a set of skills to be measured in the final written product risks undermining the critical thinking, information-seeking, and reading skills that structure the collaboration between research and writing instruction (Norgaard 127). As information literacy instruction is woven into the fabric of writing instruction and as we pay greater attention to the ways students incorporate source material, we also need to develop new ways to assess their success.

As the findings of the Citation Project suggest, students tend to produce research papers that include frequent quotation and very little summary. The ubiquity of such papers suggests that this kind of writing is being rewarded when instructors grade it. Simply reading a research paper as a finished product does not reveal the ways students misread or misuse sources. If FYW is to reward students who "re-think their assumptions about research" (Gavin 232) and change their practices accordingly, instructors need to change both the kinds of assignments they give and the ways they assess them.

One way to evaluate the research process as a whole is portfolio assessment, either a digital portfolio or a traditional folder of printed work. The advantage of the former is that it allows an exchange of work throughout the process that is more "provisional [and] . . . much more revisable than words committed to a printed page" (Howard, "Memoranda" 155), moving from teaching through the recursive process of research and writing with the student while also gathering work for a holistic assessment of the process and final product. In a digital or print project portfolio students can include a research proposal, a working or annotated bibliography, a research log, and other exploratory work in addition to the final paper. In such portfolios they also include a metacognitive essay or letter that reflects on and assesses their own writing process (Yancey). Initially, online portfolios were collected on public websites, allowing students to showcase their work but also raising intellectual property issues. The majority are now collected as part of a closed course management program such as Blackboard or Moodle or on a local or commercial password-protected Cloud server such as Dropbox. Many writing programs still prefer to collect printed copies of work in a final portfolio, partly because this is administratively easier, but also because some believe it creates a deeper sense of professionalism in the students.

Ideally, in their responses to student work, instructors explain how errors in an area of information literacy (such as source selection) lead to difficulties in developing papers (such as explaining terms or supporting claims). Similarly, no matter how diligent and thorough the research may be, murky prose style or rhetorical blunders such as inattention to audience prevent writers from sharing the found information. In tracing these connections and emphasizing the interrelatedness of writing and researching, instructors reinforce the connectedness between form and content and help students produce a "more situated, process-oriented literacy relevant to a broad range of rhetorical and intellectual activities" (Norgaard 125) and perhaps a "genuine intellectual engagement" (124).

✷✷✷✷

Emerging from the long-established critiques of the traditional FYW term paper is a significant discipline-wide trend toward affirming the need for research instruction and the need for researched assignments that value knowledge production and critical thinking over rote performance of pre-established conventions of researched writing. Schick's is an important voice in articulating this movement: "What I advocate . . . is not to dispense with teaching students how to use sources but rather to abandon our fixation on the form rather than the function of source attribution." College courses are finite; will a course, unit, or assignment on research be consumed with transmitting and practicing citation conventions, or will it be focused on rationales and methods for the pursuit and production of knowledge? The answer from Davis and Shadle (*Teaching*), from Ballenger, from Schick, and from now legions of writing instructors is clear: Research will be taught, it will be taught more successfully than it was using the hoary term paper assignment, and it will be assessed in ways sensitive to its goals.

BIBLIOGRAPHY

Adler-Kassner, Linda, and Heidi Estrem. "Rethinking Research Writing: Public Literacy in the Composition Classroom." *WPA: Writing Program Administration* 26.3 (2003): 119–31. Print.

Alvarez, Barbara, and Nora Dimmock. "Faculty Expectations of Student Research." *Studying Students: The Undergraduate Research Project at the University of Rochester.* Ed. Nancy Foster and Susan Gibbons. Chicago: Association of College and Research Libraries, 2007. 1–7. PDF file.

Anson, Chris M. "Citation as Speech Act: Exploring the Pragmatics of Reference." *Research Writing Revisited: A Sourcebook for Teachers.* Ed. Pavel Zemliansky and Wendy Bishop. Portsmouth: Heinemann, 2004. 203–13. Print.

Association of College and Research Libraries. "Information Literacy Competency for Higher Education: Standards, Performance Indicators, and Outcomes." American Library Association, 2000. PDF file.

Austin, Barbara. "A Revision Technique for Research Papers." *Teaching English in the Two-Year College* 30.1 (2002): 83. *Proquest Central New Platform.* Web. 27 June 2012.

Ballenger, Bruce. *Beyond Notecards: Rethinking the Freshman Research Paper.* Portsmouth: Heinemann, 1999. Print.

Bean, John C. *Engaging Ideas: The Professor's Guide to Integrating Writing, Critical Thinking, and Active Learning in the Classroom.* San Francisco: Jossey-Bass, 1996. Print.

Behrens, Laurence, and Leonard J. Rosen. *Writing and Reading across the Curriculum.* Boston: Little Brown, 1982. Print.

Bizup, Joseph. "BEAM: A Rhetorical Vocabulary for Teaching Research-Based Writing." *Rhetoric Review* 27.1 (2008): 72–86. *EBSCO Host.* Web. 22 Mar. 2009.

Blum, Susan D. *My Word! Plagiarism and College Culture.* Ithaca: Cornell UP, 2009. Print.

Carr, Nicholas. *The Shallows: What the Internet Is Doing to Our Brains.* New York: Norton, 2011. Print.

Chappell, Virginia, Randall Hensley, and Elizabeth Simmons O'Neill. "Beyond Information Retrieval: Transforming Research Assignments into Genuine Inquiry." *Journal of Teaching Writing* 13.1–2 (1994): 209–24. Print.

Conference on College Composition and Communication (CCCC). "Objectives and Organization of the Composition Course." The Report of Workshop No. 3. *College Composition and Communication* 1.2 (May 1950): 9–14. *JSTOR.* Web. 5 Apr. 2012.

———. "Writing from Source Materials: The Documented Paper." The Report of Workshop No. 10. *College Composition and Communication,* 6.3 (Oct. 1955): 143–45. *JSTOR.* Web. 5 Apr. 2012.

Corbett, Patrick. "What About the 'Google Effect'? Improving the Library Research Habits of First-Year Composition Students." *Teaching English in the Two-Year College* 37.3 (2010): 265–77. *Proquest Central.* Web. 5 Apr. 2012.

Council of Writing Program Administrators. "Defining and Avoiding Plagiarism: The WPA Statement on Best Practices." Jan. 2003. Web. 21 Jan. 2003.

———. "WPA Outcomes Statement for First-Year Composition." July 2008. Web. 29 July 2012.

D'Angelo, Frank J. "Rhetorical Criticism." *Encyclopedia of Rhetoric and Composition: Communication from Ancient Times to the Information Age.* Ed. Theresa Enos. New York: Garland, 1996. 604–608. Print.

Davis, Robert L., and Mark Shadle. "Building a Mystery: Alternative Research Writing and the Academic Act of Seeking." *College Composition and Communication* 51.3 (2000): 417–47. *JSTOR.* Web. 15 Dec. 2007.

_____. *Teaching Multiwriting: Researching and Composing with Multiple Genres, Media, Disciplines, and Cultures*. Carbondale: Southern Illinois UP, 2007. Print.

Deitering, Anne-Marie, and Sara Jameson. "Step by Step through the Scholarly Conversation: A Collaborative Library/Writing Faculty Project to Embed Information Literacy and Promote Critical Thinking in First Year Composition at Oregon State University." *College and Undergraduate Libraries* 15.1–2 (Spring 2008): 47–59. Print.

Dirk, Kerry. "The 'Research Paper' Prompt: A Dialogic Opportunity for Transfer." *Composition Forum* 25 (Spring 2012). Web. 29 July 2012.

Eadie, Tom. "Immodest Proposals: User Instruction for Students Does Not Work." *Library Journal* 115.17 (1990): 42–45. *Academic Search Premier*. Web. 28 July 2012.

Farrison, W. Edward. "Those Research Papers Again." *Journal of Higher Education* 16.9 (Dec. 1945): 484–87. *JSTOR*. Web. 5 April 2012.

Fister, Barbara. "The Research Processes of Undergraduate Students." *Journal of Academic Librarianship* 18.3 (1992): 163–69. Web. 8 May 2012.

Ford, James E., ed. *Teaching the Research Paper: From Theory to Practice, From Research to Writing*. Lanham: Scarecrow P, 1995. Print.

_____, Sharla Rees, and David L. Ward. "Research Paper Instruction: Comprehensive Bibliography of Periodical Sources, 1923–1980." *Bulletin of Bibliography* 39 (1982): 84–98. Print.

Foster, Helen. "Growing Researchers Using an Information-Retrieval Scaffold." *Teaching English in the Two Year College* 31.2 (2003): 170–78. *Proquest Central*. Web. 27 July 2012.

Foster, Nancy, and Susan Gibbons. Eds. *Studying Students: The Undergraduate Research Project at the University of Rochester*. Chicago: Association of College and Research Libraries, 2007. PDF file.

Gavin, Christy. "Guiding Students along the Information Highway: Librarians Collaborating with Composition Instructors." *Journal of Teaching Writing* 13.1–2 (1995): 225–36. Web. 28 July 2012.

Head, Alison J., and Michael B. Eisenberg. "Assigning Inquiry: How Handouts for Research Assignments Guide Today's College Students." *Project Information Literacy Progress Report: University of Washington Information School.* 13 July 2010. 1–41. Web. 27 July 2012.

_____. "Lessons Learned: How College Students Seek Information in the Digital Age." *Project Information Literacy Progress Report: University of Washington Information School.* 1 Dec. 2009. 1–42. Web. 10 Dec. 2012.

Holliday, Wendy, and Fagerheim, Britt. "Integrating Information Literacy with a Sequenced English Composition Curriculum." *PORTAL: Libraries and the Academy* 6.2 (2006): 169–84. *Project Muse*. Web. 27 July 2012.

Hood, Carra Leah. "Ways of Research: The Status of the Traditional Research Paper Assignment in Assignment in First-Year Writing/Composition Courses." *Composition Forum* 22 (Summer 2010). Web. 29 July 2012.

Howard, Rebecca Moore. "Bibliographies." *Rebecca Moore Howard: Writing Matters*. n.d. Web. 5 Jan. 2013.

_____. "Comp 1 Applications of Citation Project Research." *Chenango Metonymy*. 22 Feb. 2013. Web. 25 Feb. 2013.

_____. "A Plagiarism *Pentimento*." *Journal of Teaching Writing* 11.3 (Summer 1993): 233–46. Print.

_____. "Memoranda to Myself: Maxims for the Online Portfolio." *Computers and Composition* 13.2 (1996): 155–67. Print.

Howard, Rebecca Moore, Tanya K. Rodrigue, and Tricia C. Serviss. "Writing from Sources, Writing from Sentences." *Writing and Pedagogy* 2.2 (Fall 2010): 177–92. Print.

Jacobs, Heidi L. M., and Dale Jacobs. "Transforming the Library One-Shot into Pedagogical Collaboration: Information Literacy and the English Composition Class." *Reference & Users Quarterly* 49.1 (2009): 72–82. Web. 12 Dec. 2012.

Jacobson, Trudi E., and Thomas P. Mackey. Eds. *Information Literacy Collaborations That Work*. New York: Neal-Schuman, 2007. Print.

Jamieson, Sandra, and Rebecca Moore Howard. "Sentence-Mining: Uncovering the Amount of Reading and Reading Comprehension in College Writers' Researched Writing." *The New Digital Scholar: Exploring and Enriching the Research and Writing Practices of NextGen Students*. Ed. Randall McClure and James P. Purdy. Medford: Information Today, 2013. 111–33. PDF file.

Jones, Leigh A. "Podcasting and Performativity: Multimodal Invention in an Advanced Writing Class." *Composition Studies* 38.2 (2010): 75–91. Web. 29 July 2012.

Kantz, Margaret. "Helping Students Use Textual Sources Persuasively." *College English* 52.1 (Jan. 1990): 74–91. *JSTOR*. Web. 1 Nov. 2012.

Kennedy, Mary Lynch. "The Composing Process of Students Writing from Sources." *Written Communication* 2 (October 1985): 434–56. Print.

Kesselman, Martin A., and Sarah Barbara Watstein. "Creating Opportunities: Embedded Librarians." *Journal of Library Administration* 49.4 (2009): 383–400. *EBSCO Host*. Web. 29 July 2012.

Kleinfeld, Elizabeth. "Writing Centers, Ethics, and Excessive Research." *Computers and Composition Online* (Fall 2011). Web. 31 July 2012.

Kolowich, Steve. "What Students Don't Know." *Inside Higher Ed* 22 Aug. 2011. Web. 15 Jan. 2012.

Larson, Richard L. "The 'Research Paper' in the Writing Course: A Non-Form of Writing." *College English* 44.8 (Dec. 1982): 811–16. *JSTOR*. Web. 5 Apr. 2012.

Leckie, Gloria J., "Desperately Seeking Citations: Uncovering Faculty Assumptions about the Undergraduate Research Process." *Journal of Academic Librarianship* 22.3 (Mar. 1996): 201–208. *Academic Search Premier*. Web. 3 May 2012.

Leverenz, Carrie Shively. "Citing Cybersources: A Challenge to Disciplinary Values." *Computers and Composition* 15.2 (1998): 185–200. Print.

Manning, Ambrose N. "The Present Status of the Research Paper in Freshman English: A National Survey."*College Composition and Communication* 12.2 (1961): 73–78. *JSTOR*. Web. 5 April 2012.

Marsh, Bill. *Plagiarism: Alchemy and Remedy in Higher Education*. Albany: SUNY P, 2007. Print.

McCormick, Kathleen. "'On a Topic of Your Own Choosing . . .'" *Writing Theory and Critical Theory*. Ed. John Clifford and John Schilb. New York: Modern Language Association, 1994. Print. 33–52.

McKinney, Jackie Grutsch. "The American Scholar Writes the 'New' Research Essay." *Journal of Teaching Writing* 20.1–2 (2002): 71–86. Print.

Mellon, Constance A., ed. *Bibliographic Instruction: The Second Generation*. Littleton: Libraries Unlimited, 1987. Print.

Norgaard, Rolf. "Writing Information Literacy: Contributions to a Concept." *Reference and User Services Quarterly* 43.2 (2003): 124–30. *Proquest Central*. Web. 27 July 2012.

Pegram, David M. "'What If?' Teaching Research and Creative-Thinking Skills through Proposal Writing." *English Journal* 95.4 (Mar. 2006): 18–22. *JSTOR*. Web. 13 July 2012.

Perry, Alan E. "*PowerPoint* Presentations: A Creative Addition to the Research Process." *English Journal* 92.6 (July 2003). *JSTOR*. Web. 31 May 2012.

Roig, Miguel. "Plagiarism and Paraphrasing Criteria of College and University Professors." *Ethics and Behavior* 11.3 (July 2001): 307–324. Print.

Rowlands, Ian, David Nicholas, Peter Williams, Paul Huntington, and Maggie Fieldhouse. "The Google Generation: The Information Behavior of the Researcher of the Future." *Aslib Proceedings: New Information Perspectives* 60.4 (2008): 290–310. Web. 15 Dec. 2012.

Russell, David R. *Writing in the Academic Disciplines, 1870–1990: A Curricular History.* Carbondale: Southern Illinois UP, 1991. 2nd ed. 2002.

Schick, Kurt. "Citation Obsession? Get Over It!" *Chronicle of Higher Education* 30 Oct. 2011. Web. 31 Oct. 2011.

Schmidt, Sarah. "Term Papers Axed to Obliterate Plagiarism." *Calgary (Canada) Herald* 31 Mar. 2004. Web. 4 Apr. 2004.

Schwegler, Robert A., and Linda K. Shamoon. "The Aims and Process of the Research Paper." *College English* 44.8 (Dec. 1982): 817–24. *JSTOR*. Web. 5 Apr. 2012.

Shi, Ling. "Textual Borrowing in Second-Language Writing." *Written Communication* 21.2 (Apr. 2004): 171–200. Print.

Shirley, Sue. "The Art of Paraphrase." *Teaching English in the Two-Year College* (Dec. 2004): 186–89. Print.

StudentHacks.org. "How to Write a Great Term Paper in One Evening." 30 Oct. 2007. Web.

Turnitin.com. "Plagiarism and the Internet." n.d. Web. 17 July 2003.

Valentine, Barbara. "The Legitimate Effort in Research Papers: Student Commitment Versus Faculty Expectations." *Journal of Academic Librarianship* 27.2 (2001): 107–15. *Academic Search Premier.* Web. 17 May 2012.

———. "Undergraduate Research Behavior: Using Focus Groups to Generate Theory." *Journal of Academic Librarianship* 19.5 (Nov. 1993): 300–304. *Academic Search Premier.* Web. 17 May 2012.

"What Is Plagiarism?" The Citation Project. n.d. Web. 5 Jan. 2013.

Yancey, Kathleen. *Reflection in the Writing Classroom.* Logan: Utah State UP, 1998. Print.

Rhetoric and Argumentation

David Fleming

Like many compositionists of my generation, I fell into the field by accident. I had been an English major at a liberal arts college in the South, reading Shakespeare, Austen, and Whitman and writing my own (rather feeble) fiction and poetry. After graduation, my life moved in a more worldly direction. I taught English and history at a secondary school in East Africa and tracked education policy for a youth advocacy organization in Washington, DC. So when, at twenty-six, I went back to school to get an MA in English, it wasn't long before I thought I had made a terrible mistake. Reading literature had once been the center of a series of concentric circles that also included journalism, politics, and social action; now I felt that vision narrowing, and I worried that my heart wasn't in this more focused activity.

Then, something fortunate happened—I stumbled onto a part of English I didn't know existed. In a course titled Rhetorical Theory and Practice, I read Aristotle's *Rhetoric* and Erika Lindemann's *A Rhetoric for Writing Teachers*. I learned about language acquisition and process theory. And I designed my own writing course, a task I found deeply engaging. Though there were no other classes like that for me to take, I stayed in the program, writing a thesis on the use of collaborative writing projects in the classroom. Later, I taught first-year composition at a community college and, after two years, entered a PhD program in "comp-rhet," the kind I teach in now.

Looking back, the move from literature to composition must have appealed to me for a number of reasons: My focus changed from Great Authors to ordinary writers; my attention turned from the *analysis* of texts to their *production*; and, perhaps most important of all, the center of my generic universe shifted from "creative writing" to *argument*. Now, having spent a year in a developing country and two years in a city on the front lines of socioeconomic change, I knew that argument was a rich and vital activity. But I had never studied it, and I had no models for its development. In this, I was like nearly every other graduate of our school system. Even as the Common Core State Standards call for expanded attention to argument in K-12 instruction, the language arts there remain dominated by literature.

If, then, we're interested in teaching our students about argument, we will likely need to teach ourselves about it first.

WHAT *IS* AN "ARGUMENT," ANYWAY?

In common usage, the word *argument* has two very different meanings. On the one hand, it refers to a set of propositions consisting of a claim and one or more reasons offered in its behalf (Fleming, "Pictures"). Argument in this sense is one of the signal achievements of human intelligence, reflecting our species' capacity not just to assert our opinions but to substantiate them. We see this meaning in the Common Core's definition of the word: "An argument is a reasoned, logical way of demonstrating that the writer's position, belief, or conclusion is valid" (Appendix A 23). But the word "argument" also has a very different meaning, denoting a social interaction characterized by disagreement. In this sense, one *has* an argument, rather than makes one, a situation that says less about our capacity for reason than our tendency to differ and dispute. Here, "argument" is about confrontation, something most people find highly stressful.

The difference between these two meanings is so striking that, thirty-five years ago, communication scholar Daniel O'Keefe proposed that we distinguish them, calling the first "argument$_1$"; and the second, "argument$_2$". Of course, the two meanings are related. Argument$_1$ only makes sense in the context of argument$_2$. We support our claims with reasons, after all, because we're trying to persuade skeptical others that they are valid. At the same time, argument$_2$ depends on argument$_1$ if it is to be productive. Social conflict is a natural expression of human autonomy and diversity, but it can be threatening. Reason helps facilitate, manage, even resolve it.

Unfortunately, school tends to reduce and flatten argument. Students are frequently asked to make an argument without being part of a situation that actually calls for one, without what rhetoricians call an exigence: "an imperfection marked by urgency" (Bitzer). Outside school, meanwhile, argument is often identified with opposition: with attacking others and defending ourselves. The fact is, we have no shared vocabulary for talking about the space where reason and conflict intersect, a space especially crucial in politics, the activity of living with people who are different from us. For that activity, what we need is practice not in rationalizing our opinions, or in defeating our opponents, but in *reasoning with others*. I call that activity "argumentation": the process of *making* an argument in the context of *having* an argument.

Now, "argument" and "argumentation" were originally terms in the ancient art of *rhetoric*, a discipline developed to help people compose, deliver, and respond to public discourse. I first encountered rhetoric when I was introduced to Composition Studies. The more I learned, the more it appealed to me—as a writer, teacher, and citizen. Rhetoric makes argumentation the heart of public life, but it orients that activity to the goal of persuasion, to influencing others' beliefs, moving their passions, and inciting their will to act. It sees human beings as autonomous and rational but also as situated and embodied. It is the art *par excellence* of *homo politicus*, a creature driven by the forces of identification and division and thus wracked by argument, inside and out.

CLASSICAL RHETORICS

The Greek word *rhētorikē* was probably coined by Plato in the early fourth century BCE, to denote something he was deeply suspicious of: the art of the *rhētōr*, or "public speaker" (Schiappa). The prominence of *rhētores* in democratic Athens (508–322 BCE) reflected the vital role played there by verbal skill. Of course, eloquence has always been important for leadership—the Homeric heroes are often described as "honey-tongued" and "wise in council." What was new in Athens was the *setting* of eloquence: No longer the battlefield, it was now the *polis*, with its popular assemblies, people's courts, and boards of magistrates (Hansen). In these *political* fora, audiences ruled the state by listening to opposed speeches and deciding the issues before them. *Rhētores* thus not only had to compose texts and deliver them from memory, they had to ingratiate themselves to people who were neither really their friends nor strangers. To do that, they couldn't just point to some "truth" of the matter; they had to make their case by appealing to the beliefs and values of others. In a democracy, after all, *the people* decide, even if what they decide is competition among elites (Ober).

The goal of rhetoric was thus to move one's audience. This meant not just establishing or increasing their adherence to some belief; it meant stirring their emotions and eliciting their actions. Reason-giving discourse was important in that endeavor, but rhetoric's mode was never exclusively "logical." It was an art attuned to the whole situation of political speech. Inevitably, a teaching profession arose to help people learn that art. In Athens, itinerant "sophists" gave demonstrations in verbal skill, and even Plato incorporated rhetoric in his school. Eventually, the art of rhetoric settled into two streams: the Isocratean and Aristotelian (Solmsen).

The first stream is named for the Athenian *rhētōr* Isocrates (436–338 BCE), who developed a way of teaching eloquence that began with the parts of a speech, a scheme meant to help speakers prepare texts by anticipating their performance.[1]

The most common scheme had six parts:

1. Introduction (*exordium*)
2. Statement of facts (*narratio*)
3. Division (*partitio*)
4. Proof (*confirmatio*)
5. Refutation (*refutatio*)
6. Conclusion (*peroratio*)

Other schemes added (or subtracted) parts: for example, *propositio* before *partitio*. But most rhetoricians believed that what was crucial was the *function* of the parts, not their number. For example, if "proof" was about logically supporting one's

---

[1]The Isocratean tradition is sometimes referred to as the sophistic or Ciceronian tradition (Conley; Walker).

position, the introduction sought "to make our hearers well disposed to us, receptive, and attentive" (Cicero, *De Oratore* 2.80), and the conclusion, to "kindle" their emotions (2.332). *Narratio*, meanwhile, was where one laid out the facts of one's case. (Teachers today tend to separate argument and narrative, but in the classical tradition, they were part of the same art and oriented to the same goal: persuasion of one's audience [Fahnestock and Secor, "Classical" 116].)

The "parts" doctrine thus asked rhetors to imagine auditors *experiencing* their speech: What kinds of thoughts and emotions did you want them to have? in what order? How could you secure their attention at the beginning? inspire them to act at the end? (If there's continuity here with modern "arts" like the five-paragraph theme, it's tenuous: The latter provide students with inflexible discourse containers, dictating their thinking rather than helping them compose a text based on the case at hand.)

This focus on performance in Isocratean rhetoric can also be seen in the priority given to style in that tradition. But the key stylistic virtue was *decorum*, the aptness of one's words to one's purpose, audience, and occasion, factors summed up by the Greek word *kairos*.[2] The point, in other words, was not to express oneself ornately but *appropriately*. Classical pedagogy thus helped students build up a rich repertoire of verbal resources and the discernment to use them well *in situ*. The touchstone of such pedagogy is Erasmus' *On Copia*, which provides 195 variations on the Latin sentence *tuae litterae me magnopere delectarunt* ("your letter pleased me greatly").[3]

If all this seems merely playful, the real-world power of Isocratean rhetoric can be seen in its emphasis on two-sided argument (in Greek, *dissoi logoi*; in Latin, argument *in utramque partem*). Where modern liberalism assumes that dispassionate interlocutors can ultimately agree on the questions that divide them, traditional rhetoric assumed that people *always* disagree—about everything—and always will. The function of rhetoric was thus to *facilitate* controversy, not to suppress it (Garsten, *Saving* 6). As a teaching technique, *dissoi logoi* instilled in students the habit of opposing every argument with a counterargument, every counterargument with a rebuttal.[4] If we moderns are uncomfortable with such agonism, we should remember that the ancient art was more about persuading a *third* party, the judges, than confronting one's opponents. In rhetoric, "[t]he audience is courted, not vanquished" (Fahnestock and Secor, "Classical" 107).

Aristotelian rhetoric differed from Isocratean in, among other things, the way it ordered the art. If the organizing frame for Isocrates was the parts of a speech, for Aristotle it was the "offices" of the rhetor, the stages he or she went through in preparing a speech. Eventually, a standard division of five stages emerged:

1. Invention
2. Arrangement

---

[2] A useful resource on classical rhetoric is Gideon Burton's "Forest of Rhetoric" website: http://humanities .byu.edu/rhetoric/silva.htm

[3] Isocratean rhetoric was not, however, without a theory of content, especially regarding the question at issue, which was taught through the doctrine of "stasis" (Fahnestock and Secor, "Stases").

[4] Arguing in *utramque partem* is also a powerful invention technique, the rhetor anticipating the arguments of others when developing his own (Greene and Hicks; Sloane).

3. Style
4. Memory
5. Delivery

Aristotle (384–322 BCE) thus organized rhetoric "under categories representing essential qualities or functions of any speech" (Solmsen 38). Even today, the system can help students divide up rhetorical problems into manageable tasks and practice the several powers needed for full rhetorical competence.

The most important "office" or "canon" of rhetoric, for Aristotle, was invention; and the heart of invention was proof, or *pistis*. Aristotle defined rhetoric, in fact, as the ability, in each case, *to see* the available proofs (1.2). The focus was thus not on producing words but on instilling belief in one's audience—or at least on *seeing* what that would take. Belief had three sources: the truth, or apparent truth, of the matter at hand (*logos*); the character of the speaker as constructed in the speech (*ēthos*); and the emotions of the audience (*pathē*). Although Aristotle faulted other arts for neglecting "logical" persuasion (1.1), he himself claimed that *ēthos* was the most authoritative proof (1.2), and he devoted much of Book 2 to the *pathē*. Why? Because "rhetoric is concerned with making a judgment," and it is necessary therefore not only that the argument be persuasive but that the speaker be seen as a certain kind of person and the judge be prepared to act in a certain way (2.1). This holistic quality of Aristotelian rhetoric makes it not only more realistic than exclusively "logical" theories of argumentation but also more ethical, since it respects the situated, embodied nature of humans' motivations: "Even if we hope to draw citizens into deliberating reasonably with one another, we cannot help but begin by appealing to them as we find them—opinionated, self-interested, sentimental, partial to their friends and family, and often unreasonable" (Garsten, *Saving* 4–5).

The three sources of persuasion in Aristotelian rhetoric are often represented by a triangle, which can also serve to indicate the three elements of the rhetorical situation itself: speaker (ethos), subject (logos), and audience (pathos).[5]

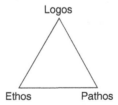

The triangle is a useful reminder to students to consider all the available proofs in composing—and analyzing—arguments (Heinrichs 38–45).

Aristotle nonetheless made *logical* demonstration—that is, showing through inductive or deductive inference that something is true or apparently true—the "heart" of his rhetorical art (1.1). For induction, he focused on the *example*; for deduction, the *syllogism*, which he defined as a discourse (*logos*) in which, certain things being

---

[5]A classic statement on balancing writer, subject matter, and audience is Booth.

stated, something other follows.[6] Unfortunately, "syllogism" later became associated with the highly formal inference pattern Aristotle called "apodictic": for example, "If A is predicated of all B, and B of all C, A must be predicated of all C."[7] Of course, people don't argue that way in the real world; that's why Aristotle also considered the kinds of reasoning people use, together, in situations of radical uncertainty.

The form that deductive reasoning takes in rhetorical situations Aristotle called the *enthymeme*, perhaps the most powerful argumentative tool to come out of classical rhetoric. It is, in essence, a rhetorical syllogism, one that concerns probabilities and contingencies, appeals to emotions and character, and is directed toward judgment. What has most impressed theorists, however, is its truncation. When arguing before a mass audience, one often leaves steps out, not just because the audience can't be expected to follow a long chain of reasoning, but because letting them supply premises themselves can be seductive. If I argue that the president should resign because he had an extramarital affair, the argument works via a "suppressed" premise which might be rendered, "Having an extramarital affair makes one unfit to be a leader."

The enthymeme has been taken up in contemporary pedagogy most passionately by John Gage, who defines it as an assertion accompanied by a because clause. But since such argument is always co-constructed by its audience, it actually has *four* parts:

THE RHETOR'S SHARE	THE AUDIENCE'S SHARE
assertion	question-at-issue
because clause	assumption

The two items in the left-hand column imply the two in the right (Gage, "Enthymeme" 224). This makes the enthymeme not just a form of argument but also a tool of inquiry "because it responds to a 'question at issue' and because its claim and reasons are subject to revision . . . based on the responses of an audience that shares the question" (Gage, "Reasoned" 15).

Such "bilateral" reasoning, says Gage, can be used to organize a whole essay:

Beginning: The reader is introduced to a problem that is of shared interest because it needs a solution: this is *the question at issue.*

Middle: The solution depends on the reader and writer sharing a common understanding or value: *the assumption*; given this assumption, an answer to the problem can be developed if a condition is shown to be the case: *the because clause.*

End: Given both assumption and condition, the solution follows: *the assertion.*

For example, I might argue that date rape occurs too often on our campus; we need to do something to reduce its incidence. Informing students that *all* forced sex is rape and punishable as such can help reduce such incidence. Therefore, we should require all students to undergo education about date rape (Gage, *Shape* 103ff).

---

[6] *Prior Analytics*, 1.1.
[7] Ibid., 1.4.

If the enthymeme was Aristotle's main theory of rhetorical *form*, the *topics* was how he accounted for rhetorical *content*. The key source (*topos*) of content, for Aristotle, was *politics*, what people argue about in civic situations. There are three kinds of civic situations, defined by the audiences who rule them: namely, judges of both past and future events and spectators of the present. The taxonomy gives us the three genres of Aristotelian rhetoric: forensic, deliberative, and epideictic (1.3). Each genre is associated with its own "topics"; in deliberation, for example, there are recurring arguments about national defense. After exhaustively cataloging these "special" topics, Aristotle enumerated twenty-eight lines of argument, or "common" topics, applicable *across* rhetorical situations, e.g., the topic of division ("All people do wrong for one of three reasons: x, y, or z; if not x or y, it must be z") (2.23).[8]

Given the richness of classical rhetorical *theory*, whether Isocratean or Aristotelian, it may be surprising to learn that, according to the ancients, "art" was less important as a source of skill than natural capacity and practice.[9] Practice was itself divided into imitation, exercise, and declamation. In "exercise," students began with short, simple narratives and worked their way up to longer, more complicated arguments. As they progressed, they not only built up a repertoire of rhetorical moves, they developed confidence and internalized cultural values. Eventually, a standard sequence of exercises emerged (see Fleming, "The Very Idea"). Following is my version of the third exercise, the *chreia*, in which the student amplifies a saying attributed to a famous person:

The *Chreia* Exercise

"Men hate each other because they fear each other; they fear each other because they don't know each other; they don't know each other because they can't communicate with each other; and they can't communicate with each other because they are separated from each other."

—Martin Luther King, Jr.

In a short essay, amplify the saying above through the following topics:

1. Praise the author (panegyric)
2. Re-state the saying (paraphrase)
3. Defend the saying, showing how it is true (proof by cause)
4. Refute its opposite (proof by contrast)
5. Support it by analogy (proof by illustration)
6. Support it by anecdote (proof by example)
7. Support it by testimony (proof by authority)
8. Exhort readers to emulate the author (epilogue)

---

[8] Aristotelian rhetoric continues to impress (Allen; Garsten, *Saving Persuasion*), even as Isocrates enjoys a renaissance (Walker); but rhetoricians increasingly merge the two streams: see, e.g., Fahnestock and Secor, "Classical."

[9] On this triad, see Fleming, "Rhetoric"; Isocrates, *Antidosis* 188.

Rhetoric's long reign at the center of the liberal arts suggests that the curriculum worked, producing individuals with discursive ingenuity, discernment, and accountability (Lausberg 502–503). Latter-day rhetoricians have seen these traits as the very dispositions needed in "a genuine and open-ended democracy" (Lanham 693).

NEW RHETORICS

Alas, in the Early Modern period, rhetoric declined as an educational force. Philosophers grew suspicious of its emotional appeals and copiousness. And they were newly confident about the methodical quest for certainty. In this emerging worldview, rhetoric was not just "trivial"—it was dangerous. At the same time, practitioners of the "new science" focused on discovering facts rather than circulating the "commonsense" of their polis (Crowley, *Methodical*). To communicate those facts, they sought a plain, truth-revealing language, one fixed and spatialized by print (Ong). In the new nation-states, meanwhile, politics was all about representation, not participation. And in the romantic era, eloquence was reserved for poetry, an "art" inaccessible to technique.[10]

There were socioeconomic factors at work, too: namely, the rise of an industrial society run by a professional middle class that defined itself through *specialized* rather than general education. If the old order needed rhetors for the senate, bar, and pulpit, the new order needed engineers and accountants. And it needed a new kind of language art, one centered on writing and aimed at clarity, rather than eloquence.

Of course, the rhetorical tradition was never completely lost. Professors of public speaking rediscovered its techniques, and professors of literature recognized its historical importance. There was also growing interest, after World War I, in *general* education, a response to the increasing complexity of society. By midcentury, with higher education expanding and the Cold War intensifying, a new "democratic" rationale for the teaching of composition emerged, one in which rhetoric played a growing role.

However it happened, the years 1950–1980 saw the birth of a host of "new rhetorics" in U.S. English Departments. No text epitomized the revival better than Edward P. J. Corbett's *Classical Rhetoric for the Modern Student*. Largely Aristotelian, it was later joined by Sharon Crowley's *Ancient Rhetorics for Contemporary Students*, more Isocratean in flavor. But *new* rhetorics also emerged, especially to help students discover content for their writing. "Most teachers know that rhetoric has always lost life and respect to the degree that *invention* has not had a significant and meaningful role," Elbert Harrington wrote in 1962 (qtd. in Lauer 74). One of the first new systems came out of the University of Chicago, where Manuel Bilsky and his colleagues proposed a new set of argumentative *topoi*—genus, consequence, similarity, and authority—to help students "say something intelligible" about the world (Bilsky, Hazlett, Streeter, and Weaver 211). More innovative was Richard Larson's questioning method, meant to show students "what is of interest and value in their experiences" (127).[11]

---

[10]See Bender and Wellbery for an influential treatment of rhetoric's decline.
[11]See also the "tagmemic" procedure developed by Young, Becker, and Pike.

Another technique widely used at this time was the "pentad" of Kenneth Burke (1897–1993). According to Burke, "In a rounded statement about motives, you must have some word that names the *act* (names what took place, in thought or deed), and another that names the *scene* (the background of the act, the situation in which it occurred); also, you must indicate what person or kind of person (*agent*) performed the act, what means or instruments he used (*agency*), and the *purpose*" (*Grammar* xv). David Blakesley later proposed "ratios" of the terms to help students generate arguments. For example, the 1999 Columbine shootings (the *act*) could be read through their suburban *scene*, a place where success is measured in terms of popularity and privilege (38).

Writing in the middle of a violent century, Burke saw more in rhetoric, though, than invention techniques. According to John Ramage and his colleagues, he was the first figure since Aristotle to "encompass the full scope of rhetorical theory" (Ramage, Callaway, Clary-Lemon, and Waggoner 67). Rhetoric was useful, thought Burke, because it helps us "traverse division" (Blakesley 61) by paradoxically encouraging the "parliamentary wrangling of our differences" (Ramage et al. 129). Though located in "the region of the Scramble, of insult and injury, bickering, squabbling, malice, and lie" (Burke, *Rhetoric* 19), rhetoric also facilitates *identification* (20). After all, in trying to change an audience's opinion in one respect, a rhetor "can succeed only insofar as he yields to that audience's opinions in other respects" (56).

Other rhetoricians were less sanguine about the "Human Barnyard." For them, the emphasis of the new rhetoric should be "problem-solving or problem-reduction rather than persuasion" (Herbert Simons, qtd. in Brent 453). A key figure here was U.S. psychotherapist Carl Rogers, who wrote in 1951 that "[T]he major barrier to mutual interpersonal communication is our very natural tendency to judge, to evaluate, to approve or disapprove, the statement of the other person" (284–85). We need to learn "empathic understanding—understanding *with* a person, not *about* him" (286). Rogers' proposal: "The next time you get into an argument . . . institute this rule. 'Each person can speak up for himself only *after* he has first restated the ideas and feelings of the previous speaker accurately, and to that speaker's satisfaction'" (286).

Richard Young, Alton Becker, and Kenneth Pike later proposed a "Rogerian argument" with the following "phases" (283):

1. An introduction to the problem and a demonstration that the opponent's position is understood.
2. A statement of the contexts in which the opponent's position may be valid.
3. A statement of the writer's position, including the contexts in which it is valid.
4. A statement of how the opponent's position would benefit if he were to adopt elements of the writer's position. If the writer can show that the positions complement each other . . . so much the better.

Rogerian argument was one of the more influential theories to come out of the mid-century rhetoric revival. In a way, it was a forerunner to those rhetorics of understanding that emerged in the 1980s and 1990s, many from feminist theorists.

Sonja Foss and Cindy Griffin's "invitational rhetoric," for example, viewed audience members "as equal to the rhetor and as experts on their own lives." Similarly, Catherine Lamb explored ways of managing conflict outside of the "male mode" of persuasion (157), using techniques of mediation and negotiation.

The twentieth century also saw the rise of a whole new *philosophical* approach to argument. Two figures are key here. The first, Chaïm Perelman (1912–1984), was a Belgian philosopher who, with Lucie Olbrechts-Tyteca, published *La Nouvelle Rhétorique* (*The New Rhetoric*) in 1958—according to David Frank, "the most important system of argument produced in the twentieth century" (267).[12] The book rejected modern logic, turning instead to Aristotle's *dialectical* reasoning, which aimed not to deduce impersonal consequences from self-evident premises but "to elicit or increase the adherence of the members of an audience to theses that are presented for their consent" (9). The audience is thus *everything*: "There is only one rule in the matter: adaptation of the speech to the audience, whatever its nature" (25).

But it was another mid-century thinker, Stephen Toulmin, whose theory had the most impact on postsecondary writing pedagogy. Toulmin (1922–2009) was a British philosopher who also rejected the modern quest for certainty and advocated the recovery of Aristotelian dialectic. And, like Perelman, he published his key work in 1958. That book, *The Uses of Argument*, contrasted the immutable criteria of formal logic with the diversity of arguments put forth in everyday life. According to Toulmin, the grounds we use to justify our claims are *field-dependent*. But the shape and force of our arguments, what Toulmin called their "layout," are *field-invariant*. The main thing we do when we argue is make an assertion, committing ourselves to the CLAIM (on others' attention and to their belief) that this involves. The merits of that claim depend, of course, on the arguments produced in its support—what Toulmin called DATA. But other things happen when we argue. Sometimes we are asked to explain *how it is* we get from data to claim; we are thus called upon to identify the WARRANT that authorizes our argument. Warrants differ from data in two ways: They are usually implicit rather than explicit, and they are expressed as rules, not facts. A warrant can usually be written in the form "if D, then C" and is thus implied by the argument itself.

Warrants confer varying degrees of force on claims; Toulmin was thus concerned to add QUALIFIERS—words like "presumably" or "certainly"—and conditions of REBUTTAL (e.g., "You should never vote for an adulterer *unless* . . .") to his layout. And there was a sixth feature that was important to him—it had to do with the support provided for the warrant itself. Sometimes we are asked: Why should *this* warrant be accepted as an authority? Why, for example, are adulterers unfit for public office? Unlike warrants (and like data), the BACKING of an argument can be expressed substantively. But like a warrant (and unlike data), it need not be

---

[12]According to Crosswhite, its appearance was "the single most important event in contemporary rhetorical theory" (35).

made explicit. Backing for our argument about the adulterous politician, for example, might be the Seventh Commandment of the Mosaic Law, a proscription against adultery.

Following is a diagram of the complete model using one of Toulmin's own examples:

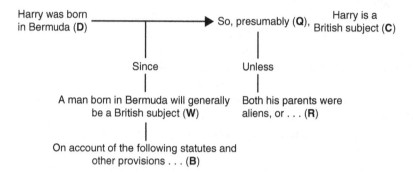

Harry was born in Bermuda (D) ────────► So, presumably (Q), Harry is a British subject (C)

Since

A man born in Bermuda will generally be a British subject (W)

Unless

Both his parents were aliens, or . . . (R)

On account of the following statutes and other provisions . . . (B)

Toulmin went to great pains to contrast his six-part layout with the traditional three-part syllogism, which he thought insufficiently "candid." Classical logic, he wrote, failed to distinguish two kinds of major premises, warrants and backing. It thus made validity a *formal* matter (118ff): after all, provided the correct *warrant*, any argument could be expressed in the form "D, W, C" and thus be valid.[13] Toulmin's model has other advantages: It employs the argumentative language people use in everyday life; the accompanying visual "layout" makes it easy for students to understand; and the model highlights how the different parts of an argument fit together.

RHETORIC AND ARGUMENTATION TODAY

By the early 1980s, composition teachers not only had several *classical* rhetorics with which to teach, but a whole slate of *new* rhetorics. Unfortunately, the space for writing instruction itself had contracted. Starting in the 1960s, first-year composition in many schools was reduced to a single semester, an unfortunate trend for argument since it had often been the focus of the second course. In addition, the success of the process movement meant that "personal" writing had become more prominent. Still, the teaching of argument was on the rise in the 1980s and 1990s, as cultural divisions in the academy and society grew. Perhaps the peak year was 1996, when four key books on the topic were published.[14] But the momentum didn't last. Here I part company with Ramage et al., who claim that we are in the

---

[13]Melvin Hall and I found some years ago that appropriations of the Toulmin model in composition textbooks typically emphasize only the first three parts of the "layout"—claim, data, and warrant—and neglect the other three—qualifiers, rebuttals, and backing. The elision of backing is especially pernicious, we argued, because, for Toulmin, backing statements are what makes real-world arguments *substantial*—that is, non-amenable to formal assessments of validity—and *field-dependent*—that is, particular to the "logic" of specific communities.

[14]See Berrill; Crosswhite; Emmel, Resch, and Tenney; and Fulkerson.

midst of a "golden age" in argument instruction (5). The events of the last ten to fifteen years—the terrorist attacks of 2001, the rise of Web 2.0, the Great Recession—have put enormous pressure on public reason. Other than Ramage et al., there has been no major book on argument by a compositionist since Barnett in 2002. There has even been a falling off of interest in Toulmin (Bizup). Rhetoric remains one of the richest approaches to writing instruction, but the "golden age" of argument, in my opinion, has passed—at least for now.

In fact, the "argument culture" that the new rhetoricians sought to build is now often seen as a *bad* thing. As Deborah Tannen put it in an oft-cited newspaper column:

> Everywhere we turn, there is evidence that, in public discourse, we prize contentiousness and aggression more than cooperation and conciliation. . . . [The resulting animosity] erodes our sense of human connection to those in public life—and to the strangers who cross our paths and people our private lives.

Today, ambivalence about argument shows up in many ways. Research increasingly shows flaws in everyday reasoning;[15] and contemporary public deliberation does not offer promising examples of reason-giving discourse: "Argumentative norms, like listening to both sides of an issue before forming an opinion, making transparent the moves from evidence to warrants and claims, and maintaining civil relations with co-arguers, often do not appear to prevail" today (Pfister 64).

There's also growing evidence about how difficult argument is to do and how late is its development. Children produce fewer words in argumentative tasks than in narrative ones, both orally and in writing (Bereiter and Scardamalia), with the big jump in argument skill taking place between ages eleven and fifteen relatively late for language acquisition (Piéraut-Le Bonniec and Valette). And experiments show that, even after age twelve, children tend to see argument as a matter of justification, not refutation (Coirier, Andriessen, and Chanquoy). It's only from ages fifteen to seventeen that teenagers begin to produce counterarguments (Golder and Coirier). Given this research, we shouldn't be surprised that the NAEP Writing Report Card consistently shows lower performance for persuasive vs. informative and narrative tasks.[16]

That said, thesis-driven prose remains the heart of the academy, the key genre of political life, and perhaps the apogee of humans' sociocognitive development. In a 2012 essay, compositionist John Duffy argued that the abysmal state of public discourse today makes first-year composition—one of the few places in the curriculum where students practice the skills of argument—crucial. In making a claim, Duffy writes, students learn to develop trust with readers; in providing evidence for claims, they acknowledge their audience's rationality; in considering counterarguments, they show tolerance of other points of view. And argument remains a key term in political philosophy. If theorists in the liberal tradition remain focused on institutions and procedures, there is growing interest in the habits that *citizens* need (Allen; Garsten, "Rhetoric Revival"). Neta Crawford has even argued that argument's political stock is rising: "Gradually displacing the role of brute force coercion,

---

[15]See, e.g., Kuhn; but cf. Mercier and Sperber.
[16]See http://nces.ed.gov/nationsreportcard/writing/

the increased importance of political argument . . . is one of the most significant changes in world politics over approximately the last 350 years" (103).

And yet the current moment offers challenges for argument and its teaching. "Non-rational" forms of public interaction, for example, seem to be on the rise. As one critic put it in 2002, "What we see all around us . . . is less the use of argument and more a pervasive enactment of the statement" (Bay 694). But the rise of a world characterized by "image and spectacle" (DeLuca and Peeples 129) is not necessarily a sign of argument's decline, though citizens who want to participate in that world need to understand the importance of communicating in the "discourse of images" (136). That discourse has begun to seep into composition instruction, as have the practices of new *interactive* media. Brian Jackson and Jon Wallin claim, for example, that the "back-and-forthness" of rhetoric on Web 2.0 sites like YouTube has potential for encouraging political participation among students, acclimating them "to a public ecology in which the single-authored, one-time essay has lost its significance" (W376). Similarly, Andrew Sullivan argues that the blogosphere "has exposed a hunger and need for traditional writing that, in the age of television's dominance, had seemed on the wane" (285). Teaching written argument in the networked era, in other words, need not be an exercise in futility (Pfister 64).

In fact, the biggest challenge for argument today may be continued resistance to the idea itself. If textbooks increasingly define argument in terms of "inquiry, discovery, or communication," rather than opposition and persuasion (Knoblauch 249), teachers still too often treat it in formal terms, as a matter of thesis statements and other propositions. Such an approach does not invite students to ask *why* one argues in the first place (Kastely). As James Crosswhite has written, we need to help students see "argumentative reasoning for the wonder that it is" (6).

How do we do that? I'd like to close with a recommendation: that teachers of written argument design classroom activities the way self-governing communities design resolution of their conflicts—by letting members themselves deliberate *together* about the paths before them. This is a messy, unpredictable, but *democratic* activity. For me, the pedagogical breakthrough came when I began to see my class as a kind of jury, to which I presented cases, provided resources for exploration, organized debates so different sides could be aired, and asked for a final *decision*, all while giving practice in complex, sophisticated, argumentative literacies.[17] Here are the steps I use:

1. **Begin with a problem.** In my course, I give students cases from actual or mock trials: "real-world" problems, organized by opposed claims. But problems need not be framed adversarily—see, e.g., George Hillocks's crime scene for ninth graders—though students *do* need an exigence that can generate wonder, inquiry, and difference.

2. **Defer position-staking.** Heather Dubrow has written about how teachers ask for thesis statements too early in the writing process. An antidote to this, advocated by Barry Kroll, is to ask students to first write "issue briefs" which describe the situation and survey the options before they actually take a stance.

---

[17]See http://people.umass.edu/dfleming/english236.html

3. **Provide scaffolding.** For these early steps, students need tools and resources to help organize their learning and externalize their thoughts. Use Toulmin diagrams or synthesis maps (Kaufer, Geisler, and Neuwirth): intermediate products that can help students see how arguers build their cases.

4. **Set up a debate.** According to Hugo Mercier and Dan Sperber, human reasoning improves in argumentative settings where disagreements can be aired (62). When one is alone or with people who hold similar views, arguments will not be critically evaluated, and the "confirmation bias" will lead to poor outcomes (65). But in "arguments among people who disagree but have a common interest in the truth," the confirmation bias can contribute to an efficient division of labor since people will hear (and thus evaluate) both sides of a case even if they only produce one.[18]

5. **Ask the group to decide the issue.** At the end of each unit, I ask the students, *as a group*, to "resolve" the issue at hand, however provisionally or contingently, unanimously or contentiously. This can be done by voting; but it need not be a zero-sum game. Kroll outlines integrative and reconstructive strategies that can harmonize values or recast problems in ways that reveal new solutions. Each student turns in his or her own argument affirming or dissenting from the group decision.

6. **Publish and circulate final opinions.** Susan Wells has written that in most argument assignments, "students inscribe their positions in a vacuum since there is no place within the culture" where student writing on public issues is of general interest. "'Public writing' in such a context means 'writing for no audience at all.'" So, I try to publish my students' work in class journals or weblogs. Let them read each other's opinions. And help them find "outside" audiences who might care about their work.

7. Finally, **encourage reflection.** We need to give students practice not just in *doing* argument but in *talking and thinking about it.* Designing a course with multiple projects or cases means that students can reflect, alone and together, on their growth over each case and across the semester.

I hope I've made my own case here for the teaching of argument. The bibliography includes ideas for more reading on this topic. In addition, there are organizations where new teachers and scholars can find professional and intellectual support. A good place to begin is the Rhetoric Society of America, which has a biennial conference and a student membership rate. There are also numerous journals worth browsing:

Argumentation	*Pre/Text*
Argumentation & Advocacy	*Rhetorica*
Informal Logic	*Rhetoric and Public Affairs*
Kairos	*Rhetoric Review*
Philosophy and Rhetoric	*Rhetoric Society Quarterly*

---

[18]On the benefits of structured classroom debate for learning, see Light 47–50, 119–126.

BIBLIOGRAPHY

Allen, Danielle. *Talking to Strangers: Anxieties of Citizenship since Brown v. Board of Education*. Chicago: U of Chicago P, 2004. Print.

Aristotle. *Prior Analytics*. Trans. A. J. Jenkinson. Internet Classics Archive. Web. 28 July 2013.

_____. *On Rhetoric: A Theory of Civic Discourse*. 2nd ed. Trans. George A. Kennedy. New York: Oxford UP, 2006. Print.

Barnett, Timothy, ed. *Teaching Argument in the Composition Course: Background Readings*. Boston: Bedford, 2002. Print.

Bay, Jennifer L. "The Limits of Argument: A Response to Sean Williams." *JAC* 22.3 (2002): 684–97. Print.

Bender, John, and David E. Wellbery. "Rhetoricality: On the Modernist Return of Rhetoric." *The Ends of Rhetoric: History, Theory, Practice*. Ed. John Bender and David E. Wellbery. Stanford: Stanford UP, 1990. 1–39. Print.

Bereiter, Carl, and Marlene Scardamalia. *The Psychology of Written Composition*. New York: Routledge, 1987. Print.

Berrill, Deborah P., ed. *Perspectives on Written Argument*. New York: Hampton, 1996. Print.

Bilsky, Manuel, McCrea Hazlett, Robert Streeter, and Richard Weaver. "Looking for an Argument." *College English* 14.3 (1953): 210–216. Print.

Bitzer, Lloyd. "The Rhetorical Situation." *Philosophy and Rhetoric* 1.1 (1968): 1–14. Print.

Bizup, Joseph. "The Uses of Toulmin in Composition Studies." *College Composition and Communication* 61.1 (2009): W1–W23. Web. 24 Feb. 2013.

Blakesley, David. *The Elements of Dramatism*. New York: Longman, 2002. Print.

Booth, Wayne. "The Rhetorical Stance." *College Composition and Communication* 14.3 (1963): 139–45. Print.

Brent, Doug. "Young, Becker and Pike's 'Rogerian' Rhetoric: A Twenty-Year Reassessment." *College English* 53.4 (1991): 452–56. Print.

Burke, Kenneth. *A Grammar of Motives*. 1945. Berkeley: U of California P, 1969. Print.

_____. *A Rhetoric of Motives*. 1950. Berkeley: U of California P, 1969. Print.

Cicero. *On the Ideal Orator [De Oratore]*. Trans. James M. May and Jakob Wisse. New York: Oxford UP, 2001. Print.

Coirier, Pierre, Jerry Andriessen, and Lucile Chanquoy. "From Planning to Translating: The Specificity of Argumentative Writing." *Foundations of Argumentative Text Processing*. Ed. Pierre Coirier and Jerry Andriessen. Amsterdam: Amsterdam UP, 1999. 1–28. Print.

Common Core State Standards for English Language Arts. Washington: National Governors Association and Council of Chief State School Officers, 2010. Web. 24 Feb. 2013.

Conley, Thomas. *Rhetoric in the European Tradition*. New York: Longman, 1990. Print.

Corbett, Edward P. J. *Classical Rhetoric for the Modern Student*. New York: Oxford UP, 1965. Print.

Crawford, Neta C. "*Homo Politicus* and Argument (Nearly) All the Way Down: Persuasion in Politics." *Perspectives on Politics* 7.1 (2009): 103–124. Print.

Crosswhite, James. *The Rhetoric of Reason: Writing and the Attractions of Argument*. Madison: U of Wisconsin P, 1996. Print.

Crowley, Sharon. *Ancient Rhetorics for Contemporary Students*. New York: Longman, 1998. Print.

_____. *The Methodical Memory: Invention in Current-Traditional Rhetoric*. Carbondale: Southern Illinois UP, 1990. Print.

DeLuca, Kevin Michael, and Jennifer Peeples. "From Public Sphere to Public Screen: Democracy, Activism, and the Violence of Seattle." *Critical Studies in Media Communication* 19.2 (2002): 125–51. Print.

Dubrow, Heather. "Thesis and Antithesis: Rewriting the Rules on Writing." *Chronicle of Higher Education* 6 Dec. 2002: B13. Print.

Duffy, John. "Virtuous Arguments." *Inside Higher Ed* 16 March 2012. Web. 24 Feb. 2013.

Emmel, Barbara, Paula Resch, and Deborah Tenney, eds. *Argument Revisited; Argument Redefined: Negotiating Meaning in the Composition Classroom*. Thousand Oaks: SAGE, 1996. Print.

Erasmus, Desiderius. *On Copia of Words and Ideas*. Trans. Donald King and David Rix. Milwaukee: Marquette UP, 1963. Print.

Fahnestock Jeanne, and Marie Secor. "Classical Rhetoric: The Art of Argumentation." Emmel, Resch, and Tenney 97–123.

_____. "The Stases in Scientific and Literary Argument." *Written Communication* 5.4 (1988): 427–43. Print.

Fleming, David. "Can Pictures Be Arguments?" *Argumentation and Advocacy* 33.1 (1996): 11–22. Print.

_____. "Rhetoric as a Course of Study." *College English* 61.2 (1998): 169–91. Print.

_____. "The Very Idea of a Progymnasmata." *Rhetoric Review* 22.2 (2003): 105–120. Print.

Foss, Sonja, and Cindy L. Griffin. "Beyond Persuasion: A Proposal for an Invitational Rhetoric." *Communication Monographs* 62.1 (1995): 2–18. Print.

Frank, David. "Argumentation Studies in the Wake of *The New Rhetoric*." *Argumentation and Advocacy* 40.4 (2004): 267–83. Print.

Fulkerson, Richard. *Teaching the Argument in Writing*. Urbana: National Council of Teachers of English, 1996. Print.

Gage, John T. "Enthymeme." *Encyclopedia of Composition and Rhetoric*. Ed. Theresa Enos. New York: Garland, 1996. 223–25. Print.

_____. "The Reasoned Thesis: The E-word and Argumentative Writing as a Process of Inquiry." Emmel, Resch, and Tenney 3–18.

_____. *The Shape of Reason*. 4th ed. New York: Longman, 2005. Print.

Garsten, Bryan. "The Rhetoric Revival in Political Theory." *Annual Review of Political Science* 14 (2011): 159–80. Print.

_____. *Saving Persuasion: A Defense of Rhetoric and Judgment*. Cambridge: Harvard UP, 2006. Print.

Golder, Caroline, and Pierre Coirier. "Argumentative Text Writing: Developmental Trends." *Discourse Processes* 18.2 (1994): 187–210. Print.

Greene, Ronald Walter, and Darren Hicks. "Lost Convictions: Debating Both Sides and the Ethical Self-Fashioning of Liberal Citizens." *Cultural Studies* 19.1 (2005): 100–126. Print.

Hall, Melvin, and David Fleming. "Reductions of the Already Reduced: The Neglect of Qualifiers, Rebuttals, and Backing in Appropriations of the 'Toulmin Model' in Contemporary Composition Pedagogy." Ontario Society for the Study of Argumentation, Hamilton. 21 May 2005.

Hansen, Mogens Herman. *The Athenian Democracy in the Age of Demosthenes: Structures, Principles, and Ideology*. Trans. J. A. Crook. Norman: U of Oklahoma P, 1999. Print.

Heinrichs, Jay. *Thank You for Arguing*. New York: Three Rivers, 2007. Print.

Hillocks, George, Jr. "Teaching Argument for Critical Thinking and Writing: An Introduction." *English Journal* 99.6 (2010): 24–32. Print.

Isocrates. *Against the Sophists, Antidosis*, and *Panathenaicus. Isocrates, Vol. II*. Trans. George Norlin. London: Heinemann, 1962. Print.

Jackson, Bryan, and Jon Wallin. "Rediscovering the Back and Forthness of Rhetoric in the Age of YouTube." *College Composition and Communication* 61.2 (2009): W374–96. Web. 24 Feb. 2013.

Kastely, James. "From Formalism to Inquiry: A Model of Argument in *Antigone*." *College English* 62.2 (1999): 222–41. Print.

Kaufer, David, Cheryl Geisler, and Christine Neuwirth. *Arguing from Sources: Exploring Issues through Reading and Writing*. San Diego: Harcourt Brace Jovanovich, 1989. Print.

King, Martin Luther, Jr. "A Look to the Future." Highlander Folk School, New Market, TN. 2 September 1957. The Martin Luther King Jr. Center for Nonviolent Change. Web. 28 July 2013.

Knoblauch, A. Abby. "A Textbook Argument: Definitions of Argument in Leading Composition Textbooks." *College Composition and Communication* 63.2 (2011): 244–68. Print.

Kroll, Barry. "Arguing about Public Issues: What Can We Learn from Practical Ethics?" *Rhetoric Review* 16.1 (1997): 105–119. Print.

Kuhn, Deanna. *The Skills of Argument*. Cambridge: Cambridge UP, 1991. Print.

Lamb, Catherine E. "Other Voices, Different Parties: Feminist Responses to Argument." Barnett 154–165.

Lanham, Richard. "The Q Question." *South Atlantic Quarterly* 87.4 (1988): 653–700. Print.

Larson, Richard L. "Discovery through Questioning: A Plan for Teaching Rhetorical Invention." *College English* 30.2 (1968): 126–34. Print.

Lauer, Janice M. *Invention in Rhetoric and Composition*. Anderson: Parlor P and WAC Clearinghouse, 2004. Print.

Lausberg, Heinrich. *Handbook of Literary Rhetoric: A Foundation for Literary Study*. Trans. Matthew T. Bliss, Annemiek Jansen, and David E. Orton. Ed. David E. Orton and R. Dean Anderson. Leiden: Brill, 1998. Print.

Light, Richard J. *Making the Most of College: Students Speak Their Minds*. Cambridge: Harvard UP, 2001. Print.

Lindemann, Erika. *A Rhetoric for Writing Teachers*. 2nd ed. New York: Oxford UP, 1987. Print.

Mercier, Hugo, and Dan Sperber. "Why Do Humans Reason? Arguments for an Argumentative Theory." *Behavioral and Brain Sciences* 34.1 (2011): 57–111. Print.

Ober, Josiah. *Mass and Elite in Democratic Athens: Rhetoric, Ideology, and the Power of the People*. Princeton: Princeton UP, 1989. Print.

O'Keefe, Daniel J. "Two Concepts of Argument." *Journal of the American Forensic Association* 13.3 (1977): 121–28. Print.

Ong, Walter S. *Orality and Literacy: The Technologizing of the Word*. London: Routledge, 1982. Print.

Perelman, Chaïm, and Lucie Olbrechts-Tyteca. *The New Rhetoric: A Treatise on Argumentation*. 1958. Trans. J. Wilkinson and P. Weaver. Notre Dame: U of Notre Dame P, 1969. Print.

Pfister, Damien Smith, ed. "Introduction to Special Issue: Public Argument/Digital Media." *Argumentation and Advocacy* 47.2 (2010): 63–66. Print.

Piéraut-Le Bonniec, Gilberte, and M. Valette. "The Development of Argumentative Discourse." *Language Bases . . . Discourse Bases: Some Aspects of Contemporary French-Language Psycholinguistics Research*. Ed. Gilberte Piéraut-Le Bonniec and Marlene Dolitsky. Amsterdam: John Benjamins, 1991. 245–67. Print.

Ramage, John, Micheal Callaway, Jennifer Clary-Lemon, and Zachary Waggoner. *Argument in Composition*. Anderson: Parlor P and the WAC Clearinghouse, 2009. Print.

Rogers, Carl R. "Communication: Its Blocking and Its Facilitation." 1951. *Rhetoric: Discovery and Change*. Young, Becker, and Pike 284–89.

Schiappa, Edward. *Protagoras and Logos: A Study in Greek Philosophy and Rhetoric*. Columbia: U of South Carolina P, 1991. Print.

Sloane, Thomas O. "Reinventing *Inventio*." *College English* 51.5 (1989): 461–73. Print.

Solmsen, Friedrich. "The Aristotelian Tradition in Ancient Rhetoric." *American Journal of Philology* 62.1/2 (1941): 35–50, 169–90. Print.

Sullivan, Andrew. "Why I Blog." *The Atlantic Monthly* Nov. 2008. Web. 24 Feb. 2013.

Tannen, Deborah. "For Argument's Sake: Why Do We Feel Compelled to Fight about Everything?" *The Washington Post* 15 March 1998: C1, C4. Print.

Toulmin, Stephen. *The Uses of Argument*. Cambridge: Cambridge UP, 1958. Print.

Walker, Jeffrey. *The Genuine Teachers of This Art: Rhetorical Education in Antiquity*. Columbia: U of South Carolina P, 2011. Print.

Wells, Susan. "Rogue Cops and Health Care: What Do We Want from Public Writing?" *College Composition and Communication* 47.3 (1996): 325–41. Print.

Young, Richard E., Alton L. Becker, and Kenneth L. Pike. *Rhetoric: Discovery and Change*. San Diego: Harcourt Brace Jovanovich, 1970. Print.

Second Language Writing Pedagogy

Paul Kei Matsuda
Matthew J. Hammill

Second language writing pedagogy is ubiquitous. Unlike other types of pedagogies, it is not site-specific; it happens wherever second language (L2) writers are, including basic writing courses, first-year composition courses, advanced composition courses, professional writing courses, writing centers, and courses across the disciplines. Nor is it optional. L2 writing pedagogy is enacted whenever a teacher interacts with an L2 writer—and some teachers are more prepared than others to work with L2 writers. The goal of this chapter is to provide the background knowledge and resources to help all writing teachers enact L2 writing pedagogy with a greater degree of confidence and competence. To this end, we explore what it means to integrate an L2 perspective into various writing pedagogies, many of which are represented in this book. We begin with an overview of the characteristics and experiences of a wide variety of L2 writers. We then discuss aspects of those characteristics and experiences in detail. We also offer some strategies that teachers and tutors can use to address those issues. The discussion in this chapter focuses primarily on first-year composition courses, but many of the issues and strategies are also applicable in other types of writing courses.

FROM THE MONOLINGUAL NORM TO THE MULTILINGUAL NORM

The presence of L2 writers in U.S. higher education has become an undeniable reality. As the CCCC Statement on Second Language Writing and Writers points out, L2 writers "have become an integral part of writing courses and programs." Most—if not all—writing courses are multilingual by default. In fact, it is unusual for writing courses other than first-year composition to offer separate sections just for L2 writers. Even when those sections are available, there may not be enough room to accommodate all L2 writers who really need the additional support and resources. In some cases, the number of L2 writers in each writing course may be small, but that does not mean the presence of one or two students can be ignored; if one student suffers, that is one too many.

Traditionally, U.S. college composition courses have been designed primarily for monolingual native users of a dominant variety of English who share more or less similar cultural and educational backgrounds. In fact, the WPA Outcomes Statement—a set of guidelines articulating what first-year composition courses nationwide are to accomplish—does not seem to provide provisions for a range of issues, especially language issues, that many L2 writers face in those courses (Matsuda and Skinnell). The tendency to exclude from learning objectives those issues that are not relevant to the traditionally dominant student population— namely, first language (L1) writers—seems to reflect the "myth of linguistic homogeneity," the assumption that all students in those classes already possess the English language proficiency typical of monolingual users of dominant varieties of English (Matsuda, "Myth" 638).

The monolingual assumption, which was more or less accurate in the late nineteenth and early twentieth centuries, is no longer tenable as L2 writers now enroll in U.S. institutions of higher education in large numbers. In order to provide adequate instruction to all students in writing courses of various kinds, all writing teachers—regardless of their previous training, experience, or interest— need to be prepared to work with a linguistically diverse student population (Ferris, *Teaching College Writing*).

CHARACTERISTICS AND EXPERIENCES OF L2 WRITERS

In general, the term *second language writers* refers to individuals who are writing in languages they are actively learning. L2 writers in U.S. college composition courses can be classified broadly into two categories based on their immigration status, including *international students*, who are attending U.S. institutions of higher education on student (F-1) or exchange (J-1) visas, and *U.S. resident students*, who are permanent residents and refugees as well as naturalized and native-born citizens. The resident students are sometimes further divided into two subcategories— early arrival and late arrival—to reflect their differing needs related to the length of residency in the United States (Ferris, *Teaching College Writing*). The distinction can be important, because age and the length of exposure to the *target language* (i.e., the language being learned) often affect the process of L2 acquisition. Sometimes the term *generation 1.5* is used in referring to a subset of L2 writers, usually late-arrival resident students (Ferris, *Teaching College Writing*). We choose to avoid this term, however, because it has been defined and used rather inconsistently, creating unnecessary confusion even among L2 writing specialists (Matsuda and Matsuda, "Erasure" 58–61). Instead, we provide descriptions based on relevant student characteristics, as needed.

While the distinction between international and resident students does not always accurately capture the different characteristics and needs, there are general characteristics that are often associated with these groups of students. In general, international students tend to have had limited exposure to English—especially spoken English—compared to resident students. Resident students are more likely to be able to rely on their language intuition in addressing their own language issues (e.g., reading aloud to identify errors), whereas international L2 writers may resort to metalanguage in identifying and revising sentences (e.g., applying explicit knowledge of grammar and conventions). In contrast to resident students, international students tend to be less familiar with the U.S. educational system and classroom culture as well as pop-culture references. Some international students might not have a problem being identified as "international" or "ESL," while resident students may resist these labels in an attempt to maintain their identity position as U.S. residents (Ortmeier-Hooper, "English").

Due to the differences in previous experience with the English language, some students have different levels of proficiency in spoken and written English. Some students who cannot communicate well face-to-face may be able to produce texts that seem much more advanced; the discrepancy between students' spoken and written performance, therefore, is not necessarily an indication that the student has plagiarized. Conversely, students whose speech is indistinguishable from L1 writers may struggle in producing grammatical sentences. To make appropriate placement and instructional decisions, it is important to account for both spoken and written proficiency levels.

These descriptions are generalizations based on typical characteristics, but individual student characteristics vary widely. There are resident students who have had limited exposure to English (Fu); likewise, there are international students who have previously lived in English-dominant contexts. Some international students may also have attended English-medium schools. Some international students resist being singled out for their differences, while some resident students choose to highlight their linguistic and cultural differences as a coping strategy. It is important to keep in mind that these characterizations provide a general frame of reference for understanding a range of student characteristics; they cannot be used in predicting any individual student profiles, attitudes, or behavior (see Matsuda, "Myth").

While L2 writers differ from their L1 counterparts to varying degrees, they are also similar in many ways to monolingual English users. In fact, even L1 writers—especially speakers of nondominant varieties of English such as African American English (AAE) or Appalachian English—often struggle with similar sets of issues, and texts written by L2 writers may resemble, at least on the surface, those written by L1 basic writers. Yet those similarities can be deceptive. Although L1 writers may also make errors similar to those made by L2 writers, the reasons for making those errors might be quite different (Leki, *Understanding*). While some scholars have argued that academic writing is a second language even in one's native language, it is important to keep in mind that L2 writers go through the same struggle while literally learning another language (Matsuda and Jablonski). L1 and L2 writers' background knowledge about subject matters, cultural contexts, and educational systems may be vastly different, and L2 writers may rely on a different set of linguistic or cultural resources to develop textual features, such as word choice (collocations), idioms, sentence structures, and paragraph organization, that are sometimes different from typical texts written by L1 writers (Silva).

One of the distinguishing characteristics of L2 writers in U.S. college composition courses is that they are in the process of developing *communicative competence* (Bachman) in English. Communicative competence involves not only the knowledge of grammar and discourse but also the awareness of appropriate ways of creating and maintaining social relationships with the audience as well as strategic knowledge, such as the knowledge of writing processes. While L1 writers also continue to develop their communicative competence, they have had a head start. In working with L2 writers, it is important to bear in mind that L2 development does not happen overnight—or by taking one or two semesters of intensive English courses or prerequisite writing courses designed to facilitate their language development. The process is also complicated by individual L2 writers' language backgrounds, including their native language background, prior language learning experience, age of language learning, and the level of metalinguistic knowledge and awareness (Ortega).

Another important characteristic is the varying level of knowledge and experience with literacy practices in various languages. While some L2 writers have limited or no literacy in their native language, most L2 writers do bring some levels of literacy experiences and practices from their previous language learning and use—whether in their native language or other languages. While many aspects of literacy practices and strategies may carry over to English literacy, literacy practices in some languages are drastically different, and when they are transferred to English it may create miscommunication (Connor). Some of the differences are readily apparent—for example, many non-Indo-European languages, such as Arabic, Chinese, Japanese, Hebrew, Korean, and Russian, use different writing systems. Other differences are subtler, such as the extent to which written texts are valued and trusted. While some of the differences in student text can be evidence of a student's developing competence in writing in general, it may also reflect the writer's background in rhetorical education (Matsuda, "Contrastive").

Although the use of L1 literacy strategies can facilitate communication and learning in a second language, some of the genre-specific differences may detract from L2 students' attempts to communicate. A well-known example is the contrast between Japanese and English business letters (Jenkins and Hinds). While English business letters often begin by stating the purpose of the letter (ostensibly to get the reader's attention quickly), formal Japanese letters often begin with highly conventionalized salutations that include seasonal references. If students transfer these features to English business letters for a U.S. audience, it might be considered inappropriate, and the teacher's job may include pointing out the expectations of the U.S. audience and explaining the rationale—keeping in mind that those conventions are not universally applicable. In fact, not all Japanese business letters these days include seasonal salutations, especially for internal correspondences or informal business letters. Conversely, some English business letters are supposed to be less direct—as in the case of rejection letters and other "bad news" letters.

While awareness of the possible differences is important, it can be problematic to attribute them solely to linguistic or cultural differences (Kubota and Lehner; Matsuda, "Contrastive"). One way to avoid overgeneralizing about L2 writers is to ask students during writing conferences to explain their rhetorical decisions in their own words, which can help teachers understand more about their students' work without assuming that perceived differences are necessarily rooted in linguistic or cultural differences. New composition teachers also need to keep in mind that they are not solely responsible for raising students' awareness of academic discourse conventions; L2 writers will also be learning these expectations through their disciplinary coursework. (See Thaiss and McLeod, this volume, for more discussion of L2 issues in disciplinary writing.)

L2 writers' prior educational background also plays an important role in their experience in U.S. higher education. While some L2 writers have previously been exposed to U.S. educational systems, others may have been educated in different systems with different assumptions and expectations about educational goals, approaches to learning, appropriate classroom behavior, and the teacher–student relationship. Some students have been through school systems that do not encourage questioning, collaboration, or active participation by students; a student from Yemen once told us that even the idea of asking questions of a teacher seems socially inappropriate. Peer feedback, which can be a challenge even to U.S.-educated students, can also pose a particular problem for students from non-U.S. school backgrounds who are not used to the idea of talking to other students in class or criticizing other students' work. In a mixed group of L1 and L2 writers, some L2 writers may not feel comfortable asserting themselves because of the social roles they had been assigned in their previous classroom experience (Zhu, "Interaction"). In order to facilitate learning among students from various backgrounds, it is important not to assume that students are familiar with any particular mode of learning or classroom interaction, and to provide explicit instructions (with examples) about the rationale, goals, procedures, and desired outcomes for classroom activities. (For descriptions of trained peer feedback for L2 writers, see Berg; Stanley; Zhu, "Effects".)

The presence of students with these characteristics calls for a reassessment of pedagogical objectives, instructional practices, and assessment practices. It does not mean abandoning all the previous assumptions and practices. Teaching writing to second language writers is not fundamentally different from teaching writing to native English users (Leki, *Understanding*). Many of the pedagogical strategies that writing teachers use can help second language writers develop various aspects of their literacy. Yet there are particular challenges that L2 writers tend to encounter because of their linguistic, cultural, and educational backgrounds. In the following sections, we discuss some of those challenges and ways of addressing them.

CULTURAL ISSUES IN L2 WRITING

L2 writers bring a wealth of diverse cultural backgrounds, values, assumptions, and practices into the composition classroom. Their experiences as language learners and previous exposure to different cultural traditions can certainly be helpful in broadening classroom discussion. However, L2 writers vary in how they view themselves in relation to the different cultures they are a part of (Chiang and Schmida). For example, resident L2 writers may identify more with U.S. culture than that of their heritage culture (or vice versa). Teachers can provide opportunities for L2 writers to discuss cultural issues, but they should not assume students' cultural identifications based on their names, ethnicity, language proficiency, or length of time spent in the United States.

In classrooms using cultural studies pedagogy (see George, Lockridge, and Trimbur, this volume), it is important to keep in mind that L2 writers may not be familiar with or identify with U.S. popular culture. Notions such as the "culture of everyday life" and "the larger culture" (George and Trimbur 82), which implicitly refer to the dominant U.S. culture, may be elusive for students who grew up in other cultural contexts. Tapping into the knowledge base of the dominant student population—such as in the analyses of pop culture or social issues—can be particularly challenging to students who have been living in other cultural contexts. The gap may be narrowing with the global spread of pop culture and the rise of the international youth culture; yet the ways in which the same pop culture is experienced, interpreted, and discussed could be drastically different from one cultural context to another.

For cultural studies pedagogy to work with L2 writers, it is important to provide all the background knowledge necessary to succeed. Yet students who are already familiar with the dominant culture may find the background information unnecessary. One of the strategies for keeping all students engaged may be to ask students to articulate the assumptions of their own cultures during class discussions. Doing so can help heighten students' cultural awareness while also benefitting those who are not familiar with those assumptions. In addition, L2 writers may find it helpful to have access to supplementary background readings in the forms of articles, websites, and such.

Asking students to talk about their "home" language or culture may be a good way of encouraging some students to tap into their resources (Ortmeier, "Project Homeland"), but it can also backfire. Some students may not like being singled out or may feel that the teacher has come to a conclusion about their identity prematurely. U.S. resident students tend to want to identify with the U.S. culture rather than being constructed as perpetual foreigners. Other students are eager to share and may even foreground their "foreign" identity as a coping strategy (Leki, "Coping Strategies"). Yet other students, particularly refugee students, may have had traumatic experiences in leaving their "home" countries, and they may not want to remember—much less write about—them. Teachers should also keep in mind that "sensitive topics, such as sexuality, criticism of authority, political beliefs, personal experiences, and religious beliefs, are subject to differing levels of comfort among students of different cultural and educational backgrounds" (CCCC Statement). However, new writing teachers should not feel intimidated by working with L2 writers because of these complex cultural issues. If students are willing to write or speak about culturally sensitive issues out of their own initiative, then teachers can support these efforts.

TAPPING INTO LINGUISTIC
AND CULTURAL RESOURCES

As U.S. higher education becomes increasingly diverse, and as the need for all students to develop global literacy becomes clear, another important challenge—and opportunity—for writing teachers is to tap into the rich linguistic and cultural resources that L2 writers bring to the classroom. One of the most obvious resources L2 writers have is access to their native language—and perhaps additional languages they may have learned. They may also be experts in language learning strategies because they have learned at least one language (i.e., English) at a level that is far more advanced than the foreign-language-learning experience of many U.S.-educated native English users. Students who have learned English through explicit instruction may also have extensive meta-knowledge of the English language that native English users do not often have. Since students who are native English users do not often believe that people who are learning English as a second language could possibly know more about the English language than they do, it may be useful to point it out explicitly in a general discussion of language learning (rather than in reference to a specific student or specific incidents that have already happened in class).

Another important resource is the lived knowledge of various cultural values, assumptions, and practices. L2 writers have lived in language communities with different sets of values and practices, and learning about them can be interesting and beneficial for other students. Because of their experience outside the English-dominant communities, they may also be able to understand and analyze the cultural values, assumptions, and practices from different perspectives. In addition, they can read and comment on texts written by monolingual English users from a different perspective. In classes where students write for international or multilingual audiences, they can serve as cultural and linguistic informants.

Tapping into these strengths requires some effort and care on the part of the teacher. While some students consciously and sometimes strategically use these resources, others may be reluctant to do so. Some students do not speak up simply because they are not sure if their perspectives would be valued by the teacher or their peers; other students, however, may prefer not to share information that might call attention to their differences. Without singling out specific students, the teacher can create opportunities for students to speak up—if the students so choose—by choosing topics for reading, discussion, and writing that are related to various languages, cultures, and places around the world. This practice can also contribute to U.S. students' development of global competence. It is also important to keep in mind that students can contribute individual perspectives but not, in most cases, a comprehensive understanding of any given topic—or speak for others. (For an example of pedagogy that taps into L2 writers' linguistic and cultural resources, see Matsuda and Silva.)

LEARNING STRATEGIES AND RESOURCES

Although most L2 writers come to U.S. college classrooms with advanced proficiency in the English language—enough to graduate from high school or to obtain certain scores on proficiency tests—they will likely continue to develop their English proficiency throughout their college years. Writing courses play a particularly important role in L2 writers' overall language and literacy development. In order to achieve these goals, L2 writers need to maximize their use of effective learning strategies and resources available to them. Writing teachers may not be experts in language learning strategies, but we can direct students to useful resources and teach them how to use them responsibly.

Many L2 writers use learner's dictionaries, which provide language learners with grammatical information, usage guides, and example sentences that are more useful for them than those found in traditional dictionaries written with native speakers in mind. Commonly used dictionaries include the *Oxford Advanced Learner's Dictionary*, the *Longman Dictionary of Contemporary English,* and the *Cambridge Learner's Dictionary*. These days, many students prefer to use learner's dictionaries accessible through their cell phones or other portable devices, which will put them at a disadvantage if classroom policies forbid the use of such devices. L2 writers also benefit from developing their own self-editing skills by using resources such as *Grammar Troublespots: A Guide for Student Writers* (3rd ed.) by Ann Raimes and *Problem/Solution: A Reference for ESL Writers* by Patricia Byrd and Beverly Benson.

L2 writers may use translation as a strategy for drafting. Traditionally, translation was frowned upon by English teachers because it was considered to slow down the development of L2 fluency and to encourage negative transfer from their L1. Yet translation can also be a useful strategy in generating texts, especially for less advanced students (Kobayashi and Rinnert). Even for advanced writers, translation can be a handy tool, especially if they already have substantial knowledge of the subject matter in another language. Translation at the word level is especially helpful for technical terms that are defined more or less the same way across languages. At the level of idiomatic phrases or sentences, however, translation may not produce appropriate results that suit the particular context.

Students can use their first language as a resource to be used strategically in their process of developing their English writing proficiency. It may be helpful for some L2 writers to work through the process of invention in their first language, especially if they are writing about a topic of their own choice or based on their knowledge or experience gained in their L1. Of course, teachers may not be able to understand the languages that students use to perform these tasks; if this is a concern, asking students to provide a brief summary in English might be appropriate. Some L2 writers may prefer to write only in English; not all L2 writers are comfortable using their L1 in the composition classroom.

Writing centers can be a helpful resource for L2 writers; however, writing centers should not be seen as a place to send L2 writers to get their papers "fixed" (see Lerner's chapter on Writing Center Pedagogy in this collection). Rather, it is an additional resource that can be incorporated into students' repertoire of learning strategies.

TEXTUAL BORROWING PRACTICES

In U.S. higher education, plagiarism is considered a serious violation of academic integrity, and the penalties for students can be severe. Universities have explicit policies about the penalties and consequences students will face, but it is not always the case that students understand the line between plagiarism and legitimate textual borrowing. Composition teachers are tasked with teaching students to use and cite sources according to the standards of U.S. higher education. However, L2 writers from diverse cultural backgrounds may bring different beliefs and attitudes to the composition classroom about plagiarism that may conflict with U.S. cultural norms.

While L2 students' cultural backgrounds may affect their intertextual practices to some degree, it is important to avoid cultural stereotypes about plagiarism. While plagiarism has sometimes been explained in terms of certain cultural backgrounds, others have pointed out that plagiarism is not culturally acceptable in those cultures (Ha; Liu). Composition teachers should also be aware of how textual borrowing can facilitate the learning of language usage that is specific to the rhetorical context. *Patchwriting*—the copying of words and grammatical structures from source texts—can be a useful transitional strategy that students use to mimic and learn the practices of a target discourse community (Howard 788–806).

When learning a second language, social interaction is crucial, and learners are rarely penalized for incorporating others' spoken language into their own linguistic repertoire. However, when L2 writers use similar strategies in writing— such as seeking help from their roommates and friends—it is sometimes viewed as a form of academic dishonesty. Some L2 writers may see getting their work checked or rewritten by a native speaker as an important learning strategy, if not a coping strategy. To avoid unnecessary conflicts, it would be useful to establish clear guidelines regarding what kind of help is appropriate under what circumstances. Most teachers probably have these guidelines in their syllabi already, but it would be useful to review those guidelines with L2 writers in mind.

An effective strategy for promoting a more nuanced understanding of plagiarism and how to avoid it is showing students examples of intertextual practices in different genres and rhetorical contexts, including texts written by students. Students can then understand the boundaries between acceptable and unacceptable intertextual practices, and how writers successfully navigate these boundaries. Teachers can also discuss how collaborative writing in social media contexts, professional writing, and journalistic writing differ from traditional academic writing in terms of citation practices and notions of textual ownership.

THE ROLE OF GRAMMAR IN L2
WRITING DEVELOPMENT

One of the key differences between first and second language writers is the extent to which the structure of the target language (English in this case) has been internalized. (For overviews, see Lightbown and Spada; Ortega.) Native users of dominant varieties of English have an internalized sense of the language structure; this knowledge enables them to compose grammatical sentences and to judge the grammaticality of sentences intuitively—without studying the rules of the language explicitly. In contrast, second language writers are in the process of actively acquiring the grammar of English as a second language. Since most measures of writing quality assume grammatical competence that L2 writers do not necessarily have, it is important to facilitate grammar development as part of composition instruction.

This is not to say that L1 writers do not make "mistakes" in grammar. *Mistakes*, as S. Pit Corder put it, are "errors of performance," while "errors" are reflections of internalized structures of the English language that deviate from the dominant form (167). While performance errors can also happen to L2 writers, many of the L2 errors reflect the internalized structures that are different from those of native English users. The evolving grammar in the L2 user's mind is often referred to as an *interlanguage* (Selinker 214). For L2 writers whose mental grammar is still evolving, it is not possible to produce sentences or evaluate their grammaticality the way highly proficient L1 and L2 writers can. For these reasons, L2 errors are sometimes considered to be "windows" into L2 users' minds (Raimes, "Errors")—an opportunity to assess where students are and where they need to go.

The situation is somewhat different for users of underprivileged varieties of English, such as African American English. While features of those varieties are sometimes treated as "errors," they are not *interlanguage* features but reflections of a different grammar; in fact, those features are perfectly grammatical to users of those varieties. The issue of language differences for users of nondominant varieties of English requires different explanations and different responses, which is beyond the scope of this chapter.

For L2 users of English, some of the common issues include word choice, incorrect usage of count and noncount nouns, transitive and intransitive verbs, verb tenses, number agreement, prepositions, and articles. Dana Ferris has suggested that some errors that students make in these areas are rule-governed (such as subject/verb agreement and the simple past tense) and therefore "treatable"; other errors (such as word choice, idioms, and prepositions) are idiosyncratic and thus "untreatable" (*Treatment*). For the latter, Ferris suggests providing the answers rather than having students self-correct. Some researchers have suggested that some error correction and reformulation (i.e., rewriting parts of students' texts) may be helpful for students, in that it serves as useful *input* (Krashen) as well as providing opportunities for *noticing* (Schmidt), which occurs when learners perceive gaps in their intended meaning and their actual language output.

Despite the best effort on the part of the writing teachers to provide feedback, however, the same set of errors may persist from one writing project to another (Truscott and Hsu). The persistence of these errors is not necessarily due to the lack of effort on the part of the students; rather, it reflects the recursive and complex nature of L2 development. For college-age L2 writers, the process of developing the mental grammar of the target language is a slow and incremental one. Working with language development takes much patience.

The efficacy of error correction has been a point of contention in recent years among L2 writing researchers. In 1996, John Truscott published a controversial synthesis article that echoed the prevailing argument among mainstream composition teachers—that error correction was not only ineffective but also harmful to L2 writers. Ferris and others have replied to Truscott's challenge and have produced a growing body of scholarship devoted to the effects of various types of error correction and written feedback. While the debate is still ongoing, Ferris makes the case that teachers should continue to provide feedback on errors because students expect it and it is likely to be beneficial for their language development (Ferris, "The Case for Grammar Correction"; " 'Grammar Correction' Debate"). More recent research has begun to amass some evidence showing the long-term efficacy of error correction and language acquisition (Bitchener; Bitchener and Knoch). (For an overview of research on error feedback and practical suggestions for providing feedback, see Ferris, *Treatment*.)

Although some L2 writers have developed some level of metalinguistic awareness through prior experience with explicit grammar instruction, composition teachers who are L1 users (or L2 users who did not receive formal language instruction) may not be able to explain the rules of English grammar to these students in ways that build on their prior knowledge. Knowledge of pedagogical grammar—a set of teachable and learnable rules—allows teachers to describe and explain common language errors to L2 writers who are still in the process of developing their linguistic proficiency (e.g., Azar and Hagen; Celce-Murcia, Larsen-Freeman, and Williams; Swan; Thornbury).

Even without extensive background in pedagogical grammar, composition teachers can facilitate L2 writers' grammar development using a number of strategies. For example, focusing on the effects—rather than the rules—of particular errors (e.g., "I got confused here" or "Who are you referring to with 'they' here?") may be effective in developing students' sense of how a reader might respond to their work. This can help students focus their attention on both the form and function of language, which is crucial for developing their linguistic and rhetorical knowledge (Matsuda and Cox).

Another strategy is reading aloud. Some L2 writers with a high level of oral proficiency (often resident L2 students) may be able to identify and correct their errors by reading aloud. For students lacking the intuition of what "sounds" right, however, having them read aloud will not be helpful. For some L2 writers, reading aloud may cause them to focus too much on their own pronunciation, which detracts from their ability to work with the text itself. In those cases, the teacher can read aloud the text while the student pays attention to places where the teacher seems to lose his or her understanding of the writer's meaning and purpose.

Collaborative activities can provide L2 writers with opportunities for interaction that will help facilitate their language development. Meryl Swain has argued that collaboration allows L2 learners to engage in discussions that promote metalinguistic awareness, notice gaps in their linguistic knowledge, and negotiate their own roles and objectives in a communicative setting, all of which will be beneficial for L2 writers' overall development of language proficiency (see also Storch,

"Collaborative"; "Two Heads"). Online feedback and other activities using various forms of technology, such as e-mail, discussion board posts, blogs, and wikis, can also be beneficial for L2 students, who may require additional time and resources that cannot be provided during regular classroom sessions.

NEGOTIATING LANGUAGE DIFFERENCES

While it is important for L2 writers to develop the knowledge of grammar in order to function in English-dominant communicative contexts, they also need to develop strategies to negotiate language differences to capitalize on their multilingual resources that can enrich their own writing. How can writing teachers help students balance the seemingly conflicting goals of learning the dominant language use, on the one hand, and learning to use their multilingual resources, on the other hand? Aya Matsuda and Paul Kei Matsuda have articulated the principles of teaching writing that could guide writing teachers as we help students develop strategies for negotiating language differences. They include the following:

- Teach dominant language forms and functions.
- Teach nondominant language forms and functions.
- Teach the boundary between what works and what does not.
- Teach the principles and strategies of discourse negotiation.
- Teach the risks involved in using deviational features. ("World Englishes" 372–73)

The first three principles can be realized by providing examples of dominant uses and alternative uses of language and discourse, and by engaging students in the discussion of what is effective, what is not effective, and why. The fourth principle is somewhat more challenging, but the principles of discourse negotiation include rhetorical appropriateness, *ethos*, and intentionality. Rhetorical appropriateness and *ethos* are already familiar to those who use rhetorical pedagogy.

The last principle is especially important in creating space for student agency. In exposing students to dominant and nondominant forms and functions, it is important to keep in mind that students are the ones who have to make the decision to adopt those resources. The teacher's job is not to decide what is best for them but to provide a wide range of discursive resources and to guide students in making sensible decisions. Although the "choice" may not seem like a real choice in academic contexts where students are being evaluated by the teacher, it is possible to help students make informed decisions.

ASSESSING SECOND LANGUAGE WRITING IN THE COMPOSITION CLASSROOM

Assessment is a challenging issue for any writing class, but it may pose a special challenge in classes that include L2 writers because their texts often include features that are different from those found in texts written by L1 writers. Assessment is another area in which the monolingual assumption in the writing classroom becomes problematic because of the various differences that L2 writers bring, such as interpersonal styles, organizational strategies, rhetorical appeals, and language structures. While it is important to help students develop repertoires that are appropriate for the English-dominant audience, writing teachers also need to keep in mind that the audience—faculty across the disciplines, editorial boards, and participants in online interactions—are becoming increasingly international and multilingual.

While some of the differences that are found in L2 writers' texts may add to the richness of the text, other differences, especially differences in grammar features, may distract the readers from focusing on the meaning and the overall strengths of the text. We have even seen cases in which teachers fail students for not being able to eliminate all grammar errors, despite obvious strengths in other areas of writing.

If there are clear and reasonable course goals and objectives, and if appropriate instructions are provided to help all students reach those goals and objectives, it would be appropriate to hold all students accountable. In most cases, however, assessment criteria for U.S. college writing courses are based on what L1 writers should be able to accomplish at the end of the semester—or even the beginning of the semester. Furthermore, most writing teachers are not professionally prepared to teach the English language to L2 writers. Even when the teacher has a background in language teaching, it is not possible to guarantee language development because language learning, unlike learning basic facts, is a slow and incremental process. For these reasons, it would not be advisable to punish L2 writers by failing students for grammar errors.

If grammar has to be part of the grade, it would be important to set a reasonable level of attainment in the course objectives, to provide appropriate instruction that facilitates language development, and to establish clear criteria for assessing language development—not just by counting the number of errors. To do any less would be to fail the students unfairly for conditions that are beyond their control. One way to safeguard against failing students unfairly would be to assign a certain percentage of the grade to language issues. The grammar portion of the grade should be proportional to the amount of attention given to grammar issues in the course goals and objectives stated in the syllabus *and* in the actual instruction. (For more detailed discussion of the importance of aligning learning objectives, instruction, and assessment as well as strategies for fair assessment practices for L2 writers, see Matsuda, "Let's Face It.")

PROFESSIONAL DEVELOPMENT

To work effectively with a growing and shifting population of L2 writers in the writing classroom, writing teachers need to tap into various resources. Here are some of them. The CCCC Statement on Second Language Writing provides a succinct statement covering various aspects of second language writing instruction, assessment, and program administration. The *Journal of Second Language Writing*, established in 1992, publishes research on various issues related to second language writing and writers. In addition, the *Journal* also regularly publishes annotated bibliographies of publications on second language writing. Parlor Press's series on Second Language Writing publishes cutting-edge, state of the art books that advance the knowledge of second language writing, and the Michigan Series on Teaching Multilingual Writers (published by the University of Michigan Press) provides overviews and syntheses of various topics in second language writing instruction. Leki, Cumming, and Silva's *A Synthesis of Research on Second Language Writing in English* provides a comprehensive overview of research insights into L2 writers and writing, and Leki's *Undergraduates in a Second Language* provides an intimate account of undergraduate L2 writers' experiences in learning to write in U.S. higher education. Dana Ferris's *Teaching College Writing to Diverse Student Populations* provides excellent resources in understanding various types of L2 writers and how to work with them.

There also are a number of conferences where writing teachers and writing program administrators can gain additional insights. The Symposium on Second Language Writing, an annual international conference that began in 1998, provides a forum for the discussion of various issues related to second language writing theory, research, and instruction (http://sslw.asu.edu/). Presentations and workshops on instructional and research issues can also be found at conferences such as the Conference on College Composition and Communication, American Association for Applied Linguistics, and TESOL: An International Association (formerly Teachers of English to Speakers of Other Languages). In addition, an increasing number of graduate programs are beginning to offer coursework on L2 writing theory, research, and instruction. Other courses that might be relevant include second language acquisition and pedagogical grammar.

L2 writers already are an integral part of U.S. higher education, and the number will likely continue to rise, posing challenges to the monolingual assumptions behind existing composition pedagogies. To respond to this major shift in demographics, all composition teachers need to be prepared to integrate second language writing pedagogy into their existing pedagogical practices. We hope this chapter provides an entry point into this ongoing and collective effort.

BIBLIOGRAPHY

Azar, Betty Schrampfer, and Stacy A. Hagen. *Understanding and Using English Grammar*. 4th ed. White Plains: Pearson Longman, 2009. Print.

Bachman, Lyle F. *Fundamental Considerations in Language Testing*. Oxford: Oxford UP, 1990. Print.

Berg, E. Cathrine. "The Effects of Trained Peer Response on ESL Students' Revision Types and Written Quality." *Journal of Second Language Writing* 8.3 (1999): 215–41. Print.

Bitchener, John. "Evidence in Support of Written Corrective Feedback." *Journal of Second Language Writing* 17.2 (2008): 69–124. Print.

Bitchener, John, and Ute Knoch. "The Contribution of Written Corrective Feedback to Language Development: A Ten Month Investigation." *Applied Linguistics* 31.2 (2010): 193–214. Print.

Byrd, Patricia, and Beverly Benson. *Problem/Solution: A Reference for ESL Writers*. Boston: Heinle & Heinle, 1994. Print.

CCCC Committee on Second Language Writing. "CCCC Statement on Second Language Writing and Writers." *Conference on College Composition and Communication.* Rev. ed. National Council of Teachers of English. Nov. 2009. Web. 15 June 2012.

Celce-Murcia, Marianne, Diane Larsen-Freeman, and Howard Alan Williams. *The Grammar Book: An ESL/EFL Teacher's Course.* 2nd ed. Boston: Heinle & Heinle, 1999. Print.

Chiang, Yuet-Sim D., and Mary Schmida. "Language Identity and Language Ownership: Linguistic Conflicts of First-Year University Writing Students." *Generation 1.5 Meets College Composition.* Ed. Linda Harklau, Kay M. Losey, and Meryl Siegal. Mahwah: Erlbaum, 1999. 81–96. Print.

Connor, Ulla. *Contrastive Rhetoric: Cross-Cultural Aspects of Second-Language Writing.* New York: Cambridge UP, 1996. Print.

Corder, S. Pit. "The Significance of Learner's Errors." *International Review of Applied Linguistics* 5 (1967): 161–70. Print.

Ferris, Dana R. "The Case for Grammar Correction in L2 Writing Classes: A Response to Truscott (1996)." *Journal of Second Language Writing* 8.1 (1999): 1–11. Print.

_____. The "Grammar Correction" Debate in L2 Writing: Where Are We, and Where Do We Go from Here? (And What Do We Do in the Meantime. . .?)" *Journal of Second Language Writing* 13.1 (2004): 49–62. Print.

_____. *Teaching College Writing to Diverse Student Populations.* Ann Arbor: U of Michigan P, 2009. Print.

_____. *Treatment of Error in Second Language Student Writing.* 2nd ed. Ann Arbor: U of Michigan P, 2002. Print.

Fu, Danling. *An Island of English: Teaching ESL in Chinatown.* Portsmouth: Heinemann, 2003. Print.

George, Diana, and John Trimbur. "Cultural Studies and Composition." *A Guide to Composition Pedagogies.* Ed. Gary Tate, Amy Rupiper, and Kurt Schick. New York: Oxford UP, 2001. 71–91. Print.

Ha, Phan Le. "University Classrooms in Vietnam: Contesting the Stereotypes." *ELT Journal* 58.1 (2004): 50–57. Print.

Hornby, A. S. *Oxford Advanced Learner's Dictionary.* 8th ed. Oxford: Oxford UP, 2010. Print.

Howard, Rebecca Moore. "Plagiarisms, Authorships, and the Academic Death Penalty." *College English* 57.7 (1995): 788–806. Print.

Jenkins, Susan, and John Hinds. "Business Letter Writing: English, French, and Japanese." *TESOL Quarterly* 21.2 (1987): 327–50. Print.

Kobayashi, Hiroe, and Carol Rinnert. "Effects of First Language on Second Language Writing: Translation Versus Direct Composition." *Language Learning* 42.2 (1992): 183–215. Print.

Krashen, Stephen D. *The Input Hypothesis: Issues and Implications.* New York: Longman, 1985. Print.

Kubota, Ryuko, and Al Lehner. "Toward Critical Contrastive Rhetoric." *Journal of Second Language Writing* 13.1 (2004): 7–27. Print.

Leki, Ilona. "Coping Strategies of ESL Students in Writing Tasks across the Curriculum." *TESOL Quarterly* 29.2 (1995): 235–60. Print.

_____. *Undergraduates in a Second Language: Challenges and Complexities of Academic Literacy Development.* Mahwah: Erlbaum, 2007. Print.

_____. *Understanding ESL Writers: A Guide for Teachers.* Portsmouth: Heinemann, 1992. Print.

Leki, Ilona, Alister Cumming, and Tony Silva. *A Synthesis of Research on Second Language Writing in English.* New York: Taylor & Francis, 2008. Print.

Lightbown, Patsy M., and Nina Spada. *How Languages Are Learned*. 3rd ed. New York: Oxford UP, 2006. Print.

Liu, Dilin. "Plagiarism in ESOL Students: Is Cultural Conditioning Truly the Culprit?" *ELT Journal* 59.3 (2005): 234–41. Print.

Longman Dictionary of Contemporary English. Upper Saddle River: Pearson Education, 2009. Print.

Matsuda, Aya, and Paul Kei Matsuda. "World Englishes and the Teaching of Writing." *TESOL Quarterly* 44.2 (2010): 369–74. Print.

Matsuda, Paul Kei. "Contrastive Rhetoric in Context: A Dynamic Model of L2 Writing." *Journal of Second Language Writing* 6.1 (1997): 45–60. Print.

_____. "Let's Face It: Language Issues and the Writing Program Administrator." *Writing Program Administration* 36.1 (2012): 141–63. Print.

_____. "The Myth of Linguistic Homogeneity in U.S. College Composition." *College English* 68.6 (2006): 637–51. Print.

Matsuda, Paul Kei, and Aya Matsuda. "The Erasure of Resident ESL Writers." *Generation 1.5 in College Composition: Teaching Academic Writing to U.S.-Educated Learners of ESL*. Ed. Mark Roberge, Meryl Siegal, and Linda Harklau. London: Taylor and Francis, 2009. 50–64. Print.

Matsuda, Paul Kei, and Michelle Cox. "Reading an ESL Writer's Text." *ESL Writers: A Guide for Writing Center Tutors*. 2nd ed. Ed. Shanti Bruce and Ben Rafoth. Portsmouth: Boynton/Cook Heinemann, 2009. 42–50. Print.

Matsuda, Paul Kei, and Jeffrey Jablonski. "Beyond the L2 Metaphor: Towards a Mutually Transformative Model of ESL/WAC Collaboration." *Academic.Writing* 1 (2000): n. p. Web. 20 June 2012.

Matsuda, Paul Kei, and Tony Silva. "Cross-Cultural Composition: Mediated Integration of US and International Students." *Composition Studies* 27.1 (1999): 15–30. Print.

Matsuda, Paul Kei, and Ryan Skinnell. "Considering the Impact of the *WPA Outcomes Statement* on Second Language Writers." *The WPA Outcomes Statement: A Decade Later*. Ed. Nicholas N. Behm, Gregory Glau, Deborah H. Holdstein, Duane Roen, and Edward White. Anderson: Parlor P, 2012. 230–41.

Ortega, Lourdes. *Understanding Second Language Acquisition*. London: Hodder Education, 2009. Print.

Ortmeier-Hooper, Christina M. "English May Be My Second Language, but I'm Not 'ESL.'" *College Composition and Communication* 59.3 (2008): 389–419. Print.

_____. "Project Homeland: Crossing Cultural Boundaries in the ESL Classroom." *TESOL Journal* 9.1 (2000): 10–17. Print.

Raimes, Ann. "Errors: Windows into the Mind." *College ESL* 1.2 (1991): 55–64. Print.

_____. *Grammar Troublespots: A Guide for Student Writers*. 3rd ed. New York: Cambridge UP, 2004. Print.

Schmidt, Richard. "The Role of Consciousness in Second Language Learning." *Applied Linguistics* 11 (1990): 129–58. Print.

Selinker, Larry. "Interlanguage." *International Review of Applied Linguistics* 10 (1972): 209–41. Print.

Silva, Tony. "Toward an Understanding of the Distinct Nature of L2 Writing: The ESL Research and Its Implications." *TESOL Quarterly* 27.4 (1993): 657–77. Print.

Stanley, Jane. "Coaching Student Writers to Become Effective Peer Evaluators." *Journal of Second Language Writing* 1.2 (1992): 217–33. Print.

Storch, Neomy. "Are Two Heads Better Than One? Pair Work and Grammatical Accuracy." *System* 27.3 (1999): 363–74. Print.

_____. "Collaborative Writing: Product, Process, and Students' Reflections." *Journal of Second Language Writing* 14.3 (2005): 153–73. Print.

Swain, Merrill. "The Output Hypothesis and Beyond: Mediating Acquisition through Collaborative Dialogue." *Sociocultural Theory and Second Language Learning*. Ed. James P. Lantolf. Oxford: Oxford UP, 2000. 97–114. Print.

Swan, Michael. *Practical English Usage*. 3rd ed. New York: Oxford UP, 2005. Print.

Thornbury, Scott. *How to Teach Grammar*. Harlow: Pearson ESL, 2000. Print.

Truscott, John. "Review Article: The Case against Grammar Correction in L2 Writing Classes." *Language Learning* 46.2 (1996): 327–69. Print.

Truscott, John, and Angela Yi-ping Hsu. "Error Correction, Revision, and Learning." *Journal of Second Language Writing* 17.4 (2008): 292–305. Print.

Woodford, Kate, Elizabeth Walter, and David Shenton. *Cambridge Learner's Dictionary*. 3rd ed. Cambridge: Cambridge UP, 2007. Print.

Zhu, Wei. "Effects of Training for Peer Response on Students' Comments and Interaction." *Written Communication* 12.4 (1995): 492–528. Print.

_____. "Interaction and Feedback in Mixed Peer Response Groups." *Journal of Second Language Writing* 10.4 (2001): 251–76. Print.

The Pedagogy of Writing in the Disciplines and Across the Curriculum

Chris Thaiss

Susan McLeod

ORIGINS OF WAC/WID

As an educational reform movement, WAC (Writing Across the Curriculum) has been around more than forty years in the United States. It was born in the 1970s during a time of curricular and demographic change in higher education. The widespread use of the "objective" multiple-choice/true-false test in public education meant that many students had little practice with extended writing tasks by the time they got to college; at the same time, the rapid growth of higher education coupled with open admissions at some institutions brought a new population of first-generation college students. Faced with what looked like declining skills, faculty felt the need to do something, anything, about the state of student writing.

The first WAC faculty seminar came about in 1969–1970 at Central College in Pella, Iowa (Russell, *Writing* 283). English teacher Barbara Walvoord organized a regular meeting of faculty to discuss issues of student writing. She went on to write the first book on teaching writing that was aimed at faculty in the disciplines, *Helping Students Write Well: A Guide for Teachers in All Disciplines.*

All of us who have been involved in WAC since its beginnings have a story to tell about how we got started facilitating faculty seminars; the story usually involves faculty colleagues like Barbara's who were at their collective wits' end trying to deal with the student writing problems they were encountering. Here is Susan's:

> One day I was cornered just outside my office by a friend who taught History, who was furious with me and with (it appeared) not only the English Department but the entire discipline of English. "Why can't you people teach these students how to write?" he thundered. I was defensive—of course I was teaching them how to write. I had stacks of papers waiting to be graded to prove it. After we had both finished harumphing and started to listen to each other, I asked to see the papers he was so distressed about. Among them was a paper from a former student of

mine, one who had done reasonably well in my freshman comp class the previous semester. He was right; it was abysmal. He had asked for analysis and discussion of historical data, and she had responded with vague generalities and personal opinion. Like all progressive writing teachers at that time, I was trying to help my students find their authentic voices. But my History colleague was not interested in this student's authentic voice; he wanted her to try to think and write like an historian. My class, based as it was on literary notions of what good writing was, had not helped her figure out how to do that.

Out of cross-disciplinary faculty conversations like this one, out of seminars like the one Walvoord started, the WAC movement was born.

WHAT ARE WAC AND WID?

Like general education programs, WAC programs are defined in part by their intended outcomes—helping students to become critical thinkers and problem solvers as well as developing their communications skills. WAC is uniquely defined by its pedagogy. Indeed, one might say that WAC has been aimed at transforming pedagogy at the college level, at moving away from the lecture mode of teaching (the "delivery of information" model) to a model of active student engagement with the material and with the genres of the discipline through writing, not just in English classes but in all classes across the university. WAC draws on pedagogical techniques used in first-year writing classes—in particular "writing as process." But, whereas first-year composition might focus on learning the general features of what we term *academic discourse*, WAC focuses not on writing skills per se but on learning (1) the content of the discipline and (2) the particular discourse features and rhetorics used in writing about that content.

WID (Writing in Disciplines) is related to WAC by its emphasis on the features that distinguish writing in one field from writing in another. But where WAC implies the *institutional move to have teachers from across fields become involved* in helping students learn through writing, WID emphasizes the distinct disciplines, the discursive and rhetorical features that characterize them, research that studies these characteristics, and appropriate genres and writing pedagogies. That the two terms have come to be used almost interchangeably in the names of WAC and WID programs shows their similarities.

When we speak of WAC/WID pedagogy, we are talking about two somewhat different approaches: We may think of these under the headings Writing to Learn and Writing to Communicate. Based on the theories of language and learning articulated in the 1970s by James Britton and Janet Emig and reinforced by more recent research in cognitive science (Reynolds, Thaiss, Katkin, and Thompson), Writing to Learn pedagogy encourages teachers to use frequent writing exercises, often informal and ungraded, to help learners probe what they know, what they need to learn, and ways to think about what they study. Writing to Communicate is pedagogically more complex. It is based on theories of the social construction of knowledge, summarized for early WAC developers in Kenneth Bruffee's article "Collaborative Learning and the 'Conversation of Mankind'" (1984). One obvious pedagogical manifestation of this approach is the use of peer groups in the classroom. A second is the application of "process pedagogy," including commentary by peers and/or teachers to writing in progress, with the opportunity for the writer to revise the work to communicate more successfully. A third manifestation is WID appreciation for analysis of the discourses of diverse disciplines: Who are the audiences of writers in this field of study? What main purposes do they try to serve? What modes of thinking are particular to this field, and in what genres are they embodied? These and other questions have been explored, for example, in Carolyn Miller's concept of "genre as social action" (1984) and Charles Bazerman's groundbreaking work on the rhetoric of science (1988).

Most of us who have been involved in WAC programs from the beginning see Writing to Learn and Writing to Communicate as two complementary, even synergistic, approaches to Writing Across the Curriculum.

WRITING TO LEARN

Writing to Learn pedagogy encourages teachers to use writing as a tool for learning as well as a test for learning. This branch of WAC has its roots in the Language across the Curriculum movement in British secondary schools, sparked by James Britton and his colleagues. In *Language and Learning*, Britton argued that language is central to learning because it is through language that we organize our representations of the world (214). The analog for this kind of student writing is the expert's notebook—the scientist's lab book, the engineer's notebook, the artist's and architect's sketchbook. It is not polished work intended for an outside audience; sometimes it is comprehensible only to the writer.

The teacher does respond, but as a facilitator and coach rather than as a judge. The most popular assignment early in the WAC movement was the journal. In *The Journal Book*, Toby Fulwiler gathered together more than forty different versions from teachers across the disciplines: for example, French teacher Karen Wiley Sandler describes the journal in the foreign language class as a place to experiment and make mistakes (as we all do when learning a language) without fear of penalty (312–20). Stephen Bemiller describes the mathematics notebook, in which students do their practice work—explorations of possible solutions to problems, discussions of the course challenges, questions, outlines of concepts, and self-tests of comprehension (359–66).

Of course, the journal is not the only assignment teachers have integrated into their pedagogical repertoire. Another way to facilitate writing as a mode of learning is the "quick write" or "focused free-write" (popularized by Angelo and Cross in *Classroom Assessment Techniques* as the "minute paper" [148–58]). The technique is simple: In the middle or at the end of a lecture or discussion, students might be asked to type or jot the most important points they have gleaned, plus what puzzled them about the material. These quick-writes, usually no more than 100 to 200 words, give the students the chance to articulate their perceptions—and gives the teacher, if she wishes to read the results, instant feedback on what issues may need clarification.

There are many other ways to use writing-to-learn assignments. John Bean, in the second edition of the popular *Engaging Ideas: The Professor's Guide to Integrating Writing, Critical Thinking, and Active Learning in the Classroom* (2011), devotes parts of several chapters to varieties of writing-to-learn exercises. These include versions of the journal and the minute paper as well as creative approaches (having students write an imaginary dialogue between historical figures) and practice pieces for what will eventually be graded writing (e.g., dry-run essay exams). Bean also answers common objections teachers have to using this kind of writing (it will take too much time; students will regard it as busy work; if it's not corrected, it will promote bad writing habits) and provides useful suggestions for responding to the assignments and managing the reading load.

Teachers who are concerned about their students' learning pick up WAC techniques and use them successfully. These exploratory writing assignments all provide feedback to teachers on the progress of student learning, allowing them to adjust their teaching.

WRITING TO COMMUNICATE

Interconnected with Writing to Learn, Writing to Communicate has these differences: It focuses on writing to an audience outside the self, usually for a formal purpose, for example to persuade; writing is therefore crafted, revised, and polished. Writing as process is still central to this communicative emphasis, but there is also emphasis on the "product" of this process that intended readers see. Writing to Communicate uses the styles and vocabulary of a particular discourse community or shifts language for a different purpose and audience. The notion of discourse communities is commonplace now in the field of rhetoric and composition, but it was not so obvious to composition teachers in the 1980s. Then, as now, conversations with faculty in different disciplines helped us understand differences in disciplinary discourses—which embody their different objects of study and ways of thinking. We learned through these conversations that the person who knows better how to initiate the newcomer in a specialized discourse is not usually the composition teacher but the teacher who is already grounded in the content of the field and who is fluent in the disciplinary discourse—the History teacher, the Biology teacher, the Math teacher. In Thaiss and Zawacki's *Engaged Writers and Dynamic Disciplines*, interviews, focus groups, surveys, and analysis of student reflections show the vital role of disciplinary faculty, whose mentoring of student writing acculturates writers to the discourses of their majors.

WAC/WID IN THE WRITING COURSE

This is not to say that writing teachers can't make students aware that there are different discourse communities and teach them some strategies for asking the right questions about discourse expectations in their other classes. Linton, Madigan, and Johnson (and Madigan, Johnson, and Linton), for example, describe in two essays how such a class might be set up: teaching students to observe disciplinary patterns in the way discourse is structured, helping them understand the various rhetorical moves that are accepted within particular discourse communities, explaining conventions of reference and of language. Composition teachers, the authors argue, are no strangers to teaching discourse analysis; we just need to enlarge our notions of what discourses we should be helping students analyze.

But there's the rub: Since the number of academic discourses is so great and our students in a typical first-year writing class represent so many of them, which do we teach? WAC/WID pedagogical theory says that the composition teacher and course can only be part of a developmental process for the student *that must include other teachers* who take some role in this discursive, epistemological education. As recent longitudinal observation of students across disciplines has shown (e.g., Carroll; Herrington and Curtis), students become versatile and agile in academic discourse only through experience and practice across diverse writing environments—experience facilitated by teachers, usually in their majors, who take care to help them grow. For WAC/WID pedagogy to work in a first-year writing class, teachers must be aware of ways in which student writing and learning are happening in the rest of the institution. More on that later in the chapter.

However, we are not saying that a teacher of Biology or Mechanical Engineering is necessarily prepared to take on mentoring of their students in writing. That academics are so grounded in their own disciplinary discourse conventions is an advantage to the students, but it is also an immediate challenge, precisely because those conventions seem so natural to those fluent in them that it is difficult for them to see why students struggle as they learn them. For example, literature professors who move effortlessly among close reading strategies may be bewildered by students who are ignorant of the concept of textual analysis. If these same students are fluent in mathematics, they may wonder why the literature professor never uses the language of equations nor performs statistical tests. Fortunately, to help students learn discourse conventions in diverse disciplines, and to help their teachers learn how to talk about these conventions to their students, there are many resources, many of these written by colleagues in those disciplines. For example, excellent guides to writing in STEM fields (sciences, technologies, engineering, math) have been written by Bahls; Day; Pechenik; Penrose and Katz; and Porush. Chris has co-authored guides to writing in law enforcement (Thaiss and Hess) and in theater (Thaiss and Davis) with experts in those fields. Moreover, a number of guides to writing in various disciplines have developed rapidly on WAC/WID program websites for teachers to introduce to their students. The WAC sites of Oregon State and George Mason University are among those that have commissioned guides from faculty in diverse fields. The number one WAC/WID resource site, the WAC Clearinghouse at *http://www.colostate.edu*, has collected an impressive array of materials and grows steadily. The site publishes and republishes an expanding array of WAC/WID books, answers frequently asked questions about WAC, provides links to other WAC sites on the Web, and publishes searchable databases of articles.

Writing to Communicate involves more than just learning genres and discourse conventions, however. It also involves learning the processes by which experts in the field develop and disseminate knowledge. All of the aforementioned guides take this epistemic rhetorical approach to genre. David Russell argues the matter thus:

> [Since writing is] a matter of learning to participate in some historically situated human activity that requires some kind(s) of writing, it cannot be learned apart from the problems, the habits, the activities—the subject matter—of some group that found the need to write in that way to solve a problem or carry on its activities. ("Vygotsky" 194)

Once teachers in the disciplines begin to see the teacher/student relationship as one of professional/apprentice, and once they also begin to view their classrooms as social systems that model the methods and the discourse of their particular disciplines, it is not a large step for them to see that it makes sense for apprentices to follow the same process that the experts do when writing articles. *If the experts draft and revise according to readers' and editors' comments, students should become familiar with this process.* One of the most interesting quiet revolutions that has taken place on college campuses as a result of successful WAC programs is the use across disciplines of what we have come to think of as the "process approach" in teaching writing—not only allowing revision of student work but requiring it, often using peer groups in the classroom to respond to drafts.

FILAMENTS OF GROWTH IN WAC/WID: INFLUENCES ON TEACHING

Since 2000, teaching Writing Across the Curriculum has been further shaped by five interrelated influences, which we explore now in the rest of this chapter. These "filaments" grow and intertwine, and will, we believe, transform the teaching of writing—both across disciplines and in the composition class.

Filament One: Redefining WAC/WID through Technological Innovation

When we began, years ago, talking with fellow teachers across disciplines about Writing to Learn and "writing as process," those conversations meant writing limited to print (or even handwriting) and assignments produced on paper. Writing for research meant helping students negotiate library stacks and periodical rooms, and that meant going with a class to the library, and even then not being able to observe students grappling to interpret a text. Integrating writing within a course in, say, Psychology or Calculus, meant thinking with a teacher about, for example, scheduling enough time between drafts for comments to be written on the papers (legibly, we hoped), those papers to be returned, and new drafts to be written and retyped. If a teacher wanted to have students keep an informal journal of, say, responses to assigned readings, those journals would likely be shared only with the teacher, and the teacher would need to write back to each student. If the teacher wanted to have journal entries shared with other students in the class, that interaction would have to occur during class time, or students would have to bring their journals to class, distribute them to one colleague each, and have responses written for homework. Frequent questions in faculty workshops would include "How much credit do I take off for poor handwriting?" "Should I accept handwritten pieces?" "What if a student loses another student's journal?" "How would I know that all the entries weren't written the night before I collect the journals?" "How much time should I spend with each journal? Can I afford that time?"

It was little wonder that teachers might be heavily resistant to including assignments that would require response time. "Handling the paper load" was the number one concern in faculty workshops in the early days of the WAC movement, and for good reason.

Today's teachers across disciplines are still concerned with time management and how to integrate writing into a crowded course schedule. But the technologies available on almost all campuses and to most students (though not all) have made student writing far easier to integrate into course learning, greatly increased student and teacher efficiency in building a community of writers in a class, and greatly lessened teacher time in needing to respond to each writer.

In workshops and individual consultations with colleagues across disciplines these days, Chris is likely to ask early on if (and how) they use the university's web-based course management system (CMS) to build writing into their teaching. Over the years that the current CMS has operated on his campus, it has added tools to enhance active learning through writing both within and outside class time.

For example, colleagues in sociology, music, chemistry, and plant sciences (among other fields) are using "forums," "chats," and "wikis" to carry out regular informal writing exercises that enable students to write to the entire class or to designated project teams. Students in a large introductory-level sociology course in popular culture write weekly to fellow students their reactions/reflections on lectures and course readings, then students—not the teacher or TAs—respond to their colleagues' opinions and ideas. Instructors browse the entries and identify patterns that they can discuss during class time or in general responses to the class, but not to each student. Teacher and TA response time is reserved for the longer analytical essay written in three stages: proposal, first draft, revised draft. In the introductory general education course in music history, taken by several hundred students across many disciplines, weekly forums give students regular practice in writing critiques of musical events and seeing how fellow students respond to the same events. These regular, less formal assignments give these non-majors models and confidence to take on longer critiques required later in the course. At the graduate level, a law professor has for several years managed a course blog that is read and responded to not only by her current students but also by graduates who were her students from years past. A colleague in plant sciences and biotechnology recently shared with Chris his students' creative forum responses—in verse!—to a reading about phages. Again, these students now write as much for each other as for the teacher, and the building of classroom community through the writing is as much an advantage of the WAC pedagogy as is the opportunity to improve each student's own performance by having seen what one another produces.

In his own practice, Chris uses these collaborative tools in diverse time-efficient ways in his junior-senior course Writing in Science, which enrolls students from the life and physical sciences, math, engineering, and agriculture. He uses the CMS tools to inspire and manage class writing in several ways; for example:

- To carry on real-time opinion exchanges on such topics as "Technical Writing Pet Peeves" and "Rhetorical Strategies Science Journalists Use"
- To do quick analyses of sample readings, e.g., the Discussion section of a peer-reviewed science article; these spark conversation about better ways to craft such discussions
- To build Team Forums that allow three-person research teams to manage their sharing of data collected for their research reviews

How do these technologies address the ever-present concern by teachers regarding lack of time to give students responses? Most important, *the concept of the online forum or blog makes each student a reader and potential respondent to every other writer in the class.* As Chris's students frequently say, "I learn a lot about my own writing from seeing how the other students responded to the question."

Second, the teacher may craft the blog/forum assignment to make giving *direct* feedback an explicit task. For example, the assignment might include this instruction:

> For your second entry of the week, reply to the ideas of another writer in the class, or reflect on ideas that seem to be emerging in the discussion. Feel free to quote another writer.

If teachers across disciplines wish to make assessment of student written performance more detailed, formal, and explicit, there are other technology options that also involve peer response. The best-known of these is Calibrated Peer Review (CPR; http://cpr.molsci.ucla.edu/Home.aspx), developed by Chemistry professor Arlene Russell for use in the sciences, especially in large-enrollment classes; now, a dozen years later, it has been adapted in over 5,000 courses at all college levels and across the sciences, social sciences, and humanities ("Calibrated Peer Review"; Likkel). The primary goal of CPR is *to make substantial student writing possible even in large classes*—and its evaluation more accurate and consistent. Successful use of such tools requires a teacher to carry out the significant "frontloading" responsibilities of (1) detailed assignment design, (2) building of a rubric related to the learning goals of the course, and (3) training of students to conduct helpful peer review. The CPR website offers teachers instruction and models for all three tasks. Basically, what the online assessment management system contributes is storage and organized presentation of all the writing from the students, plus facilitation, storage, and presentation of all peer reviews and student self-evaluations. Through the iterative process managed by the system, teachers and students learn not only how to improve their drafts but how to improve their feedback.

One by-product of the technological revolution, therefore, has been the willingness of an increasing number of teachers across disciplines to make writing a part of their curriculum. The teacher of first-year composition who wants to prepare students for the writing they will encounter in courses across general education and their majors can be confident that indeed they will be writing in many of those venues.

Filament Two: The Internationalizing and Translingualizing of Faculties and Student Populations

Until the past decade, little explicit attention in the WAC/WID literature has been paid to the steady growth in multilingual students and faculty in courses across disciplines throughout the United States. Part of the reason for this neglect has been the artificial separation between so-called mainstream composition scholarship and scholarship in the teaching of English to multilingual students for whom English is a second or later language. The collection by Matsuda, Cox, Jordan, and Ortmeier-Hooper is helping to change this trend, as is the CCCC "Statement on Second-Language Writers." Earlier essays by Johns; Leki (a series of articles beginning in 1995); Matsuda and Jablonski; and Villanueva, among others, had critiqued conventional WAC teaching for its neglect of English L2 student backgrounds and needs. But it was not until 2011 that an issue of the influential journal *Across the Disciplines* published a special issue on "WAC and Second Language Writers," with pedagogy and programmatic articles devoted to WAC/WID in multilingual environments. An anthology of research and pedagogy on this topic (Cox and Zawacki) appeared in 2013.

The basic complaint in the literature has been, as Cox says in her essay in the *Across the Disciplines* special issue, that "WAC has increased emphasis on writing across undergraduate programs without creating mechanisms that help L2 students succeed as writers and without creating faculty development programs that offer training in working with L2 writers." Indeed, WAC pedagogy going back to the 1970s, to the extent that multilingual writers were mentioned at all, saw one goal of WAC as very similar to the goal of required composition courses at that time in regard to English L2 writers: to help them progress toward achieving native-like fluency and correctness. While theory and pedagogy in first-year composition studies underwent the "social turn" beginning in the 1980s—a move toward programmatic respect for cultural and linguistic diversity in the writing classroom (see, e.g., the CCCC "Statement on Students' Right to Their Own Language" [1974; 2006])—WAC pedagogy had no similar move. This was ironic, given that many of the same program leaders who were redirecting required writing programs toward respect for diversity were also initiating WAC on their campuses.

How to account for this disjunction? The distinction came from the basic contrast in what the respective programs expected of writing faculty vs. what was expected of teachers in WAC settings. Namely, writing faculty were expected to work more fully with students, and with greater respect for language differences, because literacy was their primary responsibility. Teachers in other fields, whose first responsibility was to the content and epistemology of their disciplines, could not be expected to devote the same care and breadth of concern for all their students in regard to their writing. The problem, say the critics, is that when teachers in any setting are untrained to read and respond to versions of English that they do not regard as "standard," they are likely to underestimate the quality of thinking expressed in the writing *and* perhaps to pay too much attention in their responses to what they perceive to be linguistic error. The research studies in the Cox and Zawacki anthology show numerous examples of this reaction by WAC faculty. As a result, multilingual students are penalized by the uses of writing in the course, and so writing, which was always intended in WAC theory to deepen student learning in courses, becomes an occasion of failure.

The need, say the authors in the special issue of *Across the Disciplines*, is for WAC workshops to emphasize writers' "multicompetancies" (e.g., Hall and Navarro, 2011) rather than the differences in their writing from a perceived "standard." An example of this shift in perspective is given in Lavelle and Shima, in which history faculty at Uppsala University in Sweden are trained in WAC workshops to look past nonstandard versions of English usage and style. Readers concentrate on how students' writing reveals their understanding and application of course content and disciplinary modes of thought. Another manifestation of the "multicompetencies" approach is assignments that encourage multilingual students to draw on the richness of their cultural backgrounds to address research questions in their majors. While WAC/WID pedagogy has always tried to emphasize Writing to Learn, the multilinguality of students in contemporary higher education gives particular urgency to teachers' avoiding hyperawareness of perceived language errors in order to concentrate on how that diversity can contribute to increasing knowledge in any field.

Just as WAC/WID pedagogy in the United States has begun to respect the linguistic diversity and cultural depth of students across disciplines and institutions, so have WAC/WID scholars just begun to pay attention to ways that this pedagogy is enacted in diverse language contexts outside monolingual English education. The spread of Writing to Learn and process pedagogies transnationally by websites and listservs (as well as by international conferences) over the past dozen years has demonstrated again and again that WAC/WID pedagogy translates well across languages. The anthology *Writing Programs Worldwide: Profiles of Academic Writing in Many Places* (Thaiss, Bräuer, Carlino, Ganobcsik-Williams, and Sinha) contains many such examples. In one, De Micheli and Iglesia describe how they came to use writing assignments in "constructivist" ways in their biology classes, taught in Spanish, at the University of Buenos Aires. Assignments ask students to interpret and apply concepts from course readings: "We confront students with different problems and challenge them to write about these problems" (38). Having learned through practice over five years that responding to these writings with suggestions, rather than with corrections, produces better student engagement and learning, De Micheli and Iglesia have come to regard these interactions through writing to be "an unbeatable resource in learning the subject from a systemic viewpoint" (38).

Filament Three: International Program Development in Writing, and Effects on U.S. Teaching Practice

Teachers of writing in the United States, many of whom receive training to work in self-contained classes within required first-year writing programs, should understand that outside the United States such constructs as "first-year writing" and "general education" are rare. In *Writing Programs Worldwide* (Thaiss et al.), Lisa Ganobcsik-Williams, who studied and has taught both in the United States and in England, reflects on her education "as an American student in a UK university." She realizes that she "had not been looking for a composition class, but for guidance on expectations for writing in a higher education culture in which, at that time, students learned to write (or didn't) through acculturation" in the areas of study in which they concentrated (500). Ganobcsik-Williams goes on to describe the emergence of a broad range of structures for such "guidance" in universities in Europe, New Zealand, and Australia, many of these structures organized under the broad concept of "writing centre"—and most quite different from the United States' understanding of a writing center as (quoting Lisa Emerson) part of "a whole institutional infrastructure around writing" (Emerson 314). Teachers in the centers that Ganobcsik-Williams and Emerson describe don't see writing instruction as existing separately from the ways of thought, content, and goals for learning in the rest of the university, but as working in concert "ethnographically" with faculties across disciplines. In *Writing Programs Worldwide* are examples from six continents of center staff collaborating with teachers in such fields as the arts, biology, business, chemistry, history, law, mathematics, mechanical engineering, and political science.

Among lessons that U.S. writing teachers can take from center designs and pedagogy in transnational contexts are (1) that teachers in other disciplines care about writing and about student proficiency, though they are usually not trained in writing pedagogy, and (2) students want their writing education to be connected to their disciplinary learning goals. What might these lessons mean for pedagogy in the traditional self-contained American writing class?

One application of a "writing across disciplines" pedagogy involves drawing readings and models for writing from different disciplines. Over the several decades of the WAC movement in the United States, numerous textbooks with titles that include "across the curriculum" or "in the content areas" have been published to facilitate such an approach in first-year or advanced writing courses.

Now, myriad such writings can be found in online blogs and magazine websites. Students may be asked to compare different disciplinary perspectives on a timely common issue (e.g., how would an economist and a sociologist write differently about the 2007–2009 spike in unemployment?). Another option in the self-contained writing class is to assign students to become beginning ethnographers of the disciplines in which they are majoring or are thinking of majoring. The *case studies* they write could include (1) interviews with faculty, graduate students, or undergraduate majors in the target field regarding methods of research and characteristics of successful writing in that discipline; (2) analysis of articles in journals in the field about how writers design research, identify evidence, and draw conclusions. An advantage of these WAC/WID approaches is that students get to explore areas of interest and begin to appreciate the importance of writing to what they are passionate about. Students will more likely see the relevance of the writing course to the rest of their education.

The ethnographic approach may be facilitated by understanding the "academic literacies" theory developed in the United Kingdom (e.g., Jones, Turner, and Street; Lea and Street). An "academic literacies" approach sees writing in any field of study as a complex interaction of genres, personalities, institutional policies, cultures, and languages. It moves far away from a simplistic notion of "writing in the disciplines" as consisting of a few formats for "typical" writing in, say, sciences or the arts.

In all these ways, the self-contained writing class is "opened up" as a portal to becoming more aware of the rest of the university and its diverse learning cultures. The technologies described in Filament One can be used to deepen and expand this inquiry, through investigation of disciplinary program websites, blogs, and research sites—as well as student online sharing with one another of their investigations into disciplinary cultures.

Filament Four: Writing "in the Disciplines" as Preparing Students to Write "Beyond the Curriculum"

The 2006–2008 survey of U.S. WAC programs by the International WAC/WID Mapping Project showed that 36 percent of all programs reporting had "upper-division courses in WID taught by the English department or writing program" (Thaiss and Porter). This statistic supports the optimism expressed in the collection *Coming of Age: The Advanced Writing Curriculum* (Shamoon, Howard, Jamieson, and Schwegler), in which teachers from many U.S. writing programs described courses and pedagogies for students beyond the first year. That optimism is also reinforced in the increasing number of majors and minors in writing studies; majors are captured in the CCCC Web resource "Committee on the Major in Writing and Rhetoric." These programs often include capstone courses looking toward life after graduation, as well as many professional writing emphases specifically directed toward careers in fields across the disciplinary spectrum. (The writing program at UC Davis, for example [*http://writing.ucdavis.edu*], includes more than thirty courses focused on writing in such fields as business, law, film studies, ethnic studies, the sciences, human development, engineering, health professions, and journalism.) Such courses frequently include assignments to write background and goals statements suitable for graduate school, job, or professional school applications; the building of portfolios of written work to support these applications; and investigation assignments to study the communication climates and needs of workplaces. Internship courses reinforce this "beyond the curriculum" move.

All these examples support the idea that WAC/WID pedagogy should, to varying degrees, interpret the concept of "discipline" as extending through time. Even first-year writing students are not too inexperienced to imagine themselves after graduation, perhaps in the careers they dream of. Indeed, for the huge percentage of college students who come back to school after having gained work experience, or who attend school while working, a first-year writing course is an ideal place to have students write about their college plans, the links between their majors and their hoped-for careers, and the place of writing, current and imagined, in the several parts of their lives. In their study of graduating seniors looking back on their college writing courses, Jarratt, Mack, Sartor, and Watson strongly recommend such past-present-future literacy narrative assignments. Anne Beaufort, in her longitudinal study *College Writing and Beyond*, describes first-year literacy autobiography assignments as part of a whole-course philosophy that prizes students learning to map the many discourse communities—academic, work-related, personal—of which they are a part. She teaches students (and teachers) how to discern metacognitively the larger idea structures that connect the parts of these maps, in order to help students transfer current learning into the future. Necessarily, such a course is cross-disciplinary, as first-year students occupy diverse curricular spaces.

The pedagogy of WAC as Writing to Communicate invites teachers to think about how they might place students in rhetorical situations that approximate those they will encounter as professionals in their fields and learn to use the appropriate genres and discourse conventions. For example, the College of Engineering at Susan's institution has a capstone course in which students form teams that become consulting firms; they must go out into the community, find a client, and work up a project for that client, who then has a say in their final grade for the class. Business schools pioneered the use of the case method for situated learning, giving students a narrative describing a realistic scenario in which they might find themselves in their work and asking them to provide possible solutions to the problem described; this method has been used successfully by teachers in other disciplines to create writing assignments like the ones students will encounter in their professions (Hutchings).

Filament Five: The Steady Expansion of "Writing Intensive" Requirements in U.S. Higher Education, and Implications for Teaching

The U.S. survey of the International WAC/WID Mapping Project reports that 58 percent of WAC/WID programs (2006–2008) include a required course structure variously named "writing intensive," "writing in the major," "writing enriched," "writing emphasis," or something similar. Described by Farris and Smith and by Townsend, such courses fulfill general education requirements by assigning students to write a substantial amount in relation to their study of the particular subject of the course, whether it be in, say, music, political science, education, or physics. Though policies vary somewhat from institution to institution, proposals for such courses are usually approved by a cross-disciplinary committee; criteria usually include (1) a minimum number of graded words/pages, or a percentage of the course grade to be determined on the basis of student writing; (2) multiple assignments during a term or work written in stages; (3) instruction in how to complete the assignments and feedback to students during the process. Though goals statements for such requirements also vary, one goal is almost always to ensure that students have opportunities *in addition to their required composition course(s)* to do significant writing during their college careers—and to receive some guidance in that writing from their teachers.

Teaching methods in these courses don't differ significantly from the types described earlier. Technology tools (Filament One) can facilitate the communication, community-building, and response to writing in these courses; WI teachers need to be equally aware of the strengths and needs of a multilingual student population (Filament Two); writing process pedagogy is as useful here as in any other course; and so on. We regard WI courses here because the presence of these structures offers composition teachers a different kind of opportunity for pedagogy design.

Knowing that certain courses and teachers have also made the commitment to work with student writers can open possibilities for collaboration. For example, the "ethnographic" assignments described in Filament Three might enlist the cooperation of WI faculty in other departments—their interest in student writing may make them more ready to agree to interviews by students about their writing and about their perceptions of writing in the discipline. Further, they might also be interested in more formal collaborations with writing faculty, such as the "linked" or "clustered" courses arrangements that occur in some WAC/WID programs, by which sections of writing courses are paired with specific courses in other disciplines. The Mapping Project statistics showed that 27 percent of programs had some degree of linked arrangement. Essays by Graham and by Zawacki and Williams describe examples of teaching in these "learning communities."

In some U.S. colleges and universities, the idea of writing instruction based completely across disciplines—with no separate English composition requirement—flourishes (Gladstein and Regaignon; Gottschalk and Hjortshoj). Indeed, this model, often called the "Freshman Seminar" or "Cornell" model (since that university has been influential in sharing its ideas with other schools), has been for many years popular in smaller colleges, where commitment to WAC and WID principles took root early and sparked the WAC/WID movement from the 1970s onward.

THE FUTURE OF WAC/WID PEDAGOGY?

Technology continues to present us with ever more accessible tools to encounter the rich diversity of discourses and rhetorics in and across disciplines, in and across cultures. Social media spark unprecedented interest in peer-to-peer writing—and "peers" (e.g., "friends") are redefined in terms of the media communities themselves. Through these tools "writing" is being redefined as blends of written words, pictures, video, and audio. One effect of these trends is that teaching in all disciplines will be irrevocably transformed. Although the large lecture model of higher education still hangs on in many institutions, the "lecturer" is becoming a multimedia presenter, with "content" coming from many web-available sources and "lectures" being recorded as video sources for any-time playback.

Hence, for the first time, "flipping the classroom" (Alvarez)—to the active learning model WAC/WID visionaries have always recommended—may become the norm in education, with "homework" being watching/listening to lectures, slide shows, and video feeds, while "class time" becomes both face-to-face and social media interactions among participants. As we write this essay, the biggest story in higher ed curriculum is MOOCs—Massive Open Online Courses—in the sciences, social sciences, technical professions, humanities, and arts, with enrollments in some courses at over one hundred thousand worldwide. Coursera, a company founded by Daphne Koller and Andrew Ng (https://www.coursera.org/), is thus far the largest creator of such courses, and operates in collaboration with universities, who provide the lectures *and* curriculum tools such as tests, assignments, rubrics for grading student work and guiding peer-to-peer interactions. Coursera courses are active learning environments, a twenty-first-century example of Writing to Learn and Communicate pedagogy using advanced technologies. Though MOOCs have not yet shown that they can be a viable means to generate college credit, they demonstrate that WAC/WID pedagogies put forward in the 1970s, most easily realized in small classes, and adapted since to large courses in research universities, are scalable through digital, multimedia technology to worldwide "communities."

Whether or not MOOC companies like Coursera succeed in their current forms, they exemplify the pressure that the filaments of growth described in this chapter are putting on traditional higher education across disciplines—including the self-contained writing classroom. Will there any longer be an excuse for first-year writing classes to ignore the diversity of the disciplinary interests represented in their classrooms, when tapping those disciplinary resources is so easy for the student and the teacher? Will there any longer be an excuse for large-enrollment courses across disciplines to ignore the writing-to-learn-and-communicate tools that have been shown to facilitate learning among thousands of students? Will there any longer be an excuse for designing courses for a monolingual student body when the reach of instruction is transnational?

While WAC/WID pedagogy proponents in the 1970s and 1980s struggled to convince teachers that they could use writing and respond to writers, current proponents help to show how new tools can facilitate a new *cross-disciplinary* paradigm of learning that may in the future be the new norm for the teaching of writing.

BIBLIOGRAPHY

Alvarez, Brenda. "Flipping the Classroom: Homework in Class, Lessons at Home." National Education Association, 2012. Web.

Angelo, Thomas A., and K. Patricia Cross. *Classroom Assessment Techniques: A Handbook for College Teachers*. 2nd ed. San Francisco: Jossey-Bass, 1993. Print.

Bahls, Patrick. *Student Writing in the Quantitative Disciplines: A Guide for College Faculty*. San Francisco: Jossey Bass, 2011. Print.

Bazerman, Charles. *Shaping Written Knowledge: The Genre and Activity of the Experimental Article in Science*. Madison: U of Wisconsin P, 1988. Print.

Bean, John. *Engaging Ideas: The Professor's Guide to Integrating Writing, Critical Thinking, and Active Learning in the Classroom*. 2nd ed. San Francisco: Jossey-Bass, 2011. Print.

Beaufort, Anne. *College Writing and Beyond: A New Framework for College Writing Instruction*. Logan: Utah State UP, 2007. Print.

Britton, James. *Language and Learning*. London: Penguin, 1970. Print.

Britton, James, Tony Burgess, Nancy Martin, Alex McLeod, and Harold Rosen. *The Development of Writing Abilities (11–18)*. London: Macmillan, 1975. Print.

Bruffee, Kenneth A. "Collaborative Learning and the 'Conversation of Mankind.'" *College English* 46 (1984): 635–52. Print.

"Calibrated Peer Review: 21st Century Pedagogies." PKAL. 2004. Web.

Carroll, Lee Ann. *Rehearsing New Roles: How College Students Develop as Writers*. Carbondale: Southern Illinois UP, 2002. Print.

Conference on College Composition and Communication (CCCC). Committee on the Major in Writing and Rhetoric. http://www.ncte.org/cccc/committees/majorrhetcomp Web.

Conference on College Composition and Communication (CCCC). "Statement on Second-Language Writers." 2009. Web.

Conference on College Composition and Communication (CCCC). "Statement on Students' Right to Their Own Language." 1974; 2006. Web.

Cox, Michelle. "WAC: Closing Doors or Opening Doors for Second Language Writers?" *Across the Disciplines*, 8 (2011). Web.

Cox, Michelle, and Terry Myers Zawacki, eds. WAC and Second Language Writers: Research towards Linguistically and Culturally Inclusive Programs and Practices. Anderson: Parlor P, and Fort Collins: The WAC Clearinghouse, 2013. Print and web.

Day, Robert. *How to Write and Publish a Scientific Paper*. Phoenix: Oryx, 1994. Print.

De Micheli, Ana, and Patricia Iglesia. "Writing to Learn Biology in the Framework of a Didactic-Curricular Change in an Argentine University." Thaiss et al., 35–42. Print.

Emerson, Lisa. "Developing a 'Kiwi' Writing Centre at Massey University, New Zealand." Thaiss et al. 313–24. Print.

Emig, Janet. "Writing as a Mode of Learning." *College Composition and Communication* 28 (1977): 122–28.

Farris, Christine, and Raymond Smith. "Writing Intensive Courses: Tools for Curricular Change." McLeod and Soven. 52–62. Print.

Fulwiler, Toby. *The Journal Book*. Portsmouth: Boynton/Cook-Heinemann, 1987. Print.

Ganobcsik-Williams, Lisa. "Reflecting on What Can Be Gained from Comparing Models of Academic Writing Provision." Thaiss et al. 499–512. Print.

Gladstein, Jill, and Dara Regaignon. *Writing Program Administration at Small Liberal Arts Colleges*. Anderson: Parlor P, 2012. Print.

Gottschalk, Katherine, and Keith Hjortshoj. *The Elements of Teaching Writing: A Resource for Instructors in All Disciplines*. Boston: Bedford, 2004. Print.

Graham, Joan. "Writing Components, Writing Adjuncts, Writing Links." McLeod and Soven. 78–93. Print.

Hall, Jonathan, and Nela Navarro, "Lessons for WAC/WID from Language Learning Research: Multicompetence, Register Acquisition, and the College Writing Student." *Across the Disciplines* 8 (2011). Web.

Herrington, Anne and Marcia Curtis. *Persons in Process*. Urbana: National Council of Teachers of English, 2000. Print.

Hutchings, Pat. *Using Cases to Improve College Teaching: A Guide to More Reflective Practice*. Washington: American Association of Higher Education, 1993. Print.

International WAC/WID Mapping Project. http://mappingproject.ucdavis.edu. Web.

Jarratt, Susan C., Katherine Mack, Alexandra Sartor, and Shevaun E. Watson. "Pedagogical Memory: Writing, Mapping, Translating." *Writing Program Administration* 33.1–1 (2009): 46–73. Print.

Johns, Ann. "ESL Students and WAC Programs: Varied Populations and Diverse Needs." McLeod et al. 141–64. Print.

Jones, Carys, Joan Turner, and Brian Street. *Students Writing in the University: Cultural and Epistemological Issues*. Amsterdam: John Benjamins, 1999. Print.

Lavelle, Thomas, and Alan Shima, "Writing Histories: Lingua Franca English in a Swedish Graduate Program." Cox and Zawacki, 2013. Print.

Lea, Mary, and Brian Street, "Student Writing and Staff Feedback in Higher Education: An Academic Literacies Approach." *Studies in Higher Education* 23 (1998): 157–72. Print.

Leki, Ilona. "Coping Strategies of ESL Students in Writing Tasks across the Curriculum." *TESOL Quarterly* 29.2 (1995): 235–60. Print.

Likkel, Lauren. "Calibrated Peer Review™ Essays Increase Student Confidence in Assessing Their Own Writing." *Journal of College Science Teaching* 413 (2012): 42–47. Print.

Linton, Patricia, Robert Madigan, and Susan Johnson. "Introducing Students to Disciplinary Genres: The Role of the General Composition Course." *Language and Learning across the Disciplines* 1 (1994): 63–78. Print.

Madigan, Robert, Susan Johnson, and Patricia Linton. "The Language of Psychology: APA Style as Epistemology." *American Psychologist* 50 (1995): 428–36. Print.

Matsuda, Paul, Michelle Cox, Jay Jordan, and Christina Ortmeier-Hooper, eds. *Second-Language Writing in the Composition Classroom: A Critical Sourcebook*. Boston: Bedford/St. Martin's, 2011. Print.

Matsuda, Paul Kei, and Jablonksi, Jeffrey. "Beyond the L2 Metaphor: Towards a Mutually Transformative Model of ESL/WAC Collaboration." *Academic Writing: Interdisciplinary Perspectives on Communication Across the Curriculum*. 2000. Web.

McLeod, Susan H., and Margot Soven, eds. *Writing Across the Curriculum: A Guide to Developing Programs*. Newbury Park: Sage, 1992. Print.

McLeod, Susan, Miraglia, Eric, Soven, Margot, and Christopher Thaiss, eds. *WAC for the New Millennium: Strategies for Continuing Writing-Across-the-Curriculum Programs*. Urbana: National Council of Teachers of English, 2001. Print.

Miller, Carolyn. "Genre as Social Action." *Quarterly Journal of Speech* 70 (1984): 151–67. Print.

Pechenik, Jan. *A Short Guide to Writing about Biology*. 7th ed. New York: Longman, 2009. Print.

Penrose, Ann, and Steven Katz. *Writing in the Sciences: Exploring Conventions of Scientific Discourse*. 3rd ed. New York: Longman, 2010. Print.

Porush, David. *A Short Guide to Writing about Science*. New York: HarperCollins, 1995.

Reynolds, Julie, Christopher Thaiss, Wendy Katkin, and Robert Thompson. "Writing-to-Learn in Undergraduate Science Education: A Community-based, Conceptually Driven Approach." *CBE—Life Sciences Education* 11 (2012): 17–25. Web.

Russell, David. *Writing in the Academic Disciplines, 1870–1990*. Carbondale: Southern Illinois UP, 1991. Print.

Russell, David R. "Vygotsky, Dewey, and Externalism: Beyond the Student/Discipline Dichotomy." *Journal of Advanced Composition* 13 (1993): 173–97. Print.

Shamoon, Linda, Rebecca Howard, Sandra Jamieson, and Robert Schwegler, eds. *Coming of Age: The Advanced Writing Curriculum*. Portsmouth: Heinemann, 2000. Print.

Thaiss, Chris, and John Hess. *Writing for Law Enforcement*. Boston: Allyn and Bacon, 2000. Print.

Thaiss, Chris, and Richard Davis. *Writing about Theater*. Boston: Allyn and Bacon, 2000. Print.

Thaiss, Chris, and Tara Porter. "The State of WAC/WID in 2010: Methods and Results of the U.S. Survey of the International WAC/WID Mapping Project." *College Composition and Communication* 61.3 (2010): 534–70. Print.

Thaiss, Chris, and Terry Myers Zawacki. *Engaged Writers and Dynamic Disciplines: Research on the Academic Writing Life*. Portsmouth: Heinemann, 2006. Print.

Thaiss, Chris, Gerd Bräuer, Paula Carlino, Lisa Ganobcsik-Williams, and Aparna Sinha, eds. *Writing Programs Worldwide: Profiles of Academic Writing in Many Places*. Anderson: Parlor P and Fort Collins: The WAC Clearinghouse, 2012. Web.

Townsend, Martha. "Writing Intensive Courses and WAC." McLeod et al. 233–58. Print.

Villanueva, Victor, Jr. "The Politics of Literacy across the Curriculum." McLeod et al. 165–78. Print.

"WAC and Second Language Writing: Cross-field Research, Theory, and Program Development." Special issue. *Across the Disciplines* 8 (2011). Web.

Walvoord, Barbara Fassler. *Helping Students Write Well: A Guide for Teachers in All Disciplines*. 2nd ed. New York: Modern Language Association, 1986. Print.

Zawacki, Terry Myers, and Ashley Williams. "Is It Still WAC? Writing within Interdisciplinary Learning Communities." McLeod et al. 109–40. Print.

Writing Center Pedagogy

Neal Lerner

The claim that "writing center pedagogy" is somehow different from writing classroom pedagogy—and thus should merit a dedicated chapter—might seem bold. After all, writing centers seem to augment the work that goes on in classrooms, offering a separate-but-familiar space for students to receive one-to-one writing instruction. And in this physical or virtual space, students and writing center staff are engaged in practices intended to improve students' writing, a kind of happy ending for all involved: tutors, students, and classroom instructors who will be grading that final product.

Well, in that idealized description lurk histories, ideologies, politics, and, simply, the complexities of teaching and learning, all of which make the writing center a unique context, one well worth understanding in its own right and one that has much to offer classroom teachers and researchers about the one-to-one teaching of writing. Almost every two- and four-year post-secondary institution in the United States has a writing center of some sort, whether aligned with an academic department or student services. However, the mere presence of a writing center does not guarantee its stability nor provide the resources it would need to fulfill a capacious role. That presence might instead offer mere symbolic assurance that an institution is doing something about the "problem" of underprepared writers, without a full commitment to making writing and writing instruction a central feature of an academic program (for more on the institutional relationships of writing centers, see Mauriello, Macauley, and Koch).

This chapter offers a reading of the complexity of writing center pedagogy, from its history, to its primary features, to its theoretical foundations. Next, I describe the connections between writing centers and other sites of writing (for example, the writing center's role in Writing Across the Curriculum) and the long-standing relationship of writing centers to technology. Finally, a review of writing center assessment studies explores efforts to understand the effectiveness of teaching writing in writing center settings.

A subject not covered in this chapter but one vitally important to the larger educational enterprise is writing centers in secondary schools and earlier grades (see Farrell; Fels and Wells; Kent). When students have had writing center experiences before they come to higher education (whether as students or peer tutors), not only will those students most likely be well prepared but college and university writing centers also benefit.

Throughout this chapter, I argue that writing centers are innovative spaces, offering tutors, students, teachers, and researchers a window into both the promise of literacy learning and the long-standing tension between access and excellence. An understanding of writing center pedagogy offers future writing center tutors, classroom teachers, and writing program administrators an idea of how to make writing central to an institution's teaching and learning efforts.

WHERE DID IT ALL START?
HISTORY OF WRITING CENTER PEDAGOGY

While writing centers might seem to be relatively contemporary features of an institution's support structure for student writers, their physical presence and their pedagogical approach are long standing. In terms of the physical presence, accounts of early writing "laboratories" and "clinics" appeared in the professional literature throughout the first half of the twentieth century. In his 1929 survey of first-year composition practices throughout the United States, Warner Taylor of the University of Wisconsin noted the "inauguration of English 'clinics,'" which he defined as "a systematized method of compelling students found delinquent in English after having received credit for the Freshman course to take extra work under supervision to bring them abreast of a normal standard of correctness" (31). This approach, steeped in notions of first-year writing as the first defense against the ills of slovenly writing, is an unfortunate legacy of writing center—and composition's—history (see Rose).

However, not all accounts in this era described writing clinics and laboratories as places for students to be punished for language transgressions. The University of Minnesota General College Writing Laboratory, founded in 1932, was marked by a progressive approach that would fit well into twenty-first-century practices, particularly the rejection of drill-and-practice grammar work. As described by its founding director, Francis Appel,

> At first, feeling that good writing depended largely upon a knowledge of grammar, we assigned a self-instructing, self-testing manual of grammar; but when it became apparent that there was but little demonstrable correlation between a knowledge of grammar and the ability to write, the manual was discarded. (281)

The dual appeal of early writing centers—punishment for violators of language conventions versus possibilities for meaningful individualized instruction (see Lerner, "Punishment and Possibility")—stems from what Elizabeth Boquet has described as the duality of writing centers as a place and writing centers as a pedagogy ("Our Little Secret"). As a place, writing centers have long offered a physical space to send writers underprepared for the demands of college writing. As a pedagogy, however, writing centers have represented an alternative to the limits of classroom writing instruction, particularly when that instruction was based on memorization of rules, correction of "daily themes," and completion of drill-and-practice grammar exercises. As a 1950 Conference on College Composition and Communication workshop described, "The writing laboratory should be what the classroom often is not—natural, realistic, and friendly" ("Organization and Use" 18).

U.S. writing centers as a type of pedagogy have their roots in late-nineteenth-century notions of "laboratory" methods of instruction (Carino; Lerner, *Idea*). The tenets of this approach—individualized learning, the need for practice, and the role of the teacher as a guide rather than a sage—offered a powerful alternative to the lecture and recitation methods that dominated teaching at the time. As higher education enrollments rapidly expanded into the twentieth century, and as these newly enrolled students were far more diverse and often less prepared than previous generations of students, laboratory methods of instruction made a great deal of sense. For teachers of writing, the move was away from what Albert Kitzhaber has described as "a mass of principles to be committed to memory" (219). Instead, the emphasis was on practice. In a description in *The Dial* in 1894, influential rhetoric scholar Fred Newton Scott of Michigan declared that "the teaching of composition is properly *laboratory work*" (84, emphasis in original). Moving these laboratories from the classroom to stand-alone entities was an inevitable outcome.

In the happy version of this history, writing centers and their institutional colleagues worked as equal partners in the larger enterprise of teaching students to write. In reality, the relationship between writing centers and the institution has not featured equality. While writing centers as a place and as a type of pedagogy have flourished in many ways, particularly as access to higher education has increased and students have come to campus underprepared for writing, the politics of remediation and writing centers' association with remedial practices continue to create tension. In 1984, Stephen North decried this circumstance in "The Idea of a Writing Center," essentially arguing to his English Department colleagues that writing centers were far more than grammar garages. Over thirty-five years later, writing center directors continue to have to make arguments about their centers as hubs of writing-related activities on their campuses (though, ironically, many centers find comfort in the niche of the "downtrodden"—see Boquet and Lerner). Contemporary writing centers are usually relatively small operations, with staffing and hours of operation far under proportion to the number of students who are writing at any given moment. Historically, then, writing centers have long been recognized as valuable, but translating this value into resources commensurate to the charge to support all writers continues to be challenging.

Amid this history of growth and change, one relatively stable function of writing center pedagogy is the meeting of student writer and tutor. That meeting contains key features that differentiate writing center pedagogy from teacher–student or peer-to-peer conferencing that might take place in the classroom, yet it also provides models for those non-writing-center instructional sites, as the next section describes.

WHAT DOES IT LOOK LIKE?
INSIDE OF A WRITING CENTER TUTORIAL

At the heart of a writing center session is conversation about student writing (North 446). This conversation is quite different from one-to-one teacher–student conferencing, especially when the tutor is an undergraduate peer. The peer-to-peer dynamic offers insider knowledge and empathy that teacher–student conferences might lack, and the non-evaluative aspect of writing center work—in that the tutor is not grading the student's paper—frees the interaction from a significant constraint. That's not to say that the presence of the classroom instructor or the outcome of a final grade does not have a presence in a writing center tutorial—indeed, those factors are strong influences. However, the writing center as a relatively "safe" space to practice and put aside—at least for a while—impending deadlines and final grades offers great potential for productive work and makes writing center conferencing quite different from the peer review students might offer in a classroom (Harris).

While *conversation* is a term that implies shared responsibility, mutual turn-taking, and symmetric power relations, most guides to writing center tutoring do not take as a given that peer-to-peer interaction in the writing center will naturally ensure such equality (e.g., Gillespie and Lerner; Murphy and Sherwood; Ryan and Zimmerelli). Instead, many inexperienced tutors are quite accustomed to the role of editing their fellow students' texts (and are usually quite good editors), so a starting premise is that tutors need to adopt a more facilitative role. As a result, question asking is typical of writing center pedagogy as opposed to directives and strong handling of a student's text (Brooks). Also, setting an agenda is particularly important (Newkirk), as what happens in a session is a negotiation between a student's goals and the tutor's sense of responsibility within the ethos of a particular center. For example, most writing centers stress in their mission that they do not edit or proofread students' texts, that they're not a drop-off service for papers to be corrected or cleaned up; instead, writing center tutors help writers learn how to best to improve a text. The long-range goal is the *development of students as writers*, captured succinctly by Stephen North in his oft-repeated adage that

> in a writing center the object is to make sure that writers, and not necessarily their texts, are what get changed by instruction. In axiom form it goes like this: Our job is to produce better writers, not better writing. (438)

In practice, this ideal is complicated by several factors: (1) students' experiences with and expectations for writing center interaction (usually shaped by their experience with classroom writing teachers, many of whom have played a very directive role); (2) the role of time, whether that's the time allotted for a session—anywhere from twenty minutes to one hour at most writing centers—or the time before a student's paper is due (see Geller); (3) the context for a student's writing task, for example, whether or not the task is in response to a class assignment or is the student bringing a nonclass task such as a resume or statement of purpose; and (4) whether the visit to the writing center is required or voluntary. The last factor is particularly confounding: While an instructor might well know that having her students seek out assistance at the writing center is a good thing, requiring that attendance could result in disgruntled students not engaging in their writing center sessions or a center overwhelmed with a long line of students there merely to have a form checked off as proof of participation. The ideal goal of a student writer's development, however, speaks to the need for communication between instructors and writing center directors and a negotiation to balance resources available and assignment and writing cycles (see Clark for a study of the effects of required visits).

Overall, our understanding of effective practice in the writing center easily translates to effective practice for any context in which teaching and learning writing might be taking place: the need for tutors/instructors to listen fully and carefully, to respond as readers, and to allow the space for writers to be in control of the session and their texts; the need for writers to learn to articulate meta-language about whatever it is they're writing, that is, to be able to describe goals, intended readers, purpose of individual sections and approaches, and areas needing revision. Thus, writing center pedagogy is a model for writing classroom pedagogy, as well as any class in which writing instruction might take place, a lesson that is too often a "little secret" (Boquet, "Our Little Secret"), but one deserving of far more exposure.

WHY DOES IT WORK? THEORETICAL BASIS FOR WRITING CENTER PEDAGOGY

Writing center pedagogical interactions all occur within particular theoretical contexts, essentially models for teaching and learning in writing center settings. These models attempt to explain why writing center pedagogy works, as well as what it shares with, and how it is distinct from, other writing pedagogies.

Mary Louis Pratt's notion of "contact zone" or "social spaces where cultures meet, clash, and grapple with each other, often in contexts of highly asymmetrical relations of power" (34) has often been employed to describe contemporary writing centers (e.g., Sloan, "Collaborating"). Given the wide variety of potential encounters in a writing center—between disparate disciplines, native and non-native English speakers, undergraduates and graduate students, students and faculty—the writing center is a window into a wide variety of issues, including language (Thonus, "What Are the Differences"), authority (Kail and Trimbur), identity (Denny, *Facing*), race and racism (Greenfield and Rowan), gender (Carter), sexuality (Denny, "Queering"; Sloan, "Closet"), professionalization (Hughes, Gillespie, and Kail), creativity (Dvorak and Bruce), and literacy (Grimm). Thus, rather than a sort of "purified space" (Petit) marked by a straightforward encounter between tutor and student over a piece of student writing, writing centers are complex spaces, marked by the complications that teaching and learning always hold and that literacy education is particularly known for, and which makes writing centers particularly rich sites for theory, research, and practice.

At the theoretical center of writing center pedagogy is the belief that learning to write is a social process (Ede; Lunsford). The terms *social* and *process* are essential to these beliefs. As far as the social aspect, rather than the romantic ideal of the isolated writer calling upon an elusive muse, writing center pedagogy is predicated on the idea that interaction is at the heart of any act of writing. In one sense, this interaction is based in rhetorical theory or the idea that any writer needs to consider purpose, audience, context, and content for any writing task. In another sense, the basis for these beliefs draws on developmental learning theory, particularly the ideas of Soviet psychologist Lev Vygotsky, who saw writing development as starting with the social and moving to the internal, rather than the opposite. Vygotsky is also influential in his notion of the "zone of proximal development" or the idea that learners are capable of higher achievement if working alongside a more experienced peer or instructor (Bruffee).

Contemporary social theories of learning that influence our beliefs about writing center interaction and why it works are predicated on notions of "cognitive apprenticeship" (Collins, Brown, and Newman) and "legitimate peripheral participation" (Lave and Wenger). Social learning theorists view tutor–student interaction as occurring between an expert and a novice. Writing center tutors have expertise in teaching writing and academic literacies—whether through their experience as writers or the specific training they might receive—and students are novice writers with the intention of learning expert behaviors. However, this interaction is not merely one way but is instead mutual. After all, student writers most often have expertise in their topic or content (or in the context for their writing task), so in writing center sessions, the writer must often teach that content to the novice writing center tutor (see Lerner, "Situated Learning").

Learning in a writing center setting is "socially situated" in the sense that, as described by literacy theorist James P. Gee, "knowledge and intelligence reside not solely in heads, but, rather, are distributed across social practices (including language practices)" (181). Tutors have the expertise to offer and model these language practices and to reveal their use in particular social settings, such as school-based settings. Further, a student's role in writing center sessions is ideally active and participatory, a kind of learning by doing that is essential to social theories of learning and the development of expertise (see also Boquet, *Noise*; Geller, Eodice, Condon, Carroll, and Boquet; Shamoon and Burns).

In terms of *process*, writing center pedagogy is predicated on the idea that any writer needs to address the rhetorical elements of any communication situation: task, audience, purpose, context, and content. A writer does not necessarily address these elements in linear stages as "the writing process" sometimes gets interpreted, but instead in recursive rounds. The writing center's involvement in this process might come at any point: when a writer is brainstorming ideas or engaging in classical rhetoric's notion of *invention*; or when the rhetorical demands of *arrangement* are in focus and the writer is determining how best to organize content for a given audience and purpose; or when a writer needs to engage in revision, best enabled through feedback; or when a writer is focusing on *style* and rewording sentences and making language-level corrections. Unfortunately, given many writing centers' association with remediation and helping only struggling writers—as well as many faculty and student perceptions that feedback is equal to correction—writing centers are commonly associated with the final type of language-level intervention, and it often takes a strong effort of public relations to inform an academic community that all writers need feedback at all points of a composing process.

An influential concept of writing center pedagogy strongly shaped by this need is the distinction between "higher order" and "lower order" concerns in giving writers feedback. First popularized by Reigstad and McAndrew in their guide for writing center tutors, the idea is that writing center sessions are most useful to students when they focus on higher order concerns, such as choosing a topic, supporting an argument, or re-organizing a text. Lower order concerns are ones that operate at the language level: punctuation, grammar, usage, and wording. In some views, instruction in these areas is not the best use of time in a writing center session. In practice, however, this simple bifurcation gets complicated; in many instances students will want the focus to be on lower order concerns, particularly if this agenda is set by a classroom instructor's previous feedback on the student's writing. Further, many (but certainly not all) English-language learners and non-native English speakers with relatively low proficiency will have language-level needs as primary (Blau and Hall; Myers; Severino; Thonus, "Tutors"). Because of these complications, some guidebooks use the term *later order concerns* (Gillespie and Lerner) to indicate that language-level issues are important to any writing task, but that they're best addressed once a writer has clarified a text's focus, evidence, and organization. Still, the growing presence of English-language learners in writing centers challenges these priorities when language-level instruction is perhaps the best use of tutoring time (Myers).

Overall, the theories that have guided writing center pedagogy are also valuable outside of the walls of the writing center. Whether it is teacher–student conferencing or the use of peer review, fundamental to these activities are theories of writing and language development as a social, active process, as well as novice–expert learning models. On many campuses, writing center pedagogy strongly influences these additional sites for writing instruction, as the next section describes.

HOW DOES IT CONNECT? INTERSECTIONS OF WRITING CENTER PEDAGOGY WITH MULTIPLE SITES OF WRITING

Two areas in which writing centers can make larger connections are through Writing Across the Curriculum initiatives and working with libraries. These connections seem a natural fit, given the wide variety of students from a wide variety of classes and contexts who come to the writing center. The task for writing center sessions might vary from a personal statement for graduate school to a scientific research article to a PowerPoint presentation to a senior thesis. And the writers who come to the writing center seeking feedback might not be only students but will include faculty, staff, and alumni (or the writing center itself might serve the community; see, for example, the Salt Lake Community College Community Writing Center at http://vvww.slcc.edu/cwc/). This multiplicity is both a challenge and an opportunity. The challenge is to offer a pedagogy that will be flexible enough to contribute to these many writers and contexts. The opportunity is to be involved in the many sites of writing that educational community members might inhabit, both in and out of classrooms.

Many writing centers are closely aligned with Writing Across the Curriculum (WAC) or Writing in the Disciplines (WID) efforts at an institution, particularly as many colleges and universities recognize the importance of writing for learning disciplinary content, as well as communicating that content (see Thaiss and McLeod in this volume). Boquet's distinction between writing centers as a physical space and writing centers as a type of pedagogy is particularly important when instruction moves into specific disciplines and classes ("Our Little Secret"). As a type of teaching and learning, writing center pedagogy has long been seen as potentially central to a WAC program (e.g., Barnett and Blumner; Haviland), and the writing center is often the *de facto* "WAC program" at an institution when there is no formal arrangement. This role can often be seen in the staffing of writing centers when students—both graduate and undergraduate—are recruited from a wide variety of disciplines and majors.

A specific practice often associated with writing centers and WAC is the use of "writing fellows" (Haring-Smith) or "classroom-based tutors" (Spigelman and Grobman). In many of these formulations, the writing center assigns one or more tutors to specific classes to work closely with that instructor and its students. The writing fellow brings expertise on writing pedagogy in these settings, particularly when a disciplinary instructor is unaccustomed to teaching with writing. Ideally, this partnership involves co-teaching as the writing fellow and instructor shape writing assignments and their teaching, and the writing fellows meet regularly with that class's students via individual or small-group meetings.

While these arrangements have great promise to expand the reach of a writing center and contribute to the larger mission of teaching writing, they're not without complication. In particular, writing tutors might not have shared affinity with student writers, particularly for writing fellows programs set up to work with developmental writers (DiPardo). Further, the relationship between writing fellows and classroom instructors is key to the success of these arrangements (Hughes and Hall), and that relationship takes careful cultivation and consistent support. Finally, the teaching the writing fellows are asked to do might be considerable and time-consuming, particularly if they are meeting individually and regularly with all students in a relatively large class (Zawacki). Thus, any writing fellows program needs to be established with much planning and continual monitoring.

In addition to partnerships with writing in the disciplines, a relatively recent development in the partnerships that writing centers might establish is the academic library. Many of the most impressive physical examples of contemporary writing centers are housed in campus libraries, and such institutional positioning offers centrality to student activity—essentially going to where writers are—as well as alliance with another campus entity devoted to student learning: the library (Elmborg and Hook). Ideally, students are one-stop shopping, conducting library research on their writing projects before and after writing center sessions, as well as using the technological and space resources that many libraries have available.

Along these lines, "learning commons" are becoming an increasingly popular way to bring together library, writing, and technological instruction in one physical space but with a menu of expertise (Bennett). Going to where writers are, then, increasingly means central teaching and learning spaces in which activity reflects the many facets of composing: combining resources, technology, and assistance to help students succeed with their writing projects.

WHAT HAPPENS WHEN IT'S WIRED?
TECHNOLOGY AND THE WRITING CENTER

Technology is not new to writing centers when one defines technology broadly, including the humble pencil (see Baron). Historically, writing centers have often been intertwined with certain types of technology, whether the "drill pad," the precursor to drill-and-practice worksheets, or "programmed instruction," a behaviorist psychology approach first popularized in the early 1960s (see Lerner, "Drill Pads"). Technology's role in education has long been as way to make things "easier" for students and instructors (Dilger), and, in that sense, the entire enterprise of writing centers is a kind of technology as applied to the challenges of writing instruction.

Still, the development of digital technologies over the last twenty-five years has re-shaped writing center pedagogy in fundamental ways. The use of synchronous and asynchronous online tutoring is part of the repertoire of many writing centers. In some instances, that simply means offering e-mail response to students' papers, or in others it also means consulting in some sort of virtual environment (McKinney), such as Google+, Adobe Connect, or WCOnline, in terms of currently available options. While early debates on the merits of online technologies centered around whether they were superior or inferior to face-to-face consulting (Kimball), the reach and depth of online technology has pushed writing center scholars to go beyond the question of whether or not we should go online, but to examine what happens when we do and how best to prepare for it (see Hewett).

While the technology itself has changed from early virtual chat rooms to Google+, these practices offer an interesting challenge to long-standing practices of writing center pedagogy. For example, if the pedagogy is fundamentally about conversation with students about their writing, how does one create "conversation" when asynchronous consulting might consist of students e-mailing their papers along with some contextual notes and questions and receiving a consultant's response? Similarly, how is the hands-off-student-papers approach (lest one succumb to the temptation to edit for students) challenged when that student's paper itself is largely driving an online tutoring session, whether synchronous or asynchronous? Such circumstances have offered opportunities to re-examine many accepted tenets of writing center pedagogy and to consider if online consulting gives rise to completely different approaches to working with students and their texts (McKinney; see also Hobson; Sheridan and Inman).

Of course, online technologies have not only influenced the teaching of writing; they play an increasingly strong role in students' production of texts as multimodal composing has become an increasingly common activity in first-year writing and beyond. The response of writing centers to these practices has, on the whole, been slow to take shape (Pemberton, "Planning"). Nevertheless, many writing centers now assist with multimodal assignments, and, as pointed out in the previous section, are increasingly forming partnerships with educational technology colleagues to address both composing and technology issues.

Additionally, multimodal composing is not solely the province of first-year writing or digital humanities. Students in science and engineering have long needed to communicate in visual forms—whether in a graph, table, or drawing— and contemporary writing centers that intend to work with students across the college or university need to build expertise in the many visual forms of composing and the many technologies being used to communicate in those forms. The prevalence of one such technology—PowerPoint or other presentation software— means that writing centers that offer response to students' oral communication practices will often need to develop expertise in slide design and data visualization. Such expertise most often comes from the staff itself, especially when that staff comes from diverse disciplines with multiple forms of composing. However, this area also offers opportunities for collaboration with colleagues in the sciences or engineering or other fields with strong visual and digital composing practices. And collaboration is a writing center pedagogy of long standing.

DOES IT WORK? ASSESSMENT OF WRITING CENTER OUTCOMES

With a long history as a partner in the teaching of writing, one would think that the need for writing centers to "prove" their effectiveness would have passed long ago. Unfortunately, for many writing centers, arguments for funding need to be repeated in each budget cycle, and struggles for adequate space take constant negotiations. Such circumstances point to the need for assessment to demonstrate the value of ongoing use of the writing center to students and faculty.

Assessing writing center effects on students is quite complex (as is true for most educational practices) but also potentially quite powerful to better understand what students gain from their educational experiences. For example, it might seem simple to compare a student's paper before and after writing center visits, but many additional influences might play a strong (or stronger) role in the kinds of revisions a student might make (Jones). Or, perhaps, one might compare final grades between students who used the writing center and those who did not to see if the writing center made a difference (see, e.g., Lerner, "Counting Beans"; Newmann; Williams and Takaku); however, final grades (whether on a paper or in a course) are a product of a wide variety of factors, one of which might be the writing center, and that effect might only be small. Another approach is to survey students for their perceptions of writing center effectiveness, and these quick, end-of-session surveys are common practice (Bell). One limitation is that they offer only a snapshot of students' attitudes, a snapshot that might change over time or even once students receive grades on their papers (Morrison and Nadeau). Additionally, tracking the writing center's effects on student retention is particularly important in those institutions with poor retention rates (Griswold), and the writing center has great promise to provide the kind of contact with an institutional representative that research has shown is a vital component in retaining at-risk students (Tinto). Finally, examining the writing center's potential contribution to more internal student factors, such as self-efficacy (Williams and Takaku) or procrastination (Rapp Young and Fritzsche), offers promising directions to trace writing center effects.

What students might draw from their writing center visits is just one facet to assess, however. Another is what the tutoring staff might gain from their experiences, particularly undergraduate peer tutors. Hughes and his colleagues have led a large-scale survey of these effects via the Peer Writing Tutor Alumni Research Project (http://www.writing.wisc.edu/pwtarp/), which has revealed impressive, long-lasting effects of their writing center experiences on peer tutors. A writing center's contribution to its campus community is another effect that can be difficult to capture but is vital to demonstrate (Lerner, "Writing Center Assessment"; Thompson).

Overall, the opportunities to show off the good work of the writing center are many, though methodological and rhetorical considerations can be constraining factors (Johanek). It is quite common for writing center directors to be very good at counting things up: How many students visited, how many sessions held, how many questions fielded on the grammar hotline, how many workshops conducted. However, these counts are not necessarily sufficient to make the case for increased resources and a more central role in the enterprise of teaching students to write. Indeed, most writing centers are relatively small operations given the size of their student bodies. Fulfilling Stephen North's charge in 1984 to make writing centers "the centers of consciousness for writing on our campuses" (446) will require assessment in a wide variety of ways for a wide variety of audiences.

CONCLUSION: HOW CAN I LEARN MORE?

Writing centers are thriving in the present moment. Rather than resources only for developmental and first-year writing students and their instructors, writing centers are in a position to be true centers for writing instruction for an entire campus community, and they are increasingly involved in a wide range of activities (Pemberton, "A Finger"). In a sense, the writing center is no longer contained within its walls (whether physical or virtual) and has much to offer the rest of the institution.

As a professional field, writing centers have also achieved significant progress in organizing themselves via the International Writing Centers Association, or IWCA (http://writingcenters.org) and twelve regional writing center associations, including one in northern Africa and one in Europe (http://writingcenters.org/about/regional-organizations/). The IWCA holds conferences every two years, and most regional WCAs hold annual conferences, all of which provide key opportunities to meet and learn from writing center professionals from a wide variety of contexts.

Also, the two publications dedicated to writing centers issues—*Writing Center Journal* (http://www.cas.udel.edu/writing-center/journal/), a biannual, peer-reviewed publication; and *Writing Lab Newsletter* (https://writinglabnewsletter.org/), published five times per year—have been in existence for more than thirty years, while newer peer-reviewed publications such as *Praxis: A Writing Center Journal* (http://praxis.uwc.utexas.edu/) offer additional venues for writing center scholarship. The listserv WCenter (wcenter@lyris.ttu.edu), first established in 1991, continues to be a forum for writing center professionals to address concerns and discuss common issues. Additionally, the growing number of dissertations focusing on writing centers and the steady stream of published book-length monographs all attest to a field that continues to grow and mature.

In terms of finding many of these resources, the CompPile database (http://comppile.org/) is a comprehensive bibliographic source for writing center scholarship—including all articles that have appeared in *Writing Center Journal* and *Writing Lab Newsletter* and every dissertation or thesis written about writing centers up to 2011. Within CompPile are also specific research bibliographies on specific writing center-related topics, including an annotated list of articles on writing center tutoring published from the late nineteenth century to 1977 (Lerner, "Chronology"). The WAC Clearinghouse at Colorado State is also an excellent online resource, particularly on the subject of Writing Fellows Programs (http://wac.colostate.edu/fellows/).

Perhaps the best way to find out more is to gain experience working in a writing center, whether one connected to a university or one serving the community. The experience of one-to-one teaching of writing is unlike any other: the opportunity to connect with a writer who might be struggling to find her way with words, the mutual benefit for both tutors and writers, the tangible contribution that one can make in a very short period of time, the preparation for a wide range of teaching contexts, including classroom teaching. These are powerful potential outcomes of writing-center experiences; add in the rich opportunities for writing centers as research sites to explore the complexities of literacy learning, and it is easy to see why the field as a whole has persisted for a very long time and continues to grow. That's not to say that the political and financial constraints on writing centers are easily ignored. Quite the contrary; those factors make writing center directors particularly savvy administrators and call for a new generation of writing center scholars to take up the call for centrality rather than marginalization. Simply put, the writing center is a unique window into teaching and learning writing and the many intertwined contexts in which that teaching and learning take place.

BIBLIOGRAPHY

Appel, Francis S. "English Studies." *The Effective General College Curriculum*. Ed. Committee on Education Research of the University of Minnesota. Minneapolis: U of Minnesota P, 1937. 274–300. Print.

Barnett, Robert W., and Jacob S. Blumner. *Writing Centers and Writing Across the Curriculum Programs: Building Interdisciplinary Partnerships*. Westport: Greenwood, 1999. Print.

Baron, Dennis. "From Pencils to Pixels: The Stages of Literacy Technology." *Passions, Pedagogies, and 21st Century Technologies.* Ed. Gail Hawisher and Cynthia Selfe. Logan: Utah State UP, 1999. 15–33. Print.

Bell, James H. "When Hard Questions Are Asked: Evaluating Writing Centers." *Writing Center Journal* 21.1 (2000): 7–28. Print.

Bennett, B. Cole. "Private Writing, Public Delivery, and Speaking Centers: Toward Productive Synergies." *Praxis: A Writing Center Journal* 9.1 (2012). Web. 10 July 2012.

Blau, Susan, and John Hall. "Guilt-Free Tutoring: Rethinking How We Tutor Non-Native-English Speaking Students." *Writing Center Journal* 23.1 (2002): 23–44. Print.

Boquet, Elizabeth H. "'Our Little Secret': A History of Writing Centers, Pre- to Post-Open Admissions." *College Composition and Communication* 50.3 (Feb. 1999): 463–82. Print.

_____. *Noise from the Writing Center.* Logan: Utah State UP, 2002. Print.

_____ and Neal Lerner. "After 'The Idea of a Writing Center.'" *College English* 71.2 (2008): 170–89. Print.

Brooks, Jeff. "Minimalist Tutoring: Making the Student Do All the Work." *Writing Lab Newsletter* 15.6 (1991): 1–4. Print.

Bruffee, Kenneth. "Peer Tutoring and the 'Conversation of Mankind.'" *Writing Centers: Theory and Administration.* Ed. Gary A. Olson. Urbana: National Council of Teachers of English, 1984. 635–52. Print.

Carino, Peter. "Early Writing Centers: Toward a History." *Writing Center Journal* 15.2 (1995): 103–115. Print.

Carter, Shannon. "The Feminist WPA Project: Fear and Possibility in the Feminist 'Home.'" *Identity Papers: Literacy and Power in Higher Education.* Ed. Bronwyn T. Williams. Logan: Utah State UP, 2006. 42–56. Print.

Clark, Irene Lurkis. "Leading the Horse: The Writing Center and Required Visits." *Writing Center Journal* 5.2/6.1 (1985): 31–35. Print.

Collins, Allan, John Seely Brown, and Susan E. Newman. "Cognitive Apprenticeship: Teaching the Crafts of Reading, Writing, and Mathematics." *Knowing, Learning, and Instruction: Essays in Honor of Robert Glaser.* Ed. Lauren B. Resnick. Hillsdale: Erlbaum, 1989. 453–94. Print.

Denny, Harry. *Facing the Center: Toward an Identity Politics of One-to-One Mentoring.* Logan: Utah State UP, 2010. Print.

_____. "Queering the Writing Center." *Writing Center Journal* 25.2 (2005): 39–62. Print.

Dilger, Bradley. "The Ideology of Ease." *The Journal of Electronic Publishing* 6.1 (2000). Web. 19 February 2013.

DiPardo, Anne. "'Whispers of Coming and Going': Lessons from Fannie." *Writing Center Journal* 12.2 (1992): 125–45. Print.

Dvorak, Kevin, and Shanti Bruce, eds. *Creative Approaches to Writing Center Work.* New York: Hampton, 2008. Print.

Ede, Lisa. "Writing as a Social Process: A Theoretical Foundation for Writing Centers." *Writing Center Journal* 9.2 (1989): 3–15. Print.

Elmborg, James K., and Sheril Hook, eds. *Centers for Learning: Writing Centers and Libraries in Collaboration.* Chicago: American Library Association, 2005. Print.

Farrell, Pamela. *The High School Writing Center: Establishing and Maintaining One.* Urbana: National Council of Teachers of English, 1989. Print.

Fels, Dawn, and Jennifer Wells, eds. *The Successful High School Writing Center: Building the Best Program with Your Students.* New York: Teachers College P, 2011. Print.

Gee, James P. "The New Literacy Studies: From 'Socially Situated' to the Work of the Social." *Situated Literacies: Reading and Writing in Context*. Ed. David Barton, Mary Hamilton, and Roz Ivanic. London: Routledge, 2000. 180–209. Print.

Geller, Anne Ellen. "Tick-Tock, Next: Finding Epochal Time in the Writing Center." *Writing Center Journal* 25.1 (2004): 5–24. Print.

_____, Michele Eodice, Frankie Condon, Meg Carroll, and Elizabeth H. Boquet. *The Everyday Writing Center: A Community of Practice*. Logan: Utah State UP, 2007. Print.

Gillespie, Paula, and Neal Lerner. *The Longman Guide to Peer Tutoring*. 2nd ed. New York: Pearson/Longman, 2008. Print.

Greenfield, Laura, and Karen Rowan, eds. *Writing Centers and the New Racism: A Call for Sustainable Dialogue and Change*. Logan: Utah State UP, 2011. Print.

Grimm, Nancy Maloney. *Good Intentions: Writing Center Work for Postmodern Times*. Portsmouth: Boynton/Cook-Heinemann, 1999. Print.

Griswold, Gary. "Writing Centers: The Student Retention Connection." *Academic Exchange Quarterly* (Winter 2003): 277–81. Web. 10 July 2012.

Haring-Smith, Tori. "Changing Students' Attitudes: Writing Fellows Programs." *Writing Across the Curriculum: A Guide to Developing Programs*. Eds. Susan H. McLeod and Margot Soven. Newbury Park: SAGE, 1992/2000. 123–131. Print.

Harris, Muriel. "Collaboration Is Not Collaboration Is Not Collaboration: Writing Center Tutorials vs. Peer-Response Groups." *College Composition and Communication* 43.3 (1992): 369–383. Print.

Haviland, Carol Peterson. "Writing Centers and Writing-Across-the-Curriculum: An Important Connection." *Writing Center Journal* 5.2/6.1 (1985): 25–30. Print.

Hewett, Beth L. *The Online Writing Conference: A Guide for Teachers and Tutors*. Portsmouth: Heinemann/Boynton-Cook, 2010. Print.

Hobson, Eric. H., ed. *Wiring the Writing Center*. Logan: Utah State UP, 1998. Print.

Hughes, Brad, and Emily B. Hall. "Guest Editors' Introduction." *Across the Disciplines* 5 (2008, March 29). Web. 10 July 2012.

Hughes, Bradley, Paula Gillespie, and Harvey Kail. "What They Take with Them: Findings from the Peer Writing Tutor Alumni Research Project." *Writing Center Journal* 30.2 (2010): 12–46. Print.

Johanek, Cindy. *Composing Research: A Contextualist Paradigm for Rhetoric and Composition*. Logan: Utah State UP, 2000. Print.

Jones, Casey. "The Relationship between Writing Centers and Improvement in Writing Ability: An Assessment of the Literature." *Education* 122.1 (Fall 2001): 3–20. Print.

Kail, Harvey, and John Trimbur. "The Politics of Peer Tutoring." *Writing Program Administration* 11.1–2 (1987): 5–12. Print.

Kent, Richard. *A Guide to Creating Student-Staffed Writing Centers, Grades 6–12*. New York: Peter Lang, 2006. Print.

Kimball, Sara. "Cybertext/Cyberspeech: Writing Centers and Online Magic." *Writing Center Journal* 18.1 (1998): 30–50. Print.

Kitzhaber, Albert. *Rhetoric in American Colleges, 1850–1900*. Dallas: Southern Methodist UP, 1990. Print.

Lave, Jean, and Etienne Wenger. *Situated Learning: Legitimate Peripheral Participation*. Cambridge: Cambridge UP, 1991. Print.

Lerner, Neal. "Chronology of Published Descriptions of Writing Laboratories/Clinics, 1894–1977, WPA-CompPile Research Bibliographies, No. 9." *WPA-CompPile Research Bibliographies*, July 2010. Web. 10 July 2012.

_____. "Counting Beans and Making Beans Count." *The Writing Lab Newsletter* 22.1 (Sept. 1997): 1–4. Print.

_____. "Drill Pads, Teaching Machines, and Programmed Texts: Origins of Instructional Technology in Writing Centers." *Wiring the Writing Center*. Ed. Eric H. Hobson. Logan: Utah State UP, 1998. 119–36. Print.

_____. *The Idea of a Writing Laboratory*. Urbana: Southern Illinois UP, 2009. Print.

_____. "Punishment and Possibility: Representing Writing Centers, 1939–1970." *Composition Studies* 31.2 (2003): 53–72. Print.

_____. "Situated Learning in the Writing Center." *Marginal Words, Marginal Work? Tutoring the Academy in the Work of Writing Centers*. Ed. William J. Macauley, Jr., and Nicholas Mauriello. New York: Hampton, 2007. 53–73. Print.

_____. "Writing Center Assessment: Searching for the 'Proof' of Our Effectiveness." *The Center Will Hold: Critical Perspectives on Writing Center Scholarship*. Ed. Michael A. Pemberton and Joyce Kinkead. Logan: Utah State UP, 2003. 58–73. Print.

Lunsford, Andrea. "Collaboration, Control, and the Idea of a Writing Center." *Writing Center Journal* 12.1 (1991): 3–11. Print.

Mauriello, Nicholas, William J. Macauley, Jr., and Robert T. Koch. *Before and after the Tutorial: Writing Centers and Institutional Relationships*. New York: Hampton, 2011. Print.

McKinney, Jackie Grutsch. "New Media Matters: Tutoring in the Late Age of Print." *Writing Center Journal* 29.2 (2009): 28–51. Print.

Morrison, Julie Bauer, and Jean-Paul Nadeau. "How Was Your Session at the Writing Center? Pre- and Post-Grade Student Evaluations." *Writing Center Journal* 23.2 (Spring/Summer 2003): 25–42. Print.

Murphy, Christina, and Steve Sherwood. *The St. Martin's Sourcebook for Writing Tutors*. 4th ed. Boston: Bedford/St. Martin's, 2011. Print.

Myers, Sharon A. "Reassessing the 'Proofreading Trap': ESL Tutoring and Writing Center Instruction." *Writing Center Journal* 24.1 (2003): 51–70. Print.

Newkirk, Thomas. "The First Five Minutes: Setting the Agenda in a Writing Conference." *Writing and Response: Theory, Practice and Research*. Ed. Chris M. Anson. Urbana: National Council of Teachers of English, 1989. 317–31. Print.

Newmann, Stephen. "Demonstrating Effectiveness." *The Writing Lab Newsletter* 23.8 (April 1999): 8–9. Print.

North, Stephen M. "The Idea of a Writing Center." *College English* 46 (1984): 433–46. Print.

"Organization and Use of a Writing Laboratory: Report of Workshop No. 9." *College Composition* and *Communication* 2 (1951): 17–18. Print.

Pemberton, Michael. "A Finger in Every Pie: The Expanding Role of Writing Centers in Writing Instruction." *Writing and Pedagogy* 1.1 (2009): 89–100. Print.

_____. "Planning for Hypertexts in the Writing Center . . . or Not." *Writing Center Journal* 24.1 (2003): 9–24. Print.

Petit, Angela. "The Writing Center as 'Purified Space': Competing Discourses and the Dangers of Definition." *Writing Center Journal* 17.2 (1997): 111–23. Print.

Pratt, Mary Louise. "Arts of the Contact Zone." *Profession* (1991): 33–40. Print.

Rapp Young, Beth, and Barbara A. Fritzsche, "Writing Center Users Procrastinate Less: The Relationship between Individual Differences in Procrastination, Peer Feedback, and Student Writing Success." *Writing Center Journal* 23.1 (Fall/Winter 2002): 45–58. Print.

Reigstad, Thomas J., and Donald A. McAndrew. *Training Tutors for Writing Conferences*. Urbana: National Council of Teachers of English, 1984. Print.

Rose, Mike. "The Language of Exclusion: Writing Instruction at the University." *College English* 47 (1985): 341–59. Print.

Ryan, Leigh, and Lisa Zimmerelli. *Bedford Guide for Writing Tutors*. 5th ed. Boston: Bedford/ St. Martin's, 2009. Print.

Scott, Fred Newton. "English at the University of Michigan." *The Dial: A Semi-Monthly Journal of Literary Criticism, Discussion, and Information* 16 (16 Aug 1894): 82–84. Print.

Severino, Carol. "Approaches to Teaching Non-Native English Speakers across the Curriculum." *Writing Center Journal* 20.1 (1999): 78–81. Print.

Shamoon, Linda K., and Deborah H. Burns. "A Critique of Pure Tutoring." *Writing Center Journal* 15.2 (1995): 134–52. Print.

Sheridan, David, and James A. Inman, eds. *Multiliteracy Centers: Writing Center Work, New Media, and Multimodal Rhetoric*. Cresskill: Hampton, 2010. Print.

Sloan, Jay. "Closet Consulting." *Writing Lab Newsletter* 21.10 (1997): 9–10. Print.

_____. "Collaborating in the Contact Zone: A Writing Center Struggles with Multiculturalism." *Praxis: A Writing Center Journal* 1.2 (2004). Web. 27 December 2012.

Spigelman, Candace, and Laurie Grobman, eds. *On Location: Theory and Practice in Classroom-Based Writing Tutoring*. Logan: Utah State UP, 2005. Print.

Taylor, Warner. "A National Survey of Conditions in Freshman English." *Bureau of Educational Research Bulletin*, No. 11. Madison: U of Wisconsin P, 1929. Print.

Thompson, Isabelle. "Writing Center Assessment: Why and a Little How." *Writing Center Journal* 26.1 (2006): 33–61. Print.

Thonus, Therese. "Tutors as Teachers: Assisting ESL/EFL Students in the Writing Center." *Writing Center Journal* 13.2 (1993): 13–27. Print.

_____. "What Are the Differences? Tutor Interactions with First- and Second-Language Writers." *Journal of Second Language Writing*, 13.3 (2004): 227–42. Print.

Tinto, Vincent. "Research and Practice of Student Retention: What's Next?" *Journal of College Student Retention* 8.1 (2006-07): 1–19. Print.

Vygotsky, Lev S. *Mind in Society: The Development of Higher Psychological Processes*. Cambridge: Harvard UP, 1978. Print.

Williams, James D., and Seiji Takaku. "Help Seeking, Self-Efficacy, and Writing Performance among College Students." *Journal of Writing Research* 3.1 (2011): 1–18. Web. 10 July 2012.

Zawacki, Terry Myers. "Writing Fellows as WAC Change Agents: Changing What? Changing Whom? Changing How?" *Across the Disciplines* 5 (2008, March 29). Web. 10 July 2012.

CONTRIBUTORS

Chris M. Anson is University Distinguished Professor and Director of the Campus Writing and Speaking Program at North Carolina State University, where he helps faculty in nine colleges to use writing and speaking in the service of students' learning and improved communication. Most of his scholarly work focuses on the development and teaching of writing abilities, particularly across the curriculum; it includes fifteen books and over one hundred journal articles and book chapters. He has spoken at conferences and universities across the United States and in twenty-seven other countries. He is currently Chair of the Conference on College Composition and Communication. More at http://www.ansonica.net.

Collin Gifford Brooke is Associate Professor of Rhetoric and Writing at Syracuse University. He is the author of *Lingua Fracta: Towards a Rhetoric of New Media* (Hampton P, 2009), winner of the 2009 Computers and Composition Distinguished Book Award. His work on rhetoric and technology has appeared in a wide range of edited collections and journals such as *CCC*, *JAC*, *Kairos*, and *Enculturation*. Brooke is the current Director of Electronic Resources for the Rhetoric Society of America and blogs at http://www.cgbrooke.net.

Chris Burnham, Regents Professor of English, has served at New Mexico State University (NMSU) since 1981. Formerly Department Head and Writing Program Director in the English department, his academic specialties and publications cover writing and the teaching of writing, Writing Across the Curriculum, rhetoric, and assessment. He has conducted Writing Across the Curriculum seminars for university faculty at NMSU since 1981. He serves as Director of the *Borderlands Writing Project*, a National Writing Project–affiliated site providing professional development for teachers from kindergarten through university levels. For more information check http://www.nmsu.edu/~english/faculty/burnham.html.

Amy Devitt (Ph.D. University of Michigan) is Professor of English, Frances L. Stiefel Teaching Professor, and Chancellors Club Teaching Professor at the University of Kansas, where she teaches courses in composition, rhetoric, and English language studies. She has received six teaching awards, including the Kemper Fellowship and the CLAS Graduate Mentor Award. She has directed the University of Kansas's writing program and served as Associate Director of the Writing Across the Curriculum program. Her research specialties have included language standardization and genre theory, resulting in three books: *Writing Genres* (Southern Illinois UP, 2004); *Scenes of Writing: Strategies for Composing with Genres,* with Anis Bawarshi and Mary Jo Reiff (Pearson Longman, 2003); and *Standardizing Written English: Diffusion in the Case of Scotland 1520–1659* (Cambridge UP, 1989). She has published articles in *College Composition and Communication, College English,* other journals, and several edited collections.

Christine Farris is Professor of English and former Director of Composition at Indiana University. She is the author of *Subject to Change: New Composition Instructors' Theory and Practice* (Hampton, 1996); co-editor with Chris Anson of *Under Construction: Working at the Intersections of Composition Theory, Research, and Practice* (Utah State UP, 1998); and co-editor with Judith H. Anderson of the MLA volume *Integrating Literature and Writing Instruction: First-Year English, Humanities Core Courses, Seminars* (2007). Her most recent book, co-edited with Kristine Hansen, *College Credit for Writing in High School: The "Taking Care of" Business* (NCTE, 2010), won the Council of Writing Program Administrators (WPA) Best Book Award in 2012.

David Fleming is Professor of English at the University of Massachusetts Amherst, where, from 2007 to 2011 he was also director of its award-winning writing program. From 1998 to 2006, he was Assistant and Associate professor of English at the University of Wisconsin–Madison, where he also directed the intermediate and freshman composition programs. He is the author of *City of Rhetoric: Revitalizing the Public Sphere in Metropolitan America* (SUNY P, 2008) and *From Form to Meaning: Freshman Composition and the Long Sixties, 1957–1974* (U of Pittsburgh P, 2011), which won the 2011 MLA Mina P. Shaughnessy Prize and the 2012 CCCC Outstanding Book Award.

Ann George, Professor of English at Texas Christian University, teaches undergraduate and graduate courses in rhetorical theory and criticism, composition, and style. She is coeditor of *Women and Rhetoric between the Wars* (Southern Illinois UP, 2013) and coauthor of *Kenneth Burke in the 1930s* (U of South Carolina P, 2007). She is currently working on a book titled *A Critical Companion to Kenneth Burke's Permanence and Change.* Her articles have appeared in *Rhetorica* and *Rhetoric Society Quarterly.*

Diana George is Professor of rhetoric and writing and currently serves as Director of the Writing Center at Virginia Tech. She is a past recipient of the Richard Braddock Award with Marilyn Cooper and Dennis Lynch. Her work on public rhetoric and the dissident press has appeared in a number of journals and book collections, most recently in *Reflections: A Journal of Public Rhetoric, Civic Writing, and Service Learning* (New City Community Press, 2010), and, with Paula Mathieu, in John Akerman and David Coogan's *The Public Work of Rhetoric: Citizen Scholars and Civic Engagement* (U of South Carolina P, 2010).

Eli Goldblatt is Professor of English and former Director of First-year Writing at Temple University. Through New City Writing, the outreach arm of the writing program, he has helped to support Open Borders Project, Tree House Books, Temple Writing Academy, and other projects in collaboration with community partners. Goldblatt was the founding director of the Community Learning Network, the office to support community-based learning at Temple. Among other scholarly and creative publications, he is the author of *Because We Live Here: Sponsoring Literacy beyond the College Curriculum* (Hampton Press, 2007), and *Writing Home: A Literacy Autobiography* (Southern Illinois UP, 2012).

Matthew J. Hammill is a doctoral candidate in the Ph.D. program in applied linguistics at Arizona State University. He teaches first-year writing courses at ASU and has taught a wide range of ESL courses at intensive English programs, community colleges, and overseas in Japan. His research focuses on second language writing in U.S. higher education contexts. His work has appeared in the *CATESOL Journal, International Multilingual Research Journal,* and the *Encyclopedia of Applied Linguistics.*

H. Brooke Hessler is Professor of English and Eleanor Lou Carrithers Chair of Writing and Composition at Oklahoma City University. She teaches undergraduate and graduate courses in rhetoric, composition, and digital storytelling and serves as Assistant Director of the Red Earth MFA in creative writing. She is a recipient of numerous teaching awards, including a DaVinci Fellowship for pedagogical innovation. Her scholarship on composition pedagogy has appeared most recently in *Community Literacy Journal* and the *International Journal for the Scholarship of Teaching and Learning.*

Beth L. Hewett is Co-Chair of the CCCC Committee for Effective Practices in Online Writing Instruction, an educational consultant, and adjunct Associate Professor for the University of Maryland University College. Beth was the initial developer of the OWI program at Smarthinking, Inc. and redesigned the TutorVista OWI program. Individual publications include *Reading to Learn and Writing to Teach: Literacy Strategies for OWI* (Bedford, 2014), *The Online Writing Conference: A Guide for Teachers and Tutors* (Heinemann, 2010), and the *Good Words for Grief* series (Grief Illustrated P, 2010–2013). Co-edited/authored publications include *Virtual Collaborative Writing in the Workplace: Computer-Mediated Communication Technologies and Processes,* with Charlotte Robidoux (IGI Global, 2010); *Preparing Educators for Online Writing Instruction: Principles and Processes,* with Christa Ehmann (NCTE, 2004); and *Technology and English Studies: Innovative Career Paths,* with James A. Inman (LEA, 2005).

Rebecca Moore Howard is a graduate of West Virginia University who has taught at Texas Christian, Cornell, Colgate, and Binghamton Universities and is now Professor of writing and rhetoric at Syracuse University. She has written and edited a number of scholarly and pedagogical books and essays, including *Standing in the Shadow of Giants: Plagiarists, Authors, Collaborators* (Praeger, 1999) and *Writing Matters: A Handbook for Writing and Research,* 2nd ed. (McGraw-Hill, 2013). With Sandra Jamieson, she is a principal researcher in the Citation Project <citationproject.net>, a collaborative, multi-site, data-based study of college students' use of research sources.

Sandra Jamieson is Director of Writing Across the Curriculum at Drew University and a principal researcher in the Citation Project, a multi-institution study of student researched writing. Her publications include *The Bedford Guide to Writing in the Disciplines: An Instructor's Desk Reference* (with Rebecca Moore Howard; Bedford/ St. Martin's, 1995), *Coming of Age: The Advanced Writing Curriculum* (co-edited with Linda K. Shamoon, Howard, and Robert Schwegler; Heinemann, 2000), and articles on reading, plagiarism, information literacy, the vertical writing curriculum, WAC, textbooks, and multicultural education. She is Chair of the CCCC's Committee on the Major in Writing and Rhetoric and has served on the CCCC's executive board.

Laura Julier wrote the chapter on community-service pedagogy in the first edition of *A Guide to Composition Pedagogies.* She currently directs the Professional Writing program at Michigan State University, where she teaches courses in editing and publishing, grammar and style, and environmental and place-based nonfiction. She also edits *Fourth Genre: Explorations in Nonfiction,* an award-winning international literary journal published by Michigan State UP. She received a Michigan Campus Compact Community Service Learning Outstanding Faculty award and is a former Lilly Endowment Teaching Fellow.

Krista Kennedy is Assistant Professor of Writing and Rhetoric at Syracuse University, where she teaches courses in rhetorical theory, digital rhetorics, technical communication, and history of technology. Her work on distributed authorship has appeared in *College English* as well as several edited collections. She is currently completing a book-length historical comparison of authorship and rhetorical agency in the *Chambers' Cyclopædia* and *Wikipedia*.

Steve Lamos is Associate Professor in the Program for Writing and Rhetoric at the University of Colorado–Boulder. His publications include *Interests and Opportunities: Race, Racism, and University Writing Instruction in the Post-Civil Rights Era* (Pittsburgh UP, 2011), articles in *CCC, CE, JBW*, and *WPA*, and a chapter in *Writing Studies Research in Practice: Methods and Methodologies* (Southern Illinois UP, 2012). Lamos' current book project examines the role of non-tenure-track writing instruction in the neoliberal academy.

Neal Lerner is Associate Professor of English and Director of the Writing Center at Northeastern University in Boston, Massachusetts. He is the author of *The Idea of a Writing Laboratory* (Southern Illinois UP, 2009), which won the 2011 NCTE David H. Russell Award for Distinguished Research in the Teaching of English; co-author (with Mya Poe and Jennifer Craig) of *Learning to Communicate in Science and Engineering: Case Studies from MIT* (MIT, 2010), which won the 2012 CCCC Advancement of Knowledge Award; and co-author (with Paula Gillespie) of *The Longman Guide to Peer Tutoring*, 2nd ed. (Longman, 2007). He writes about the history, politics, and practices of teaching writing in classrooms, writing centers, and science laboratories.

Kathleen Livingston spent years working with youth and adults at Affirmations, an LGBT community center in metro-Detroit. She currently teaches community-engaged and nonfiction writing courses, primarily in the first-year writing program at Michigan State University. She has essays on consent as queer feminist practice forthcoming in several edited collections. She has presented and performed her work on consent at *CCCC, Feminisms and Rhetorics, AWP, Michigan Women's Studies Association*, and Detroit's *Allied Media Conference*, among others. She is also a longtime zinester.

Tim Lockridge is Assistant Professor of Digital Media Studies at Saint Joseph's University. He is the 2012 recipient of the *Computers and Composition* Hugh Burns Best Dissertation Award. His work on digital media and circulation has appeared in several edited collections, including, with Diana George and Dan Lawson, *The New Work of Composing* (Computers and Composition Digital P & Utah State UP, 2012), and, with Dan Lawson and Evan Snider, *Guns, Grenades, and Grunts: First-Person Shooter Games* (Bloomsbury Academic, 2012). He is Co-Director of the Beautiful Social Community Media Collaborative and a Senior Editor of Computers and Composition Digital Press.

Paul Kei Matsuda is a Professor of English and Director of Second Language Writing at Arizona State University. Founding Chair of the Symposium on Second Language Writing and editor of the Parlor Press Series on Second Language Writing, his work appears in journals such as *College Composition and Communication, College English, English for Specific Purposes, Journal of Basic Writing, Journal of Second Language Writing, TESOL Quarterly, Writing Program Administration,* and *Written Communication*.

He has presented lectures and workshops at conferences and universities in various countries, including China, Hong Kong, Hungary, Israel, Japan, Korea, Malaysia, Mexico, Qatar, Spain, Taiwan, Thailand, United Arab Emirates, and throughout the United States.

Susan H. McLeod is Research Professor and Writing Program Distinguished Scholar at the University of California, Santa Barbara. Her scholarship includes ten books and numerous articles on Writing Across the Curriculum, writing program administration, and the affective domain in the writing classroom. She is the editor of the Perspectives on Writing book series with the WAC Clearinghouse (http://wac.colostate.edu/books/perspectives.cfm), and co-editor (with Margot Soven) of the Writing Program Administration series with Parlor Press (http://www.parlorpress.com/wpa.html).

Laura R. Micciche teaches writing, rhetorical theory, and writing pedagogy at the University of Cincinnati. She has written on feminist theory and pedagogy in *Doing Emotion: Rhetoric, Writing, Teaching* (Heinemann, 2007) and in essays for *College English, Composition Studies, jac, Rhetoric Review, Rhetorica in Motion* (University of Pittsburgh, 2010), and other venues. Effective July 2013, she is the editor of *Composition Studies*.

Deborah Mutnick is Professor of English and Co-Director of LIU Brooklyn Learning Communities. She is author of *Writing in an Alien World: Basic Writing and the Struggle for Equality in Higher Education* (Heinemann, 1996), recipient of the W. Ross Winterowd Award, and has published on basic writing, narrative, critical pedagogy, oral history, and place-based composition studies. She also serves on the editorial boards of *Science & Society* and the *Journal of Basic Writing*. At present, she is completing an NEH Digital Humanities Startup Grant for the Pathways to Freedom Digital Narrative Project documenting civil rights history in Brooklyn, New York.

Rebecca Powell is a graduate student in rhetoric and professional communication at New Mexico State University, where she is finishing a dissertation on high school students' writing experiences and place. Rebecca's research interests include literacy studies, composition pedagogy, and critical regionalism. Her publications include: "Bad Mothers, Good Mothers and Mommy Bloggers: Rhetorical Resistance and Fluid Subjectivities" in *MP: Online Feminist Journal*; "Mapping Literacies: Land Use Planning and the Sponsorship of Place" in *Environmental Rhetoric and Ecologies of Place*; and "Developing Curriculum for a Multi-Course Interdepartmental Learning Community to Promote Retention and Learning for Underprepared Engineering Students" in *Xchanges*.

Kurt Schick teaches writing and rhetoric at James Madison University. He has published scholarship on teaching writing, faculty development, and writing centers. With Laura Schubert, he coauthored *So What? The Writer's Argument* (Oxford UP, 2014).

Amy Rupiper Taggart is Associate Professor of English at North Dakota State University, formerly Director of First-year Writing. As a writing studies specialist, she teaches a range of undergraduate and graduate courses in writing and literacy studies. Her research focuses on issues in composition pedagogy, including community-engagement, formative assessment, student and teacher reflection, and teacher preparation. Her articles have appeared in varied journals and edited collections, including, most recently, the *International Journal for the Scholarship of Teaching and Learning* and *WPA: Writing Program Administration*. She co-authored the textbook *Research Matters* (McGraw-Hill, 2013) with Rebecca Moore Howard.

Gary Tate taught English for three decades at Texas Christian University. He helped establish the discipline of composition through his editorial work, including collections such as *Teaching Freshman Composition* (co-edited with Edward P. J. Corbett; Oxford UP, 1967), *Teaching Composition: 10 Bibliographical Essays* (Texas Christian UP, 1977), *The Writing Teacher's Sourcebook, 4/e* (co-edited with Corbett and Nancy Myers; Oxford UP, 1999), and this collection. In 1972, Tate created an independent journal for exchanging practical ideas about teaching composition, *Freshman English News*, later renamed *Composition Studies*. Tate also wrote an influential exchange with Erika Lindemann about the value of literature in first-year writing (*College English*, 1993) and co-edited *Coming to Class: Pedagogy and the Social Class of Teachers*, with John McMillan and Alan Shepard (Heinemann, 1998).

Chris Thaiss is Clark Kerr Presidential Chair and Professor in the University Writing Program of the University of California, Davis, where he also directs its Center for Excellence in Teaching and Learning. Thaiss coordinates the International Network of Writing Across the Curriculum Programs and serves as a consultant/evaluator for the Council of Writing Program Administrators. He teaches undergraduate courses in writing in the disciplines and graduate courses in writing pedagogy, research, and administration. Author, co-author, or editor of twelve books and many chapters and articles, his most recent book is *Writing Programs Worldwide: Profiles of Academic Writing in Many Places* (Parlor, 2012), co-edited with an international team.

John Trimbur is Professor of Writing, Literature & Publishing at Emerson College. He has won a number of awards, including the Richard Braddock Award (2003), with Bruce Horner, for "English Only and U.S. College Composition" (*College Composition and Communication*, 2002), and the James L. Kinneavy Award (2001) for "Agency and the Death of the Author: A Partial Defense of Modernism" (*JAC*, 2002). A collection of his essays, *Solidarity or Service: Composition and the Problem of Expertise,* appeared in 2011 (Heinemann).

Author Index

Ackerman, John M., 56, 101
Adams, John L., 215
Adams, Katherine H., 215
Adams, Peter, 28, 30
Adler-Kassner, Linda, 56, 60, 233
Ahmad, Aijaz, 102
Alexander, Jonathan, 65, 137, 139, 201
Allen, Christopher, 189
Allen, Danielle, 254, 259
Alvarez, Barbara, 234, 239
Alvarez, Brenda, 297
Anderson, Daniel, 189
Anderson, Judith H., x, 163, 169, 170, 171, 172, 173
Anderson, Virginia, 89
Andrew-Vaughan, Sarah, 152
Andriessen, Jerry, 259
Angelo, Thomas A., 285
Annas, Pamela J., 130
Anson, Chris M., 5, 14–15, 46, 66, 115, 213, 218, 219, 221, 234
Appel, Francis S., 302
Appleby, Bruce C., 130
Arca, Rosemary, 60
Aristotle, 12, 119, 121, 194, 251–254, 256–257
Aronowitz, Stanley, 79
Artemeva, Natasha, 158
Ashton-Jones, Evelyn, 133
Association of College and Research Libraries, 238
Atkinson, Dwight, 118
Austin, Barbara, 237

Autostraddle, 63
Azar, Betty Schrampfer, 276

Baca, Damián, 104
Bachman, Lyle F., 269
Bacon, Nora, 57–60, 67
Bahls, Patrick, 287
Baker, Edith M., 172
Baker, Sheridan, 212
Ball, Eric L., 61
Ballenger, Bruce, 236–237, 243
Baltodano, Marta P., 91
Banks, Adam J., 99
Banks, William P., 121
Barker, Thomas T., 43
Barnes, Luann, 133
Barnett, Robert W., 308
Barnett, Timothy, 259
Baron, Dennis, 194–195, 309
Baron, Henry, 217
Barrios, Barclay, 138
Barthes, Roland, 37, 99, 104
Bartholomae, David, 22–25, 27, 123, 167–169, 217
Barton, Matt, 50, 201
Bastian, Heather, 155
Batt, Thomas A., 199
Bauer, Dale M., 134
Baumgardner, Jennifer, 129
Bawarshi, Anis, x, 147, 150, 152–156, 158–159
Bay, Jennifer L., 260
Bazerman, Charles, 146, 285

Beach, Richard, 219
Bean, Janet, 137
Bean, John C., 241, 286
Beaufort, Anne, 151, 159, 295
Becker, Alton L., 223 , 255–256
Becker, Anne, 219
Bedore, Pamela, 38
Beech, Richard, 46
Behrens, Laurence, 241
Belanoff, Pat, 126
Belenky, Mary Field, 118
Bell, James H., 310
Bender, John, 255
Benkler, Yochai, 45
Bennett, B. Cole, 309
Benson, Beverly, 273
Bereiter, Carl, 259
Berg, E. Cathrine, 270
Berger, John, 104
Bergmann, Linda S., 172
Berlin, James A., 2, 4, 17, 20, 78, 89, 97–98,
    100, 104, 113, 117, 119, 121, 170,
    215, 225
Bernstein, Susan Naomi, 28
Berrill, Deborah P., 258
Berry, Patrick W., 100
Berthoff, Ann, 132, 223
Bessette, Lee Skallerup, 184
Bhabha, Homi K., 102
Bickford, Donna, 70
Bilsky, Manuel, 255
Birkenstein, Cathy, 167
Bishop, Wendy, 11, 111, 121, 124
Bitchener, John, 276
Bitzer, Lloyd, 249
Bizup, Joseph, 236, 259
Bizzell, Patricia, 83–84,
Blaauw-Hara, Mark, 23
Blair, Kristine, 135
Blakesley, David, 256
Blau Susan, 307
Bleich, David, 52–54
Blitz, Michael, 86, 89
Blommaert, Jan, 103
Blum, Susan D., 235
Blumner, Jacob S., 308
Boese, Christine, 135
Boler, Megan, 136
Bolker, Joan, 130
Bolter, Jay David, 98, 178
Booth, Wayne, 164, 252

Boquet, Elizabeth H., 302–303,
    305–306, 308
Borton, Sonya C., 190
Boucher, Michel, 138
Bowdon, Melody, 70
Boyd, Patricia Webb, 206
Boyd, Stowe, 190
Boyer, Ernest, 4
Boylan, Hunter, 28
Braddock, Richard, 219
Brady, Laura, 173
Branch, Kirk, 69
Brandt, Deborah, 20, 68, 101
Brannon, Lil, 87
Bräuer, Gerd, 292
Braxton, John, 67
Brent, Doug, 223, 256
Brereton, John, 212
Breuch, Lee-Ann Kastman, 40,
    46, 197
Bridwell-Bowles, Lillian, 132
Brier, Stephen, 179
Britton, James, 112, 115–117, 122, 166, 220,
    284–285
Brizzee, H. Allen, 202
Broad, Bob, 140
Brody, Miriam, 130
Brooke, Collin Gifford, 14, 16, 45, 50,
    99–100, 122, 197
Brookfield, Stephen D., 9
Brooks, Jeff, 304
Brooks, Kevin, 151, 155
Brown, John Seely, 306
Bruce, Shanti, 305
Brueggemann, Brenda Jo, 137, 140
Bruffee, Kenneth A., 37, 219, 284, 306
Bryant, Lizbeth A., 120
Bui, Kara, 199
Bullock, Richard, 93, 105
Bump, Jerome, 43
Bunting, Ben S., Jr., 47
Burgess, Tony, 126, 227, 298
Burgstahler, Sheryl, 203
Burke, Kenneth, 11–12, 77, 90–91, 182,
    218, 223, 256
Burnham, Christopher C., 13, 112
Burns, Deborah H., 306
Burns, Hugh Lee, Jr., 43
Butin, Dan, 56
Butler, Judith, 138
Byrd, Patricia, 273

Callaway, Michael, 256
Campus Compact, 67
Canagarajah, Suresh, 30, 103
Cargile Cook, Kelli, 207
Carino, Peter, 303
Carlino, Paula, 292
Carr, Nicholas, 240
Carrick, Tracy Hamler, 60
Carroll, Lee Ann, 287
Carroll, Meg, 306
Carter, Shannon, 25, 305
Celce-Murcia, Marianne, 276
Centre for Contemporary Cultural Studies, 95, 106
Chang, Ching-Fen, 203
Chanquoy, Lucile, 259
Chappell, Virginia, 237
Charney, Davida, 38
Chiang, Yuet-Sim D., 271
Ching, Kory Lawson, 38
Chiseri-Strater, Elizabeth, 104
Cicero, 194, 250–251
Clark, Brooks, 222
Clark, Irene Lurkis, 152 , 305
Clark, J. Elizabeth, 196–197
Clark, Michael P., 173
Clark, Suzanne, 42
Clarke, John, 96
Clarke, Melinda, 67
Clary-Lemon, Jennifer, 256
Cleary, Michelle Navarre, 60
Clifford, John, 164
Clinchy, Blythe McVicker, 118
Coe, Richard M., 147, 152–154, 155
Cohen, Dan, 179
Coirier, Pierre, 259
Coles, William E., Jr., 113, 115, 221, 223
College Composition and Communication
    Committee for Best Practices in
    Online Writing Instruction, 209
Collins, Allan, 306
Colombo, Gary, 104
Comer, Denise, 38
Comley, Nancy R., 165, 168–169
Committee on the Major in Writing and
    Rhetoric, 295
*Common Core State Standards for English
    Language Arts*, 262
Condon, Frankie, 306
Conference on College Composition and
    Communication, 165, 221, 279

Conley, Thomas, 250
Conniff, Brian, 58
Connor, Ulla, 269
Connors, Robert J., 165, 215–216, 222
Coogan, David, 56, 101–102
Cooper, David D., 55
Cooper, George, 199
Cooper, Marilyn M., x, 133
Cope, Bill, 149
Corbett, Edward P. J., xiv, 223, 255
Corbett, Patrick, 238
Corbett, Stephen, 199
Corder, Jim W., 124
Corder, S. Pit, 275
Council of Writing Program
    Administrators, xiv, 221, 233
Cox, Michelle, 276, 291–292
Crawford, Neta C., 259
Critcher, Chas, 106
Crooks, Robert, 56
Crosswhite, James, 257–258, 260
Crowley, Sharon, 37, 113, 163, 165–167, 225, 255
Crunk Feminist Collective, 63
Cruz, Nadinne I., 56, 67
Cullen, Robert, 104
Cumming, Alister, 279
Cummings, Robert E., 49–50
Cunningham, Ward, 48
Curtis, Marcia, 120, 287
Cushman, Ellen, 56, 61–64, 68–69, 184
Cyganowski, Carol Klimick, 44

D'Angelo, Frank J., 221, 241
Daiute, Colleen, 220
Danielewicz, Jane, 126
Darder, Antonia, 88
Davi, Angelique, 28, 66
Davidson, Cathy, 177
Davis, Andréa, 45
Davis, Richard, 287
Davis, Robert L., 232, 234, 236–237, 243
Dawkins, John, 23
Day, Robert, 298
de Acosta, Martha, 71
de Certeau, Michel, 99–100
de Courtivron, Isabelle, 131
De Micheli, Ana, 293
Dean, Deborah, 148
Deans, Thomas, 56–57
Declair, D. P., 195

Deitering, Anne-Marie, 239
Delpit, Lisa, 26, 118, 147
DeLuca, Kevin Michael, 260
DeMers, Kathleen Dunn, 34
Denny, Harry, 305
DePew, Kevin Eric, 195, 199
Desmet, Christy, 135
Devitt, Amy J., 8, 12, 150–151, 153,
    155, 170
DeVoss, Dànielle Nicole, 45, 50, 99, 184,
    201, 208
Dewey, John, 7, 55–56, 58, 79, 82, 117,
    123–124
Dewitt, Scott Lloyd, 190
diGennaro, Kristen, 30
DiGrazia, Jennifer, 138
Dilger, Bradley, 309
Dimmock, Nora, 234, 239
Dingo, Rebecca A., 103
DiPardo, Anne, 308
Dirk, Kerry, 236
Dirlik, Arif, 102
Doe, Tannis, 203
Doheny-Farina, Stephen, 43
Dolmage, Jay, 139
Donahue, Christiane, 139
Downs, Doug, 15, 225
Dubisar, Abby M., 190
Dubrow, Heather, 260
Dudley-Evans, Tony, 150
Duffelmeyer, Barbara B., 84
Duffy, Cheryl Hofstetter, 58
Duffy, John, 259
Duin, Ann Hill, 44
Dunn, Patricia A., 31–32, 140, 185
Duttagupta, Chitralekha, 28
Dvorak, Kevin, 305

Eadie, Tom, 238
Eberly, Rosa A., 100
Ede, Lisa, 38–40, 42, 133, 225, 305
Ehmann, Christa, 195, 207–208
Eichhorn, Jill, 131
Eidman-Aadahl, Elyse, 201
Eisenberg, Michael, 232, 236, 239
Elbow, Peter, 1, 38, 56, 77, 111, 113–115,
    117–120, 123–125, 165, 217–218,
    221–223, 240
Eldred, Janet C., 101
Ellsworth, Elizabeth, 84
Elmborg, James K., 308

Emerson, Lisa, 293
Emig, Janet, 112, 166, 213–214, 220, 284
Emmel, Barbara, 258
Enoch, Jessica, 90
Eodice, Michele, 306
Erasmus, Desiderius, 251
Estrem, Heidi, 233
Evans, Donna J., 47
Ewald, Helen Rothschild, 136
Eyler, Janet, 56, 67, 69

Fagerheim, Britt, 239
Fahnestock, Jeanne, 251, 254
Faigley, Lester, 97–98, 104, 121, 195
Farrell, Pamela, 302
Farris, Christine, 169–170, 172–173, 296
Farrison, W. Edward, 235
Feez, Susan, 148
Fels, Dawn, 302
Ferrari, Joseph R., 72
Ferreira-Buckley, Linda, 2
Ferris, Dana R., 267, 275–276, 279
Fieldhouse, Maggie, 240
Fish, Stanley, 84
Fishman, Stephen M., 123–124
Fishman, T. A., 209
Fister, Barbara, 238
Fitts, Karen, 2, 10
Flanigan, Michael C., 213–214, 216, 219
Fleckenstein, Kristie S., 16, 197
Fleischer, Cathy, 152
Fleming, David, 12, 249, 254,
Flower, Linda, 5, 9–10, 42, 56, 58, 68,
    101, 220
Flynn, Elizabeth A., 130–131
Fontaine, Sheryl I., 39
Fontaine, Sheryl I., 39
Forbes, Cheryl, 40
Ford, James E., 231–232
Forman, Janis, 44
Foss, Sonja, 257
Foster, Helen, 236, 239
Foster, Nancy, 238
Foucault, Michel, 37, 87, 171
Fox, Janna, 158
Fox, Thomas, 21, 25, 40
Frank, David, 257
Fraser, Nancy, 101
Freadman, Anne, 148
Freedman, Aviva, 148–149, 154, 157
Freel, Penny, 28

Freire, Paulo, 20, 56, 58–59, 78, 80, 83, 85–87, 90, 124
Fritzsche, Barbara A., 311
Frydenberg, Mark, 66
Fu, Danling, 268
Fulkerson, Richard, 12, 117, 258
Fulwiler, Toby, 112, 166–167, 285

Gage, John T., 253
Gale, Irene, 90
Gannett, Cinthia, 118, 130
Ganobcsik-Williams, Lisa, 292–293
Garsten, Bryan, 251–252, 254, 259
Gavin, Christy, 239, 242
Gay, Pamela, 23
Gearhart, Sarah, 28
Gebhardt, Richard C., 219
Gee, James Paul, 2, 26, 99, 306
Geisler, Cheryl, 261
Geller, Anne Ellen, 304, 306
George, Ann, 1, 13, 157
George, Diana, 16, 26, 78, 100–102, 104–105, 271
Gere, Anne Ruggles, 38, 100–101, 133
Gerstle, Val, 41
Gervin, Cari Wade, 222
Gibbons, Susan, 238
Gil-Gomez, Ellen M., 135
Giles, Dwight E., Jr., 56, 67, 69
Gillespie, Paula, 304–305, 307
Gilroy, Paul, 96, 102
Gilyard, Keith, 26
Giroux, Henry A., 58, 78–80, 82, 84
Gitelman, Lisa, 178–179
Gladstein, Jill, 296
Glau, Greg, 28, 30
Gleason, Barbara, 28
Glenn, Cheryl, 136
Goeglein, Tamara, 173
Goen-Salter, Sugie, 30
Gold, David, 215
Gold, Matthew K., 179
Goldberger, Nancy, 118
Goldblatt, Eli, 9, 13, 56, 58, 61–62, 64, 68, 101
Golder, Caroline, 263
Gonçalves, Zan Meyer, 138
Goodburn, Amy, 89
Gore, Jennifer, 87–88, 135
Gorzelsky, Gwen, 90
Gottschalk, Katherine, 296

Gouge, Catherine, 195–197, 202
Grabill, Jeffrey T., 56, 68–69, 184, 200
Gradin, Sherrie L., 118, 123
Graff, Gerald, 164, 167–169, 171–172
Graham, Joan, 296
Grant-Davie, Keith, 207
Graves, Heather Brodie, 130
Gray, Charlene J., 69
Greco, Norma, 58
Green, Bill, 154
Green, Erik, 71
Greenbaum, Andrea, 134
Greenberg, Karen, 27–28
Greenblatt, Stephen, 170
Greene, Nicole Pipenster, 21
Greene, Ronald Walter, 251
Greene, Stuart, 219
Greenfield, Laura, 305
Grego, Rhonda, 27–28
Griffin, Cindy L., 257
Griffin, June, 198, 203
Griffin, Susan, 32
Grimm, Nancy Maloney, 305
Griswold, Gary, 311
Grobman, Laurie, 308
Gruber, Sibylle, 132
Gulati, Girish, 66
Gurak, Laura J., 43–45

Ha, Phan Le, 274
Habermas, Jürgen, 101
Hagen, Stacy A., 276
Hairston, Maxine, 26, 84, 215
Hall, Emily B., 308
Hall, John, 307
Hall, Jonathan, 292
Hall, Stuart, 95–96, 102
Halloran, S. Michael, 195
Hammill, Matthew J., 13, 29–30, 150
Handa, Carolyn, 178, 195
Hansen, Craig, 44
Hansen, Mogens Herman, 250
Haraway, Donna, 98
Hardaway, Francine, 219
Haring-Smith, Tori, 308
Harkin, Patricia, 172
Harl, Allison, 23, 25
Harris, Jeanette, 115
Harris, Joseph, 104, 165, 168–169, 171
Harris, Muriel, 217, 224, 304
Haviland, Carol Peterson, 308

Hawisher, Gail E., 99–100, 195, 201–202
Hawk, Byron, 119, 151
Hawkins, Thom, 219
Hayes, John R., 5, 10, 220
Haynes, Janell, 65
Hea, Amy Kimme, 191
Head, Alison, 232, 236, 239
Heard, Matthew, 225
Heath, Shirley Brice, 72
Hebdige, Dick, 96, 99
Heineman, David S., 45
Heinrichs, Jay, 252
Hellebrandt, Josef, 67
Hensley, Randall, 237
Herrington, Anne, 120, 287
Herzberg, Bruce, 56, 58, 60, 66
Hesford, Wendy S., 103, 135
Hess, John, 287
Hessler, H. Brooke, 9
Hewett, Beth L., 14, 195–200, 202–203, 206–208, 309
Hicks, Darren, 251
Hicks, Troy, 46, 201
Higgins, Lorraine, 56, 68
Hill, Carolyn Erikson, 118
Hillocks, George, Jr., 220, 260
Hilst, Joshua, 120
Himley, Margaret, 60, 62
Hindman, Jane, 120–121
Hinds, John, 269
Hinshaw, Wendy Wolters, 136
Hjortshoj, Keith, 296
Hoang, Haivon, 65–66
Hobson, Eric. H., 309
Hocks, Mary E., 191
Hoggart, Richard, 95, 98, 100
Holland, Barbara, 67
Holliday, Wendy, 239
Hollis, Karyn L., 131
Honnet, Ellen Porter, 59
Hood, Carra Leah, 232, 236
Hook, Sheril, 308
hooks, bell, 56, 78–80, 112, 119, 124–125, 134
Hoover, Ryan, 180
Horner, Bruce, 25, 30, 87–88, 103, 139
Horner, Winifred, 164
Horning, Alice S., 22–23, 25, 219
Horton, Marjorie, 40
Howard, Jeffrey P. F., 74

Howard, Rebecca Moore, 14, 39, 45, 197, 233–234, 238, 240, 241, 243, 274, 294
Howe, Florence, 130
Hoy, Cheryl, 202
Hughes, Brad, 305, 308, 311
Hughes, Linda K., 40
Hull, Glynda A., 22–23
Hunter, Susan M., 39
Huntington, Paul, 240
Hunzer, Kathleen, 52
Huot, Brian, 29, 187
Hurlbert, Mark M., 86, 89
Hutchings, Pat, 295
Hyland, Ken, 150, 157
Hyon, Sunny, 147, 158

Iglesia, Patricia, 293
Inman, James, 309
International WAC/WID Mapping Project, 296
Irigaray, Luce, 131
Isocrates, 12, 83, 194, 250–251, 254

Jablonski, Jeffrey, 268, 291
Jackson, Bryan, 260
Jackson, Phoebe, 47
Jackson, Shirley, 170
Jacobi, Tobi, 60, 65, 101
Jacobs, Dale, 239
Jacobs, Heidi L. M., 239
Jacobson, Trudi E., 239
Jameson, Sara, 239
Jamieson, Sandra, 14, 234, 294
Janangelo, Joseph, 42
Jarratt, Susan C., 102, 129, 134, 295
jayarr, 181
Jefferson, Tony, 96
Jenkins, Henry, 99–100
Jenkins, Susan, 269
Jin, Li, 203
Johanek, Cindy, 311
Johns, Ann M., 146, 149, 153, 291
Johnson-Eilola, Johndan, 44
Johnson, Cheryl L., 134
Johnson, Richard, 94–96
Johnson, Susan, 286
Jolliffe, David A., 23, 25
Jones, Carys, 294
Jones, Casey, 310
Jones, Leigh A., 242

Jordan, Jay, 291
Julier, Laura, 9, 13, 62, 66
Jung, Julie, 120, 132, 139

Kachru, Braj B., 103
Kail, Harvey, 305
Kalantzis, Mary, 149
Kameen, Paul, 4, 119
Kantz, Margaret, 240
Kastely, James, 260
Katkin, Wendy, 284
Katz, Steven, 287
Kaufer, David, 261
Keith, Philip M., 221, 223
Kells, Michelle Hall, 73
Kemp, Fred, 43
Kendrick, J. Richard, 67
Kennedy, Krista, 14, 45, 197, 238, 240
Kennedy, Mary Lynch, 237
Kent, Richard, 302
Kent, Thomas, 170, 223, 225
Kephart III, John M., 45
Kerschbaum, Stephanie L., 202
Kesselman, Martin A., 238
Kimball, Sara, 309
Kinneavy, James, 112, 115–116, 221
Kittle, Peter, 46
Kitzhaber, Albert, 303
Kleinfeld, Elizabeth, 237
Kluge, Alexander, 101
Knoblauch, A. Abby, 260
Knoblauch, C. H., 87
Knoch, Ute, 276
Knoeller, Christian, 214
Kobayashi, Hiroe, 273
Koch, Robert T., 301
Kolb, David A., 7
Kolowich, Steve, 237
Kopelson, Karen, 89
Kozol, Jonathan, 79
Kozol, Wendy, 103
Krashen, Stephen D., 275
Kress, Gunther, 99
Kroll, Barry M., 217, 260–261
Krug, Steve, 49
Kubota, Ryuko, 270
Kuhn, Deanna, 232, 259

Lackey, Dundee, 45
Ladson-Billings, Gloria, 89
LaDuc, Linda M., 135

Lai, Alice, 61
Lalicker, William, 28
Lamb, Catherine E., 131, 257
Lamos, Steve, 12, 21
Lanham, Richard, 178, 255
Laquintano, Tim, 100
Larsen-Freeman, Diane, 276
Larson, Richard L., 217–218, 235, 255
Lathan, Rhea Estelle, 73
Lather, Patti, 80, 87–88, 90
Lauer, Claire, 178
Lauer, Janice M., 218, 255
Lausberg, Heinrich, 255
Lave, Jean, 306
Lavelle, Thomas, 292
Lea, Mary, 294
Leckie, Gloria J., 235
LeCourt, Donna, 1, 133, 135
Lee, Alison, 161
Lee, Amy, 81–84, 86
Lee, Carmen K. M., 191
LeFevre, Karen Burke, 38
Lehner, Al, 270
Leki, Ilona, 268, 270–271, 279, 291
Lerner, Neal, 8, 15, 199, 273, 302–304,
    306–307, 309–312
Lessig, Lawrence, 45, 100
Lettner-Rust, Heather, 195
Leuf, Bo, 48
Leverenz, Carrie Shively, 232
Lewiecki-Wilson, Cynthia, 28,
    138, 140
Light, Richard J., 261
Lightbown, Patsy M., 274
Likkel, Lauren, 290
Lindemann, Erika, 165–166, 168, 170,
    216, 248
Lindquist, Julie, 137
Linton, Patricia, 286
Lisle, Bonnie, 104
Liu, Dilin, 274
Livingston, Kathleen, 9, 13
Lloyd-Jones, Richard, 219
Lockridge, Tim, 16, 26, 78, 271
Logan, Shirley Wilson, 101, 133–134
Logie, John, 45
Long, Elenore, 68
Longo, Bernadette, 94
Looser, Devoney, 130
Losh, Elizabeth, 100, 173
Lowe, Charles, 191

Lu, Min-Zhan, 23, 25–26, 30, 88, 102–103, 131
Lugones, Maria, 134
Luke, Allan, 148, 156
Luke, Carmen, 135
Lund, Michael, 40
Lundin, Rebecca Wilson, 197, 201
Lunsford, Andrea A., 22, 38–40, 42, 102, 133, 218, 305
Lutkewitte, Claire, 16
Lynch, Paul, 83
Lynn, Marvin, 89
Lynn, Robert, 203
Lyons, Mark, 73

Maasik, Sonia, 104
Macauley, William J., Jr, 301
Macedo, Donaldo, 79
Mack, Katherine, 295
Macken-Horarik, Mary, 147–148
Mackey, Thomas P., 239
Macrorie, Ken, 56, 113–114, 217, 221, 223
Madigan, Robert, 286
Mahoney, Kevin, 101
Malinowitz, Harriet, 138
Manning, Ambrose N., 232
Manovich, Lev, 191
Mao, LuMing, 103
Maranto, Gina, 201
Marks, Elaine, 131
Marr, Vanessa, 64
Marsh, Bill, 234
Marshall, James, 217
Martin, J.R., 147–148, 154
Martin, Nancy, 126, 227
Martinez, Aja Y., 30, 139
Massey, Lance, 219
Mathieu, Paula, 56, 64, 68, 94, 100–102
Matsuda, Aya, 277
Matsuda, Paul Kei, 13, 29–30, 103, 150, 224–225, 267–270, 272, 276–278
Matsuhashi, Ann, 220
Mauriello, Nicholas, 301
McAlexander, Patricia J., 21
McAndrew, Donald A., 307
McCarthy, Lucille P., 123–124
McClintock, Anne, 102
McCormick, Kathleen, 234
McCracken, Nancy Mellin, 130
McCurrie, Matthew Killian, 30

McDonald, Catherine, 158
McGrath, Laura, 208
McGuiness, Ilona M., 74
McIntosh, Peggy, 63
McKinney, Jackie Grutsch, 309
McLaren, Peter, 58, 77, 79, 82
McLeod, Alex, 126, 227, 298–299
McLeod, Susan H., 15, 116, 221, 270
McLuhan, Marshall, 10
McNenny, Gerri, 27
McRobbie, Angela, 96
Medway, Peter, 148–149, 154
Mellon, Constance A., 238
Meloncon, Lisa, 203
Menendez, Diane S., 219
Mercier, Hugo, 259, 261
Merriam, Sharan B., 31
Merton, Thomas, 112
Meyer, Sheree L., 132
Micciche, Laura R., 78, 114, 132, 137
Michel, Anthony, 45
Middleton, Joyce Irene, 134
Miller-Cochran, Susan, 202–203
Miller, Carolyn R., 4, 6, 146, 156, 285
Miller, Richard E., 120–121
Miller, Robert, 28
Miller, Susan, 131, 185
Minter, Debbie, 198–203
Miraglia, Eric, 300
Mitchell, Tania D., 64
Moddelmog, Debra A., 137
Moffett, James, 221
Monberg, Terese Guinsatao, 55, 62–63
Moneyhun, Clyde, 168, 173
Monroe, Barbara, 191
Moran, Charles, 177, 183, 188
Moraski, Brittney, 190
Morgan, Meg, 40
Morris, Richard, 192, 211
Morrison, Julie Bauer, 310
Mortensen, Peter, 101
Morton, Keith, 74
Murphy, Christina, 304
Murphy, James J., 225
Murray, Elizabeth, 187
Murray, Donald, 113–115, 117, 165, 216–217, 221, 223
Mutnick, Deborah, 12, 21, 28
Myers, Nancy, 3
Myers, Sharon A., 307

Nadeau, Jean-Paul, 310
Nakamura, Lisa, 99
National Council of Teachers of
    English, 172, 207
National Writing Project, 116, 118,
    187, 221
Navarro, Nela, 292
NeCamp,Samantha, 139
Negt, Oskar, 101
Nelms, Gerald, 215, 225
Nelson, Mark Evan, 191
Neuwirth, Christine, 261
Newkirk, Thomas, 217, 304
Newman, Susan E., 306
Newmann, Stephen, 315
Nicholas, David, 247
Nissenbaum, Helen, 45
Norgaard, Rolf, 238, 242–243
North, Stephen M., 87, 218–219,
    303–304, 311
Nowacek, Rebecca S., 159
Nystrand, Martin, 219

O'Gorman, Marcel, 192
O'Keefe, Daniel J., 249
O'Sullivan, Brian, 38
Ober, Josiah, 250
Odell, Lee, 218
Olbrechts-Tyteca, Lucie, 257
Olson, Gary A., 90
Ong, Walter J., 194, 255
Ortega, Lourdes, 269, 274
Ortmeier-Hooper, Christina M., 268, 291
Oswal, Sushil K., 203

Palmeri, Jason, 16, 179
Palmquist, Michael E., 206
Paltridge, Brian, 150
Parker, Laurence, 89
Parks, Stephen (Steve), 74, 102
Patchan, Melissa M., 38
Payne, Michelle, 136
Pearson, Melissa, 190
Pechenik, Jan, 287
Peck, Wayne C., 56, 68
Peeples, Jennifer, 260
Pegram, David M., 241
Pemberton, Michael, 310–311
Pennycook, Alastair, 103
Penrod, Diane, 191
Penrose, Ann, 287

Perelman, Chaïm, 257
Perl, Sondra, 22, 166, 220, 224
Perry, Alan E., 241
Peters, Brad, 155
Peterson, Linda H., 131
Peterson, Patricia Webb, 195
Petit, Angela, 305
Petrosky, Anthony, 23–24, 167–169
Pew Research Center, 192, 209
Pfister, Damien Smith, 259–260
Phillipson, Mark, 50
Phillipson, Robert, 103
Piéraut-Le Bonniec, 259
Pigott, Margaret B., 130
Pike, Kenneth L., 223, 255–256
Plato, 119, 124, 194
Platt, Michael D., 217
Pollard, Nick, 74
Pompa, Lori, 70
Pope, Adam R., 203
Porter, James E., 44
Porter, Tara, 294
Portillo, Manuel, 73
Porush, David, 287
Postman, Neil, 99, 111
Pough, Gwendolyn D., 65, 102, 134
Poulsen, Susan J., 59
Powell, Rebecca, 120
Poynter, Kerry John, 63
Pratt, Mary Louise, 25, 305
Prendergast, Catherine, 98
Prensky, Marc, 196, 202
Progoff, Ira, 217
Purves, Alan, 219

Qualley, Donna J., 134

Racism School, 63
Rafferty, Steven F., 45
Rafoth, Bennett A., 37
Raimes, Ann, 273, 275
Ramage, John, 256, 258–259
Ramanathan, Vai, 127
Rampton, Ben, 103
Ratcliffe, Krista, 136–137
Rawson, K.J., 142, 144
Readings, Bill, 172
Reagan, Sally Barr, 52–54
Rees, S., 232
Regaignon, Dara, 296
Reichert, Pegeen, 131

Reiff, Mary Jo, 147, 150, 152–156, 158–159
Reigstad, Thomas J., 307
Reinheimer, David A., 197–198
Ren, Jingfang, 202
Resch, Paula, 258
Restaino, Jessica, 56, 64
Reynolds, Julie, 284
Reynolds, Nedra, 27, 98, 132
Rhoads, Robert A., 56
Rhodes, Jacqueline, 65, 132
Rice, Jeff, 192
Richardson, Elaine B., 101
Ridolfo, Jim, 45, 50
Riedner, Rachel, 101
Rife, Martine Courant, 99
Rigolino, Rachel, 28
Riker, Linda, 199
Rinnert, Carol, 273
Ritchie, Joy, 130
Ritter, Kelly, 20, 84
Robby, Matthew A., 75
Roberts, Anne, 28
Roberts, Brian, 96
Robinson, William S., 23
Robison, Lori, 170
Roche-Smith, Jeeva, 191
Rodrigo, Rochelle L., 185, 202–203
Rodrigue, Tanya K., 233
Rogers, Carl R., 256
Rogers, Priscilla S., 54
Rohman, D. Gordon, 217
Roig, Miguel, 241
Romberger, Julia E., 199
Ronald, Katharine, 82, 136
Roozen, Kevin, 29
Rose, David, 147–148, 154
Rose, Mike, 23, 33, 218, 302
Rose, Shirley K., 101
Rosen, Harold, 126, 227, 298
Rosen, Leonard J., 241
Rosinski, Paula, 185
Roskelly, Hephzibah, 82, 136
Rosteck, Thomas, 94
Roswell, Barbara, 56
Rousculp, Tiffany, 69, 102
Rouse, John, 23
Rowan, Karen, 305
Rowlands, Ian, 240
Royster, Jacqueline Jones, 30, 101, 133
Rubin, Donald L., 37
Rubin, Donnalee, 131

Russell, David R., 232, 283, 288
Rutz, Carol, 221
Ryan, Leigh, 304
Ryder, Phyllis M., 101

Said, Edward W., 109
Salvatori, Mariolina, 21
Salvo, Michael J., 185, 202
Samuels, Robert, 192
Sandy, Marie, 67
Sapp, David Alan, 197, 200–202
Sartor, Alexandra, 295
Scardamalia, Marlene, 259
Scenters-Zapico, John, 100
Schafer, John C., 217
Scheinfeldt, Tom, 179
Schell, Eileen E., 131
Schiappa, Edward, 250
Schick, Kurt, 243
Schilb, John, 97–98, 164
Schmida, Mary, 271
Schmidt, Adeny, 75
Schmidt, Richard, 275
Schmidt, Sarah, 233
Schoer, Lowell, 227
Scholes, Robert, 165, 168–169, 171
Schunn, Christian D., 38
Schuster, Charles, 105
Schwegler, Robert A., 234–235, 294
Scott, Fred Newton, 303
Scott, J. Blake, 94
Scott, Tony, 86
Secor, Marie, 251, 254
Seitz, David, 81, 85
Seitz, James, 164
Selber, Stuart, 183
Selfe, Cynthia L., 16, 40, 99–100, 178, 183,
　　195, 201–202, 207
Selinker, Larry, 275
Serviss, Tricia C., 233
Severino, Carol, 307
Sewell, Donna N., 191
Shadle, Mark, 232, 234, 237, 243
Shamoon, Linda K., 234–235, 294, 306
Shaughnessy, Mina, 22, 217
Shenton, David, 273
Sheridan, David, 45, 47, 309
Sherwood, Steve, 304
Shi, Ling, 241
Shima, Alan, 292
Shipka, Jody, 179

Shirley, Sue, 241
Shor, Ira, 27, 77–84, 86–87, 90
Sidler, Michelle, 192
Silva, Mary Lourdes, 201
Silva, Tony, 269, 272, 279
Silver, David, 186
Simon, James, 197, 200–202
Simon, Roger, 79
Sinha, Aparna, 292
Sirc, Geoffrey, 193
Skinnell, Ryan, 267
Sloan, Jay, 305
Sloane, Thomas O., 251
Smagorinsky, Peter, 220
Smith, Cheryl C., 31
Smith, Elizabeth Overman, 192, 211
Smith, Jane Bowman, 121–122
Smith, Jeff, 85–86
Smith, Raymond, 296
Smith, Summer, 156
Smitherman, Geneva, 21
Smudde, Peter M., 91
Snart, Jason Allen, 197, 201
Soliday, Mary, 28, 149
Solmsen, Friedrich, 250, 252
Solomon, Jack, 104
Sommers, Nancy, 22, 220, 224
Sorapure, Madeleine, 186
Soven, Margot, 299–300, 314
Spada, Nina, 274
Spear, Karen, 38
Sperber, Dan, 259, 261, 264
Sperling, Melanie, 218
Spigelman, Candace, 38, 121, 131, 308
Spivak, Gayatri C., 102
Stahl, Norman A., 28
Stanley, Jane, 20, 270
Stanton, Timothy K., 56
Stenson, Christine M., 69
Stine, Linda, 31
Storch, Neomy, 276
Stovall, David O., 89
Street, Brian, 26, 294
Stroupe, Craig, 192
Stygall, Gail, 133
Suarez, John, 67
Sullivan, Andrew, 260
Sullivan, Laura L., 133
Sullivan, Patricia A., 144
Sunstein, Bonnie Stone, 104
Surman, Karen Paley, 120

Sutton, Brian, 149
Swain, Merrill, 276
Swales, John M., 149, 151, 154, 156
Swan, Michael, 276
Swiss, Thom, 46

Taggart, Amy Rupiper, 10, 19, 52, 73, 143,
   191, 230, 280
Takaku, Seiji, 310–311
Takayoshi, Pamela, 16, 135, 178
Tannen, Deborah, 259
Tapscott, Don, 49
Tardy, Christine M., 158
Tarule, Jill Mattuck, 118
Tassoni, John Paul, 28
Tate, Gary, 1, 10, 165–166
Taylor, Todd W., 192
Taylor, Warner, 302
Tenney, Deborah, 258
Thaiss, Christopher, 15, 116, 270, 284,
   286–287, 292–294, 308
Thompson, E.P., 95, 98
Thompson, Isabelle, 311
Thompson, Nancy, 27–28
Thompson, Robert, 284
Thonus, Therese, 199, 305, 307
Thornbury, Scott, 276
Tingle, Nick, 120
Tinto, Vincent, 311
Tobin, Lad, 124, 214, 217
Tompkins, Jane, 132
Torres, Rodolfo D., 88
Toulmin, Stephen, 12, 257–259, 261
Townsend, Martha, 296
Trainor, Jennifer Seibel, 89
Trifonas, Peter Pericles, 89
Trimbur, John, 16, 26, 30, 42, 78, 97–98,
   100, 103–104, 224–225, 271, 305
Truscott, John, 275–276
Tubbs, Nancy Jean, 63
Tuell, Cynthia, 131
Turkle, Sherry, 98
Turner, Joan, 294
Turnley, Melinda, 192
Tuzi, Frank, 203

Ulmer, Gregory L., 165, 168–169, 187

Vaidhyanathan, Siva, 100
Valentine, Barbara, 235, 238
Valette, M., 259

Van Leeuwen, Theo, 99
Vernon, Andrea, 75
Vie, Stephanie, 201
Villanueva, Victor, Jr., 40, 85, 102, 291
Vygotsky, Lev S., 306

Waggoner, Zachary, 256
Walker, Jeffrey, 250, 254
Wallace, David L., 136
Wallin, Jon, 260
Walsh, Lynda, 41
Walter, Elizabeth, 273
Walvoord, Barbara Fassler, 283–284
Ward, D.L., 232
Ward, Irene, 192
Ward, Kelly, 75
Wardle, Elizabeth, 15, 29, 158, 225
Warner, Michael, 101
Warnick, Barbara, 53
Warnock, Scott, 197, 200, 202, 207
Warnock, Tilly, 124–125
Waterman, Alan S., 56, 62
Watson, Sam, 122
Watson, Shevaun E., 295
Watstein, Barbara, 238
Watters, Ann, 56
Webb, Suzanne, 45
Weingartner, Charles, 111
Weiser, Irwin, 74, 101
Weissman, Jordan, 20
Welch, Nancy, 102
Wellbery, David E., 255
Wells, Jennifer, 302
Wells, Susan, 100, 261
Wenger, Etienne, 306
West, William W., 219
White, Edward M., 29
Whithaus, Carl, 193
Whithaus, Carl, 193
Wichman, Nanette, 23
Wiederhold, Eve, 172
Wiemelt, Jeffery, 219
Williams, Anthony D., 49
Williams, Ashley, 296

Williams, Bronwyn, 99, 122, 310–311
Williams, Howard Alan, 276
Williams, James D., 316
Williams, Nicole, 187
Williams, Peter, 240
Williams, Raymond, 95
Williams, Terra, 191
Willis, Paul, 96
Wills, Katherine V., 94
Wilson, James C., 145
Winans, Amy E., 136–138
Winterowd, Ross W., 218
Wolf, Maryanne, 202
Wolfe, Eric A., 170
Wolfe, Joanna, 39
Women's Study Group, Centre for
        Contemporary Cultural Studies, 110
Woodford, Kate, 273
Worrall, Laurie, 67
Worsham, Lynn, 136
Writing in Digital Environments (WIDE)
        Research Center Collective, 188
Wu, Tim, 100
Wurr, Adrian, 56, 67
Wyatt, Christopher Scott, 41
Wysocki, Anne Frances, 193

Yancey, Kathleen Blake, 29, 121–122, 124,
        218, 243
Yi-ping Hsu, Angela, 275
Young, Art, 166–167
Young, Beth Rapp, 311
Young, Morris, 103
Young, Richard E., 215, 218, 223, 255–256
Young, Robert, 102
Young, Vershawn Ashanti, 30, 139
Youngkin, Betty Rodgers, 58

Zappen, James P., 43
Zawacki, Terry Myers, 130, 132, 286,
        291–292, 296, 308
Zdenek, Sean, 185
Zhu, Wei, 203, 270
Zimmerelli, Lisa, 304

Subject Index

Abject identity, 137
Ableism, 63, 137
Academic discourse/Academic writing
  and awareness of injustice, 83
  and basic writers, 21–24, 29
  challenges to, 169–70
  and citation, 274
  and Current-Traditionalism, 113
  and expressivism/personal writing,
    120–21, 125, and feminism, 131–33
  and L2 writers, 268, 270
  and online writing, 182
  and process, 217
  and students of color, 118
  and WAC/WID, 284, 287
  and Writing about Writing (WaW), 225
Accelerated Learning Program (ALP),
  28, 30
Access/Accessibility (see also Universal
  Design)
  community partner access to higher
    education resources, 67
  technological, 7, 31, 44, 49, 177, 183–85,
    188, 195, 199, 203, 205–07, 297
  for disability, 41–42, 139–40, 205
  to higher education, 20–21, 27, 32, 303
  for learning differences, 139–140, 203
Activism
  digital, 16
  and expressivism, 112, 114–15
  and feminist pedagogy, 128–29, 133
  and media consumption, 99
  and service learning, 60–61, 65–66

and socio-political pedagogies, 13, 86
and students, 80
and technology, 100
Advanced writing/Upper-division writing,
  8, 15, 152, 173, 242, 294
Advertising/Advertisement, 5, 58, 99,
  156, 171
Affect (see Emotion), 136–37
After-class group, 81
Agonism, 132, 251
Alliance of Digital Humanities
  Organizations, 188
American Dream, 79, 85
American Association for Higher
  Education, 221
American Educational Research
  Association, 221
American Indian nations, 63
Analysis (see also Rhetorical analysis)
  and academic initiation, 24, 167
  and basic writers, 21
  and community-engaged courses, 60
  critical, 58, 88, 129
  and cultural studies, 98, 103
  dialectical, 194
  of discourse and text, 3, 135, 149, 163,
    168, 171, 173
  error, 22
  and genre critique, 154–56
  models for, 8, 149, 153
  papers, as antecedent genres, 150
  and reading, 240
  self-, 137

Analysis (*Continued*)
   students, of their own writing, 23
   and studio models, 28
   and WAC/WID, 285, 287, 294
Annotated bibliography, 180, 243
Antigenres, 155, 160
Appeals (*see* Rhetorical appeals)
Argument/Argumentation, 12, 21–22, 24,
      167, 218, 232–34, 240–41, 248–65
   to create identification across
      difference, 125
   essay, 130–131
   feminist rejections of, 134
   and the personal, 121, 130
   and mediation/negotiation, 131
   as mode, 213, 216
   Rogerian, 42
ARPANET (Advanced Research Projects
      Agency Network), 43
Assessment, evaluation of writing, 20, 217,
      220, 290
   and basic writing, 29–30
   and community-engaged writing, 66–70
   and critical pedagogy, 81–82
   and expressive pedagogy, 113
   diagnostic, 158
   and digital tools, 47, 49
   formative/classroom assessment
      techniques (CATs) (*see also*
      Feedback) 187, 217, 285
   and genres, 156, 157–59
   and L2s (second language learners),
      270, 277–78
   multimodal, 187
   portfolio, 8, 218, 243
   self-, 121–22, 291
   standardized, 218
   and teaching with technology, 186–87
   timed-writing as
   and writing centers, 310–11
Association of Internet Researchers, 188
Asynchronous learning/courses, 199–02,
      04–06
Audience, 21, 23–24, 46, 50, 57, 59, 114,
      120, 122, 148, 155, 170, 179, 181,
      188, 196, 206, 217, 219–20, 235, 241,
      243, 253–57, 259, 261, 269, 306
   in Classical Greece and Rome, 250–52
   and L2 writers, 272, 278
   students as, 201–05
   and WAC/WID, 285–86

Audio response, 140
Authority, 13, 113, 254–57, 305
   students', 59, 82
   teachers', 81, 83–85, 134, 198, 212
Authorship, 37–39, 44, 49, 82, 85, 99, 133,
Autism, 41

Back to basics, 79
Banking model of education, 78
Basic writing pedagogy (*see Pedagogy,
      Basic writing*)
Bitch pedagogy, 134
Borderlands, 102, 104
Blogs, 44, 47–8, 51, 63, 65–6, 148, 197, 201,
      261, 277

CCCC (*see* Conference on College
      Composition and Communication)
Calibrated Peer Review, 290
Canons of rhetoric, 165, 218
Capitalism, capitalist culture, 79, 86–87, 90,
      96, 103, 135
Centre for Contemporary Cultural Studies,
      The (CCCS), 95, 97
Citation Project, The, 231–39, 242
Citizen Scholars Program, 64
Citizenship, education for, 78
Civic discourse, 84
Class (*see* Social class)
Class discussion (*see* Discussions)
Cognitive psychology, cognitivists, 5, 16,
      22–25, 165, 220, 224, 284
Collaboration, 8, 10, 14, 37–54, 99–100,
      113, 133–34, 39, 140, 149–50, 166,
      169, 197, 206, 274, 276, 290,
   dialogic and hierarchical, 40, 238
Collaborative
   learning, 37, 43, 50, 284
   pedagogy, (*see* Pedagogy, Collaborative)
Commons-based peer production
      (CBPP), 45
Communicative competence, 269
Community college, 21, 28, 30, 32,
      79, 307
Community engagement,
   community-engaged pedagogy
      (*see* Pedagogy, Community
      engagement; *see also* Service-
      learning)
Community Literacy Center, 58, 75
Complexity thesis, 168

Composing-aloud protocols, 220
CompPile, 312
Computer classroom, 41, 82, 184, 188, 205
Computers and Writing Conference, 189
Conferences with students, 21, 131, 140,
    159, 202, 206, 270, 304
    peer group, 219
Conference on College Composition and
    Communication (CCCC), 16,
    221, 279
CCCC Committee for Best Practices in
    Online Writing Instruction, 14, 209
Consensus, 42
Consortium for the Study of Writing in
    College, 5
Content management system (see also
    Course management system), 12,
    44, 48
Context (writing/rhetorical), 99, 114,
    119–20, 131, 149–59, 164, 170, 187,
    274, 277, 306
Contingent writing teachers, 131
Conventions, 23–24, 32, 113, 121, 146, 149,
    151, 172, 217, 243, 268, 270, 287–88,
    295, 302
Correctness, 29, 165, 215, 291, 302
Counterevidence, 42, 240
Counterpublic, 102
Course management system, 12, 43–44, 46,
    178, 289
Craft of writing and rhetoric, 26, 84, 149,
    166, 168
Creative Commons, 48
Creative writing, 146, 151, 157, 212–13,
    286, 290
Creativity, 24, 123, 138, 150, 165, 217, 305
Critical
    consciousness (conscientização), 20, 60,
        78, 83, 86, 88, 124, 150
    essay, 169, 171
    pedagogy, (see Pedagogy, Critical)
    Race Theory (CRT), 88
    reading, 58, 239–40, 242
    thinking, 17, 23–4, 26, 59, 118, 124,
        138, 140, 194, 239, 242–43
Cultural critique, 25, 77, 79, 89, 104, 128
Cultural studies, 13, 77, 79, 94–110, 118,
    170, 271
Current-traditionalism, 2, 9, 100, 113–14,
    120, 165, 215
Cyberliteracy, 84

Database, 12, 48, 179, 233, 236, 287
    created texts, 45
Dayton Literacy Project, 58
Democracy, 32, 79, 82, 84, 86, 250
Description (see also Modes), 165
Developmental writers (see also Basic
    writing pedagogy), 203, 205
Dialectic, 194. 257
Dialectical notebook, 132
Digital forums (see Discussion boards)
Digital humanities (DH), 179, 310
Digital Humanities Summer Institute, 189
Digital immigrants and natives, 196
Disability, 31, 41–2, 129, 137, 139–40
Discourse
    analysis, 3, 135, 149, 163, 168, 171, 173
    community, 32, 123, 138, 166, 274,
        286, 295
    expressive, 115–16
Discussion boards, 43, 47, 135, 277
Discussions, small- and large-group, 29,
    131, 218
Diversity, 11, 17, 21, 26, 29, 62, 65, 84, 123,
    249, 291–92
Document-sharing applications, 47
Doubting and believing game, 1, 38, 114
Drafting, 22, 46–7, 111, 115, 165, 215,
    223–24, 273

Editing, 8, 41, 45, 47, 48, 82, 157, 200, 217,
    223, 273, 304
Electracy, 187
Embodiment, 119, 136, 137, 139, 140
Emotion, 30, 129, 132, 135–37, 140, 167,
    250–53, 255
Empowering pedagogy, 77
Empowerment, 81, 87, 125
Engaged pedagogy, 56–57, 124–25
Engfish, 114, 217
English Studies, 125, 163, 166, 169, 170
Enthymeme, 253–54
Epistemology, 4, 98, 113, 115, 117, 292
Error (grammatical), 12, 21–26, 29, 31, 32,
    217, 268, 275–78, 292
    analysis, 22
Essay, the, 16, 24, 29, 46, 56, 104, 130–32,
    136, 156, 169, 170, 171, 179, 181–82,
    185–87, 195, 197, 201, 214–20, 222,
    231, 237, 243, 253, 260, 289
    five-paragraph, 14, 148, 212
    rhetorical, 253–54

Essentialism, 130
Ethic of care, 131
Ethnocentrism, 96
Ethnography, ethnographic research,
    microethnography
  about amateur and student writers, 29,
    81, 84–85, 90, 94, 98–100, 104, 120,
    158, 220, 293
  by students, 78, 104, 149, 153,
    294, 296
Ethos, 113, 119, 120, 188, 240, 252, 277
Evaluation (*see* Assessment)
Exegesis, 168
Experiential learning, 56, 59, 62, 82
Exposition, expository writing (*see also*
    Modes), 212, 223
Expression, expressive function of
    language, 31, 60, 68, 84, 104, 111,
    113, 115, 116, 138, 166, 217
Expressivism (*see also* Pedagogy,
    expressive), 13, 56, 111–27, 217
Extracurriculum, 100–01

Facebook (*see also* Social networking), 44,
    181, 187, 188
Faculty development (*see* Professional
    development)
Feedback (*see also* Peer review), 8, 14, 21,
    44, 49, 65, 114, 128, 197, 198, 206,
    256, 270, 276–77, 285–86, 290–91,
    296, 306–07
Feminism, 87–88, 96, 98, 103, 118, 120,
    128–45
  first-wave, 128–29
  second-wave, 128–29, 132
  third-wave, 129
  fourth-wave, 129
  sex-positive, 129
  transnational, 103
Feminist pedagogy (*see* Pedagogy, feminist)
FERPA (Family Educational Rights and
    Privacy Act), 46
Fieldwork, 104
First-generation college students, 150
First-year composition (FYC; *see* First-year
    writing)
First-year writing (FYW), 15, 55, 101,
    158–59, 166, 197, 201, 231, 284, 287,
    293, 295, 302, 309–10
*Framework for Success in Postsecondary
    Writing*, 226

Freewriting, 111, 113–15, 120, 219, 222
Freirean pedagogy, 78, 80, 86–89

Gadugi, 63
Gaming, 94, 99, 201, 203
Gatekeeping, 43, 85
Gender, 25, 40, 60, 78, 88, 96, 98, 118,
    128–40, 164, 172, 305
  bias, 131
  equity, 129–30
Generative themes, 78
Genre, 4, 29, 57, 60, 82, 120, 122, 146–60,
    166, 173, 197, 216, 254, 269, 284–85,
    295
  awareness, 133, 151–54, 274
  blurred, 155
  critique, 8, 154–57, 173
  digital, 132, 148, 181, 185, 197, 241–42
  hybrid/multigenre texts, 132, 155,
    167–69
  multimodal (*see* Multimodal)
  patterns, 4, 152–53, 171
  research paper as, 232–37
  studies, 146–47, 164
  theory, 4, 146, 170, 216
G.I. Bill, 20, 97
Globalization (*see also*
    Internationalization)
Grading (*see also* Assessment), 10, 82, 242,
    278, 284, 286, 295, 296, 297, 304
  and collaboration, 43
  contracts, 81
  criteria, 43, 82
  portfolio (*see* Portfolio assessment)
Grammar (*see also* Error), 29, 275
Group work (*see* Collaboration)

Harvard Study of Undergraduate
    Writing, 168
Heteroglossia, 82
Heterosexism, 135
Heuristics, 8, 9, 14, 121, 183, 218, 240
Hierarchy (*see* Labor)
History of composition and rhetoric, 2–3,
    16, 20, 98, 104, 119, 164, 172, 179,
    194, 214–224, 255, 293–94, 302–03
Homophobia, 135, 138
Humanism, 32, 37, 96, 166, 171
Humanities, Arts, Sciences, and
    Technology Advanced
    Collaboratory, 189

Humanities and Technology Camp,
   The (THAT Camp), 189
Hybrid
   courses and pedagogy, 31, 179, 189,
      194–208
   literacy, 22, 103
   texts 146, 151, 153, 155, 167
Hypertext, 48, 133, 151, 155–56,
   173, 177

Identity, 60, 84, 88, 114, 116, 122, 129, 137,
      154, 271, 305
   civic/cultural, 9, 59, 268
   disciplinary, 163, 166
   gender, 137–40
   online, 99
   personal/self, 119
   race and, 88
Ideology, 26, 60, 78, 80, 82, 84–86,
      96, 117, 129, 133, 136, 137, 154, 234
Information literacy, 232, 237–43
Inquiry, 42, 59, 64, 98–99, 104, 121, 136,
      166, 168, 170–71, 220, 232–42
Instant messaging (IM), 47, 200
Intellectual property, 99–100, 243
Internet, 43, 45, 84, 181–84, 195–96, 203
International Society for Technology in
      Education, 189
Internationalization (see also
      Globalization), 61, 102–04, 196,
      266–67, 272, 291–94
Internship, 62, 295
Interpretation, 24, 164–65, 167, 170, 173,
      203, 234, 271, 288
Interruption, 131–32
Interviews (as writing assignments), 58,
      104, 149, 153, 213, 294
Invention (see also Prewriting), 38, 114,
      119, 181, 218, 223, 224, 273
   and collaboration, 38–39
   as a canon of rhetoric, 119, 165, 218–19,
      251–52, 255–56, 306
Interlanguage, 22, 275
Intersectionality, 88
Intertextuality, 82, 167–68, 274

Journaling, 111, 115
Journals
   for formative assessment and reflection,
      66, 114, 128, 187, 289
   blogs as, 48, 261

professional and scholarly, 75, 94, 95,
      121, 125, 177, 179, 189, 261, 294

Kairos
   rhetorical term, 112, 181, 251
   scholarly journal, 177, 189

L2 writers (see Second language writers)
Labor (see also Working Class)
   of Composition instructors, 131,
      163, 188
   of Writing Program Administrators, 16
   writing as, 67, 109
LatCrit pedagogy, 88
Learning cycle, Kolb's, 7
Learning Management System (LMS; see
      Course Management System)
Lecture, as pedagogical practice, 169,
      201, 212–15, 218, 241, 284, 285, 289,
      297, 303
LGBTQ (Lesbian, Gay, Bisexual, Trans,
      Queer), see also Gender, Sexuality,
      55, 61–63, 65–66, 129, 137–138
Liberal arts, 163, 255
Liberatory pedagogy, 59, 77, 112
Liberatory rhetoric, 77, 113
Liberation, 78, 86–87, 121
Linguistics, 4, 103, 116, 147–49, 279
Listening
   gendered communication practice, 131
   pedagogical and rhetorical (see also
      Mutuality), 132, 136–37, 259
Literacy, 3, 20–21, 58, 154, 164, 165,
      194–95, 219–220, 225–26, 238,
      269, 306
   civic/community, 9, 58, 61, 62, 65, 68,
      100–02
   crisis, 165
   critical, 25–26, 58, 78–80
   media and technology, 31, 99–100,
      179, 182–83, 185, 207
   digital, 46–47
   information, 232, 237–43
   narratives, 100, 103–04, 146, 157, 295
   and second-language writers, 269–70,
      272–73
   sponsorship, 20, 68
   tutoring, 58
Literary criticism, 116, 173
Literary Studies, 95, 130, 163–64, 167–68
Literary theory, 37, 164, 218

Literature, 6, 95, 116, 131, 163–73, 216, 248, 287
Logic, 163, 250, 252, 257–58

Manifesto, 132
Marxism, 95–96
Massive Open Online Courses (MOOCs), 38, 206, 297
Meaning-making (*see also* Writing to Learn), 115, 124, 133, 178, 237
Mechanics (*see* Grammar)
Media (*for primarily digital media, see* New Media; *see also* Social media)
  consumption/mass media, 79–80, 100
  contrasted with modality, 201
  mass media coverage of writing instruction, 21–22, 89, 233
  studies, 100
  for teaching and writing, 65, 84, 104, 133
Mediation, 63, 78, 104, 131–32, 257
Memoir, 81
Mestiz@ rhetoric, 104
Metaphor, 168–69, 172
Metacognition, 15, 158, 182
Metis, 89
Minority opinions, 42
Mobile devices (*see* New media)
Modes (of writing), 131, 165, 173, 213, 215–16
Modeling, Models of writing, 8, 38, 42, 68, 104, 131–33, 149–51, 153, 164–66, 216, 289, 294
MOOs (MUD Object-Oriented), 43
MUDs (Multi-User Dungeons), 43
Multiculturalism, 25–27, 102
Multigenre texts,132, 168
Multilingual writers (*see also* Second language writers), 30–31, 103, 118, 203, 205, 241, 266–67, 272, 277–79, 291–92, 296
Multiliteracies, 103–04, 139, 178, 183
Multimedia (*see* New media or Multimodal composition)
Multimodal composition, multimodality, 16, 45, 94, 98, 179, 309–10
  assessment, 187
  differentiated from multimedia, 16, 99
  genres, 148
  pedagogy, 48–49, 122, 178–79, 187, 242

research, 99, 242
Mutuality (*see also* Listening, rhetorical), 60, 70, 136

Narration
  as a mode of writing, 165, 213, 216
National Council of Teachers of English (NCTE), 125, 145, 172, 207
National Institute for Technology in Liberal Education, 189
National Writing Project, 116, 118, 187, 189, 221
Native American pedagogy (*see* Red pedagogy)
National Survey of Student Engagement (NSSE), 5
Negotiation, 65, 131–32, 149, 257, 277
New City Writing, 58
New Left, 95–96
New London Group, 178
New media/Digital media (*see also* Social media)
  for teaching and writing, 14, 16, 38, 45, 50, 94, 105, 122, 132–33, 151, 177–89, 201, 236–37, 260, 297
  studies, 98–100
No Child Left Behind Act, 20, 91
Non-human and human interaction, 133
Nontraditional learners (*see* Students, nontraditional)

Online teaching and learning (OTL; *see* Online writing instruction)
Online writing instruction (OWI), 31, 40–50, 66, 99–100, 122, 132–33, 135, 177–93, 194–211, 242, 290, 294, 297, 309–10
Online writing lab (OWL), 199
Open admissions. 20, 22, 97, 283
Oppression, 27, 69, 78, 85, 88–89, 135
Outcomes Statement (WPA), 267

Partner, community, 57–69
Patchwriting, 223–4, 274
Pedagogy
  as critically reflective practice, 9
  as evaluation of existing practices (*see also* Assessment), 8
  as heuristic for new practices, 8
  as heuristic for writing theory, 9–10
  as personal, 6

as research-based, 5
as response to student needs, 7–8
as rhetorical, 5–6
as a social force, 10
as theory, 3–4
basic writing, 20–36, 132–33, 167,
    182, 203, 205, 217–18, 268–69,
    303, 308
collaborative, 37–54, 82, 113,
    132–34, 139, 149–50, 182, 197,
    206, 219, 236, 276–77,
    284–85, 290
critical, 59, 77–93, 113, 134
cultural studies, 77–78, 79, 94–110,
    170, 271
community engagement, 47, 55–76,
    100–01
current-traditional, 9, 100, 113–14,
    165, 215
defined, 2–3
digital, 179
expressive, 56, 104, 111–27, 129, 132,
    134, 197, 217, 224
feminist, 63, 78, 84, 87–88, 96, 98, 103,
    112, 114, 118, 120, 123–24, 128–45,
    217, 257–58
genre, 4, 8, 48, 57–58, 60, 122,
    132–33, 146–62, 164, 168, 170,
    173, 197, 216, 231–37, 241–42,
    259, 284–85
literature, 61, 163–76
new media, 45–46, 98–100, 122, 129,
    177–93, 201
of hope, love, and possibility, 77
online and hybrid, 31–32, 38, 43–50,
    122, 132, 135, 177, 194–211, 290,
    297, 309–10
process, 49, 115–17, 121, 130–31, 140,
    165–70, 181–83, 212–30, 231–32,
    238, 243, 260, 284–85, 288, 305–07
Red (Native American), 88
research, 65, 78, 86, 104, 149, 152,
    180–83, 231–47, 294
rhetoric/argument, 24, 42, 121, 130–32,
    134, 164, 167, 197–98, 218, 234, 241,
    248–65
second language, 26, 102, 158, 266–82
Writing Across the Curriculum (WAC),
    166–67, 238, 283–300, 308
writing center, 207, 218, 237, 273, 293,
    301–16

Peer response/peer review (see also
    Calibrated Peer Review;
    Collaboration), 14, 37–8,
    46–8, 114, 197, 214, 219–20,
    270, 290
Performativity, 138
Pentad, 218, 256
Personal
    experience, 24, 56, 60, 114–16, 119,
        129–30
    writing, 100, 121, 136, 258
Photo sharing, 44, 47, 48
Pictography, 104
Plagiarism, 99, 231, 233–35, 268, 274
    detection software, 178, 233
Poetics, poetic writing, 97, 116–17,
    169–70
Popular culture, 99, 122
Portfolio assessment (see also Assessment),
    29, 43–44, 218, 243, 295
Post-colonial studies, 102
Postmodernism, 44, 98, 113, 119, 131
Post-process theory, 170, 224–26
Post-structuralism, 37, 80, 87–88, 131
Praxis, 78, 124
Pre-writing (see Invention)
Prison writing, 101
Privacy, 45–47, 49
Problem-based teaching and learning,
    199, 256
Process
    movement, 165, 212–30, 258
    v. product, 82, 151, 166, 180, 183, 198,
        215–18, 242–43
    wheel, 224
Professing, 25–26, 112
Progressive pedagogy, Progressivism,
    77–79, 117, 123–24, 222, 284, 302
Public pedagogy, 79–80
Public rhetoric, public sphere, 56–59, 65,
    68, 82, 100–02, 138

Queer pedagogy, 137–39

Race, 21, 25, 40, 60, 80, 88, 96, 103, 119,
    128–30, 134, 164, 172, 305
Racialization, 88
Racism, 63, 84–85, 88, 96, 134
Radical pedagogy/education, 77–91,
    97–98, 123, 132
Reader-response theory, 131

Reading, 6, 23, 29–30, 50, 56, 58, 65, 82, 104,
    123, 131–32, 158, 163–73, 197–98,
    202–03, 237, 239–41, 287, 294
Reciprocity, 60–61
Red (Native American) pedagogy
    (*see* Pedagogy, Red)
Reflection (*see also* Self-assessment), 1, 7,
    9, 26, 28, 59, 60, 64, 66, 78, 80, 90,
    112–14, 120–22, 124–25, 134, 152–3,
    149, 182–83, 185–88, 221, 243, 261,
    286, 289, 290
Religion, 88, 129
Remediation
    of struggling writers, 21, 29–30, 303, 306
    as a digital literacy practice, 98, 151,
Remix, 45, 100
Research
    assignment, paper, project, 24, 48–49,
        57, 65–66, 113, 149, 152, 180,
        231–47, 294
    methods (*see* specific types:
        Composing-aloud protocols,
        Ethnography, Fieldwork, Interviews,
        Observation, Think aloud protocols,
        Usability testing)
Response, student (*see* Peer review)
Response, teacher (*see* Feedback)
Retention (*see* Student retention)
Revising, revision, rewriting, 38, 86,
    114–15, 132, 154, 169, 198, 206,
    214–15, 219–20, 224, 261, 286, 288,
    305–06
Rhetoric
    classical, 113, 119, 218, 250–54
    current-traditional, 113–14, 165, 215
    New, 218, 255–60
    Society of America, (RSA), 221, 261
Rhetorical
    analysis, 153, 240–41
    appeals, 152, 278
    flexibility, 157
    situation, 146, 252–54, 295
    velocity, 45
    uptake, 45, 154
Rhizomatic travel, 45
Rogerian argument, Rogerian rhetoric, 42,
    256–57
Romantic authorship, romanticism, 37,
    117–19, 255, 306
Rubrics, 8, 187, 242, 290, 297

Scaffolding, 9, 21, 236, 261
Second language (L2) writers, 267–71, 291
Self-assessment, 121–22, 153, 182–83,
    186–88, 261, 289
Semantic integrity, 197–99
Semiotics, 99
Service courses (*see* Labor)
Service-learning (*see* Community
    engagement)
Sexism, 63, 83, 134
Sexuality, 65, 137–39
Signifier/signified, 99
Social activism (*see* Activism)
Social class, classism, 20–22, 60, 63, 79, 88,
    95–96, 134, 137, 195
Social construction, 37, 123, 136, 139,
    197, 284
Social context (*see* Context)
Social epistemic rhetoric, 117, 288
Social media, 31, 44–46, 181, 187–88,
    274, 297
Social turn, 23, 58, 135, 165, 224, 291
Sophistic rhetoric, 134, 250
Stasis theory, 89, 222, 251
Street papers, 101
Student-centered pedagogy, student-
    centered instruction, 21, 56, 77,
    82–83, 131, 134, 183, 218, 221
Students
    international, 267–78, 291–93
    nontraditional, 60, 202
    retention of, 30, 67, 198, 200, 311
Subjectivity, 119, 131–33, 165
Synthesis, 24, 39, 180, 223

Tagmemics, 223
Taste (cultural), 98, 165
Teaching-learning cycle, 148–49
Technical writing, 44, 49
Testing, 20, 25, 218
Textbooks, 113–14, 165, 195, 222–23, 241,
    258, 260, 295
Textuality, 167–70
Texting, 47
Think-aloud protocols, 5, 9
Threaded discussion (*see*
    Discussion boards)
Topics, *topoi* (rhetorical), 218, 254–55
Toulmin model of argument, 258
Transactional writing, 116–17

Transgender (*see* LGBTQ)
Transfer, transferability of learning, 60,
    151, 153, 157–59, 173
Translanguaging, 29, 30–31
Transnational (*see* Globalization)
Transphobia, 63
Trivium, 163, 168
Turnitin.com, 223
Tutoring, 58, 199, 204, 304–07, 309–10
Twitter, 44, 50, 181, 186–88

Universal Design, 31–2, 139, 185
Usability testing, 44, 46, 49, 185,
    202–03, 207
Usage, 25, 165, 215, 274, 292, 307

Vernacular texts, 98–100
Veterans (military), 29, 41
Video, 49, 65, 100, 181, 297
conference, 47, 199–202, 204–05
Visual texts, 99, 105, 151, 169–71,
    242, 310
Vitalism, 119
Vocationalism, 163
Voice, 65, 81–84, 113–15, 119–20, 123, 132,
    150, 172, 217, 237, 241, 284

Weblogs (*see* Blogs)
Whiteness, 135–37
Wikis, 44–45, 48–50, 197, 201, 277, 289
Witnessing, 135
Womanist rhetoric, 134
Women's writing groups, 101
Working class, 95–96, 137
Workshop, writing, 28, 111, 218–19, 237
Writer's block, 218
Writing about Writing (WaW), 15, 225
Writing Across the Curriculum (WAC),
    116, 149, 166–67, 238, 283–98,
    307–09
Writing conference (*see* Conference,
    see also video conference)
Writing majors, 15, 294–95
Writing program administrators, Council
    of (CWPA), 16, 221, 231, 297
Writing Studies, 15–17, 44, 56, 101,
    238, 294
Writing theory (*see also* Theory),
    4, 9–10, 164
Writing to communicate, 286, 295
Writing to learn, 167, 284–86, 292

Zines, 57, 99

Ideas

"Vertical writing program"
- Required writing course at 1st & 3rd year

. Lit Auto.

- Practice Pedagogy (Presentation)

. Peer study — composition Case study

. Final research essay
  options:
  - Craft criticism
  - key word
  - other

. Blog: weekly Rks + comments